THE COMPLETE
VEGETABLE
GARDENER'S
SOURCEBOOK

DUANE NEWCOMB AND KAREN NEWCOMB

THE COMPLETE VEGETABLE GARDENER'S SOURCEBOOK

New and Revised

PRENTICE HALL PRESS

New York London Toronto Sydney Tokyo

Prentice Hall Press
Gulf + Western Building
One Gulf + Western Plaza
New York, New York 10023

Copyright © 1980 By Duane Newcomb
Copyright © 1989 by Duane Newcomb and Karen Newcomb

PRENTICE HALL PRESS and colophon are registered
trademarks of Simon & Schuster, Inc.

Library of Congress Cataloging in Publication Data
Newcomb, Duane G.
The complete vegetable gardener's sourcebook. new and
revised edition.
    Includes index.
    1. Vegetable gardening. 2. Vegetable gardening—Equip-
ment and supplies—Catalogs. D. Newcomb, Karen.
SB321.N44   1989   635   89-25875

ISBN 0-13-612110-1

Designed by *In the Can*

Manufactured in the United States of America

10 9 8 7 6 5 4 3 2 1

First Prentice Hall Press Edition

Contents

ACKNOWLEDGMENTS

WE WISH TO EXPRESS thanks to our agent Jane Jordan Browne who has believed in and worked with this project for a number of years, to the many people within the garden industry, and the Cooperative Extension Services, who helped with the assembly of the original material. And to Helene McMahan, for additional research.

NOTE

The following abbreviations are used in several of the tables in this book:

- (A)   Annual
- (B)   Biennial
- (HP)   Hardy Perennial
- (P)   Perennial
- (TP)   Tender Perennial.

Introduction

IN PUTTING TOGETHER EIGHT gardening books and as avid gardeners ourselves, we have seen new products by the hundreds become available to help solve any number of gardening problems.

The frustrating part, however, was that while we knew there were a number of new items on the market, we could seldom find out just what they were or even where to buy them. In truth, only a fraction of the available home garden products can be found in any one nursery or garden catalog.

Suppose, for instance, you read about a new mini variety of cauliflower and decide to try it. Often, no one at the local nurseries has even heard of that particular variety. The only real way to find it is to send for as many individual garden catalogs as possible, then thumb through them looking for a seed source.

Or, you may be a novice gardener looking for a backyard greenhouse. There are dozens of types available today in a wide range of materials. Just where can you find the information you need to make a decision? Until this sourcebook was first published in 1980, there was no single source that allowed you to make a comprehensive comparison of products or even a complete list of manufacturers' addresses.

As we initially began to look for home-garden supply manufacturers to include in this sourcebook, we discovered that there were hundreds of them producing literally thousands of products, many more than would be possible to include here. As a result we decided to present an overview of each garden area and to include products that represent basic types.

With tractors, for instance, we try to show what's available, from the simplest to the most complex, explaining the basic differences between types and the jobs each performs best.

With hand tools, we describe the uses of each tool and the choices available.

For transplanting, we provide a summary of both commercial and noncommercial devices.

This approach is carried through in the chapter reviewing vegetable varieties (Chapter 13). Since this sourcebook was first published the number of varieties available in most vegetable groups has almost doubled. The choice today is huge.

With ordinary radishes, for instance, you have a choice of round red to one-third white, to two-thirds white round, to all-white long, plus several unusual-combinations. In addition, there are a number of oriental types available.

Eggplant is available in the familiar plumb oval or long cylindrical varieties; color variations include purple, green, yellow, white and near-black. Even zucchini comes in dark green, medium-green, green-black, gray, yellow, white, round and striped (cocozelle type) varieties.

This sourcebook allows the gardener to visualize the variation within each vegetable group and also charts the vegetable varieties available through over 100 seed catalogs.

The sourcebook itself is intended primarily as a guide to available choices and to help you decide what's best for you.

If you are considering the purchase of a rototiller, you might conclude from the sourcebook that both general front end and rear end tillers are too heavy but that a compact tiller is exactly what you need. Having made that decision, send for literature from several manufacturers listed in this sourcebook. Then, using the dealer addresses these manufacturers provide, go look at some machines. By this time, using both the sourcebook and the manufacturer's information, you should be well-equipped to make a final choice as to which one is right for you.

Gardening is not only great fun but also a practical way to provide yourself with vegetables. This sourcebook is intended to take some of the load off your shoulders. We think you will find it an essential reference tool, a real help in making the good choices and decisions that turn vegetable gardening into a truly enjoyable endeavor.

Figure 1.01

NUMBER OF PLANTS NEEDED PER PERSON

Vegetable	Plants per person
Asparagus	20
Beans, snap (bush)	2-3
Beans, snap (pole)	1-2
Beans, lima (bush)	1-2
Beans, lima (pole)	1-2
Beets	10-20
Brussels sprouts	1
Cabbage	2
Cabbage, Chinese	2-3
Cardoon	1
Carrot	40-60
Cauliflower	8-12
Celeriac	1
Celery	2-3
Chard, Swiss	2
Collards	3-5
Corn, sweet	4
Cucumber	1-2
Eggplant	1
Florence fennel	1
Garlic	1-3
Horseradish	1-2
Kale	2-4
Kohlrabi	5-6
Leeks	6-10
Lettuce, head	3-4
Lettuce, leaf	4
Muskmelon	2
Mustard	4-6
Okra	1-2
Onion	20-30
Parsnips	15
Peas, sugar snap	3-4
Peppers	1-2
Potato	1-2
Pumpkin	1
Radish	30-60
Rutabaga	5-10
Salsify	3-10
Shallot	4-10
Spinach	3-6
Spinach, Malibar	5-10
Spinach, New Zealand	5
Squash, summer	1
Squash, winter	1-2
Sweet potato	2-3
Tomato	1-2
Turnip	8-15
Watermelon	1

Figure 1.02

SAVINGS

Vegetable	Spacing of Row	Yield	Retail Value	Savings
*Cucumbers (6 plants on trellises)	2 ft.	60 cucs.	$0.40	$24.00
*Tomatoes (9 plants)	2 ft.	100 lbs.	0.80	80.00
*Zucchini (5 plants)	2 ft.	40 lbs.	0.60	24.00
*Bell Peppers (9 plants)	2 ft.	40 lbs.	1.20	48.00
Cabbage (2 plantings)	2 ft.	24 heads	0.70	16.00
Lettuce (2 plantings)	1½ ft.	48 heads	1.00	48.00
Beans (2 plantings)	2 ft.	25 lbs.	0.80	20.00
Chard	1½ ft.	48 lbs.	0.88	42.24
Beets (2 plantings)	1 ft.	36 lbs.	0.65	23.40
Carrots (2 plantings)	1 ft.	36 lbs.	0.79	28.44
Spinach (2 plantings)	1 ft.	12 lbs.	1.00	12.00
Radishes (2 plantings)	1 ft.	24 bunches	0.39	18.76
Parsley	1 ft.	48 bunches	0.79	37.92
Green Onions (sets)	½ ft.	24 bunches	0.29	6.96
Leeks	½ ft.	28 bunches	1.00	28.00
*Broccoli	2 ft.	24 heads	0.89	11.36
*Cauliflower	2 ft.	12 heads	0.89	11.36
Peas (sugar snaps)	2 ft.	15 lbs.	1.69	25.35
*Brussels sprouts	2 ft.	60 pints	1.40	84.00

*Use hybrid variety   Total $523.79

Figure 1.03

WORK SAVER TIPS

- Drive stakes to support your cucumbers and tomatoes before you plant them. This prevents damage to the plant roots.
- Keep weeds and grass mowed around the edge of the garden so pests don't have a place to hide and breed.
- Visit your garden once a day to check for problems before they get out of hand.
- Store seeds in coffee cans with plastic lids; the cans are insect- and rodent-proof.
- Place trellis and stakes so that the plants lean against them when the prevailing wind blows.
- Measure rainfall with a gauge posted near the garden so you'll know when to water. Gardens need about one inch of rain a week.
- Don't spray on windy days, to avoid wasting pesticide.
- Grow transplants in pots. Cut plastic trash bags into small squares to fit inside the pot. Poke holes in the bottom of the plastic for drainage. Fill with soil and seed. When it's time to transplant, just lift the plastic out.

I. Vegetable Gardening Today

VEGETABLE GARDENING HAS TAKEN on dimensions unimaginable when the current boom began back in the early 1970s. At that time, one out of every four vegetable gardeners was brand, spanking new. Today, only one in fifteen gardeners is just starting out.

That, of course, doesn't mean that a tremendous number of new gardeners won't be turning over their first shovelful of dirt in the late 1980s. It does mean, however, that America today has a great many experienced vegetable gardeners who are looking to extend their experience, to try new things. According to the National Gardening Association, home vegetable gardening today has become a vast and almost invisible enterprise spread across 1.7 million acres in 29 million backyard and community plots, in flower borders and in boxes on apartment terraces and rooftops. In 1987, the National Gardening Association estimated the gross national home-garden product at $12 billion.

Why is the vegetable gardening boom still accelerating at full speed?

The reasons are somewhat complex. According to a Gallup survey, all or many of these home gardeners claim they raise vegetables to save on food bills. But perhaps a more fundamental motive is that vegetables picked fresh from the home garden taste a lot better than the stiff, often overripe, vegetables found in the supermarket. Corn, for instance, reaches a peak of sweetness, then holds it only two to five days. Other vegetables hold their peak taste only a short time after picking. And, says Joseph Williamson, managing editor of *Sunset* magazine, "a really good-tasting tomato is so tender you couldn't carry it around the block."

Some gardeners feel they obtain a healthier product from their own garden. There are no commercial grade chemicals used on home garden vegetables and no forced ripening by ethylene gas.

Gardening is also therapeutic and is playing an increasingly important part in treating many of the maladies of our modern age; it alleviates stress, helps the recovery of stroke victims, the rehabilitation of alcoholics and is often an ingredient in convalescent programs. "There's something about planting and working with the soil," said Pam Neace of the Chicago Botanic Garden, which over the past ten years has helped 50 institutions start plant therapy programs. "We have worked with nursing homes, rehab settings in hospitals and amputee patients. It really helps." In addition, gardening has become recreation for two-income families who need relaxation on weekends. It has also become a fashion statement in some circles, as mini vegetables began to appear in innovative restaurants such as Chez Panisse in Berkeley, California and specialty food markets such as Balducci's New York. Currently, tiny gardens of mini-vegetables are popping up on patios and in the small backyard gardens of gourmet cooks and hostesses almost everywhere.

Indeed, gardening is an avocation that gives pleasure to millions. For those who would like to start a vegetable garden of their own, it is first necessary to know a few fundamentals.

Planning your garden

The first step to a more productive garden is selecting the location. Be sure to pick a spot that will receive six to eight hours of sunlight per day. The soil should be fertile, well-drained, and located several feet from trees and other vegetation that might rob your plants of nutrients. Start your garden in January or February by laying it out on paper. Select your favorite vegetables from seed catalogs or garden shops. Then, using a sheet of graph paper, sketch in the garden's vital statistics.

Garden size depends primarily on space available. A standard plot should be no less than 100 square feet (10 x 10 feet). With a garden this size, you can plant as many as fifteen different types of vegetables, including corn, lettuce, beets, radishes, carrots, tomatoes and green beans. If your family is large and the space is available, a standard garden 25 x 50 feet, when properly tended, can provide all the fresh vegetables five people are likely to eat in an entire season; so can smaller gardens when intensive techniques are used.

In plotting your rows, it is best to run them from north to south to maximize sun exposure. Place tall plants at the north end so they don't shade other vegetables in your garden. Large plants should also be placed against a fence whenever possible. Fences make nice trellises for tall plants like cucumbers and green beans.

How much of each crop to plant will depend in part, on your plans for canning or freezing. If you want just enough for immediate consumption, 25 feet or less of each vegetable will probably be enough. (See Figures 1-01 and 1-05.)

Selecting the tools

After you've determined the size and 'lay' of your garden, you're ready to collect the tools you'll need to do the job. To minimize the time and effort you'll spend, proper tool selection is vital. (See Chapters 4 and 5.)

For the small garden (less than 100 square feet), only the basic tools will be needed—spading fork, rake, hoe, trowel, tape measure, garden hose, string and label stakes. If your garden is larger, you should also think about investing in a rotary tiller.

Preparing the soil

Local weather conditions usually dictate the best time for you to begin tilling. Dig up a trowelful of dirt and squeeze it with your hand. If it packs solidly, the soil is too wet. If it crumbles, the soil is too dry. If it just holds together nicely, conditions are right for tilling to begin.

To give proper richness and texture to the soil, commerical fertilizers or manure should be applied using a tiller or a shovel until the ground is a workable consistency. (See Chapter 2.)

After the initial tilling or digging job is completed, rake or harrow the soil. Break up any larger clumps that may be left, but do not granulate the soil. Fine soil will crust after a hard rain, making it difficult for plant sprouts to push through.

Planting

Different types of vegetables need to be planted at different times because some will withstand temperatures while others will not. As a rule, the best time to plant sensitive crops is usually two or three weeks after the last freeze in your area. For more specific information on proper planting times, contact your county extension office or local garden shop.

After you've determined the proper planting time, you're ready to begin the actual planting process. Check seed packets for any special instructions, then stake out your garden area. Set up stakes at either end to ensure straight rows. Then begin making your rows with a hoe or till and furrow opener accessory.

Plant the seeds and cover them with a thin layer of soil. Firm the soil with your hand or foot. Then label each row stake with the empty seed packet.

Consider planting companion crops of early- and late-maturing plants in the same row. For example, radishes can be planted with carrots, and harvested and replanted before the carrot plants mature.

Green beans, tomatoes, cucumbers and certain other plants require only a third to half the normal space when properly staked or trellised. Staking and trellising should be considered, especially in smaller gardens.

Garden care

For higher yields and tastier vegetables, correct garden care is essential. Proper care includes watering, cultivating, mulching and fertilizing. For maximum growth, your garden should receive no less than one inch of water per week, about 120 gallons per 12-by-15-foot area. (See Chapter 7.) Water between furrows until rows are soaked. It's far better to water thoroughly once a week than to water lightly every third or fourth day. A weekly soaking allows plant roots to grow deeply into the soil. Then, if a drought should occur, the plant's deep root system lets it draw from the 'water table' for continued growth.

Cultivate your garden whenever the need arises with a tiller or a hand cultivator.

Proper mulching and fertilizing also improve plant yield. Compost placed between the rows helps prevent weed growth, conserves moisture and provides added nutrients for the soil. (See Chapter 3.) Fertilizer stimulates root growth and produces fleshier, healthier fruit.

Postharvest tilling

Working the soil in the fall pays big dividends the following spring. Use a rotary tiller or spading fork to turn undersurface refuse-weeds, stalks and dead leaves. A tiller used in fall also accelerates the breakdown of soil-building materials that occurs naturally during the winter. That means richer, more workable soil the following spring.

That's one classic method of establishing and maintaining a vegetable garden. Other ways have been developed, and are worth consideration by all gardeners.

THE GARDENING METHOD EXPLOSION

So popular has vegetable gardening become today, that not only are millions of new gardeners growing vegetables, but dozens of different gardening methods are springing up all across the country. These methods differ in one way or another from the conventional way of planting vegetables in wide rows in a fairly large garden. Here are a few.

Small-Space Intensive Gardening

A good method for city gardeners who have only

small flowerbed type spaces. After intensive cultivation utilizing compost and manure, seeds are broadcast across the bed, utilizing all the space. The system uses dynamic plant groupings with key producer plants surrounded by secondary and tertiary plantings. Vine crops, including squash and watermelons, are grown in the air on a trellis. This method produces a tremendous yield while requiring fifty percent less labor and water.

Reference: The Backyard Vegetable Factory *by Duane G. Newcomb (Rodale, Emmaus, PA).*

Square-foot gardening

A system for laying out, planting and maintaining a productive, attractive garden in any amount of space. The garden is based on a grid of 1 x 1 foot squares with single seeds or plants placed in carefully determined spacings. The square-foot system lets you make the most of your garden to conserve the amounts of water, soil conditions and labor needed to produce a maximum amount of food in that space.

Reference: Square Foot Gardening *by Mel Bartholomew, (Rodale, Emmaus, PA).*

Raised-bed method

Beds approximately 20 feet long and 5 feet wide are made up by double-digging in large amounts of compost or aged manure, then adding bone meal and wood ash. Seeds are broadcast across the beds so that the plant leaves touch as they grow. This creates a mini-climate under the soil that helps hold moisture and reduce weed growth.

Reference: How to Grow More Vegetables Than You Ever Thought Possible on Less Land Than You Can Imagine *by John Jeavons (Ten Speed Press, Berkeley, CA).*

Depressed-bed method

One- to two-foot-wide beds are planted between two ridges with two to three rows of vegetables planted in each bed. Organic material is dug into each of these beds with a spading fork. Advantages: the soil in the

Figure 1.04

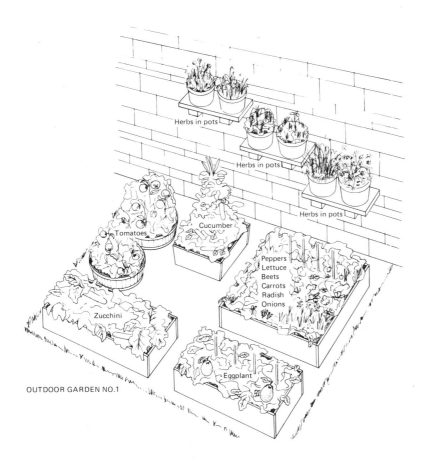

Herbs in pots

Herbs in pots

Herbs in pots

Tomatoes

Cucumber

Peppers
Lettuce
Beets
Carrots
Radish
Onions

Zucchini

Eggplant

OUTDOOR GARDEN NO.1

Garden variety
Vegetable gardens today often consist of a combination of raised beds and container vegetables. This type of garden can easily be fitted into an area if almost any size and shape.

Figure 1.05

A home-grown vegetable garden will provide a tremendous harvest. Here's a guide to help you estimate the yield you can expect from your garden:

ESTIMATED YIELD OF VEGETABLE CROPS & SUGGESTED SPACING BETWEEN ROWS		
Crop	**Pounds (or Units) per 100 ft. row**	**Row spacing (Inches)**
Asparagus	30	48-60
Beans, Lima (bush)	25	30-36
Beans, Snap (bush)	100	30-36
Beets	275	36
Broccoli	75	30-36
Carrot	275	36
Cabbage	150	30-36
Cauliflower	100	30-36
Chard	75	24-30
Corn	120 (ears)	30-36
Cucumber, Slicing	275	48-60
Cucumber, Pickling	180	48-60
Garlic	40	30-36
Eggplant	100	30-36
Kohlrabi	75	30-36
Lettuce, Head	100 (heads)	36
Lettuce, Leaf	100	30-36
Muskmelon	100 (fruits)	60
Mustard	150	30-36
Okra	110	30-36
Onion, Bulb	230	36
Pea	20	30-36
Pepper, Bell	130	30-36
Potato, White	240	30-36
Potato, Sweet	200	30-36
Spinach	130	30-36
Squash, Summer	350	36-48
Squash, Winter	300	60
Tomato	280	48-60
Turnip	180	30-36

beds stays moist longer, and the beds are protected from the winds by ridges in between,

Vertical vegetable growing

Utilizing limited patio areas, vegetables are now being grown in upright vertical containers. Here are a few:

The **vegetable tree** is made of wire filled with planting mix, along an eight foot-high board with tomatoes at the bottom, cucumbers above, then radishes and carrots. **Vegetable pot** trees are baskets supported on a 5 x 7 foot post that has been anchored with bags of sand. There are also many types of **roll-around bookcase vegetable planters** being used. (See Chapter 10 for details.)

Reference: Gardening Shortcuts (Ortho Books, Chevron Chemical Co., San Francisco, CA).

Wide-row gardening

Wide-row planting is planting in extra-wide rows of up to three or more feet. Vegetable seeds are then broadcast across the rows.

Reference: The Joy of Gardening by Dick Raymond (Storey Publishing, Pownal, VT).

Which method for you? That depends on your gardening conditions. But if your time and space are limited, consider either small-space intensive or wide-row gardening. If you are interested primarily in organic gardening, and want to try a more productive method, consider either the raised-bed or depressed-bed method. If you live in an apartment or townhouse with a patio, try container vegetable gardening. There are, of course, many other methods besides these—one of the great joys of gardening, as you become more experienced, will be to experiment with the many methods and to decide for yourself which best suit your needs or goals.

Figure 1.06

TEST YOUR VEGETABLE/VITAMIN KNOWLEDGE

Think you know which vegetable is the 'best' for you? Spinach, right? Not necessarily; take this quick quiz and you may be surprised. (Answers at end of chapter.)

1. What yellow garden vegetable grown from seed, has the lowest amount of sodium?
2. Guess which leafy vegetable has the highest calcium content.
3. This one vegetable was found to be highest in both Vitamin A and C; can you guess which it is?
4. This one's easy. The vegetable with the lowest number of calories is _____?
5. The seeds of which two vegetables have the highest amount of iron?
6. This delicious seed is highest in fiber and fat content. Can you name it?

HOW MUCH IS YOUR GARDEN REALLY WORTH?

Surprisingly, even a small garden is worth quite a bit. A few years ago several national garden organizations worked out the production from a 'small' conventional 25 x 15 foot backyard plot. At that time the total amount saved came to $480.60 at 1984 prices. Today that same garden is worth $545.79 and going up.

The costs were basically as follows: fertilizer and insecticide, $28.00; nursery transplants, $29.00; seedlings $26.30; for a total of $83.30. (See Figure 1-02.)

CHOOSING A GARDEN SITE

Selecting the right site for your vegetable garden is important. Here are a few points to consider:

1. Select a site with loamy or sandy loam soil instead of clay whenever possible. (See Chapter 2).
2. Choose a garden spot that receives at least six hours of direct sunlight a day (eight to ten hours is ideal). Vegetables should be planted away from buildings, trees and other objects that shade the garden. If part of your garden is in the shade, plant that part with leafy vegetables such as lettuce, spinach and similar plants.
3. Don't plant your garden near trees—their roots can compete with vegetables for water and nutrients. Generally, the tree roots take food from the soil in a circle as far out as the tree's widest-reaching branches; plants usually do poorly within that circle.
4. Place the garden on high ground rather than in a depression at the base of a hill. Low spots warm up slowly in the spring. High ground allows vegetables to escape borderline freezes.
5. Locate the garden away from low or soggy areas where water stands in puddles after rains.
6. Use contour rows or terraces on hillside gardens. Rows run across a slope help catch the rain.
7. Do not plant your gardens in a windy location.
8. Your garden should be close to a water supply. This eliminates having to drag a hose long distances. Also try to put the garden as near your tool storage as possible.
9. Locate your garden fairly near the back door. This makes it easier to reach for weeding, watering, planting, picking and other chores.

COMMUNITY GARDENING

If you don't have space for your own garden, group gardening may well be your path to growing your own vegetables.

A few years ago, surveys indicated that over 30 million Americans would like to grow their own food but couldn't because of lack of space. Since that time, literally hundreds of communities have begun garden projects almost everywhere across the United States.

The group garden itself is simply a piece of land divided into individual plots that are rented or given to people who don't own their own land. In any project there may be as few as six gardeners or as many as several hundred,

In the Troy-Albany-Schenectady, New York, area, for instance, gardeners rent plots in sites coordinated by the Capital District Community Gardens, Inc.

In Burlington, Vermont, the Burlington Parks Commission divided a half-acre site into 24 plots at Cliffside Park. To supplement this, the Burlington Parks Commission ran ads in the local paper asking for free garden plots. The Cliffside project attracted a side cross-section of people, including retirees, a stock-broker's wife, medical students, businessmen and others. More recently, the Burlington Department of Parks and Recreation began a project called the Burlington Area Community Gardens, six rent-free sites within the Burlington city limits.

In Boston, Fenway Gardens, composed of four hundred 15 x 30 foot plots, was established a number of years ago in the Back Bay area. There is no charge for gardening here, but the gardeners are encouraged to become members of the Fenway Garden Society.

"Without these gardens," says the Administrative Secretary of the Boston Parks Department, "a lot of people in the city would never get out of the house."

Besides communities and nonprofit organizations, many business organizations also sponsor community gardening projects. In Louisville, Kentucky, the Citizen's Fidelity Bank recently began a project that attracted over 3,000 gardeners. "These gardens," the bank estimates, "saved over a quarter of a million dollars based on retail food prices."

Numerous large companies also offer group gardening opportunities for their employees. Dow Chemical Company employees, for instance, have been gardening on company land for 34 years, and at RCA's David Sarnoff Research Center, employees share 120 garden plots that are plowed in the spring by the company.

In many cases, these group gardens are sponsored or coordinated by the City Parks and Recreation Department. In others, they are backed by local businesses, the YWCA, churches, and many other organizations. In Appleton, Wisconsin, the Sacred Heart Church's garden project rented seven acres of land (tagged "The Papal Gardens') from a local farmer and divided it into 259 10 x 100 foot plots. And in Asheville, North Carolina, an enthusiastic local gardener convinced the YWCA to transform a weed lot into a community garden project for retired people.

In some cases, University Extension Services, various local government agencies, and even the Department of Health, Education and Welfare, get involved, giving expert advice and money. And the National Gardening Association, a nonprofit organization with offices in Burlington, Vermont, publishes information, considers research, and provides consulting services to community garden projects all across the country.

Community gardening is not expanding as it once was, but it is still going strong in many areas. If you are interested in joining one of these projects in your own area, call your local Parks and Recreation Department. If it does not sponsor a gardening program, it will be able to refer you to a group gardening project within your own community.

Figure 1.07

	Food													
NUTRITIONAL VALUE FOR GARDEN VEGETABLES														
100-Gram (3.5 oz) Sample Raw, Edible Portion	Food Energy Cals.	Protein Grams	Fat Grams	Fiber Grams	Cal-cium ML	Iron ML	Sodium ML	Potas-sium ML	Vit A IU	Vit B$_1$ ML	Vit B$_2$ ML	Nia-cin ML	Vit C ML
1. Green bean	32	1.9	0.2	1.0	56	0.8	7	243	600	.08	.11	0.5	19
2. Beets	43	1.6	0.1	0.8	16	0.7	60	335	20	.03	.05	0.4	10
3. Beet greens	24	2.2	0.3	1.3	119	3.3	130	570	6100	.10	.22	0.4	30
4. Brussel Sprouts	45	4.9	0.4	1.6	36	1.5	14	390	550	.10	.16	0.9	102
5. Chard, Swiss	25	2.4	0.3	0.8	88	3.2	147	550	6500	.06	.17	0.5	32
6. Collards	45	4.8	0.8	1.2	250	1.5	—	430	9300	.16	.31	1.7	152
7. Corn, Sweet	96	3.5	1.0	0.7	3	0.7	Trace	280	400	.15	.12	1.7	12
8. Cress, garden	32	2.6	0.7	1.1	81	1.3	14	606	9300	.08	.26	1.0	69
9. Eggplant	25	1.2	0.2	0.9	12	0.7	2	214	10	.05	.05	0.6	5
10. Kale, leaves with stems	38	4.2	0.8	1.3	179	2.2	75	378	8900	—	—	—	125
11. Muskmelon—Cantaloupe	30	0.7	0.1	0.3	14	0.4	12	251	3400	.04	.03	0.6	33
12. Okra	36	2.4	0.3	1.0	92	0.6	3	249	520	.17	.21	1.0	31
13. Parsley	44	3.6	0.6	1.5	203	6.2	45	727	8500	.12	.26	1.2	172
14. Parsnips	76	1.7	0.5	2.0	50	0.7	12	541	30	.08	.09	0.2	16
15. Peppers, hot, immature green	37	1.3	0.2	1.8	10	0.7	—	—	770	.09	.06	1.7	235
16. Peppers, red, no seeds	65	2.3	0.4	2.3	16	1.4	25	564	21600	.10	.20	2.9	369
17. Pumpkin	26	1.0	0.1	1.1	21	0.8	1	340	1600	.05	.11	0.6	9
18. Squash, summer, all varieties	19	1.1	0.1	0.6	28	0.4	1	202	410	.05	.09	1.0	22
19. Squash, winter, all varieties	50	1.4	0.3	1.4	22	0.6	1	369	3700	.05	.11	0.6	13
20. Tomatoes, green	24	1.2	0.2	0.5	13	0.5	3	244	270	.06	.04	0.5	20
21. Watermelon	26	0.5	0.2	0.3	7	0.5	1	100	590	.03	.03	0.2	7

Compiled from USDA Handbook No. 8, *Composition of Foods.*

Figure 1.08

Cooking Vegetables — What's Best For You

With most vegetables you'll get the most food value by eating them raw. Cooking vegetables in water causes the water-soluble vitamins and minerals to break down or leach out.

Raw sweet corn is especially delicious when eaten uncooked, fresh off the plant. Other vegetables which have good raw flavor include broccoli, peas, summer squash and green beans. Serve them with a dip as a finger food for snacks or hors d' oeuvres.

Figure 1.09

THE NEW GARDEN SPOT

Select a spot in full sunlight near a water hose, on well-drained soil, away from weeds and tree roots.

- Remove sod with a spade and put in a compost pile to decay or rot.
- Spread compost or rotted manure.

If you have begun your new garden in the fall, your next step is to plow, spade or roto-till your garden deeply (8 to 10 inches).

If you have begun your new garden in the spring, your next step is to spade or roto-till the soil about 4 to 6 inches deep to prepare a bed for your seeds.

Quiz Answers: 1. Sweet Corn 2. Kale 3. Hot Red Peppers 4. Crisphead Lettuce 5. Pumpkin and Squash Seeds
6. Sunflower seeds
Source: National Garden Bureau

2. Soil

SOIL FOR GROWING VEGETABLES is not just an accumulation of dirt and rock. It is a combination of organic material, living organisms, air, water and minerals. An ideal soil for vegetables contains 50 percent of solid matter and 50 percent pore space. with water occupying about half of the latter area.

Basically there are three types of soil—clay, sand and loam. (Some classifications also include silt, an intermediate grade between clay and sand, consisting of gritty, hard-packed particles.) We will follow that system in this discussion.

TYPES OF SOIL

Clay: is composed of fine, flat, waferlike particles that fit together tightly and take in water slowly. Chemically, clay is primarily silicon and aluminum in composition, with small amounts of sodium, magnesium, iron, calcium and potassium.

Once the clay particles absorb moisture, they hold it so tightly that it is almost impossible for plants to get any use out of it. Beyond this, there is no space for air to penetrate. When clay dries, it is difficult to work, and plant roots have a hard time penetrating downward.

Rubbed between your fingers, wet clay soil feels smooth, soft and slippery.

Sand: has particles at least 25 times larger than the largest clay particles. Pure sand, while high in mineral content, contains almost no nutrients and has almost no capacity to store moisture. Air penetrates sand deeply, and water moves through too rapidly, dissolving away many nutrients.

Sand thus dries out quickly and sometimes reflects enough heat to damage vegetable crops. Most sandy soils contain enough clay and silt to retain some water and nutrients.

Rubbed between your fingers, sand feels grainy and gritty. Silt is a kind of intermediate stage between clay and sand. Silt particles pack down hard, almost like clay, but they are considerably larger. Their size is about halfway between the size of sand and clay particles. Silt topsoils are often found over dense layers of clay. They are often not fertile.

Rubbed between your fingers, silt feels a bit slippery, with a grainy texture.

Loam: is made up of clay, sand, silt and a good supply of decomposed organic material called humus. The grains have good structure built by the combined action of root growth, insects, worms and bacteria. This type of soil drains well, yet retains enough water for good plant growth. Air can circulate freely, and there is plenty of room for roots to grow.

Very few soils are ready to grow vegetables; most soils need to be worked before they will yield as they should. If soil has a high clay content, or too much sand or silt, it's got to be improved. Fortunately, it is possible to change the structure, drainage and circulation of most types of soil by the addition of organic material and inert materials such as gypsum. This is also dealt with under *Organic Gardening* in Chapter 3. Organic additives should be the first alternative considered by the gardener.

ORGANIC ADDITIVES

In clay soils, the coarse organic particles hold the compacted soil particles apart, breaking up the heavy soil. The fine organic particles help hold the clay particles together in small crumbs. This improves the drainage, allows the soil to 'breathe,' and adds nutrients.

Organic material added to sandy soil holds water and nutrients where plants can use them. Organic matter also keeps sandy soils from warming up quickly and prevents damage to vegetables. In order to be effective, at least one-third of the final mix must be organic.

In addition, the minute organic material is added, microorganisms in the soil begin to break it down into forms plants can use. The rate of decomposition and the products of decay depend on the material itself.

There are four general types of organic soil conditioners:-

Manures: have good water- and nutrient-holding ability, useful for changing soil structures. Manures can be obtained directly from a farm or stable or purchased in sacks as a commercial product from a garden center or nursery. Fresh manure should be allowed to rot before it is used in the garden. Commercial dried and packaged manures often have fairly high levels of soluble salts.

Peat moss: is high in water- and nutrient-holding ability, fair for changing soil structure. The better peats come from Canadian bogs. They are long-lasting but provide little nor no nutrient value.

Figure 2.01

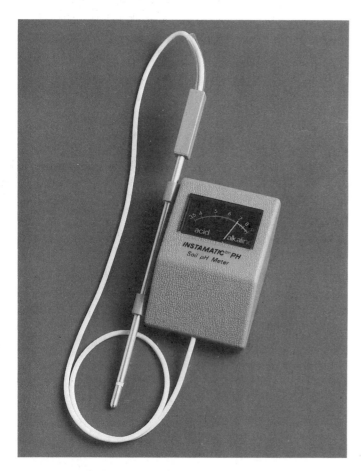

Instamatic pH soil meter

Soil pH levels are vital to successful gardening as pH controls the food available to plants. Some vegetables prefer acid, others alkaline soil. Most need a neutral pH, around 7. This probe will read the pH of soil, compost or potting mix to instantly determine pH levels from 3.5 to 9.0.

LUSTER LEAF PRODUCTS, INC.
P.O. Box 1067
Crystal Lake, IL 60014

Figure 2.02

WHAT A SOIL ANALYSIS WILL TELL YOU

1. pH
2. Electrical conductivity
3. Nitrate nitrogen
4. Ammonium nitrogen
5. Phosphorus
6. Potassium
7. Calcium
8. Magnesium

Micronutrients (trace and minor elements) such as zinc, manganese, copper and iron can also be requested. The proper use of fertilizer will produce better plant growth because the elements required by your plants will be provided in proper balance.

WHAT CHEMICAL SOIL TESTING WILL NOT TELL YOU

The chemical analysis will not diagnose plant problems resulting from:-

1. Pathological organisms such as fungus, soil insects or nematodes.
2. Abnormal plant growth resulting from excessive soil moisture.
3. Reduced growth resulting from soil chemical sterilants.
4. Poor growth resulting from subnormal weather conditions.

Figure 2.03

OPTIMUM pH RANGE FOR VEGETABLES	
pH	**Vegetable**
6-8	Asparagus, beets, cabbage, muskmelons
6-7.5	Peas, spinach, summer squash
6-7	Cauliflower, celery, chives, endive, horse-radish, lettuce, onions, radishes, rhubarb
5.5-7.5	Pumpkins, corn, tomatoes
5,5-6.8	Beans, carrots, cucumbers, parsnips, peppers, rutabagas, winter squash
5.5-6.5	Eggplant, watermelons
4.8-6.3	Potatoes

Figure 2.04

CHANGING SOIL pH			
		Additional lbs / 1000 Square feet	
From	**To**	**Limestone**	**Sulfur**
4.5	6.5	175	
5.0	6.5	140	
5.5	6.5	100	
6.0	6.5	66	
7.0	6.5		4
7.5	6.5		20
8.0	6.5		38

Wood by-products: are fair in water- and nutrient-holding ability, excellent for altering soil structure. These by-products include leaf mold, wood shavings, sawdust and ground bark. These have a high ratio of carbon in relation to the amount of nitrogen present, which means that the nitrogen is used up by the micro-organisms in the decay process, making it unavailable to growing vegetables. Thus, nitrogen must often be added to these mixtures. Frequently, commercial wood by-products have nitrogen added in the manufacturing process.

Organic by-products (Rice hulls, cottonseed meal): have poor water- and nutrient-holding ability, but are good for altering soil structure at low cost.

Partially decomposed organic material (compost), which is discussed at length in Chapter 3, has good moisture-holding and nutrient-holding ability. It quickly adds humus to the soil, along with nutrients in usable form.

Which additive you use in your garden depends on your own soil conditions and preferences. In general, sandy soils benefit from spongy materials like peat that hold water and nutrients well. Clay soils benefit most from bulky additions such as bark, hulls and similar materials that separate the clay particles.

INORGANIC ADDITIVES

Inorganic additives generally are used in heavy clay soils to break up the soil structure and to allow greater penetration of air and water. You can utilize inert substances, which mechanically hold the particles apart, or chemical conditioners. (See Figure 2.05.)

Clay soil can be broken up by the addition of gypsum (calcium sulfate). Clay in its natural state generally becomes packed and airless because an excess of sodium in each clay particle strongly attracts water. As the water drains away, the particles are left tightly packed. Gypsum removes the sodium by exchanging the sodium ions for calcium ions. The clay particles are then soon separated into large crumbs with ample pore space. Gypsum should be spread on the soil surface at the rate of about 50 pounds per 1,000 square feet. Sand added to clay will not improve it, will not prevent it from baking hard.

ACID-ALKALINE SOIL

Soils are often acid (sour) or alkaline (sweet). This is expressed in terms of pH (the degree of alkalinity or acidity) on a scale of 1 to 14—7 is neutral, below 7 acid, above 7 alkaline. Most vegetables—with some notable exceptions like tomatoes—do best in neutral soils. (See Figure 2.03.)

Soils become acid by the leaching of calcium and magnesium ions and their replacement by hydrogen ions. This occurs naturally in regions of heavy rainfall.

Soils turn more alkaline as calcium, manganese, and sodium ions accumulate and replace hydrogen ions. This conditions occurs because of low rainfall and poor drainage. It is also prevalent in areas with native limestone deposits.

Sometimes you can tell whether the soil is too alkaline just by looking at it. Symptoms of alkalinity are yellowing leaves on vegetation, stunted growth and burning of leaf margins. Often, alkaline soils are too salty. In extreme cases, heavy brown or white.salt deposits are left on the soil surface or on the edges of water ditches.

The surest way of telling whether or not your soil is too acid or too alkaline is with a pH test. There are three ways to make this test. First, take samples of your soil and have them tested by the State Cooperative Extension Service. Usually, the agent in your county can arrange to have this done free or for a small fee. Second, you can send these soil samples

Figure 2.05

INORGANIC SOIL CONDITIONERS		
	Source	Function
MECHANICAL		
Pumice	A ground volcanic stone full of minute cavities	Holds apart massed clay particles
Sand		Useful when applied in large quantities
Vermiculite	Exploded mica	Holds 3-4 times its weight in water
CHEMICAL OR COMBINATION		
Gypsum	Naturally occurring calcium sulfate	The calcium in gypsum is capable of replacing the sodium ions in clay that make clay particles pack so hard; when the calcium ions replace the sodium, the particles group, forming large pore spaces
Lime sulfur	Sold as calcium polysulfide	Acts in a manner similar to gypsum; the most effective lime sulfur has a wetting agent that causes a deeper soil penetration
Soil sulfur		As the soil warms up, the sulfur breaks down into sulfuric acid and reacts with calcium carbonate in the soil to form soluble calcium sulfate

Figure 2.06

ORGANIC SOIL CONDITIONERS

Type	Structure-Modifying Ability	Other advantages	Nutrient & Water-Holding Capacity	Uses
Activated sludge, garden compost	Organic sludge and compost are useful for modifying soil structure	Adds nutrients to soil	Good	Useful in clay and sand
Manures	Fair	Has high nutrient content, but must be well rotted	Fair	Useful in clay and sand
Leaf Mold	Fair	Should be well decompopsed; adds usable nutrients	Fair	Useful in clay and sand
Sawdust	Good	Untreated is high in carbon, low in nitrogen, can be purchased with nigrogen added	Fair to good	Useful in sand
Rice hulls	Fair	Adds nitrogen 1/5 lb. per 10 cu. ft.	Poor	Useful in clay
Bark	Granular, easy to use; helps break up heavy soild	Needs nitrogen if untreated—1 lb. per 10 cu. ft.	Poor	Useful in clay

Figure 2.07

ALL YOU NEED TO KNOW ABOUT PLANT NUTRIENTS...AND MORE

Nutrients	Function	Symptions of soil nutrient deficiency
MAJOR NUTRIENTS		
Nitrogen (N)	Produces a dark green vigorous leaf color, vigorous root system, feeds soil microorganisms	Leaves yellow yellow-green, stunted growth
Phosphorus (P)	Stimulates early root formation, gives rapid start, hastens maturity, provides disease resistance; important for development of flowers, fruit and seed	Leaves have purple or red appearance
Potassium (K)	Important in the manufacturer of sugar and starch; influences leaf and root system development; imcreases vigor and disease-resistance	Leaves look dry or scorched at edges
SECONDARY NUTRIENTS		
Calcium (Ca)	Necessary for manufacture and growth of plant cells, promotes early root growth	Plants stunted, leaves wrinkles
Manganese (Mn)	Speedsor important for seed development	Chlorosis (yellowing) of leaves
Sulfur (S)	Maintains dark-green color—constituent of proteins	Pale-green, yellowing
MICRO-NUTRIENTS (TRACE ELEMENTS)		
Iron (Fe)	Promotes chlorophyll production; catalyst in enzyme system	Yellowing leaves, green veins
Magnesium (Mg)	Forms chlorophyll and sugar; important for seed development	Chlorosis (yellowing) of leaves
Copper (Cu)	Enzyme activator essential for chlorophyll formation	Multiple budding
Zinc (Zn).	Necessary for normal chlorophyl production and growth	Small, yellow leaves
Boron (B)	Needed for calcium utilization and normal cell division	Leaves yellowish red
Molybdenum (Mo)	Important in the utilization of nitrogen	—
Chlorine (Cl)	Essential for proper plant development	—

to the commercial laboratory for testing. There are many labs throughout the country that make this service available. Check your telephone yellow pages under *Labs-soil.*

Third, you can purchase a soil test kit at your local nursery or garden center and test the soil yourself. The procedure consists of filling a small glass container partly full of fine soil, then adding the testing solution. The result of this mixture is compared with an easy-to-read color chart. Anyone who can read and compare colors can produce practical results. Kits range from a simple pH test (about $3) to elaborate soil test kits that test for all major, secondary, and trace elements ($100). Small kits (about $15), which test for the major nutrients (nitrogen, phosphorus and potash), are satisfactory for most home gardens.

To counteract acid soil, group limestone is an effective agent, and in some areas it is used extensively. Dolomite lime contains both calcium and magnesium. Hydrated or burned lime is sometimes used, but it leaches away rapidly and can burn your hands. To correct alkaline soil, add gypsum, soil sulfur or aluminum sulfate.

SOIL NUTRIENTS

Plants need nutrients for growth. Three elements—oxygen, carbon and hydrogen—come from the air and water. The other thirteen nutrients are found in the soil. Three of these thirteen are major nutrients: nitrogen, phosphorus and potassium. Another three are secondary: calcium, manganese and sulfur. Seven are micronutrients: zinc, iron, magnesium, copper, molybelenum, boron and chlorine.

The major nutrients are needed by most vegetables in large amounts. They have a strong effect on the growth of stems, leaves, roots and fruits. You must make sure your soil has sufficient supplies of nitrogen, phosphorus and potash.

Among the secondary nutrients, calcium promotes early growth, magnesium is an important component

Figure 2.08

Soil test kit

This home gardener test kit measures the pH and three basic macronutrients using simplified test methods. Graduated plastic test tubes are used for the measurement of the soil sample and reagent solutions. The results are compared to standards on laminated color charts.

LA MOTTE CHEMICAL PRODUCTS CO.
P.O. Box 329
Chesterttown, MD 21620

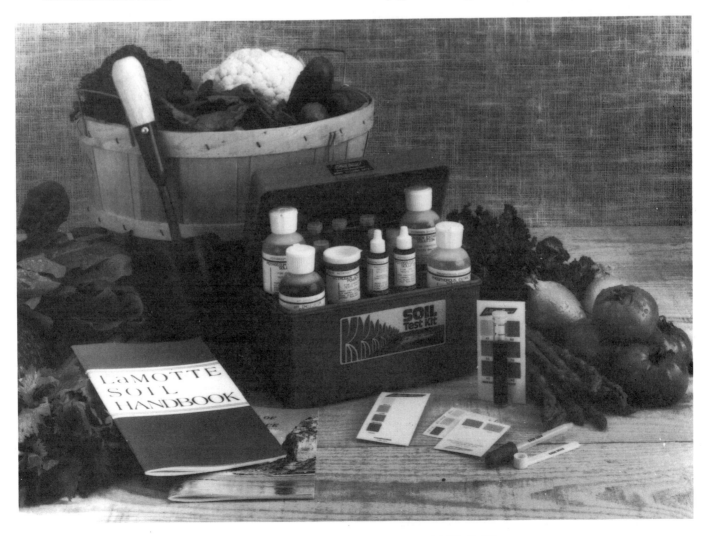

of chlorophyll, and sulfur is a constituent of protein. All are needed for healthy growth. Although the micronutrients are needed only in very small quantities they are important, and should not be overlooked.

Most garden soils are not perfect—they are generally deficient in one or several of the basic nutritional elements. For maximum production of healthy vegetables, it is therefore generally necessary to provide some kind of fertilizer to the soil.

Figure 2.09

Soil thermometer
The most accurate planting guide is soil temperature. Lettuce seed, for instance, will germinate at a soil temperature of 32° F, while most beans won't germinate until the soil temperature reaches 60° F or more.
TAYLOR TRU TEMP PRODUCTS
TCA Thermometer Corporation of America
95 Glenn Bridge Road
Arden, NC 28704

SELECTING THE RIGHT FERTILIZER

The different choices of available plant foods can be confusing. Four different kinds are used in vegetable gardens:-

Dry chemical fertilizers

Powdered: These are sold as a combination of materials in powdered form. They provide vegetables quick access to nutrient material, but blow away easily and leach out quickly.

Pelletized-granular: Powdered fertilizer is compressed into pellets. These pellets are easy to spread and release the nutrients slowly as the pellets break down.

Time-release: The fertilizer pellets are coated with resin or a similar substance. The nutrients slowly diffuse through the resin. When watered, the surface is worn away much like licking a lollipop. There is no danger of overfertilizing, but one application is generally enough for vegetables for an entire season. Time-released fertilizers are especially good for slow-maturing crops such as melons and winter squash.

Liquid fertilizers

These are sold as concentrated powders or concentrated liquids that you dilute with water. Liquid fertilizers are absorbed through the leaves, stems and branches, as well as through the roots. They can be sprayed or sprinkled on the vegetables.

Different kinds of fertilizers are prepared for different soil conditions and vegetables. Some manufacturers offer as many as twelve different formulations. Most are composed of nitrogen, phosphorus and potassium, with trace elements.

Vegetable fertilizer formulations are generally based on the following:-

Nitrogen: which promotes leaf growth, stimulates vegetative development for cabbage, lettuce, spinach, and collards.
Phosphorus: which promotes strong root growth, hastens maturity, and aids in seed and fruit development.
Potassium (potash): is necessary for new cell division in roots and buds and is important to fruit quality. Corn ears sometimes don't fill out when a plant is low in potash. Potash is also important to the ripening of tomatoes and for the development of root crops such as beans and potatoes.

The numbers you find on a fertilizer container refer to the percentage of nitrogen (N), phosphorus (P) and potassium (K) found in that particular fertilizer (in that order). A 5-10-5 fertilizer contains 5 percent nitrogen, 10 percent phosphorus and 5 percent potassium. In a 100-pound bag of this fertilizer there would be 5 pounds of nitrogen, 10 pounds of phosphorus, and

Figure 2.10

WHY AMMONIUM SULFATE?

1. Supplies both nitrogen and sulfur needs in one application.
2. All nitrogen is in the ammonium form, which resists leaching.
3. Sulfur is in the sulfate form, so that it is immediately available to plants.
   Source: USS Granular Ammonium Sulfate
   Agri-Chemicals Division
   United States Steel
   P.O. Box 1685
   Atlanta GA 30321

Figure 2.11

LAMOTTE SOIL HANDBOOK

This handy booklet explains the nature of soils, the macro-, micro- and trace nutrients needed by vegetables, soil pH (includes liming tables), the principles of soil testing and a glossary of terms.
LAMOTTE CHEMICAL PRODUCTS CO.
P.O. Box 329
Chestertown, MD 21620

Figure 2.12

	PEAT AND PEAT MOSS				
Type	**Identifying Characteristics**	**Physical Properties**	**Chemical Properties**	**Advantages**	**Disadvantages**
Sphagnum peat moss (includes related moss peats)	Light yellow to brown; extremely fibrous; readily identifiable; whole plant remains	Least decomposed or raw; highest moisture-holding capacity, lowest bulk density	Highest acidity; lowest ash content; lowest nitrogen content; highest in organic matter	Highest water-holding capacity; lowest volume weight; high acidity; desirable for acid-loving plants such as conifers; very sterile—free from plant disease and noxious weed seeds	Tends to decompose faster than other types; problems in mixing with soil because of light, fibrous structure; difficult to wet; high acidity can injure acid-intolerant plants; tendency to blow away
Reed-sedge peat (also called fibrous peat)	Dark brown to reddish brown; variable in fibrosity; identifiable plant remains	Most favorable state of decomposition for immediate soil benefit; intermediate moisture-holding capacity and bulk density	Low cellulose content; high in organic matter, mild acidity; low ash content; high nitrogen content	Two to three times the nitrogen content of sphagnum; contains organic acid in its original moist condition; mixes smoothly with soil; free of weed seed; does not suffer the rapid uneconomic decomposition of sphagnum	Does not hold quite as much moisture as sphagnum; bacterially active when applied
Peat Humus	Very dark brown to black; advanced state of decomposition; few if any fibers; no identifiable plant remains	Very low moisture-holding capacity; highest bulk density; almost completely decomposed	Highest nitrogen and ash content; variable acidity; lowest in organic matter	Lowest but most stable organic matter	Very dusty when dry; drying difficult to apply; may have impaired rewettability; may contain noxious weed seed

Figure 2.13

		NATURAL PLANT FOODS				
Type	**Source**	**Composition (%)**				
		N	**P**	**K**	**CA**	**MG**
Animal manures (fresh)	Cattle	0.53	0.29	0.48	0.29	0.11
	Chicken	0.89	0.48	0.83	0.38	0.13
	Horse	0.55	0.27	0.57	0.27	0.11
	Sheep	0.89	0.48	0.83	0.21	0.13
Animal manures (dried)	Cattle	1.00	0.50	1.00	—	—
	Horse	1.50	1.00	1.00	—	—
	Sheep	1.50	1.00	1.00	—	—
Animal tankage	Dried blood meal	13.00	1.50	1.00	—	—
	Bone meal	3.50	15.00	—	—	—
	Dried fish scrap	10.00	4.50	—	—	—
	Fish emulsion	7.50	—	—	—	—
Pulverized rock powders	Rock phosphate	—	30.00	—	—	—
	Limestone	—	—	—	40.00	—
	Green Sand	—	1.35	6.00	—	1.63
Vegetable residues	Coffee grounds	2.00	0.40	2.50	—	—
	Cottonseed meal	6.50	2.00	1.50	—	—
	Seaweed	1.70	0.80	5.00	—	—
	Soybean meal	6.50	1.00	2.00	—	—
	Wood ashes	—	2.00	5.00	23.00	—
	Oak leaves	0.80	0.40	0.20	—	—
	Maple leaves	0.50	0.10	0.50	—	—

5 pounds of potassium.

Manufacturers make up different formulations depending on use. A good general fertilizer suitable for spring fertilizing might be 5-10-5 or 10-10-10. A fertilizer meant for potatoes might have the formulation of 0-20-20, and one meant especially for tomatoes might be low in nitrogen, high in phosphorus and medium in potassium, such as 5-10-5.

The following nitrogen materials are also used by home gardeners: ammonium sulfate, ammonium nitrite, urea sulfate, ammonium nitrate, nitrate of soda, ammonium phosphate and calcium nitrate.

Sidedressing

In order to achieve optimum growth, many crops, such as asparagus, corn, and tomatoes, need additional amounts of nitrogen in the form of ammonium nitrate during the season. (See Figure 2.17 for amounts and times.) Do not allow fertilizer to come into contact with plant leaves and stems. Apply ammonium nitrate in a band along the side of the row or around transplanted crops, 4 to 6 inches away. Water lightly if rain is not expected.

Application of dried fertilizers

If you have not tested your soil you can apply a general fertilizer containing nitrogen, phosphorus (P205) and soluble potash (K20), rather than a specific analysis for each vegetable. These three grades give excellent results with most garden crops: 6-12-12, 10-10-10 and 5-10-15.

You can either broadcast the fertilizer before planting and work it into the soil or apply it in bands at seeding time. If you broadcast the fertilizer, work it into the soil fairly soon, either mechanically or by

Figure 2.14
How to sow seeds

A triangular how works well for digging a straight furrow.

Tap the seeds out of the packet. When the seedlings appear, thin to the correct spacing. Large seeds can be placed in the bottom of the furrow in groups of two, at the recommended spacing.

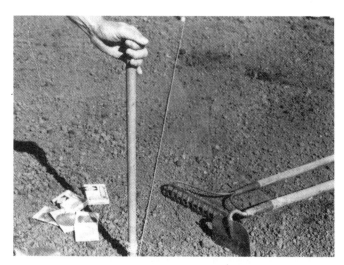

Preparing the seed bed is very important for good germination. Loosen the soil and rake smooth to pulverize and level the surface soil. Use two poles and some twine to mark the row and to use as a guide for straight sowing.

A gentle tapping of the soil with the back of a how will help to ensure soil/seed contact. Follow with a gentle watering, keeping the soil moist until the seeds germinate.

Credit: National Garden Bureau, Inc.

hand.

To band a fertilizer, first determine where you are going to plant the seeds or plants. Mark the row with a small furrow or a string tied from one end of the row to another. Dig a shallow trench 2 to 4 inches to one side of the row and 2 to 4 inches below where the seed is to be placed. Place the fertilizer in the bottom of the trench and cover it with soil.

SELECTED SOIL AND pH TEST KITS

LaMOTTE CHEMICAL PRODUCTS COMPANY, P.O. Box 329, Chestertown, MD 21620, offers many sophisticated test kits including greenhouse, hydroponic, and complete nutrient test outfits. LaMotte can be reached by phone at 1-800-344-3100 (778-3100 in state).

The Importance of a Guide for Your Garden

- **Avoids Hidden Hunger:** Visible symptoms of nutrient deficiency indicate severe starvation. Plant health and productivity begin to deteriorate long before symptoms appear.
- **Maximizes Productivity:** Properly nourished plants are more resistant to disease, drought and inclement weather. Plants require nutrients throughout all stages of growth. Periodic soil testing enables the gardener to monitor changing soil conditions.
- **Greater Economy:** By determining specific soil nutrient requirements you can make more efficient use of fertilizer additions. A soil test also allows the gardener to evaluate mineral levels in the soil.

The following kits are best suited for the home gardener:-

Model B, Code 5803: A basic test kit for pH that will determine the alkaline, neutral or acidic nature of soil and whether lime or alum is required to adjust soil to the proper pH level. The color developed in the test tube is compared with a laminated color chart.

Model EL Code 5679: Offers accurate analysis of pH and three basic macronutrients using simplified test methods. Graduated plastic test tubes are used for measurment of the soil sample and reagent solutions. All results are compared to standards on laminated color charts.

Model EM Code 5934: Tests for pH, nitrogen, phosphorus and potassium. This kit is for the analyst who requires a greater number of tests on a larger sized plot of land.

LaMotte Soil Handbook: This handbook offers an excellent discussion of soils, macronutrients, micronutrients, trace nutrients, the pH prefereence of a wide number of plants and a glossary of soil terms and more.

Figure 2.15

PLANT FOOD ABC'S

Properly balanced feeding is as vital to all living plant life, particularly young newly established growth. Federal and State regulations require that every package of plant food state plainly the number of contained units of plant food and their origin. The numbers you find on fertilizer containers refer to the percentage of nitrogen (N), phosphorus (P), and postasium (K). The following: 4-8-4, 5-5-5, 5-10-10, 6-10-4, 7-7-7, 8-10-4 and 10-6-4 are field and garden proved, balanced formulations, each providing the minimum necessary 15 units of plant food.

Figure 2.16

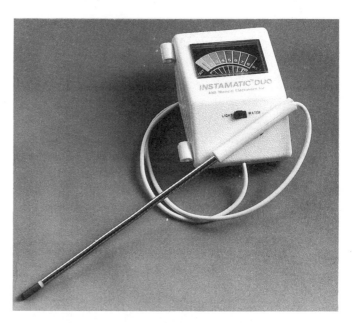

Instamatic Duo-Plant light and water meter

Use this electronic meter to test for moisture and light. The moisture reading is obtained from the tip of the probe, at root level. Gives a precise numerical reading which correlates with the watering requirements of a list of plants. The light meter uses a solenoid photocell and built-in chromatic filter to measure whether the plants are receiving the correct quality as well as quantity of light.

LUSTER LEAF PRODUCTS, INC.
P.O. Box 1067
Crystal Lake, IL 60014

SOURCES OF SOIL ADDITIVES

Bark

BOISE CASCADE
Wood Products Division
P.O. Box 50
Boise, ID 83707

GREENLIFE PRODUCTS, INC.
142 Lee St.
West Point, VA 23181

MEAD PAYGRO
P.O. Box 221
Dayton, OH

Chemicals

LEFFINGWELL CHEMICAL
COMPANY
111 S. Berry St.
Brea, CA 92611

Gypsum

AMERICAN PELLETIZING
CORP.
P.O. Box 3628
Des Moines, IA 50322

BANDINI FERTILIZER
4139 Bandini Blvd.
Los Angeles CA 90023

BENWOOD LIMESTONE
P.O. Box 68
Benwood WV 26031

LESCO, INC.
20005 Lake Rd.
Rocky River, OH 44116

LIMESTONE PRODUCTS
CORP.
P.O. Box 217
Sparks, NJ 07871

OLD DUTCH MATERIALS CO.
350 Pingston Rd.
Northbrook, IL 60062

PAX CO.
580 W. 1300 St.
Salt Lake City, UT 84115

UNITED STATES GYPSUM
COMPANY
101 S. Wacker Drive
Chicago, IL 60606

Limestone

AMERICAN PELLETIZING
CORP.
P.O. Box 3628
Des Moines, IA 50322

BENWOOD LIMESTONE
P.O. Box 68
Benwood, WV 26031

BROWN GOLD FLORAL
SUPPLY
50 E. 25th St.
Paterson, NJ 07514

CHIPMAN, INC.
400 Jones Rd.
Stoney Creek, Ont.
Canada L8G3Z1

DRAGON CHEMICAL CORP.
P.O. Box 7311
Roanoke, VA 24019

GOOD EARTH ORGANICS
CORP.
5960 Broadway
Lancaster, NY 14086

JAMES RIVER LIMESTONE
CO.
P.O. Drawer 617
Buchanan, VA 24066

KOOS, INC.
4500 13th Ct.
Kenosha, WI 53140

H. LILLY, CHASE CO.
7737 N.E. Killingsworth
Portland, OR 97218

LUTTRELL MINING CO.
P.O. Box 11705
Knoxville, TN 37919

ROBINSON FERTILIZER CO.
1460 N Red Gum
Anaheim, CA 92806

SUNNILAND CORP.
P.O. Box 1687
Sanford FL 32771

Mineral Soil Conditioners

SET PRODUCTS INC.
23700 Chagrin Blvd.
Freeway Dr.
Cleveland, OH 44122

Packaged Cow Manures

GREENLIFE PRODUCTS INC.
West Point, VA 23181

Peat Moss

ASB GREENWORLD LTD.
Pointe Sapin, Kent C.O.
Canada E0A2A0

ANCO PRODUCTS
P.O. Box 24343
Dayton, OH 45424

ATKINS & DUBROW
P.O. Box 55
Port Colborne, Ont.
Canada L3K5V7

BANDINI FERTILIZER
4139 Bandini Blvd.
Los Angeles, CA 90023

BLACK MAGIC PRODUCTS
8137 Elder Creek Rd.
Sacramento, CA 95824

CHEEK GARDEN PRODUCTS,
INC.
2035 Shadywood Lane
Shreveport, LA 71105

COLBY, ELL CO.
P.O. Box 248
Lake Mills, IA 50450

DESCHENES & MARTIN LTD.
212 Queen St.
Suite 401
Fredericton, NB
Canada E3B1A8

CONRAD FAFARD, INC.
P.O. Box 3033
Springfield MA D1101

GOOD EARTH ORGANIC
CORP.
5960 Broadway
Lancaster, NY 14086

GREENLIFE PRODUCTS CO.
P.O. Box 72
West Point, VA 23181

THE HEFFLIN CO.
P.O. Box 1485
Rockville, MD 20850

A.H. HOFFMAN INC.
Landsville, PA 17538

LEONI'S POWER-O-PEAT
Box 958
Gilbert, MN 55741

MICHIGAN PEAT CO.
Box 66388
Houston, TX 77006

VALLEY ENTERPRISE
7009 Taylorsville Rd.
Dayton, OH 45404

WEGRO
P.O. Box 288
Grand Rapids, OH 43522

J.M. WERLING & SONS
2800 E. 13th
Kansas City, MO 64127

Perlite

CAREFREE GARDEN
PRODUCTS
Box 383
West Chicago, IL 60185

GRACE HORTICULTURAL
PRODUCTS
W.R. Grace Co.
62 Whitemore Ave.
Cambridge, MA 02140

LEONI'S POWER-O-PEAT
P.O. Box 956
Gilbert, MN 55741

WHITTEMORE PERLITE CO.,
INC.
79 Beacon Lawrence
MA 02140

Vermiculite-Terralite

GRACE HORTICULTURAL
PRODUCTS
W.R. Grace Co.
62 Whitmore Ave.
Cambridge, MA 02140

LEONI'S POWER-O-PEAT
Box 956
Gilbert, MN 55741

MICHIGAN PEAT CO.
P.O. Box 66388
Houston, TX 77006

SOURCES OF LIQUID FERTILIZERS

ASB GREENWORLD LTD.
Pointe Sapin, Kent C.O.
Canada E0A 2A0

AGRO-K CORP
1401 NE Marshall St.
Minneapolis, MN 55413

AQUA 10 CORP
P.O. Box 818
West Beaufort Rd.
Beaufort, NC 28516

BIO CHEMICAL, R & D
210 Eye St.
Harlington, TX 78554

BLACK MAGIC PRODUCTS
8137 Elder Creed Rd.
Sacramento, CA 95824

BONIDE CHEMICAL CO., INC.
2 Wurz Ave.
Yorkville, NY 13495

BRANDT CHEMICAL CO.,
INC.
P.O. Box 277
Pleasant Plains, IL 62677

BRIT-TECH CORP
P.O. Box 1130
Britt, IA 50423

H.D. CAMPBELL, CO.
238 N Main
Rochelle, IL 61068

CLAREL LABORATORIES,
INC.
513 Grove
Deerfield, IL 60015

CHACON CHEMICAL CO.
2600 Yates Ave.
City of Commerce,
CA 90040

CHEVRON CHEMICAL CO.
Ortho Consumer Products
Div
575 Market St.
San Francisco, CA 94105

CHIPMAN, INC.
400 Jones Road
Stoney Creek, Ont.
Canada L8G 3Z1

DEXOL INDUSTRIES
1450 W. 228th St.
Torrance, CA 90501

THE FARNAM COMPANIES,
INC.
301 W Osborn Rd.
Phoenix, AZ 85002

GERMAIN'S, INC.
4820 E. 50th St.
Los Angeles, CA 90058

GOOD EARTH ORGANICS
CORP.
5960 Broadway
Lancaster, N.Y. 14086

GRACE HORTICULTURAL
PRODUCTS
W.R., Grace Co.
62 Whittmore Ave.
Cambridge, MA 02140

HETTICH MFG CO.
P.O. Box 157
Dousman, WI 53118

HORTOPAPER GROWING
SYSTEMS
4111 N. Motel Dr.
Suite 101
Fresno, CA 90711

HY-TROUS CORP.
3 Green St.
P.O. Box 299
Woodburn, MA 01801

LESCO, INC.
20005 Lake Rd.
Rocky River, OH 44116

H. LILLY, CHASE CO.
7737 N.E. Killingsworth
Portland, OR 97218

MINNTRALIA MFG INC.
P.O. Box 135
Garfield MN 56332

NACCO AGRICULTURAL
CHEMICALS NATIONAL
RESEARCH & CHEMICAL
CO.
14439 S. Avalon Blvd.
Gardena, CA 90248

PARROTT AGRO
INDUSTRIES, INC.
16 Sunnyside Ave.
Stamford, CT 06902

PLANT RESEARCH LABS
P.O. Box 18498
Irvine, CA 92713

RA-PID-GRO CORP
575 Market St.
San Francisco, CA 94105

RINGER CORP
9959 Valley View Rd.
Eden Prairie, MN 55344

ROSS DANIELS, INC.
P.O. Box 66430
West Des Moines, IA 50265

SUDBURY LABORATORY,
INC.
6 October Hill Rd.
Hilltop, MA 01746

WR RESEARCH
7 Commercial Blvd.
Novato, CA 94947

ZOOK & RANK, INC.
Rt 1 Box 243
Gap, PA 17527

Figure 2.17

SIDEDRESSING FERTILIZER — AMOUNTS AND TIMES

Vegetable Crop	Oz per 10 ft. row, Ammonium Nitrate 33-0-0	Time of Application
Asparagus	3½	Before growth begins in spring
Beans and peas	1½	After heavy bloom and set of pods
Beets, carrots, sweet potatoes, watermelon	None	Sidedressing of nitrogen not needed
Broccoli, cabbage, cauliflower	1½	Three weeks after transplanting
Cantaloupe, cucumber	1½	One week after blossoming begins
Corn	1½	When plants are 12-18 inches tall
Eggplant, peppers	1½	After the first fruit sets
Kale, mustard, spinach, turnip greens	1½	When plants are about a third grown
Lettuce, parsnips, turnips	1½	Two weeks after transplanting, four weeks after sowing seed
Onion (mature)	1½	One to two weeks after bulb formation
Potato	2½	After tuber formation starts
Tomato	1½	One to two weeks before first tomato ripens

SOURCES OF DRY FERTILIZERS

ACME-BURGESS, INC.
Rt 83
Graystake, IL 60030

ACME MFG CO.
P.O. Drawer Z
Filier, ID 83328

AGRICHEM, INC.
P.O. Box 237
Ft Lupton, CO 80621

AMERICAN PELLETIZING
CORP.
P.O. Box 3628
Des Moines, IA 50322

ANCO PRODUCTS
P.O. Box 24343
Dayton, OH 45424

THE ANDERSON
P.O. Box 119
Maumee, OH 43537

BANDINI FERTILIZER
4139 Bandini Blvd.
Los Angeles, CA 90023

BONIDE CHEMICAL CO., INC.
2 Wurz Ave.
Yorkville, N.Y. 13495

BROWN GOLD SOIL CORP.
50 E. 25th St.
Paterson, NJ 07514

H.D. CAMPBELL, CO.
402-410 Dewey Ave.
Rochelle, IL 61066

CAREFREE GARDEN
PRODUCTS
P.O. Box 27
West Chicago, IL 60185

CHEVRON CHEMICAL CO.
Ortho Consumer Products
Div.
575 Market St.
San Francisco, CA 94105

CHIPMAN, INC.
400 Jones Rd.
Stoney Creek, Ont
Canada L8G 3Z1

DEXOL INDUSTRIES
1450 228 St.
Torrance, CA 90501

DRAGON CHEMICAL CORP.
P.O. Box 7311
Roanoke, VA 24019

ESPOMA CO.
6 Espoma Rd.
Milville, NJ 08332

GARDEN RESOURCES, INC.
P.O. Box 2537
Garnada Hills, CA 91344

GARFIELD-WILLIAMSON,
INC.
1072 West Side Ave.
Jersey City, NJ 07360

GROW FORCE FERTILIZER,
INC.
P.O. Box 3445
Bellevue, WA 98009

A.H. HOFFMAN, INC.
Landsville, PA 17538

INTERNATIONAL SPIKE, INC.
P.O. Box 1750
Lexington, KY 40593

KAISER AGRICULTURAL
CHEMICALS
P.O. Box 246
Savannah, GA 31402

LESCO, INC.
20005 Box 956
Rocky River, OH 44116

H. LILLY, CHASE CO.
7737 NE Killingsworth
Portland, OR 97218

ROD MCLELLAN CO.
1450 El Camino Real
S. San Francisco, CA 94080

NACCO AGRICULTURAL
CHEMICALS NATIONAL
RESEARCH & CHEMICAL
CO.
14439 S. Avalon Blvd.
Gardena, CA 90248

NUTRI-SOL CHEMICAL CO.,
INC.
P.O. Box 15124
Tampa, FL 33684

PARKER FERTILIZER CO.,
INC.
P.O. Box 540
Sylacauga, AL 35150

PAX CO.
580 W. 13th St.
Salt Lake City, UT 84115

PLANTABBS CORP.
P.O. Box 397
Timonium MD 21093

PRONTO PLANT FOOD, INC.
P.O. Drawer V
Wisner, LA 71378

RIGO CO.
P.O. Box 89
Buckner, KY 40010

ROCKLAND CHEMICAL CO.,
INC.
P.O. Box 809
W Caldwell NJ 07006

SCHULTZ CO.
11730 Northline Blvd.
St. Louis, MO 63043

SEA-BORN, INC.
2000 Rockford Rd.
Charles City, IA 50616

SIERRA CHEMICAL CO.
1001 Yosemite Dr.
Milpitas, CA 95035

TEX-GRO FERTILIZER CO.
P.O. Box 1712
Pecos, TX 79772

USS AGRI-CHEMICALS DIV.
P.O. Box 1685
Atlanta, GA 30321

Figure 2.18

Vegetables fall into three categories with regard to their fertilizer requirements. If you have a large garden, you can group vegetables according to their requirements. This makes fertilizing easier.

VEGETABLE FERTILIZER REQUIREMENTS

HEAVY FEEDERS	MEDIUM FEEDERS	LIGHT FEEDERS	VERY LIGHT FEEDERS
Artichoke	Asparagus	Beet	Southern Peas
Cabbage	Beans	Carrots	
Celery	Broccoli	Radishes	
Onion	Cantaloupe	Rutabaga	
Sweet potato	Cauliflower	Turnip	
Tomato	Corn		
	Cucumber		
	Eggplant		
	Herbs		
	Kale		
	Mustard		
	Okra		
	Peas		
	Pumpkin		
	Rhubarb		
	Swiss Chard		
	Watermelon		

Beans and Peas help improve soil fertility. The bacteria living in the nodules on the roots of legumes take soil nitrogen in unusable forms and combine it with sugars from the legumes to produce ammonia, a nitrogen compound that plants can use. Legumes actually conserve and restore soil.

3. Organic Gardening

THE MOST IMPORTANT FEATURES of organic gardening are related to care of the soil and management of pests. In some ways these two subjects are intertwined, based on the following set of facts: healthy plants resist insects and disease better than unhealthy plants; one of the best ways to grow plants is to take good care of the garden soil; and to maintain the soil in excellent condition, it must be supplied with nutrients found in such organic matter as compost.

Soil care is the main topic of this chapter. Since mulching is an important aspect of soil care, especially in organic gardening, that subject is also covered here. Chapter 8 (Pest Management) deals with bugs, diseases weeds and other garden plagues in detail.

ORGANIC SOIL CARE

Reduced to its basics, organic gardening is a system of maintaining the soil's fertility by replenishing it, not with chemicals, but with organic materials in the form of humus and compost. Organic gardening stays true to the natural life cycle in which soil, water, plants and animal life all work in harmony, one having a part in the nourishment of the others.

When decomposed plant and animal remains are returned to the earth, they help produce healthy soil structure and good aeration. This in turn results in good drainage and water and nutrient retention. Plants thrive in this environment, with the oxygen present in the loose soil structure being used by the microorganisms therein to burn organic matter, releasing carbon dioxide and nutrients needed by plants.

Organic gardening is almost as old as the earth itself. Our current system, however, was developed early in the twentieth century by Sir Albert Howard, an English agricultural expert working in India. It was not until the 1940s that this system reached the United States, introduced by Jerome I. Rodale. He attracted a loyal group of followers who believed in the importance of good soil.

DEVELOPING GOOD SOIL

A soil in which vegetables can thrive generally contains solid matter and pore space in approximately equal measure. Moisture should occupy about half the pore space, air the other half. Most of the sold matter, about 43 to 45 percent of the entire soil makeup, should be mineral; the rest of the solid matter (5 to 7 percent of the soil composition) should be animal and vegetable organic material.

Most garden soils start out being either too sandy or too clayish. Sand has too much air, clay too little, and both lack organic material. When this deficiency is corrected by the addition of compost or similar material, the soil becomes a rich source of nutrients for plants.

Organic matter is composed of a number of elements, most particularly carbon and nitrogen. Bacteria in the soil use the nitrogen in breaking down the carbon. This bacterial action proceeds normally when the ratio of carbon to nitrogen is about ten to one. When the organic material is higher in carbon and lower in nitrogen, the bacteria 'borrow nitrogen from the soil, depriving the growing plants. A symptom of this is yellowing of leaves.

There are several ways to avoid this problem. For one thing, you can add nitrogen to the soil, perhaps in the form of manure, at the same time as you are adding nitrogen-poor organic matter. Or you can add organic material to the soil before you plant, so that any carbon/nitrogen imbalance will have been corrected by the time you're ready to plant. Perhaps the best method of all—and the one used by millions of gardeners—is to make compost outside the soil, in a separate bin or pile. The organic material is then broken down before it is turned into the soil.

Compost

Organic waste that has been allowed—in some cases, encouraged—to decay is called compost. When you put compost into your soil, your plants can immediately make use of the nutrients it contains.

There are a number of ways you can obtain compost. You can make it yourself, in a large pile, in a bin or a can, or in a commercial unit manufactured for the purpose. In addition, ready-made compost can be purchased in sacks from nurseries and garden-supply stores.

Making your own compost is a fairly simple matter. First, every garden produces quite a bit of waste—leaves, decaying plants, weeds, hedge trimmings, and so on. Second, every kitchen produces suitable compost material, such as vegetable and fruit scraps, eggshells, coffee grinds, and the like (but don't use meat, fat, bones, etc.). Instead of throwing away all of this garbage, tote it all to one corner of the yard, which you plan to devote to your compost pile.

There are several ways of constructing a compost pile or bin, just as there are various recipes favored by gardeners in different parts of the country. Before discussing them, we should consider the five basic principles of decomposition, the process of nature that is at the heart of composting:

1. The smaller the particle size, the faster, generally speaking, the rate of decomposition, because bacteria can attack more surface area more quickly. If the leaves, stems and other materials are shredded into small pieces before being added to the compost pile, they'll decay quicker and be ready sooner.
2. The bacteria in the pile need nitrogen. Too much organic material (carbon) in proportion to the available nitrogen will slow the bacteria and the speed of decomposition. Evidence of this will be poor heat production in the compost pile. You can correct this by adding nitrogen in the form of fresh manure or blood meal here and there throughout the pile.
3. A compost pile must heat up for good bacterial action to occur. The degree of heat depends on the size of the pile. If the pile isn't high enough, it will lose heat and bacterial action will slow down. Too high a pile is also bad because it will then be compressed, shutting off too much of the air supply to the bacteria.
4. Every pile needs moisture for decomposition to take place. A moisture content of 40 to 50 percent is about right; more than this cuts down on the oxygen available to the bacteria. You can keep your pile at about the right moisture level by making sure that it remains about as wet as a squeezed-out wet sponge. Just put your hand in the pile and feel (watch out, however, for it can be really hot—about 130 to 160 degrees F). If it doesn't seem moist enough, just add water with a hose until it reaches the right

consistency.
5. A compost pile also needs turning. Using a manure fork or a shovel, turn it so that the top and side

Figure 3-01

COMMON COMPOSTING PROBLEMS

Lack of moisture

This is the most common problem in starting and maintaining a compost pile. Piles tend to dry out during hot, sunny weather. Without adequate moisture microorganisms cease to function and decompostion stops. Add water whenever moisture is less than a squeezed-out sponge.

Unpleasant odors

When the pile has been overwatered and packed too tightly, oxygen is unable to penetrate and aerobic microbes are unable to function. Anaerobic micro organisms take over, causing unpleasant fermentation odors. Do not 'stomp down' materials when added. A working pile will shrink naturally from the addition of water and the activity of microorganisms. Compaction can also result from using all fine materials. Mix coarse materials with fine. A compost pile that develops an unpleasant odor should be turned over and aerated.

Overwatering

An overwatered pile will compact and not allow air to penetrate. This condition encourages anaerobic bacterial activity and fermentation odors.

Improperly activated pile

Microorganisms cause decomposition. If the pile is not properly activated with a broad spectrum of microbes, decomposition will be slow. If your pile doesn't seem to be decomposing, add a compost booster.

Freeze-up

Small home compost piles freeze in winter and are slow to get started in the spring. Microbes become inactive below 40° F. In order to start up the pile faster in the spring, add one cup of sugar and mix into the pile by turning over the surface material.

Figure 3-02

MAIL ORDER ORGANIC SUPPLIERS

Products	Source*
Bio Organic Boosters	TWI
Electric garden shredders	PAR
Compost Maker	PIN
Garden Green Manure	STO
Composters	BUR, HEN, PAR, STO
Natural Plant Foods	BUR, JOH, HEN
Organic Legume-Aid	TWI
Organic Soil Conditioners	JUN, MEY, LET, LIB
Sea Weed Products	NIC, PIN, STO, LIB

*See Figure 13.01, Chapter 13 for catalog names

materials become the center. This allows air penetration and also brings raw matter to the center when more action is taking place.

When finished, or 'ripe', the materials placed in the compost pile will have been converted into a crumbly brown substance with the fragrance of good earth. It's then ready to use. The volume of organic materials will have decreased. As decomposition proceeds, most piles shrink to about half their original size.

Building a Compost Pile

You should develop an individual approach to compost-making based on how much space you have, how much compost you need for the garden bed, and how elaborate a layout you're inclined to construct. As a guide, following are five different approaches to setting up a compost pile, using a range of devices from a simple plastic bag to a permanent group of bins.

Plastic bag compost:

1. Buy a dark-colored plastic bag, the kind used to line 20- or 30-gallon garbage cans.
2. Inside, put a 2-inch layer of soil or peat moss.
3. Add randomly any kind of waste kitchen materials (as noted before) and maybe occasionally garden wastes.
4. When full, set the bag out in full sunlight for about three weeks. The compost will then be ready to use.

Garbage can method:

1. Buy a galvanized garbage can (a 20- or 30-gallon size), and punch several small holes in the bottom. Put the can up on a few bricks, and place a pan underneath to catch any liquid that might drain from the moisture contained in the decaying garbage that you will be adding.
2. Put a 3-inch layer of soil or peat moss on the inside bottom of the can.
3. If you like, buy some red worms—the fishing kind—and add them to the soil at the bottom.
4. Add 2 to 3 inches of kitchen garbage, then a 2-inch layer of grass clippings and leaves, another layer of kitchen garbage, a layer of grass clippings and leaves, and so on until the can is full.
5. Put the lid on the can. The ripe compost will be ready in about 3 or 4 months. If you start the can in the fall, the compost will be ready to add to your garden by spring. (You don't have to worry about the moisture content of this kind of pile, nor does it need to be turned.)

Conventional compost pile:

1. Clear off a 5- or 6-foot square ground area.
2. On top of the cleared area put down a 6-inch layer of fairly coarse material—twigs, brush, a few corn stalks, sunflower stalks, and so on. This provides ventilation underneath the pile.
3. Start building the main body of the heap in layers. Put down a 6-inch layer of waste vegetation—grass clippings, leaves, weeds, vegetable remains, organic garbage, and so on. On top of this greenery, add

a 2-inch layer of fresh manure. (You can also add rock phosphate and a thin layer of limestone to improve bacterial action and hasten the decomposition.)
4. For every two or three layers of vegetation (and manure), add a 1-inch layer of soil. This soil contains bacteria that will help break down the organic material. Now wet down the pile until it is just moist, not saturated.
5. Repeat this procedure until the pile reaches a height of about 5 feet.
6. When finished, add a thin covering of soil to the pile to help seal in the moisture. You must also keep air flowing throughout the pile in order to keep bacterial action high; take a stick or thin pole and punch vertical holes from the top of the pile, reaching all the way to the bottom. Make the holes 2 to 3 feet apart.
7. Always keep the moisture content of the pile at 40 to 60 percent—about the consistency, as we've said, of a squeezed-out wet sponge. Check the moisture by feeling inside the pile with your hand, and then add water whenever necessary. Watering may be required every 4 to 5 days in hot weather.
8. Except for watering, let the pile sit undisturbed for two to three weeks. Then turn it, putting the material from the top and sides into the middle. Turn it again at three-week intervals. When the inside materials turn brownish and crumble on touch, you can be sure that the compost is ready for your garden. This usually takes 3½ to four months.

The University of California quick method: In 1953, the University of California at the Organic Experimental Farm developed a composting method that's just great for the impatient because the compost is ready in just 14 days. The decomposition is speeded up by shredding the materials and mixing them all together so that the bacteria have many surfaces to work on at once.

1. Mix together one part fresh manure and two parts other compost ingredients (leaves, grass clippings, cut-up corn stalks, table scraps, and so on). You can obtain fresh manure from a local riding stable. It must be fresh, not processed.
2. Using a rotary lawnmower, shred everything completely. (You have to catch the shreddings in a grass bag, naturally.) Just put down a small pile of waste and run the lawnmower over it. Then put down another pile and repeat the process. Better yet, use a power shredder. Either way, the material must be shredded into very small particles for this method to work well.
3. Mix everything together, and form the mixture into a 4 x 6 foot heap, four feet high.
4. By the second or third day, the middle of the pile should have heated up to around 130 to 160° F. If it hasn't, add more manure.
5. Turn the heap on the fourth day. Make sure it's warm and moist. Simply put your hand inside, but watch for the heat. If it isn't moist to the touch, (again, about like a squeezed-out wet sponge) add water.
6. Turn the heap again on the seventh day.

7. Turn it once more on the tenth day. The heap should now have started to cool off, for it's almost ready.
8. It's ready on the fourteenth day. It won't look like fine humus, but the materials will have broken down into a dark, rich, fairly crumbly substance. You can let it rot further if you wish, or you can use it in your garden right away.

Compost bins: You can make a good compost bin with a few boards. Twelve planks of boards—each 12 inches wide, 1 inch thick and 30 inches long— will work fine. Take four of the boards and nail them together to make a frame or bottomless box. Using the remaining boards, make two more frames. You then set one frame on the ground and stack the other two on top to make a tall bin. Next, just chop up the whole material with your lawnmower and load the shredded matter into the bin. You then proceed, using whatever composting method suits you—either 'The Big, Conventional Pile' or 'The University of California Quick Method.'

You can multiply your bins easliy by taking off the top tier after the compost has sunk below its level. Place it on the ground beside the original, now lower, bin and start to fill it with new materials for compost. As the compost in the first bin subsides some more, you should be able to take the second tier of the frame off and place it on top of your fledgling second bin, then, by building one new tier, form another.

A compost bin actually can be made from almost anything. Just make it about 3 feet high and about 2½ feet square. A neighbor of ours nailed four window screens together with a screen over the top to keep out flies. Let your imagination run!

Figure 3-03

Commercial composters

Can-type composters come in a variety of shapes. These four turn out ripe compost in as little as four weeks.

Figure 3.04

COMPOSTING SYSTEMS

These three types of compost makers add a broad spectrum of microorganisms to your compost pile:-

Brown leaf compost maker

Works in 20 to 60 days to turn brown leaves into rich humus containing basic nutrients in a form readily usable by your plants.

Grass clippings compost maker

Works in 10 to 30 days to turn grass clippings into rich, moist humus. Allow nutrients in grass clippings to be returned to the soil rather than to be bagged and disposed of.

Compost plus

Developed for use with hard-to-compost materials such as sawdust, wood chips, pine needles, twigs and pine cones. Works in 60 to 90 days.

COMMERCIAL COMPOST MAKERS

There are basically three types of commercial compost-makers on the market: bins; upright, canlike containers; revolving drums.

Bins: These are usually three to four feet high, constructed of plastic or wire mesh. Two recent models to have been introduced are made with aluminum corner posts and wood or aluminum cross-pieces. Odorless compost is removed from the bottom.

Upright cans: These round, canlike containers made of heavy plastic come in many variations. **The Soilsaver** compost bin is made of polyethylene with thermal insulated walls and a translucent plastic top that is engineered to trap the soil heat. To use, just lift the top and add food waste, grass clippings, leaves and weeds. The finished compost comes out the bottom in four to eight weeks.

The Grass Eater is a heavy, U.V. stabilized polyethylene can-type designed to turn grass-clippings into compost in about eight weeks. This composter snaps together and, using an add-on kit and a leaf-eater activator, allows you to compost fall leaves. **The Rotocrop** has individual sliding panels with round holes for ventilation. This container is fed from the top, and finished humus is taken from the bottom. A good feature of a can like the Rotocrop is that it doesn't have to be filled all at one time. "Start with at least 12 inches of materials," the company says, to provide enough bulk for heating up. Thereafter add materials at least once a week whenever you have collected enough materials for a 2- to 3-inch layer. Ultimately, you can add fresh material at the top, remove mature compost at the bottom. You can buy models that will produce 21 feet of compost.

Drums: These are simply drums with turning handles and vents to allow air to enter. The tumbler is filled with shredded material (shred with a rotary type lawnmower, catching in a bag or a shredder/grinder); flanges inside ensure that compost tumbles as it is rotated (one to five times a day). This turning and shredding speeds up decomposition to about fourteen days. These are not as popular as they once were.

Other essential equipment includes:

- **A compost tool**. This is a long tube with four inch blades on the end that close as you insert them into the compost, open as you withdraw. As you pull the blades out they turn and aerate the pile.
- **A handy-hoop bag**. This comes with a lock-on ring which holds a plastic bag for collection of garden refuse for composting.
  Contact:
  D.F.S., INC.
  P.O. Box 103,
  Scotch Plains, NJ 07076.
- **Ringer's Compost Maker.** This contains high concentrations of selected microorganisms that charge the compost pile and accelerate decomposition. There are several different types: Brown Leaf Compost Booster—for speeding up decomposition of brown leaves; Grass Clippings Compost Booster—for grass and other green materials; Compost Plus—for twigs, wood chips, hay, straw and other difficult materials; and Compost Pile Recharger—to speed up and 'recharge' composting after winter dormancy.
  Contact:
  RINGER CORP.
  9959 Valley View Rd.
  Eden Prairie, MN 55344

Other organic nutrients

Many organic gardeners feed their plants other organic nutrients, in addition to compost, to improve vegetable growth. Such waste materials as peanut hulls, seaweed, manures, cottonseed meal and wood ashes are good sources of the basic nutrients plants need. As explained previously, the three most important elements for healthy plants are nitrogen, phosphorus and potassium. The following are major sources of these nutrients, most readily available to organic gardeners:-

Nitrogen:
- Blood meal is 7 to 15 percent nitrogen and can be applied in liquid form.
- Cottonseed meal is 6 to 9 percent nitrogen and is especially good for acid-loving plants.
- Fish meal and fish emulsion contain up to 10 percent nitrogen, along with some phosphorus.
- Activated sewage sludge, the solid product of sewage treatment, is high in nitrogen and provides a wealth of trace elements.

Phosphorus:
- Bone meal is 22 to 35 percent phosphoric acid, also containing up to 5 percent nitrogen.
- Phosphate rock is a finely ground rock powder that is about 30 percent acid and many trace elements.

Potassium:
- Granite dust is about 8 percent potash and may contain trace elements.
- Ashes of hardwood contain about 10 percent potash; of soft wood, about 5 percent.

Animal manures

Many animal manures are moderately rich in nitrogen, phosphorus and potassium. However, they are not as potent as chemical fertilizers. Generally,

Figure 3.05
Leaf Eater
The Vorando Leaf Eater shreds leaves wet or dry as fast as they can be loaded into the bushel-sized hopper. Shreads leaves down to one tidy bundle. Use for composting or as a fall garden mulch.
VORANDO POWER PRODUCTS, INC.
386 Park Ave. South
New York, NY 10016

Figure 3.06

IMPROVING SOIL WITH FALL LEAVES

Rather than throw away or burn fall leaves, collect them with a sweeper-shredder or a power lawnmower with a lawnmower bag, You can then:-

1. Sheet compost by tilling the leaves into the garden soil with a rotary tiller. If you till the leaves into the soil in the fall, they will be decomposed by spring. Sprinkle fertilizer (10-5-5) over the leaves at thje rate of about 10 to 15 pounds per 1,000 square feet of garden. The nitrogen will feed the decay organisms.

2. Compost in a heap using one of the methods described above. A compost starter will help speed up the process. Work into the soil in the spring.

HANDY-HOOP

Keeps plastic bags open. Good base for rain cover.

Figure 3.09 ▶

Handy-Hoop

Handy-Hoop is a metal hoop that is easily snapped into a large 3 to 4mm plastic bag. It comes in handy for picking up leaves and garden waste to dump into the compost. The bag is held open for easy refilling every time.

D.F.S., INC.
P.O. Box 103
Scotch Plains, NJ 07076

Figure 3.07

COMPOSITION OF ANIMAL MANURES

Manure Type	%N	%P205	%K20	%Ca	%MG
Fresh Cattle	0.53	0.29	0.48	0.29	0.11
Fresh Chicken	0.89	0.48	0.83	0.38	0.13
Fresh Horse	0.55	0.27	0.57	0.27	0.11
Fresh Sheep	0.89	0.48	0.83	0.21	0.13
Fresh Swine	0.63	0.46	0.41	0.19	0.03
Dried Cattle	2.00	1.80	2.20	—	—
Dried Sheep	1.40	1.00	3.00	—	—

Figure 3.08

COMPOSITION OF COMPOST

Compost Material	Nitrogen %N	Phosphorus %P205	Potassium (Potash) %K20
Banana skins (ash)	—	3.25	41.76
Cantalope Rings	—	9.77	12.21
Cattail reeds	2.00	0.81	3.43
Coffee grounds	2.08	0.32	0.28
Corncob ash	—	—	50.00
Corn stalks, leaves	0.30	0.13	0.33
Eggs, rotten	2.25	0.40	0.15
Feathers	15.30	—	—
Fish scraps	2.0-7.5	1.5-6.0	—
Grapefruit skins	—	3.58	3C.60
Oak leaves	0.46	0.35	0.21
Pine needles	4.15	0.12	0.03
Tea grounds	4.15	0.62	0.40
Wood ashes	—	1.00	4.0-10.00

you should use rotted manure, not fresh. The bacteria in your soil will need extra nitrogen to break down fresh manure and may divert some of the nitrogen from your plants. Moreover, like organic materials that have been composted, manure that has already rotted or decomposed is in a form your plants can use more easily. You can obtain rotted manure by placing fresh manure in a pile, covering it with a thin layer of dirt, or letting it stand a few months.

Do not buy steer manure, because it is high in salt content which offsets any benefit that the manure might have. While the salt can be leached out by watering, the leaching process also washes the nitrogen out of the manure.

Hen, horse, sheep, and rabbit manures are know as 'hot manures' because of their high nitrogen content. Cow and hog manures are called 'cold manures' because they are fairly low in nitrogen and break down slowly. (For information on other animal manures, see Figure 3-07.)

THE EVER-PRESENT EARTHWORM

By burrowing, feeding and excreting, earthworms break up the soil particles and let air and moisture in. They usually don't go very deep, but the minute that plants start taking root, earthworms go with the roots, improving the soil.

The gray pink worms *(Helodrilus caliginosus* and *Helodarilus trapezoides)* are important to your garden. The red one *(Eisenia foetida),* the fishworm, is not so beneficial—it wants to fool around in damp spongy places instead of getting down to work. This red worm is, however, good for compost piles.

Figure 3.11
The Soil Saver composter
This composter combines quick decomposition with attractive backyard design. Toss in your garden refuse, kitchen garbage, grass clippings or spoiled fruit. The Soil Saver Composter turns organic waste into rich, nutrient-filled compost in as little as four weeks.
The insulated walls hold heat inside, keep cool air outside. It is made of extra tough, UV-stabilized plastic. Built-in air slots speed up aerobic decomposition. Measures 28 x 28 x 30 inches.
BARCLAY HORTICULTURE MFG LTD.
949 Wilson Ave.
Downsview, Ontario
Canada M3K 1G2

Figure 3.10

THE B.D. COMPOST STARTER

This is a concentrated mixture of several cultivated strains of beneficial oil bacteria, enzymes, and plant growth-promoting factors. These bacteria have been isolated from the most fertile humus soils. Under the proper condition of moisture, aeration and organic matter, the B.D. Compost Starter will:-
- *Quickly decompose* raw organic matter and wastes by breaking down into simpler compounds.
- *Reassemble* these simple compounds into complex, lasting substances-humus.
- *Fix nitrogen* from the air and make it available.
- *Increase the availability* of minerals in the soil and transform unavailable minerals into their available form.
- *Hold the soil* and improve its structure.
- *Prevent leaching* and washing away.
  Contact:
  THE PFIEFFER FOUNDATION, INC.
  Laboratory Div.
  Threefold Farms
  Spring Valley, NY 10977

Figure 3.12

HOMEMADE ORGANIC FERTILIZER

This brew utilizes fresh chicken manure—which can be dangerous because of the high amonia content. It is perfectly safe for vegetables, however, if handled properly. Place a shovelful of fresh chicken manure into a cloth bag. Submerge the bag in a bucket containing 2½ gallons of water from 2 to 3 days. Store mixture in an airtight container. To use, dilute 12 ounces of the liquid in one gallon of water.

Figure 3.13

VALUE OF EARTHWORMS

Chemical analyses of parent soil without earthworms and the same soil after being worked by earthworms have shown an increase of the following:-

Chemical Nutrient	% Increase
Nitrate of Nitrogen	500
Available phosphorus	700
Exchangeable potassium	1,200
Exchangeable calcium	150
Organic Carbon	200

The earthworm enriches the soil in the process of swallowing it and later expelling it in the form of castings. It takes in the soil, grinds it up, mixes it with calcium carbonate, pulverizes it, sends it on through the intestine to be digested by enzymes and then excreted. The final earthworm casting contains nitrogen, phosphorus and potassium, the three elements that vegetables most need.

Chemical fertilizers seem to decrease the number of earthworms in the soil, killing them or driving them off; ammonium sulfate is especially harmful. Many insects sprays are toxic to earthworms.

Earthworms are good soil builders. But you can't put earthworms in infertile or hard clay soils and expect results. Where possible. dig up earthworms from other parts of the yard.

GREEN MANURING

Green manuring is the process of growing and turning under foliage crops solely for their fertilizing and soil-conditioning values.

Plants with long tap roots tap deep-buried nutrients and trace minerals, break up the soil, and return to earth nutrients that are used in growing.

Plants utilized as green manure include grasses, grains, and legumes, ryegrass and buckwheat. These plants generally grow rapidly, producing a lot of organic material quickly. Legumes fix nitrogen—that is, microbes in the soil are attracted to their roots and extract nitrogen and convert it into forms usable by plants. To ensure that nitrogen-fixing microbes are present, it is recommended that you inoculate legume seeds. The inoculant comes in a dark powder and is available from a number of seed firms.

DIFFERENT ORGANIC METHODS

There are many schools of thought within the organic gardening community. Some organic gardeners garden in moderation; that is, while they prefer compost and organic fertilizers, sometimes they also use chemicals in controlling insects. Other gardeners treat organic gardening like an exacting and exact science. Between these extremes fall several other variations, including:-

Biodynamic gardening: A rather strict discipline of gardening in balance with Nature, based on the principles of Rudolph Steiner and developed in the early 1900s. Compost is constructed according to a specific formula using a bacterial starter. For more information contact:
THREEFOLD FARM
Spring Valley, NY 10977.

French intensive method: First developed in France in the 1890s and written about in 1913. Vegetables are planted in equal distances from each other across raised beds rather than in rows at such spacing that leaves overlap on maturity, creating a microclimate.

Biodynamic/French intensive method: Combining elements of the above two methods, this was developed by Australian master gardener Alan Chadwick. It generally produces about four times as many vegetables as conventional methods, takes one-third less water and requires less weeding.
Contact:
ECOLOGY ACTION OF THE MIDPENINSULA,
2225 El Camino Real,
Palo Alto, CA 94306.

MULCHING

It used to be called 'trash gardening,' this practice of spreading peat moss, hay or some other material—generally organic, but not always—over the garden soil. Within the last twenty years, mulching has taken on new respectability, as experience has shown how valuable it can be in many environments.

In general, mulches modify and protect the growing environment, especially the soil, of plants. Mulches conserve soil moisture, keep soil temperature moderate, help control weeds (thereby reducing root injury from hoeing and cultivation, which are often unnecessary after mulch has been applied), maintain good soil structure (thereby helping to retard erosion) and improve soil fertility. Let's examine these benefits to see how mulches might be of help in your own vegetable plot.

Benefits of mulching

Conserves soil moisture: All mulches slow down evaporation of water from the upper 6 to 8 inches of soil. Since they shade the soil (but not the plants) from the sun, evaporation is reduced by a good 70 to 90 percent. In addition, mulching tends to promote the distribution of water evenly over the soil area that it covers.

Moderates soil temperatures: Mulching tends to insulate the soil from the weather conditions 'outside,' and thus helps prevent baking, freezing, and so on. In addition, organic materials and some inorganic mulches like paper and materials with shiny surfaces reflect or inhibit the sun's rays. This keeps the temperature of the covered soil as much as 10 degrees below that of the surrounding, exposed soil.

Controls weeds: Organic mulches that are at least two inches thick will generally inhibit weed growth. Many weeds simply can't make it through the mulch to get at light and air. However, persistent perennial weeds will come through most organic mulches, and so must be pulled by hand. Inorganic mulches, expecially black plastic, virtually eliminate weeds.

Enhances soil structure: Soil frequently develops a surface crust because of the compacting pressure from rain or from sprinkler irrigation. A mulch breaks this water pressure and allows the earth's pore spaces to remain open. In addition, mulch slows water runoff and thus helps to hold the soil in place. (A subsidiary benefit is that mulch holds maturing vegetables off the moist ground and thus helps prevent premature rotting).

Improves soil fertility: Organic mulch decomposes slowly, thus functioning as a kind of time-release fertilizer for the soil it covers. Each day a little bit of organic matter is added to the soil, improving its texture and providing it with nutrients.

Disadvantages of mulching

Despite what you may think from reading the preceding paragraphs, mulching is not the answer to every gardener's prayer. For one thing, if the soil is not in very good shape, a mulch may do more harm than good by keeping it hidden from view. For another, organic mulches are high in carbon, and the microorganisms breaking them down will use up some of the soil's nitrogen to restore the balance. There is also a danger that in damp areas certain kinds of mulches will provide the perfect home for slugs and similar pests. Inorganic mulches, like black plastic, have their disadvantages, too, and they are discussed below.

Mulches are not a cure-all. Nothing is. But used properly, mulches can be of great benefit to both large and small gardens.

Figure 3.14

ORGANIC MULCHING MATERIALS			
Organic Mulches	**Rating**	**Application**	**Remarks**
Bagasse-baled crushed sugar cane	Good	Apply 2-3" thick.	By-product of sugar manufacturing; great water-holding capacity.
Buckwheat hulls	Fair	Apply 2" deep.	Lightweight, high in potash, lasts several years.
Chunk bark	Fair	Small bark chunks used infrequently in vegetable gardens.	Makes a durable mulch that stays in place well; especially effective in combination with polyethylene film.
Cocoa bean shells	Fair	Spread 2" deep.	Has a cocoa color.
Coffee grounds	Poor-fair	Apply lightly.	Slightly acid.
Compost	Excellent	Take partially decomposed grass clipings and plant tops from your compost bin.	Save the more decomposed compost to place directly in the soil.
Corncobs (ground)	Good	Apply 3" thick.	Inexpensive, will decay and add nutrients, must add a nitrogen fertilizer.
Cornstalks (chopped)	Good	Apply 2" deep.	Add nitrogen fertilizer.
Lawn clippings	Good	Mow grass before the seed ripens to prevent the introduction of weeds and grass seed; apply in a thin, 1-2" layer, cultivate into top of soil.	Green clippings build up heat if applied too thickly.
Leaves	Good	Run through a chipper before applying 2-3" deep.	Decomposes slowly, ties up nitrogen.
Manure	Excellent	Apply partially decomposed.	Fresh manure can burn plants; steer manure can contain salts and weed seeds.
Mushroom compost	Good		Often available from commercial mushroom growers
Pecan shells Peanut shells Rice hulls	Good	As purchased, apply 1-2" deep.	Inexpensive, becoming more available, high in nitrogen
Peat moss	Good	Use the larger sized particles; wet before spreading.	Dry peat moss tends to blow away allowing water to run off surface.
Pine needles	Fair to good	Can be used on vegetable gardens.	Good for acid-loving plants, does not affect the soil pH.
Sawdust	Good	Add nitrogen to the soil before applying; new sawdust is high in carbon, low in nitrogen, will draw nitrogen from the soil.	Covers the soil well; some bagged sawdust manufactuers add nitrogen.
Straw, hay, cured grasses	Good	Add nitrogen 2-3" deep.	Long lasting, breaks down slowly; high carbon/nitrogen ratio; used for winter protection.
Wood chips, shavings	Good	Add nitrogen to keep plants from turning yellow.	Chips decompose slowly, can be obtained from local mills.

Organic Mulches

Almost any organic material will make a usable mulch (see Figure 3-14) if it provides some insulation and is porous enough to permit moisture and air to penetrate to the soil. Organic mulches have an almost immediate effect on the garden. Aeration is improved in clay soils, as is the water-retaining propensity of sandy soils. Organic material as it decomposes also plays an important role in soil granulation.

In addition to the standard products, many unusual and economical mulches such as rice hulls, are often available locally. To find the materials listed in Figure 3-14, check your nurseries, newspapers, stables, woodworking plants, and any type of fiber processing plant. Many of the potential sources can be found simply by checking the telephone yellow pages. Writing the manufacturers listed on page 33 should get a list of local dealers for manufactured mulches.

Rules for organic mulching:

1. Apply fine organic materials at least 2 inches thick, coarse or fluffy materials should be 3 to 4 inches thick.
2. Don't apply mulch to seedlings. In certain climates it may keep them too damp and promote rotting. Wait several weeks after setting out seedlings before using mulches.
3. In general, keep mulch away from root crops; it may cause crown rot.
4. Watch out for insects. Mulch can provide a hiding place for bugs and other troublemakers.
5. Don't apply a mulch until after the soil has warmed up.

Plastic Mulching

Over the past several years, agricultural experiment stations and manufacturers have conducted extensive research on the use of plastic (polyethylene) film, aluminum foils, brown asphalt paper, and a whole series of woven and perforated plastic films that allow penetration of air and water. Plastic mulch is excellent for crops that have trailing plants with fruit on the ground, such as melons, pumpkins, squash. Plastic is also good for peppers and eggplant. It keeps down weeds and prevents the fruit from spoiling. Consider the following:

Ordinary polyethylene film: 1½ mm thick, comes in rolls 3 to 6 feet wide. Clear plastic heats the soil about 10° F; black plastic 3 to 6 degrees. Use clear plastic to promote the early germination of cool-season crops. Black plastic is effective for accelerating the growth and increasing the yield of most warm-season crops. You can double the size of the plants in a given period by using black plastic. It can extend the seasons two to three weeks for such crops as tomatoes, eggplant and peppers. The problem with polyethylene is that it restricts the flow of air and traps moisture, which can promote disease and insect problems. As a result, many gardeners have tried and then abandoned it in favor of plastic mulches that allow air and water to penetrate.

Sky-blue plastic: Can be used to heat the soil in beds 5 to 8 degrees. It has the additional advantage of repelling some insects.

Ordinary kitchen foil: Increases light intensity, helping to grow vegetables in shady parts of your garden. Foil lowers the soil temperature about 10° F and helps keep lettuce from going to seed during hot weather. Experiments show that kitchen foil is an effective control against aphids because the insects seem to dislike light reflected under leaf surfaces.

Nonwoven polyester (or nonwoven polypropylene): Has good air and water penetration and can be cut with scissors. Both come in UV-resistant formulas.

Biodegradable paper: This thick, dark material holds down weeds for an entire season. Instead of removing it at the end of each garden year, work it into the soil.

Perforated plastic: Has small holes every inch or so allowing air and water to reach the soil easily. It only lasts one season unless you cover it with soil or gravel.

Woven plastic: Also allows air and water to penetrate. It can be used for several years.

Figure 3.15

AVERAGE PLANT FOOD CONTENT OF ORGANIC FERTILIZER MATERIALS					
Organic Materials	%N	%P205	%K20	Availability	Acidity
Basic slag	—	8.0	—	quickly	alkaline
Bone meal	3.5	22.0	—	slowly	alkaline
Castor pomance	5.0	1.8	1.1	slowly	acid
Cocoa shell meal	2.5	1.0	2.5	slowly	neutral
Cotton seed meal	6.0	2.5	1.5	slowly	acid
Dried blood	12.0	1.5	0.8	moderately	acid
Fish meal	10.0	4.0	—	slowly	acid
Green sand	—	1.0	6.0	very slowly	neutral
Ground rock phosphate	—	33.0	—	very slowly	alkaline
Guano	10.0	4.0	2.0	moderately	acid
Hone and hoof meal	12.0	2.0	—	moderately	neutral
Milorganite	6.0	2.5	—	moderately	neutral
Peat moss	1.5	0.25	—	slowly	acid
Seaweed	1.0	—	4.0-8.0	slowly	neutral
Sewage sludge	4.0	2.5	0.4	slowly	acid
Soybean meal	7.0	1.2	1.5	slowly	neutral
Wood ashes	—	2.0	4.0-10.0	quickly	alkaline

Figure 3.17 ▶

Tomahawk chipper/shredder

This powerful chipper handles branches up to 2 inches thick. The high speed shredder instantly pulverizes brush, twigs and leaves into a light, even-textured mulch and compost material. Choice of 8, 5, and 2½ horsepower models. Optional bar grate available for shredding wet materials.

GARDEN WAY MFG.
102nd St. & 9th Ave.
Troy, NY 12180

Figure 3.16

Compost shredder/grinder

The Mighty Mack *shredder/grinder will easily shred and grind tree prunings one inch thick. The balanced rotor has 24 hardened, free-swinging knives (hammers). Each knife has four cutting edges so when one wears smooth, you can turn the knife around for a new, sharp surface. Remove the screens and the shredder will handle wet materials such as wet manure, wet leaves and green stalks.*

AMERIND-MACKISSIC, INC.
P.O. Box 111
Parker Ford, PA 19457

SHREDDER/GRINDERS

For gardeners who want to make quick compost, create mulch, or condition the soil organically, a shredder/grinder is a must.

For mulching and soil conditioning: Finely chopped vines, corncobs, hay, leaves and manure make better mulch than coarse raw material, because their fine texture pemits them to retain moisture more effectively.

For composting: A shredder both speeds and eases complete decomposition through bacterial action by reducing the size of the individual particles of matter.

Most models utilize steel tines (hammers) on a shaft that sweeps across grate bars or a perforated plate. The standard types are either fixed hammers (attached solidly to the shaft) or free-swinging hammers. Inexpensive models utilize blades; older types include a rotating square gate and grinding belt.

The size of the hopper, the type of material used in the frame, and the quality of the hammers vary considerably between models.

There are also an increasing number of small shredders and shredder/chippers on the market that can be stored easily. One unusual one uses a flywheel and large cutting discus instead of a blade. The **Steinmax Electric Shredder** is a light-weight electric shredder that is easy to move around and store. The **Lescha electric chipper/shredder** uses a high performance 1.54 hp. motor and razor-sharp steel cutting blade that spins vertically on a heavy flywheel. It will swallow branches up to one inch thick. The **Leaf Eater** is specifically designed for shredding leaves. It takes piles of wet or dry leaves and turns them into finely-textured leaf mulch. It is available from:

GARDENER'S SUPPLY
133 Elm St.
Winsooki, Burlington, VT 05401.

Some tractors and tillers offer shredder/composter combinations. Also available are leaf mills, into which leaves are fed, chopped up by a blade, and collected in a bag for compression or use in compost.

SUPPLIERS AND MANUFACTURERS OF SHREDDERS/GRINDERS

AMERIND-MACKISSIC, INC
P.O. Box 111
Parker Ford, PA 19457

ARMSTRONG INTERNA-
TIONAL
Flowtron Div.
2 Main St.
Melrose, MA 02176

BARCLAY ROTHSCHILD MFG
949 Wilson Ave.
Downsview, Toronto
Canada

THE C.S. BELL CO.
170 W. Davis St.
Tiffin, OH 44883

LINDIG MFG CORP.
1875 W. Country Rd. C
St. Paul, MN 55113

MTD PRODUCTS, INC.
P.O. Box 360900
Cleveland, OH 44136

NATIONAL GREENHOUSE
CO.
400 E. Main St.
Pana, IL 62557

PIQUA ENGINEERING, INC.
P.O. Box 605
Piqua, OH 45356

PROMARK PRODUCTS, INC.
330 9th
Industry, CA 91746

ROBO HOE LAWN &
GARDEN EQUIPMENT
8125 Main
Newbury, OH 44065

ROVER-STOTT BONNER LTD.
P.O. Box 292
Allendale, NJ 07401

ROYER FOUNDER &
MACHINE CO.
158 Pringle St.
Kingston, PA 18704

SGK, INC.
2 Davis Ave.
Frazer, PA 19355

STERLING ASSOCIATES,
INC.
687 Seville Rd.
Wadsworth, OH 44281

TRANS-SPHERE CORP.
P.O. Box 1564
Mobile, AL 36633

W-W GRINDER, INC.
P.O. Box 4029
Wichita, KS 67204

WHEEL HORSE PRODUCTS,
INC.
515 W. Ireland Rd.
South Bend, IN 46614

WHITE OUTDOOR
PRODUCTS
White Farm Equipment
2625 Butterfield Rd.
Oak Brook, IL 60521

WINONA ALTRITION
MILL CO.
1009 W 5th St.
Winona, MN 55987

THE YARD MAN CO.
P.O. Box 36940
Cleveland, OH 44136

Figure 3.18

THE FULL-TIME MULCH

Mulching can be a permanent proposition. As soon as your vegetables come up and look vigorous, spread a hay, straw, grass or leaf mulch 8 to 19 inches thick everywhere, between the rows and around all plants.

Next season, don't till the soil; just push back the mulch and make the row plantings. Then when the plants have sprouted, push the mulch back around them. The soil beneath this permanent mulch will stay loose and friable. Add more mulch the second year to maintain a 4 to 7 inch depth.

A disadvantage is that soil under the mulch stays cool. This delays planting of the warm-weather plants.

Figure 3.19

HAMMERS

Solid hammers
Advantage: Heavy hammers will crush or break fairly heavy materials.
Disadvantages: Will sometimes break or twist when processing heavy twigs or rocks. Rigid hammers often wrap heavy vines around hammer mills.

Swinging hammers
Advantages: Hammers will release on impact with heavy material and rocks.
Disadvantages: Hard to balance. Takes more power. Heavy strain and wear on pivot points.

MANUFACTURERS OF SYNTHETIC MULCHES

AGROTECH
P.O. Box 857
Houlton, MA 04730

ALLIED PLASTICS, INC.
1663 Hargrove Ave.
Gastonia, NC 28052

ANDERSON BOX CO., INC.
2130 Stout Field W. Dr.
Indianapolis, IN 46241

AVERY CORP.
3500 N. Kimball Ave.
Chicago, IL 60618

ASSOCIATED BAG CO.
160 S. 2nd St.
Milwaukee, WS 53204

CENTRAL STATES
   DIVERSIFIED, INC.
9332 Manchester Rd.
St. Louis, MO 63119

CHAPLEWSKY'S, INC.
1618 Commercial St.
Bangor, WI 54614

COLUMBIA BURLAP
   & BAG CO.
Nursery Supply Div.
999 Bedford
N. Kansas City, MO 64116

CORDAGE PACKAGING
66 Jenny Rd.
Dayton, OH 45404

DALLAS BAG &
   BURLAP CO., INC.
153 Leslie St.
Dallas, TX 75207

DEWITT CO. INC.
Polypropylene Fabric Div.
Hwy 61 South
Sikeston, MO 63801

DURA PRODUCTS, INC.
417 N. Main St.
P.O. Box 1068
Houston, TX 77001

EASY GARDENER, INC.
P.O. Box 2105
Waco, TX 76703

J.C. EHRICH CHEMICAL
   CO., INC.
840 William Lane
Reading, PA 19612

FESCO PLASTICS CORP., INC.
2850 Festival Dr.
Kanakee, IL 60901

GARDEN TECH LTD.
P.O. Box 612
Needham, MA 02192

GRIFFOLYN CO.
P.O. Box 33248
Houston, TX 77233

GRO GROUP, INC.
Five Shawsheen Ave.
Bedford, MA 01730

INSUL-RIB, INC.
P.O. Box 447
Castle Rock, MN 55010

JADERTOON CO., INC.
P.O. Box 685
Irmo, SC 29063

KENBAR, INC.
24 Gould St.
Reading, MA 01867

KEYSTONE STEEL & WIRE CO.
7000 W. Adams
Peoria, IL 61641

LINDO INDUSTRIAL
   PRODUCTS, INC.
40 Queen Elizabeth Blvd
Toronto, Ont
Canada M87 1M2

MALLOW CORP.
1835 S. Nordic Ave
Mt. Prospect, IL 60056

NORTH AMERICAN PLASTIC
   CORP.
921 Industrial Dr.
Auroa, IL 60506

PARAMOUNT PERLITE CO.
16236 S. IL
Paramount, CA 90723

PENURKE PRODUCTS
13 Linden Ave. E.
Jersey City, NJ 07305

PRESTO-PRODUCTS, INC.
P.O. Box 2399
670 N. Perkins St.
Appleton, WI 54913

RAVEN INDUSTRIES, INC.
P.O. Box 1007
Sioux Falls, SD 57117

RELIANCE PLASTIC &
   CHEMICAL CORP.
110 Kearney St.
P.O. Box 2627
Paterson, NJ 07509

SERVICE CANVAS CO., INC.
149 Swan St.
Buffalo, NY 14203

STAR-TEX CORP.
P.O. Box 20
645 Washington St.
Hanover, MA 02339

UNITED BAGS, INC.
2508 N. Broadway
St. Louis, MO 63102

WARP BROS.
4647 W. Augusta Blvd
Chicago, IL 60651

ZARN, INC.
P.O. Box 1360
Reidsville, NC 27320

Figure 3.20
   Combo chipper/shredder
   *This versatile chipper/shredder/mulcher oper-
ates standing up or lying on its side. Yard and
garden debris is reduced to one-tenth its original
volume for clean, economical disposal or for use
as mulch and compost.*
   VORANDO POWER PRODUCTS, INC.
   386 Park Ave. South
   New York, NY 10016

MANUFACTURERS AND DISTRIBUTORS OF ORGANIC FERTILIZERS AND OTHER ORGANIC PRODUCTS

THE ANDERSON
P.O. Box 119
Maumee, OH 43537

B.C.A. PRODUCTS
P.O. Box 325
Sleepy Eye, MN 56085

BANDINI FERTILIZER
4139 Bandini Blvd.
Los Angeles, CA 90023

BARZEN ENTERPRISES, INC.
455 Harrison St. N.E.
Minneapolis, MN 5413

BONIDE CHEMICAL CO.
2 Wurz Ave.
Yorkville, NY 13495

BROWN GOLD SOIL CORP.
50 E. 25th St.
Paterson, NJ 07514

CHEVRON CHEMICAL CO.
Ortho Products Div.
575 Market St.
San Francisco, CA 94105

CHIPMAN, INC.
400 Jones Rd.
Stoney Creek, Ont.
Canada L8G 3Z1

DOUGLASS FERTILIZER
& CHEMICAL, INC.
P.O. Box 2811
Lake Mary, FL 32714

ESTECH, INC. (VIGORO LAWN
& GARDEN PRODUCES)
One Southern Illinois
Bank Bldg
Fairview Heights, IL 62208

GARFIELD-WILLIAMSON, INC.
1072 West Side Ave.
Jersey City, NJ

GOOD EARTH ORGANICS
CORP.
5960 Broadway
Lancaster, NY 14086

HOME GARDENING
NATURALLY
Div. of Progressive
Agri-Systems, Inc.
201 Center St.
Stockertown, PA 18083

J&L ADIKES, INC
182-12 93rd Ave.
Jamaica, NY 11423

KCI PRODUCTS
2535 Pilot Knob Rd.
Mendota Hts., MN 55120

LESCO, INC.
20005 Lake Rd.
Rocky River, OH 44116

LOFT'S SEED, INC.
Chimney Rock Rd.
Bound Brook, NJ 08805

MILAZZO INDUSTRIES
1609 River Rd.
Pittston, PA 18640

MOUNTAIN SPRING RANCH,
INC.
P.O. Box 53
Carlsbad, CA 92006

ORGANIC CONSERVATION
CORP.
P.O. Box 249
Altura, MN 55910

PACIFIC AGRO CO.
903 House Way N.
P.O. Box 326
Renton, WA 98027

PAYGRO, INC.
11000 Huntington Rd.
South Charleston, OH 45386

PRO-AG, INC.
2072 E. Center Circle
Minneapolis, MN 55441

RID-A-BUG
P.O. Box 6246
10 W. Adams St.
Jacksonville, FL 32236

RINGER CORP.
9959 Valley View Rd.
Eden Prairie, MN 55344

STA-GREEN
Parker Fertilizer Co.
P.O. Box 540
Sylacauga, AL 35150

SEA-BORN
200 Rockford Rd.
Charles City, IA 50616

SOIL ENTERPRISE CORP.
P.O. Box 81333
Mobile, AL 36689

SUDBURY LABORATORY,
INC.
6 October Hill Rd.
Holliston, MA 01746

SUNNILAND CORP.
P.O. Box 996
930 Riverside
Wichita, KS 67201

SUTHERLAND INDUSTRIES,
INC.
11781 Lee Jackson
Memorial Hwy
Fairvax, VA 22033

TEX-GRO FERTILIZER CO.
P.O. Box 1712
Pecos, TX 79772

U.S. FETRO-CORP.
P.O. Box 111
Spanish Fork, UT 84660

VERMA GROW PRODUCTS
Rt. 3, Box 402
Salem, VA 24153

ZOOK & RANCK, INC.
Rt. 1, Box 243
Gap, PA 17527

4. Hand Tools

A TOOL IS A TOOL is a tool...right?

Wrong!

Scratch twelve gardeners and you'll find a dozen different opinions on which tools to use for a particular job. What's more, try selecting even something as simple as a garden shovel, and you'll be faced with hundreds of choices.

As a result, many gardeners, even experienced ones, wind up with a shedful of tools they never really use. These implements look good in the store, but when you get them out in the garden, they turn out to be worth very little indeed. Fortunately, with a little planning, some luck and the help of this chapter, you should be able to avoid wasting valuable cash and even more valuable storage space.

CHOOSING YOUR TOOLS

When figuring out what tools you need, first make a list of the jobs that have to be done around the garden—this chapter and others in this book ought to help you there. Then try to estimate how frequently each job is likely to come up—this will depend to a great extent on the size of your garden and the type of vegetables you intend to grow. Armed with the results of this homework, select only those tools that you need for the tasks you are likely to encounter, giving priority to those that can be used for more than just the odd minor job.

In a typical garden the chores fall into four basic categories: (1) digging and planting; (2) materials handling (i.e. moving stuff from one place to another); (3) raking; and (4) weeding and cultivating. Theoretically at least, you should be able to handle all these jobs with little more than a shovel, trowel, rake and hoe—supplemented perhaps by a cart or wheelbarrow. That seems straightforward enough, until you visit your local garden supply store to be confronted by the huge choice of styles available nowadays in even the simplest implements. A shovel, for instance, can be designed specifically for digging in rocky soil, can be reinforced for heavy-duty work over an extended period of time, or can be made out of lightweight materials for the convenience of those gardeners who don't think of themselves as another Arnold Schwarzenegger. There are, of course, many other variations on the basic shovel, just as there are hundreds of types to choose from among rakes, hoes and other standard hand tools.

Two important considerations in the purchase of tools are quality and price. In most cases, when one is high, so is the other—just as often, cheap equals junky. Some mail-order firms categorize their tools as good, better and best, and price them accordingly. Your target should be to match the quality of the tools with the job you expect them to perform. If you've got a small garden and give your tools relatively light use, you should be able to get good service and value from a medium-priced tool. (Experts tend not to recommend really low-end tools because, more often than not, they're complete trash. But if you run across a low-priced tool that looks and feels right, don't be afraid to buy it for your light-duty work.) If you have a large garden, however, and if you expect to give your tools lots of use, then give careful consideration to the more expensive, more sturdily-constructed tools.

Let's take a look at the wide variety of tools available, their different uses and idiosyncrasies.

DIGGING AND MATERIALS-HANDLING TOOLS

Some gardeners use one tool for all their digging; others have a range from which to choose. Before going any further consider the following:

Will your use of the tool be light or heavy? Shovels are constructed in one of three basic ways—hollow-back, closed-back, or solid-shank, hot-tapered. The type of construction determines their strength, the amount of abuse they will withstand and, naturally, their price.

Figure 4.01
Plastic hand tools
These indoor/outdoor hand tools are lightweight, durable and made of tough, molded plastic. They are immune to garden chemicals and weather. The trowel has a built-in depth scale to help in planting.
ALLEN SIMPSON MARKETING & DESIGN LTD.
Albert Street
Eden Mills, Ontario, Canada, N0B 1P0

Hollow-back shovels and spades derive their name from a ridge stamped into the center of the blade for strength and reinforcement. This type of shovel is generally least expensive and holds up reasonably to light-to-moderate garden use.

Closed-back (or fast-back) shovels are completely closed in back by a strap welded over the conventional back area. This reinforces the blade and prevents drag and deadweight from mud and dirt. A closed-back shovel is stronger than a hollow-back shovel and is well-suited for moderate to heavy garden use.

A solid-shank, hot-tapered shovel is forged from a single piece of steel. Blade and socket are one piece, with no welds or seams—this is the most durable type of construction. There are several grades of solid-shank shovels designed for different conditions, from home-garden to heavy-duty industrial use. These shovels are not cheap, but they will stand up for long time under a heavy workload.

Do you need a shovel for digging, for moving materials, or for both? A standard round-point shovel will do an excellent job of digging and a passable job of moving peat moss and similar material. If you intend to move sawdust, gravel, straw, leaves, and the like, you should consider buying one of the more specialized shovels or forks described below.

Do you have a soil condition that requires a specialized tool? You can handle light to medium soil with a standard shovel, but if your soil is extremely hard or if it contains lots of rocks or roots, consider a spade or mattock. For cutting through roots you

can purchase a shovel with a serrated rather than a standard blade.

Types of shovels

With the answers to the above questions in mind, read through the following descriptions of different shovels and select the model or models that best meet your particular needs.

Round-point shovel: Most gardeners say this is the best all-around tool for digging, scooping and shoveling. The blade is set at a slight angle to the handle. These shovels are manufactured with several variations. The clipped-point and caprock patterns, for instance, are flatter across the end than standard models. Some gardeners believe that these blunted points dig better in moist, wet soil. Other types of shovels include the deep-bowl and the semiflat bowl, which vary in their capacity to carry earth and other material, and the irrigation shovel, which has a straight instead of an angled shank. Some people find it easier to use an irrigation shovel when digging holes or ditches with straight edges.

At the back edge of the round-point shovel's blade (called a step), the shovel is cut off square—sometimes part of the back edge is extended beyond the shovel and turned backward, forward, or rolled to form a smooth step, forward-turn step, or rolled step. They simply make it easier to place a foot on the back portion of the shovel for digging.

Anyone who has tried to cut through roots knows it's an impossible job with a standard round-point shovel. A serrated point is the solution. A shovel with a serrated point will easily cut through hard soil, soil laced with masses of small roots and heavy roots an inch thick and more. In addition, a shovel with a serrated point will clean out roots from ditches and other areas where you would otherwise have to use an axe.

Square-blade shovel: This shovel digs only moderately well, but it holds a good-sized load when you need to move soil, peat moss and other materials. It is useful for picking up the last of a pile of rotted manure or similar material and for leveling areas around the garden.

Spade: This is stronger than most shovels. A spade has an almost flat blade and straight sides. Many gardeners use it to dig and turn the soil, to work in fertilizers, manures, sawdusts, etc., to dig trenches or to cut straight edges into the ground. A long-bladed spade is good for turning soil to a good depth or for digging deeply in one spot.

Scoop shovels: A deep blade for moving bulk materials such as bark, sawdust, gravel and similar material is the outstanding feature of scoop shovels. They are available in many variations of sizes and weights. The blades are made of either aluminum (to make them lighter for heavier jobs) or high-carbon steel. They are generally hollow-backed in design and construction.

Forks and other tools

A spading fork is better than a shovel for digging hard soil, rocks or roots; a spading fork is also useful for loosening around plants and working in soil amendments. The standard mode, which has 11-inch diamondback shaped tines, works well in most soils. The English pattern, which has inch-long square tines, is used for heavy soils. An 11-inch, six-tine clam fork with sharp, rounded tines is also available for working with light soil.

Barn and manure forks: These round-tined forks are the equivalent of a scoop-shovel. They're excellent for moving light material such as leaves, partially decayed compost, manure and coarse straw. The prongs pierce the mass and hold it together so that you can move a large pile in one piece. Round-tined forks come with anywhere from three to ten tines; 4- to 6-tined models are used for most garden jobs. The more tines a fork has, the better it can pick up wet or heavy material. Heavy forks are available for picking up rocks and stones.

Mattocks: A modified pickaxe, the mattock is a double-bladed tool. One blade is shaped like a big, 3½-inch-wide chisel, and serves to fracture hard soil and to perform other brute-force tasks in the soil. For the other blade you generally have a choice of a pencil-shaped pick end, which is good for chopping in rocky and clay soils, or an axe-shaped end, which can chop through the roots of such tough plants as bamboo or ivy.

Figure 4.03
Nit-Picker
The concave blade makes it ideal for pricking out and transplanting seedlings or for seeding and fertilizing. Useful as a seed drill. Made of semi-polished stainless steel.
ALLEN SIMPSON MARKETING & DESIGN LTD.
Albert Street
Eden Mills, Ontario, Canada N0B 1P0

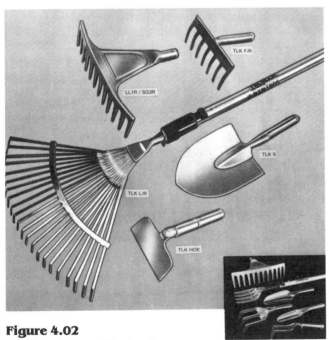

Figure 4.02
Interchangeable tools
Five different garden tools can be plugged into this handle: two rakes, a hoe, shovel and lawn rake. In addition, five different hand tools fit the handle to eliminate bending while weeding or transplanting. All tool-heads are securely clamped into the handle.
ALLEN SIMPSON MARKETING & DESIGN LTD.
Albert Street
Eden Mills, Ontario, Canada N0B 1P0

Rakes

The rake is another apparently simple tool that comes in an astounding array of shapes and sizes. It is a key implement, but so common that most people grab the first one they see on sale at the right price. That's often a mistake. It's as important to match the right style of rake to the task at hand as it is to use the right wrench on a mechanical repair job.

Level head: With its head fastened directly to the handle, this rake is useful for removing small clods of earth, twigs and similar material. It has a flat side for leveling.

Bow design: A fond favorite with gardeners (so called because the rake head it attached to the handle by a bow-shaped piece of metal), the bow rake has a spring action that helps with the removal of small clods of earth and the like.

Floral: A small (usually about 8 inches wide), flat-headed rake that is useful in the garden for raking cultivated soil and for working small beds.

Multipurpose: A large tool, this has triangular-shaped teeth on both sides, useful for cultivating soil

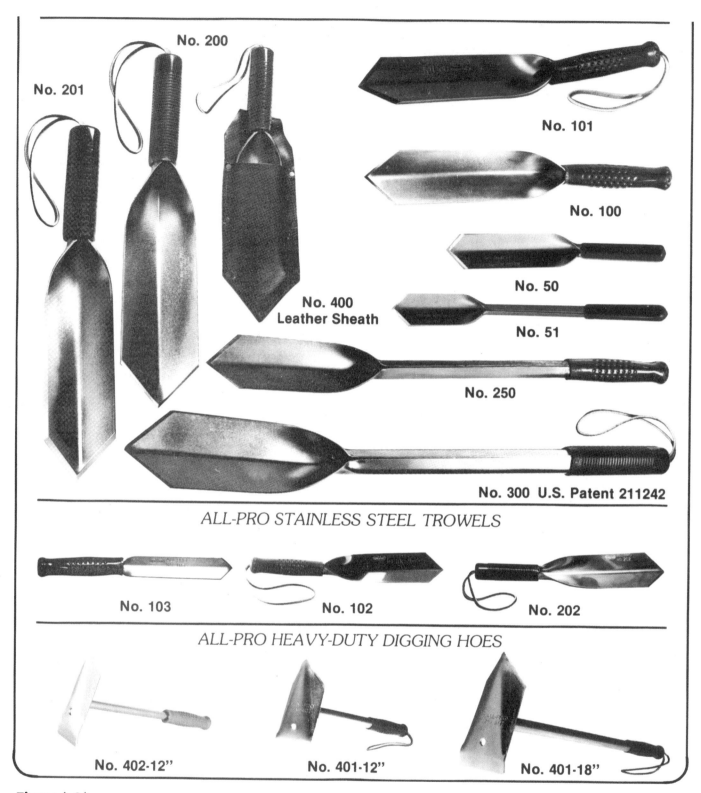

No. 201

No. 200

No. 101

No. 100

No. 50

No. 51

**No. 400
Leather Sheath**

No. 250

No. 300 U.S. Patent 211242

ALL-PRO STAINLESS STEEL TROWELS

No. 103

No. 102

No. 202

ALL-PRO HEAVY-DUTY DIGGING HOES

No. 402-12"

No. 401-12"

No. 401-18"

Figure 4.04

All-Pro digging tools

These unusual stainless steel gardening tools are excellent for working with all types of vegetables. The narrow blade widths make it extremely easy to use around closely planted vegetables. Handy for heavy-clay soils. Each is especially designed for cultivating, transplanting and weeding.

WILCOX ALL-PRO TOOLS & SUPPLY
Montezuma, IA 50171

and cleaning lawns.

Heavy-duty: These flat-headed rakes are designed for raking large stones or for smoothing asphalt. They can be useful in heavy soils or when puting in garden walks and paths.

WEEDING AND CULTIVATING TOOLS

Hoes

Traditionally an important tool for all gardeners, the hoe is a versatile piece of equipment. There are many sizes and models available, each is designed to accomplish different tasks around the home garden. The following is a description of the most common hoes and their primary uses:

All-purpose garden hoe: The standard hoe, useful for turning up soil and for some weeding.

Warren cultivator hoe: A heart-shaped hoe with a point, useful for making short rows or hills to plant seeds. Turn the hoe point up and use the other face to hill dirt over new seeds.

Weeding hoe: This has a flat blade on one side and one or two prongs on the other; extremely useful for cultivating around plants.

Nurseryman's hoe: This resembles a standard hoe but with a tapered top; useful for many garden jobs.

Scuffle hoe: It has a flat blade that can be used to cut the tops off of weeds simply by pushing the hoe along the ground or slightly underneath. Also comes with an open center, so weeds can be cut by either a pushing or a pulling action.

Action hoe: An easy-to-use cultivator-weeder and edger, this comes with a sharp double-edge blade that cuts weeds and grass in both directions. It will cut right up to the edge of bricks and other border materials.

Cultivators

There are two basic kinds of cultivators—the small hand-type, which we'll deal with here, and the larger mechanical variety, which is covered later in this chapter.

A cultivator is a pronged, forklike tool used to cultivate or turn over the dirt between plants. It is available in three or four pronged, curved-tine style or in a three prong, adjustable one. The cultivator will not slice off weeds that have gotton a good start, but it does an excellent job of loosening the soil. If used regularly, the cultivator will keep the soil open and discourage weeds from growing.

Trowels

Some gardeners who manage to make do with the smallest number of tools claim that they get along very well without a trowel. Others consider these small shovel-type tools a necessity. A trowel is handy for digging small holes in which hot-weather plants like tomatoes can be set out. And for quick, one-step transplants, the proper trowel is indispensable. Trowels are also useful for many other minor but necessary digging jobs. Besides the **standard trowel** there are several other designs to consider.

A **long-handled trowel** ($7-15) has a handle of two feet or so, and is the choice of gardeners who have trouble stooping. It helps to reach into hard-to-reach spots in a vegetable factory bed.

A **steel-bladed trowel** ($5-18) has a sharp blade that cuts easily into the soil. Many of them use a thin connecting rod, in the handle, that bends easily with heavy use.

The narrow cupped blade of the **transplant trowel** ($3-8) makes it excellent for transplanting tomatoes, cauliflower, cabbage and other seedlings into the garden. It is not useful for general digging.

Aluminum trowels ($5-10) are usually one piece, with plastic covered handles for extreme sturdiness. Aluminum trowels are not nearly as sharp or as strong as those of steel.

The **offset trowel** ($7-10) has a pointed blade that is good for digging out seedlings from flats.

An **aluminum trigger trowel** ($6-8), with a hook under the handle, is especially useful for anyone with arthritis or a weak grip.

Figure 4.05

Heavy duty cultivators/diggers

These heavy duty tools are perfect for heavy or rocky soils. They hold up well under all types of soil and gardening conditions.

VILLAGE BLACKSMITH
1219 S. Los Angeles St.
Glendale, CA 91204

SHARPENING YOUR DIGGING TOOLS

When you're finished using any digging tool, a good way to clean it is to plunge it into a bucket of sand. If anything is stuck to the blade, scrape it first. If you're particularly care-conscious, wipe the blade with an oily rag. Also, periodically wipe down wooden handles with linseed oil and resharpen the blades with a small flat file.

GARDEN HANDCARTS

Garden carts have taken over where the wheelbarrow left off. Today's modern garden cart is so well balanced that it will handle bulky materials with complete stability and without a lot of musclepower. Unlike the wheelbarrow, carts allow you to move even the heaviest of loads with minimal effort.

Manufacturers have begun to make a wide variety of carts, from small-wheeled, wedge-shaped models with with a capacity of four cubic feet to large, 26-inch wheel carts designed to carry anything from leaves to sacks of mulch to four or five bales of hay.

Some manufacturers provide these carts in the form of do-it-yourself kits. To assemble at home, some kits require additional materials such as plywood paneling. The saving on these kits is in the region of $15 to 20.

Figure 4.06

Versatile garden cart

This card has four load-carrying features: (1) the raised front panel allows it to move big bulky loads; (2) the open back makes it easy to carry heavy, long loads such as an extension ladder; (3) the swinging dump front allows you to dump compost and wood chips easily; (4) the cart's flat sides makes it possible to use the entire bed space for carrying bales of hay and similar items.
GARDEN WAY CARTS
102nd Street & 9th Ave.
Troy, NY 12180

PLASTIC HAND TOOLS

To many a gardener, "them's fightin' words!" They'd sooner eat plastic-wrapped tomatoes than be caught with a plastic tool in the garden. To many other gardeners, however, the brightly colored, lightweight, and inexpensive plastic tools are just what they want. These tools can handle any garden chore a metal tool can, yet are immune to garden chemicals and the weather—no crust, no rust, no fuss. And since these tools are cheaper than their metal counterparts, it's no big deal if you lose one now and then. Especially useful are the trowels, transplanters, hand rakes, and hand hoes. One manufacturer has a complete line in attractive colors including red, green, blue, orange, yellow and gray:
NORTH CENTRAL PLASTICS, INC.
Ellendale, MN 56026.

MAGNESIUM AND ALUMINUM RAKES

Rakes made of magnesium and aluminum are lightweight yet extremely rugged. Such rakes can be manufactured four feet wide with 3⅜-inch teeth without becoming too heavy to handle easily. This extra width speeds up the raking of larger vegetable gardens. A complete line of magnesium and aluminum rakes is manufactured by:
WHITE METAL ROLLING & STAMPING CORP.
80 Moultrie Street
Brooklyn, N.Y. 11222

BICYCLE-TYPE PLANTER

These seeders do 'all' planting operations, from opening the soil to pressing it over the planted seed. Seeders come with up to 21 different plates that allow you to adjust the planting depth for any vegetable variety.
Contact:
Lambert's Golden Harvest Garden Seeder
LAMBERT CORPORATION
519 Hunter Ave.
Dayton, OH 45404

Earthway Precision Garden Seeder
ESMAY PRODUCTS, INC.
P.O. Box 547
Bristol, IN 46507

MECHANICAL CULTIVATORS

Mechanical cultivators are still popular with many gardeners. The high- and low-wheel types work in much the same manner as the old horse-drawn plow. Instead of pulling, you push the plow through the soil. Both types can be used effectively in large gardens. Most cultivators come with several attachments: fint-tine cultivator-weeders, a moldboard plow that turns the soil, and a double-end shovel that forms furrows on either side. Some cultivators come with a slicing hoe that cuts weeds below the surface. Most cultivators have an adjustment that allows changes in cutting angle and depth.

Contact:
ESMAY PRODUCTS, INC.
P.O. Box 547,
Bristol, IN 46507

RITEWAY-DOMINION MFG. CO.
200 Old River Rd.,
Bridgewater, VA 22812

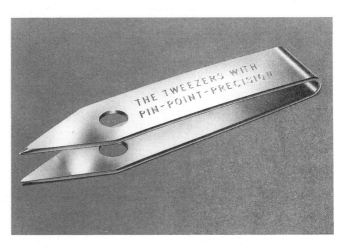

Figure 4.08
Plant tweezers
Excellent for pricking out seedlings. The large size makes them easier to handle and control.
EL MAR, INC.
43 Cody Street
West Hartford, CT 06110

Model No. 1800

Figure 4.07
Seeder
This hand seeder efficiently plants up to 28 different vegetable seeds. The seeder opens the soil, spaces and plants the seed, packs the soil and marks the next row. It utilizes a seed plate for spacing individual vegetables.
ESMAY PRODUCTS, INC.
P.O. Box 547
Bristol, IN 46507

Figure 4.09
High-wheel cultivator
These high-wheel cultivators are still popular among many gardeners. They will cultivate, plow, cut furrows, and slice weeds below the surface. The over-the-axle frame design lightens handle load and improves operating stability.
ESMAY PRODUCTS, INC.
P.O. Box 547
Bristol, IN 46507

Figure 5.01

John Deere lawn garden tractor

This tractor has an overhead valve engine that provides greater fuel economy. Standard features on all models include full pressure lubrication, electric start, headlights, electric PTO switch, 3-gallon fuel tank, parking brake and toolbox.

JOHN DEERE
Moline, IL 61265

Figure 5.02

HOW AND WHERE TO ORDER MAIL-ORDER GARDEN TOOLS

Hard-to-find and heavy-duty garden tools are often available through specialized mail order firms. These firms offer a wide variety of tools not usually available frum nurseries or garden centers.

ALSTO COMPANY
Rte 150 East
Galesburg, IL 61401

BROOKSTONE CO.
127 Vose Farm Rd.
Peterborough, NH 03458

CLAPPERS
Box A
West Newton, MA 02165

GARDENER'S SUPPLY CO.
133 Elm St.
Winooski, VT 05404

GREEN RIVER TOOLS
Box 1919
Brattleboro, VT 05301

DAVID KAY GARDEN
& GIFT CATALOG
4509 Taylor Lane
Cleveland, OH 44128

A.M. LEONARD, INC.
Box 816
Piqua, OH 45356

MELLINGER'S, INC.
2310 W. South Range
North Lima, OH 44452

WALTER NICKE
Box 667
Hudson, NY 12534

THE PLOW & HEARTH
560 Main St.
Madison, VA 02727

RINGER CORP.
9959 Valley View Rd.
Eden Prairie, MN 55344

SMITH & HAWKIN
25 Corte Madera
Mill Valley, CA 94941

5. Power Tools

EVERYONE WHO NOW HAS or is thinking of taking on a large vegetable plot should consider supplementing his or her collection of garden tools with some power tools. They multiply by many times the amount of work a gardener can do.

This chapter examines a representative selection of the best power tools currently on the market. The first major category, rototillers, is of greatest interest to vegetable gardeners. The second category is the largest; tractors are made by dozens of different companies, and there are thousands of different attachments. A third major category, shredder-grinders, has been covered in Chapter 3.

THE USES OF POWER TOOLS

In the right places and at the right times, power tools can be invaluable to the home gardener. With a power rototiller, for instance, you can break up and pulverize large quantities of soil with relative ease. Cultivation becomes much less back-breaking, and you can even furrow a hill! With a garden tractor you can haul large amounts of material around the garden and with the proper attachments you can disc-plow, cultivate, grind, compost, plant and make light work of many other garden chores. With the proper power tools a gardener can effectively manage a vegetable planting three or four times the size that can be handled by a gardener working only with hand tools. Even at times when gasoline and other sources of power are expensive or in short supply, it is still worthwhile considering the purchase of the right kind of power tools. If you've got a good-sized plot of land, the amount of your own energy that these tools can conserve is far more than the relatively small amounts of oil they'll burn up. There is probably no more controversial decision in gardening, however, than whether to use power tools or not; so, after weighing the pros and cons and considering what's best for your garden, you'll have to make up your own mind.

ROTOTILLERS

The principal purpose of the rototiller is to break up the earth—to till the soil—in preparation for planting. There are two basic types of tillers, front-end and rear-end. The difference between them is simply that one has the tines in front of the wheels, the other has them in back of the wheels. Front-end tillers are powered through the movement of the tines. An adjustable drag bar is used to make the tines dig in, and the operator can use this to control both speed of the tiller and depth that the tines dig. On rear-end tillers, power is applied through the wheels. The weight of the machine

Figure 5.03

Mang tillers

Mang tillers, both rear and front end tilling, are designed for easy operator control and maneuverability. All models feature a durable chain drive, slasher tines and instant release safety clutches. Built for professional use and an amateur's abuse.
OREGON MANUFACTURING COMPANY, INC.
6920 S.W. 111th Ave.
Beaverton, OR 97005

Figure 5.04
Snapper tillers

The Snapper front-end tiller converts quickly to a walking tractor. Walking tractor attachments include a hiller-furrower, and plow/cultivator. Has a reinforced chain-and-gear transmission. The rear-end tiller has a standup bar and engine guard that allows you to stand it on end for easy access to tines.

SNAPPER POWER EQUIPMENT
P.O. Box 777
Mcdonough, GA 30253

Figure 5.06
Roto-Hoe rear-end tiller

This lightweight rear-end tiller is designed to meet the needs of individuals with small gardens looking for rear tine performance in a compact design. Model 904 features one forward and one reverse speed. Attachments include a furrow plow, a row maker and a transport wheel for moving the tiller over hard surfaces.

ROTO-HOE
Newbury, OH 44065

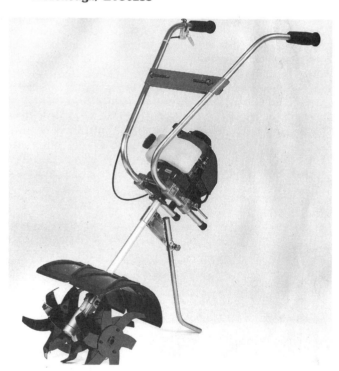

Figure 5.05
Little Wonder cultivator

This 20 pound cultivator features 9-inch wide steel tines that can weed at depths of 1 to 3 inches or up to ten inches. The tines are reversible. Good for tight spaces, yet rugged enough for big gardens.

LITTLE WONDER
Division of Schiller-Pfeiffer, Inc.
1028 Steet Road
Southampton, PA 18966

Figure 5.07
Troy-Bilt rear-end tillers

The 'Horse' has 4 speeds and a tine disconnect that allows you to stop the times from turning while you transport the machine. The rear tilling section comes off to allow access to the power take-off. The power take-off can power a log splitter, home generator and chipper shredder.

GARDEN WAY MFG.
102nd St. & 9th Ave.
Troy, NY 12180

is distributed so that the tines dig in without pressure from the operator.

Front-end rototillers

Advantages:
1. Lighter and generally less expensive than rear-end.
2. Mover maneuverable, can turn in less space, making it easier to work garden beds.
3. Good digging capability. Takes fewer passes to get the soil in good shape.

Disadvantages:
1. Some compacting occurs, since wheels pass over soil that tines have tilled.
2. Not easy to control without strength and effort. Jumps and bucks in heavy soil or when rocks are hit.

Rear-End rototillers

Advantages:
1. Easy to operate. Can be guided with one hand. Good for people without the strength necessary to run a front-end model.
2. More efficient for breaking ground in heavy soils over large areas.

Disadvantages:
1. Generally more expensive than front-end, although not prohibitively so.
2. Less maneuverable than front-end.
3. Digs only six to nine inches deep.

Characteristics of tillers

There is a wide variation among tillers in their horsepower and engines, speed, size, type of tines, tilling width and depth, handles, and available accessories. The greatest choice is found among front-end tillers, with many different models on the market. Rear-end tillers tend to be somewhat similar in construction, ranging in horsepower from 4 to 10; front-end models range from 2 to 8 hp.

Engines: Offered in two- or four-cycle models. The former are fueled by oil and gas mixed together; the later have separate gasoline and oil chambers, like an automobile. Another choice is between gear drive and chain drive; the latter is more expensive initially but is up to 35 percent more efficient.

Speed: The less expensive machines are one-speed, good for average-to-loose soil and for cultivation. Two-speed operation helps in deep digging and is faster in churning soil and in mixing several ingredients. A few expensive tillers have four speeds, one each for heavy, medium and light soil, and for cultivating.

Size: Small, medium and large are the obvious variations here. Of interest is a relatively new idea, the compact tiller with foldable handle. This variant can be easily transported in a car trunk or stored in a small space; it is excellent for tilling easy, workable soil, but not good enough for heavier work.

Tines: There are generally three choices—spring-steel, bolo and slasher—for different uses. Spring-steel

Figure 5.08

John Deere tillers
The steel tines of this tiller are driven by a worm gear syswtem constructed with long-lasting anti-friction roller bearings. The depth bar setting and wheel adjustment control tilling depths and forward speed. Reverse drive allows it to back away from fences and tight spots without having to be lifted.
JOHN DEERE
Moline, IL 61265

Figure 5.09

Adjustable tiller
A versatile tiller that can work narrow or wide areas. The tilling width can be adjusted from 7 to 22 inches – useful for weeding between rows. Has a chain drive and steel tines.
FORD NEW HOLLAND
New Holland, PA 17557

tines are all-purpose, made of special heat-treated steel that absorbs the impact of stones and rocks. They can penetrate hard soil, blend in organic material, and do a good job of bordering and cultivating. Bolo tines are narrow and curved, good for deep tilling and shallow weed control. Slasher tines provide brute strength for tough soil and roots.

Tilling width and depth: Many models give you only one width (often 20 inches), while others have adjustable widths from 6 to 32 inches. (One model has expansion tines to 5 feet!) On most front-end models depth capability varies from 7 to 12 inches. Most machines are adjustable, utilizing adjustable wheels, a depth stick, or a combination of both. On some models the depth can be controlled from the handle while tilling.

Handles: In addition to the folding handles on compact tillers, other models have tilt handles, allowing the operator to walk alongside, not behind, the tines and thus not leave any footprints in the newly cultivated soil. And some handles can also be adjusted up and down.

Accessories: A wide and ever-increasing variety of attachments are offered. With some, your tiller can be converted into a tractor for plowing, cultivating, leveling and even snow removal and other such jobs.

Figure 5.10

Yard Marvel

These tillers are extremely versatile. The sod stripper attachment makes it easy to remove the soil to create a vegetable garden. The trencher attachment digs ditches. It also has dual purpose tines with pick points for faster digging action. The tine sets can be reversed for surface cultivation.
YARD MARVEL MFG CO., INC.
5509 N. Market St.
Spokane, WA 99207

SMALL CULTIVATORS

The latest power development for gardeners is the power cultivator/hoe/tiller. Both electric and gas power models can be used to cultivate small gardens even among tightly spaced plants and vine crops. They can weed shallow depths at 1 to 3 inches, or till up to 10 inches deep. All weigh under 30 pounds and are much easier to handle than the standard size rototiller.

LAWN/GARDEN TRACTORS

Garden experts say you should consider four points when deciding whether to purchase a lawn garden tractor:-
1. Can you afford it?
2. Do you have a lot of different jobs to perform?
3. Are you growing vegetables seriously in large quantities?
4. Is it impossible to find inexpensive labor in your neighborhood?

Figure 5.11

Electric weeder/cultivator

The Green Machine's electric Weeder/Cultivator's oscillating steel tines churn up, loosen and aerate the soil. Lightweight and easy to handle, this cultivator is perfect for cultivation of mini-gardens and large garden areas. it is especially useful for mixing soil amendments like peat moss, compost and manure into the top six inches of the soil.

Garden tractors with their attachments can perform many functions. They are good for seed bed preparation, tilling, cultivating, planting and more. They can be used as mowers, and they are helpful in leaf and grass disposal, utilizing sweepers, vacuum units, composters. They are good for grading; they will load materials, haul, spray, dig and do many other chores.

There are, of course, many models on the market. Here are some points and the variations to consider when purchasing a tractor:

Horsepower: There are three broad categories: Tractors with under 10 hp. are used primarily for tending a yard under one acre and for light snow removal; those with 10 to 14 hp. are good for preparing a good-sized vegetable garden and are able to handle a variety of cultivating equipment; those with 16 to 20 hp. are designed for heavier-duty, large garden work, and utility chores.

Transmission controls: Tractors in the 10 to 14 hp. category usually have gearshift transmissions. Some have 3 or 4 speed transaxles or, combined with a high/low range selector, 6 speeds forward, one speed backward; one model allows a variable control speed in each range without clutching. Tractors in the 16-hp. and above class generally use hydrostatic drive, which is like automatic transmission. There is just one lever, which provides forward and reverse. One tractor model has a foot-operated hydrostatic pedal that requires uniform foot pressure. A hand control mounted through the dash panel is generally the most convenient system.

Some tractors offer almost vibration-free operation achieved by proper balancing or isolating the engine on rubber mounts. Many new tractor models also have completely enclosed engines, which reduce noise levels.

Interiors: Best is a welded steel, one-piece design. Some tractors have a two-piece frame that is bolted and riveted together.

Axles: Best are solid cast iron. Some models have hollow axles of shaped steel: these are not durable.

Steering spindle: A 1-inch spindle is the mark of a well-built tractor. Steering spindles of ¾-inch diameter have less bearing surface for the front wheels to turn on, allowing heat to build up.

Operator's section: The station should be uncluttered so you can get in and out without hindrance. Controls should be within convenient reach from the seat. Best are color-coded controls for easier identification. The seat should be padded with a high backrest. Brake and clutch pedals should be wrapped in rubber.

Figure 5.13

TILLING CLAY SOIL

Since clay is extremely hard, start tilling at a very shallow depth. On each succeeding pass go down a couple of more inches until you reach the depth you want. It is difficult to work clay when it is wet. If you do, it will lump together and become extremely hard as it dries out. An especially heavy clay soil may be quite slow to dry out below the surface. To solve this problem, till at a depth of 3 to 4 inches, let the plot dry out for a day then till deeper.

Figure 5.12

Snapper garden tractors
Snapper garden tractors featur a high/low dual range transmission. Disc drive lets you shift on the go. Other standard features include 8-position tilt steering wheel, adjustable seat, electric front PTO clutch and a 9 position lift.
SNAPPER POWER EQUIPMENT
P.O. Box 777
Mcdonough, GA 20253

Figure 5.14

Ford garden tractor
Hydrostatic drive in some models provides an infinite range of forward ground speeds from 0 to 6 mph. Heel-toe pedal lets you speed up, slow down and change direction without clutching or shifting gears. a 26 to 40 inch rotary tiller can be attached for easy seed-bed preparation.
FORD NEW HOLLAND, INC.
New Holland, PA 17557

Figure 5.15
Speedy hoe
  This 23 pound tiller/cultivator is designed for spot tilling and weeding. Powered by a 1.6 HP 2-cycle engine, it is especially useful for working the soil in small gardens.
  GARDEN WAY MFG
  102nd St. & 9th Ave.
  Troy, NY 12180

Figure 5.16
Mainline Lady Bug
  The Mainline engine is mounted directly to the all gear drive transmission resulting in a low center of gravity. Can be used in smaller gardens. Optional attachments include a dozer blade, snow thrower, log splitter, sickle bar mower, bulk liquids pump, sprayer, trailer dump cart, hiller/furrower, power platform pulley, and one- and two-way plows.
  CENTRAL STATES MAINLINE
  Box 348
  London, OH 34140

MANUFACTURERS OF FRONT-END TILLERS

AMERICAN HONDA MOTOR
  CO., INC.
Box 50
Gardena, CA 92047

ARIENS CO.
655 West Ryan St.
Brillion, WI 54110

ALLIS CHALMERS
Box 512
Milwaukee, WI 53201

ATLAS TOOL & MFG CO.
5151 Natural Bridge Rd.
St. Louis, MO 63115

AUTO HOE, INC.
Box 121
DePere, WS 53074

BOLENS-FMC
215 S. Park St.
Port Washington, WI 53074

DAYTON ELECTRIC MFG
5959 W. Howard St.
Chicago, IL 60648

JOHN DEERE
John Deere Rd.
Moline, IL 61265

FELDMAN ENG & MFG
639 Monroe St.
Sheboygan Falls, WI 53085

GILSON BROTHERS
Box 152
Plymouth, WI 53073

HAHN, INC.
Outdoor Products
1625 N Garvin St.
Evansville, IN 47717

HEALD, INC.
Box 1148
Benton Harbor, MI 49022

INTERNATIONAL
  HARVESTER
401 N. Michigan Ave.
Chicago, IL 60611

JACOBSEN
Div. of Textron, Inc.
1721 Packard Ave.
Racine, WI 53403-2561

MAGNA AMERICAN CORP.
Box 90
Raymond, MS 39154

MASSEY-FERGUSON, INC.
1901 Bell Ave.
Des Moines, IA 50315

MCDONOUGH POWER
  EQUIPMENT
McDonough, GA 30253

MONO MFG CO.
P.O. Box 2787
Commercial St. Station
Springfield, MO 65803

MTD PRODUCTS, INC.
P.O. Box 36900
Cleveland, OH 44146

THE MURRAY OHIO MFG CO.
P.O. Box 268
Brentwood, TN 37027

ROPER SALES
1905 W. Court St.
Kankakee, IL 60901

SIMPLICITY MFG CO.
500 N. Spring St.
Port Washington, WI 53074

SOLO MOTORS, INC.
Box 5030
Newport News, VA 23605

THE TORO CO.
8111 Lyndale Ave. S.
Minneapolis, MN 55420

MANUFACTURERS OF REAR-END TILLERS

ARIENS CO.
655 West Ryan St.
Brillion, WI 54110

CENTRAL STATES MAINLINE
Box 348
London, OH 43140

GARDEN WAY MFG. CO., INC.
102nd St. & 9th Ave.
Troy, NY 12180

GIANT VAC MFG CO.
South Windham, CT 60033

HOWARD ROTOVATOR
Howard, IL 60033

OREGON MFG CO.
6920 S.W. 111th Ave.
Beaverton, OR 97005

PRECISION VALLEY MFG CO.
Springfield, VT 05156

ROTO HOE
100 Auburn Rd.
Newbury, OH 44065

YARD MAN CO.
Box 2741
Cleveland, OH 44111

MANUFACTURERS OF COMPACT TILLERS

ARIENS CO.
655 W. Ryan St.
Brillion, WS 54110

ATLAS TOOL & MFG CO.
5151 Natural Bridge Rd.
St. Louis, MO 63115

FELDMAN ENGINEERING
639 Monroe St.
Sheboygan Falls, WI 53085

GILSON BROS. CO.
Box 152
Plymouth, WI 53073

MTD PRODUCTS, INC.
P.O. Box 36900
Cleveland, OH 44136

ROPER SALES
1905 W. Court St.
Kankakee, IL 60901

SIMPLICITY MFG CO.
500 No. Spring St.
Port Washington, WI 53074

THE TORO CO.
8111 Lyndale Ave. S.
Minneapolis, MN 55420

MANUFACTURERS OF GARDEN TRACTORS

ALLIS CHALMERS CORP
Box 512
Milwaukee, WI 53201

ARIENS CO.
655 W. Ryan St.
Brillion, WI 54110

BOLENS-FMC
215 S. Park St.
Port Washington WI 53074

J.I. CASE CO.
Winnecone, WI 54986

DEERE & CO.
Deere Rd.
Moline, IL 61265

ENGINEERING PRODUCT
    CO.
P.O. Box 284
Waukeska, WI 53186

FORD TRACTOR
    OPERATIONS
Troy, MI 48084

FERRARI
6104 Avenida Encinas
Carlsbad, CA 72008

GILSON BROTHERS CO.
Box 152
Plymouth, WI 53030

GRAVELY, INC.
One Gravely Lane
Clemmons, NC 27012

HOMESTEADER-
    ANDERSON'S CUSTOM
    TRAILER MFG CO.
P.O. Box 207
Clinton, AR 60611

INTERNATIONAL
    HARVESTER
401 N. Michigan Ave.
Chicago, IL 60611

JACOBSEN
Div of Teltron, Inc.
1721 Packard Ave.
Racine, WI 53403-2561

KUBOTA TRACTOR CORP.
300 W. Carob St.
Compton, CA 90220

MASSEY-FERGUSON, INC.
1901 Bell Ave.
Des Moines, IA 50315

MTD PRODUCTS, INC.
P.O. Box 36900
Cleveland, OH 44136

Figure 5.17
Hiller/furrower
This hiller/furrower mounts on the back of any Troy-Bilt tiller without tools. It is used for digging trenches or furrows, for forming raised beds and for hilling corn and potatoes.
    GARDEN WAY MFG.
    102nd St. & 9th Ave.
    Troy, NY 12180

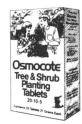

Osmocote® Osmocote® Osmocote®

SIERRA Sierra Chemical Company, P.O. Box 4003, Milpitas, CA 95035-2003. Tel. 408/263-8080 • TWX 910/338-0565
© 1988 Sierra Chemical Company, Milpitas, CA 95035. Osmocote* is a registered trademark of Sierra Chemical Company for its brand of controlled release fertilizers.

SCR-222/18

6. Transplanting

AFTER A YEAR OR two of vegetable growing, many gardeners decide to steal a march on Nature by planting seeds indoors during late winter and early spring. Later, when the weather has warmed up, they transplant their homegrown seedlings to the outdoor garden. By doing this they not only lengthen their growing season, they also avoid the expense and risk of buying seedlings from a nursery.

Many vegetables benefit from transplanting. For instance, it is very difficult to start such vegetables as tomatoes, eggplant, and peppers outdoors as seeds. Other vegetables such as lettuce, onions, melons, squash and corn can be started indoors or outdoors.

THE METHODS OF TRANSPLANTING

There are many techniques that can be used with transplants, and the most important will be discussed in this chapter. Warming the soil electrically can hasten the germination and growth of seeds indoors. Outdoors, coldframes and hotbeds can be used as intermediate stopovers between the indoor seedling bed and the garden—or, as the weather gets warmer, as places where seeds can be eased through the first weeks of life. The techniques of English cloche gardening can be used to protect tender seeds that have been planted directly in the garden soil.

Starting transplants inside

Many gardeners have not tried their luck with seedlings because they think the whole process is difficult and time-consuming. In fact, it's quite simple. To start, all you need is: (a) a growing medium; (b) warmth and moisture; and (c) adequate light. There are two general methods to choose from—the two step and the one step.

Two-step method:

You can start quantities of plants in containers and transplant them later into individual pots. Plant initially in commercial plastic flats or half-flats, in shallow wooden crates or in such household items as aluminum meat loaf pans, milk cartons cut lengthwise, large frozen food containers, cut-off gallon bleach containers and the like. Following is an outline of the procedure:-

Step 1:
1. Fill the container with vermiculite, commercial soil mix or a homemade soil mix. Scrape off the excess, mix with a flat knife or stick, then press down the remaining soil lightly.
2. Make furrows with a pencil or similar tool.
3. When using large flats, water from above before planting seeds. With smaller containers, water from the bottom after planting. You can put one or two inches of water in a sink and place the container in it. When the surface of the vermiculite becomes moist, take the container out and allow it to drain.
4. Sow seeds directly from the package, about an inch apart. Sow more seeds than the number of plants you'd lke to end up with. Then, when they come up, thin out the weak plants by clipping with a small pair of scissors.
5. Slip the trays into a plastic bag (a bread bag will do fine), and keep as close to 70 degrees Fahrenheit. as possible. Don't water again until after germination—that is, after you see the little sprouts poking up through the soil—and after that add only enough water to keep the soil mix damp.

Step 2:
When the first true leaves have formed (the first two leaflike growths are not leaves, the third and succeeding ones are), dig the seedlings out and put them into pots; handling them carefully by the seed leaves. When they are five or six inches high, you can transfer them into the garden plot or large container.

Figure 6.01

STARTING VEGETABLES		
Method	**Type of Vegetables**	
Start directly from seed in garden	Beets Carrots Corn salad Cress, Garden	Okra Parsnip Radishes	Rutabagas Salisfy Turnip
Start indoors, transplant to garden	Broccoli Brussel sprouts Cabbage Cardoon	Cauliflower Celeriac Celery Eggplant	Florence Fennel Peppers Tomatoes
Start indoors or outdoors	Chinese cabbage Chard Collards Corn	Endive, Escarole Kale Kohlrabi	Leeks Lettuce Mustard
Start from seed in garden or start indoors in individual biodegradable containers to protect sensitive root systems	Beans Cucumbers Muskmelons	Peas Pumpkins	Squash Watermelons
Start in other ways	Artichokes: start from root divisions	Onions: start from sets seeds, or small plants	Potatoes: start from potato pieces

Figure 6.02

COOL- AND WARM-SEASON CROPS			
Cool-Season Crops		**Warm-Season Crops**	
Very hardy (plant 4-6 weeks after last frost-free date	Hardy (plant 2-4 weeks before frost-free date)	Not cold-hardy (plant on frost-free date)	Needs hot weather (plant 1 week or more after frost-free date)
Asparagus Broccoli Cabbage Lettuce Onions Peas Radishes Rhubarb Spinach Turnips	Beets Carrots Chard Mustard Parsnips Potatoes	Beans, Snap Corn New Zealand Spinach Okra Pumpkins Soybeans Squash Tomatoes	Beans, Lima Cucumbers Eggplant Peppers Sweet potatoes

But before you complete this step you must be sure that the weather conditions are suitable. The time to transplant cool-season crops such as lettuce and celery is when the outside temperature averages 55 to 75° F. For warm-season crops such as tomatoes and peppers, the time to transplant is when the average outside temperature is in the 65 to 80° F range. (For a breakdown of cool- and warm-season crops see Figure 6.02.)

One-Step Method:

Seeds can also be sown directly into small pots or cubes made of biodegradable material. Generally it's one seed to a pot. After the plants have come up, and when the temperature is right for the particular vegetable (see above), you can plant each of these containers directly into the garden bed or larger container. Roots grow right through the wall of the pots and spread into the surrounding soil.

One of the major advantages of this procedure is that it avoids the root shock that besets many vegetables when they are transplanted. Large-seeded plants such as squash and melons should always be handled in this way; their root systems do not tolerate

transplanting well.

Pots and pellets

There are several kinds of small pots, pellets, cubes and other small containers available for use in transplanting. **Jiffy-7** pellets are compressed sterile sphagnum peat and soil with added fertilizer, all enclosed in a plastic net. The pellet expands to form a small container (1¾" x 2") when placed in water. The seed is planted directly in the pellet just before this watering. Jiffy pots are available in several forms: Jiffy-7 Special, with a preformed quarter-inch hole, ideal for cuttings; Jiffy-7 Trays, prepackaged pellets in green plastic trays; and Jiffy-9, which is held together with a binder instead of a net.

Other brands include **BR-8 Gro-Blocks**, which are fiber blocks containing fertilizer; **Fertil-Cubes and Gro-Blocks**, which are made from a blend of mosses, plant food and vermiculite, and each of which has a depression for planting seed; **Peat Pots**, which are made of fiber and should be filled with synthetic soil. These latter are square or round and come in multiple break-apart strips. **Cell Pots** or **Paks** are light plastic pots, filled with synthetic soil, for growing individual

Use Jiffy-7s® to start seedlings.
Photo Credit: Carefree

Use Jiffy-7s® to root cuttings of indoor plants.
Photo Credit: Carefree

Use Jiffy-7s· to root cuttings for outdoor use.

There's no transplant shock when started in Jiffy-7s®.
Photo Credit: Carefree

Figure 6.03

Jiffy-7s

Jiffy-7 pellets are compressed sterile sphagnum peat and soil with added fertilizer, all enclosed in a plastic net. The pellet expands to form a small container when placed in water. The seed is planted directly in the pellet, then watered.
CAREFREE GARDEN PRODUCTS
P.O. Box 338
West Chicago, IL 60185

"pop-out" transplant. They are available as single cells or in units of 2, 3, 4 or 12 cells. There are also larger sizes.

Seed starter kits

Several companies now offer vegetable and herb starter kits. Each kit contains everything you need to grow healthy seedlings to transplant size. These kits vary from containers already planted with individual vegetable seeds to kits with cubes, fertilizers, trays, heating cables and clear plastic tops to keep in the moisture (these latter are often referred to as indoor greenhouses; for some examples see Chapter 10).

TIMING YOUR INDOOR PLANTING

If you put your seeds in containers too early, the plants may grow too large for their containers. As they sit inside waiting for the proper time to be transplanted, they may grow weak. If, on the other hand, you plant too late, your seeds will not be mature enough to cope with the move out-of-doors. So you've got to know what you're doing—timing is everything.

The two most important factors in the indoor-planting equation are the climate of your area and the time your seeds need for germination, leaf development and growth. You should be able to get this latter information from individual seed packets. (For a general idea about early and late varieties of various vegetables refer in this book to Chapter 13.)

Take onions as an example. If your seeds take eight weeks to become mature enough for transplanting, and if the middle of May is the proper time in your area to set out onions, then start them indoors in the middle of March.

Figure 6.04 ▶

Seed Starter Kit

Several companies now offer vegetable and herb starter kits. Each kit contains everything size. Most can be purchased at your garden center.

HARDENING THE TRANSPLANTS

Before actually planting the seedlings in the garden bed or in a patio or balcony container, you should get them used to outdoor conditions. Adjust the young plants by placing them outside, in their pots, around the middle of the day. Don't overexpose them, especially at first, but gradually increase the time they are left out in the fresh air. Be sure to bring them indoors whenever frost seems likely, especially overnight. In one way or another, expose your seedlings to lower temperatures for about two weeks before setting them out in the garden bed.

PROTECTIVE DEVICES

You can easily protect vegetables from the weather by placing a cover over individual plants, a section of the garden, or an entire Vegetable Factory bed. These devices make it possible to raise the garden temperature 5 to 15° F or more. This allows you to start crops earlier and to extend the season for such warm-season crops such as tomatoes and eggplant by two to four weeks.

A *cloche* is any covering that admits the sunlight to warm a bed. In a Vegetable Factory garden this might mean anything from a Dixie cup turned upside down over a single plant to a bed-wide greenhouse.

When the sun's rays pass through the glazed surface, they are stored in the soil as energy. This heat energy has a longer wavelength than light energy and will not pass back out through the glazing. The trapped heat raises the temperature of the soil and air under the cover. As a result, even simple cloches made from household materials will extend the growing season by at least a few weeks.

Hot caps and *hot tents* are the simplest devices to use in a Vegetable Factory bed. They are slightly translucent, and let in enough light to support plant growth. You can buy hot caps and hot tents at garden centers or nurseries or from seed catalogs. Or you can make your own by cutting the bottoms off plastic jugs, and by turning plastic containers (such as cake covers) over individual vegetables.

Soft plastics (most commonly polyethylene) are lightweight and inexpensive, and are useful for covering a variety of cloches you intend to move around the garden. A drawback is that they don't last as long as rigid plastics. Here are some ideas for making soft plastic cloches:-

- Stretch polyethylene coathanger wickets to make a plastic tent. Hold down the plastic with rocks.
- Cover a hinged A frame with polyethylene. It can be easily moved about the garden and folded for storage when not in use.

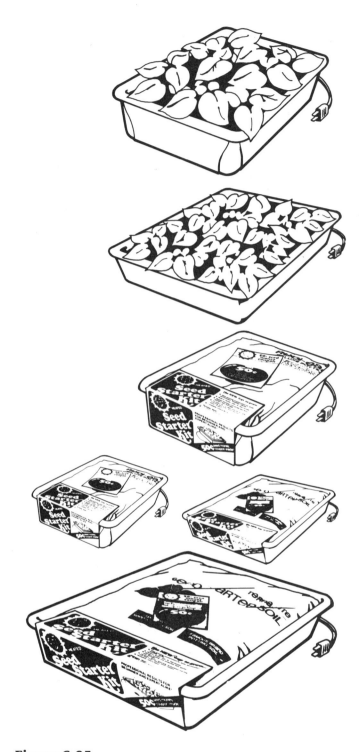

Figure 6.05

PLANTING IN PEAT KUBES USING AN ELECTRIC SOIL WARMER

Wet the soil thoroughly and plant the seedlings according to the directions on the seed package. The healthy seedlings with strong roots, well-developed stems and full leaves will show the benefits of soil warming during the germination and early stages of growth. The seedlings in peat pots can be placed directly into prepared holes in your garden or into permanent pots indoors.

- Cover the entire bed or a portion of the bed with a 'Wicket Tunnel'. This tunnel is made of construction wire covered with clear plastic. Construction wire is heavy wire mesh used in pouring concrete foundations. Buy it at any lumberyard or building supply store. Cut the wire to fit you bed.
- For plants normally grown in vertical cages, simply wrap polyethylene sheets around the cage and staple it in place.

Rigid plastics (often fiberglass) can be bent over a frame and aren't damaged by wind and rain. One cloche design can be made by drilling a pair of holes in rectangular sheets of acrylic and fastening them together at the top by passing notebook rings through the holes. These can be moved around easily and folded for storage.

Or create a cucumber incubator from a flexed sheet of translucent ribbed fiberglass. This incubator traps growth-enhancing heat and carbon dioxide to speed up seed-to-harvest time for melons, pumpkins, squash and cucumbers.

The **Floating Row Cover** requires no wire support. It consists of soft, lightweight polypropylene fabric that allows light and water to pass through. As your crops grow, they lift the cover along with them. Simply roll it out loosely over the seedbed and secure the edges with soil or mulch.

One word of warning about plastic: on warm, sunny days, the air heat under the plastic cover can quickly become too great for plants. It is therefore essential to provide good ventilation and to check the temperature regularly. The easiest way to do this is to place a thermometer inside the device. When temperature rises 10° F or more above the maximum for the specific vegetables, remove or open the protective device. Replace or close it only on cooler days.

COLD FRAMES

Cold frames and hotbeds mark the next step in Vegetable Factory evolution. A cold frame is an

Figure 6.06

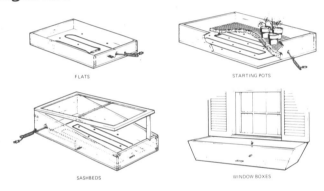

FLATS   STARTING POTS

SASHBEDS   WINDOW BOXES

Four Flats where heating cables can be used
Heating cables can be used with a variety of containers. Make sure the bottom surface is evenly covered.

There are several devices on the market you might want to consider.

Portable roll greenhouses can simply be laid out over the whole bed or a portion of the bed. A **three-piece miniature-greenhouse**, resembling a clear plastic garbage can with a shower-cap cover, allows you to set out tomatoes, peppers and eggplant at least five weeks early; as the plants grow, you remove the dome lid.

The **Wallo' Water** consists of a plastic ring of sectioned, cylindrical tubes filled with water. The liquid will hold heat from the day's sun to warm the plants at night. If the water should freeze, heat is still released as the water cools. This device protects plants to 16° F and allows you to water and fertilize without removing the cloche.

The **Sunhat** is a rigid plastic cone that has alternating clear and green stripes. The transparent stripes let sunshine in, and the colored stripes provide shade.

unheated box-like glass- or clear plastic-covered structure for protecting plants. A hotbed is a cold frame with an added heat source. Cloches are designed for short-term use, cold frames and hotbeds can be used for year-round gardening.

A Vegetable Factory cold frame consists of a wooden or masonry box with a plastic or glass top. For maximum exposure to the sun, the cold frame should face due south. This is easy if you orient your cold frame directly north and south. It doesn't matter if you are slightly off—the orientation can be varied as much as 20 degrees east or west without significantly inhibiting the cold frame's solar gain.

The top should be slanted so that the sun's rays strike it as near as possible to a 90-degree angle. Because the sun's path through the sky changes daily there is no way to set the top so that is perpendicular to the sun at all times.

The rule of thumb is, add 20 degrees to your latitude to arrive at the best angle from the horizon. If you

Figure 6.07

FROM SEED TO PLANT

Days For Seed to Emerge at Different Temperatures (degrees F)

Crop	32°	41°	50°	59°	68°	77°	86°	95°	104°
Asparagus	0	0	52.8	24.0	14.6	10.3	11.5	19.3	28.4
Bean, Lima	0	0	0	30.5	17.6	6.5	6.7	0	0
Bean, Snap	0	0	0	16.1	11.4	8.1	6.4	6.2	0
Beet	0	42.0	16.7	9.7	6.2	5.0	4.5	4.6	0
Cabbage	0	0	14.6	8.7	5.8	4.5	3.5	0	0
Carrot	0	50.6	17.3	10.1	6.9	6.2	6.0	8.6	0
Cauliflower	0	0	19.5	9.9	6.2	5.2	4.7	0	0
Celery	0	41.0	16.0	12.0	7.0	0	0	0	0
Corn	0	0	21.6	12.4	6.9	4.0	3.7	3.4	0
Cucumber	0	0	0	12.0	6.2	4.0	3.1	3.0	0
Eggplant	0	0	0	0	13.1	8.1	5.3	0	0
Lettuce	49.0	14.9	7.0	3.9	2.6	2.2	2.6	0	0
Muskmelon	0	0	0	0	8.4	4.0	3.1	0	0
Okra	0	0	0	27.2	17.4	12.5	6.8	6.4	6.7
Onion	135.8	30.6	13.4	7.1	4.6	3.6	3.9	12.5	0
Parsley	0	0	29.0	17.0	14.0	13.0	12.3	0	0
Parsnip	171.7	56.7	26.7	19.3	13.6	14.9	31.6	0	0
Pea	0	36.0	13.5	9.4	7.5	6.2	5.9	0	0
Pepper	0	0	0	25.0	12.5	8.4	7.6	8.8	0
Radish	0	29.2	11.2	6.3	4.2	3.5	3.0	0	0
Spinach	62.2	22.5	11.7	6.9	5.7	5.1	6.4	0	0
Tomato	0	0	42.9	13.6	8.2	5.9	5.9	9.2	0
Turnip	0	0	5.2	3.0	1.9	1.4	1.1	1.2	0
Watermelon	0	0	0	0	11.8	4.7	3.5	3.0	0

Source: Department of Vegetable Crops, University of California, Davis.

Figure 6.09

Figure 6.08

Juwel cold frame

   The latest in cold-frames. The gabled roof form permits higher growth and allows the soil to be worked earily by lifting up the window from below. Double-ribbed panels with air chambers store the heat. The frame can be limitlessly extended with an extension kit.

Sauna bath for seeds

   Homemade tunnels of clear plastic stretched over wire create a warm moist greenhouse for sprouting seeds. In the spring, use tunnels to collect solar heat and protect seedlings from cold temperatures and drying winds. Leave the tunnels in place until the weather becomes warm. Close the ends only during cold weather.

photo credit: National Garden Bureau

live in northern California as we do, or in northern Colorado, southern Nebraska, central Illinois, Indiana, Ohio, Pennsylvania or New Jersey, you're near the 40-degree parallel. So you should slant the top 60 degrees from the horizon. In northern Oregon, southern Minnesota, and northern Wisconsin through central Maine, you will need to slant the top 65 degrees from horizontal.

To construct a cold frame or hotbed, enclose a bed or a portion of it with 2 x 8 or 2 x 10-inch boards, forming a box. The box can sit on the bed frame if it has one, or directly on the ground. Make the cover out of 1 x 3-inch boards glazed with either two layers of windowglass, two layers of polyethylene plastic, or a combination of both. You can also use double-pane recycled windows if you can find a size that fits your bed.

Figure 6.11
Tomato Gro-Bags

Tomato Gro-Bags increase yields and allow tomatoes to be set out earlier in the spring. The consistent warm, moist atmosphere within the bag fosters more abundant growth while protecting tender plants from driving rains, hail and unexpected late frosts. The perforations are designed to allow proper air circulation and prevent overheating.
EASY GARDENER, INC.
P.O. Box 21025
Waco, TX 76702

Figure 6.10
Plastic fabric mulches

The newer plastic mulches overcome the disadvantages of conventional plastic sheets. Landscape fabrics come with thousands of tiny funnels molded into the fabric. They gather and channel water to the soil, allowing maximum air and water movement while at the same time blocking out direct light necessary for weed growth. This reduces compaction and water evaporation.
EASY GARDENER, INC.
P.O. Box 21025
Waco, TX 76702

Soft plastic used for glazing is lighter and cheaper than glass. Rigid plastic can be more expensive. Most plastics, however, deteriorate rapidly when exposed to the sun and atmosphere. You can fasten polyethylene films and rigid plastics directly to the frame with nails, screws or staples.

In our own area, the winters are so light that we frequently use single glazing for cold frames. In cold winter climates, many expert gardeners build the lid

Figure 6.12

CHOOSING THE CORRECT CABLE LENGTH

Lowest Temp Reading F	Square Feet of Soil to be Heated									
	1	2	3	4-5	6	7-8	9-11	12-16	17-22	23-25
Below 0°	6'	12'	24'	36'	48'	60'	80'	120'	160'	200'
0 - 15°	6'	12'	24'	36'	36'	48'	60'	80'	120'	160'
15 - 30°	6'	12'	12'	24'	36'	36'	48'	60'	120'	120'
Above 30°	6'	12'	12'	24'	24'	24'	36'	48'	60'	80'

Figure 6.13

PLANT GROWING TEMPERATURE RANGE

Minimum Growing Temp °F	Optimum Temp° F	Maximum Temp° F	Crop
30	75	85	Asparagus, rhubarb
35	75	85	Garlic, leek, lettuce, mustard, onion, parsley, peas spinach
40	85	90	Beet, broccoli, brussel sprouts, cabbage, carrot, cauliflower, celery, chard, collard, kale, kohlrabi, parsnip, potato, radish
50	85	100	Corn
60	85-90	95-100	Bean, cucumber, eggplant, melon, okra, pepper, pumpkin, squash
65	80-85	95	Tomato

HOTKAPS®
Plant Protectors
6" High—
11" Diameter at Base

Figure 6.14

SEED GERMINATION TEMPERATURE NEEDS

Crop	Minimum °F	Optimum Range, °F
Asparagus	50	60-85
Beans, Lima	60	65-85
Beans, Snap	60	60-85
Beets	40	50-85
Cabbage	40	45-95
Carrots	40	45-85
Cauliflower	40	45-85
Celery	40	60-70
Chard	40	50-85
Corn	50	60-95
Cucumbers	60	65-90
Eggplant	60	75-90
Lettuce	35	40-80
Muskmelon	60	75-95
Okra	60	70-95
Onions	35	50-95
Parsley	40	50-85
Parsnips	35	50-70
Peas	40	40-75
Peppers	60	65-95
Pumpkins	60	70-90
Radish	40	45-90
Spinach	35	45-75
Squash	60	70-95
Tomatoes	50	60-85
Turnips	40	60-105
Watermelon	60	70-95

Source: Department of Vegetable Crops, Universith of California, Davis

Figure 6.15

VEGETABLE LIGHT NEEDS

Partial Sun	Full Sun
Beets	Beans
Carrots	Broccoli
Cauliflower	Brussel sprouts
Chard	Cabbage
Lettuce	Corn
Onions	Eggplant
Parsley	Muskmelons
Peas	Peppers
Radishes	Pumpkins
Spinach	Squash, Summer
	Squash, Winter
	Tomatoes

Figure 6.16

Hotkaps

Commercial paper protectors come in a number of shapes and sizes: Standard 'Hotcaps', 'King-sized hotkaps', 'Hotents' and 'Super Hotents'.

Figure 6.17

Use following table to plan your seeding optimum yield and quality:-

Crop	Approx. No. of Seed per gram	per ounce	Final plant spacing in row (inches)	Suggested seeding rate/ foot of row
Beans, bush		100	3-4	4
Beans, pole		100	6-8	4
Beans, lima		20-70	6-8	4
Beets	60	1,600	3-4	8
Broccoli	320	9,000	9-12	6
Brussels sprouts	300	8,500	18	6
Cabbage	300	8,500	12-14	6
Carrots	800	2,300	2	12
Cauliflower	350	10,000	14-18	6
Swiss Chard	40	1,200	10-12	6
Corn		100-200	10-12	2
Cucumbers	35	1,000	12	2 (H)
Endive	880	25,000	10-12	6
Lettuce	8800	25,000	10-12	6
Melons	35	1,000	12	2 (H)
Okra		5,000	8-12	6
Onion, Dry bulb	330	9,500	3-4	12
Parsnip	420	12,000	3-4	8
Peas		2,000	3-4	6
Pepper	160	4,500	12-14	6
Pumpkin		100	24	2 (H)
Radish	70	2,000	1-2	12
Spinach	100	2,800	3-4	6
Squash, Summer		100	18	2 (H)
Squash, Winter		400	18	2 (H)
Tomato	380	11,000	12	6
Turnip	460	13,000	3-4	8
Watermelon		200-300	24	2 (H)

(H) Plant in hills, not rows.

Figure 6.18

Wallo' Water

The Wallo' Water enables you to start tomatoes, eggplants, squash or other warm-weather vegetables six to eight weeks earlier without fear of freezing. During the day, the water held between the plastic layers absorbs heat, moderating the temperature inside the tepee. As the water cools at night, it releases up to 900,000 calories of heat to warm plants. Wallo' Water protects vegetables from outside temperatures as low as 10° F.
TERRACOPIA, INC.
2365 South Main
Salt Lake City, UT 84115

with glass on the outside and plastic inside. This insulates better, and the glass screens out ultraviolet rays that damage plastic. What's more, the plastic protects the bed if the glass is broken.

In areas with cold winters, you need to insulate cold frames. We line them with two-inch thick foam sheets because they are easy to cut and handle. Since foam deteriorates with exposure to water and sunlight, paint exposed surfaces with a white latex paint. The frame should be as tight as you can make it. Fill the gaps, corners, seams and other joints with silicone caulking compound. Make sure you seal air spaces around glass or plastic glazing panels.

In really cold climates, you can add a two-inch thick foam panel to the inside of the lid. For large cold frames, glue the foam to the back of half-inch plywood, and cut to fit the inside of the lid. Put the panel inside the lid at night to insulate your plants from the cold, and remove it during the day to allow sunlight to enter.

Ventilation is vital. Direct sun can overheat your cold frame. Waste gasses may also increase to harmful levels, and carbon dioxide levels can decrease, slowing plant growth. Humidity builds inside the frame and condensation inside the box encourages mildew, fungus and bacterial diseases.

On warm or sunny days, open the top of the frame to allow air to circulate. Be careful, though, if it is extremely cold outside—exposing your vegetables to prolonged cold is harmful. The best way to overcome this problem is to buy automatic vent controllers (about $25), the kind used for greenhouse ventilation panels; they are available from a number of catalog seed firms. (See Figure 13.01, Chapter 13.) These vent controllers open automatically when the atmosphere in the frame becomes too hot, and close when the temperature lowers.

If overheating is a consistent problem, place cheesecloth or burlap over the top or paint the glazing white.

You may want to consider buying a ready-made cold frame. A new design from Austria has a peaked roof with four hinged top panels. The top and side panels are made of strong weatherproof polycarbonate plastic. The lid is double-glazed. You can add units to make the frame bigger as your garden grows.

HOTBEDS

A cold frame with an added heat source becomes a hotbed. By heating the soil in beds, you can speed up the seed germination of most vegetables. The seeds of cool-season crops sprout eagerly at soil temperatures as low as 50⁰ F. Seeds of warm-season crops 'sulk' and rot when soil temperatures remain below 65 degrees. Within these two categories, each vegetable has its own temperature requirements for seed germination. (See Figure 6.14 for seed germination temperatures of commonly grown vegetables.)

The most efficient methods of heating are by cable or mats. Most come with a built-in thermostat that makes it easy to monitor the soil temperature and keep it constant. To install cable in a bed, lay the cable out on the ground within the frame and spread it evenly over the entire area in large loops. Cover the cable with 2 to 3 inches of sand and then with 3 to 6 inches of garden soil.

To heat the frame naturally, place it on top of a pit containing about 18 inches of green organic material (grass clippings or other vegetation) or fresh manure, The bacterial action involved in the rotting of the material will supply heat to the frame. You can also heat a frame by placing one or more light bulbs in the box. This is not a particularly efficient method, but it does work.

Figure 6.20

THE RIGHT SOIL MIX

The soil mix used makes a tremendous difference in seedling growth. A recent study using tomato plants showed that seedlings planted in ordinary potting mix had the least growth in a six week period. Plants grown in perlite and vermiculite did a little better. Seedlings grown in pure sand grew twice as fast as seedlings grown in potting mix, perlite or vermiculite. Plants grown in either Cornell or University of California mix did best. In six weeks tomato plants grown in potting mix were barely an inch high.

Figure 6.19

SEED GERMINATION

Crop	Minimum federal standard germination percent	Seeds per ounce (average)	Relative longevity (years)
Asparagus	60	1,400	3
Bean, Lima	70	20 - 70	3
Bean, Snap	75	100	3
Beet	65	2,000	4
Broccoli	75	8,100	3
Brussel sprouts	70	8,500	4
Cabbage	75	7,700	4
Carrot	55	22,000	3
Cauliflower	75	8,600	4
Celeriac	55	50,000	3
Celery	55	76,000	3
Chard	65	1,500	4
Chicory	65	20,000	4
Chinese cabbage	75	7,000	3
Corn	75	140	2
Cucumber	80	1,100	5
Eggplant	60	7,200	4
Endive	70	17,000	5
Kale	75	10,000	4
Kohlrabi	75	9,200	3
Leek	60	9,900	2
Lettuce	80	26,000	6
Muskmelon	75	1,100	5
New Zealand spinach	40	430	3
Okra	50	500	2
Onion	70	8,500	1
Parsley	60	18,000	1
Parsnip	60	6800	1
Pea	80	50 - 230	3
Pepper	55	4,500	2
Pumpkin	75	200	4
Radish	75	3,100	4
Rutabaga	75	11,000	4
Salsify	75	2,000	1
Spinach	60	2,900	3
Squash	75	180 - 380	4
Tomato	75	10,000	4
Turnip	80	14,000	4
Watermelon	70	320	4

Source: J.F. Harrington, University of California, Davis

Figure 6.21

TRANSPLANTING AIDS

Additives	Sources
Cold Frames	
Cold frames	PAR
Automatic cold frame	JUN, LED, PAR
Automatic openers	JUN, HEN
Fiber-Seed Starters	
Fiber trays	EAR, WILL
Fiber garden paks	BUR, EAR
Organic Starters	
Fertil-cubes	BUR, BURG, FAR, HAS, HEN, NIC, PAR, PER
Fertilepots	NIC
Hy-Fiber cubes	HAS
Jiffy-7 peat pellets	BUR, EAR, FAR, HAS, LET, LIB, STO, TWI, WET
Jiffy-9	EAR, HEN, LET, STO
Jiffy peat pots	EAR, JUN, LET, PER, TWI, WET, WIL
Jiffy strips	LIB, LET, PAR, TWI, WET
Jiffy paks	LET
Peat pots	BUR, FAR, HEN
Protective Devices	
Hotkaps	BUR, EAR, FAR, GUR, JUN, HEN, LED, LET
King-sized hotkaps	GUR
Sun Hats	BURG, EAR, GUR, HEN
Tomato Gro-bags	EAR, PAR
Wall O' Water	EAR, HEN, PIN
Plastic Seed Starters	
Germinating trays	LIB, LET, PER, TWI
Plastic growing cells	HAS, JUN, PAR, TWI
Polystrene flats and paks	EAR
Pro-trays	JOH
Plastic trays	LET, LIB, VES, WET
Plastic Cloches	
Greenhouse tunnels	FAR, PER, PIN, VIS
Greenhouse film	EAR, FAR, PIN
Starter mats	EAR
Seed Starter Kits	
Mini-electric greehouses	GUR, HEN, STO
Mini-greenhouses	PER, STO, VES
Seed kits	JOH, JUN, LIB, WIL PAR
Seed domes	JOH
Window greenhouses	EAR, STO, VES, WET
Soil Cables	
Heating cables/tapes	EAR, FAR, JOH, JUN, HEN, LED, PAR
Heating mats	EAR, JOH, JUN, LED
Seeding Mediums	
Perlite	WIL
Redi-earth	WIL
Seed starter mix	JOHN, JUN, PAR, STO
Vermiculite	WIL
Vegetable Tapes	
Vegetable seed tapes	BUR

[See Figure 13.01 Chapter 13 for explanation of source codes.]

Figure 6.22

Commercial cold frame
This cold frame has 8 mm-thick hollow chamber panes. Winder levers at the top to be adjusted to different positions at different levels.

7. Watering

PROPER WATERING IS EXTREMELY important to any garden. In fact, according to U.S. government studies, "water is the most frequent factor limiting plant growth." This is particularly true of vegetables, because most of them are constituted principally of water. Beyond this, water is essential to the manufacture of food and to its movement through a plant's circulatory system. Both oxygen and carbon dioxide enter and leave plants in water solution. In this chapter we will describe the best techniques and products available to help gardeners ensure that their vegetables receive the proper amount of water.

HOW MUCH WATER IS NEEDED?

In most areas of North America a rule of thumb is that vegetables need about an inch of rainfall per week. If Nature doesn't provide, then it's up to the home gardener to fill the gap. A 15 x 25 foot plot needs about 225 gallons of water per week. A plot double that size needs double the volume of water, and so on. If it rains a bit, you can reduce your watering a bit. But be careful. Although it's better to water too much than too little, try to do neither. A deluge may result in insufficient oxygen for the plant and interfere with root growth and function.

When you saturate the soil, you add water until it reaches 'field capacity'—that is, the point at which the air spaces in the soil can hold no more water. Ideally,

◀ **Figure 7.01**
Water Wand
This wand, manufactured by Scotts, allows you to reach into the middle of wide beds and under leaves. It helps keep the moisture off upper vegetable leaves.
O.M. SCOTTS & SONS
Marysville, OH 43041

you should keep your garden soil somewhere between this condition and the point at which moisture is so scarce that plant roots can no longer take water from the soil.

How often you water is as important as how much. If you sprinkle for a brief period each day, you will only wet the upper few inches of the soil. Light watering like this should be avoided because it causes roots to grow too close to the surface, adding the risk that a sudden hot spell will severely damage plants. The soil should be wet to a depth of 6 to 12 inches each time you water. Then it need not be watered again until the top few inches begin to dry out. You can take a trowel to dig in and check. If it rains, don't water until this trowel test shows that watering is needed. For many gardens, a good soaking once a week is just right.

METHODS OF WATERING

In addition to rain, which is not easy to control, there are two basic ways of bringing water to your garden. Some gardeners insist that the best way of watering vegetables is right on the ground, using some kind of irrigation system. Others believe that watering from above more closely approximates rain and is therefore better for vegetables. We'll discuss both methods.

Watering from above is generally the easiest method. However, a fair amount of water is lost through evaporation. Another disadvantage to this method is that it can damage some hot-weather crops—tomatoes, for instance, may crack. This can be prevented by watering overhead until the plants start to produce fruit, then watering on the ground thereafter. Overhead watering can also encourage mildew, especially if you live along the coast or a region with lots of fog where humidity tends to be high during the growing season. You can overcome this problem by watering in the morning, so that plants dry out by evening and do not sit overnight in ground that is continuously wet.

Watering from below takes less water, but it involves more work. It is not easy to set up and maintain this type of irrigation. However, in recent years a drip system has been developed that does an excellent job of providing plants with a good water supply, and in addition is not difficult or expensive to install. (More about this anon.)

Overhead watering

In addition to simple sprinklers, today's overhead watering devices can be divided into five major groups: pulsating sprinklers, oscillating sprinklers, rotating sprinklers, hand-held sprays (nozzles) and sprinkler spray heads (irrigation systems).

Pulsating sprinkler: This is the well-known 'rainbird' type, where water striking an arm moves the sprinkler around in a circle. Each sprinkler will cover an area 50 to 75 feet in radius and can be adjusted to water in a full circle or part circle. It is available in brass or less expensive plastic. Pulsating sprinklers can be used with a stationary underground pipe system and screwed into a standing pipe or utilized with a portable spike or sled base. One operating alone in a full circle is enough for a small garden. *Rated excellent for vegetable gardens.*

Oscillating sprinkler: This sprinkler is operated by water, moving back and forth to cover an area of 50 to 60 feet. It can also be set for varying coverage within that area. Oscillating sprinklers are available with timing devices that allow you to dial the total amount of water you want up to 1,200 gallons. These sprinklers spray in squares or rectangles—the shape of most gardens. *Rated good for vegetable gardens.*

Rotating sprinkler: There are many types of rotating sprinklers on the market. Generally, they consist of rotating arms or small rotating blades propelled by a spray of water. They will water in a circle from 5 to 50 feet. Some types will also fertilize while they water. Traveling sprinklers are generally the rotating type and can be made to travel along a hose laid down the middle of the garden. These will water an area up to 15,000 square feet. Some water can be wasted by these sprinklers because most water in a circle (although some are manufactured to water in a square. *Rated fair to good for vegetable gardens.*

Hand-held sprayer (nozzles, wands): Some gardeners insist that vegetable gardens must be hand watered. There is a wide variety of hose nozzles on the market today, including **aqua hand gun nozzles**, **straight nozzles**, **fan hand sprays** and **bubblers** for ground use. In addition, there are many water wands available—ranging from 24 to 52 inches long—that allow you to put the water exactly where you want it. These are available with special seeding nozzles, which produce a very fine mist that won't disturb vegetable seeds, or soft rain irrigator nozzles, which keep water from splashing and cut down runoff. *Wands with special nozzles are excellent for hand watering vegetable gardens.*

Sprinkler spray head (irrigation systems): Ground level or pop-up sprinker spray heads are used

Figure 7.02
Rain Wand
The soft-flow nozzle produces a full flow, soft concentrated water stream. Expecially useful for spot-watering individual plants.

Figure 7.03
Rain Guard
The Rain Guard automatically turns your watering system off if approximately an inch of rain falls. The system will start again automatically when the rainfall evaporates.

extensively for shrubbery and lawns. Sprayheads are used with PVC plastic pipe to form extensive underground irrigation systems. The heads can be made of plastic or brass and offer varying patterns: quarter-half-, three-quarter- and full-circle. There are two general types—stationary (including the pop-up) and rotating (gear-driven). These systems can be automated with timers connected to moisture sensors.

A significant disadvantage to these systems is that the underground pipe makes cultivating vegetable gardens almost impossible, unless it is placed deep. However, underground irrigation systems can be used in small gardens by laying the pipe outside the garden area, on the sides and corners. Unfortunately, the efficiency of these systems reduces as the garden reaches maturity.

The big news in sprinkler spray heads is **low precipitation rate nozzles** that allow an entire garden to be irrigated with less water. These sprinklers improve uniformity and reduce runoff.

The **basic spray nozzle** applies water at the rate of 1½ to 2½ inches per hour with a radius range of 7 to 16 feet. The **multiple-stream gear rotor** applies ½ to ⅞ inches per hour. The spray radius is 15 to 40 feet. Interchangeable disks determine spray pattern. The **single-stream rotor** applies water at the

Figure 7.04

SPRINKLER HEADS - THE 8 MOST POPULAR MODELS

	Coverage in feet	Discharge in G.P.M.	Pressure at nozzle P.S.I.	Spacing maximum
SQUARE PATTERN HEADS				
Small Square. Adjustable from 6'x6' up to 18'x18' 836C or 36C	18'x18'	2.5	25	18'
	17'x17'	2.2	20	17'
	15'x15'	1.8	15	15'
	11'x11'	1.5	10	11'
	8'x8'	1.2	7.5	8'
Medium Square. Adjustable from 18'x18' up to 25'x25' 866C or 66C	25'x25'	5.8	25	25'
	24'x24'	5.2	20	25'
	22'x22'	4.5	15	22'
	20'x20'	4.0	12	20'
	18'x18'	3.5	10	18'
PARKWAY AND STRIP HEADS				
Parkway. Covers an area up to 5'x40' 851C or 51C	5'x40'	3.8	30	40'
	5'x38	3.5	25	38'
Strip. Covers an area up to 5'x38' 852C or 52C	5'x25'	2.8	30	25'
	5'x23'	2.6	25	23'
FULL CIRCLE PATTERN HEADS				
Small Circle. Adjustable from 10'x24' diameter 855C or 55C	24' Diam	2.6	30	16'
	22' Diam.	2.3	25	15'
	19' Diam.	2.0	20	14'
	16' Diam.	1.8	15	12'
	14' Diam.	1.4	10	10'
Medium Circle. Adjustable from 24' up to 34' diameter 855C or 55C	34' Diam	6.5	25	24'
	32' Diam.	5.9	20	21'
	28' Diam.	5.2	15	18'
	25' Diam.	4.5	10	16'
HALF- AND QUARTER-CIRCLE HEADS				
Half Circle. Adjustable from 5' up to 12' radius 832C only	12' Radius	1.7	25	16'
	11' Radius	1.5	20	15'
	10' Radius	1.3	15	14'
	9' Radius	1.1	10	12'
	8' Radius	1.0	8	10'
Quarter Circle. Adjustable from 5' up to 12' Radius 831C only	12' Radius	1.2	25	used in corners on odd shaped areas
	11' Radius	1.1	20	
	10' Radius	1.0	15	

**NO. 500
SS P RANGER**

THOMPSON MANUFACTURING COMPANY
a division of Jennison Enterprises, Inc.
P.O. BOX 1500, 4832 Chino Avenue, Chino, California 91708
(714) 591-4851

**NO. 505
SS P RANGER**

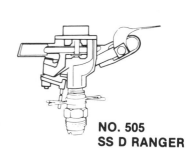

**NO. 505
SS D RANGER**

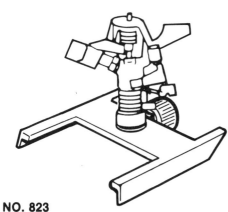

**NO. 821
BRASS IMPACT ON BASE**

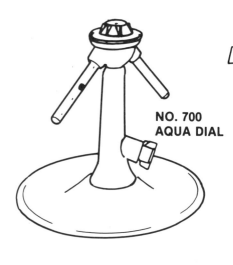

**NO. 700
AQUA DIAL**

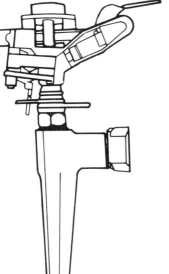

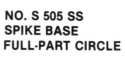

**NO. S 505 SS
SPIKE BASE
FULL-PART CIRCLE**

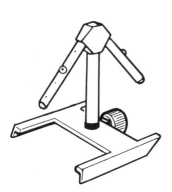

**NO. 823
BRASS IMPACT WITH
CONTROL SPRAY ARM ON BASE**

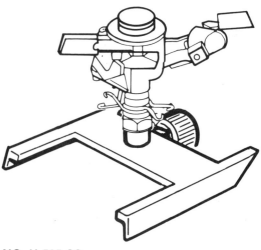

**NO. H 505 SS
SLED BASE/FULL-PART CIRCLE**

**NO. 710
RAIN WHIRL**

rate of one-tenth to one-half inch per hour. Radius is 18 to 15 feet. The pattern and the radius are adjustable. Impact (or impulse) sprinklers work like the familiar 'rain-bird' type. They apply water at the rate of about one-half inch per hour. The water distribution is heaviest closest to the sprinkler.

Matched precipitation rate nozzles are available for almost every type of system. This means that a sprinkler covering 180 degrees puts out one half as much water as a 360 degree head. This conserves water by allowing coordinated coverage.

UNDERGROUND SPRINKLER SYSTEMS

It is worthwhile taking all the time you need to shop around for different products and to plan the layout very carefully before you install a sprinkling system. There are a great many different products on the market, and one of them should be just right for your particular situation. Do some research, following the leads given in this chapter.

You'll want to determine the number of circuits you need and the number of sprinkler heads per circuit. Find out how many gallons per minute are available through your water system, and how many gallons per minute are used by the various sprinkler heads you're interested in. Sprinkler heads need a certain volume of water to maintain coverage. The total amount of water needed by the heads should not exceed the volume that is available if the system is to work efficiently.

For instance, if you have 17 gallons per minute available and if all your sprinkler heads use a total of 20 gallons per minute, you will need to eliminate some sprinkler heads from the system—or divide the system into two circuits. For information on the eight most popular models of sprinkler heads, see Figure 7.04.

It's worth bearing in mind that small- and medium-sized gardens can be watered by sprinklers located at the perimeter of the bed. This keeps the pipe from interfering with cultivation. For this layout, heads in the corners are ¼-pattern, while at the sides they are ½-pattern.

Bottom watering

Vegetables can be watered from the bottom by such simple methods as a ditch between the rows, an open-ended pipe or a hose bubbler. Far better today, however, are the drip-trickle irrigation systems. These work by providing small amounts of water to your vegetables along the root zone. Most cut water dosage by up to fifty percent by putting water exactly where it is needed and by slowing evaporation.

There are four ways of getting water to your garden based on the drip-trickle method:-

Drip hose (soaker/oozer): This operates like the familiar lawn soaker hose. Perforated or porous hose or tubing allows water to trickle from the entire length of the soaker hose at a uniform rate. This can be attached directly to the water supply, and the hose laid down the rows. Most systems allow several hoses to be attached together. In some systems, separate control valves and lines are used for deep-rooted plants like tomatoes and shallow-rooted plants like lettuce. The lines that run down each row may be placed on top of the soil.

Twin wall (variation of the drip hose): Several manufacturers market a double tube. Some utilize an inner water-supply flow chamber with an outer ooze chamber, others have side-by side twin tubes. One tube receives the water and transfers it to the ooze/trickle chamber. Some double-drip hoses are prepunched for spacings of 4, 8, 12 and 36 inches. These systems are not as popular as they once were.

Drip emitter (microdripper): This system consists of ½-inch polyethylene pipe tubing laid throughout the beds. Emitters have a preset flow rate and are installed exactly where needed along the row. Snap-on emitters can be attached anywhere along the line and are often available with various length extensions. A variation of this system utilizes screw-in spray heads (available in preset spray arcs). Spray heads vary from a coarse spray to a fine mist and fit into holes punched with an awl.

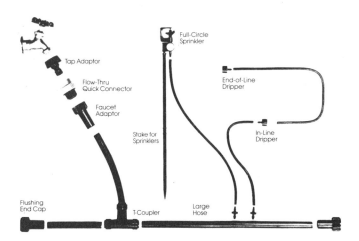

Figure 7.06

Drip system

All parts of this system are made to be snapped or threaded together. Drippers and adjustable mini-sprinklers put the water just where you want it. Can be used for vegetable gardens as well as shrubs and flower beds. Once the system is laid out, all you do is turn on the faucet. Enlarge the entire system at will by simply snapping additional units together.

O.M. SCOTTS & SONS
Marysville, OH 43041

◄ **Figure 7.05**

Impact or impulse sprinklers

Water striking an arm moves the sprinkler around in a circle. Each sprinkler will cover an area of 50 to 75 feet. They can be used on a free-standing pipe or on a sled or spike base.

Figure 7.07

Soaker hose
Made from recycled rubber, this hose oozes water from tiny pores distributed over its entire length. It is flexible enough to follow the shape of your garden beds, but can be buried under 12 inches of ground.

Spaghetti or microtube systems: Holes are punched into a ½-inch polyethylene tubing and small spaghetti tubes, ⅛-inch or less in diameter, are then inserted into the tubing and run out to individual plants. There are many variations. Spaghetti systems use a spaghetti tube, a rigid stand-up tube with a spray head and tubes with stick-in sprayers, drop-in bubblers and water loops of various sizes.

Spaghetti systems are particularly good for watering the planter boxes, tubs and hanging containers discussed in Chapter 10. Tubes are run to each container and connected to stick-in sprayers, bubblers, or similar devices. Most gardeners today use a system combining the drip emitter with spaghetti tubes. Emitters are used with such plantings as carrots and beets, while spaghetti tubes with or without an emitter are run to large individual plants such as tomatoes, squash, eggplant and similar vegetables.

Water-supply regulators: Every drip setup utilizes one or more regulators or accessories to make the system work better. A **filter strainer** prevents small particles from clogging the system; an **antisyphon valve** prevents dirt and foreign matter from draining in to the system (this may be required by local plumbing regulations); a **ball valve** regulates flow rate; a **pressure regulator and pressure gauge** precisely controls pressure; a **solenoid valve** is utilized with a time clock. All systems can be hooked to an automatic timer.

Automatic sprinker controllers: It's important to control watering to keep it at optimum efficiency. There are a number of automatic controllers on the market, incorporating many different features, though, essentially, every controller uses a clock that turns the water on and off for a specified period of time.

The simplest type of controller uses a mechanically times hose bibb valve. Screw one end to the house outlet, the other end to a hose, then set the timer to shut off the water flow after a specified time.

Electric timers have become increasingly sophisticated. A clock timer that can be set to operate a valve which simply turns on the water for a given number of minutes a day is considered rudimentary by today's standards. The more complex timers have multiple clocks that allow watering every day, every third day, every sixth day, and similar combinations. Some allow a different program to be set each day, others offer repeated watering several times a day. Yet more intricate controllers allow operation of three, six, eleven, fourteen and even more stations (or circuits) at any one time.

More and more gardeners today are switching to the new *electronic* solid state digital systems. Each zone or system of can be placed on its own watering schedule. You can, for instance, water your vegetable garden once a day for an hour, at 8 A.M. each morning, water the flowerbeds at 2 P.M. and the lawn at an entirely different time. You can also repeat this schedule several times a day.

Moisture sensor systems: Another way of regulating the amount of water your garden receives is through the use of a sensor system. A sensing device is buried in the root zone of the plants in order to determine the moisture content of the soil. When the content gets below a certain level that has been pre-set on a controller, the sensor activates another part of that same controller, which then 'orders' an electric valve to turn on the water. After a predetermined time, the water is shut off.

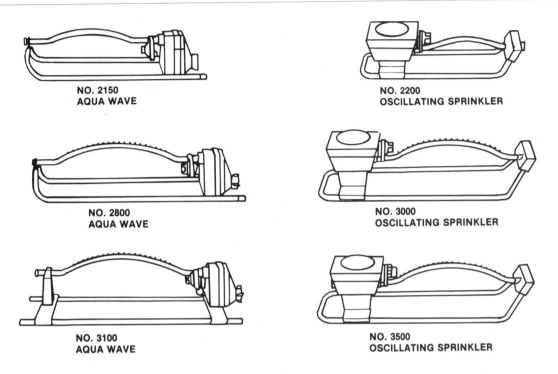

NO. 2150
AQUA WAVE

NO. 2200
OSCILLATING SPRINKLER

NO. 2800
AQUA WAVE

NO. 3000
OSCILLATING SPRINKLER

NO. 3100
AQUA WAVE

NO. 3500
OSCILLATING SPRINKLER

▲**Figure 7.08**
Oscillating sprinklers
These sprinklers can be set for various coverages within the water area. The sprinklers spray in squares or rectangles.

▼**Figure 7.09**
Traveling sprinklers
These are best for use on a lawn, but they also could be made to run down the middle of garden paths.

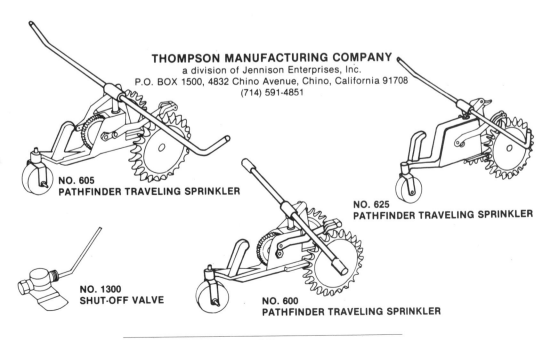

THOMPSON MANUFACTURING COMPANY
a division of Jennison Enterprises, Inc.
P.O. BOX 1500, 4832 Chino Avenue, Chino, California 91708
(714) 591-4851

NO. 605
PATHFINDER TRAVELING SPRINKLER

NO. 625
PATHFINDER TRAVELING SPRINKLER

NO. 1300
SHUT-OFF VALVE

NO. 600
PATHFINDER TRAVELING SPRINKLER

SPRINKLER MANUFACTURERS

ACME-BURGESS, INC.
Rte 83
Grayslake, IL 60030

ALLSTATE LAWN
PRODUCTS, INC.
3010 Ranchview Land
Minneapolis, MN 55447

ARMSTRONG
ENVIRONMENTAL
INDUSTRIES, INC.
2104 E. 15th St.
Los Angeles, CA 90804

BARCO MFG CO., INC.
7 Jackson St.
Worchester, MA 01608

BROWN GOLD SOIL CORP.
50 E. 25th St.
Paterson, NJ 07514

BURCH MFG CO., INC.
618 First Ave. N.
Fort Dodge, IA 50501

CASCADES, INC.
53057 Marina Dr.
Elkhart, IN 46514

CHAMPION SPRINKLER
SYSTEMS
1460 N. Naud St.
Los Angeles, CA 90012

CLOVER GARDEN
PRODUCTS
P.O. Box 847
Smyrna, TN 37167

DEERE & CO.
John Deere Rd.
Moline, IL 61265

THE DRAMM CO.
P.O. Box 528
Manitowock, WI 54220

DRIP IRRIGATION GARDEN
P.O. Box 5253
Ventura, CA 93003

FLEXON INDUSTRIES CORP.
One Flexon Plaza
Newark, NJ 07114

GARDENA, INC.
6005 Culligan Way
Minnetonka, MN 55345

GERING PRODUCTS
909 E. Glendale Rd.
Sparks, NV 89431

GREEN GARDEN, INC.
P.O. Box 351
Johnstown, PA 15907

GREENLAWN
SPRINKLER CO.
1301 S. Chjerokee
Denver, CO 80223

GROGROUP, INC.
Five Shawsheen Ave.
Beford, MA 01730

HUB INTERNATIONAL
53 Fargo St.
Boston, MA 02210

KING BROS INDUSTRIES
27114 Henry Mayo Dr.
Valencia, CA 91355

LAFAYETTE BRASS CO.,
INC.
409 Lafayette St.
New York, NY 10003

MELNOR INDUSTRIES
1 Carol Place
Moonachie, NJ 07074

NATIONAL MFG CO.
Division of TMCO, Inc.
544 J St.
P.O. Box 30228
Lincoln, NE 68508

L.R. NELSON CO.
7719 N. Pioneer La.
Peoria, IL 61615

PROEN PRODUCTS CO.
2777 9th St.
Berkeley, CA 94710

RAIN BIRD NATIONAL
SALES CORP.
145 N. Grand Ave.
Glendora, CA 91740

RAIN JET CORP.
27671 LaPaz Road
Laguna Niquel, CA 92677

RAINMATIC CORP.
P.O. Box 3321
Omaha, NB 68103

RAIN-O-MAT SPRINKLERS
P.O. Box 151
Whittier, CA 90608

ROVER-SCOTT BONNAR
LTD
P.O. Box 292
Allendale, NJ 07410

SALCO PRODUCTS, INC.
4463 W Rosecrans Ave.
Hawthorne, CA 90250

SARLON INDUSTRIES
775 NW 71st St.
Miami, FL 33150

TEKNOR APEX CO.
505 Central Ave.
Pawtucket, RI 02862

THOMPSON MFG. CO.
4832 Chino Ave.
Chino, CA 91710

TRI-CON INC.
27331 Tungsten
Cleveland, OH 44132

TUFF-LITE, INC.
216 Tingley, Lane
Edison, NJ 08817

WATERWAND CO.
865 Lind Ave.
P.O. Box 757
Renton, WA 98055

WEATHER TEC
5645 E. Clinton
Fresno, CA 93727

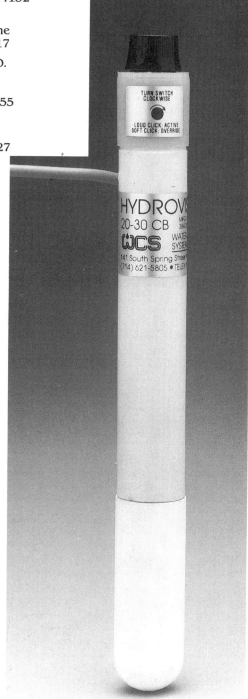

Figure 7.10

Hydrovisor
Hydrovisor directly measures water availability in the soil and reacts to pre-set root stress to automatically turn on the water when needed. Saves up to 60 percent on irrigation water use.

SUPPLIERS/MANUFACTURERS OF IRRIGATION SYSTEMS

AG-RAIN INC.
600 S. Schrader
Havana, IL 62644

THE AMERICAN GRANBY CO.
1111 Vine St.
Liverpool, NY 13088

AMETEK, PLYMOUTH
PRODUCTS DIV.
502 Indiana Ave.
Sheboygan, WI 53081

AQUATIC IRRIGATION
SYSTEMS
619 E. Gutierrez St.
Santa Barbara, CA 93103

AQUA/TRENDS
Blair Bldg.
215 N. Federal Hwy.
Boca Raton, FL 33432

JOHN BLUE CO.
2800 Bob Wallace Ave.
Huntsville, AL 35802

CLOVER GARDEN PRO-
DUCTS
P.O. Box 874
Smyma, TN 37167

DIETRICH'S
P.O. Box 777
Valley City, ND 58072

THE DRAMM CO.
P.O. Box 528
Manitowoc, WI 54220

DRIP IRRIGATION GARDEN
1264 W 2nd St.
Los Angeles, CA 90026

DRIP IRRIGATION
SPECIALISTS
P.O. Box 5253
West Los Angeles, CA 93003

DYCKES PLASTICS
149 Jessop Ave.
Saskatoon, Sask.
Canada S7N 1Y3

GALCON, INC
6400 Variel Ave.
Woodland Hills, CA 91367

GARDEN AMERICA CORP.
P.O. Box A
Carson City, NV 89702

GILMOUR MFG CO.
P.O. Box 838
Somerset, PA 15501

GREENLAWN SPRINKLER CO.
1301 S. Cherokee
Denver, CO 80223

HARDIE IRRIGATION
27671 Lapaz Rd.
Laguna Niquez, CA 92656

HYDROFLO CORP.
P.O. Box 539
Plumsteadville, PA 18949

IMPERIAL SPRINKLER
SYSTEMS
13555 W. 107th St.
P.O. Box 14666
Lenexa, KS 66215

IRRIDELCO DRIP CORP.
3081 E. Hamilton
Fresno, CA 93721

IRR-TROL MFG, INC.,
Irrigation Control Systems
27940 Beale Court
Valencia, C 91335

JADERLOON CO., INC.
P.O. Box 685
Irmo, SC 29063

KING BROS INDUSTRIES
27781 Hopkins Ave.
Valencia, CA 91355

LESCO, INC.
20005 Lake Rd.
Rocky River, OH 44116

TED MAHR CO.
P.O. Box 930
Cape Coral, FL 33910

L.R. NELSON CORP.
7719 N. Pioneer La.
Peoria, Il 61615

RAINDRIP, INC.
14675 Titus St.
Panorama City, CA 91402

RAIN JET CORP.
27671 La Paz Road
Laguna Niquel, CA 92677

RAINMATIC CORP.
1227 S. 22nd St.
P.O. Box 3321
Omaha, NB 3321

RAIN-O-MAT SPRINKLERS
P.O. Box 151
Whittier, CA 90606

RICHEL, INC.
P.O. Drawer A
1851 Oregon St.
Carson City, NV 89701

ROBERTS IRRIGATION
PRODUCTS, INC.
700 Ranchros Dr.
San Marcos, CA 92069

SALCO PRODUCTS, INC.
4463 West Rosecrans Ave.
Hawthorne, CA 90250

SEA-BORN, INC.
2000 Rockford Rd.
Charles City, IA 50616

SEAMAN-PARSONS CORP.
P.O. Box 25309
Milwaukee, WI 53225

SPECIALTY MFG CO.
2356 University Ave.
St. Paul, MN 55114

SPOT SYSTEMS
5812 Machine Dr.
Huntington Beach, CA
92649

SUBMATIC IRRIGATION
SYSTEMS
P.O. Box 246
Lubbock, TX 79408

THIRST QUENCHER
SYSTEMS
1151 N. Kraemer Place
Anaheim, CA 92806

THOMPSON MFG CO.
4832 Chino Ave
Chino, CA 91710

THOMPSON MFG CO.
5075 Edison Ave.
Chino, CA 91710

TIDY GROW PRODUCTS CO.
8 Charles Plaza
Suite 805
Baltimore, MD 25200

TRICKLE SOAK SYSTEMS
8733 Magnolia
Suite 109
Santee, CA 92071

WATERGUARDE
SUBSURFACE
IRRIGATION CO.
P.O. Box 1222
LaMesa, CA 92044

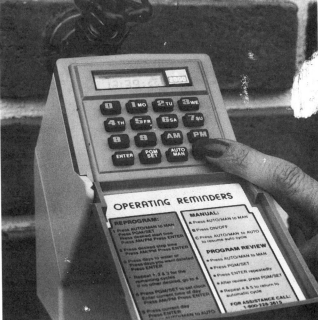

Figure 7.11

Automatic water controller
Set your own schedule 1 to 14 days ahead with as many as 8 variable length-cycles per day. The keyboard displays the day and exact start times. You key in your program. Fits any existing hoses.
RAINMATICCORP
1227 S. 22 St.
Omaha, NB 68103

Figure 8.01

Fungal damage

1 **Sooty molds and smuts.** *Sooty mold shows up as unsightly superficial dark brown or black blotches. It causes little damage. Smuts produce brown to black sooty-looking spore masses inside swollen white blisters.*

2 **Rusts.** *Rusts appear as bright yellow, orange, red, reddish-brown or black powder pustulates (blisters) on the underside of leaves.*

3 **Mildews.** *Powdery mildew appears as superficial white to light grayish patches on the upper surfaces of leaves and buds. Downy mildews produce pale green or yellow areas on the upper leaf surface with light gray or purplish patches below.*

4 **Rots.** *Plants with root rot lose vigor, the leaves become pale. The rot area in fruits and leaves may be mushy and spongy.*

5 **Cankers.** *Dead areas on stem. They are oval or irregular, sunken or swollen. Some completely girdle the stem.*

6 **Fungal leaf sports.** *The center of the spots may fall out. They may also enlarge to form big blotches.*

7 **Wilts.** *Fungal wilt (fusarium and verticillium) invades and plugs up the water- and food-conducting vessels inside the plants. Wilting starts at the base and proceeds upward.*

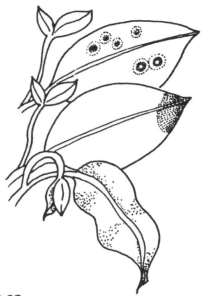

Figure 8.02

Bacterial disease

A plant is diseased when it doesn't develop normally because it is being attacked by some living organism. A typical leaf or stem infection has the following appearance: a sunken, brown center, bordered by a tan or yellow area surrounded by a pale yellow border.

Often you can tell what's wrong with your plants by looking at the leaves. These examples illustrate the typical 'look' for each type of disease:-

1. **Bacterial spots.** *Bacterial spots may start as dark green spots or streaks on leaves and stems. later turn gray, brown and ooze a gelatinous fluid. The spots may drop out.*

2. **Soft bacterial rots.** *The infected area is generally bordered by a lighter yellow or tan area. Advanced infection causes large dark areas on the fruit.*

3. **Bacterial wilts.** *Bacteria invade and plug up water-conducting tubes. The stem will ooze a gelatinous fluid if you slice the stem.*

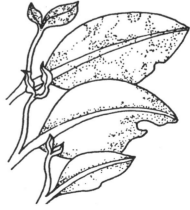

Figure 8.03

Viruses

Viruses are often identified by what they do. They frequently show up as (a) mottling, (b) distortion of the leaves, flowers and fruit, and (c) dwarfing.

8. Pest Management

IT DOESN'T TAKE A vegetable gardener long to find himself or herself facing the problem of controlling bugs and other pests. There are essentially two approaches to this problem—organic and chemical. While a few people still rely solely on one or the other method, most gardeners try a little of both. Though wary of the dangers of manufactured chemicals, they recognize their unique benefits in certain situations. Pest control systems come in the form either of sprays or traps.

Different insects and different disease organisms affect different vegetables. The tables in this chapter will help you diagnose the various pest problems your garden is likely to face as well as suggest a cure.

TECHNIQUES

During the last two decades, the attitude of most Americans toward bugs, diseases and chemical controls has undergone quite a change. It used to be the common feeling that the only good bug was a dead bug—that with modern super-strong chemicals it was just a matter of time before insects, germs and other pests were eradicated from the face of the Earth.

Of course, that didn't happen. In fact, reports began to appear suggesting that some manufactured 'miracle cures' were creating more problems than they were solving. Rachel Carson wrote her landmark study, *Silent Spring*, about the effects of DDT and other chemicals on the environment. People began paying more attention to the organic gardeners and farmers, some of them turned the tables on the advocates of chemicals by demanding that manufactured pesticides, herbicides and other unnatural substances be eradicated from the face of the Earth.

The verbal battles between the users of chemicals and promoters of the organic approach have had some

useful results. Many discoveries have been made and many new products have come on the market that have made vegetable gardening much easier for the amateur gardener. There are still some gardeners—not many to be sure—who run for the spray can every time they see a bug. And there are some strict disciples of the organic method who swear that *all* chemicals are dangerous—hazardous to the lives of plants and animals alike. But most gardeners fall somewhere in between these two extremes. There are in fact wide gradations of toxicity and effectiveness among chemicals. Some of them, like chlordane, are quite powerful and long-lasting. Others, like malathion, are relatively mild and last about a week. But all chemicals are dangerous to some degree and need to be handled with care.

In this chapter we outline contrasting methods of pest management, involving both organic and chemical approaches. For the most part, they're more complimentary than contrasting, and most gardeners happily make selective use of both. We take the view that organic methods are always to be preferred, and that resort should only be had to chemicals where the pest problem is seriously out of hand.

ORGANIC INSECT MANAGEMENT

Insect infestation in your garden can come and go. There are many factors that determine whether or not a particular pest will attack your plants. Insects move from one place to another and are often influenced by weather, day length, what your neighbors are doing, what crops you are raising (and what stage of life they are in), and many other factors. Almost any change can send insects out of your garden and off in another direction. Furthermore, the insects' own life cycles figure in the equation. If you're aware of what these are likely to be in your area, you can schedule planting accordingly. If a garden is started at a certain time of the year, it may be overwhelmed with pests; a few weeks later, and it might escape virtually scot-free.

Figure 8.04
Insect predators

Praying Mantis: *Praying mantises consume quantities of beetles, caterpillars and grasshoppers. The young eat aphids and other insects.*

Green lacewing-lacewing larvae: *The larvae of the lacewing (the aphidlion) devour many insects.*

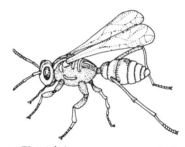

Wasp: *The trichogramma wasp helps destroy more than 200 insect pests.*

Convergent lady beetle: *The lady beetle (ladybug) eats two and a half times its own weight each day in aphids, mealybgugs, moth eggs and spider mites. The larva is a blackish spiny-bodied insect with six short legs and red, blue or yellow spots.*

Robber fly: *Robber flies eat everything from grasshoppers to beetles.*

If you intend to control insects organically, learn to live with some insects. A few holes in a cabbage leaf aren't very important—and you won't get rid of all bugs no matter what you do.

In trying to keep garden pests under control, always start with the simplest, least intrusive methods, move on to more aggressive controls only if necessary. Here are the steps to follow:-

Keep your garden clean: Get rid of all dead weeds, clean up piles of trash, and remove crop residue. This debris provides a place for disease and insects to multiply and hibernate during the winter. If you have severely diseased plants or rotted fruit, don't put them in the compost, as the problem may eventually find its way back into your garden.

Start with healthy plants and seed: Buy disease-free seed and healthy-looking transplants. Disease-free seed can be purchased through seed catalogs and at garden centers, and it will be "certified disease free." Many growers treat their seed with Captan, a powdered fungicide, but you can buy untreated seed from Nichol's Garden Nursery,

Johnny's Selected Seeds and others.

Most nurseries sell healthy plants. To make sure, select only vigorous looking plants without spots on the leaves.

Beware of overhead watering: Mildew and other diseases frequently occur on leaves that stay wet. Water in the morning so the sun dries the foliage quickly, by hand watering under the leaves or by using a ground level drip irrigation system.

Plant resistant varieties and repellent plants: You can avoid many diseases and insects by growing resistant varieties. Certain types of beans, for example, are rust resistant, and several tomato varieties are resistant to nematodes, and fusarium and verticillium wilts.

Some plants are not attractive to insects; others, such as marigolds and garlic, contain oils that repel insects. Still others are not affected by insect attack.

Rotate your crops: If you grow vegetables in the same spot year after year, certain diseases may spread rapidly. Cabbage, broccoli and cauliflower are particularly prone to club root, for example. In a Vegetable

Figure 8.05

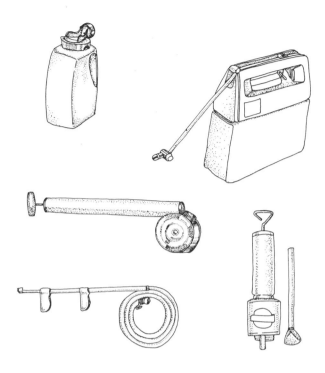

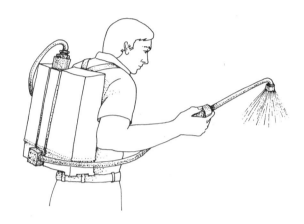

Sprayers and dusters

Small handsprayers and hose-end sprayers are extremely useful for small gardens.
Use slide sprayers for fruit trees.
Piston dusters are effective in small gardens.
Electric sprayers using rechargeable batteries take the work out of pumping.

Sprayers and dusters

Backpack sprayers, which hold about 4 gallons of liquid, are especially useful for large gardens. Most gardeners use these for a combination vegetable garden/home orchard.

Factory garden, rotate the vegetables within the bed. Plant zucchini where the cabbage was and cabbage in place of eggplant.

Watch your timing: Time your plantings to avoid peak insect buildups. Insects generally appear at about the same time every year. In some areas, flea beetles will destroy radishes and turnips planted in early summer, but if you hold off a few weeks until the adult (beetle) stage has passed, your crop will suffer little damage. Many other insects can be avoided in this same manner.

Even if you have the best soil and the healthiest plants, some pests may find their way into your garden. If you see any large crawling insects, such as the tomato hornworm, feeding on your plants, simply pick them off into a wide-mouth jar. The same goes for caterpillars and other large bugs. Pick off pieces of leaf that contain colonies. Spray small bugs and flying insects with a hard, direct stream of water from the garden hose.

Many insects can be lured into home-made traps. Some beer or other fermenting carbohydrates in a glass jar, cooking pan or similar receptacle will trap many moths and bores. Earwigs will crawl into rolled-up newspapers, from which they can be dumped each morning into a pail of hot water. Another method of trapping earwigs—and snails, slugs, grubs and cutworms—is to place pieces of ripe fruit and vegetables around the garden. The bugs will gather for the feast, especially at night, and you can dispose of them in the morning.

If insects are especially bad, cover plants with a netting and enclose fruit in a plastic bag. Or you might consider using a spray of some kind.

DO-IT-YOURSELF ORGANIC SPRAYS

There are many home-made concoctions that work well to eliminate or reduce insect populations. One idea is to mix about 20 tablespoons of soap flakes (like Ivory) in six gallons of water. Soap (not detergent) can be sprayed on the plants without danger of hurting them, and it will help control aphids and some other insects.

Figure 8.06

PEST DIAGNOSIS AND REMEDIES

Vegetables	Symptoms	Pests	DIAZINON	DYLOX	MALATHION	METHOXYCHLOR	PYRETHRUM	ROTENONE	RYANIA	SEVIN	NICOTINE SULFATE	SABADILLA	THIODANENDOLSUFAN	THURICIDE
Artichokes	Colonies of insects on leaves and buds.	Aphids			•		•	•		•	•		•	
	Trails of silver slime.	Slugs, snails					See Figure 8.09							
Asparagus	Shoots channeled, leaves eaten by larvae of beetles.	Asparagus beetle					•	•	•	•			•	
Beans	Colonies of black sucking insects on leaves.	Aphids			•		•	•			•		•	
	Circular holes eaten in leaves.	Bean leaf beetles	•		•			•	•				•	
	Hopping, running insects that suck sap from leaves.	Leafhoppers			•	•				•				
	Lower surface of leaves eaten between veins; skeletionized.	Mexican bean beetles			•			•	•	•				
	Scaly nymphs on underside of leaves; white adults flutter when disturbed	Whiteflies.			•				•					
Beets	Leaves eaten leaving trail of slime.	Snails, slugs					See Figure 8.09							
Broccoli	Colonies of small green insects on leaves.	Aphids			•		•	•	•	•	•			
	Plants sickly; maggots attack underground parts of plants.	Cabbage maggots		•										
	Holes in leaves eaten by larvae.	Cabbage worms, loopers			•		•						•	•
	Small plants cut off at soil level at night.	Cutworms	•	•						•			•	
Brussels sprouts	Colonies of small insects on leaves.	Aphids			•		•	•	•		•			
	Maggots attack underground parts of plants.	Cabbage maggots		•										
	Holes eaten in leaves by larvae.	Cabbage maggots, loopers			•		•			•			•	•
	Small plants cut off at soil level at night.	Cutworms	•							•			•	
Cabbage	Colonies of small green insects on leaves.	Aphids			•			•	•	•		•	•	
	Plants sickly; maggots attack underground parts of plants.	Cabbage maggots		•										
	Holes in leaves eaten by larvae.	Cabbage worms, loopers			•		•			•			•	
	Small plants cut off at soil level at night.	Cutworms	•							•			•	
Cauliflower	Colonies of small green insects on leaves.	Aphids			•		•	•	•		•			
	Plants sickly; maggots attack stems & underground parts of plant.	Cabbage maggots		•										
	Holes in leaves eaten by larvae.	Cabbage worms, loopers			•		•			•				
Corn	Silks cut off at ear; kernels destroyed by fairly large larvae.	Corn earworms							•	•			•	
	Ears and stalks tunneled by larvae.	Corn borers								•				
	Small plants cut off at soil level at night.	Cutworms	•							•			•	
Cucumber	Colonies of small insects on underside of leaves.	Aphids			•		•	•	•		•		•	
	All parts eaten.	Cucumber beetles	•	•				•		•			•	
	All parts of vines eaten.	Pickleworm	•		•			•		•			•	•
Eggplant	Plant defoliated (beetle—black striped larvae—brick red)	Colorado potato beetles.	•				•	•					•	
	Colonies of small insects on underside of leaves.	Aphids			•		•	•		•	•		•	
	Colonies on underside of leaves.	Eggplant lacebug			•		•						•	

Vegetables	Symptoms	Pests	DIAZINON	DYLOX	MALATHION	METHOXYCHLOR	PYRETHRUM	ROTENONE	RYANIA	SEVIN	NICOTINE SULFATE	SABADILLA	THIODANENDOLSUFAN	THURICIDE
Lettuce	Colonies of small insects on leaves.	Aphids			•		•	•		•	•		•	
	Leaves eaten by pincer bugs.	Earwigs												
	Wedge-shaped insects found on leaves—tips of leaves turn brown.	Leafhoppers			•		•	•	•	•				
	Leaves eaten, leaving trails of silver slime.	Snails, slugs					See Figure 8.09							
Kale	Colonies of small insects on leaves.	Aphids			•		•	•	•				•	
	Small pin-size holes chewed in leaves.	Flea beetles	•				•	•	•				•	
Melons	Colonies of small insects on under-side of leaves.	Aphids			•		•	•	•		•		•	
	All parts eaten.	Cucumber beetles	•				•	•	•	•			•	
Mustard greens	Colonies of small insects on leaves.	Aphids			•		•	•	•					
	Leaves with holes eaten by larvae.	Cabbage worms						•		•				
	Plants sickly; maggots attack root and stem underground.	Root maggots	•											
Onions	Older leaves wither; small yellow insects feed at base of leaves.	Onion thrips			•			•	•	•				
	Plants sickly; maggots attack parts below ground.	Onion maggots	•											
Okra	Holes eaten in pods.	Corn earworms							•	•				
Peas	Terminals deformed; colonies of small insects on leaves.	Pea Aphids			•		•	•	•		•		•	
	Beetles feed on blooms: larvae bore through pod and enter young peas.	Pea weevils	•		•			•						
Peppers	Colonies of small insects on leaves.	Aphids			•		•	•	•		•		•	
	Plants defoliated by orange and yellow-bodied beetles.	Blister beetles					•	•	•				•	
	Small plants cut off at soil level at night.	Cutworms	•							•				
	Leaves and fruit eaten.	Pepper weevils								•			•	
Radishes	Plants sickly; maggots attack plants below ground.	Root Maggots	•											
Spinach	Colonies of small insects on leaves.	Aphids			•		•	•	•		•		•	
	Larvae tunnel through leaves.	Leaf miners	•											
Squash	Colonies of small insects under-neath the leaves.	Aphids			•		•	•	•		•		•	
	All parts eaten.	Cucumber beetles	•				•	•	•	•				
	Plants wilted (brownish flat bugs).	Squash bugs					•	•	•	•		•	•	
	Sudden wilting of runners; holes in stem near base.	Squash vine borers								•				
Swiss chard	Colonies of small insects on leaves.	Aphids			•		•	•	•		•		•	
Tomatoes	Colonies of small insects on leaves.	Aphids			•		•	•	•		•		•	
	Small plants cut off at soil level.	Cutworms	•							•				
	Many shot-sized holes in leaves.	Flea beetles	•				•	•	•	•			•	
	Leaves eaten (large green worm with horn)	Tomato hornworms.					•	•		•			•	•
	Scalelike nymphs attached to underside of leaves.	Whiteflies			•		•	•						
Turnips & Rutabagas	Maggots attack plant below ground.		•							•				
		Cabbage loopers			•			•		•				•

Another spray can be made from plants with pungent aromas, such as garlic, marigolds and chives. One 'recipe' is to put the cloves, petals, leaves or whatever into a pot, add enough water to cover, bring the mixture to boiling point, remove from the stove and strain off the solid matter. Dilute the remaining liquid with four or five parts of water, stir for five to ten minutes, and spray. Another method is to liquify the raw material, adding water to cover, in a blender. Strain off solid particles, mix the remaining liquid in the proportion of two or three teaspoons to a quart of water, and spray.

Other simple formulas include the following:

- Tomato stems and leaves boiled in water destroy aphids, etc.
- Lime mixed with wood ashes prevents maggot damage.;
- Hot pepper mixed with equal amounts of water and soap powder is effective against tomato worms.

PREDATOR AND PARASITIC INSECTS

Many gardeners assume that every bug they see is destructive. The truth is that of the approximately 80,000 species of insects in North America, over half are beneficial. Most of these insects work in two ways to help keep the destructive insects in your garden under control.

First, predator insects, mites and molluscs destroy garden pests. Some of these insects have large mouthparts that allow them to tear up and devour their prey. Others have piercing mouthparts with which to suck the body fluids from other insects. Predators include antlions, dragonflies, a few true bugs and a number of beetles: blister beetles, carrion beetles, ladybugs, net-winged beetles, soldier beetles, soft winged beetles and tiger beetles.

You can often identify predacious beetles by sight. If a beetle's jaws are short and chunky, it is a plant eater. If the jaws are long and pointed with sharp cutting edges, it destroys other insects. Although most true bugs are destructive, a few are extremely helpful. Pirate bugs feed on small insects and mites. Some stink bugs are predacious on the Colorado potato beetle. And assassin bugs attack Japanese beetles and other harmful insects.

Parasitic insects deposit their eggs on or in other insects. Many have an egglaying device called an ovipositor that allows them to pierce the bodies of other insects to lay eggs. When the eggs hatch, the larvae feed inside the victim's body. Some of these parasitic insects lay their eggs in a number of host species, but others attack only one.

Probably the most popular commercially available parasite is the trichogramma wasp. It lays eggs in more than two hundred harmful species. Thousands of other wasps (some are called flies) are useful in controlling garden pests—ichneumon flies, braconid wasps, aphid wasps and pelecinid wasps to name a few. Although almost everyone considers flies obnoxious household

SUPPLIERS OF BENEFICIAL INSECTS

ALLAN'S AQUARIUM &
EXOTIC BIRDS
845 Lincoln Blvd.
Venice, CA 90291
ladybugs

BIO-CONTROL CO.
Route 2, Box
Auburn, CA 95603
ladybugs, praying mantises

W. ATLEE BURPEE CO.
Warminster, PA 18974
fly parasites, green lacewings, ladybugs, praying mantis egg cases, trichogramma wasps

CALIFORNIA GREEN
LACEWINGS, INC.
P.O. Box 2495
Merced, CA 95340
lacewings, trichogramma wasps

CONNECTICUT VALLEY
BIOLOGICAL CONTROL
CO.
Valley Rd.
South Hampton, MA 01073
*damselfly nymphs
dragonfly nymphs*

EASTERN BIOLOGICAL
CONTROL CO.
Rte 5, Box 379
Jackson, NJ 08527
praying mantises

GOTHARD, INC.
P.O. Box 370
Canutillo, TX 79835
praying mantises, trichogramma wasps, whitefly parasites

GURNEY SEED AND
NURSERY CO.
Yankton, SD 57079
fly parasites, facewings, ladybugs, praying mantises

HENRY FIELDS SEED
AND NURSERY CO.
Shenandoah, IA 51602
ladybugs, green lacewings, praying mantises, trichogramma wasps

KING LABS
P.O. Bo 69
Limerick, PA 19468
green lacewings, praying mantises

LAKELAND NURSERY SALES
340 Poplar
Hanover, PA 17331
ladybugs, praying mantises

NATURAL PEST CONTROLS
8864 Little Creek Dr.
Orangeville, CA 95662
green lancewings, ladybugs, mealybug destroyers, parasitic wasps, predatory mites, whitefly parasites

NATURE'S PESTS
CONTROLS
8864 Little Creek Dr.
Medford, OR 97501
green lacewings, ladybugs, mealybug destroyers, parasitic wasps, predatory mites

ORGANIC PEST
MANAGEMENT
Box 55267
Seattle, WA 98135
green lacewings, ladybugs, mealybug destroyers, parasitic wasps, predatory mites, whitefly parasites

RINCON VITOVA
INSECTARIES, INC.
P.O. Box 95
Oak View, CA 93022
fly parasites, lacewing flies, ladybugs, trichogramma wasps

ROBERT ROBBINS
424 N. Courtland St.
East Stroudsburg, PA 18301
praying mantises

UNIQUE INSECT CONTROLS
P.O. Box 15376
Sacramento, CA 95851
green lacewings, ladybugs, mealybug destroyers, parasitic wasps, predatory mites, whitefly parasites

pests, there are a number of predacious and parasitic fly families including syrphid flies, robber flies, aphid flies and tachina flies.

Here are the most important beneficial insects you can obtain commercially:-

The larvae of the **green lacewing** are active against mealybugs, scale and aphids. Once introduced into the garden as eggs, they hatch in a few days and feed for about three weeks, pupate and emerge as adults. Adults feed on the so-called honeydew that aphids excrete. Lacewings are shipped from the insectory as eggs in rice hulls.

Ladybugs eat two and a half times their weight each day in aphids, mealybugs, moth eggs and spider mites. The larvae also consume a number of insects. Ladybugs are probably most popular of all beneficial insects. Unfortunately, most will leave your garden within a few days of being released.

The **mealybug destroyer** is a member of the ladybug family that prefers mealybugs. The larvae consume aphids as well.

Parasitic nematodes attack borers and soil-borne grubs. A few firms offer them for sale.

Of the parasitic wasps, **Encarsia formosa** attacks the common whitefly larvae, **Aphytis melinus** attacks red scale and **Trichogramma** parasites the eggs of corn earworm, cabbage worms and other larval pests.

The **praying mantis**, a large, dramatic-looking insect, consumes huge quantities of beetles, caterpillars, and grasshoppers. The young eat aphids, flies and other small insects.

Predatory mites feed on plant-damaging spider mites. They are most effective when a mixture of species is released. To encourage beneficial insects to prey and parasitize in your yard, grow pollen-rich flowers around the garden. Strawflowers attract ladybugs. Goldenrod hosts over 75 beneficial species. Dandelion, wild carrot, lamb's quarters and evening primrose are also useful.

You can buy a yeast-sugar insect food sold as artificial nectar. Spray it across the garden and yard. Beneficial insects such as ladybugs and adult lacewings will feed on it just as they do on honeydew secreted by pests or flower nectar. You can make your own solution by combining equal parts of brewer's yeast and sugar with enough water to dissolve them completely. Apply either solution with a hand-pump sprayer.

BACTERIAL CONTROLS

Some bacterial agents are extremely effective against garden insect pests. **Bacillus thuringiensis**, sold under the names Thuricide, Biotrol, Agritrol and Dipel, produces a toxin that paralyzes the digestive system of caterpillars including cabbage loopers and tomato hornworms. It does not harm birds, bees, pets or humans.

Bacillus popilliae (sold under the names Doom and Milky Spore Disease) helps control the beetle grub.

Grasshopper Spore contains a natural parasite that attacks grasshoppers. The effect of this parasite is slower to show results, but can be effective if used over several seasons.

BOTANICAL SPRAYS

Plants themselves are the source of some of the strongest insecticides around.

Pyrethrum is made from the dried and powdered flowers of Chrysanthemum cineraefolium, a close relative of the garden chrysanthemum. Pyrethrum is extremely effective against aphids, leafhoppers, thrips and leaf miners.

Rotenone is an insecticide derived from the roots and stems of tropical shrubs and vines in the genera Derris and Lonchocarpus. Rotenone acts on contact and is also a stomach poison. It controls many sucking and chewing insects including beetles, caterpillars, leaf hoppers, thrips and aphids.

Ryania is derived from the ground stems of Ryania *speciosa*, a tropical South American shrub. It is especially effective against the European corn borer as well as a variety of other insects.

Sabadilla, made from the seeds of a lilylike Mexican plant (Schoenocaulon *officinale*) is sold as wettable powder. It works as both a contact and a stomach poison against squash bugs.

Figure 8.07

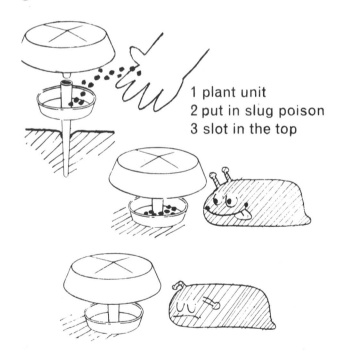

1 plant unit
2 put in slug poison
3 slot in the top

Slugtrap

Slugs can't resist climbing into this saucer and cover. Just plant the unit in the ground so the little saucer rests on the ground. Pour in almost any meal or pellet slug bait, and add the top. Can be placed almost anywhere.

WALTER F. NICKE
P.O. Box 71G
Hudson, NY 12534

COMPANION PLANTING

Many gardeners have come to the conclusion that some plants attract insects, others repel them. And for this reason some types of plants do especially well in combination with certain other types. For instance, nasturtiums often attract aphids. If your melons, say, have been bothered by aphids in past years, nasturtiums planted right next to the melon plot might attract all the aphids away from the melons. On the other hand, garlic repels aphids; planted next to a melon patch it might just be able to keep all the aphids away. The results of companion planting are unscientific and depend on trial and error, but enough people have enjoyed success with it to make it worthwhile trying. Here are some additional beneficial plants:-

- Leeks repel carrot flies.
- Marigolds repel nematodes, bean beetles, Japanese beetles.
- Radishes repel striped cucumber beetles.
- Rosemary repels Mexican bean beatles.
- Sage repels cabbage worm butterflies.
- Tansy repels several different kinds of beetles.
- Thyme repels cabbage worm.

CHEMICALS IN THE GARDEN

There is no doubt that the use of simple organic techniques can be effective in the management and control of all kinds of garden pests. They have been considered first in this chapter because most gardeners prefer to consider organic methods before resorting to chemicals. There is a time and place for everything, however, and when pest problems get truly out of hand you may feel the need to turn to laboratory-developed assistance.

It is important for the gardener thinking of using any of the available chemical sprays and powders to find out as much as possible about them. Some of the dangers inherent in their use can be avoided through intelligent planning and careful application. Overkill can be as damaging to the pocketbook, in these days of high prices, as it may be to the plants

Figure 8.08

PROPER USE OF INSECTICIDES

1. Select an insecticide that can be used on a wide variety of crops.
2. Read the instruction label carefully and follow directions exactly when preparing and applying insecticides.
3. Never use an insecticide on a crop that is not listed on the label.
4. Never use more than the specified dosage.
5. Store insecticides out of reach of children.
6. Dispose of the container in a safe manner; do not break or puncture the pesticide container. Wrap in a newspaper and place in the trash or bury at least 18 inches deep in the ground.

and animals (including humans) subjected to it.

There are three major categories of chemicals used in the garden: pesticides, to control insects; fungicides, to control fungus-borne plant diseases; and herbicides, to control weeds. There are also bacteriocides to prevent or cure bacterial diseases; nematicides, to control nematodes; and rodenticides, to control rodents.

While all of these categories will be discussed in this section, emphasis will be given to the first two.

INSECTICIDES

Insecticides used in the garden come either in solid or liquid form. Dusts, baits and granules are applied dry. Baits are mixed by the manufacturer with a pest attractant; dusts and granules are mixed with an inert carrier. Three types of insecticides are applied wet: emulsifiable concentrates (EC), soluble powders (SP), and wettable powders (WP). These last are mixed with water and transferred to spray apparatus.

When applying either dusts or sprays, it is important to make sure that they cover all surfaces of the infested plants. It's also important not to apply them to yourself or to anyone else. Cover your body with protective clothing; wear a broad-brimmed hat and gloves too. Try not to get any of the liquid or powder on your skin; if you should, wash it off right away.

The chemical insecticides most frequently used in the garden are carbaryl, malathion and diazinon. (These are generic names; different manufacturers may give them different brand names. For instance, a popular make of carbaryl is Sevin.) Two other chemicals, trichlofon and methoxychlor, are also used at times, along with a host of minor preparations. Some manufacturers put out preparations combining two or more ingredients.

Slug and snail control

Most standard snail and slug control baits contain metaldehyde. Unfortunately, these are ineffective in wet weather. But slug baits based on methiocarb will destroy slugs and snails even in the damp.

Two good ones are: **mesurol (Slug-geta)** and **Snail Snare**. The latter dehydrates pests rather than poisoning them. You can also exercise preventive control by utilizing chemical compounds based on zectran or mesurol.

Nematode control

Nematodes are tiny microscopic worms that live in the soil and on the insides of plant roots. Nematode root knot disease can be a serious problem in home garden. Here's how to control it:-

Nonchemical controls:
1. Move the garden every two or three years.
2. Make sure purchased transplants do not show tiny root swellings or knots on the roots.
3. Place mulch around the base of plants to keep the soil from drying out, and make sure the soil stays moist during dry weather.

4. Destroy the roots by pulling up and destroying after harvest.
5. Use resistant varieties where possible.

Chemical controls: Several chemicals (nematicides) can be used to kill nematodes in the soil:

Figure 8-10

NEMATICIDES	CROPS
D-D or Telone II	Any vegetable crop
Fumazone 86% liquid EC or Nemagon 86% liquid EC	Beans, broccoli, cantaloupes, cabbage, carrots, okra, squash, tomatoes, melons

(Do no use granular formulation of Fumazone or Nemagon for snap beans, eggplant, peppers, onions, and sweet potatoes.)

Figure 8.09

COMMON HOME GARDEN INSECTICIDES AND THEIR USE

Insecticide	Use and Comments
Chlordane	Chlorinated hydrocarbon that kills by contact and stomach action; effective for control of ants and earwigs; do not use on any vegetables.
Cygon-dimethoate	Kills aphids, spider mites and serpentine leaf miner.
Diazinon	Organic phosphate recommended primarily for use in the soil to control cutworms, grubs, wireworms and other ground pests; toxic to fish and honey bees; has a brief residual action.
Dipel-Thuricide (Bacillus thuringiensis)	Bacterial organism that paralyzes the digestive system of such leaf-chewing worms as caterpillars, cabbage loopers and tomato hornworms without having any toxic effect on bees, pets or humans.
DOOM (Milky Disease Spoor Powder)	Ordorless powder containing the living spores of the organism which produces the milky disease of the grubs of the Japanese beetle—effective for control of the Japanese beetle.
Dormant oil	Highly refined petroleum oil mixed with water; some formulas contain fish or vegetable oils; effectively smothers scale and other sucking insects.
Dylox (Trichlorfon)	Contact and stomach insecticides useful for controlling cutworms.
Kelthane (Dicofol)	Effective miticide that kills red spider and clover mites; for control of mites on ornamentals, house plants, fruits and vegetables.
Lindane	Chlorinated hydrocarbon with action similar to DDT—effective on ants; do not use on any vegetables.
Malathion	Contact phosphate compound that is useful on all sucking insects such as aphids; used extensively in home gardens.
Methoxychor (Mariate)	Contact and stomach insecticide that effectively controls a wide range of chewing insects; has a residual action—not recommended by many gardeners.
Mirex	Kills ants; do not make more than one application every 2 months or three applications in 12 months.
Nicotine sulfate	Organic insecticide made from the waste products of tobacco; especially useful on aphids; very poisonous.
Pyrethrum	Organic insecticide made from the dried, powdered flowers of certain plants of the chyrsanthemum genus; effective against aphids, leafhoppers, thrips, leaf miners.
Rotenone	Insecticide derived from the roots and sometimes stems of certain New World tropical shrubs and vines of the genera Derris and Lonchocarpus; effective against beetles, caterpillars, leaf miners, thrips, aphids.
Ryania	Insecticide derived from the ground stems of a tropical South American shrub, Patrisia Pryrifera; used effectively against the corn borer.
Sabadilla	Contact insecticide made from the seeds of a lilylike Mexican plant; sold as a wettable powder; useful for squash bugs, stink bugs and harlequin bugs.
Sevin (Carbaryl)	Contact phosphate that is useful to control over 170 chewing insects; widely used by home gardeners.
Systemic insecticides	A systemic insecticide is absorbed by the plant's roots and circulated through the vascular system, killing chewing and sucking insects as they feed; not used on vegetables.
Thiodan endosulfan	Used for the control of a wide range of insects.

FUNGICIDES

Chemical fungicides are effective in preventing and controlling vegetable disease. Because fungicides can be blown or washed off plants, they must be reapplied at regular intervals while the disease is active. The following chemicals are often used in vegetable gardens.

Figure 8-11

CHEMICALS	SOME TRADE NAMES
BENOMYL (1-butylcarbamoyl-2-benzimidazole carbamate	Benlate, Tersan 1991
Bravo	Bravo 75%, Bravo 6F
Bordeaux: A mixture of copper sulfate and spray lime in water	Bordo-Mix
Captan (N-trichlorme-thylmer-capto-4-cycolhex-ene-1,2 dicarboximide	Orthocide 50 W, Orthocide, Garden Fungicide
Ferban (Ferric dimethyl dithocarbamate)	Fermate, Ortho Ferban, Stauffer Ferban
Fixed copper (Copper oxychloride sulfate)	Basic Copper Fungicide, Corona 53, Ortho Copper 53 Fungicide, Triangle Brand
Basic Copper Sulfate, Tribasic Copper Sulfate (Copper hydroxide)	Kocide 101
(Copper ammonium carbonate)	Cal-Cop 10
(Copper salts of fatty and rosin acids)	Citcop 4E, Copoloid 6, TL-90
Folbet (Phaltan, N-trichloro-methylthio-pthallmide)	Chevron Folpet 75W, Fungitrol 11, Ortho Rose and Garden Fungicide, Stauffer Folpet 75W
Karathane (Dinocap, Dinitor crotonate)	Karathane WD, Mildex
Lime sulfur 26-30% solution of calcium polysulfides	Orthorix spray, Security Lime Sulfur
Maneb Fungicide; with zinc added, Dithane M-22 Special, Manzate D.	Dithane M-22, Manzate Maneb, Vancide Maneb
Zinc-Ion Maneb	Dithane M-45, Manzate 200
Streptomycin Zineb (zinc ethylene bisdi-thiocarbamate)	Dithane Z-78, Ortho Zineb Wettable, Parzate C, Vancide Zineb, Stauffer Zineb, Orchard Brand Zineb

Figure 8.13

Birchmeier sprayers

Birchmeier sprayers are Swiss quality products. They have a pressure relief valve that prevents the tank from being overpressurized, a funnel tank top opening that helps prevent spills, and a plastic nozzle and flexible plastic wand.

TREBOR CORP.
4045 A Jonesboro Rd.
Forest Park, GA 30050

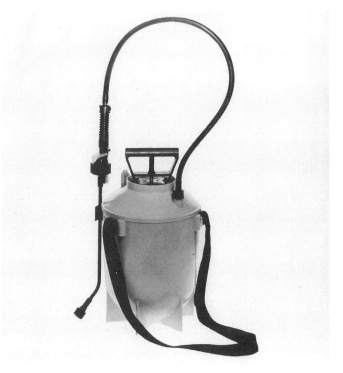

Figure 8.12
Polypropylene tank

This lightweight polypropylene tank is impact-resistant and corrosion-proof. The wide-mouth funnel top fills fast. The pressure builds in a few short strokes of the pump.

BURGESS VIBROCRAFTERS, INC.
Graystake, IL 60030

Figure 8.14
Hand-held sprayer
This two quart pressure sprayer has a built-in pump. Adjusts for mist or stream. Lightweight and easy to handle.
TOLCO CORP.
1920 Lindwood Ave.
Toledo, OH 43624

HERBICIDES

Weed killers (herbicides) are not all that useful for the home gardener. Most herbicides are practical only for large-scale agricultural and for single-crop fields. A chemical that is safe for one kind of vegetable may severely injure or destroy another. Weeds can be controlled more effectively in the home garden by a heavy mulch, by cultivating or by hand weeding.

Chemical weed killers can be classified as selective and non-selective—that is, they are selective and attack only one plant or group of plants, or they are non-selective and attack all vegetables.

Some non-selective herbicides are Aminotriazole, Diuron, Monouron, Silvex, 24D and Simazine. These are not for use within the garden. **Silvex** is found in most herbicides used to control chickweed, bent grass, clover, spurge and similar weeds. It does not harm lawn grass. **Octyly Ammonium Methyl Arsonate** (AMA) is the universally recommended chemical to kill crabgrass in all stages. **Amitrole** is recommended for poison ivy, poison oak, clump grass and similar vegetation.

Some selective herbicides are Betasan, Casoran, Chloro IPC, Dachthal, Trifluralin, Eptam and Chloramben. **Chloramben** can be used around tomatoes and peppers as a pre-emergence weed killer to control weeds and grasses. **Dachthal** (DCPA) can be used among certain vegetables as a pre-emergence weed control.

A good reference on weed control is the booklet *Chemical Weed Control Bulletin 516*, from:
KANSAS AGRICULTURAL EXPERIMENT STATION
Manhattan, KS 66502.

SPRAYERS

Sprayers are essential for the application of pesticides and fungicides in the garden, for spraying liquid fertilizer, for administering weed killer, for applying dormant sprays to fruit trees, and for many other purposes. Today, there are many improved designs on the market, offering different applicators and differing modes of operation.

Small hand sprayers or atomizers come in various types. There are some for small jobs that are like a Windex bottle—you simply pump the top with your fingers. These are especially useful if you want to spot-spray, keeping your application to a very limited area. Another type of hand sprayer is the old familiar standby, consisting of a hand pump (like a bicycle pump) mounted on top of a metal or glass container. There are single-action models, in which the spray stops at the end of each stroke, and continuous-action models, in which the spray is uninterrupted as long as you keep pumping. Many of these sprayers have a nozzle that adjusts for either a fog or a residual-type spray. It's best to choose a sprayer with an adjustable nozzle that is made of a non-corrosive material and can be easily cleaned.

Figure 8.15
No-pumping sprayer
For gardeners tired of hand-pumping. Just attach a gaden hose to fill, and automatically pressurize the tank. The household water pressure does all the work.

Figure 8.16
Solo Knapsack Sprayer
Solo manufacturers an all-plastic backpack sprayer. It can be used with a wide variety of jet nozzles and other accessories such as a pressure control gauge kit.
SOLO KLEINMOTOREN GMBH
D-7032 Sindelfingen 6
West Germany

Figure 8.17

Crank dusters

The crank duster operates with a hand crank that forces the insecticide into a fan where it is blown out over the vegetables. Crank dusters are only practical when you are cultivating large acreage.

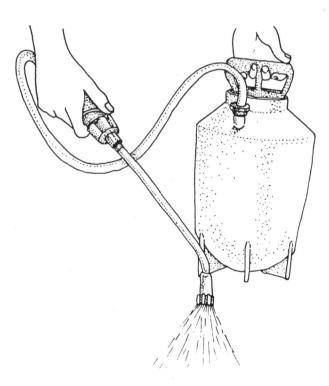

Figure 8.18

Compressed-air sprayers

These are made of galvanized steel or plastic and are pumped by hand to create air pressure. They are available in sizes of from 1 to 15 gallons or more. Most have adjustable nozzles. A long wand allows you to reach easily under the leaves.

Hose end sprayers consist of a nozzle, a holding jar and a female hose end that can be attached to your garden hose. The chemicals can be diluted or mixed in proper proportions right in the jar. Some of these sprayers come with an adjustable nozzle that allows you to mix chemicals and water in whatever proportion you desire during the spraying action. And some models are equipped with a pistol grip handle for each operation. These sprayers are fine for applying chemicals to small gardens.

Slide sprayers sometimes called trombone sprayers, utilize a small, round, brass slide pump. There is no tank; the hose end is placed in a bucket or some other open source of water. These sprayers sometimes come with adjustable brass nozzles and will reach to a distance of about 35 feet. Most are double-action and give a continuous spray.

Compressed-air tanks are usually made of galvanized steel or plastic and are pumped by hand to create air pressure that forces out the spray. They are highly adaptable and range in capacity from one to fifteen gallons; the usual size is two gallons. The smaller tanks are often carried by a shoulder strap. The larger ones use a golf-bag type of caddy. Compressed-air tanks can handle both oil-based sprays and wettables, and are excellent for use in large gardens.

Back pack sprayers are fairly large metal or plastic containers that are designed to be strapped to the user's back. Most hold about four gallons of liquid and are pumped with a hand lever. Some are equipped with a small gas-operated compressor.

Electric sprayers are quite similar to the other large sprayers, but utilize a rechargeable battery for compressor power.

Power sprayers There are a number of large-volume all-purpose, power-drive sprayers on the market with tanks that hold ten gallons of liquid and more. Some models are designed to be pulled by a garden tractor, others are self-propelled.

DUSTERS

Some gardeners prefer to apply insecticides in dry dust rather than liquid form. Dusters actually are an extremely convenient and effective method of applying chemicals to vegetables. There two basic types available: The **Piston Duster**, for small-to-medium-sized gardens, stores the dust in a dust chamber. The dust is forced out by hand action of the piston. These small dusters hold up to two quarts of dust. **Crank Dusters** are large enough for use on eight to ten acres. They are operated by a hand crank which forces the dust into a fan where it is blown out over the vegetables. Extension tubes put the dust exactly where is is needed. Some large dusters utilize a power source.

ANIMALS

Some species of animal can be an extreme nuisance in the garden.

Gophers can be driven out using a gopher-mole windmill, which essentially sets up a vibration in the ground that gophers and moles can't tolerate. Mothballs or moth flakes can also be used to keep gophers out of the garden. Rabbits can be held off completely by surrounding your plot with a chicken wire fence.

Birds are a mixed blessing. They feed on damaging insects which is why many gardeners build birdhouses to attract them. On the other hand, some birds will eat seedlings of such fruit as tomatoes. One defense: hang up metal foil strips on strings extended two or three feet over the garden. An extreme measure would be to enclose the garden completely with gauze of chicken wire held up by posts and a frame.

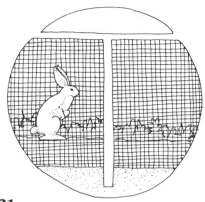

Figure 8.21
Rabbit fences
Rabbit fences should be extended below ground level. This is found to be 100 percent effective.

Figure 8.19

Spot cages
These can be used to protect individual crops. Simply place them over vegetables that are being attacked by animals.

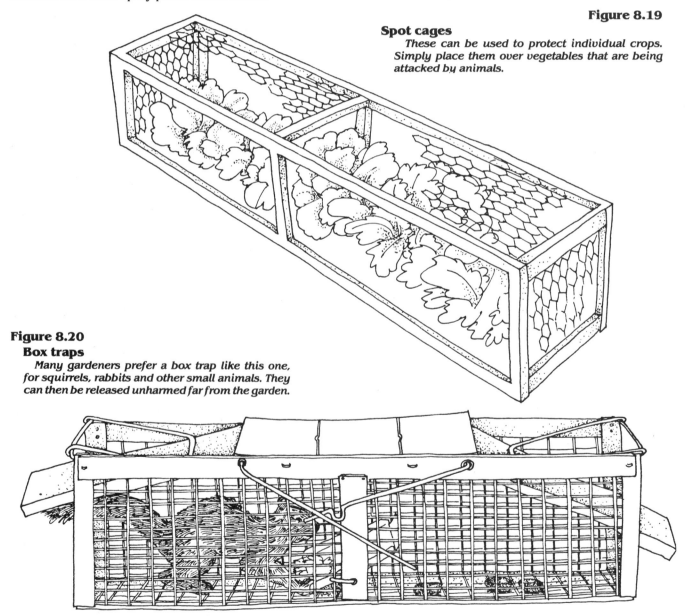

Figure 8.20
Box traps
Many gardeners prefer a box trap like this one, for squirrels, rabbits and other small animals. They can then be released unharmed far from the garden.

Figure 8.22

CHEMICAL CONTROLS FOR LARGER PESTS

Moles-Gophers	Rabbits-Deer	Dogs-Cats	Mice-Rats
Black Leaf Products 667 N. State Elgin, IL 60120	Panogen Co. Ringwood, IL 60072 Improved Z.I.P.	Associate Laboratories 1771 Massachusetts Ave. Cambridge, MA 02138 Skat Stix, does not wash away	Chemper Chemical Co. 269 Madison Ave. New York, NY 10016 Rozoi—mouse killer
Carajon Chemical Co. Inc. Fremont, MI 49412 Force's Gopher Killer: whole-grain oats–strychnine alkaloid Force's Mole Killer	Pensalt Chemicals Corp. Box 1297 Tacoma, WA 98401	Chevron Chemical Co. 200 Bush St. San Francisco, CA 94105 Scram-Dog repellent, easy to use aerosol	Colonial Products, Inc. 1830 10th Ave. N. Lake Worth, GI 33460 32, 42 rat and mice killer, dry pellets
Cooke Laboratory Products Pico Rivera, CA 90660 Gopher tabs with strychnine	State College Laboratories 800 Hiesters Ln. Reading, PA 19605 Magic Circle rabbit and deer repellent	Johnson Nurseries Box 411 Dexter, NY 18640 Scent Off	Cooke Laboratory Products poisoned barley—special formula attracts rats
Great Lakes Chemical Corp. El Dorado, KS 67402 Meth-O-Gas-100% Methyl Bromide	Sudbury Laboratory Inc. Sudbury, MA 01776 Chaperone rabbit & deer repellent	Samuel J. Milazzo Co. Pittston, PA 18640 Animal Chaser	Nott Manufacturing Pleasant Valley, NY 12569 Rat Nots-kill rats overnight—a saline additive directs rats outside: Mouse Nots are tasty poison seeds; Sia Rat is an anti-coagulant deadly to rats
Nott Manufacturing Co. Pleasant Vallley, NY 12569 Smoke' em generates sulfur smoke		Sudbury Laboratory, Inc. Sudbury, MA 01776 Chaperone liquid dog and cat repellent	
Gopher-Mole Chaser 420 N. Bloomfield Rd. Nevada City, CA Windmill vibration frightens moles and gophers	Allock Mfg Co. North Water St. Ossining, NY 10562 17 different Humane (Havahart) animal trap for garden predators, dogs, squirrels, skunks, rabbits, etc.		Allock Mfg. Co. North Water St. Ossining, NY 10562 Katch-All Rat traps made of No. 2 galvanized hardware cloth, electrically welded

Figure 8.23

Scarecrows
They are especially useful for keeping birds out of the garden. Just use your imagination to design a scarecrow that appeals to you.

Figure 8.24

VEGETABLE DISEASE CONTROL RECOMMENDATIONS

Crop	Disease	Description	Remedy
Beans (snap, lima)	Anthracnose	Dark, sunken, circular or oval pod spots; brown borders and salmon-colored ooze in spots; leaves and stems also infected.	Spray with Maneb or Zineb or dust with Maneb at first sign of disease and weekly thereafter; also, use Bordeaux mixture.
	Bacterial blight	Brown or tan spots or blotches with a yellow border on leaves; pods may have brick-red or brown sunken blotches.	Use disease-free seed.
	Damping-off	Seeds fail to grow; young plants die.	Treat seeds with Captan dust, or apply Captan to soil at planting time.
	Root and stem rot	Plant wilts and dies; plant is decayed on lower roots and stem.	Apply Captan to soil at planting time.
	Rust	Brown spots (pustules) on leaves.	Use Maneb or Bravo. Sulfur dust can also be applied at weekly intervals.
Broccoli, brussels sprouts, cabbage, cauliflower, and other "cole" crops	Club root fungus	Roots become enlarged; plants wilt and finally die.	Grow only in well-drained soil.
	Yellows	Leaves turn yellow; plants are often deformed.	Choose resistant varieties.
	Black rot	Infections make leaves yellow or tan; leaf veins and vascular ring in stem may be black; head may decay.	Rotate cabbage with other crops; plant disease-free seed; use Bordeaux mixture.
	Blackleg		Keep garden tools clean; remove debris; follow crop rotation.
	Damping off; stem rot	Young plants die; seeds may rot.	Treat seed with Captan dust; work Captan into soil in accordance with instructions.
Corn	Bacterial wilt	Long pale-green or tan dead streaks on leaves; may cause stunting and death of plants.	The disease bacteria is carried by flea beetles, so use insecticides to control; use resistant varieties.
	Smut	Galls on leaves, stems, ears or tassels continue to enlarge, turn black and break open.	Cut off the galls before they break open and destroy.
Cantaloupe, cucumber, pumpkin and watermelon	Anthracnose	Dark sunken, circular or oval pod spots; brown borders and salmon colored ooze in center, on fruits, stems and borders.	Spray with Maneb at first sign of disease and continue weekly as needed.
	Bacterial wilt	Vines wilt and die.	The bacteria is transmitted by cucumber beetle—use insecticide to control the beetles.
	Fruit rot	Rotted fruit; gray, moldy growth; decay at blossom end of squash.	Spray with Maneb at the first sign of disease and continue weekly.
	Powdery mildew	White, powdery growth on surface of leaves and stems.	Spray with Karathane or Benomyl…at weekly intervals sulfur dust.
Peas	Damping off	Seeds fail to grow; young plants die.	Buy treated seed; treat seed with Captan dust or apply to soil at planting time.
	Downy mildew	White mode on underside of leaves.	Grow resistant varieties.
	Fusarium wilt	Seedlings wilt and die; older plants growth is stunted.	Grow resistant varieties.
Pepper	Bacterial spot	Irregular tan or dark-brown spots on leaves.	Spray with fixed copper at first sign of disease and then weekly as needed.

▶

◀ Crop	Disease	Description	Remedy
Potato	Black leg	Stems decayed and blackened at or below ground line; tops grow poorly.	Plants disease-free tubers. Do not plant cold potatoes into cold soil.
	Late blight	Dead areas on leaves—brown or dark purple; white or gray moldy growth on leaf underside.	Plant disease-free tubers; spray foliage at first sign of disease with zinc-ion, Maneb, Zineb, fixed copper, or Bravo.
	Scab	Black, rough, scabby patches appear on the skin.	Grow resistant varieties.
Squash	Bacterial wilt	Leaves suddenly start to wilt; cucumber beetles in evidence, especially on young plants.	Dust with Sevin or Diazinon; may be necessary to destroy all infected plants.
	Blossom end rot	Flowers become rotted, deformed.	Spray blossoms with Maneb or Zineb.
	Leaf Spot	Dried brown spots on leaves soon become holes.	Spray with Zineb or Captan.
	Fruit rot	Rot attacks squash resting on moist ground.	Prevent by growing on black plastic.
	Powdery mildew	Powdery white material appears on leaves.	Dust with sulfur.
	Scab	Brown holes in fruit.	Spray with Maneb.
Sweet Potato	Scurf	Irregular purple-brown discoloration.	Use only disease-free potato roots.
Tomato	Blossom end rot	Leathery black or dark-brown decay on the blossom end of fruit.	Can be cut down or eliminated by maintaining a uniform soil moisture.
	Early blight	Dark-brown spots with concentric rings on leaves, stems and fruits.	Spray foliage with zinc-ion Maneb, Maneb, Zineb, fixed copper or Bravo at first signs of disease and at weekly intervals.
	Fusarium and verticillium wilt	Leaves turn yellow and fall on one side of the plant before the other; vascular tissue may have dark discoloration; leaves wilt.	Use resistant tomato varieties; rotate garden crops.
	Late blight	Brown or dark-purple dead areas on leaves; white or gray moldy growth on leaf underside.	Use partially resistant varieties; apply zinc-ion Maneb, Maneb, Zineb, fixed copper or Bravo at the first signs of disease and at weekly intervals.
Vegetables in general	Southern stem blight	Decay of stem near ground line; often heavy white fungus growth.	Rotate crops.
	Virus	Mottling, mosaic yellowing of leaves or fruits; some malformation in shape of leaves or fruit.	Use resistant varieties; clean up weeds and garden residue.

Figure 8.25

ROUNDUP OF SUPPLIERS OF PEST CONTROLS

FUNGICIDES

Benomyl	JUN, PER
Bonide	JUN
Bordo	EAR, PER
Captan	JOH, JUN, PER
General purpose	EAR, WET
Lime sulphur	FAR, JUN, PER
Maneb	FAR, JUN, PER
Zineb	EAR

CHEMICAL INSECTICIDES

Black Leaf 40	EAR, JUN
Bonide (border and miner killer)	JUN
Combination insecticide	GUR
Diazinon	EAR, JUN, PER, WET
Earwig destroyer	PER
Malathion	EAR, JUN
Sevin	EAR, FAR, GUR
Slug destroyer	MET, PER, WET
Special purpose insecticides	MEY, TWI

MECHANICAL DEVICES

Garden Monster	HAS
Owl	BUR, FAR, PAR
Scarecrow	HAS
Snakes	BUR, PAR
Traps	BUR, BURG, FAR

PEST CONTROLS

Dog and Cat Repellent	EAR, FAR
Mouse/Rat baits	MEY
Squirrel repellent	EAR

ORGANIC INSECTICIDES

Grasshopper spore	GUR
Insecticidal soap	BUR, GUR, JUN, NIC, VER
Pyrethrum	BUR, JOH, NIC, PIN
Rotenone	EAR, JON, JUN, PER, PIN
Special purpose	JOH, VER, VES
Thuricide	EAR, JOH, JUN, NIC, PIN, VER

WEED CONTROL

Dacthal	GUR
General weed control	BURG, FAR, MEY, PER, WET

See Figure 13.01, Chapter 13 for explanation of source codes

Figure 8.26

Deer fences

Regular deer fences need to be at least 8 feet high to prevent deer from entering the garden. An alternative is a 4-foot-high fence with outriggers. Just drop 2-by-4s from the top of the fence to the ground as shown, and string single wires between the 2-by-2 diagonals.

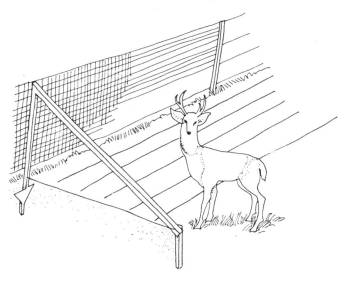

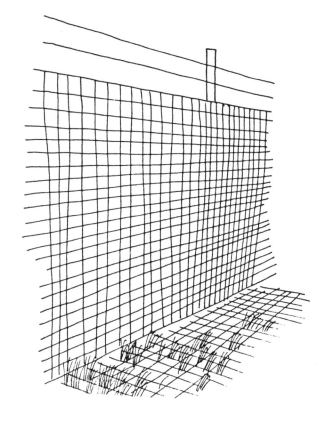

9. Greenhouses

THE MOST POPULAR TYPE of greenhouse today is the sunroom-greenhouse, but there are many other types available for the home gardener. This chapter focuses on the dozen or so leading styles of modern greenhouse, and describes some of the major greenhouse accessories, from heaters to cooling systems.

GREENHOUSES ARE PRACTICAL

More people than ever before are growing vegetables, and they want them year round. Greenhouse manufacturers have capitalized on the boom and increased sales all over the country. Economies of scale and the growing use of plastics, fiberglass and other inexpensive materials have brought greenhouse prices within the reach of millions—some small units sell for as little as $100. Even the grander, aluminum-and-glass styles cost only around $1,000. Furthermore, a marriage of experience and modern technology has enabled an increasing number of companies to offer greenhouse kits that can be built and installed in a single weekend. For the adventurous and handy consumer, these offer an opportunity to save a tidy sum in construction costs.

The multiplicity of choice available to the home gardener nowadays is mind-boggling. Structural alternatives include inflatable, lean-to, free-standing, quonset-hut, gothic, dome-shaped—and a hundred variants in between. Structural materials range from steel to aluminum to wood; coverings from glass to soft plastic to rigid plastic and other futuristic materials. Accessories include heaters, humidifiers, water systems, time controls, vents and many more.

The good news is that greenhouses are a practical proposition just about everywhere in the United States today (though, with recent and continuing increases in the price of energy, special attention needs to be given to keeping heat loss to a minimum).

Temperature is a key factor in the operation of a greenhouse. As a general rule, for each square foot of surface of a greenhouse that faces the outside, you need 1.4 BTUs (British Thermal Units) per hour for every degree Fahrenheit of difference between the outdoor temperature and the level of heat you wish to maintain within. For example, if a greenhouse has 80 square feet of surface area and you want to keep the inside temperature at 50^0 F, you will have to produce over 3,360 BTUs per hour if the outside temperature is 20^0 F. Double glazing and other forms of insulation will reduce this figure.

In general, then, the greater the surface area of your greenhouse, the greater will be the heat loss. (Other factors like materials and insulation will be discussed later in the chapter.) A quonset-like structure uses less than the regular rectangular greenhouse of the same length because it is curved and therefore has less surface area. By the same token, a round or dome-shaped greenhouse also has less surface area than a square structure whose sides are equal to the diameter of the round greenhouse.

Another factor affecting heat loss is the greenhouse's placement on your property. You can minimize heat loss by placing the greenhouse in a protected area—the downwind side of a row of trees, hedges, a fence, or any other barrier. If you're on more or less flat land and the wind is an important weather factor, it might be worthwhile to construct or plant some kind of windbreak. Take care, though, not to restrict the greenhouse's access to light. Some people add a piece of clear plastic to the north side of their greenhouse, thus reducing heat loss without cutting down significantly on the light.

GREENHOUSE CONSTRUCTION

All the different types of greenhouses have their individual advantages and disadvantages, depending on the circumstances of their intended use. The following should help you determine which type is most suitable for you.

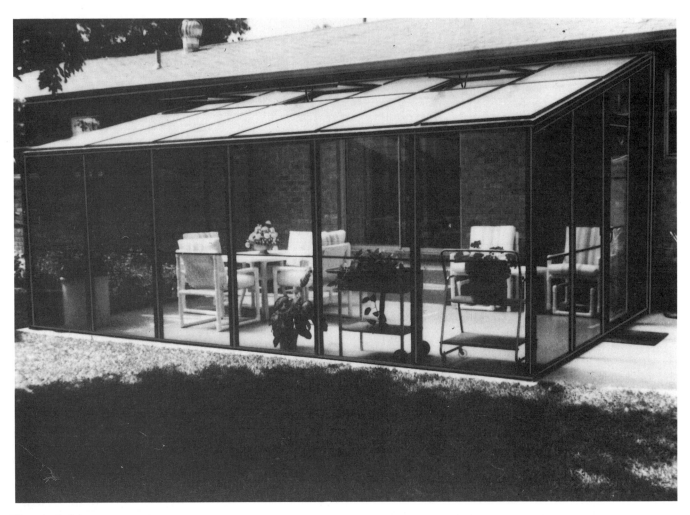

Figure 9.01

Convertible greenhouse

Designed for year-round use, the new Sun-Porch *model is an insulated winter greenhouse that converts to a summer screened room.*

It features heavy-duty bronze-finish aluminum framing with 1-inch insulated glass-clear or bronze-tinted Plexiglas. Do-it-yourself assembly.

VEGETABLE FACTORY, INC.
71 Vanderbilt Ave.
New York, NY 10169

Window models: The smallest permanent unit you would want to consider is a window greenhouse. Often you can leave the original window in place and use it to regulate the supply of air and heat in your window unit. Window greenhouse frames can be made of aluminum or wood. The basic structure is attached to the outside of the window, and sections of glass or plastic are then installed within this framework. Sunlight enters on the two short sides and through the large front. You can build a window unit facing any direction as long as the window is not badly shaded by trees. An obvious disadvantage of these greenhouses is that you can grow only limited quantities of vegetables.

Conventional models: The typical even-span greenhouse looks like a tent with a high center ridge. (The Dutch variation has sloping sides.) Its advantages are: good growing space (even under the benches); even

circulation of air; and fairly even, good light. Sections can be added easily if you want to expand. The main disadvantage is the extensive heat loss due to its large surface area. (The Dutch style is more efficient.)

Lean-to: A greenhouse can be erected on the south or east side of a house, with three sides of glass or plastic and the fourth side supported by the house. These have become so popular today as sun rooms that many manufacturers now sell more of them than of any other style. Advantages: accessible from house; can utilize heat from the house; less expensive than most types; may take up less space. Disadvantages: heat gets trapped near the roof; floor space is hard to reach; provides less bench space than other types.

A-frame: The ceiling and walls are one and the same. Advantages: aesthetically pleasing; easy to build; good light transmission. Disadvantages: heat gets trapped near the floor; floor space is hard to reach; provides less bench space than other types.

Gothic arch frame: This is an attractive, popular model. Advantages: the curved shape utilizes interior space well; structurally strong; transmits more light and heat than any other types. Disadvantages: difficult to ventilate.

Quonset: Familar half-oval shape. Advantages: easy to erect; structurally strong; good light and heat absorption; plenty of growing space. Disadvantages: must be well ventilated; not many models on the market.

Dome: Looks like a mushroom. Advantages: relatively inexpensive; airy; strong; all surfaces transmit light; attractive, offers much usable space; everything is easy to reach from one spot. Disadvantages: bench space hard to brace; hard to ventilate; benches must be rounded to fit against the wall.

Inflatable: A good mode to start with. Advantages: easy to erect; relatively inexpensive; double walls give good insulation; makes good use of limited space. Disadvantages: relatively short life; not available in large walk-in size.

Figure 9.02

Lean-to greenhouse

Lean-to greenhouse sun-rooms are now one of the most popular types on the market. This Sun Valley, slant-side Janco glass-to-ground greenhouse is 10 feet wide. It can be used as a sun-room, to extend the house or as a regular greenhouse with 36-inch benches along each wall.

J.A. NEARING CO., INC.
9390 Davis Ave.
Laurel, MD 20707

Figure 9.03

WHAT TO LOOK FOR IN A GREENHOUSE

- Metal frames should be heavy-duty.
- Aluminum frames should be painted.
- Frames should be standardized throughout the greenhouse.
- Bolts and screws should be rustproof aluminum.
- Wooden frames should be bolted, not nailed or stapled.
- Greenhouses should have grooves in upper framing for hanging baskets.
- Doors should be heavy-duty.
- Ball-bearings on doors are desirable.
- Sliding doors should be nonstick.
- Glass panels should be shatterproof.
- Fiberglass should be no. 1 grade.
- Polyethylene should have some sort of non-rip connections to the greenhouse.

Pentagon-hexagon: Five- or six-sided structure. Advantages: good use of space; inexpensive. Disadvantages: difficult to ventilate; benches must be built around walls to use available space.

STRUCTURAL MATERIALS

Frames

The main alternatives for greenhouse farming are galvanized steel, aluminum and wood. **Aluminum** is most commonly used because it is light and strong, and doesn't warp. It transmits and thus loses heat, but only to a minor degree. **Galvanized steel** is very strong, but it sometimes flakes and rusts. **Wood** has been used for many years. Redwood and cypress are quite good, but construction-grade pine and fir should be checked carefully. Wood is strong, durable and good-looking, but it is bulky and prone to crack.

Covering materials

Today's greenhouses are usually covered with either glass, hard plastic or soft plastic.

Glass has been made the standard material for greenhouses for many years. It is durable and transmits light effectively. Glass is expensive, but when you install double glazing of shatterproof glass, you've got a well-insulated structure that will last a long time. Glass generally needs to be shaded in the summertime.

Hard (acrylic) plastic is another material that is now used extensively for greenhouses. Frequently, it is reinforced with strands of glass or nylon. Fiberglass-reinforced plastic (FRP) is stronger, easier to cut and fit, and less subject to breakage than ordinary glass. FRP can also be made resistant to ultraviolet light. The big disadvantage of plastic is that it turns very brittle in cold weather.

Greenhouses are constructed with flat or corrugated hard plastic sheets. The flat sheets need strong support to prevent sagging. Corrugated sheets remain firm, but they are harder to seal than the flat sheets. Double panels can be used to provide extra insulation.

There are several types of ***soft plastic*** used in the construction of today's greenhouses, including

Figure 9.04

FILON FIBERGLASS PANELS

Filon fiberglass is a top-quality brand product made with acrylic-enriched resins, fiberglass, and mineral pigment plus ultraviolet-absorbing agents for maximum color-fastness and long life.

Filon Stripes: These multicolored panels are used for many building purposes.

Cool Rib Panels: These panels are manufactured in bright pastels. They block out much of the sun's rays.

Home Greenhouse Panels: These are special panels for the backyard gardener. They have a 95 percent light transmission.

Contact:
VISTRON CORP.
12333 Van Ness Ave.
Hawthorne, CA 90250

polyethylene, mylar, lortex and others. The soft plastics are inexpensive, have good light transmission and are easy to work with. In cold weather, however, they become rigid and inflexible. A good insulation can be achieved when two layers of polyethylene are used with spacers in between. Blowers can also be used to separate and to support layers. How long soft plastic lasts depends on the quality of the material, its thickness, and the climactic conditions. You can replace it easily with soft plastic or rigid plastic sheets.

Sometimes, soft and hard plastics are used in combination. Greenhouses can have rigid plastic roofs and soft plastic or glass sides. Soft plastic can also be used to add to the insulation of a glass or rigid-plastic greenhouse.

Foundations

Styrene or styrofoam are sometimes used in the form of extruded foam boards as perimeter insulation for greenhouse foundations. There are also urethanes which vary from very hard, rigid materials to elastomers or synthetic rubbers. All have tremendous insulation value. Urethane spray-in-place kits for insulation of foundation walls are now available in hardware and similar stores.

SOLAR GREENHOUSE

Solar greenhouses work by gathering warmth and energy from the sun during the day through a south-facing wall and by storing that heat in the (opposite) north wall for use at night and during cloudy days.

Light-gathering wall: The light-gathering wall should be two layers thick with an insulating air space between. You can utilize glass, ultraviolet-resistant fiberglass, or a combination of fiberglass panel outside and polyethylene film inside.

This wall should have a south or near south exposure and should be tilted at any angle equal to your latitude *plus* 20 to 50 degrees. This will catch the low winter sun but keep out the high summer sun. In summer, when there is too much heat, the greenhouse needs to be shaded and vented. In winter,

Figure 9.05
Gothic Arch Greenhouse
   This greenhouse is engineered to withstand extremes of wind and weather. The glazing panels are of fiberglass reinforced, acrylic modified plastic. Comes complete to the last bolt. Extras include heating, evaporative cooling, shade cloth, automatic clock-controlled water systems and benches.
   GOTHIC ARCH GREENHOUSES
   P.O. Box 1564
   Mobile, AL 36601

especially on extremely cold nights, many solar greenhouse owners use some sort of screen inside the light-gathering wall to slow down the heat loss.

Heat-absorbing wall: Since the sun lies to the south, the greenhouse must utilize a heat-absorbing storage mass at the north wall. This storage mass must be struck directly by sunlight and should be a foot thick or more. It can be constructed of rock, masonry, concrete, adobe or other heat-storing materials. You can also utilize water stored in 50-gallon black-painted drums (the black paint helps absorb heat).

The back of the north wall should be well insulated on the outside so the stored heat won't escape. The north wall can be curved to reflect added light onto the plants and keep them from bending toward the lighter south wall. (You can also store heat in a thick, well-insulated floor.)

Solar greenhouses can retard temperature loss for several days or longer, and the concept has been used successfully in the Pacific Northwest and Minnesota. In colder climates, especially where it may be cloudy for several weeks at a time, a solar greenhouse will need backup heat.

One New Mexico solar greenhouse, however, held 52° F during a -2-degree night. A Pacific Northwest greenhouse held above 50° F over a ten-day cloudy period.

GREENHOUSE ACCESSORIES

Your greenhouse actually is a compact artificial eco-system that needs warmth, humidity, water and fresh air if it is to grow vegetables. This means that you must provide some means of heating, cooling, ventilating and watering to your greenhouse as well as instrumen-

tation and facilities such as benches and bins or shelves for storage.

Nowadays, you can find a tremendous range of accessories on the market designed to handle each of these needs. With choice comes the burden of making sure that you get the right equipment for the job at hand and—just as important—that you don't waste you money on unnecessary or inefficient items.

Heating

Greenhouses are heated with electricity, gas, oil, L.P. gas or solar energy. Each has its good points and its bad.

Electrical heaters tend to be least expensive. Small, portable units, they are easy to install but expensive to use, often creating pockets of heat. Besides standard heaters, you can use soil heating cables or infrared bulbs directly above your plants. They supply an even, constant warmth to mature plants, cuttings or seedlings.

Gas or oil heaters are useful for larger greenhouses, but such units take up quite a bit of room. In general, they are less expensive to operate than electric heaters, but fans are needed to keep the warm air circulating.

Solar heaters take care of most greenhouse needs for growing vegetables at no operating cost as long as there is adequate sun. In most cases, they would need a backup heater for use on very cold nights and during long periods of overcast. Doubtless, technological advances will remedy this in the near future.

Ventilation

Every greenhouse needs some sort of mechanism, whether automatic or hand-operated, to allow regu-

Figure 9.06
Santa Barbara greenhouse
   The standard model fiberglass greenhouse has four sets of vents and a pre-assembled Dutch door frame. The frame is top-quality California redwood. Individual parts are pre-assembled at the factory.
   SANTA BARBARA GREENHOUSES
   1115J Ave Acaso
   Camarillo, CA 93010

lation of the air through the structure. If fresh air is not taken in periodically, the old internal air can become overheated and its moisture content reduced. Greenhouses can be ventilated with either vents or fans.

Most common vents are located at the peaks on either end or along the upper portion of the roof of a greenhouse. These vents may be simple flaps, louvered windows or movable panels. They can be operated by hand or power-driven. Many automatic systems are hooked in tandem with an exhaust fan. When the temperature rises, the fan draws out the warm air and the vent opens to allow fresh air in.

Figure 9.08 ▶

Turner greenhouses

The energy efficient 'Dutch design' is 14 feet wide and available with either fiberglass or polyethylene glazing (cover). It can be installed on a variety of bases: wood beam, combination wood and concrete block base, a wood and earthen base, or a concrete footing with concrete blocks or bricks. This greenhouse is large enough for almost any use. It will accommodate a 3-foot wide bench against each wall, and a 2-foot wide bench or potting table in the center (Figure 9.07).

Figure 9.07

Figure 9.09

REDWOOD GREENHOUSE FRAMES

From an aesthetic standpoint, redwood is probably the best material for a home greenhouse. It blends well with residential architecture and landscaping, whereas metal frames generally distract from the appearance of a home.

There are many advantages to redwood. It is easy to insulate for winter use and transmits heat less readily than aluminum. Expansion and contraction are significant with redwood. It is extremely easy to work. Minor modifications and additions for shelves, hanging basket brackets and special vents are easy to make. Redwood does not have to be painted.

Figure 9.10

VARISHADING

Varishading is a permanent variable greenhouse shading which transmits more light in winter than summer. Applied to the interior of a glass or plastic house, it is transparent when kept wet by winter condensation. In summer, when no condensation occurs, it is dry and opaque. The amount of varishade coating applied determines the degree of shading. When used on the outside of glass, rain will make it transparent.

Contact:
SOLAR SUNSTILL, INC.
Setuket, NY 11733

Figure 9.11
Automatic opener
Responds to inside temperatures and can be adjusted to open at any temperature from 60 to 85 degrees. Raises up to 12 pounds. Full opening is 17 inches.

Small fans keep the air moving throughout the greenhouse and help maintain an even temperature. This prevents stagnation with accompanying mildew and other diseases.

Shade

Plants frequently receive too much intense light during the long summer days. An excess of light causes wilting and leaf burn. There are a number of ways to shade your greenhouse, involving adjustable shades made from aluminum, wood or vinyl, or a shading compound that can be applied directly to the glass surface.

Wooden shades resemble large window blinds. They can be extended and retracted by a system of ropes or pulleys. *Aluminum panels* are composed of slats fastened to a wooden or aluminum frame. There is also an aluminum roll-up type of cover that can be easily adjusted from the outside. *Vinyl plastic shades* are semitransparent and flexible, reducing light by as much as 65 percent. *Shading paint* or *shading powder* (which is mixed with water) can be sprayed on the glass wall.

Cooling system

Your greenhouse will need some kind of cooling system. This may be anything from a simple hose to an evaporator swamp cooler to a refrigeration unit. A hose can be used to sprinkle water on the plants, benches and floors, cooling the area by evaporation. Humidity is not all that important a factor in the cultivation of vegetables. However, there are blowers that will put out a fine mist of water into the greenhouse from a unit measuring the humidity. This action helps to cool the area and to maintain the proper level of humidity. For larger greenhouses, an evaporator cooler that sucks air out through wet pads is a better choice. Refrigeration units are not as commonly used as they once were.

Watering system

You can water by hand with a hose (taking care of cooling at the same time) or install an automated system. One popular automatic setup consists of a flexible plastic hose with spray nozzles that can be attached along the bench. Another uses a length of plastic hose perforated with many tiny holes laid on the surface of the soil.

Instrumentation

Since most vegetables have an optimum growing temperature range from 60° to 80° F, it is important not only to keep track of the temperature in all areas of the greenhouse, but also to have the means to keep it stable within the safety range. (See Figure 6.02 on page 52 for the requirements of cool-season and warm-season vegetables.)

Thermometers placed around the greenhouse will record surprising variations in temperature. A high-low thermometer is essential to let you know what's happening in the greenhouse day and night even though you are not on the scene. It marks the high and the low points registered during a specified period of time. Another vegetable instrument is a temperature alarm, to warn you when it gets too hot or too cold in the greenhouse.

Thermostats help keep the temperature consistent by regulating the source of heat. When installing a thermostat, bear in mind that is should be kept away from bright sun or from direct exposure to any other source of heat. Check your thermostat against the temperature in the greenhouse from time to time. You may find a **humidistat**, indicating the relative humidity, useful. Even though humidity levels are not as critical with vegetables as with most other types of plants, many greenhouse gardeners like to know what the humidity in their greenhouse is. When temperature rises, humidity should rise correspondingly, and a humidistat can be coupled with a mister or humidifier for automatic action.

Figure 9.13

HOBBY GREENHOUSE ASSOCIATION

The Hobby Greenhouse Association is a group of amateur gardeners who either own a greenhouse or who want to own one. The group puts out a newsletter *The Planter,* a swap center where members may exchange seeds, plants and cuttings; they have established a lending library, where members may borrow books by mail, and a film library where members may obtain instructive slides and movies of how to assemble an aluminum frame greenhouse. They also make available seeds and samples and other services. Dues: $5.00 a year.

HOBBY GREENHOUSE ASSOCIATION
Box 695-F
Wallingford, CT 06492

Figure 9.12

Janco freestanding greenhouses

These free-standing Janco models provide the ideal growing environment for the vegetable gardener. The entire frame is constructed of maintenance-free aluminum. Standard sizes of 24 inch glass are used throughout. Factory-sealed insulated glass is available as an optional item.

J.A. NEARING CO., INC.
9390 Davis Ave.
Laurel, MD 20707

Other Equipment

Besides the bare essentials, you will need benches (to support plant pots), storage bins and possibly lights (as supplements during bouts of overcast weather). (See Figure 9.17.)

Benches should be sturdy enough to support heavy pots and shaped so as to take advantage of the available space in the greenhouse. Bench tops should allow for air circulation, easy cleaning and disinfecting. There are many commercially made benches that are worth consideration.

Storage bins or containers for soil amendments and fertilizers are essential for a neat and efficient greenhouse. You will also need dry storage facilities for seeds and fertilizers.

BUILDING YOUR OWN GREENHOUSE

Building your own greenhouse gives you more greenhouse for your money and more flexibility to have the size, shape and design that you want.

A homemade greenhouse can be anything from a window annex to a 70-foot superdome! It can be built

Figure 9.15

CO-RAY-VAC

This infrared vacuum-gas heating system consists of an overhead burner connected to an infrared heat emitting pipe. The invisible infrared rays radiate in straight lines to all surfaces. Heated surfaces transfer warmth to the air. Gas-operated.

Contact:
ROBERTS-GORDON CORP.
44 Central Ave.
Buffalo, NY 14206

Figure 9.14

Instant greenhouse structures

Barclay Horticulture offers a whole series of small, instant greenhouses made of tear-resistant woven polyethylene and durable aluminum frames. Sizes range from 5 feet 10 inches by 4 feet 8 inches to 11 feet 8 inches by 17 feet 8 inches. Both the freestanding and lean-to structures can be used as a greenhouse spring, summer and fall, and as additional storage in winter.

BARCLAY HORTICULTURE MFG LTD.
949 Wilson Ave.
Downsview, Ontario, Canada M3K 1G2

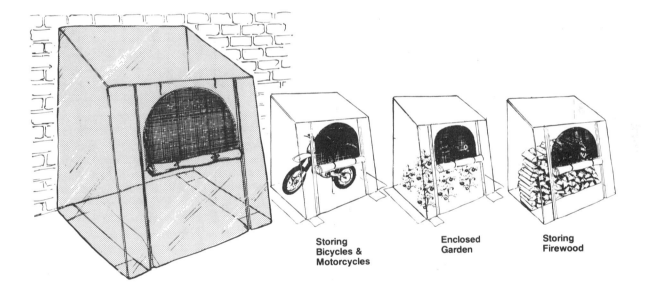

Storing Bicycles & Motorcycles

Enclosed Garden

Storing Firewood

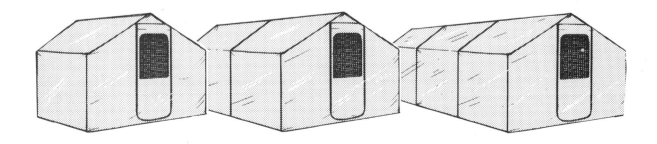

on a wood, pipe or structural metal frame. It is even possible to make a greenhouse from recycled or salvaged materials.

Most experts recommend experimenting with a modest unit before tackling a more ambitious project. But anyone who can saw straight and hammer a nail, can build a greenhouse–all it takes is some spare time and as little as about fifty bucks.

Kits—precut greenhouse

Most models of greenhouses on the market today come as knocked down structures that must be assembled on the spot. It is only a short step away to buy a greenhouse kit.

The kit industry generally has become much more reliable in recent years than it once was, and relatively few buyers of greenhouse kits complain nowadays about the way their kits fit together. Metal/wood, glass or fiberglass kits are well designed and quite easy to assemble. The less expensive, soft plastic greenhouses (from $150) can sometimes cause more problems.

Larger units (over 20 feet in length) tend to become a construction problem because they need a poured foundation and built-up sides. It may make sense to have a local contractor with greenhouse experience help you with a large installation–ask your local nurseryman for advice and a recommendation.

Figure 9.16
Do-It-Yourself

Most greenhouses today require do-it-yourself installation. Those with glazing in place go together faster than unglazed systems. Both aluminum frame and wood frame greenhouses are bolted together. Some firms offer a hot-line for do-it-yourselfers who need help.

photo credit: Pacific Coast Greenhouse Mfg Co.
8360 Industrial Ave., Cotati, CA 94928

GREENHOUSE MANUFACTURERS

ALENCO, DIV OF REDMAN
INDUSTRIES
P.O. Box 3309
Bryan, TX 77801

ALUMINEX, INC.
1920 Riverside Dr.
Los Angeles, CA 90039

AMERICAN NURSERY
PRODUCTS CO.
P.O. Box 768
Tahlequah, OK 74464

BARCLAY ROTHSCHILD
MFG
949 Wilson Ave.
Downsview, Toronto
Ontario, M3K 1G2, Canada

CLOVER GARDEN
PRODUCTS
P.O. Box 874
Murfreesboro, TN 37167

COMANCHE STEEL
PRODUCTS, INC.
P.O. Box 20128
San Antonio, TX 78220

EDMUND SCIENTIFIC CO.
7082 Edscorp Bldg.
Camden, NJ 08007

ENGLISH GREENHOUSES
PRODUCTS CORP.
1501 Admiral Wilson Blvd.
Camden, NJ 01802

FABRICO MFG CO.
4222 S. Pulaski Rd.
Chicago, IL 60632

FLEX PAX CO.,
GREENHOUSE
PRODUCTS DIV.
25330 Interchange Ct.
Farmington Hills, MI 48018

FOUR SEASONS SOLAR
PRODUCTS CORP.
425 Smith St.
Nassau, Suffolk NY 11735

GARDENER'S DELIGHTS,
Div. of Garey Properties Ltd.
5345 Munro Ct.
Burlington, Ontario
Canada L7L 5M7

GARDEN RESOURCES, INC.
P.O. Box 3537
Granada Hills, CA 91344

GREENHOUSE SPECIALTIES
CO.
9849 Kimker Lane
St. Louis, MO 53127

HANSEN WEATHER-PORT
CO.
P.O. Box 477
Gunnison, CO 81230

INSUL-RIB, INC.
P.O. Box 447
Castle Rock, MN 55010

JADERLOON CO., INC.
P.O. Box 685
Irmo, SC 29063

LASCO DIV. PHILLIPS
INDUSTRIES, INC.
3255 Miraloma Ave.
Anaheim, CA 92808

LORD & BURNHAM
P.O. Box 255
Irvington, NY 10533

MANUMARK, INC.
P.O. Box 997
Chatsworth, GA 30705

MC NEIL INDUSTRIES
P.O. Box 1110
Quincy, FL 32351

MIDWESTERN NURSERIES,
INC.
P.O. Box 768
Tahequah, OK 74464

MR. CHAIN, DIV. OF M-R
PRODUCTS, INC.
P.O. Box 1584
Troy. MI 48099

NATIONAL GREENHOUSE
CO.
P.O. Box 100
Lincoln, NB 68503

J.A. NEARING CO.
9390 Davis Ave.
Laurel, MD 20810

PACIFIC COAST
GREENHOUSE MFG CO.
8360 Industrial Ave.
Cotati, CA 94028

JOHN RUDI & SONS
Box 233, Rt. 31
Glen Gardner, NJ 08826

SANTA BARBARA
GREENHOUSES
390 Dawson Dr.
Camarillo, CA 93010

SOLAR SHELTERS, INC.
9900 Hwy 620 N.
Austin, TX 78750

SUNSHINE INDUSTRIES, INC.
P.O. Box 279
Abbeville, SC 29620

TEXAS GREENHOUSE CO.
2717 St. Louis Ave.
Ft. Worth,TX 76110

TRANS SPHERE CO.
Gothic Arch
Greenhouses
P.O. Box 1564
Mobile, AL 36633

TURNER GREENHOUSES
Hwy 117 South
Goldsboro, NC 27530

VEGETABLE FACTORY, INC.
P.O. Box 2235
New York, NY 10163

W.W. MFG CO., INC.
60 Rosenhayn Ave.
Bridgeton, NJ 08302

WINDOW GREENHOUSES

ALUMINEX, INC.
1920 Riverside Dr.
Los Angeles, CA 90039

ALUMINUM GREENHOUSES,
INC.
P.O. Box 11087
Cleveland, OH 4111

BRIGHT SPOT, INC.
4800 Wingate St.
Philadelphia, PA 19136

ENGLISH GREENHOUSE
PRODUCTS CORP.
1501 Admiral Wilson Blvd.
Camden, NJ 01802

GENERAL ELECTRIC CO.
PLASTICS GROUP
One Plastics Ave.
Pittsfield, MA 01201

HARVESTER ALLWEATHER
GREENHOUSES
275 Main St.
Chatham, NJ 07928

NATIONAL GREENHOUSE
CO.
400 E. Main
Taylorville, IL 62557

J.A. NEARING CO.
9390 Davis Ave.
Laurel, MD 20707

JOHN RUDI AND SONS
26 Evelyn Ave.
Vineland, NJ 08826

SEALED AIR CORP.
Park 80 Plaza E.
Saddle Brook, NJ 07662

Figure 9.17

GREENHOUSE ACCESSORIES AND SOURCES

Source	Heat	Ventilation Cooling	Water	Instrumentation	Shelves, Storage Etc.
Birmid Qualcast Coleridge St. Sunnyill, Derby DE 3 7JT, England	Electric	Shading panels	Mist, trickle, overhead systems		
Comanche Steel Products Inc. 343 N. White Rd. San Antonio, TX 78220	Fan-type wall heaters	Automatic exhaust fan	None	None	Shelf units Shelf brackets
D & M Enterprises P.O. Box 739 Wildomar, CA 92395	Arvin/Titan electric, hot-water, & gas heaters	Coolers, humidifiers, shutters, exhaust fans		Several kinds	Hardware
Environmental Dynamics 12615 S. La Cadena Dr. Colton, CA 92324	Electric heater systems, J, soil cables	Fans, shuters, coolers, humidifier systems, $150 to $300	Several types	Thermometers, humidity meter, temperature alarms, others	Benches
Everlite Aluminum Greenhouses Inc. 14605 Lorain Ave. Cleveland, OH 44111	Electric, gas, hot-water heaters, heating systems, soil cables	Fans, vents, automatic humidifier	Automatic watering/ misting nozzles	Thermometer, others	Several kinds of shelves/ benches
Gothic Arch Greehouses P.O. Box 1564 Mobile, AL 36601	Electric 5 KW heaters—electric, gas, kerosene, oil, hot water	Exhaust fans			
Lord & Burnham Irvington-on-Hudson, NY 10533	Several kinds of heaters—electric, gas, kerosene, oil, hot water	Shades, plastic, films, shading powder, automatic venting	Misting/ watering systems	Several kinds	Shelves/tubs
Maco Products Box 109 Scio, OR 97374	Titan heaters, ground cables	Ventilator fans	None	None	None
National Greenhouse Company Box 1000 Pana, IL 62557	126-p. catalog of all kinds of greenhouse parts and accessories; fiberglass accessories available	Several types	Several types	Several types	Several types
J.A. Nearing Co. 9390 Davis Ave. Laurel, MD 20810	Janco - fan jet environmental-control system—heating, cooling, ventilating, dehumidifying	Manual and automatic	Bench misting and other types	Thermometers, humidty indicators	Benches
Edward Owen Engineering Snow Shoe, PA 16874	Titan 220 V heater	Vent opener $62	None	None	Aluminum benches $60 to $100
Pacific Coast Greenhouse Mfg. Co. 430 Burlingame Ave. Redwood City, CA 94063	Electric & gas heaters—15,000 to 310,000 BTU's, heat cables, soil thermostat	Evaporative coolers, fog humidifiers, automatic vent openers, fans, shutters	Water valves	Maximum-minimum thermometer, other	Benches
The Plantworks Tiffany Industries, Inc. 145 Weldon Pkwy. Maryland Heights, MO 63043	Four season system with hydro/environmental control $900; individual components available	Automatic exhaust, evaporate cooler			

Source	Heat	Ventilation Cooling	Water	Instrumentation	Shelves, Storage Etc.
Peter Reimuller 980 17th Ave. Santa Cruz, CA 95060	Electric heaters, $29 to $70, 1200 cu. ft. kerosene heater, $65; has greenhouse accessories packages which include heater, fan, thermometer, shutters—$69 to $105	Exhaust fan inlet shutters, humidifier	Nozzles	Maximum-minimum thermometer, humidity meter	Benches
Santa Barbara Greenhouses 390 Dawson Dr. Camarillo, CA 93010	Electric, $30	Automatic airflow shutters, shutter-mounted exhaust fans	Watering nozzles	Several	Redwood benches
Shelter Dynamics P.O. Box 616 Round Rock, TX 78664	Electric	Exhaust fan, cooler/ humidifier, shading, roof panels	None	None	Cedar benches
Sun America Corp. P.O. Box 125 Houston, TX 77001		Louver window autovent	Rain barrel		Shelves, benches
Sunglo Greenhouses 4441 26th Ave. West Seattle, WA 98199	Elec./gas, $26 to $165	Automatic wall shutters, blowers, shutter-mounted exhaust fan	Watermatic garden kit	Thermometers, light meters	Vinyl-coated ventilated shelving
Texas Greenhouse Co. 2717 St. Louis Ave. Fort Worth, TX 76110	Electric, gas, $21 to $800	Evaporate coolers, fans, shutters	Water kits, other	Complete line	Benches, fiberglass, panels, hardware
Turner Greehouses Hwy. 117 S. Goldsboro, NC 27530	Electric, gas, soil cables	Automatic fan, ventilating systems	Watering and misting equipment, timers	Thermometers, etc.	Slat benches, asbestos-cement growing benches
Vegetable Factory 100 Court St. Copiague, NY 11726	Electric, $35 to $95, soil cables	Cooling & venting system, square	None	Maximum-minimum thermometer, hygrometer	Benches

10. Growing Vegetables in Containers

MILLIONS OF ENTHUSIASTIC GARDENERS are growing a rich array of vegetables for their dinner tables, even though they have little or no tillable ground. Container gardens can be planted indoors or out, on small suburban patios and on the balconies of high-rise city homes, bringing a sense of the land to even the most confined space.

CONTAINERS FIT EVERYWHERE

In the heart of downtown San Francisco, a couple from the midwest grow corn, beans, squash and other tasty crops on the roof of their ultramodern apartment house. In Chicago, a 60-year-old widow tends a profusion of greens in one small, south-facing window. And in New York City, a working man grows a huge crop of lettuce, carrots, tomatoes and more under lights in a four-by-seven closet.

Vegetable gardening in containers is astonishingly simple; no matter where you live, there is no reason not to enjoy vegetables the year round, fresh-picked from your own (container) garden. The prerequisites are very basic: containers and somewhere to put them, a suitable growing medium (potting soil or other mixture), light and water, and maintenance. Just add the right kind of seeds—many catalogs list varieties

◀ **Figure 10.01**

Gardening in containers
There's no need to give up gardening if you live in an apartment, condominium or mobile home without a plot of land. Pots and hanging baskets with ready-made potting soil quickly convert a balcony or courtyard into a vegetable garden.
photo credit: National Garden Bureau

bred especially for container growing—and a healthy measure of intelligent planning.

The choice of containers is as broad as your imagination. From recycled coffee cans to large patio planters, from cut-down milk cartons to redwood boxes to wicker baskets to plastic garbage cans, there are containers to suit every space and pocketbook. Depending on the size of your containers and the material used to make them, you will buy ready-to-use soil or you will mix up your own blend. The amount and frequency of watering will also depend on the type of containers used. In this chapter we will consider each of these aspects of container gardening separately and in relation to each other.

AN INFINITE VARIETY OF CONTAINERS

The first consideration in choosing containers is size. Where do you want to put them, and how much room do you have? The larger and deeper the container, the larger the yields...up to a point. Eight inches of soil is enough for just about any vegetable. (See Figures 10.03 and 10.04 for each plant's specific requirements.) If you've got fairly small containers in mind, and you want to grow tomatoes, stay with the smaller patio-type plants; the larger varieties of this great favorite require up to 20 gallons (3 cubic feet) of soil to produce a decent crop.

With size comes weight. Will your plants be moved around at all? You can, of course, easily carry the lighter containers from place to place, but the large pots are quite heavy when full of soil. So place them in a permanent position, not somewhere from which you expect to have to move them for watering, to put them in better light or for whatever reason. There are ways around this problem if mobility is important. You can increase the mobility of your heavy containers by installing casters on the bases. You can stand them on a moving man's dolly or, if you have smooth floors, on a throw rug that can be pulled easily around the room. Another alternative is to place several containers on a child's wagon, locking the wheels in place until you want to move it. Suitable containers can be made of many different kinds of material. Wooden containers hold moisture well and need less watering than clay pots. The same is true for styrofoam pots. Nonporous containers, such as those made of stone, glass, ceramics and plastic, reduce the need for watering even more.

Drainage

No matter what the container is made of, no matter how big or small it is, there must be an outlet for excess water that percolates through the soil. Without adequate drainage, the excess water will damage the plant. Holes should be drilled or punched through the bottoms of strong containers, such as those made of wood, or through the sides (about ½ inch above the base) of plastic and softer metal containers (which would be weakened—and might not be able to support the weight of soil—if holes were bored in the base).

It's important for containers to have adequate drainage, but just as important that it not be excessive.

Figure 10.02

Container Spot Spitter systems
Spot spitters used at the end of spaghetti tubes can be utilized to water vegetables in individual planters or pots.
ROBERTS IRRIGATION PRODUCTS
700 Rancheros Drive
San Marcos, CA 92069

As a general rule, containers less than ten inches in diameter need only one half-inch drainage hole. Larger pots need anywhere from two to four holes each a bit bigger than a half inch in diameter.

Two final points on drainage. First, it's a good idea to cover the drainage holes with a layer of gravel, pieces of clay or other coarse material to prevent soil from being washed away with the excess water. Second, it's obviously wise to place a dish or other receptacle under the container to catch the escaping water.

Wooden containers

Because wood has a high insulating value, containers made of wood keep the soil from drying out quickly and require less watering than other types. You can buy ready-made wooden planters in a wide variety of shapes and sizes, or you can build them yourself. To build a planter that is one foot square, for instance, purchase five 12 x 12 x 1-inch pieces of lumber, two running feet of 2 x 1-inch stock and a couple dozen penny nails. Nail the pieces together, four sides atop the base. Then cut the 2 x 1-inch piece into four equal lengths and nail them to the four corners as legs. Boxes of any size can be built in a similar manner.

Containers made of redwood or cedar will resist decay for many years, and for that reason have proven popular with gardeners. For other types of wood, you can line the interior of the container with black plastic, or you can coat the wood with a preservative paint or asphalt compound available at hardware and other stores.

Figure 10.03

HOW MUCH CAN YOU GROW IN A CONTAINER?

Vegetables	No. of Plants in 4-inch Pots	No. of Plants in 8-inch Pots
Beets	2-4	8-20
Carrots	2-4	12-24
Garlic	2-4	4-16
Green onions	4-8	16-30
Looseleaf lettuce	1	2
Mustard greens	1	3
Radishes	4-8	16-30
Spinach	1	2
Turnips	2-4	2-16

Figure 10.04

SPACING VEGETABLES IN A CONTAINER

Vegetables	Space Between Each Plant
Artichokes	Plant singly.
Beans	3-9 inches.
Beets	2-3 inches.
Broccoli	10 inches (5 gal. soil per plant).
Brussels sprouts	10 inches (5 gal. soil per plant).
Carrots	1-2 inches.
Cauliflower	12 inches (5 gal. soil per plant).
Eggplant	15 inches (5 gal. soil per plant).
Kale	Thin to 16 inches apart.
Lettuce	4-10 inches.
Melon	15 inches (5 gal. soil per plant).
Mustard greens	Thin to 4 inches apart.
Okra	20 inches (5-10 gall. soil per plant).
Peas	2 inches.
Peppers	8 inches (2½ gal. soil per plant).
Potatoes	6 inches
Radishes	1 inch.
Rhubarb	12 inches (5 gal. soil per plant).
Spinach	Thin to 5 inches.
Squash	12-20 inches (5 gal. of soil per plant).
Tomatoes	½ inch (5 gal. soil per plant).
Turnips	3 inches.

Figure 10.05

Bushel basket containers

Vining cucumbers love the warm, well-drained conditions provided by large containers such as bushel baskets, half barrels and 7-gallon tubs. Containers should be filled with artificial soil purchased ready-made or Sourcebook Vegetable potting soil.

photo credit: National Garden Bureau.

Another popular and attractive container is the half whiskey barrel. By law, barrels used for making whiskey must be discarded after just one distilling. Many nurseries sell used whiskey barrel halves for use as planters. The size of these containers is one of their principal assets—being roughly 22 inches across, they hold enough soil to support good vegetable growth. A single barrel half can hold seven to eight corn plants, two or three zucchini plants and two or three tomato plants. Some gardeners even intercrop their barrel halves—that is, they plant a low, quick-maturing crop right along with a larger, slow-maturing vegetable. Thus, corn may be planted with spinach, radishes and green onions, tomatoes may be planted with radishes, green onions and lettuce. There's no crowding out of one by the other because you pick the faster-growing vegetables before the slower-growing ones become very large.

Plastic pails

They may not win many design awards, but plastic pails are inexpensive and practical containers for use in vegetable gardening. You can buy the 2- or 3-gallon type at the local variety store, or you might be able to pick up larger, 5- or 10-gallon models that have been tossed away after use at construction sites. There are many ways to doll up these plastic eyesores, such as covering them with metal foil or placing them inside larger wicker baskets.

Some companies, such as **Rubbermaid**, manufacture attractively designed plastic containers specifically for gardeners. These ready-to-use pots come in many different sizes and shapes and have found a wide market among apartment farmers.

Other simple containers

Paper pulp pots: An all-around good vegetable container, this type of pot can be carried from place to place easily. The most popular sizes are 12 and 18 inches in inside diameter. In the larger, you can plant eggplant, tomatoes and other large vegetabes; the smaller are good for carrots and similar plants.

Wooden fruit boxes: You can still occasionally pick up an orange crate or similar wooden box outside the supermarket or vegetable store. Recycle it into a container by lining it with black plastic into which some drainage holes have been punched. Filled with good soil, one of these containers will hold several tomato, zucchini or corn plants—or almost any other variety you'd like to grow.

Bushel baskets: Some people find these more attractive than the wooden fruit boxes. Aside from that, everything we said about the fruit boxes holds true for bushel baskets. But act fast—the age of cardboard and plastic is upon us, and the old wooden baskets and boxes are becoming scarce.

Wicker baskets: As wood becomes rare, wicker seems to be becoming more common. Well-designed containers are availabe in countless styles and sizes at many 'import' and other variety stores. Use plastic liners as noted above.

Windowsill containers

The list of common household items that, with a little imagination, can be drummed into service as containers for windowsill gardens is almost infinite. Here are a few of the more widely used:-

Coffee cans: These make fairly sturdy containers for plants. Just punch a few holes in the sides, close to the base, for drainage, fill with soil, and you're ready to grow.

Milk cartons: These plastic-coated, paperboard containers won't last as long as cans, but they'll do quite nicely for one crop. Cut them off 6 to 8 inches above the base and punch out four holes for drainage with a pencil.

Freezer containers: One-pint plastic freezer containers are excellent windowsill containers. Lightweight, durable and inexpensive, they'll last through many plantings.

Flowerpots: The classic four-inch clay flowerpot is not as cheap as it used to be, but it fits very nicely onto most windowsills and is large enough to grow beets, carrots, radishes and similar leafy and root vegetables.

Vertical containers

One of the most innovative developments of recent years is vertical vegetable gardening. This adds a new concept to balcony or patio gardening—height. Now you can plant gardens that climb up the walls for as high you can plant and harvest. Following are some of the variations on this basic theme:-

Vegetable trees: You can build one of these without a great deal of hassle. For backing, use 2 x 12-inch board of any length (six to eight feet is most common). Cut standard chicken wire into two-foot widths that are as long as the board you're using. (See Figure 6.07.) Nail the wire lengthwise to each side of the board. Cut a semicircular board to fit at the base of the wire, and secure it in place. Line the wire and the boards with black plastic. Fill with soil, and you're ready for planting.

When using a vegetable tree, it's possible to garden in combination—that is, tomatoes at the base, topped by cucumbers, then lettuce, then carrots, with radishes at the top. You can use a number of these containers, placed along a wall or at the edge of a patio or balcony.

Figure 10-06

WATERPROOFING BASKETS

Buy clear polyester resin and hardener (separately) and a brush from a craft store. Be sure to use the hardener according to the instructions. Tear some newspapers into long strips about five inches wide. Brush the polyester resin on the basket bottom and sides, then line with the newspaper strips until you have filled the entire basket. Continue the resin-paper process until you've lined the basket with six coats of paper. When finished, add an additional coat of resin.

Hanging basket trees: First, buy or make hanging baskets, half-round in shape, which can be attached to a flat backing. Set up a 1 x 12-inch board as above, probably six to eight feet long. Attach the baskets to the board, about two feet apart. Line them with sphagnum moss or black plastic, place a pie tin or other device at the base, and fill these pouches with soil.

Vegetable pot trees: This is another interesting and easy-to-make variation of the tree format. Anchor four posts, 4 inches by 7 foot, to a base such as a Christmas tree stand. Keep the posts in place with sandbags. Mount 8-inch pots alternately up the posts on hooks strong enough to hold the weight As an alternative to the base, you can nail or mount the posts directly onto a balcony railing.

Bookshelf containers: These are probably the most visually interesting and useful of all vertical containers. You can put them in stationary positions or set them on heavy-duty wheels to make them mobile. Mount 2 x 10-inch side boards on a base of the same size. A good length for the sides is four to five feet, but this can be varied somewhat to suit individual requirements. Drainage holes are drilled in the base. The sides can be joined on both ends by construction wire or by crossed laths. (See Figure 10.07.) The container thus formed is lined with black plastic and filled with soil mix. Leave the top open because you are going to water from there, from halfway down, and from two-thirds of the way down.

It's important with this type of container to use hardy transplants. Insert them through the wire mesh. Keep them moist, and feed them frequently with a liquid plant solution.

A-frame gardens: This setup is second in versatility only to the bookshelf, and is even easier to construct. First, make two A-frame sides using 2 x 4-inch standard boards and a metal sawhorse clamp (a workable design utilizes boards five foot long spread five feet apart). The A-frame should be joined by another five foot long 2-by-4. This structure will become even sturdier when the A-frames are joined by three shelves, preferably of 2 x 8-inch board, mounted on large shelf brackets and braced by 2-by-4 boards. As shown in Figure 10.07, the shelves are wide toward the base, narrow at the top. On these shelves you can place a number of 8-inch or similar-size pots and create a varied, pleasing container garden.

Hanging Gardens

You can add significantly to your overall vegetable production by utilizing hanging containers on the patio, balcony, or almost anywhere. You can hang cherry tomatoes two feet apart under the eaves, or a whole garden of carrots, radishes and similar plants. Hanging containers will grow all medium-sized vegetables well, including the smaller tomatoes and cucumbers. In most cases you should avoid planting them with larger vegetables such as squash, cantaloupe, cabbage and the like.

Here are a couple of types of hanging containers:-

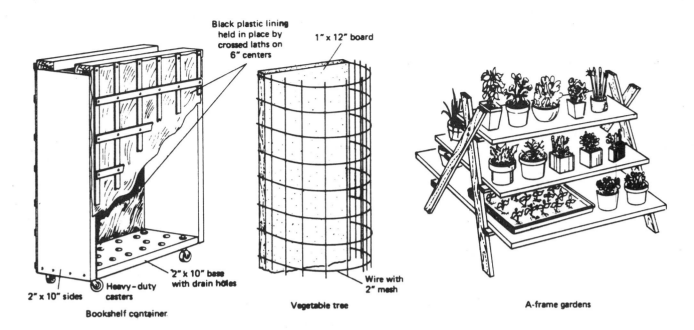

Figure 10.07

Hanging wire baskets: Wire baskets make fine containers for lettuce, radishes, even small tomato plants. Place an aluminum pie plate in the bottom to keep soil from the washing out. Stuff the open wire frame with moist sphagnum moss. You can add burlap if you like. Fill with soil and pot as you would any other container. A hanging basket dries out quickly, so it should be watered daily. To water, immerse in a pail of water. You can buy these baskets from most nurseries.

Long baskets: To make these attractive containers, cut standard-width chicken wire into 3- or 4-foot lengths and put the long edges together to form a 3-foot-long cylinder. Place a small plastic basket at one end and tie in place with twists of wire. Line the entire container with black plastic. Fill with soil mix, punch holes in the plastic, and plant vegetables from top to bottom.

VEGETABLES IN RAISED BEDS

Raised bed gardening is becoming more and more popular today. The raised soil is framed with stone walls, bricks, logs, adobe, railroad ties, redwood boards or something similar. Raised beds solve a number of gardening problems, especially those associated with backyard gardens. For instance, they:-

- Allow you to mix a light right soil on top of the ground that is perfect for root crops. This solves the problem of hard, infertile soil.
- Warm up the soil in the beds before the soil in the surrounding ground warms up. This allows you to plant earlier in the spring. Covered with clear plastic, a raised bed also becomes a coldframe to protect tender plants.
- Drain better than other types of gardens. The soil in raised beds never becomes too wet or too soggy.

- Allow the soil in the bed to be cultivated with kitchen utensils instead of standard garden tools.
- Eliminate the gopher problem when ½-inch mesh wire is place across the underneath of the bed.
- Make clear, workable gardens. The entire surface of a small raised bed can be reached from the garden paths.
- Make neat, uniform, attractive gardens that are more aesthetically pleasing than many other types of garden.

PLANTING MIXES

Some gardeners simply go out and dig common garden soil to fill their vegetable containers. In most cases this won't do. An ideal soil for growing vegetables has fifty percent solid matter and fifty percent air space. Most garden soils are either too sandy or too clayey, giving a less than ideal balance. In addition, in a contained space even a good garden soil becomes compacted more easily than it does in the ground, thus closing the air spaces and causing water to run almost straight through. It also dries out faster and often drains poorly, creating a root-rot problem. It is best, therefore, to use a special container soil for vegetable gardening.

Potting mixes

A good potting mix must be loose enough to let the roots develop freely. It must provide enough air space (despite container compacting) to allow good air and water circulation; it must have the right pH balance; and it must retain nutrients and water yet still drain well.

To fulfill these requirements, most potting mixes are a good combination of organic matter and minerals. The organic component may be peat moss, compost, bark, redwood sawdust, shavings, or any combination of these. The mineral element may be vermiculite, perlite, pumice, builder's sand, or a combination of ingredients.

Garden stores everywhere sell 'synthetic soil' or 'soiless mixes' under various trade names: Redi-Earth, Jiffy Mix, Metro Mix, Super Soil, Pro Mix, and many others. Most also contain a balance of nutrients. The exact formula may vary depending on what you intend to grow.

Jiffy Mix, for instance, is composed of equal parts of shredded sphagnum, peat moss and fine grade vermiculite plus just enough nutrients to sustain initial plant growth.

A tomato formula contains a balance of fast- and slow-release nutrients formulated for tomatoes plus sphagnum moss, vermiculite and solid soil matter.

Two of the most popular mixes were perfected at Cornell University and at the University of California. The California formula is available under the names **First Step** and **Super Soil**.

If you'd rather make your own potting mix here's the formula for the Cornell mix.

Vermiculite	8 quarts
Shredded peat moss	8 quarts
Superphosphate	2 level tablespoons
Limestone	2 tablespoons
Dried cow manure or steamed bone meal	8 tablespoons

Measure and place all ingredients in a garbage can liner. Shake vigorously. Since the Cornell mix has no smell, you can place it in plastic bags and store it in the back of a closet.

Mixing your own vegetable potting soil

Although it is possible to grow vegetables in one of these potting mixes, they generally do better in a combination of soil, potting mix and other ingredients. Vegetables in soil mixes require less frequent feeding than those in potting mixes. Furthermore, a combination soil-potting mix holds water better.

All-Purpose Vegetable Soil Mix: One part each of:

> Commercial potting mix
> Compost (homemade or purchased) or vermiculite
> Common garden soil.

Purchased soil is already sterilized. Soil from the ground is not, and you might want to sterilize it to destroy weed seed and nematodes and to avoid passing on fungus and disease.

You can sterilize your soil be spreading it out in a shallow pan and baking it at 275º F for an hour. To overcome the odor problem, soak the soil thoroughly before putting in the oven. (It should be noted that some gardeners prefer to take their chances with disease. They will not bake soil because it destroys all the microorganisms, thus making the soil 'dead.' The compost, of course, brings it back to life.)

WATERING TECHNIQUES

There are a number of ways to water containers. In general, pots less than eight inches in diameter should be watered from above. The entire container can also be half submerged in a pail of water. When the bubbles stop rising, take the container out and let it drain.

Water larger containers from above with a watering can or a hose; there are a number of specialized types of watering cans on the market. To keep the stream of water from a hose from hurting your plants, use a gentle stream or one of the water-breaking nozzles. (See Chapter 7 for complete information on watering.)

Water all vegetables until the soil is completely saturated. Don't water again until the soil is dry to a depth of 1 or 2 inches. To check, poke a finger an inch or two into the earth, take some soil from this depth and rub it between thumb and index finger. If the soil is dry to your touch, it's time to water. If the soil is mud-coated or feels wet, don't water for at least another four hours.

Figure 10.08
Container tomatoes
You can enjoy a bountiful tomato harvest without a garden. New varieties for patio containers can be grown in 4-inch windowsill pots. Three of the new varieties are Florida Lanai, Florida Petite and Florida Basket.

photo credit: Ball Seed Company

Figure 10.09

HALF WHISKEY BARRELS

When buying a tub or half whiskey barrel, look for a nursery that keeps them stacked upside down; this keeps the bands from slipping toward the base. Barrels must be coated inside or they will rot within a few years. Make sure the barrel is completely dry, then cover the inside with asphalt roof patching compound.

Figure 10.10

PREPARING HANGING BASKETS

Hanging wire baskets make fine containers for lettuce, radishes and even small tomato plants. Round ones can be hung from the ceiling; half round ones are attached to a wall.

To prepare a wire basket, stuff sphagnum moss between the two top wires until you have a neatly packed collar around the rim. Place burlap or an aluminum pie tin in the bottom to keep the soil from washing out. Line the basket with pieces of moss, overlapping them to better hold the soil. The basket should have an even layer of moss about two inches thick. Trim off straggly moss with scissors.

Figure 10.11

HANGING POTS

To prepare a 10- or 12-inch plastic hanging pot for planting, make four or five 1½-inch holes in the side of the pot (about halfway down) by drilling. Also punch small drain holes near the bottom of the pot. Enlarge the upper holes by melting them with a soldering iron. Cut a 3-inch square of black plastic and slip it around the stems of the plants. Tuck the plastic and the plants through the holes. Now fill the basket with soil mix, and add the remaining plants at the top.

Start all your vegetables in peat pots and then transfer them directly into the container when they are several inches high. To start the leaf and root vegetables, poke your fingers through the moss and push the plants through from the outside. Place about fifteen plants where you want them around the basket in the moss, so that the crown of each is about at the same level as the outside of the basket. Fill with soil and plant across the top of the container on the required spacing for each vegetable. This places vegetables around the outside and also across the top of the container.

Figure 10.12

CONTROLLING DISEASE

When re-using containers that have already carried previous crops, scrub them with a vegetabole brush dipped in clean, soapy water, then rinse them out in boilihg water. This prevents any disease organisms from being transmitted from one crop to the next.

You can also check to see if your container vegetables need watering with an **electric moisture tester**. These testers operate on the principle that wet soil conducts electricity better than dry. There are many models on the market, some equipped with a light meter.

There are many gadgets and systems to help water your containers. Perhaps the simplest is a plastic jug and watering wand combination. There are pots that water automatically from a built-in reservoir. In addition, there are 'plant pillows', which hold water like a sponge; when the soil becomes dry, water is drawn into the soil through a hole in the pot.

To keep hanging plants from dripping onto the carpet when watered, you can purchase an easily removed drip pan. This will fit containers of any size.

Drip irrigation water systems also make watering a number of containers fairly easy. Spaghetti tubes with drip spitters attach directly to the pots. To make watering 'work-free', the system can be attached directly to an automatic timer.

The best way to set up containers for vacation or any other long period when you'll be away is with a drip system connected to a timer. Other methods: place a few containers in a flat foil pan partially filled with water, or place containers in a bathtub or sink in two to three inches of water.

Figure 10.13

Lettuce, 'Red Sails'

Lettuce, 'Red Sails'

Leafy vegetables

Most leafy vegetables do especially well in small pots. Besides lettuce, you can grow spinach, chard, mustard and many other vegetables on a balcony or patio.

photo credit: National Garden Bureau.

For hanging containers, place a pail of water underneath the container and run a piece of soft cotton rope between the water and pot. Water will work its way up the 'wick' into the pot. You can also give each container a good soaking, slip it into a plastic bag, and seal the bottom with a tape. This forms a closed system in which the moisture given off by the plant leaves will return to the soil.

FEEDING TECHNIQUES

Container vegetables generally need supplemental feeding because the frequent watering leaches out many of the nutrients. Generally, plants need three major elements—nitrogen, phosphorus and potassium—plus minor trace elements. Each major nutrient affects vegetable growth in different ways.

Nitrogen, for instance, is important for the leafy growth of lettuce, mustard, spinach and other vegetables. Phosphorus is used in flowering and producing fruit such as tomatoes, cucumbers and eggplant. Potassium promotes strong root growth and is therefore essential for carrots, beets and radishes.

Use either time-release tomato and vegetable food or a liquid fertilizer.

If you use a time-release fertilizer, mix it with the 'soil' when you initially fill the container, at the rate of one tablespoon to each two gallons of soil. This will feed your vegetables throughout the growing season. Use liquid fertilizers every two weeks according to the instructions on the bottle.

VEGETABLE VARIETIES FOR CONTAINERS

A number of midget or minivegetables are especially suited to container gardening. Some of the most popular varieties include Dwarf Morden cabbage, Little Finger carrot, Golden Midget corn, Little Minnie cucumber, Morden Midget eggplant, Tom Thumb lettuce and Golden Midget watermelon.

In addition, a number of tomato varieties do particularly well in containers: Tiny Tim, Small Fry, Burpee Pixie Hybrid, Presto Hybrid, Patio Hybrid and others.

Many catalogs now have special sections devoted to mini vegetables. Chapter 13 of this book contains descriptions of the special properties of thousands of different kinds of seeds.

◀ **Figure 10.14**
Mist'r Sun Plant Probe
One instrument measures both moisture and light and has a special sensor for instant light reading. The probe measures moisture at the vital root level and has an extension for use with overhead plants.
KORTEX INDUSTRIES
51 El Pueblo Dr.
Scotts Valley, CA 95066

Figure 11.01

APPROXIMATE DISTRIBUTION OF COLORS IN FLUORESCENT LAMPS USED FOR PLANT GROWTH

Manufacturers	Type of Lamp	Red	Yellow-Green	Blue	Remarks
Duro-Lite Lamps Inc. Lighting Div.	Vita Lite				Provides full-spectrum light for vegetative growth; useful for starting all vegetables
Duro-Twist Corp. 17-10 Willow St. Fair Lawn, NJ 07410	Natur-Escent	37%	34%	29%	Full spectrum bulb will grow all vegetables. Grows tomatoes to fruit.
General Electric Lamp Manufacturing Div. Nela Park Cleveland, OH 44112	Gro and Sho Plant Light				Produces a balance of red and blue light; useful for starting seeds
	Bright Stik-Gro and Sho				Provides a balance of red and blue light; Can be plugged in for light in bookcases, cabinets and shelves.
	Power Groove Fluorescent lamps				Comes in cool white daylight, warm white deluxe; high output
Sylvania Light Center	Gro Lux Regular	43%	18%	38%	Developed for growing plants and flowers indoors; the output is almost entirely in the red and blue ends of the spectrum, designed for the propagation of low energy plants.
	Gro Lux Wide Spectrum	38%	32%	30%	Supplies more light in red than in the blue spectrum; excellent for starting seeds; promotes rapid vegatative growth.
Westinghouse Electric Corp. Fluorescent & Vapor Lamp Div. Bloomfield, NJ 07003	Agro-lite				A special phosphor which provides light rich in red while still providing considerable blue light; makes plants grow faster.
	Daylight	12%	48%	40%	Deficient in the red end of the spectrum, should be used in combination with Gro-Lux, Gro Lux Wide Spectrum or Agro-Lite
	Warm White	25%	55%	20%	The bulb provides more light in the red end of the spectrum; use in combination with Cool White
	Cool White	18%	52%	30%	The most comon fluourescent, deficient in red light; use with Warm White
	Natural White	26%	40%	34%	A more balanced bulb; Can be used alone or mixed with Cool White.

11. Growing Vegetables under Lights

ALTHOUGH VEGETABLES HAVE NOT been the most popular light-garden crop up to now, the development of a number of new bush vegetable varieties and 'container type' tomatoes make it possible to grow your own squash, cantaloupes and tomatoes indoors. In this chapter we take a close look at this fascinating new way to raise vegetables.

WHY LIGHT GARDENING?

Lights bring several advantages to the growing of vegetables. For one thing, they can be installed in a cupboard, closet, planter or part of a room to create a permanent garden where certain vegetables can thrive all the year round. Lights can also extend your outdoor growing season. By planting seeds indoors and exposing them to the proper amount of light, you can have healthy seedlings all ready to transplant into your garden by the time the weather and the temperature are right. (See Chapter 6 for detailed information on transplanting.)

Some vegetables do better under lights than others. Many root and leafy plants including beets, carrots, celery, Chinese cabbage, endive, lettuce, onions, radishes, spinach and watercress are quite easy to grow all the way to maturity indoors. Some herbs do quite well in this environment too, including basil, parsley, rosemary and savory.

There are other vegetables and herbs which, while not recommended for beginners, can be grown under lights with a little more difficulty. After you've had some experience, you'll be able to extend your gardening range to include such plants as bush cucumbers and small tomatoes (especially determinate varieties such as Burpee's Pixie Hybrid), herbs such as sage and

tarragon, and many other crops.

Of course, you don't need to grow the above crops to maturity indoors; they'll do beautifully grown from seed to transplant-size under lights, and then moved outside. Other vegetables are best grown under lights only to transplants. The large plants that produce edible fruit, such as beans and zucchini, should be transplanted (though bush varieties can be grown indoors in a container), as should broccoli, brussels sprouts, cabbage, cantaloupe, cauliflower and eggplant. These varieties require more light intensity to bring to maturity then is easy to generate indoors or are difficult to handle indoors because of their size.

LIGHT REQUIREMENTS

Vegetables need both visible and invisible light rays for healthy, vigorous growth. Outdoor gardeners do not have to pay all that much attention to light. They simply place their garden in good sunlight and hope that the growing season will not be excessively overcast. Indoor gardeners have to be more knowledgeable. The following brief explanation should be sufficient for most needs, but additional information can be obtained from the many recently-published books specializing in light gardening.

Natural light rays have a spectrum, rather like a rainbow, and different kinds of artificial light are made up of these colors in varying strengths. Blue light provides energy for both photosynthesis and chlorophyll synthesis: it also inhibits the elongation of cells and organs such as stems (so your plants won't get 'leggy'). Red light also provides energy for photo- and chlorophyll synthesis; it also promotes other plant responses such as seed germination, seedling and vegetative growth, cell and organ elongation, flowering and pigment formation. While the red light encourages plant growth, the far-red light causes it to stop. Thus a balance between these two types of light is desirable. There is some question about the value of green and yellow-orange light. Though they appear to be neutral, some experts believe that they do play a role, not yet fully understood, in plant growth.

A plant's need of red light is generally greater than its need for blue light. In supplying artificial light, it is vital that the proper balance between the different light colors be maintained. Fluorescent tubes and the common incandescent light bulb each produce some of the needed rays. Fluorescent lights, for instance, produce blue and red rays; incandescent bulbs produce the red and far-red rays.

HOW MUCH LIGHT?

Before buying lights for an indoor garden, you will need to learn the different light requirements of each vegetable. Leafy and root plants, such as lettuce and radishes, need about 1,000 footcandles (the equivalent of bright shade) for good growth. Vegetables from which we harvest the fruit—such as tomatoes, eggplant and squash—need a minimum of 2,500 footcandles of light to reach maturity.

Few gardeners own a light meter to check their indoor gardens. Plants, however, will become long and spindly or manifest some other abnormality if they are not receiving adequate light. (At that point it may be too late to take corrective measures.) One way to measure light without a special meter is to use a camera with a light meter built in to provide exposure settings. Set the film speed at ASA 100 and aim the meter at a white piece of paper placed so as to approximate the position of the plant's surface. The shutter speed reading that appears at F4 will correspond to the approximate foot candles of illumination. For example, if the indicated exposure is 1/250th of a second at F4, this means 250 footcandles of light are needed.

There is a light gardening rule of thumb dealing in watts per square foot. For example, a two-lamp fixture holding two 20-watt fluorescent tubes gives off a total of 40 watts. If the fixture and its bulbs cover a two square-foot area when mounted one foot from the surface, then that surface is receiving 20 watts per square foot:

$$\frac{40 \text{ watts}}{2 \text{ sq ft}} = 20 \text{ watts per sq ft.}$$

Most leafy and root vegetables need 20 watts per square foot or more, and most fruit-bearing vegetables need at least 40 watts per square foot.

WHAT KIND OF LIGHT?

There are many kinds of incandescent and fluorescent lights on the market. While the incandescent bulb is a good source of far-red light, it is deficient in the other colors. Most light gardeners, therefore, use fluorescent lights. There are some 'plant growth' fluorescent tubes that have been developed especially for use in indoor gardens. In general, these lamps reduce the output

of yellow-green light and increase the output of red and blue rays, which the plants need. Some gardeners swear by these special fluorescent lamps, while others feel their vegetables do just as well with the help of two standard tubes in tandem, one warm white and one cool white. Do not buy lamps designated *white* or *daylight;* these are not adapted for plant growth.

The standard fluorescent light fixture has two, three, or four 4-foot long 40-watt tubes in a reflector—it will light a growing area of 2 x 4 feet. Two fixtures mounted parallel to each other will illuminate an area 3 by 4. For a larger area still, 3 x 8 feet, you can use two 8-foot, two-tube industrial fixtures mounted side by side.

These fixtures come in many sizes and widths to fit different locations. A closet or bookshelf, for instance, can be lighted by narrow, boxlike, channel fixtures (without reflectors). These come in many different lengths and can be mounted according to individual requirements.

There is a wide choice of manufactured units available from most garden centers and from many seed catalogs. These units vary from simple two-bulb fittings to elaborate setups with a dozen or so trays. Some of them are quite well designed, and can double as room dividers or other pieces of furniture. Given that the plants themselves are attractive, an indoor garden can be designed to provide a handsome addition to your room decor.

SETTING UP A LIGHT GARDEN

A quick and easy way to start an indoor garden is to arrange your plants in a corner on a table about 3 x 4 feet in size. Mount two 4-foot reflector fixtures about twelve inches above the table's surface; go down as low as 6 inches if you've just planted seeds, as high as 18 inches if the plants are growing tall. If you want to produce large quantities of vegetables, use a basic A-frame, 5 feet long, 3 feet wide, with three shelves.

SPECIAL INSTRUCTIONS FOR SEEDLINGS

As noted, many avid vegetable gardeners get a jump on the season by planting seeds indoors, under lights. The healthy seedling can be transplanted to the garden bed when the weather warms up. Fluorescent lights are generally quite adequate for seedlings, but some experienced indoor-light people supplement fluorescents with two 25-watt incandescent bulbs to provide the far-red light energy that is necessary for the germination of light-sensitive seeds.

You can also sprout seeds with fluorescent lights. Simply place the seed trays (or peat pots, etc.) 3 or 4 inches below the tubes. Keep the lights on until the seedlings emerge. Then move the tubes so that they are 6 to 9 inches away from the plants. Give them 10 to 14 hours of light a day, sufficient water and nutrients, and you'll soon have a topnotch collection of seedlings.

HOW MUCH LIGHT, PART II?

There are three components in the equation that yields the optimum amount of light for plant growth. The first two involve the strength of the light (called candlepower) and the distance of the fixtures from the plants. As discussed, the needs of different plants depend largely on their relative size. The third element in the equation is time, the number of hours at a stretch that the bulbs should be on. The sun doesn't shine 24 hours a day (except in summer above the Arctic Circle) and your plant lights should not be in continuous use either.

Interestingly, plants don't only need light for proper growth—they also need darkness. The cycle is called the photoperiod, and it varies from variety to variety. Many vegetables require 14 to 18 hours of artificial light and 6 to 10 hours of darkness. Among these long-day plants are beets and spinach. Intermediate-day plants, such as celery, require 12 to 15 hours of light, while short-day plants, such as some types of onions, need only 10 to 13 hours of light. It's important to pay attention to photoperiods. If you leave your lights on too long over, say, tomatoes, you'll find that your plants will produce lots of attractive green foliage, but few tomatoes. If you don't have the kind of schedule that will enable you to control these lights manually, use one of the many good automatic timers on the market.

TEMPERATURE

Another environmental factor you've got to watch when growing vegetables under lights is temperature. Fluorescent lights don't generate much heat, but even they produce enough to take into account; incandescent bulbs, of course, give off a lot of heat for their size. Cool-season vegetables such as lettuce like temperatures that don't rise much above 65 degrees Fahrenheit. Warm-season vegetables such as tomatoes grow and mature best when the temperature is above 65° and below 90° F. And this is during the 'day'. Night temperature should be 50 to 60 degrees for leafy and root vegetables, a little higher for the warm-season varieties.

Raising lettuce and tomatoes side by side is therefore involves quite a bit of juggling, even though you probably want both for salads. You can try placing cool-season vegetables at one end of the table, warm-season vegetables at the other end, varying the temperature along the table by such trickery as putting a heat-producing incandescent bulb at the warm-season end to beef up the fluorescent bulbs.

If your temperature is unsatisfactory and the air is stagnant around your indoor light garden, investigate the possibility of installing a small fan or other device to improve the ventilation.

LIGHT GARDENS STARTER KIT

Some seed companies offer light starter kits for gardeners who want to try indoor light gardening. Here are three.

- **Burpee's Glow'n Grow Indoor Light Garden**
  A good basic unit. Two larger lighted shelves hold 48 six-paks (288 seedlings) or 72 three-inch pots. The unit moves around on casters. It features eight heavy-gauge, green plastic growing trays, and comes with two extra trays. Above each shelf is an adjustable light fixture with two fluorescent, cool-white 40 watt bulbs. Unit measures 47 inches high, 49 inches long and 19 inches deep. Cost: $249.00
  Contact:
  W. ATLEE BURPEE CO.
  Warminster, PA 18974
- **Park's Table Top Plant Light**
  Black metal hood adjusts to any angle, two plant light fluorescent tubes. Grows house plants, seedlings and cuttings in almost any location. Forty-eight-inch model is 48 x 11 and 25 inches high with two 20-watt plant light tubes. Cost: $67.95
- **Park's Garden Condo**
  Park's Garden Condo is made of white-enameled aluminum tubing and measures 49 inches long by 18 inches wide by 47 inches high. It has two growing racks that hold four plastic removable trays. A 48-inch fluorescent fixture with two 40-watt, cool-white tubes is mounted on chains above each rack. Light fixtures can be raised or lowered to provide optimum light intensity. You assemble, with instructions provided. Cost: $199.95
  For the last two kits, contact:
  PARK SEED CO.
  Cokesbury Road
  Greenwood, SC 29647

Figure 12.01

Coffee can hydroponic systems

This simple system will grow many vegetables to maturity without soil. The growing medium is inert perlite (puffed obsidian glass). Start plants in Jiffy-7 compressed peat cubes. Use any hydroponic plant nutrient available at any garden center. Change the nutrient every two weeks.

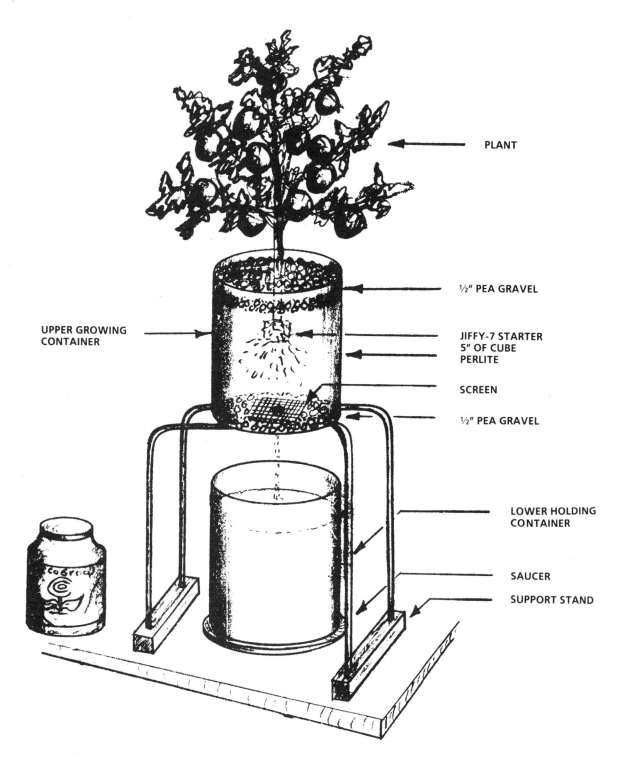

PLANT

½" PEA GRAVEL

UPPER GROWING CONTAINER

JIFFY-7 STARTER 5" OF CUBE PERLITE

SCREEN

½" PEA GRAVEL

LOWER HOLDING CONTAINER

SAUCER

SUPPORT STAND

12. Hydroponics

HYDROPONICS IS SIMPLY A method of growing plants without the use of soil. Instead, seeds (or seedlings) are planted in a growing medium, such as sand or cinders, that is periodically flooded or otherwise supplied with the nutrients necessary for plant growth. Hydroponic installations can be indoors or outdoors, in a greenhouse or on a patio. Light, air and water must be in sufficient supply, just as in the standard dirt garden.

Because of the way that they are fed, hydroponic vegetables grow bigger and faster than those in an ordinary garden. Water and fertilizer can be used over and over again. Problems of insects and disease can be kept to a minimum.

WHAT PLANTS NEED TO GROW

In Chapter 2 we explained that plants need an assortment of fifteen nutrients for growth. The three most important elements—nitrogen, phosphorus and potassium—all come from the soil (or growing medium). They are used by vegetables in relatively large amounts and have a critical effect on the growth of stems, leaves and fruit. Other necessary nutrients that come from the soil are magnesium, manganese and copper—the three secondary nutrients—and zinc, iron, sulfur, calcium, molybdenum and boron—the micro-nutrients. The last three elements—oxygen, carbon and hydrogen—come from air and water.

Each of the three secondary nutrients has a distinct role in plant growth: magnesium is an important component of chlorophyll, manganese is used by the plant enzyme system, and copper is utilized as an enzyme activator. The six microelements are essential for proper plant development, but each is required only in small quantities.

A good nutrient solution, of course, is the key to hydroponics, and regular, careful feeding produces optimum growth. It is important in using commercial mixes to follow the package directions carefully and not to burn the plants by overfertilizing.

Most solutions use one teaspoon of nutrient dissolved in one gallon of water. For starting seedlings dilute your solution to half strength, and gradually increase the dosage as the plants become bigger.

YOUR CHOICE OF HYDROPONIC METHODS

In all hydroponic methods, the plants absorb the nutrients directly from the mineral mixture dissolved in water and fed directly to the roots. You can grow your plants in sand, gravel, perlite, vermiculite, coarse sponge rock and similar material; they can even be grown directly in solution. The following are the most popular methods.

The flooding method

The growing medium is flooded one to three times a day for a period of one-half to two hours at a time. The rest of the time the roots have oxygen available through the growing medium. After flooding, the nutrient is allowed to drain back into the solution reservoir. The flooding process can be handled automatically with a pump and timer.

You can make your own flooding system (see Figure 12.02) using a plastic dishpan, a bucket and several feet of plastic tubing. Use epoxy glue to connect the system.

Once a day, fill the bucket with solution and lift the bucket so the solution goes down the hose to the growing tray. Leave the bucket on a shelf or table until the entire solution has run into the tray. After about two hours, lower the bucket so the solution can drain back into the tray.

To utilize a pump instead of gravity flow, replace the nutrient bucket with some type of plastic air-tight nutrient container (an inexpensive plastic air-tight jug will do). You will also need to purchase a simple aquarium pump (buy this at a pet store). Connect the pump to the container as shown in Figure 12.03. When

Figure 12.02

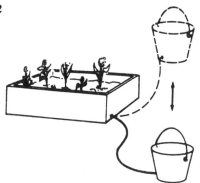

you turn on the pump, the air pressure forces the solution from the tank into the growing tray. When you turn off the pump, the nutrient drains back into the reservoir. To automate the system, hook the pump to an inexpensive timer and set it to run the pump about two hours a day.

The wick method

A synthetic fiber wick draws the water-solution into the growing medium, allowing both moisture and air to feed the plant continuously.

To make your own system, stack two plastic growing trays (plastic dishpans, for instance) one on top of the other. The nutrient solution will be placed in the top tray and the growing medium (perlite, sand or other matter) in the bottom tray. Drill small holes about three inches apart in the bottom of the top plant tray and thread pieces of fabric through the holes down into the solution. Make your wicks from synthetic fabric such as nylon, polyester or rayon. Be sure the fabric you use will draw the moisture the entire length of the wick.

After you have completed your system, fill the trays (the bottom tray with growing medium and seeds or seedlings, the top with nutrients) and wet the wicks to start the action. You will need to replenish the nutrient solution every two weeks.

The drip method

The plants, grown in a perlite/peat moss medium, are watered slowly with a nutrient solution through drip irrigation tubes. The system should be set to allow just enough solution to run so that all the moisture is absorbed by the growing medium.

Figure 12.03

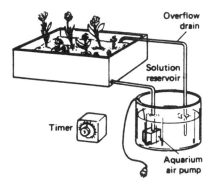

The standing solution method

This is a less common, but quite practical method. Plants are grown directly in the nutrient solution, with root aeration provided by bubbling air into the solution.

Ready-made hydroponic systems

In recent years, dozens of new firms have entered the hydroponics market, manufacturing a tremendous variety of ready-made systems. All are variations of the basic hydroponic methods outlined above, and include:

- Subirrigation gravel beds or flood systems with recycled nutrients.
- Trickle irrigation on sand beds or sand culture.
- Top-fed gravel bed systems with recycled nutrients.
- Container systems using a rigid black polyethylene container with an inert sterile growing medium.
- Nutrient film systems with no growing medium.
- Tube systems with and without growing medium.

Figure 12.04

Hydro-Greenhouse

This auto-feed hydroponic grower works indoors or out without soil. Grow vegetables and herbs year round. The table-top unit includes a planting bed, folding greenhouse incubator, one-gallon nutrient reservoir and a year's supply of nutrient mix.

UNCLE MILTON INDUSTRIES, INC.
10325 West Jefferson Blvd
Culver City, CA 90232

13. Vegetable Varieties

SINCE THIS SOURCEBOOK WAS originally published in 1980, the number of varieties available to home gardeners has more than doubled. In the past few years plant breeders, in both government and industry, have developed hundreds of new varieties.

For instance, the Sugar Snap edible podded snap pea, a new variety a few years back, proved so popular that we now have a whole category of snap peas on the market, from Snappy (the Sugar Snap's cousin) to compact varieties such as Sugar Daddy and Sugar Bon, which grow only to 24 inches. Interest in bush melons—such as cantaloupe Bush Star Hybrid—bush pumpkins—such as Bushkin—and bush squash—such as Bush Acorn Table King—has continued to grow. Entire catalogs are also now devoted to heritage and gourmet vegetable varieties.

The big news in new varieties, however, is the development of genetic baby vegetables bred for their size. Today we have baby beets, cabbage, lettuce, corn and many more.

Never before has the home gardener been given such an abundance of top-quality seeds from which to choose.

Some of the new varieties mature in a shorter time and grow in a smaller space. Others grow larger, juicier, more delicious and more colorful than ever before. Plants are also being bred with stronger resistance to disease. The choice is so wide, it's confusing. The charts in this chapter provide a comprehensive guide to what's available; we hope they'll help you select the varieties that are just right for your taste buds and growing conditions.

A complete list of seed catalogs follows. As you study the charts of vegetable varieties, you'll notice that suppliers are indicated by codes in the right hand column that refer you back to the seed catalog list.

Figure 13.01

VEGETABLE SEED COMPANIES

Code Name	Company
ABU	ABNUDANT LIFE SEED FOUNDATION P.O. Box 772 Port Townsend, WA 98368
ALL	ALLEN, STERLING AND LOTHROP 191 U.S. Route 1 Falmouth, ME 04105 (207) 781-4142 (207) 781-4143
ARC	ARCHIAS' SEED STORE P.O. BOX 109 Sedalia, MO 65301 (816) 836-1330
BAN	THE BANANA TREE 715 Northhampton Street Easton, PA 18042 (215) 253-9589
BRI	BRITTINGHAM PLANT FARMS P.O. Box 2538 Dept. VGS Salisbury, MD 21801 (301) 749-5153
BRO	BROWN'S OMAHA Lock Box 787 Omaha, TX 75571
BURG	BURGESS SEED AND PLANT CO. Dept. 89 905 Four Seasons Road Bloomington, IL 61701
BURP	BURPEE, W. ATLEE, CO. 300 Park Avenue Warminster, PA 18991-0001 (215)) 674-4915

Code Name	Company
BURR	D.V. BURRELL SEED GROWERS Rocky Ford, CO 81067 (303) 254-3318
BUT	BUTTERBROOKE FARM 78 Barry Road Oxford, CT 06483 (203) 888-2000
COM	COMSTOCK, FERRE & CO. P.O. Box 125 Wethersfield, CT 06109
COO	THE COOK'S GARDEN Box 65 Londonderry, VT 05148 (802) 824-3400
DAN	DAN'S GARDEN SHOP 5821 Woodwinds Circle Frederick, MD 21701
DEG	DE GIORGI CO., INC. 1411 Third Street Council Bluffs, IA 51502 (712) 323-2372
DIX	DIXIE PLANT FARMS P.O. Box 327 Franklin, VA 23851 (804) 562-5276
EAR	EARL MAY SEED & NURSERY L.P. Shenandoah, IA 51603 *Credit Card Holders:* 1-800-432-5858 (Iowa) 1-800-831-4193 (Outside Iowa)

▶

◀ VEGETABLE SEED COMPANIES

Code Name	Company
EARL	EARLY'S FARM & GARDEN CENTER, INC. Box 3024 Saskatoon, SASK., Canada S7K 3S9 1-800-667-1159
ECO	ECOLOGY ACTION 5798 Ridgewood Road Wilits, CA 95490
FAR	FARMER SEED AND NURSERY Dept. 77 Reservation Center 2207 East Oakland Ave. Bloomington, IL 61701 (507) 334-1623
FER	FERN HILL FARM P.O. Box 185 Clarksboro, NJ 08020
FIS	FISHER'S GARDEN STORE P.O. Box 236 Belgrade, MT 59714 (406) 388-6052
FOS	FOSTER, DEAN, NURSERIES, INC. P.O. Box 127 Hartford, MI 49057 (616) 621-2419
FRE	FRED'S PLANT FARM Rte 1, P.O. Box 707 Dresden, TN 38225-0707 (901) 364-5419
GAR	GARDEN CITY SEEDS P.O. Box 297 Victor, MT 59875 (406) 961-4837
GIL	GILFEATHER TURNIP Elysian Hills Rte 1, Box 452 Brattleboro, VT 05301
GLE	GLECKER'S SEEDMEN Metamora, OH 43540
GRA	GRACE'S GARDENS (now called RIPLEY'S BELIEVE IT OR NOT) 10 Bay Street Westport, CT 06880 (303) 454-1919

Code Name	Company
GUR	GURNEY SEED AND NURSERY CO. Yankton, SD 57079 Bank Card Holders: (605) 665-1930 Others: (606) 665-1671
HARR	HARRIS MORAN SEED COMPANY Eastern Operations: 3670 Buffalo Road Rochester, NY 14624 (716) 594-9411 Western Operations: 1155 Harkins Road Salinas, CA 93901 (408) 757-3651
HEN	HENRY FIELD'S SEED & NURSERY CO. Shenandoah, IA 51602 Credit Card Holders: (605) 665-9391 Others: (605) 665-4491
HER	HERB GATHERING, INC. 5742 Kenwood Kansas City, MO 64110 (816) 523-2653
HIG	HIGH ALTITUDE GARDENS P.O. Box 4238 Ketchum, ID 83340
HOL	M. QUISENBERRY HOLMES 4626 Glebe Farm Road Sarasota, FL 33580
HOR	HORTICULTURAL ENTERPRISES P.O. Box 810082 Dallas, TX 75381
HUM	ED HUME SEEDS P.O. Box 1450 Kent, WA 98032
JLH	J.L. HUDSON, SEEDMAN P.O. Box 1058 Redwood City, CA 94064
JOH	JOHNNY'S SELECTED SEEDS 305 Foss Hill Road Albion, ME 04910 Telephone Orders: (207) 437-4301 Customer Service: (207) 437-9294

Code Name	Company
JUN	JUNG SEEDS & NURSERY 335 S. High Street Randolph, WI 53957-0001 Bank Card Holders: (414) 326-3121
KAL	KALMIA FARM P.O. Box 3881 Charlottesville, VA 22903
KIT	KITAZAWA SEED CO. 1748 Laine Avenue Santa Clara, CA 95051-3012
LAG	LAGOMARSINO SEEDS, INC. 5675-A Power Inn Rd Sacramento, CA 95824
LAK	LAKELAND NURSERIES SALES Building 4 Unique Merchandise Mart Hanover, PA 17333
LED	LEDDEN, OROL, & SONS P.O. Box 7 Sewell, NJ 05873 (609) 468-1000
LEJ	LE JARDIN DU GOURMET West Danville, VT 05873
LEM	LE MARCHE SEEDS INTERNATIONAL P.O. Box 190 Dixon, CA 95620 (916) 678-9244
LET	LETHERMAN SEEDS COMPANY 1221 Tuscarawas Street E. Canton, OH 44707 Ohio Customers: 1-800-362-0487 Others: (216) 452-5704
LIB	LIBBY CREEK FARM P.O. Box 177 Carlton, WA 98814 (509) 997-0071
LIBE	LIBERTY SEED CO. P.O. Box 806 New Philadelphia, OH 44663
MAR	MARGRAVE PLANT CO. Gleason, TN 38229

Code Name	Company
MEY	THE MEYER SEED CO. 600 S. Caroline Street Baltimore, MD 21231 (301) 342-4224
MID	MIDWEST SEED GROWERS 505 Walnut Street Kansas City, MO 64106 (816) 842-1493
NIC	NICHOLS GARDEN NURSERY 1190 North Pacific Highway Albany, OR 97321 (503) 928-9280
PAR	PARK SEED COMPANY Cokesbury Road Greenwood, SC 29647-0001 (803) 223-7333
PEA	PEACE SEEDS 1130 Tetherow Road Wiliams, OR 97544
PEP	THE PEPPER GAL 10536 119th Ave N. Largo, FL 34643
PER	W.H. PERRON 515 Labelle Blvd Laval, Quebec, Canada H7V 2T3 332-3610
PET	PETER PEPPER SEEDS H.W. Alfrey P.O. Box 415 Knoxville, TN 37901
PIE	PIEDMONT PLANT CO. P.O. Box 424 Albany, GA 31703 (912) 883-7029
PIN	PINETREE GARDEN SEEDS New Gloucester, ME 04260
PLA	PLANTS OF THE SOUTHWEST 1812 Second Street Santa Fe, NM 87501 (505) 983-1548
PON	PONY CREEK NURSERY Tilleda, WI 54978 (715) 787-3899
POR	PORTER & SON, SEEDSMEN P.O. Box 104 Stephenville, TX 76401-0104

▶

Code Name	Company
RAW	RAWLINSON GARDEN SEED 269 College Road Truro, Nova Scotia, Canada B2N 2P6 *Bulk Orders:* 893-3051
RED	REDWOOD CITY SEED CO. P.O. Box 361 Redwood City, CA 94064 (415) 325-7333
RIS	RISPENS, MARTIN, & SONS 3332 Ridge Road (rear) Lansing, IL 60438 (312) 474-0241
ROS	ROSWELL SEED CO., INC. 115-117 South Main Roswell, NM 88201 (505) 622-7701
SEE	SEEDS BLUM Idaho City Stage Boise, ID 83706
SEED	SEEDWAY Ontario County Hall, NY 14463-0250 (714) 526-6391
SHE	SHEPHERD'S GARDEN SEEDS 7389 West Zayante Rd Felton, CA 95018 *Bank Card Holders:* (408) 335-5400
SOU	SOUTHERN EXPOSURE SEED EXCHANGE P.O. Box 158 North Garden, VA 22959
STA	STARK BROS Louisiana, MO 63353-0010 1-800-325-4180
STE	STEELE PLANT CO. Gleason, TN 38229 (901) 648-5476
STO	STOKES SEEDS, INC. Box 548 Buffalo, NY 14240 (416) 688-4300
SUN	SUNRISE ENTERPRISES P.O. Box Elmwood, CT 10058
TER	TERRITORIAL SEED CO. P.O. Box 27 Lorane, OR 97451
TEX	TEXAS ONION PLANT CO. P.O. Box 871 Farmersville, TX 75031

Code Name	Company
THO	THOMPSON & MORGAN P.O. Box 1308 Jackson, NY 08527 (201) 363-2225
TIL	TILLINGSHAST SEED CO. P.O. Box 738 La Conner, WA 98257 (206) 466-3329
TSA	TSANG AND MA 1306 Old County Rd. P.O. Box 294 Belmont, CA 94002 (415) 595-2270
TWI	TWILLEY SEEDS P.O. Box 65 Trevose, PA 19047 *PA only:* 1-800-232-7333 *Outside PA:* 1-800-622-7333
VER	VERMONT BEAN SEED CO. Garden Lane Fair Haven, VT 05743-0250 (802) 265-4212
VES	VESEY'S SEEDS LTD. P.O. Box 9000 Houlton, ME 04730-0814 (902) 892-1048
WES	WESTWIND SEEDS 2509 N. Campbell Ave. #139 Tucson, AZ 85719
WET	WETSEL SEED CO., INC. P.O. Box 791 Harrisonburg, VA 22801-0791 (703) 434-6753
WIL	WILLHITE SEED CO. P.O. Box 23 Poolville, TX 76076 (817) 599-8656
WILL	WILLIAM DAM SEEDS P.O. Box 8400 Dundas, Ontario, Canada L9H 6M1 (416) 628-6641
WIT	WILTON'S ORGANIC POTATOES P.O. Box 28 Aspen, CO 81611
WYA	WYATT-QUARLES SEED CO. P.O. Box 739 Garner, NC 27529

HERB SOURCES

Code Name	Company
APP	APPLEWOOD SEED CO. P.O. Box 10761 Edgemont Station Golden, CO 80401 (303) 431-6283
CAP	CAPRILANDS HERB FARM 534 Silver Street Coventry, CN 06238 (203) 742-7244
IND	INDIANA BOTANIC GARDENS P.O. Box 5 Hammond, IN 46325 (219) 931-2480
RIC	OTTO RICHTER & SONS LTD. Box 26 Goodwood, Ontario, Canada L0C 1A0 (416) 640-6677
STI	STILLRIDGE HERB FARM 10370 Route 99 Woodstock, MD 21163 (301) 465-8348
TAY	TAYLOR'S HERB GARDENS, INC. 1535 Lone Oak Road Vista, CA 92084 (619) 727-3485

ARTICHOKES
(Cynara scolymus)

Artichokes are bold, showy, silver-green perennial plants that really show off in a small garden or in a flower bed. This thistle-like vegetable can grow to a height of about four feet and spread as wide as six feet. The flower buds ripen into large thistle blossoms that can be used in dried arrangements. Once an artichoke plant has become productive, it will remain vigorous and productive for five to six years.

CULTURE: Home gardeners will often find it better to buy root divisions from a local nursery. Early spring is the best time to plant. Place the division in a rich

soil with the old wood stalk in a vertical position and the base of the new leafy shoot just above ground level. Space 3-4 feet apart, and leave 4-5 feet between rows.

SEASON: Artichokes require the cool days of spring to produce an edible crop. Generally, artichokes need a sunny location, but in hot-summer areas they do better in half-shade since early summer heat causes the buds to open rapidly and become tough.

HARVESTING: Initial harvest is the spring following the first planting. Cut the unripened flower heads before the bracts start to separate. Both the terminal buds and those on the side shoots are delicious.

ARTICHOKES

Variety	Heads/Plants	Remarks	Sources
EARLY GREEN PROVENCE	Small, long	Early variety with narrow green scales.	JLH
GREEN GLOBE	Large flower heads, 4 ft. plants with 6 ft. spread	Edible flower buds made up of thick flashy scales and solid centers. Best harvested when young. Not hardy.	COM DEG EARL GLE GUR HEN LAK LED LEJ LET NIC PAR RED RIC TER TIL
GREEN GLOBE IMPROVED	Large flower heads, 5-6 ft. plant	Standard variety. Reduced sharp spines.	HUM PIN THO
VIOLETTA	Elongated. Purple heads	Italian variety.	PIN

ARTICHOKES

OTHER TYPES

Variety	Heads/Plants	Remarks	Sources
ARTICHOKE SEED			TIL
CHINESE ARTICHOLKES	12-18 in. tall	Keep plant moist to produce a pearly white 2 in. root. Roots resemble pop beads. Use as you would radishes in salads or on relish trays, stir fry or pickle them.	SHE SUN THO

ASPARAGUS
(Asparagus officinalis)

Asparagus is one of the most permanent, dependable and earliest of all home-garden vegetables. It is a perennial that produces from March until June, well ahead of other vegetables. It can be planted almost anywhere in your garden or yard. Besides being a delicious food, it is as decorative as any ornamental. The only problem with asparagus is that it takes three years to come into full production from seed. However, it is worth waiting for if you are an asparagus lover. Once established, it will keep producing for up to twenty years.

CULTURE: Starting with seed in the early spring, soak the seed in water for two days. Plant seeds a half-inch deep in rows 2 feet wide; thin seedlings to 3 to 4 inches between plants. Grow these seedlings a season, and

the following year transplant to a permanent asparagus bed. Starting from crowns, buy year-old plants (or crowns) from seedsmen in the early spring. This will save a full year.

Dig a trench one foot wide and 8 to 10 inches deep, to any length that you like. Work 2 to 6 inches of steer manure into about 6 inches of soil at the bottom of the trench. Space the crowns about 12 inches apart and cover with 2 inches of loose, fine soil.

SEASON: Cool.

INSECTS/DISEASES: *HEAD/CROWN ROT*: Apply captan and PCNB.

SLUGS, WORMS, EARWIGS: Use Slug-Geta or Snail Snare.

APHIDS: Apply malathion, botanical sprays or diazinon.

HARVESTING: As the young plants grow, fill in the trench little by little. Don't harvest any spears the first year. When the foliage turns brown in the late fall, cut the stems to the ground. The second year you can harvest the 6 to 8-inch-high spears for four weeks. Cut the spears at ground level or a few inches below the soil, but never closer than 2 inches to the crowns. In the early spring cultivate the bed and feed with Complete fertilizer. The third year you can cut spears for a full season (about 6 weeks).

ASPARAGUS

Variety	Stalks	Remarks	Sources
ARGENTEUIL EARLY	Green with purple tips		LEJ
BROCK IMPERIAL (hybrid)	Large, plump, dark green fiber-free	Moderately rust-resistant.	GUR
CALIFORNIA 500	Tight, fine-green spears are free of purple tips	Adapted to the West Coast of the United States.	HEN
CONNOVER'S COLOSSAL		Grown from seed this variety will take 3 to 4 years to establish a crop. Best to use the seed among a bed already established.	ECO
GIANT WASHINGTON	Thick green stalks are large, yet remain crisp and tender	Can be eaten raw or cooked.	ARC JUN TIL
HOWARD'S GREEN (hybrid)	Large, heavy stalks	First generation hybrid. Poundage average 30% more.	FAR
JERSEY GIANT (hybrid)		Widely adapted. Rust-resistant, tolerant to fusarium wilt.	COM
LARAC (hybrid)	Uniform spears	French variety. Disease-resistant. Takes 3 years to establish from seed.	LEM
LORELLA (crowns)	Extra thick, tender spears	1 year crowns. French variety.	THO
MARTHA WASHINGTON	Large, tight spears are green with purple overcast	Resistant to fusarium rust and tolerant to fusarium wilt.	HARR RIC
MARY WASHINGTON	Medium, green tips	Prolific variety. Rust-resistant.	ALL BRI BURG BUT COM DAN DEG EAR FAR FIS FOS GAR GUR HEN HIG HUM JLH JUN LAK LED LET MEY PAR PIN PON POR RAW RED RIS ROS SEE SEED SUN THO WET WYA
MARY WASHINGTON UC 72	Tight heads with green stalks, no purple tinge	Earliest of the Mary Washingtons.	BURR MID WIL
PEDIGREED WASHINGTON	Standard variety	Asparagus seed for the home garden.	WYA
RUTGERS		Big yielder. Can withstand most kinds of stress and diseases	EAR
U.C. #72	Large, dark green spears have purple overcast	High yields. Good tolerance to fusarium wilt and rust.	TWI
U.C. #157 (hybrid)	Deep green, smooth spears, uniform scales	Tendency to cluster in 3 to 5 spears. Vigorous growth.	MID POR TWI
VIKING (MARY WASHINGTON IMPROVED)	Heavy green stalks	Rust-resistant. Good freezer.	ARC EARL FOS STO TWI VES WILL
VIKING KB3 (op)		Hardy, rust-resistant. Fusarium-tolerant.	STO
WALTHAM (hybrid)	Tighter heads than most varieties	Consistent, high quality. Easy to grow. Rust-resistant.	GUR HEN
WALTHAM WASHINGTON	Dark green with slight purple tinge	Top quality. Excellent flavor.	FOS

BEANS
(Phaseolus sp)

Beans are literally small food factories that give you your money's worth in your garden. They are rapid growers, give tremendous yields and require little attention. When you start trying to make a selection, you'll find there are beans, beans and more beans.

POLE GREEN BEANS
(Phaseolus vulgarus)

Pole beans give the best results when grown on freestanding supports at the north or east end of your garden. Many gardeners think pole varieties have a better taste than do bush-type beans.

CULTURE: Plant 1½ inches deep, 4 to 6 inches apart in rows 36 to 48 inches apart. You can also grow pole beans inside a 2 foot diameter wire cage. Plant 6 inches apart inside the cage. You may have to help them grow up the cage.

SEASON: Warm.

INSECTS/DISEASES: Same as for bush green beans.

HARVESTING: Pole beans are best harvested when the pods are still young. This is especially true of the French gourmet type bean. Keep beans picked to encourage new bean production.

SNAP POLE BEANS

Variety	Days	Pods	Remarks	Sources
ANELLINO GREEN		O shaped	Superb flavor.	LEM
ANELLI (HILLARY)			Old Indian variety. Use as fresh or dry bean.	SEE
BLUE LAKE (WHITE SEEDED) (WHITE CREASEBACK)	55-66	Oval, straight, 5½-6 in. Dark green	White-seeded. Stringless. Vigorous 5-6½ ft. plant. Use canned, fresh or frozen.	ABU ALL ARC BURP COM EAR EARL FIS GAR GUR HEN HUM JLH HUN LAG LEM LET MEY NIC PAR POR RAW ROS SHE STO SUN TER TIL VER VES WET WIL WILL WYA
BUTLER	60	12 in.	Red-flowered, runner bean. Sets well in hot weather. Stringless and meaty.	THO
CHALLENGE (BEST OF ALL)	65	Long	Heavy cropper. Fine texture, quality and flavor.	ECO
DADE	55	7-8 in. Flat, oval	White-seeded. Stringless. Resistant to rust and common southern bean mosaic.	LET VER
DESIREE	65	10-12 in.	White-flowered, runner type. Stringless. Prolific variety. Exceptional flavor and more productive under dry weather conditions.	ECO THO
EMERGO	65	8-12 in.	White-flowered, white-seeded runner bean. Large, tender, good flavored bean. Vine can exceed 10 feet. Will produce until frost.	PIN
ENORMA	65	20 in. Slender	Heavy yields. Good flavor.	LEM RAW THO
ERECTA	63	12-14 in.	Tolerant to wide range of growing conditions. White-flowered. Good freezer.	THO
GARRAFAL ORO	65	9 in. Flat	French variety. Rarely grows over 4 ft. Profusion of beans. Good freezer.	THO
GENUINE CORNFIELD (SCOTIA) (STRIPED CREASE-BACK)	70-80	5-7 in. Round, medium-green	Buff-colored seeds with brown stripes. Best harvested before the seed fills the pod. Good canner and freezer.	HEN LET RED SEE SOU VER WET WYA
GOLIATH (PRIZETAKER)	65	20 in.	Runner bean. Red flowers. Heavy cropper. Reliable. Good freezer.	THO
GREEN PAK	60	5½-6 in. Dark green	White-seeded. Resistant to bean mosaic and New York 15 strain of virus.	TWI
GREEN PERFECTION	58	6 in. Round, green	Heavy yielder. Good canner and freezer. Resistant to common bean mosaic.	TWI

Variety	Days	Pods	Remarks	Sources
HUNTER		8 in. flat	Stringless. Disease-resistant. Also suited for greenhouse growing.	WILL
KELVEDON MARVEL	65	10-12 in. Straight	Most productive if left unstaked and sprawling. Runner type bean. Good freezer.	THO
KENTUCKY WHITE WONDER	63	6-8 in. Straight, dark green	Highly productive variety. Sets pods from base to tip of vine. Stringless. White-seeded. Rust-resistant. Well adapted to Pacific Coast and Southeastern United States.	BURR PON SEED
KENTUCKY WHITE WONDER 191	60-66	6 x ½ in. Oval, silvery-green	White-seeded. Can be used as a dry shell or snap bean. Grows 60-78 in.	ARC HARR RIS VER WET WYA
KENTUCKY WONDER (OLD HOMESTEAD) (TEXAS POLE) (EGG HARBOUR)	58-74	7-9 in. Oval, silvery-green	1850s heirloom variety. Brown-seeded. Hardy climber. Stringless. Meaty and tender with distinctive flavor and texture. Good fresh or frozen.	ABU ALL ARC BURG BURR BUT COM DAN DEG EAR EARL FAR GAR GUR HEN HIG HUM JOH LAG LED LEM LET MEY MID NIC PAR PIN PLA POR RAW RED RIS ROS SEE STO SOU TER TIL TWI VER WES WET WIL WILL WYA
LAZY WIFE	80	5½ in. Straight	Heirloom variety of 1810. Spreading vine. White seeds have faint gray pattern. Stringless. Below average as snap bean, but very good shell bean.	SOU
LAZY WIFE RED	115		Drought-tolerant. Use fresh or dry.	SEE
MCCASLAN	61-66	7½ in. Flat, dark green	1930s variety. White seeds. Stringless, fleshy and brittle. Use as fresh or dry shell. Good flavor.	LET RED SOU VER WET
MISSOURI WONDER	65	Long, medium-green	Seeds are mottled tan with a brown stripe. Good variety to plant with corn.	RED VER
NECKARKONIGIN		9 in. Slim, green	German variety. Very fleshy. Pods are good for French slicing. Stringless.	WILL
NON PLUS ULTRA		6 in. Thin, flat	European type. High yields. White-seeded. Excellent flavor.	WILL
NORTHEASTERN	65	8 in. Flat, medium-green	Strong vine. Rich flavor bean. Stays tender and stringless.	JOH HIG
OREGON BLUE LAKE	60	6½ in. Oval, round	Small white seeds are good for dry shell use. Stringless. Use fresh, canned or frozen.	NIC
OREGON GIANT PAUL BUNYAN BEAN	63-68	12 in. Mottled red	Prolific climber. Large pod remains flavorful. Good also as a shell bean.	ABU GAR HUM VER
PAINTED LADY	68	9-12 in.	Runner bean. Red and white flowers. Good freezer.	THO
PHENOMEEN		7-9 in. Round	European variety. Thick and meaty. Good flavor.	WILL
PRINCESSE RACE PEVIR	60		French bean. White-seeded. Few seeds. Good taste.	HER
PRIZE WINNER	70	Large	Improved strain of Scarlet Runner Bean. Scarlet flowers. Excellent cool weather variety. Good flavor.	NIC
RATTLESNAKE	73	7 in. Round	Buff-colored seeds with purple streaks. Heavy producer in hot humid climates.	SOU
RED KNIGHT	70	Long, flat	British runner bean. Scarlet flowers. Stringless bean. Vines grow up to 12 feet. Hummingbird plant. Use as fresh or dry bean.	SHE
ROMANO (ITALIAN POLE)	64-70	5½ in. Wide, flat	Brown-seeded. Good in Italian cooking. Good canner and freezer. Nice flavor.	ABU ALL ARC BURG BURP COM DAN DEG FAR GUR HEN LAG LED LET NIC PAR PIN POR RED SEE SEED SOU SUN THO TIL VER WILL

◄ SNAP POLE BEANS

Variety	Days	Pods	Remarks	Sources
SCARLET EMPEROR	75	16 in. Smooth-textured	Runner bean with scarlet flowers. Heavy cropper. Good freezer.	ECO TER THO
SCARLET RUNNER	65-70	6 in. Flat	Runner bean. Scarlet flowers. Vines grow to 12 feet. Good crops.	ABU ALL COM EARL GAR JLH LET PIN PLA RAW RED SEE SEED SOU TIL TWI VES WET WILL
SELKA IMPROVED	60	10-12 in. Flat	French variety. White flowers. Pods have a nice aroma and flavor. Sets well in dry conditions. Stringless. Excellent freezer.	THO
SELMA STAR	60	7-8 in. Straight	Stringless. Good fresh, canned or frozen.	PAR
SELMA ZEBRA	58	Light green striped purple	Grows to 6 feet and matures as early as a bush bean. Good fresh, dried or frozen. Very tender.	PAR
SERBO	66	Round	Dutch variety. Heavy cropper. Beans borne in clusters on vigorous vines. Stringless and brittle pods.	SHE
SNIJ-PRONKER EMERGO			White flowered runner bean that should be picked when young for best flavor. Good yields.	WILL
STREAMLINE	75	16 in.	Runner type. Beans borne in clusters. Good flavor.	THO
SUNSET	60	12-15 in.	Runner bean with pink flowers. Continues to crop all season. Good flavor.	THO
TURKEY CRAW		3½-4 in.	Southeastern heirloom variety. Pods cling to the vine. Buff-colored seeds are frosted with brown on one end. Good freezer. Good drying quality.	SOU
VEITHES CLIMBING	60	Very long, narrow	Fleshy pods.	TSA
WESTLAND		4-5 in.	European type. Good yields. Stringless. Good freezer.	WILL
WHITE DUTCH RUNNER (OREGON LIMA)			Not a true lima. Short-season variety. Large white bean. Strong climber.	ABU
WHITE KNIGHT	73	8 in.	British runner bean with white flowers. Vines grow up to 12 feet. Thick, stringless green beans. If left to grow large beans can be used as shell beans.	SHE
WINGED BEAN	150		Pods and foliage are edible. Tropical climber, grows to 8 feet. Best grown as greenhouse crop.	BAN SEE THO
YARD LONG BEANS (DOW GAUK) (ASPARAGUS BEAN)	75	2-4 ft. Deep green	The GREEN POD BLACK-SEEDED variety should be picked at 12-15 inches.	SOU SUN TSA
		2-4 ft. Light green	The GREEN POD RED-SEEDED variety should also be picked at 12-15 inches. Seeds are maroon-brown with darker brown streaks. Isolate both varieties from cowpeas and other types of asparagus beans by 35 feet miniumum.	SOU SUN TSA

POLE SNAP BEANS

YELLOW AND PURPLE

Variety	Days	Pods	Remarks	Sources
ALABAMA NO. 1	67	Silver-green tinged with purple	1930 heirloom seed. Shade-tolerant. Good vigor. Nematode-resistant. Black-seeded. Stringless when young.	SOU

Variety	Days	Pods	Remarks	Sources
ANELLINO YELLOW		O shaped	Good flavor.	LEM
B.B. WAX		Yellow, straight, oval	Slow to deteriorate after maturing. White-seeded. Do not plant until ground warms. Good eating.	RAW
BLUE COCO		Purple		SEE
BLAUHILDE		9 in.	Blue bean that turns green when cooked. Stringless and fleshy. High yielder.	WILL
BURPEE GOLDEN	60	5½-6½ in.	Stringless, tender meaty pods.	BURP
CHEROKEE		6 in.	Lots of purple pods.	SEE
KENTUCKY WONDER WAX ROUND POD (GOLDEN-PODDED WAX)	60-68	7-9 in. Slightly curved	Almost stringless. Meaty and brittle. Brown-seeded.	ALL ARC BURG COM GUR HEN JUN LET MEY RAW TER VER WET
LOUISIANA PURPLE POD	67	7 in. Bright purple	Southern heirloom variety. Entire plant is purple-green with textured leaves and bright purple flowers. Harvest when young and stringless. Seeds are light to medium brown.	SOU
MERVIGLIA DI VENEZIA		Wide, flat	Italian-type bean. Great for stews, soups and stir-fries.	LEM
NECKARGOLD		9 in. Round, deep yellow	Stringless. Do not plant until soil warms. White-seeded.	WILL
PURPLE POD	65	8 in. Red-purple	Turns green when cooked. Stringless. Thick-meated.	THO
PURPLE YARDLONG		Purple	Pods stay purple when cooked.	SEE
ROBISON PURPLE POD		Purple, round	Oregon variety.	ABU
VIOLET-PODDED			Sprouts when soil is cool. Tender and fine flavored. Sets abundantly.	TER

BUSH GREEN BEANS
(Phaseolus vulgarus)

These bean plants grow to a compact 24 inches or less. They can be grown successfully in fairly short-summer areas since they need only six to seven weeks to reach maturity.

CULTURE: Plant 1½ inches deep, 4 to 6 inches apart in rows 18 to 30 inches apart. Up to 3 feet apart for mechanical cultivation. Thin plants to 4 to 6 inches apart when they are 2 to 3 inches tall. Cover seed with finer soil and tamp down firmly.

SEASON: Warm.

INSECTS/DISEASES: *APHIDS, BEAN LEAF BEETLES, FLEA BEETLES, LEAF HOPPERS, MEXICAN BEAN BEETLES, SEED CORN MAGGOTS, SPIDER MITES, WHITE FLIES, WHITE GRUBS:* Malathion, diazinon, pryethrum, rotenone, ryania, Sevin or Kelthane.

ANTHRACNOSE, BACTERIAL BLIGHT, FUNGAL BLIGHT: Captan, dichlone.

DOWNY AND POWDERY MILDEW: Maneb, zineb, sulfur or karathane.

MOSAIC-POD MOTTLE: Malathion or Sevin to control insects.

ROOT AND STEM ROT: Lanstan or PCNB.

RUST: Maneb or zineb.

HARVESTING: Pick when the pods are fairly small; the flavor is better then. Keeping the plants picked extends the season.

BUSH SNAP/SLICING BEANS

Variety	Days	Pods	Remarks	Sources
ADMIRES		1 in. Wide	Tasty bean. Resistant to common bean mosaic and anthracnose.	WILL
AIGUILLE VERT		Dark green	Very thin bean. French style.	LEJ LEM
AJAX BROAD		Long, flat	Disease-resistant. Stringless. Should be picked when young. European variety.	WILL

◄ BUSH SNAP/SLICING BEANS

Variety	Days	Pods	Remarks	Sources
ARAMIS		7-9 in.	European variety. Disease-resistant. Stringless. Must be picked young for best flavor. Very tasty.	WILL
ASTRO (ROUND POD)	50-56	Deep green	Upright, vigorous plant. Good canner.	ALL MID VER
AVALANCHE	50-57	Light green	Good for canning or freezing.	LET PAR TWI VER
BAHALORES	47	4-5 in.	French filet type. Harvest when immature and stringless for truly fine flavor.	PIN SEE
BALLACK			Sweet and tender.	SEE
BEST CROP	52	6 in. Medium-green	Stringless. Short-season variety. Resistant to common bean mosaic. Meaty and flavorful.	VER
BLACK VALENTINE	70	6½ in. Slightly flattened	Heirloom variety. Heavy yielder. Will stand cooler temperatures.	ABU JLH SEE TWI
BLACK VALENTINE RESISTANT	50	6½ in. Straight, round, dark green	Mosaic-resistant. An 1855 heirloom variety. Stringless. Makes a good soup bean.	LET SOU
BLAZER	58	Straight, green	Disease-resistant. Pods are set high off the ground.	LET TWI
BLUE LAKE BUSH	52-60	6½ in. Dark green, round	White-seeded. 18 in. plant. Stringless. Good flavor. Good freezer.	ABU ALL BURG BURR COM DEG EARL ECO FIS HEN HUM LEM MEY POR ROS STO SUN TER TIL TWI VER WILL WYA
BLUE LAKE BUSH NO. 47		Long, straight, round	Good canner or freezer. Very meaty. Resistant to common and New York 15 strain of bean virus.	LET
BLUE LAKE BUSH NO. 141	55-59	6 in. Dark green	Good fresh or frozen.	ARC PAR WET
BLUE LAKE BUSH NO. 274	58	5-6 in. Round, dark green	White-seeded. Resistant to bean mosaic and New York 15 virus.	BURP DAN EAR GAR GUR HARR JUN LAG LED LET PAR RIS TWI VER WIL WILL
BOUNTIFUL	48-51	6-7 in Flat, green	An all-purpose bean. Good freezer.	ALL BURG COM LED MEY PIN POR SEE TWI VER WET WIL WYA
BROWN DUTCH		Flat, light green	Used principally for dried beans. Also haricot French type bean. Tan-colored seed.	ECO WILL
BURPEE'S STRINGLESS	54	6 in. Medium-green	Brown-seeded. All-purpose bean. Good canner.	ALL DEG FAR MEY WET WYA
BURPEE'S STRINGLESS GREEN POD	50	5-6 in. Slightly curved, deep green	Tender, brittle pods. Good canner or freezer.	ARC BURP JLH LET TWI WIL
BURPEE'S STRINGLESS GREEN POD IMPROVED	53	6 in. Nearly round, slightly curved	Fiberless pods. Outstanding bean.	ROS
BURPEE'S TENDERPOD	50	5½ in. Round, curved	Tender, meaty and brittle. Stringless and fiberless. Good fresh, canned or frozen. Good flavor.	ROS
BUSH ROMANO	50-60	5-6 in. Flat	18 in. plant. Oval, white seeds. Use fresh, canned or frozen. Italian type.	COO DEG EAR HEN STO TWI VER
CANADIAN WONDER			Old-fashioned variety. Bushy plant. Vigorous, hardy and prolific.	ECO
CASCADE	54	5-6 in. Dark green	Resistant to common bean mosaic and New York 15 virus. Good flavored bean.	VER
CHEVERBEL	55	Lime-green, semi-round	15 in. plant.	THO

Variety	Days	Pods	Remarks	Sources
COMMODORE (NEW DWARF KENTUCKY WONDER)	58-63	Round, dark green	Heavy yielder. Stringless. Easy to pick.	COM DEG HEN MEY ROS SEE VER WYA
COMMODORE IMPROVED	58	7½-6 in. Curved, dark green	Vigorous, medium-sized plant.	ARC LET POR RAW WET
CONTENDER	42-55	5-7 in. Round, oval, medium-green	Bushy, vigorous plant. Mosaic-resistant. Reddish-purple seeds. Stringless. Widely adapted.	ARC BURR COM DEG EAR EARL ECO HEN HUM LED MEY MID PAR PON POR RAW RED RIS ROS SOU STO TWI WET WYA
CUTLASS		Flat, medium-green	Persistent green pods. White/green seeds. Good processing bean. Resistant to common bean mosaic and New York 15 virus.	HARR
CYRUS	50	Slim, round straight	16-18 in. plant. Very prolific and can pick handfuls at a time. Excellent flavor.	THO
DAISY	55	5-7 in. Medium-green	Easy to pick because pods set above the foliage. Heavy yielder. Seeds are slow to mature.	ARC BURG FAR GUR HEN LEJ LET
DANDY	54	Round, dark green	Pick when 4 in. for gourmet dining. High yielder ready to pick three weeks after they bloom. Good canner and freezer.	DEG NIC
DELINEL	48-50	7-8 in.	Erect plant habit with good vigor. Resistant to common mosaic and anthracnose.	LEM VES
DEL RAY	56	Medium, dark green	Upright vigorous plant. White seed.	LET
DELTA		Round, dark green	Persistent green pods. Erect plant habit. Resistant to bean mosaic, New York 15 and tolerant to one or more races of bean rust. Use canned, fresh or frozen.	HARR
DEMETER	55	Round, dark green	Excellent yielder. White-seeded. Tolerant to common mosaic virus and curly top virus.	BURR
DUTCH STRINGLESS GREEN POD	50		Has real bean taste. Good freezer.	WILL
EAGLE	54	Long, slender, straight	High yielding. Good fresh use.	LET
EARLI-SERVE	41-47	4 in. Slender, straight	Big yields on 18 in. plant. Tolerant to common bean mosaic. White-seeded.	GUR HIG STO WET
EARLY CONTENDER	49	6-7 in. Oval	Stringless. Vigorous plant. Heat-tolerant. Buff-colored seeds. Resistant to mosaic and powdery mildew.	GUR
EARLY GALLATIN	53	5-5½ in. Round, dark-geen	Resistant to pod mottle and New York 15 virus.	VER
EMPRESS	55	5¾ in. Straight, dark green	Plump white seeds. Stringless. Excellent freezer.	GUR
ETALON		Mottled, purple	French variety. Produces over 45 days.	LEM
EXECUTIVE	53	5½-6 in.	Firm, meaty bean good for canning or freezing.	TWI
E-Z PICK BLUE LAKE BUSH	60-75	6-6½ in. Dark green	Pods are concentrated and set high for easier picking. Good canner and freezer. 22-25 in. plant.	BURG FAR JOH SEED
FEYENOORD			Vigorous grower that produces over a long period.	WILL
FIN DE BAGNOL	63	6-7 in. Slim	14-16 in. plant. Filet French bean. Pick when very young, about 4 in.	COO HER LEJ LEM
FRENCHIE	43	3¾ in. Dark green	European variety. Texture is crisp and tender. 12 in. plant. Tolerant to common bean mosaic. White-seeded.	STO

BUSH SNAP/SLICING BEANS

Variety	Days	Pods	Remarks	Sources
GATOR GREEN	53	6-7 in. Slim, round, oval, green	White-seeded.	LET RIS VER
GATOR GREEN 15	55	6-7 in. Medium-green, round, slender	Plant Variety Patented. White-seeded. Upright plant habit. High yields. Resistant to mosaic and New York 15 virus.	HARR MEY MID TWI WET
GATOR GREEN IMPROVED	48	6 in.	Upright plant keeps pods off the ground. White-seeded. Mosaic tolerant.	STO
GOURMAND		Round, medium-green	Pods are set high on moderately erect bush. White-seeded. Resistant to mosaic and New York 15 virus. Use fresh or frozen.	HARR
GOURMET	70	3½ in. Dark green, straight	18-24 in. plant. High-yielding. Smooth and silky. Resistant to mosaic anthracnose. Delicate whole bean for canning and freezing.	TWI
GREENCROP	42-51	8 x ½ in. Flat, dark green	Stringless and brittle. White-seeded. Upright plant. Best for Frenching.	BURP DAN GAR HARR JOH LAG POR RIS SEE STO TWI VER WIL
GREEN ISLE	55	6-8 in.	Resistant to most diseases.	FAR NIC
GREEN LANTERN	53	8 in. Round, straight, dark green	Excellent tolerance to most mosaics and some strains of fall rust. Upright plant is vigorous. White-seeded.	STO
GREEN RULER	51	Long, very flat	18 in. spreading bushy vine. A bush romano type bean. Good freezer.	PIN THO
GREENSLEEVES	56	Round, dark green	Good freezer.	BURP
HARVESTER TEEPEE	51	8 in. Slender	Has teepee growth habit. Flavorful. Produces over a long period.	PIN
HYSTYLE		Medium dark green, round	Has persistent green color. Plant Variety Patented. White-green seed. Resistant to common mosaic and New York 15 virus. Tolerant to bacterial brown spot.	HARR
JUMBO BUSH	55-60	12 x 1 in. Dark bright green	Plant Variety Patented. Nearly seedless. Stringless. Romano-type gourmet bean. Heavy bearing, quick podding. Try cooked or raw.	COM FIS GAR GUR HEN JOH LET NIC PAR PIN POR RAW SEED SOU TER THO WIL
KENTUCKY WONDER BUSH (COMMODORE)	65	8 in. Round	Like the Kentucky Wonder pole, but in bush form. Crisp, meaty pods. Big yields if kept picked.	GUR HEN SEE WET
KENTUCKY WONDER BUSH 125	58	6-7 in. Flat, oval, medium-green	20 in. upright plant. High yields. Plant Variety Patented.	BURR EAR HARR JUN MID TWI
KENYA			Purple flowers. Prolific climber.	SEE
LAKE LARGO	58	6-8 in. Round, straight	Seeds develop slowly. 15-18 in. plant. Widely adapted. Resistant to common and New York 15 bean virus, and some races of rust.	JUN MID
LANCER	59	6 in. Slender, round	Erect bush holds pods off ground. Resistant to common bean mosaic virus and New York 15 virus.	COM
LIMBOURG	60		Yellow-seeded. Stringless. Mangetout type bean. Very productive. Can be eaten fresh or dried.	HER
LIMELIGHT	38	Thick, broad	12-15 in. plant. Heavy cropper if picked regularly. Fiberless. Rich, sweet flavor. Good freezer.	RAW THO

Variety	Days	Pods	Remarks	Sources
MEDALLION (8046)		Round to oval, medium-green	Vigorous bush. Shows some cold tolerance. White-seeded. Resistant to bean common mosaic virus and New York 15. Tolerant to one or more races of bean rust.	HARR
MONTANA GREEN	50	6-7 in. Round, medium-green	Stringless, crisp and tender. Light buff seeds.	FIS HIG
NIAGARA 773		Round, medium, dark green	Large bush, fleshy pods high on plant. Good processing bean. Resistant to bean mosaic and New York 15 virus.	HARR
NOORDSTER			Short-season variety. Most beans mature at the same time. Not completely stringless, but has good flavor.	WILL
OREGON	58	6½ in. Dark green	Stringless. Good canner and freezer. Resistant to Oregon rust.	VER
OREGON LAKE BUSH	55		Vigorous multi-branched bush.	NIC
OREGON TRAIL BUSH	55		Plants are vigorous and productive.	NIC
PARKER HALF RUNNER	52-90		Vigorous, bush plant with medium length runners. Seed is excellent for baking, freezing and canning. 90 days to mature, dry bean stage.	LET
PERFECT IMPROVED	50	4-5 in. Thin, green	Stringless. Good flavor.	WILL
PLANO	48	6 in. Flat	Mangetout type. Has great flavor at all stages. Stringless at snap stage. Creamy white seeds at mature stage.	HER
PRELUDE	45	Green	Stringless.	WILL
PROCESSOR	53-55	Oval, round, medium-green	Stringless. Good canner or freezer.	VER
PROVIDER	52	5¼-6 in. Round	Purple-seeded. Heavy yields. Resistant to common bean mosaic and powdery mildew.	ABU ALL EARL GAR HARR HIG JOH LED LET MEY MID PIN RAW RIS STO TER TWI VER VES WYA
PROVIDER WHITE SEEDED	52	Round to oval, medium-green	Resembles Provider but matures a few days earlier. Plant Variety Patented.	HARR LET TWI
RAINIER	50-54	6 in. Dark green	White-seeded. Holds tenderness for long time. For canning or freezing.	JOH VER
REGALFIN		Very thin	French slicing bean.	LEJ
REMUS MR	40	10 in. Round	Pods hang from the top of the 18-20 in. plant. Fiberless pods can be eaten raw. Resistant to common bean mosaic. Good freezer.	PAR THO
RESISTO	56	Round, straight, medium-green	Slow seed development allows extended harvest. Rust-resistant. High yields.	RIS WILL
RODOLFO	52	15 in. Pencil-shape	Stringless throughout the season. Good disease tolerance. Superb flavor.	THO
ROMA (ITALIAN BEAN)	53-59	4½ in. Wide, flat, thin, green	White-seeded. Resembles pole Romano. Needs no support. Use fresh or frozen.	ALL EARL GUR LET VES
ROMA 11	59	4½ in. Flat, medium-green	Distinctively flavored. Big yields. Plant Variety Patented. Upright plant holds pods off ground. Resistant to common bean mosaic virus. Use fresh, canned or frozen.	BURP COM HARR JUN LED MEY MID PAR POR RIS SEE SHE SOU TWI WET WYA
ROMANO 14	56	5½-6 in. Broad, flat, medium-green	True Romano flavor. Tan-colored seed. Use fresh, canned or frozen.	ARC WILL
ROYALNEL (FIN DE FIN)			French slicing bean.	LEJ

◀ **BUSH SNAP/SLICING BEANS**

Variety	Days	Pods	Remarks	Sources
SALEM BUSH BLUE LAKE	50	5½ in.	16 in. plant. White-seeded. Stringless and tender.	FAR
SAVOR		Round to oval, medium-green	Cold tolerance for germination. Slow seed development. Resistant to common bean mosaic and New York 15 virus.	HARR
SHAMROCK	57	6 in. Dark, glossy green	Highly productive bean. Disease-resistant.	LED
SLENDERETTE	53	5 in. Slender, dark green	White-seeded. Good quality bean. Erect plant holds huge crop off the ground. Good fresh, canned or frozen.	PAR SHE VER WET
SLENDER WHITE	56	5-6 in. Medium-green	Very productive.	VER
SLIMGREEN	60	5-5½ in. Round, light to medium-green	Extremely heavy yielder. Resistant to common bean mosaic.	VER
SPARTAN ARROW	52	5½-6 in. Oval, straight, medium-green	Heavy yielder.	HARR HEN MID RIS
SPECULATOR	48	4 in. Straight, dark green	18 in. plant holds pods off the ground. White-seeded. Easy to pick.	STO
SPRING GREEN	46	4-6 in. Round, dark green	18 in. upright plant. White-seeded. Mosaic-tolerant. Stringless. Good canned or frozen.	STO
SPRITE STRINGLESS	52	5-6 in. Straight, medium-green	Vigorous, bushy plant. Resistant to mosaic.	VER
STRIKE	45	5½ in. Round, slender, straight, medium-green	Pods set over a long period. White-seeded. Tolerant to common bean mosaic and New York 15 virus.	STO
STRINGLESS GREEN POD (LANDRETH'S)	52-54	5-6 in. Round, green	20 in. upright plant is heavy bearing. Brown, seeded. Able to tolerate drought. Good canner.	EARL GUR PLA POR SEE SUN VER WET
SULPHUR (HIGHLAND)	55		Not stringless. Good yielder. Does well in mountain areas.	WET
SUNRAY	58	5-6 in. Round, straight	High yields. Best harvested when 5-6 in. Brown-seeded. Fine flavor and texture.	PIN
TENDERCROP	52-61	5-5½ in. Straight, round	Dark-seeded. Good yielder. Resistant to pod mottle, mosaic and New York 15 virus. Stringless.	ARC BURG BURP COM GUR HARR HEN HUM LAG LET NIC PAR RIS SEED VER WIL
TENDERETTE	55	5½-6 in. Straight, rich green	White-seeded. Stringless, fiberless. Good fresh, canned or frozen.	GUR HEN LET MEY PAR SEE WET WYA
TENDERGREEN (ASGROW STRINGLESS)	52-57	6-7 in. Round, dark green	14-18 in. plant. Resistant to mosaic. Stringless. Good canner.	ABU ALL COM DEG ECO GUR LED LET MEY MID PIN THO TIL WYA
TENDERGREEN IMPROVED	53-56	6-7 in. Round	Seeds are purple-mottled tan. Meaty. Mosaic-resistant.	ARC BURG BURP BURR BUT EAR EARL FAR GUR JUN PAR SEED STO TWI WET WIL WILL
TENNESSEE GREEN POD (CASEKNIFE)	54	6-8 in. Flat	Not for northern states. Mosaic-resistant. Meaty pods.	JOH VER WET WIL WYA
THE PRINCE	55	18 in. Oval	Widely adapted. Excellent freezer. 14 in. plant.	ECO THO
TIDAL WAVE	54	6 in. Dark green	16-18 in. plant. White-seeded. Fine freezer.	VER

▶

Variety	Days	Pods	Remarks	Sources
TOPCROP	48-52	5½-6 in.	16 in. plant. Good yields. Stringless. Mosaic-resistant. Good canner and freezer.	ARC BURG BURP BURR DEG EAR FAR FIS GUR HEN HIG JUN LET MEY MID PAR PON POR ROS TWI VER WET WIL WILL WYA
TRIOMPHE DE FARCY	48-59	6-7 in. Thin, straight, mottled purple	17-18 in. plant. Good yields. Sweet flavor.	COO HER JOH LEJ
TRIUMPH	56	5¾ in. Curved slightly	18-24 in. plant with good leaf cover. Heavy yields. Plant Variety Patented. Excellent quality.	BURR FAR TWI
VENTURE	48	6½ in. Somewhat lumpy, green	White seeded. High yields. Widely adapted and easy to grow. This is an extra early Blue Lake variety. Stiff, erect stems hold pods off the ground. Sweet flavor.	GAR HIG JOH PAR
VERNANDON	55	6 in. Round, slim, deep green	French haricot vert. Full of flavor. Easy to grow. Resistant to bean virus and antracnose. Best eaten when young.	SHE
WADE BUSH	54	6 in. Round, slender	Red-brown seeds. Resistant to mosaic and powdery mildew. Stringless.	FAR WYA
WHITE HALF RUNNER (MISSISSIPPI SKIP BEAN)	60	4 in. Round, light green	Use as fresh or shell bean. Fibrous when full grown. Good fresh, canned or frozen.	BURP HARR RIS VER WET
WHITE HALF RUNNER (MOUNTAINER)	52	Round, oval, light green	Early half runner. Use for string bean or shell bean.	HEN JOH LET MEY PAR POR WET WIL WYA
WIDUCO IMPROVED	50	5-6 in. Round, green	Disease-resistant. Excellent flavor. Good freezer.	WILL

WAX BUSH BEANS

Variety	Days	Pods	Remarks	Sources
ANNIVERSARY GOLD	55	Yellow, long, straight	Plants are hardy and vigorous. Resistant to mosaic virus. Tender and brittle. Excellent freezer.	VES
BEURRE DE ROCQUENCOURT (GOLDEN ROCKY)	46-56	6-7 in. Yellow, oval, round	Black-seeded. Early bearer. 12-16 in. upright plant. Stringless. Recommended where nighttime temperatures drop under 60°. Pick regularly.	ABU COO GAR HER HIG JOH PIN RAW TER WILL
BLACK AFRICAN			Uncommon variety that bears heavily.	ABU
BRITTLE WAX (ROUND POD KIDNEY WAX)	50-58	6-7 in. Yellow	Stringless. White-seeded. Mild flavor. Vigorous vine. Good fresh, canned or frozen.	BURP DAN FAR LET RAW TIL
CHEROKEE (GOLDEN ALL-AMERICAN) (VALENTINE WAX)	49-58	6-6½ in. Oval, golden	Black-seeded. Stringless. Dependable during poor weather conditions. Resistant to mosaic and New York 15 virus.	BURG BURR COM DEG EAR FAR GUR HEN LED LET MEY MID PAR PON RIS STO TWI WYA
DRAGON LANGERIE (DRAGON TONGUE)	57	Long, flat, creamy-yellow striped purple	Dutch variety. Fine-flavored. High yielding.	COO JLH PIN SEE
EARLIWAX	50-54	5½ in. Round, straight, yellow	White-seeded. Very productive. Resistant to common bean mosaic.	LET TWI
EARLYWAX GOLDEN YELLOW	54	Slightly curved	Good flavor. Good canned or frozen.	VER
EASTERN BUTTERWAX	44-52	5-7 in. Straight, yellow	Stringless. Tender and thick-meated. 16 in. plant. Excellent freezer.	GUR JUN RAW VES
GALAGOLD	50	5-6 in. Round, rich-golden	Tender, fleshy and stringless.	FIS

◀ **WAX BUSH BEANS**

Variety	Days	Pods	Remarks	Sources
GOLDCROP	45-54	5-6½ in. Shiny-yellow	Stringless. White-seeded. Pods set at outer edges of foliage. Use fresh, canned or frozen.	ALL EAR FAR JUN LAG PAR RIS SEED STO TWI
GOLDEN BUTTER (MONT D'OR)		Medium, golden	Completely stringless. Black-seeded. Fine-textured.	ECO
GOLDEN ROD	54-56	5-6 in. Round, medium-yellow	High-yielding. Vigorous upright plant with slow seed development. Plant Variety Patented. Use fresh or processed. White-seeded. Tolerant to common bean mosaic.	HARR JUN LET STO
GOLDEN WAX	50-60	5¼ in. Heavy, flat	Rust-resistant. Stringless. Freezes well. Very productive.	ARC BURG FIS HEN HUM LED WIL
GOLDEN WAX IMPROVED	51	Flat, oval, light golden-yellow	White-seeded. Brittle and stringless. Good yielder. Good quality.	ALL COM DEG EARL FAR GUR PAR POR ROS
GOLDEN WAX TOP NOTCH	50	5 in. Flat, straight, yellow	White seed with brown eye.	MEY WET
GOLDKIST	59	Slender, golden-yellow	Superb eating quality. For best flavor harvest when young. Good yields.	PAR
GOLD RUSH	54	Straight, yellow	Pods hang in clusters around the main stem. Extra fine flavor. Excellent freezer. Resistant to common bean mosaic virus.	VES
HONEY GOLD	40	5½ in. Short, straight, round	12-14 in. plant. Stringless heavy yielder. Resistant to bean mosaic.	STO
KENTUCKY WONDER WAX	68		Flavor is the same as Kentucky Wonder. Slow to mature.	HEN SEE
KEYGOLD	54	6 in. Round, straight, yellow	Good quality, seems to hold during stressful conditions. High-yielding. Compact plant. Resistant to bean mosaic and New York 15 virus. Short-season variety.	HIG JOH MID
KINGHORN (BUTTER WAX) (IMPROVED BRITTLE WAX)	50-56	6 in. Creamy-yellow	White-seeded. Vigorous plant. Good canner and freezer.	COM EAR ECO GUR RAW SEE SEED WILL
MAJESTIC WAX	58		Slow seed development. Plant Variety Patented. Tender fleshy pods.	SEED TWI
MAJOR		Yellow, round	Haricot type. Seeds are slow to develop. Highly productive bush type. Full-flavored.	LEM
MOONGOLD	49-55	5-5¼ in.	14 in. plant. Stringless. Good yields. Disease-resistant.	GUR
PENCIL POD BLACK WAX	52-55	6-7 in. Round, slightly curved, golden-yellow	Black-seeded. Stringless. Good quality. Can withstand temperature changes better than some newer varieties.	ALL ARC EARL FAR GUR LEM LET POR SEED SOU WET WILL
PENCIL POD WAX (BUTTER BEAN)	51-54	5-6 in. Deeply curved, rich-yellow	Stringless, tender, brittle. Black-seeded. Pods are borne in profusion for a long time.	ABU BURP DAN DEG GAR PIN PON SEE VER
PUREGOLD	62	Round, golden-yellow	Everbearing. One planting will continue to yield most of the summer. Extra-fine flavor.	VES
ROCDOR	50	6½ in.	French bean. Pick when young. Black-seeded. Tolerates cooler and wetter conditions and is mosaic virus- and anthracnose-resistant. Use fresh, canned or frozen.	JOH SHE VER
ROUND POD KIDNEY WAX			Good freezer.	EARL
RUSTPROOF GOLDEN WAX	40-50	5-5½ in. Oval, flat	White seeds have reddish marks. Stringless. Productive. Rust-resistant.	NIC

▶

Variety	Days	Pods	Remarks	Sources
SLENDERWAX	58	5 in. Straight, bright golden-yellow	Tender pods with no fiber. 20 in. plant. Grows huge clusters. Vigorous. Excellent canner or freezer.	EAR HEN TWI VER
SUNDIAL	48	5½ in. Round, straight	Seeds develop slowly. White-seeded. Tolerant to common bean mosaic and bean virus 1A.	STO
SUNGOLD	45-56	5-6 in. Round, straight, bright yellow	White-seeded. Slow seed development. Good holding quality. Resistant to bean mosaic.	EARL HARR JOH STO
WAX 216		6 in. Round, straight golden-yellow	Concentrated heavy crop. Highly disease-resistant.	LED

BUSH BEANS

PURPLE/YELLOW (NON-WAX)

Variety	Days	Pods	Remarks	Sources
CONSTANZA	50	Round, golden-yellow	15 in. plant. Sweet, fleshy pods.	THO
PURPLE QUEEN		Purple	Pods turn green when cooked. Good texture and flavor. Light brown seed. Good freezer. Has cold tolerance.	RAW
PURPLE TEE PEE		Purple	Turns green when cooked. Compact plant is easy to pick.	LED PIN
ROYAL BURGUNDY	50-60	5½-6 in. Round, curved, purple	12-15 in. plant. Good variety for colder soils. Stringless. Turns green when cooked. Plant Variety Patented. Good fresh or frozen.	BURP COM COO DEG EAR EARL FIS GUR HEN JUN LAG NIC PAR SEE SHE SOU STO TER TIL TWI VER WET WILL
ROYALTY PURPLE POD	50-58	5 in. Round, curved	Unusual rich flavor. Cooks green. Stringless. Buff-colored seed. Good variety for colder soils. Good fresh or frozen.	ABU ALL ARC BURG BUT FAR GAR JLH JOH LEM LET PLA PON TWI WIL

LIMA POLE BEANS
(Phaseolus lunatus)

There are two types of lima beans: pole and bush. Both produce plump-seeded (potato lima) and small-seeded (baby lima) varieties.

CULTURE: For Pole Limas plant 1½ to 2 inches deep, 6 to 10 inches apart in rows 30 to 36 inches apart. For Bush Limas, plant 1½ to 2 inches deep, 6 to 10 inches apart in rows 24 to 30 inches apart.

SEASON: Lima beans require warmer soil conditions for germination and a longer growing season than green beans.

INSECTS/DISEASES: See green beans.

HARVESTING: Pick the pods of limas as soon as they begin to look a little lumpy and before they begin to turn yellow.

LIMA BEANS—POLE

Variety	Days	Pods	Remarks	Sources
BANDY (HOPI LIMA)			Strictly for warmer climates. Has red markings.	ABU
BURPEE'S BEST (DREER'S IMPROVED CHALLENGER) (POTATO LIMA)	87-92	4½ x 1¼ in. Broad, straight	10-12 foot plant. Strong climber. High yields. Excellent fresh or frozen. Plump 'potato' type bean seed.	BURP LET MEY
CAROLINA (SIEVA) (SOUTHERN RUNNING BUTTERBEAN)	79	3½ x 2 in. Flat, medium-green	White-seeded. Quick to bear. Heavy yields.	BURG BURP HEN RED ROS WET WIL WYA

◄ **LIMA BEANS—POLE**

Variety	Days	Pods	Remarks	Sources
CLIFF DWELLER			Purple speckled baby lima. Vigorous.	SEE
CHRISTMAS POLE (LARGE SPECKLED CHRISTMAS) (CALICO) (GIANT FLORIDA POLE)	80-88	5-6 in. Flat, raised area of dark red	A long-season bean. When cooked they turn pink-brown. High quality. Vigorous 10 foot climber. Cream-colored seed with irregular red stripes.	EAR LEM NIC PAR POR RIS ROS SEE SOU TWI VER WIL WYA
DR. MARTIN POLE LIMA				FER
FLORIDA BUTTER (FLORIDA SPECKLED BUTTER) (SPECKLED BUTTER)	85	3½ in. Medium-green, slightly curved	Averages 8 feet in height. Light buff-colored seeds splashed with maroon. Long-season producer. Good tolerance for hot, humid weather.	ARC FAR LAG LET POR RED ROS SOU VER WET WYA
HENDERSON'S EARLY LEVIATHAN	70		Strong grower. Bears until frost.	JUN
KING OF THE GARDEN (WHITE POLE LIMA)	88-90	5-8 in. Dark green	Climbs to 10 feet. A long-season producer. Seeds are thick, flat and ivory white to pale green. Wonderful freezer or shelling bean.	BURP COM DAN DEG EAR GUR HEN JUN LAG LED LIB MEY PAR RED SEE SEED STO SUN TWI VER WET WYA
PRIZETAKER	90	6 x 1½ in.	Excellent flavor fresh or frozen.	BURP LAK LED WET
RED-SPECKLED POLE	88		Large, flat bean. Excellent quality.	WET

LIMA BEANS—BUSH
SMALL-SEEDED

Variety	Days	Pods	Remarks	Sources
BABY BUSH (EVERGREEN BUSH)	67-72	Bright green	Becomes creamy white when mature. Stands hot weather very well.	BURG GUR
BABY FORDHOOK BUSH	67-70	2¾ x ¾ in. Dark green, slightly curved	14 in. plant. High quality.	ARC BURP MEY
BABY POTATO BUSH	60-65	3 in.	Excellent fresh, frozen or canned. White-seeded.	STO
BRIDGETON	76	3 in. Flat	Good freezer. Plant resistant to downy mildew.	WYA
CANGREEN BUSH	65	3 in.	16 in. plant. Stays green after cooked or canned.	EAR WET
CLARK'S GREEN SALAD	68	Small, flat, green	High quality. Good fresh or canned.	PAR
EARLY BUSH	65		Requires warm location. Very productive. Good quality for fresh eating or canned.	TIL
EASTLAND	70	Flat, medium-green	Upright plant habit. Greenish-white seed. Use fresh, canned or frozen. Resistant to races A,B,C,D of downy mildew.	HARR PAR WYA
GENEVA	85	Light green	Cool soil tolerance. Good flavor. Good freezer.	JOH
GREEN-SEEDED BABY HENDERSON (THOROGREEN BABY LIMA)	67	3 in. Flat, pale green	14-16 in. plant. Pods form in clusters. Seeds stay green in all stages. Prolific.	FAR HEN JUN LET MEY NIC PAR SEED VER WIL WYA
HENDERSON BUSH	65-81	3 in. Flat, dark green, slightly curved	Small erect plant. Good freezer and canner.	ALL ARC BURG BURP BURR DAN EAR EARL HEN JOH LAG LET MEY MID PAR PIN RIS ROS SEE TWI VER WET WYA

►

Variety	Days	Pods	Remarks	Sources
HENDERSON BUSH IMPROVED	65		Dependable heirloom variety.	DEG RED
JACKSON WONDER (CALICO) (SPECKLED BUSH)	65-83	3¼ in.	24 in. plant. Mottled purple, buff-colored seed. Adapted to all parts of the South. Heavy yields. Use fresh or dried.	ARC GUR HEN JOH PAR POR RED RIS ROS SOU VER WET WYA
THAXTER (ALL GREEN)	67	3¼ in. Small, flat	5-16 in. plant. Tolerant to downy mildew.	COM
WOOD'S PROLIFIC	68	3½ in. Green	Has tendency to throw out small runners.	WET WYA

LIMA BEANS—BUSH
PLUMP-SEEDED

Variety	Days	Pods	Remarks	Sources
BURPEE'S FORDHOOK (FORDHOOK)	75	4½ x ¾ in. Slightly curved, dark green	Dry, mealy quality and delicious chestnut flavor. 20 in. upright plant is 2 feet across.	BURP DEG JUN ROS WET WILL
BURPEE'S BUSH IMPROVED	70-75	5½ x 1¼ in. Flat, oval, medium-green	Easy to shell. White-seeded. Enormous yields. Highest quality.	ALL ARC BURP BURR DEG FAR JUN LED LET MEY STO VER WET WYA
DIXIE WHITE BUTTERPEA	70-76	Broad, oval, lightly curved	Strong, vigorous 2 foot plant. White-seeded. Will set even under hot conditions.	HEN LEM PAR POR VER WET WYA
DIXIE SPECKLED BUTTERPEA	76	3½ x ½ in. Slightly curved, medium dark green	Similar to Dixie White Butterpea. Brownish-red seed is speckled with darker brown. 16-21 in. plant. Productive in hot weather. Excellent taste.	DEG LED PAR ROS VER WET WIL
FORDHOOK IMPROVED	75	3-4 in. Pale green	Yields heavier in hot weather than 242 strain. Excellent fresh, canned or frozen.	FAR
FORDHOOK 242 (POTATO LIMA)	75-85	3-4 in.	Heat-resistant plants set pods under adverse conditions. Reliable yielder. Good fresh, canned or frozen.	ALL ARC BURG BURP BURR COM DAN DEG GUR HARR HEN JOH JUN LAG LED LET MEY MID PAR POR RIS SEE SEED STO SUN THO TWI VER WET WIL WYA
GIANT IMPROVED BUSH	75	5-6 in. Slightly curved	Bears from July until frost. East to grow. Erect, vigorous plant. High quality.	EAR

FAVA BEANS
(Vicia Faba)

Also know as English Broad Beans, Horsebeans, Windsor beans, is not a true bean but is related to vetch. Pods set in a whorl around a single stalk.

CULTURE: Plant 2½ inches deep, 3 to 4 inches apart in rows 24-30 inches apart.

SEASON: Cool.

INSECTS/DISEASES: See green beans.

HARVESTING: When pods are large and full of flat beans.

SHELL BEANS—FAVA
(ENGLISH BROADBEAN)

Variety	Days	Pods	Remarks	Sources
AQUADULCE VERY LONG POD	85-90	12-14 in. Pearl-green	Hardy 36-40 in. plant. Very productive variety.	NIC TER THO
AQUADULCE CLAUDIA		Pale green	4 foot plant. Hardy to 12° F.	TER

◀ SHELL BEANS—FAVA

Variety	Days	Pods	Remarks	Sources
BONNY LAD	75	5-6 in.	15 in. plant. 4-5 small light green beans per pod. Good freezer.	THO
BROAD LONG POD (FAVA LONG POD)	85-90	7 in. Oblong, flat, light green	Used as a substitute for limas in northern climates. Do not grow in hot weather.	ALL BURP COM DEG GUR HEN HUM LEJ LET NIC PIN PLA SUN VER
BROAD LONG POD IMPROVED	85-90	7 in. Flat, oblong	Use as green shell bean or in dry stage.	HARR LED RAW WILL
BROAD WINDSOR	65		Upright plant. Slow-growing variety.	SEE STO TIL
BRUNETTE	72	4-5 in.	18-24 in. plant. Small-seeded, thin pod walls.	THO WILL
BUNYARD'S EXHIBITION	85	12-14 in.	24-40 in. plant. Seven beans per pod.	THO
COLOSSAL	70	7-10 in.	4 foot plant. Bears so heavily the plant may need to be staked. Thrives in cold wet soil.	VER
EQUINA			Small-seeded.	SEE
EXHIBITION LONG POD		Enormous	Improved type of Windsor Bean. 5 very large beans per pod.	EARL
EXPRESS	71	7-8 in.	36 in. plant. 34 pods per plant. Winter-hardy. Good freezer. Does not discolor.	THO
FROST-PROOF BROAD BEAN	120	7 x 1½ in. Flat, straight	Upright 2½ foot plant. Good cooked fresh or as a winter shell bean.	BURG FAR
IMPERIAL GREEN LONGPOD	84	15-20 in.	36. in plant. Pods contain nine large beans. Good freezer.	THO
IPRO	78		Heat-resistant. Tolerant to top yellow virus.	GAR HIG JOH
ITE	75	6 in.	30 in. plant. Tiny pea-size beans are sweet-flavored. Heavy yields.	THO
MASTERPIECE GREEN LONGPOD	88	8 in.	30-36 in. plant. Green seed.	THO
RELON	84	17-22 in.	36 in. plant. Up to 11 green-seeded beans per pod. Great freezer.	THO
SUPRIFIN	84	8 in.	36 in. plant. Immense cropper. True Broad Bean taste. Good fresh or frozen.	THO
TEZIEROMA	80-90	10 in.	Vigorous production over long period. 7-8 enormous beans per pod. Good variety for cool summers.	LEM
TEZIERVIERA WHITE SEEDED	80-90	Large	6 white beans per pod.	LEM
THE SUTTON	84	5-6 in.	12 in. plant. Good freezer. Five small beans per pod. Space-saver variety.	THO
TOTO	63	8 in. Pendant, oval, medium-green	Beige seed. Dwarf upright plant holds pods off ground. High yields.	STO
TRUE BUSH	85	7 in. Flat, oblong	Large, erect bush plant. 5-7 large seeds per pod. Not suited to hot weather. Light brown seed.	TWI
WINDSOR LONG POD	75	Fat, flat	3½ foot plant. Frost-hardy. Use as green-shelled or dried. Dependable variety.	ABU GAR HIG JOH SEE
WITKIEM MAJOR	84	8-10 in. thick	36 in. plant. Good freezer. Green-seeded. Heavy yielder.	THO

SHELL BEANS—HORTICULTURAL

Variety	Days	Pods	Remarks	Sources
BUSH HORTICULTURAL NO. 4	64		Does well in short-season areas. Pink beans with dark red markings. Excellent freezer.	LIB
COCO NAIN BLANC		Thick, fat	French variety. White shell bean. 4-6 beans per pod. High quality. High yields. Vigorous bush plant.	LEM
COCO PRAGUE		Fiery red, mottled white	European strain. Can be used as fresh shell bean. Bush type.	LEM
DWARF HORTICULTURAL (KIEVITS) (LONG POD) (WREN'S NEST)	65	5-6 in. Thick	Carmine color at maturity.	BURP EAR FIS HARR MID PIN SEED TWI WET WILL WYA
FRENCH HORTICULTURAL (OCTOBER BEAN)	64-90		Heirloom bean. 18 in. plant. Hardy, disease-resistant. Dependable. 90 days for dry bean stage. Recommended as shell bean.	RIS SEED VER
FRENCH DWARF HORTICULTURAL	60-65	Long, straight	14-18 in. plant. Can be used as green snap bean or dried. Use fresh, canned or frozen.	ALL ARC COM HARR LET MID STO TWI
TAYLOR'S DWARF HORTICULTURAL (SPECKLED BAYS) (SHELLEY)	64	5½-6 in. Oval, cream-colored	1800s heirloom seed. Buff seed is splashed on red. Can be eaten in dry stage. Semi runner, 14-18 in. plant.	GUR HAS HEN JOH LET MEY RIS SEE SOU TER
TONGUE OF FIRE	70	6 in. flat, red streaked ivory pod	From Tierra del Fuego, South America. Large and round beans have great flavor and texture.	ABU JOH SEE
WORCESTOR HORTICULTURAL	70	7 in. flat, splashed red	Mammoth form of old fashioned Horticultural Shell or Speckled Cranberry Bean.	ALL

SOYBEANS
(Glycine soja)

Soybeans have been popular in China, Manchuria, Korea and Japan since ancient times. There are two kinds: green vegetable soybeans, which are meant to be eaten fresh, and dried soybeans. Uses of the dry soybeans are cooking, flour, soy milk, tofu, soy sauce and miso. Dry soybeans average 40% protein and 18% oil.

CULTURE: Plant 1½ to 2 inches deep, 2 to 3 inches apart in rows 24 to 30 inches apart. Upright plants are easy to cultivate.

SEASON: Warm.

INSECTS/DISEASES: See green beans.

HARVESTING: Harvest pods when the beans are plump. Green vegetable soybeans should be picked when they begin to turn from green to brown.

SHELL BEANS—SOYBEANS

Variety	Days	Pods	Remarks	Sources
BLACK JET	104	Medium jet-black	Short-season variety. 2 foot plant. High-yielding, thin-skinned bean. Use as a dry bean.	JOH
BUTTERBEAN	90		Sweet, buttery and high-yielding. 2-2½ foot stocky plant. Prolific pod set. Use as a fresh green bean. Freezes well.	GAR JOH
EDIBLE SOY BEAN	80-103	Oval, bright green	Young seeds cooked as a green shell bean. Mature seeds are used to prepare soybean milk or bean curd. 20 in. plant. Plant spring or summer.	ABU BURG EAR GUR LET POR SUN THO WIL
ENVY	75	Bright green inside and out	High-yielding. 2 foot plant. Use as fresh green bean or dried bean.	GAR JOH
FRISKELY V	70-91	Buff-yellow	18 in. upright plant. Beige seed. Not high-yielding. Can be grown in short-season areas.	ABU RAW SEE STO

◀ **SHELL BEANS—SOYBEANS**

Variety	Days	Pods	Remarks	Sources
FROSTBEATER	75	Large, shiny-green	22 in. plant. Heavy producer. Rich flavor. Use as a green shell bean also.	BURP LEJ
HAKUCHO EARLY	95		Very good variety. Bush type. Use as green shell or as you would limas.	KIT
KIM	125		30-36 in. plant. Heavy pod set.	MET
MAPLE ARROW	100	Bright yellow	Use as a dry bean. Also used for processed soy products like tofu and tempeh. Short-season variety.	JOH
PANTHER (JAPANESE KUROMAME ORIENTAL BLACK)	100-120	Large, dull black	Most easily digested. Excellent flavor. Use as a dry bean. High-yielding.	JOH
PRIZE	85-105	Large, oval	Erect bush. Use as a green shell bean or lima beans.	BURP DEG HEN KIT LIB MET NIC WET

SHELL BEANS—KIDNEY

Variety	Days	Pods	Remarks	Sources
CALIFORNIA RED KIDNEY	100	Large, light red	Hardy and high-yielding. Brown-seeded.	STO
CHARLEVOIX DARK RED	102	Large	Dark red seed. Resistant to antracnose.	JOH
DARK RED KIDNEY	95	Large, flat, waxy-green	Used as a dry cooking bean.	ABU BURG EAR JUN LET NIC
IMMIGRANT			Strain of Dark Red Kidney bean.	ABU
RED KIDNEY	95-100	Large, flat, green	20-22 in. plant. Pinkish-red to mahogany-colored. Rich bean flavor. Excellent baked, boiled in soups, salads, Spanish and Mexican dishes.	ALL ARC BURP BUT DEG FAR FIS GAR GUR HEN LED LET MEY PAR TER VER WILL
REDKLOUD	100		Early red kidney with some halo blight resistance. Good yielder. Milder than most kidney beans.	ABU RAW
ROYAL KIDNEY		Large		SEE
WHITE KIDNEY	100	Large, long	White bean is milder in flavor than red kidneys. 24 in. plant is vigorous and productive. Fine baking quality.	VER

SHELL BEANS

MISCELLANEOUS

Variety	Days	Pods	Remarks	Sources
ADZUKI	90-125	5 in.	Grown in China and Japan. Likes acid soil and cool nights. 2½ foot bushy plant. Red, rounded seeds have distinctive nutty flavor.	JLH RED SOU SUN THO VER
ANASAZI	90-95		Traced back to ancient cliff-dwelling people. Baking bean with sweet meaty texture.	PLA
AGATE PINTO	92		Rectangular, buff-colored, mottled bean. Spicy flavor when cooked.	JOH
APPALOOSA	90-110		White bean with maroon and black mottling. Bush plant which sends off runners.	ABU PLA
BLACK BEAN			Small, black beans used in Mexican cooking. Highly recommended.	JLH
BLACK COCO		Plump, black	Quick cooking. Good refried.	TER

▶

Variety	Days	Pods	Remarks	Sources
BLACK MEXICAN (FRIJOLE NEGRO)			Small oval black bean. Great soup bean.	ABU RED
BOLETA	100		Low bush plant with runners. Great-grand-daddy of the pinto bean. Used in Mexican cooking.	PLA
BOX			English variety. Purple on white.	ABU
BUCKSKIN			Buff-colored seed. For snap or dry use.	ABU
CLUSTER BEAN BARASATI			2-6 foot upright plant. Pods all up the stem. Likes sandy soil. Excellent producer. Use in East Indian cooking.	JLH
DRY ADVENTIST			Small plant. Old variety from the Idaho Mountains. Prolific.	SEE
DUTCH BROWN			Dutch variety. Brown-seeded. For dry use. Use in baking, boiling, soups and stews.	WILL
EXPRESS	118		Adzuki variety bean. Small, shiny dark red bean. Japanese type. Vigorous upright plant.	JOH
FLAGEOLET	65-100		24 in. plant. Pure white seed.	LEJ LEM NIC SEE VER
FLAMBEAU (FRENCH FLAGEOLET)	76	Long, slender	Easy shell pods have 8 to 10 vivid mint green beans. Prolific. Excellent freezer.	ABU JOH
GARBANZO (CHICK PEA)	65-100	Large, tan	Distinctive chestnut-like flavor. Good cold in salads. Erect bush plant. Suited to drought areas.	ABU BURP GUR HEN LED PAR VER
GAUCHO			Heirloom variety from Argentina. Rich tan color.	ABU
GREEN FLAGEOLET CHEVRIER	95		French variety. 12-16 in. plant. Gourmet bean. When young pods can be eaten.	HER
IMPROVED PINTO			Large and plump bean. Heavy producers.	POR
KABULI BLACK	95		Hardy variety of Garbanzo bean. Good sized black bean.	GAR
KENEARLY			White with yellow-brown eye. Good baking bean.	RAW VES
LEMON YELLOW			Light yellow beans. Real bean flavor. For dry use.	WILL
LIMELIGHT	46	3-4 in. Broad, flat, pale lime-green	Short, compact bush plant. Good shelling bean or left to dry.	JOH
MAINE YELLOW EYE (SULPHUR) (DOT EYE BEAN)	85-92	Curved, light green	18 in. plant. Good baking bean. Rounded yellow-tan dry bean. Is a dependable and prolific variety. Has a squash-like flavor.	ABU ALL COM GAR JLH JOH RED SEE VER
MARFAX	89	Round	Dependable yielder. Popular baking bean.	ABU
MIDNIGHT BLACK TURTLE SOUP BEAN	85-98		Heirloom variety. A black bean for soup or refried beans. Compact bush plant. Heavy yields.	ABU GAR GUR HEN LEM PIN SEE VER
MITLA BLACK BEAN	70		High-yielding variety from Mexico. Used in soup.	PLA
MONEY			High-yielding. From England. Red speckled.	ABU
MOTH BEAN	95		Young pods are eaten as vegetable in India. Dried beans are used like lentils. High protein. For very warm climates. Sprawling, mat-forming plant.	ABU
MUNG	120	Small, olive-green	Does well in warmer weather. Excellent as sprouts.	ABU COM EAR GUR HEN LEM LET PIN POR RAW SEE SUN THO WET WILL

◀ **SHELL BEANS**

Variety	Days	Pods	Remarks	Sources
PEREGION			Dark speckled Scotia type from eastern Oregon. Compact plant.	ABU
PINK BEAN	60-85	Long, narrow	Medium-pink bean similar to Mexican Red. True bush bean. Good in soup or chili. Holds shape well when cooked.	LED LET VER
PINTO	80-90	5 in. Short, oval, broad	Popular in Mexican cooking. Light-buff background speckled with greenish brown.	ABU ARC BURG BURP GUR HEN LAG LET PAR POR SEE TIL VER WES
PINTO, SAN JUAN SELECT	120		Staple bean of the Southwest. This variety is best used for burritos.	PLA
PLATA		Yellow	Brown-seeded sheller from Argentina.	ABU
RED EYE			Medium-small kidney-shaped white bean with red eye. From eastern Oregon.	ABU
RED MEXICAN	85	Medium-green	1855 heirloom California bean. 14 in. bush plant. Excellent baker, does not become soggy. Great in soup.	VER
RED PEANUT BEAN	50	4 in. Green, red at maturity	14 in. true bush. Grows well in dry climates. Use as green shell or dry shell.	VER
ROCKWELL			From Puget Sound. White seed with maroon markings.	ABU
SANTA MARIA PINQUITO	90		Pink, square-shaped bean. Great tasting when simmered with bacon, onion, garlic and chili salsa.	NIC RED
SCOTCH		Butterscotch-colored, flattened	Pole bean for dry use.	ABU
SOLDIER (JOHNSON)	85-90		White bean with a maroon blotch on the eye. Flavor similar to kidney, but milder, nuttier and more tender skin. New England heirloom bean. 18 in. plant. Drought-resistant.	ALL GAR JOH RED SEE TER VER VES
SPARTAN HALF-RUNNER			Stakless. Black-streaked from Appalachia.	ABU
SQUAW YELLOW	75		Heirloom variety. Yellow-buff colored beans. Short plant. Soup bean.	ABU FIS GAR
SWEDISH BROWN BEAN	85-92		Dark tan oval bean with small white eye. Semi-vining, heavy-yielding plant. Widely adapted. Hardy. Good baking bean.	ABU GAR GUR VER
TEPARY BEAN	90-110		Native of Southwest. Small bean with 30% more protein. This bean comes in brown-, green- or speckled-seeded. Drought-resistant. Requires little water. Quick producer. Prolific.	PLA RED WES
TEXAS PINK			Flat, pink seeds. Very productive. Half-runner type.	ABU
WALCHERSE WHITE			White beans used for soups and baking.	WILL

SHELL BEANS				
			NAVY	
Variety	**Days**	**Pods**	**Remarks**	**Sources**
IMPROVED NAVY	95		Pure-white seeds.	EAR
LUCAS' NAVY			Small white bean grown in Puget Sound.	ABU

▶

Variety	Days	Pods	Remarks	Sources
MICHILITI (IMPROVED NAVY SANILAC)	85	Long	Glossy-white bean. Heavy yielder. Resistant to blight.	ARC
NAVY (PEA BEAN) (WHITE WONDER) (SOUP BEAN) (SANILAC)	85-95	Long, off-green	Standard dry bean. Small white seeds. Heavy yielder. Good soup bean.	COM GAR GUR HEN LED LET VER

SHELL BEANS

RED, PURPLE, CRANBERRY

Variety	Days	Pods	Remarks	Sources
CRANBERRY BEAN	60	Egg-shaped, thick, flat	Splashed red at maturity. Rich flavor.	ABU TER
GRAMMA WALTERS			Heavy-bearing, speckled Cranberry type.	ABU
JACOBS CATTLE (TROUT BEAN) (DALMATION BEAN) (COACH DOG BEAN)	65-85		Oblong beans are red on pure white. Heirloom bean. 24 in. plant. Good baking bean, has clear, spicy flavor.	ABU GAR JOH LEM RAW RED VER
LOWE'S CHAMPION	65-72	4-5 in. Rounded, flat, green	Heirloom seed. Mahogany-brown seed. 18-24 in. plant.	ALL JOH
MEXICAN RED BEAN	85	Medium-green	14 in. plant. Excellent baking quality.	VER
MONTEZUMA	95		Bush plant. Red bean. Use dried in baking.	NIC
SPECKLED BALE			Plump Cranberry type from Oregon.	ABU
RED BEAN	95		2½ foot plant. Heavy yields. Used in Mexican cooking.	GUR
SPECKLED CRANBERRY EGG (WREN'S EGG) (KING MAMMOTH)	65	5 in. Wide, thick	Pole bean. Very productive. Excellent frozen or fresh-shelled. Disease-resistant.	SEE VER
UNCLE WILLIE'S			Bush Cranberry type.	ABU
VERMONT CRANBERRY BUSH (OLD FASHIONED) (KING'S EARLY)	60-90		Heirloom soup bean. Bush type. Maroon seed with rose tan streaks. Steak-like taste makes it useful for a meat replacement.	ABU LET RED TER TIL VER
VERMONT CRANBERRY POLE	60-90		Possesses same characteristics of the Vermont Bush Cranberry. Use as shelling bean. Will do well in all climates.	VER

SHELL BEANS

WHITE

Variety	Days	Pods	Remarks	Sources
AZTEC (DWARF WHITE)	55		Known as a potato bean. Has large plump white seeds the size of limas. Plant has short 3 foot runners. Can withstand hot days and cool nights.	PLA RED
BULLOT			Heirloom variety. Round, shiny white, dry bean.	SEE
BUMBLEBEE			Large white seed with red splotch.	SEE
GREAT NORTHERN WHITE (MONTANA WHITE)	85-90	5 in. Flat	Big white bean. Cooks one-third faster than navy beans. Heavy yielder. 1907 heirloom bean. Semi-vining. Use in soup or baking.	ARC BURG BURP DEG EARL FAR GAR GUR HEN JUN LET PON POR SEE THO VER
WHITE HAILSTONE			From Canadian maritimes. Plump white pea-bean.	ABU

◀ **SHELL BEANS**

Variety	Days	Pods	Remarks	Sources
WHITE MARROW	68-100	4½-5 in. Flat, straight	White seed. Good baker.	STO

BEETS
(Beta vulgaris)

Beets are a double-barreled vegetable because you can eat both the roots and the leaves. Beets grow rapidly from seed, are disease-free, and aren't bothered much by insects. Beets are a little slow to sprout from corky seeds but, once up, they produce a lot of food in a small space.

CULTURE: Plant seed a half inch deep in rows 12 to 18 inches apart. the beet seed is a compact ball with numerous tiny seeds. When the plants reach about 6 inches high, thin to 2 to 3 inches apart.

SEASON: Cool season. 40 degree soil temperature or more. In hot-summer regions plant in early spring or late summer. In cold regions plant in the spring as soon as the ground can be worked.

INSECTS/DISEASES: APHIDS, FLEA BEETLES, WEBWORMS, GRASSHOPPERS, LEAF MINERS: Malathion, diazinon, pryethrum, rotenone or ryania.
LEAF SPOT, DOWNY MILDEW: Maneb or zineb.

HARVESTING: Pick some beets when they are about an inch in diameter. Let others grow to about 2 inches. Large, older beets have a tendency to become woody. Delaying harvest until after frost also increases sugar content and improves keeping qualities.

BEETS
GLOBE-SHAPED

Variety	Days	Color	Remarks	Sources
AVENGER (hybrid)		Medium-red	Little zoning. Bright glossy green tops. Excellent for bunching.	HARR
BOLDET		Red	English variety, full-flavored beet. Vigorous-growing.	LEM
BOLTHARDY	58	Deep red	Stringless, sweet flesh that stays fresh.	SHE
BURPEE'S RED BALL	60	Dark red	Medium-tall tops. 3 in. round beet.	BURP WET
CARDENAL	58	Bright red	Tops are 12-14 in. and dull green. Retains root shape when crowded. Space-saver variety.	RIS
DARK RED CANNER	59	Dark red	Small, but exceptional for canning. Short tops. Great flavor.	HEN
DETROIT CRIMSON	61-63	Maroon	Good freezer and canner. Greens can also be canned.	ECO PIN THO
DETROIT DARK RED (op) MEDIUM TOP	55-60	Dark red	12 in. dark, glossy tops. Early and sweet. 3 in. diameter. Good fresh, canned or frozen.	ABU ALL ARC BURG BURP BURR DAN DEG EAR EARL FIS GAR GUR HARR HEN HUM LAG LED LET MEY MID PAR PIE PON POR RAW SEE SEED STO SOU TIL TWI VER VES WES WET WIL WILL WYA
DETROIT DARK RED IMPROVED	65	Dark red	Smooth skin, small tap root.	COM
DETROIT DARK RED (op) SHORT TOP		Deep red	Minimal zoning. Tops are dark green with maroon tinge.	HARR JUN STO
DETROIT SUPREME	65	Dark red	Fine tap root, little tendency to form interior rings. Sow from May to July.	TER
EARLY RED BALL	48	Bright red	Deep crimson interior. Short tops.	STO
EARLY BLOOD	68	Red	Good winter use beet.	WET

▶

Variety	Days	Color	Remarks	Sources
FIRE CHIEF	52-70	Deep red	Tops have a bronze tinge. Tops make good canning.	STO
FIRST CROP	45	Dark red	Tender and sweet. Tops can be used as greens.	WES
GARNET	55-60	Garnet red	Clean roots and short tops. Sweet texture. Completely free of zoning.	FAR JUN LET
GLOBE DARK RED	65	Dark red	Recommended for dehydration and pickling. Excellent quality and color.	GLE
KING RED	52	Dark red	Good canning variety.	DEG EAR EARL
LITTLE EGYPT	34	Deep red	Only as transplanting type. Short tops.	STO
MATCHLESS GREEN TOP	55	Deep red	Smooth bulb with small neck and tap root. Distinctive erect green tops.	MID
MONO-GERM (MOBILE)	45-50	Dark red	Uniform stand of beets with little thinning necessary.	JOH STO
MONOPOLY	45	Deep red	No need to thin. Good freezer.	SHE THO
NEW GLOBE	60	Dark red	Detroit type. Good freezer.	WILL
PACEMAKER II (hybrid)	52	Red	Tender and sweet even when big.	BURR THO
PACEMAKER III (hybrid)	50	Blood-red	Excellent fresh or processed. Medium size roots. 16-17 in. tops. Tolerant to leaf spot.	POR STO TWI
PERFECTED DETROIT DARK RED	58	Deep, dark red	Tender, juicy, no rings or streaks. Great canner. Pick golf-ball size beets for eating.	DEG GUR HEN
RED ACE (hybrid)	51-53	Deep red	Smooth round roots have an excellent flavor. 14 in. tops. Good fresh or processed.	BURP EAR GUR HEN HUM JOH JUN LET MEY PAR PIN SOU STO TER TIL VES WET
ROYAL DETROIT (hybrid)	52	Deep purple-red	Free of zoning. 16-17 in. light green tops.	TWI
STAYSGREEN	53	Dark red	16-18 in. glossy dark green tops. Small tap roots.	MID
STOKES SPECIAL EARLY	55	Dark red	Medium tops. Good bunching beet.	STO
SWEETHEART	58		Extra-sweet. Use fresh, canned or for storage. Medium high tops are green, shaded red.	JOH
VERMILION	63	Dark red	Smooth skin, dark crimson interior. Short green tops. Some tolerance to bolting.	STO
WARRIOR (hybrid)		Deep red	Tops are bright green to maroon. Excellent flavor for processing.	HARR

BEETS

SEMI-GLOBE

Variety	Days	Color	Remarks	Sources
BIG RED (hybrid)	55	Deep red	Excellent quality for fresh, canned or pickling use. High yields. Top-shaped.	JUN POR
CROSBY'S EGYPTIAN	42-60	Dull red	Dark red interior. 3-5 in. flattened roots. Good buncher.	DEG EARL HARR HEN LEJ LET SHE SOU VER WET
CROSBY'S GREEN TOP (op)		Dark red	Tall bright green tops. Good for bunching.	HARR
EARLY BLOOD TURNIP	50-68	Dark red	Turnip shaped beet.	WYA

BEETS

Variety	Days	Color	Remarks	Sources
EARLY WONDER STAYS GREEN (op) (GREEN TOP)	48-55	Dark red	16-18 in. tall. Stores well. Use fresh, canned or for greens. Good flavor.	ABU ALL ARC BURG BURP BURR BUT COM DEG EAR EARL FAR FIS GAR GUR HARR HEN JOH LAG LED LEJ MEY PIN PLA PON RAW RIS TWI VER WET WIL WILL
FLAT EGYPTIAN	50	Dark red	Small tops.	HER WILL
LONG SEASON (WINTER KEEPER) (LUTZ GREEN LEAF) (ALWAYS TENDER)	60-80	Deep red	Large, rough-looking but fine keeper. Sweet and tender. All-purpose beet.	ABU BURP COM DEG GAR GUR HIG HUM LAG LED LEM NIC PEA RAW SEE SEED SOU STO TER VES WES WET
RUBY QUEEN	52-60	Dark red	Short top. Greens are also good for processing. A popular variety, sweet-flavored. Somewhat elongated roots.	BURR COM DAN DEG EAR EARL FAR GUR HARR HEN JUN LAG LED LET MEY MID PAR PIN PON RAW RED SEE SEED STO TWI VER WIL
SMOOTHIE	55	Deep red	Small crown makes excellent canning beet.	FAR

BEETS

CYNDRICAL

Variety	Days	Color	Remarks	Sources
CYLINDRA (BUTTER SLICER)	55-60	Dark red	Up to 8 in. long, 1 3/4 in. across. Roots taste good and are ideal for slicing.	ALL BURG BURP BURR COM DAN DEG EAR FAR FIS GUR HEN HUM JUN KIT LAG LEM PIN PON SEE THO TIL TWI VER WET WILL
FORMANOVA (CYLINDRA IMPROVED)	50-56	6-8 x 2½ in. Dark red	Good for pickling or freezing. Tender and tasty.	ARC COO ECO JOH LET NIC RAW STO VES
FORONO	54-70		Very productive, high quality elongated beet. Flavor and quality are excellent. Tops are short. Danish variety. High sugar content.	GUR PIN TER

BABY BEETS

Variety	Days	Color	Remarks	Sources
BADGER BABY	47	Deep red	1 in. diameter. Perfect pickler. Flavorful and tender.	HEN
DWERGINA	58	Dark red	Dutch variety. Dense and smooth texture. Free of zones. Small tap roots.	HIG JOH LEM
GLADIATOR	54	Deep crimson	Golf-ball size is perfect for pickling.	GUR
LITTLE BALL	43-54	Red	Dutch variety. Root ball forms rapidly and is smooth. Harvest quickly in bunches. Plant densely in successions for crop all season long.	BURP LAG PIN SHE STO TER TIL TWI VES WILL
SPINEL BABY BEET	52-60	Red	1½ in. beet. Great for pickling or canning.	NIC THO

BEETS

OTHER COLORS

Variety	Days	Color	Remarks	Sources
ALBINO VEREDUNA	50-60	Pure white	Globe-shaped. Large roots. Spinach-type greens. Good pickler. Sweet, mild flavor.	COO HEN SEE STO TER THO

Variety	Days	Color	Remarks	Sources
BURPEE'S GOLDENBEET	55	Golden-orange	Small round beet used in salads. Good pickler or use tops for greens. Won't bleed.	ABU BURP COO EAR EARL FIS GAR GLE GUR HEN HIG JUN LAG LED LEM NIC SEE SHE STO THO WILL
CHIOGGIA		Red and white rings	Italian variety. A specialty variety.	LEM

BEETS

FOR GREENS

Variety	Days	Remarks	Sources
COME AND CUT AGAIN		Greens are cooked like chard, or use them in salads.	LEM
EARLY WONDER STAYSGREEN			JOH
ERBETTE LEAF BEET		Grown for its fine texture and flavor. Great cut and come again greens. Keep cut for a continued harvest.	COO

BROCCOLI
(Brassica oleracea italica)

Broccoli is big, easy to grow and one plant can produce a huge quantity of food. Unfortunately, broccoli is quite sensitive to heat. There are two types of broccoli, central head with many side branches and central head with few side branches. Broccoli also comes in colors.

CULTURE: Start from seed in peat pots or purchase young plants from nurseries. space the plants 18 to 24 inches apart in rows and leave 36 inches between the rows.

SEASON: Cool.

INSECTS/DISEASES: *APHIDS, CABBAGE LOOPERS, WEBWORMS, CABBAGE WORMS:* Malathion, diazinon, pryethrum, rotenone or ryania.
CLUBROOT: Lanstan.
DOWNY MILDEW, FUNGAL SPOTS: Maneb or fixed copper sprays.

HARVESTING: Cut the heads while they are hard and green—never wait until the buds begin to crack. In many varieties, the more you pick the more new shoots will be produced.

BROCCOLI

CENTRAL HEAD, SIDE SHOOTS

Variety	Days	Head Size	Remarks	Sources
BONANZA (hybrid)	55	3-5 in. diameter	Tight buds on central head. Lots of side shoots. Good raw or cooked. Good freezer.	BURP
CALABRESE (GREEN SPROUTING CALABRESE) (ITALIAN GREEN) (ITALIAN GREEN SPROUTING)	70-85	5-6 in.	Bluish-green, has many side branches. Fine-grained head. Good as buncher or freezer. 2½-3 foot plant.	ABU COM COO DEG ECO FAR JLH LET NIC SEE SEED SOU STO THO WET WIL WILL WYA
CALABRESE CORVET (hybrid)	55	2-2½ in.	Green. Profusion of side heads. Compact. Great for smaller gardens. Good flavor. 2 foot plant.	THO
CITATION (hybrid)		Medium-size	Dark green, dome shaped, tight beads. Resistant to downy mildew.	GUR HARR
CLEOPATRA (hybrid)	50-70	Large	Vigorous medium-size side shoots. Dark green heads. Cold- and drought-resistant. Good fresh or frozen.	LET PIN
CRUISER (hybrid)	58		High-yielding. Does well in hot, dry conditions. Blue-green. Prolonged secondary shoots.	VER
DANDY EARLY	90	6 in., 10 ozs.	Compact, nonspreading plant. Profusion of side shoots.	THO

◀ BROCCOLI

Variety	Days	Color	Remarks	Sources
EARLY EMERALD (hybrid)	50	5-6 in. diameter	Heavy production of side shoots. Blue-green. Great raw or cooked.	PAR
EMPEROR (hybrid)	58-64	8 in.	Tight, deep green head. Widely adapted. Highly tolerant of black rot and downy mildew. Spring or fall crop. Good side shoot production.	DIX JOH PAR SEED STO TWI WILL
GOLIATH	55-75	10-12 in.	Many good-sized side shoots. Heavy producing. Blue-green. Good fresh or frozen. 15 in. plant.	BURP PON STO WILL
GREEN MOUNTAIN	60	Large, compact	Dark green. Large side shoots over the season.	ARC
GREEN SPROUTING DE CICCO	60-70	3-6 in. Flat	Many side shoots. Tall, green. Good freezer. Old Italian variety. Some heat tolerance.	ALL BURG COM DAN DEG EVA FIS GAR JOH LAG LEM MEY PLA RED SOU TIL
GREEN VALIANT (hybrid)	70		Very dense blue-green heads. Good side shoot production. Frost-resistant. Good fall crop.	JOH MID TER TWI VES WIL
MORSES (op)	90	Large	Waltham type. Good side shoot production.	VER
NORTHWEST 29	90-140		Small buds on dark, blue-green head. Heavy yields. Fresh or frozen. Recommended for short-season areas.	HUM
OKTAL (hybrid)	84	8 in., 12 ozs.	Central head somewhat open on very long stem. Excellent side shoot production. Continues until frost.	PIN
PACKMAN (hybrid)	58-80	10 in.	Extremely uniform. Excellent side shoots after main head is cut. Large heavy head with medium beading. Good flavor.	DIX EAR GUR HEN HUM JOH LED LET LIBE MID NIC PIN POR RIS STO TWI WET WILL
PROMINENCE (hybrid)	65		Large, firm head, fine small beads. Good fresh or processed.	HARR RIS TWI
ROYAL CRUISER (hybrid)		Cone-shaped	The side shoots are almost as large as the main head. Side shoots appear over several weeks.	LEM
SEPTAL	78	11 in., 1¾ lbs.	Heads are looser and more segmented than other varieties. Good side shoot producer.	PIN TER
SHOGUN (hybrid)	93	6 in., 14 ozs.	Fall variety. Tolerance to downy mildew and black rot. Weather-tolerant. About 5 side shoots per plant. Japanese variety.	SEE SHE STO TER
SOUTHERN COMET (hybrid)		4-6 in. diameter	Japanese variety. Rapid growth of side shoots. Thin skin, tender.	TER
SOUTHERN COMFORT (hybrid)		Large	Good processor. Bright green, semi-domes. Large beads.	HARR
SPARTAN		7 in.	Dark green head. Short compact plant. Good side shoot production.	WES
SPARTAN K EARLY (op)	47-55	6-8 in.	Short, compact plant. Bluish-green. Good freezer.	BURR BUT EAR FIS GUR HEN LET MID ROS SEE SOU STE STO
TOP STAR (hybrid)	65		Fairly good-size head and side shoot production well into fall.	PIN
WALTHAM 29 (op)	74-80	4-8 in.	Slate-green. Low, compact plant. Good fresh or frozen. Lots of side shoots.	ABU ALL BURR COM FIS GAR JUN LED LET LIBE MEY MID PLA ROS SEE SEED SOU TER THO WES WET

BROCCOLI

CENTRAL HEAD, FEW BRANCHES

Variety	Days	Head Size	Remarks	Sources
ATLANTIC	65	Medium	Short, compact plant.	LET MEY
COMET IMPROVED (hybrid)			Bolts quickly if not harvested when ready.	RAW VES
COMMANDER	81	11 in.	Dark green, large beaded head.	STO
CRUSADER (hybrid)	60-92	6-12 in.	Dome-shaped green head. Smaller and more compact than standard. Flavorful and tender. Withstands heat rot.	JOH STO
GREEN COMET (hybrid)	40-78	6-9 in.	Solid central stem. Tight buds are deep, blue-green. Disease-resistant. Holds shape well. 12-16 in. plant. Good fresh or frozen.	ARC BURP COM DAN DIX EAR FAR GUR HARR LED LET LIBE MEY MID PAR PIE PIN PON POR RIS THO TWI VER WET WIL WYA
GREEN DUKE (hybrid)	69-88	7-8 in.	Dome-shaped head. Good freezer. 22-24 in. plant. For spring or summer planting.	DEG HEN JUN LAG MID PIE TWI WIL
GREEN HORNET	78	7-8 in.	No side branches. Bright green head. Good fresh or processed.	STO
PARAGON (hybrid)	75	8 in.	Blue-green head with extra long spear. Good fresh or frozen.	STO
PREMIUM CROP (hybrid)	58-82	9-10 in.	Medium blue-green. No side shoots. Disease-resistant. 16-18 in. plant. Good fresh or frozen. Good flavor.	ALL BURP COM DIX EAR FAR GUR HARR HEN HIG JOH LAG LED LIBE MID NIC PAR PIN POR SEED SHE SOU STO TWI VES WET WYA
SPRINTER (hybrid)	60-72	Medium	Fast-growing variety. Performs well under high temperatures. Dark green head. Highly disease-tolerant.	VER

BROCCOLI

OTHER TYPES/COLORS

Variety	Days	Head Size	Remarks	Sources
BRONZINO			Short-season variety. A Romanesco broccoli.	COO
CHRISTMAS PURPLE SPROUTING	120		Excellent, full-flavored.	THO
EARLY PURPLE SPROUTING	120-220	Medium	Prolific and frost-hardy. Head turns green when cooked. 3 foot plant.	ABU ECO JLH LEM TER THO
EARLY WHITE PEARL			Hardy plant. Fine white curds. Weather-tolerant.	GLE
FAT SHAN WHITE (CHINESE BROCCOLI)			Japanese variety. Delicate flavor. Very thick main stem which can be cooked along with flowerbuds. Cool weather variety.	GLE JLH RED
FLOCCOLI (hybrid)	60	1¾ lbs.	Cross between broccoli and cauliflower. Should be sown before mid-May. 12-15 in. plant. Good freezer.	THO
GREEN LANCE (hybrid)	50		Actually a member of the Chinese kale family. Seeds, flowering stalks and young leaves can be eaten. Heat- and drought-resistant.	VER
KING ROBERT PURPLE	57	Large	Turns green when cooked. Good freezer.	GLE
LATE PURPLE SPROUTING			English purple variety, bred for over wintering. Large bush.	COO ECO
NINE STAR PERENNIAL	120	Good size	Produces 6 to 9 heads a year, year after year. Good cultivation is essential.	THO

▶

◀ **BROCCOLI**

Variety	Days	Head Size	Remarks	Sources
RAAB (RAPA) (ITALIAN TURNIP) (RAPINI)	50-100	6-8 in.	Lots of branching, no central head. Rapid grower. Cut before the plant flowers. Pungent flavor. Never serve raw, steam for 5 minutes.	BURP COO HARR HUM LED LEM LET PIN RIS TWI
RAAB 7 TOP	85		Harvest at 6 in. long, before blossom opens.	THO
ROMANESCO	58-85	Conical with loads of little spears	3-foot plant produces apple-green spears that can be snapped off individually or all together. Wonderful taste and texture.	ABU COO ECO LEM SEE SHE THO
SALAD	50		Resembles Seven Top Turnip. Sends up shoots. Withstands heat and cold.	WYA
SPIRAL POINT			Olive-green spiral pointed curds. Cross between cauliflower and broccoli. Italian variety.	GLE
VIOLET QUEEN (hybrid)	70		Japanese variety. Deep purple florets turn green when cooked. Large plant.	SHE
WHITE SPROUTING	105-120	Small	Heavy cropper. White heads that look like cauliflower. Mild flavor. 3 foot plant. Good freezer.	COO ECO JLH LEM SEE THO
WHITE SPROUTING LATE	250		Has some cauliflower genes. Creamy white color. English variety.	TER

BRUSSELS SPROUTS
(Brassica oleracea gemmifera)

This member of the cabbage family produces edible sprouts that look like tiny cabbages in the axils of the leaves. Brussels sprouts are easy to grow if you live in the right climate. One plant will keep producing until you wonder if it will ever stop.

CULTURE: Purchase plants from local nurseries or start from seed in peat pots. Plant 12 to 18 inches apart, in rows 24 to 30 inches apart as soon as the soil can be worked.

SEASON: Cool.

INSECTS/DISEASES: *APHIDS, CABBAGE LOOPERS, WEBWORMS, FLEA BEETLES, CABBAGE WORMS:* Malathion, diazinon, pyrethrum, rotenone, sevin or ryania.

CLUBROOT: Lanstan.

DOWNY MILDEW, FUNGAL SPOTS: Maneb or fixed copper sprays.

HARVESTING: Pick the lowest sprouts each time you pick, and break off any leaves left below the 'sprout'. Don't remove the top leaves.

BRUSSELS SPROUTS			
Variety	Days	Remarks	Sources
ARCHILLES (hybrid)		Mid-size, tight round sprouts. Good Freezer. Harvest from October to February.	THO
ANAGOR	90	Cold-resistant.	HER
ARIES (hybrid)		English variety. Medium-size, hard, tough green sprouts. Cold-hardy. High yields from November to February.	TER
BEDFORD FILLBASKET	92	Harvest from October through December. Heavy yields of solid sprouts. Good freezer.	THO
CAMBRIDGE NO. 5		Harvest from January to March. Winter-hardy. High-quality walnut-size sprouts.	THO
CAPTAIN MARVEL (hybrid)	96	Small, hardy ¾ in. sprouts. Japanese variety. Harvest October through December. 26 in. plant.	STO TER TWI
CITADEL (hybrid)		Tight, medium-size sprouts. Good freezer. Harvest until late March.	THO

▶

Variety	Days	Remarks	Sources
DOLMIC	102	European variety. Ready late August. Dark green oval sprouts. Good yields.	STO
EARLY DWARF DANISH (op)	95-105	Large sprouts on short plant. Well-suited short-season variety.	ABU GAR HIG SEE
EARLY HALF TALL		Heavy crops. Ready by mid- to late autumn.	ECO
FIELDSTAR (hybrid)		Dutch variety. Medium-size, hard light green sprouts. Harvest from November to February.	TER
FORTRESS (hybrid)		Bred for hardiness. Dutch variety. Big yields. Harvest from December through March.	TER
HOOSA (hybrid)		Harvest from November to March. Tight, medium-sized dark green sprouts. Good freezer.	THO
JADE CROSS E (hybrid)	90-97	26 in. plant. Oval, dark blue-green pods. Good freezer. Produces twice as many sprouts as open pollinated types.	BURP DAN EAR HUM JOH LIBE MEY MID NIC RAW RIS SEED STO TWI WIL
JADE CROSS (hybrid)	80-95	24 in. plant. Oval, blue-green pods. Heavy yielder. Good freezer. Sprouts grow all the way up the stalk. Excellent flavor.	ARC BURG COM GUR HEN LAG LED LET PAR PIN PON POR RAW STO VES WET
LONG ISLAND	90-95	1 ½ in. pods. Fall frost improves flavor.	FAR WYA
LONG ISLAND IMPROVED (CATSKILL)	85-95	20 in. upright plant with 1¼ in. sprouts that cover most of the plant. Good yielder with several pickings. Good freezer.	ABU ALL ARC BURR BUT COM DAN DEG EAR HEN HUM LAG LED LEJ LET LIBE NIC PAR PIN PON RED SEE SEED SOU STO TIL WIL WILL WYA
LUNET (hybrid)		Medium-large, firm sprouts. Dutch variety. Very good flavor. Highest yields. Harvest from November and December.	TER
OLIVER (hybrid)	90	Medium-green, smooth ¾ oz. sprouts. Vigorous in diverse climates.	BURP JOH
ORMAVON (hybrid)		Harvest from November to February. Good freezer. Produces a cabbage on top of the plant. Sprouts all the way up the stem. Cabbage top can be harvested without affecting the sprouts.	THO
PEER GYNT (hybrid)	140	Dark green sprouts of high quality.	THO
PRINCE MARVEL (hybrid)	90-97	35 in. plant. Firm, smooth, rounded well spaced sprouts. Has better tolerance to bottom and center rot. Use fresh or processed.	HARR PAR PIE POR RIS STO TWI VER
ROODNERF LATE SUPREME (op)		Medium-tall plant. Yields from November to March.	TER
RUBINE RED		Plants with red foliage and red sprouts. Distinct flavor.	SEE WILL
SAILOR (hybrid)		Medium-sized green sprouts.	SEED
SEVEN HILLS		Bountiful crop is ready early winter.	ECO

◄ BRUSSELS SPROUTS

Variety	Days	Remarks	Sources
STABOLITE (hybrid)		30-36 in. plant. Dutch variety. Dense leaf cover protects sprouts. Plant in mid-May and harvest from December to April.	TER THO
STIEKEMA-VROSA ORIGINAL	100	Large uniform sprouts are medium-green. Very productive.	SEE WILL
VALIANT (hybrid)	110	Dutch variety. Heavy yields button-like sprouts. Rich flavored. Rot- and burst-resistant. Harvest late fall through winter.	SHE

CABBAGE
(Brassica oleracea capitata)

Cabbages offer a delightful number of varieties for the home gardener. Cabbage produces in great abundance and is very hardy, withstanding temperatures down to 10 or 15° F. In growing cabbage it is important to select varieties for the time of year you intend to grow. Decide whether you want to harvest in summer or late fall, then make your selections working back from the maturity period.

CULTURE: Sow the seeds a half-inch deep in flats or peat pots about six to eight weeks before you intend to set the plants outdoors. Space early varieties 12 to 16 inches apart in rows 20 to 24 inches apart. Space winter varieties 18 to 24 inches apart in rows 30 to 36 inches apart.

SEASON: Cool.

INSECTS/DISEASES: *APHIDS, BLISTER BEETLES, CABBAGE LOOPERS, WEB WORMS, CABBAGE WORM:* Malathion, diazinon, pyrethrum, rotenone, Sevin or ryania.
    CLUBROOT: Lanstan.
    DOWNY MILDEW, FUNGAL SPOTS: Maneb or fixed copper sprays.

HARVESTING: When cabbage reaches proper size for its variety pick before splitting.

CABBAGE—EARLY
TO 75 DAYS; ROUND, GREEN

Variety	Days	Head	Remarks	Sources
ASGROW BANNER (hybrid)	62	2½ lbs. 5½ in.	Compact, short-stemmed plant. Medium-size core.	LET
BADGER MARKET	70-78	2¾-3 lbs.	Dark, blue-green head holds well. Yellows-resistant.	GUR LET
BERGKABIS			Forms a head quickly. Does not stand long without bolting. Excellent raw or cooked.	RAW
CC CROSS (hybrid)	45	3lbs.	Green. Not yellows-resistant.	
CHARMANT	52-64	2½-3 lbs.	Vigorous grower. Stonehead type. Few outer leaves. Deep green. Yellows- and tip burn-resistant.	TWI
COPENHAGEN MARKET	68	3½ lbs.	All-purpose cabbage.	ARC BRO BURR DAN EAR FIS GUR HEN LAG LEJ LET MEY MID STO
COPENHAGEN MARKET LATE	70	6½ lbs. 6-8 in.	Not yellows-resistant. All-purpose.	DEG WIL
DERBY DAY	61	2½ lbs.	Holds well. Dark green.	JOH
EARLIANA	60	2 lbs. 4½-5 in.	Golden Acre type.	BURP DEG PAR
EARLY DUTCH ROUND	70-72	4-5 lbs. 7 in.	Not yellows-resistant.	MID WET

►

Variety	Days	Head	Remarks	Sources
EARLY GREEN BALL	63	2½ lbs. 4 in.	English variety. Globe-shaped head has small core. Not yellows-tolerant.	STO
EARLY MARVEL (EARLY DITMARSH)	59-65	3-4 lbs. 5 in.	Dark green round head. Short core. High eating quality. Not tolerant to yellows.	DEG STO
EARLY WONDER	60-62	3 lbs.	Dutch variety. Solid head.	WILL
EMERALD ACRE	61	3-4 lbs. 4 in.	Medium-green. Good tolerance to bolting. Not yellows-tolerant.	STO
EMERALD CROSS (hybrid)	62-67	4-5 lbs. 7 in.	Blue-green. Copenhagen Market characteristics. Japanese variety. Very attractive, space-efficient plant.	ARC BURP EAR HEN KIT PIN STO WILL
FERRY'S EARLY DUTCH ROUND	70-75	4-5 lbs. 7 in.	Blue-green.	WYA
GOLDEN ACRE	58-65	2-3 lbs.	Gray-green. Resistant to diseases. Quite sweet. Short-stemmed. Used for slaw or kraut.	ABU ALL ARC BURG DAN DEG EAR FIS GAR GRA GUR HEN HUM JUN LAG LED LET MID PIE RAW ROS SEE SOU STE TER TIL WET WIL WILL
GOLDEN ACRE RESISTANT			Some yellows tolerance.	BURR MEY RIS
GOLDEN ACRE SPECIAL	63		Yellows-resistant.	SEED
GRAND PRIZE (hybrid)		3-6 lbs. 7-8 in.	Blue-green. Excellent wrapper leaves. Resistant to fusarium and tip burn.	MID RIS
GRENADIER (hybrid)	52-63	3-5 lbs. 8 in.	Good flavor, firm texture. Prefer spring and fall growth. Not yellows-tolerant.	PIN SHE STO
GREENBACK	74	3-5 lbs. 7-8 in.	Yellows-resistant. Firm head.	BURR LET MEY MID MEY TWI
GREENBOY (hybrid)	75	5 lbs. 7 in.	Blue-green. Compact head with short core. Ball-head type. Fair tolerance to black speck. Good for sauerkraut.	BURR MID RIS TWI WIL
HANCOCK (hybrid)	70		Resistant to yellows, black rot and tip burn. Blue-green. Firm interior, short core.	JUN
HEADS UP (hybrid)	65		Globe-shaped. Bright green foliage. Resistant to yellows. Holds well.	HARR
HEAD START (hybrid)	67		Slightly flattened globe shape. Copenhagen type. Spring or fall variety.	LET
HEAVY WEIGHTER (hybrid)	75	15 lbs.	Round, slightly flattened head. Vigorous grower.	PAR
HYBRID NO. 15 (hybrid)	70		Round head. Blue-green foliage. Stands well. Compact plant, short core.	HARR
HYBRID NO. 39	65	3¾ lbs.	Yellows-resistant.	MID
JET PAK YR (hybrid)	64-66	5-6 in.	Blue-green with purpling outer leaves. Short core. Sweet taste. Yellows-tolerant.	MID RIS

◄ CABBAGE—EARLY

Variety	Days	Head Size	Remarks	Sources
LANGEDIJKER EARLY	65		Remains in good condition without splitting.	WILL
MARKET TOPPER (hybrid)	73		Blue-green. Adapted to Eastern United States. Productive and vigorous. Stands well without bursting.	HARR
MARKET VICTOR (hybrid)	65		Harvest promptly when ready. Bright blue-green foliage.	HARR PIE
MINICOLE (hybrid)	70		Small, round to slightly oval head. Short core. Can stand for months without splitting.	SEED THO VES
PEDRILLO (hybrid)	70		Round head, short core. Few outer leaves. Stands without splitting.	SEED
PERFECT ACTION (hybrid)	73	2-4 lbs.	Dark green, round dense head. Split-resistant. Yellows-resistant.	JOH
POLAR GREEN (hybrid)	56	2½-3 lbs.	Compact plant. Light-green head. Good tolerance to tip burn and low temperatures. Not yellows-tolerant.	STO
PRIMAX	63	2-4 lbs.	A larger strain of Golden Acre. Short stem and dark wrapper leaves. Resists splitting.	GAR JOH
PRIME PAK (hybrid)	74	3-4 lbs. 5-6 in.	Blue-green. Resistant to yellows.	STO TWI WIL
PRIMO	65		Compact, ball-headed. Seems to do well in any soil.	ECO THO
PRIME TIME (hybrid) YR	72	2½-5 lbs. 6¾ in.	Silvery blue-green. Good interior. Short core. Yellows-tolerant.	MID STO
PRINCESS (hybrid)	66-75	3-8 lbs. 6¾ in.	Medium, gray-green. Medium size core. Yellows-resistant.	HARR STO TER
QUICKSTEP (hybrid)	57		Sow in February for crop by June. Good flavor.	THO
QUISTO (hybrid)	70	4-5 lbs.	All-purpose cabbage. Blue-green. Firm texture.	PIN
RAPID BALL (hybrid)			Medium size.	POR
REGALIA (hybrid)	64	2-3 lbs.	Yellows-, black rot-, tip burn- tolerant. Solid interiors. Short cores. Tolerant to bursting.	STO
SALARITE	57	5½ in.	Semi-savoyed Ballhead type. Deep green. Solid buttery yellow interior. Compact plant.	GUR NIC STO TER
SHAMROCK (hybrid)	60	3½-4 lbs.	Blue-green. Crisp and sweet.	RAW THO
STOKES VIKING GOLDEN ACRE	65	2¾-4 lbs. 5½ in.	High yellows tolerance. Compact plant.	STO
STONEHEAD (hybrid)	50-70	3½ lbs. 6 in.	Blue-green. Firm head. Produces well in small area. Excellent all-purpose cabbage.	ARC BURG BURP COM DEG EAR FAR GUR JUN LED LET LIBE MEY MID NIC PIE PIN POR RAW STO THO TWI VES WET

Variety	Days	Head	Remarks	Sources
SUN UP (hybrid)	64	20 in.	Blue-green, slightly flattened head. Short core. A Copenhagen hybrid.	HARR HEN
SUPERETTE (hybrid)	66	3-7½ lbs. 8 in.	Silvery blue-green. Yellows-resistant. Does well in New York and Florida.	LET LIBE MID STO
SUPERMARKET (hybrid)	72	3½-4 lbs. 6½ in.	Dark blue-green. Short core. Strong tolerance to yellows, black rot and black speck.	TWI
TASTIE (hybrid)	68	4½ lbs.	Close substitute for Stonehead. Blue-green.	BURR VES
TITANIC 90 YR (hybrid)	73		Blue-green. Excellent for kraut.	LET SEED
TUCANA (hybrid)	62	3 lbs.	Requires proper moisture for larger heads. Will split if not harvested at maturity.	STO
VIKING EXTRA EARLY	62	4½ lbs.	Blue-green. Golden Acre type. No tolerance to yellows. Short core.	STO
WISCONSIN GOLDEN ACRE	67	6 in.	May be planted close together. Dark blue.	COM

CABBAGE—MID-SEASON
75 TO 90 DAYS; ROUND, GREEN

Variety	Days	Size	Remarks	Sources
ALL SEASONS			Solid, compact head. Heat- and drought-resistant.	WYA
ATLAS (hybrid)	75-80	4-5 lbs. 10 in.	Resists splitting and premature bolting. Resistant to black rot and damping off.	NIC
BADGER BLUE BOY	85-90		Bright, blue-green. Resembles Badger Ballhead. Stores well.	TWI
BLUE BOY (hybrid)	78	4½ lbs.	Semi-round. Deep blue-green. Short core. Yellows-resistant. Tolerant to black rot.	TWI
BLUE PAK (hybrid)	76-78	2¼-4 lbs.	Deep blue-green. Solid interior. Resistant to fusarium yellow.	LET LIBE MID STO
BLUE RIBBON	76	3½ lbs.	Round to oval shape. Deep blue-color. Yellows-resistant. Disease-tolerant.	TWI
BRAVO	85		Rugged habit. Flattened-globe shape. Gray-green. Large frame.	HARR PIE
BURPEE'S COPENHAGAN MARKET	72	4-4½ lbs. 6½ in.	Heavy yield. Solid head. White interior. Good for kraut.	BURP
CABARET (hybrid)	78		Dark blue-green. Compact, tight outer leaves. Black rot-resistant. Yellows-resistant.	HARR
COLE CASH (hybrid)	86		Blue-green. Good holding ability. Well-wrapped heads. Tolerant to yellows and tip burn.	HARR
CONDOR (hybrid)	78		Blue-green. Medium length core. Good wrapper leaves. Tolerant to fusarium yellows.	HARR

◀ **CABBAGE—MID-SEASON**

Variety	Days	Head	Remarks	Sources
ENTERPRISE (hybrid)	75		Full globe shape. Bright-green. Small core. Yellows-tolerant.	LET
ERDENO (hybrid)	88	6-8 lbs.	Blue-green. Dense interior. Frost-tolerant. Adapted to lower fertile soils.	JOH SHE
FALCON (hybrid)	80	9 lbs. 10 in.	Used for kraut, coleslaw and storage.	STO
FORTUNA (hybrid)	80	2-3 lbs.	Blue-green. Vigorous plant with good wrapper leaves.	MID
GLOBE	75-80	6 lbs. 6 in.	Yellows-resistant.	DEG MID
GLORY OF ENKHOUSEN (ENKHUIZEN)	75	6-10 lbs.	Dark green. Moderately dense interior.	DEG GAR SEE WILL
GOURMET (hybrid)	75	3-5 lbs. 5-6 in.	Blue-green. Round to flat head. Yellows-resistant.	MID PIE RIS STO WIL
GRAND PRIZE (hybrid)	75		Blue-green. Good holding ability. Yellows-resistant.	MID
GRAND SLAM (hybrid)	82	7-8 in.	Blue-green. Well-compacted head. Excellent wrapper leaves. Good fresh or for kraut. Fusarium- and yellows-resistant.	FAR LED RIS
HERCULES (hybrid)	83	8-10 in.	All-purpose cabbage. Resists splitting.	GUR WIL
HISTONA (hybrid)	75		High yields. Short core. Good kraut cabbage. Good tip burn resistance.	SEED
HYBRID NO. 5	78	3½-4 lbs.	Blue-green. Widely adapted. Yellows-resistant.	TWI
JUMBO (LARGE LATE DRUMHEAD)	78-105	12-16 lbs. 7½-9 in.	Not yellows-resistant. Dutch variety. Good keeper.	BURG STO
KING COLE (hybrid)	68-70	4-10 lbs. 7-8 in.	Blue-green. Good kraut cabbage. Yellows-resistant.	HEN LED LET LIBE MEY SEED STO
KRAUTPACKER (hybrid)	87		Dense interior. Short core. Use for coleslaw or processing. Yellows-resistant.	SEED
LITTLE ROCK (hybrid)	84	2½-7 lbs. 6-7 in.	Ball-head type. Can be harvested small or allowed to grow for kraut. Resists splitting.	JUN LET LIBE MID RIS SEED STO
MARION MARKET	70-80	5½-7 lbs. 8 in.	Blue-green. Kraut cabbage. Yellows-resistant.	ARC BURR DEG EAR LED LET MID WET
MARKET PRIZE (hybrid)	66-76		Blue-green. Resembles Early Danish variety.	DIX HARR LED PIE
MULTIKEEPER (hybrid)	86		Disease-tolerant. Short-term storer.	STO
OLYMPIA (hybrid)	85		Good wrapper leaves. For fresh or kraut use. Tip burn-resistant.	MID
PERFECT BALL (hybrid)	84		Dark, blue-green. Summer or fall crop. Short core. Yellows-resistant.	JOH

▶

Variety	Days	Head	Remarks	Sources
PRIME CHOICE	74	2½-5 lbs. 6½ in.	Dark, blue-green. Does not split easily. Yellows-tolerant.	STO
RIO VERDE (hybrid)	79-85	5 lbs. 7 in.	Blue-green, slightly flattened firm head. Yellows-resistant. Fairly cold-tolerant. Given enough space it grows into nice kraut size.	DIX HARR MEY MID RIS TWI WIL
ROUND DUTCH	75-78	3½-5 lbs. 6-7 in.	Dark blue. Cold-resistant. Does not store well.	MID WIL
ROUNDUP YR (hybrid)	76-80	3-9½ lbs.	Slightly flattened head. Good kraut cabbage as well as for slaw and cooking.	JUN LET LIBE SEED STO TWI
SHOWBOAT (hybrid)	78		Dark blue-green. Medium-short core. Holds well without bursting. Black rot-resistant.	HARR
SUPERPACK (hybrid)	78	2-6 lbs.	Blue-green. Short core, dense interior. Resistant to yellows. Tolerant to black speck.	JOH
SURVIVOR (hybrid)	85	3 lbs.	Dark blue-green. Disease-tolerant. Multi-purpose cabbage. Short-term storer.	STO

CABBAGE—LATE

90+ DAYS; ROUND, GREEN

Variety	Days	Head	Remarks	Sources
APEX (hybrid)	95	3-5 lbs.	Holds for weeks without cracking. Short core. Good frost resistance.	JOH
APRIL GREEN	99		Short-stemmed. Dark green Dutch variety. Landgenfiker type.	SEE STO VES
BARTOLO (hybrid)	115		High yield. Long-term storage. Short core. Dark green. Tolerant to gray speck and pepperspot.	SEED
BISLET (hybrid)	99	8¾ lbs.	Dark green. Solid head will store until spring. Some yellows tolerance.	STO
BRUTUS (hybrid)	105		Thrip- and gray speck-tolerant. Long storer.	SEED
BURPEE'S DANISH ROUND-HEAD	105	5-7 lbs. 7-8 in.	All-purpose cabbage. Good winter keeper.	BURP DAN
CUSTODIAN (hybrid)	95	4-6 lbs.	Storage cabbage. Bright green. Tolerates frost. Tolerant to black rot.	JOH STO
DANISH BALLHEAD	100-105	3-8 lbs.	Dark green. Long stemmed. All-purpose cabbage. Grows well in mountain sections. Good keeper.	ABU ALL BURG BURR COM DEG EAR FAR FIS GAR GUR HARR JUN LED LET MEY PIN SEE SEED TER TIL WET WILL
DECEMA (LANGEDIJKER LATE WINTER-KEEPER)	95-120		Dutch variety. Heavy yielder. Light green. Holds color well during storage.	SEED VES WILL
DECEMA EXTRA	125		A little greener than other storage-type cabbages.	SEED
EVERGREEN BALLHEAD	98		Apple green color. Heavy yielder. Storage cabbage.	STO

CABBAGE—LATE

Variety	Days	Pods	Remarks	Sources
EXCEL (hybrid)	100		Deep blue-green. Large plant. Good yields. Resistant to yellows.	HARR
GOLIATH (ZWAAN JUMBO)	105	20-25 lbs.	Give these plenty of room. Pale green. Good keeper.	GUR HEN
GREEN WINTER (op)	120		Blue-green. Tall and vigorous. Excellent long-storage type.	HARR
HARRIS RESISTANT DANISH (hybrid)	95		Blue-green. Short-stemmed. Heavy yielder. Yellows-resistant.	HARR
HIDENA (hybrid)	100		Thin leaves, dense structure and short core. Dark green. Keeps well in cold storage.	SEED
HINOVA (hybrid)	100		Gray-green leaves. Very short core. Strong grower. Yellows-resistant. Use for coleslaw or processing. Good storer.	SEED
HISTAR (hybrid)	125	12 lbs. 10-16 in.	Bred for kraut. Dutch variety. Rapid grower. White interior.	TER
HITOMA (hybrid)	100		Short core, dense interior. Used for coleslaw or processing.	SEED
HOLLANDER SHORT STEM	105	16 lbs. 6 in.	Medium, blue-green. No hollow spaces.	DEG
HOUSTON EVERGREEN			Very firm. Retains green color in storage. Has few outer leaves.	RAW STO VES
HYBRID H (hybrid)	95		Blue-green. Good wrapper leaves. Disease-resistant. Limited storage.	HARR
KRAUT KING (hybrid)	95		Short core. Use for coleslaw and sauerkraut.	SEED
LANGEDIEER LATE WHITE	95		Light green. Large, firm heads. Storage type.	WILL
LARIAT	125	5-8 lbs.	Dark green to blue-green. Well-packed interior. Needs fertile soil and early planting.	JOH
LATE DANISH (hybrid)			Round and firm head. Blue-green. Short-stemmed. Uniform and compact.	PON
LENNOX (hybrid)	105		Late-storage type. Highly productive. Short core.	SEED VES
OCALA (hybrid)	110-115	8 lbs.	Widely adapted. High yields. Solid white heads are used for kraut. Holds well. Tolerance to yellows and black rot.	BURR
PENN STATE BALL-HEAD	90-110	4-8 lbs. 7-9 in.	Whitish. For kraut. Good winter keeper. An improved short-stem Ballhead type. Good wrapper leaves and solid head.	GAR HUM LET RAW
POLINIUS (hybrid)	115		Dense structure, short core. Highly tolerant to gray speck and pepperspot. Holds well in cold storage.	SEED

Variety	Days	Head	Remarks	Sources
PREDENA (hybrid)	95		Dutch variety. Holds for long time without splitting. Dark green. Short core. Use for coleslaw.	SEED
QUICK GREEN STORAGE	90		Short-season variety. Storage type.	STO
QUINTAL D'ALSACE	120		French heirloom variety. Famed for sauerkraut. A big cabbage, so leave plenty of growing space.	LEM
RENOVA (hybrid)			Gray-green. Storage type as well as for coleslaw. Yellows-resistant.	SEED
RODOLFO (hybrid)			Very productive. Yellows-resistant. Use for sauerkraut.	SEED
SAFEKEEPER (hybrid)	95		Storage type. Heavy frame and wrapper leaves. No yellows tolerance.	STO
SANIBEL (hybrid)	90-92	10 lbs. 10-11 in.	Medium-green. Good fresh, kraut or for storage.	JUN LET LIBE POR
STONAR (hybrid)	96	8¾ lbs.	Long-term storage cabbage. Thrips- and yellows-tolerant.	STO
STONEHEAD	100	5 lbs.	One of the longest keepers.	RED
STRUCKTON (hybrid)	98		Blue-gray. Storage type. Thrips- and yellows-tolerant.	STO
SUPERIOR DANISH	98	5-8 lbs.	Harvest size in late August. Blue-green with rosy-edged wrapper leaves. Medium-term storage.	FIS JOH
WINTERKEEPER (hybrid)	93		Short core. Dark green. Some tolerance to black rot. Tolerance to bursting.	STO
WINTERSTAR (hybrid)			Flattish-round shape. Gray-green. Short-stemmed.	SEED
WISCONSIN HOLLANDER NO. 8	105-110		Excellent storer. Yellows-resistant.	DEG RIS WET
ZERLINA (hybrid)	120		Long-storage type. Good holding ability. Tolerant to rust. Use for coleslaw or long storage.	SEED

CABBAGE

SMALL

Variety	Days	Size	Remarks	Sources
ASGROW BANNER (hybrid)	62	2½ lbs. 5½ in.	Small, compact, short-stemmed. Medium-size core.	LET
BABY EARLY (hybrid)	50	2 lbs.	Red. Nice tight head. Excellent flavor.	PIN
BADGER BABY HEAD	69	2-3 lbs.	Good choice for small gardens. Good flavor and quality. Perfect for single meal.	HEN
FIRST EARLY MARKET 218	240	1-1½ lbs.	Cold-hardy English variety. Pointed, loose head.	TER
HOLLAND WINTER EXPORT	90		Popular small cabbage in England and Holland. Peel away shriveled outer leaves for white heart. Ideal for coleslaw.	LEM

◀ ## CABBAGE—SMALL

Variety	Days	Size	Remarks	Sources
LIBRA (hybrid)	85	Size of a grape-fruit	Dutch variety. Recommended for small gardens.	LEM

CABBAGE
FLAT

Variety	Days	Size	Remarks	Sources
ALL SEASONS	85-90	12 lbs. 10-12 in.	Yellows-resistant. Winter storer. Can be used for slaw, fresh or kraut.	DEG
BRUNSWICK	85-90	6-9 lbs.	Old variety. Flattened head that stores well. Use fresh or for kraut.	GAR GLE
CELTIC (hybrid)			Very cold-hardy. English variety. Sow March to May.	THO
CHRISTMAS DRUMHEAD			Sow April to June. Very hard, dwarf and compact.	THO
EARLY DWARF FLAT	71	4-5 lbs.	Good storer.	FIS WET
EARLY FLAT DUTCH	84-95		Heat-resistant. Few outer leaves. Excellent variety for sauerkraut.	ARC DEG GUR LAG MEY MID POR SOU STE WYA
LATE FLAT DUTCH	100-110	15 lbs. 6 in.	European variety. Bluish-green. Good winter keeper.	ARC DEG JUN LED LET MID ROS STE WYA
LATE PREMIUM DUTCH FLAT	100-105	8-14 lbs. 12 in.	Slow grower. Does better in cool weather.	BURG FAR HEN MEY SEE SOU TIL WET WIL
RIO VERDE (hybrid)	85		Blue-green. Flat, medium core. Large, vigorous plant. Excellent wrapper leaves.	HARR
STEINS EARLY DUTCH FLAT	75-85	5½-6 lbs. 8-9 in.	Good winter keeper.	LET MEY SEE
TRI STAR (hybrid)	76	6½-8 lbs.	For spring or fall crops. Small core. Resistant to tip burn. For slaw or kraut.	BURP
WISCONSIN ALL SEASONS	90-95	9lbs. 10-12 in.	Blue. Yellows-resistant.	BURR DEG FAR LET WET

CABBAGE
POINTED HEADS

Variety	Days	Size	Remarks	Sources
APRIL			Sow late summer or spring. Excellent cold tolerance.	ECO THO
CHARLESTON WAKEFIELD (LONG ISLAND WAKEFIELD)	70-75	4-5 lbs. 8 in.	Dark green conical head holds well.	DEG MEY POR SEE SOU WET WYA
DURHAM EARLY	62		Sow spring or late summer. Cold-tolerant. High quality.	THO

▶

Variety	Days	Size	Remarks	Sources
EARLY JERSEY WAKEFIELD	62-70	2-3 lbs.	Dark green. Reliable, well adapted old favor-ite with tight cone-shaped head.	ABU ARC BURG BURP COM DEG DIX EAR FIS GAR HEN HUM JOH LAG LED LET NIC PON POR ROS SEE SOU TIL WET WILL WYA
EXPRESS	60		Green. Firm, crisp and tender.	WILL
GREYHOUND	64		Sow February/April. Average flavor.	ECO THO
HISPI (hybrid)			Sow February/June or late July/September. All-purpose cabbage.	THO
HORNSPI (hybrid)			Grows to a huge size.	THO
JERSEY QUEEN	58-63	2-3 lbs.	Dark green. Disease-resistant.	FAR
JERSEY WAKEFIELD	58-75	2-3 lbs.	Compact plant. Yellows-resistant.	GUR JUN PAR

CABBAGE
SAVOYED

Variety	Days	Size	Remarks	Sources
ALEXANDERS NO. 1 (op)	200		English variety.	TER
BEST OF ALL			Extra-large head can be cut early winter. Stands cold well.	ECO
BLUE MAX	85	3-4 lbs.	Tender texture. Blue and lime-green in color.	JOH SEE
CANADA SAVOY	73	3½ lbs.	Small savoy. Dark green. Not yellows-toler-ant.	STO
CHIEFTAIN SAVOY	80-90	5-7 lbs. 8 in.	Blue-green. Flat globe shape. Will stand for long time without splitting. Good for slaw. Tolerant of late frosts.	ABU COM DEG DIX GAR HARR HEN HUM LED LET MEY MID PON RAW RIS SEED STO TER WET WYA
DARK GREEN SAVOY	85	3-6 lbs. 9 in.	Dark green. Slow to bolt.	RED
DES VERTUS	75	3 lbs.	French variety. Deep blue-green. Can stand heat better than most. Excellent all-around variety.	SHE
DRUMHEAD SAVOY	90		Firm, well-blanched, crisp head.	ALL
EARLY CURLY (hybrid)	74	3-4½ lbs.	Well-curled. Sweet flavor. Small core. Green.	BURP
ICE PRINCE	83	4 lbs.	Dark green. Well-savoyed.	STO
ICE QUEEN (hybrid)	80	3½-4 lbs.	Dark green. Well-crumpled. Small head.	STO
JANUARY KING	100-110	1½-5 lbs.	Dark bluish-green outside, pale green inside. Sweeter than most savoys. Will stand light frost. Use fresh or cooked. Leaves turn bright pink with cool weather.	ABU ECO LEM NIC RAW TER THO

◀ **CABBAGE—SAVOYED**

Variety	Days	Size	Remarks	Sources
KAPERTJES	65		Fine curled head for summer use.	WILL
LANGEDIJKER WINTER KEEPER			Light green. Hardy.	SEE
NOVUM, ORIGINAL	80		Very dark green. Heavily crinkled. For summer and fall. Good taste.	WILL
ORMSKIRK EARLY			Large, round dark green head with flower-like leaves. Hardy to 10 degrees.	ECO
PERFECTION DRUMHEAD	90-100	6-7 lbs. 9-10 in.	Retains green color when cooked.	DEG WILL
SAVOY ACE (hybrid)	70-90	4-5 lbs.	Deep green, almost round head. Known for withstanding summer heat.	BURG BURP DAN HARR JUN LED MEY PIE PIN TWI WET
SAVOY DE VERTUS	75		Dark green. Richly textured leaves.	LEM
SAVOY EARLY DRUMHEAD	80	3 lbs.	Short, flat, round. Dark green curly leaves.	DEG
SAVOY KING (hybrid)	82-120	4-5 lbs.	Dark green. Vigorous, high-yielding. Stands heat better than others. Semi-flat head.	ARC DEG EAR FAR GUR LAG LET NIC PAR RIS STO TER THO TWI VES WILL
SAVOY LANGEDIJKER WINTER KEEPER	80		Original variety. Light green. Good storer.	SEE WILL
SAVOY LATE DRUMHEAD	90-100	3-5 lbs.	Round. Dark green. Finely curled solid head.	DEG
SAVOY MONARCH	110	9-10 in.	Flat-topped, light green. White core. Vigorous. For slaw or salad.	TER
SAVOY PRINCESS	72	3-3½ lbs.	Semi-globe head. Medium core. Dark green. Well-crinkled leaves. Good for spring or fall crops.	TWI
SAVOY QUEEN	88	5 lbs.	Nearly the same as Savoy King. Yellows-tolerant.	STO
SAVOY WINTER KING (hybrid)	80-100	3-5 lbs.	Dark green. Very hardy. Some frost resistance.	TER WILL
SPIVOY			Exceptional flavor. Long standing and very hardy.	THO
SPRING SONG (hybrid)			Japanese variety. Grayish-green leaves are slightly ruffled. Widely adapted.	LEM
VANGUARD	70		Sweet and tender.	FIS
WINTERKEEPER			Dark green. Half hardy. Storage type.	SEE
WIROSA (hybrid)			Round. Gray-green. 6 week storage.	SEED
WIVOY	220		Dutch variety. Medium-green. Highly savoyed. Cold-resistant.	TER

RED CABBAGE

Variety	Days	Size	Remarks	Sources
APRIL RED (hybrid)	95	6 lbs.	Sow seed late April/May. Dense round heads are well wrapped.	STO
AUTORO (hybrid)	100-115		Slightly oval, medium-large. Dense dark red structure. Tolerant to cold fall weather. Cold-storage type. Use fresh or processed.	JOH SEED
LANGEDIJKER DARK-RED WINTER KEEPER	100		Strong storage quality. Solid red head.	SEE WILL
LANGEDIJKER RED, EARLIEST		2 lbs.	Ideal for small gardens.	WILL
LANGEDIJKER RED WINTER KEEPER, ORIGINAL #218			Oblong, firm head. Good keeper.	WILL
LASSO (op)	70-75	2-4 lbs.	Heads are on the small side. Very firm. Has few outer leaves. Very dependable import from Denmark. Stands well without splitting.	FIS GAR JOH PIN SEE
LUCILLE (hybrid)	75	3 lbs.	Very solid round head.	STO
MAMMOTH RED ROCK	90	5-8 lbs.	Red-purple. Stores well. Use in slaw, salads, or pickle it.	ABU GAR GUR LEJ LET NIC VES WILL
METEOR	110	6-8 in.	Bright red. Dutch variety.	STO TER
PIERRETTE	78	3½ lbs. 6 in.	Tolerant to splitting.	STO
PREKO	75	2½ lbs.	Blood-red. Compact. High quality.	STO
RED ACRE	75-85	2-5 lbs. 6-7 in.	Reddish-purple. Crisp leaves and tender core. Short stem.	ALL BURG BURP BURR COM DAN DEG DIX FAR FIS GUR HARR HEN HUM LET PON POR RAW RIS ROS SOU TIL WES WYA
RED DANISH BALLHEAD	92-97	4-6 lbs.	Solid ball-shaped head. Good storage type. Purple-red color. Fairly tolerant to yellows.	HARR RIS SEED STO
RED DEBUT	85		Deep red. Stands well without splitting. Will store for winter use. Good for slaws, salad or for pickling.	VES
RED DRUMHEAD	95	7-8 in.	Pickling type. Sow February/May. Yellows-resistant.	ECO THO
RED DUTCH	82		Fine, delicate flavor.	GUR
RED EARLIEST OF ALL	70	3-4 lbs.		MID
RED HEAD (hybrid)	80-85	3 lbs. 5-7 in.	Deep magenta color. Spherical head holds well.	BURR DEG HARR MID RIS STO
RED HOLLANDER	95-110	6½-7 in.	Similar to Round Red Dutch. Yellows-resistant.	MID
RED RIBBON (hybird)	78		Widely adapted. Solid head, medium core. Full red interior.	TWI

▶

◄ **CABBAGE—RED**

Variety	Days	Remarks	Sources	
RED ROCK	100		Good fresh, cooked or pickled.	ARC LET MEY WET
RED RODAN	140	8-10 in.	Danish variety. Hard, yet tender head. Large frame. Vigorous plant.	TER
RED STORAGE	96	7 lbs.	Globe-shaped head. Use in slaw. Storage type.	COM STO
RODE KOGEL	80		European variety. Matures late summer.	WILL
RONDY (hybrid)	70	2-4 lbs.	Good density. Short core. Holds well without splitting. For summer and for fall crops.	JOH
ROOKIE			Deep red all the way through.	LIBE
RUBY BALL (hybrid)	65-80	3-6 lbs.	Japanese variety. Cooked or raw usage. Very dependable cabbage.	EAR HARR LED LET LIBE MEY MID PIE PIN POR TER TWI WIL
RUBY PERFECTION (hybrid)	83-85	3-5 lbs. 6 in.	Deep red, round head. Slow to burst. Stores well.	BURP HARR JOH JUN MID RIS STO TWI VER
SAN MICHELE ITALIAN	100		Large red cabbage. Deeply veined and padded leaves.	LEM
SCARLET O'HARA (hybrid)	72	2-3½ lbs.	Japanese variety. Red-burgundy. Good storer. Makes great-tasting salads or sweet and sour cabbage.	SHE
SUPER RED		2-3½ lbs.	Somewhat flat shape. Grayish-green leaves. Deep purple-red head.	LET

CABBAGE
OTHER TYPES

Variety	Days	Size	Remarks	Sources
CABBAGE-SPROUTS			Cross of Golden Acre cabbage and Brussels Sprouts.	FIS
WALKING STICK		7 feet	Cabbage grows atop a stick. Cut and dry stick for a light, strong walking stick.	LAK

ORIENTAL CABBAGE
(Brassica rapa)

Oriental cabbage combines the thin crisp texture of lettuce with the fresh mustardy tang of juicy cabbage. Unlike lettuce, Oriental cabbage grows with a great deal of vigor. There are two types of Oriental cabbage. The heading, long types are taller and considered the 'Michihili' type. The heading, squat types are called 'Wong Bok'.

CULTURE: Sow seeds ¼ inches deep, 10 inches apart, in rows 24 to 30 inches apart. Thin plants to 10 to 18 inches apart.

SEASON: Direct seed planted in late spring to early summer. 40 degree soil temperature or higher.

INSECTS/DISEASES: See cabbage.

HARVESTING: When the heads feel solid.

ORIENTAL CABBAGE
HEADING, LONG TYPE

Variety	Days	Size	Remarks	Sources
CHIHFU	65-70	5-6 lbs. 10 in.	Winter-hardy. Good keeping quality.	RED
CHIHILI	73	18-20 x 3½ in.	White with fringed edges.	DEG TIL WIL
CHINKO (hybrid)	65	16 x 10 in.	Good tolerance to dry rot. Crisp leaf texture.	SEED
DYNASTY (hybrid)	65	13 x 8 in.	Good keeper. Medium-green outside, nearly white inside.	BURP
EARLY TOP	55	4-5 lbs.	Sow in summer.	SUN
GREEN ROCKET (hybrid)	70	4-5 lbs. 18 in.	Tolerant to most diseases. Tall, tightly folded head.	VER
HYBRID O-S CROSS	100	up to 20 lbs.	White, very solid and crisp. Keeps well. Fine flavor.	EAR
JADE PAGODA (hybrid)	72	16 x 5 in.	Broad and compact, extra uniform and vigorous. Slower to bolt. Deep green.	COM HARR MID PAR PIE POR RIS STO TWI
MICHIHILI (op)	70-75	4-6 lbs. 18 x 4 in.	Dark green, resembles celery and cos lettuce. Sow in summer.	ABU ALL ARC BURG BURR BUT COM DAN DEG EAR FAR GAR HUM KIT LED LET MEY MID PIN PON POR RAW RIS ROS SEED STO SUN THO TWI WES WET WIL WILL WYA
MONUMENT (hybrid)	70-80	17-18 in.	Tolerant of speckling. White interior. Vigorous plant. Heavy yields. Bolts quickly in spring.	JOH LEM STO TWI
PE-TSAI	75	12 in.	Pale green. Sow in mid-summer.	ECO STO
SHOSAI	86		Green outside, white inside. Best sown in fall and winter. For salads, stir fries or pickling.	LEM
SOUTH CHINA EARLIEST	45	1 lb. 10 x 14 in.	Tender, compact head. Creamy-white. Tolerates summer heat and bad weather. Sow July to September. Japanese variety.	GLE JOH RED
TIP TOP (hybrid)	65	4-5 lbs.	Sow in spring.	SUN
TWO SEASONS (hybrid)	62	10 x 7½ in.	Matures quickly to form a large solid head. Stands a long time before bolting to seed. Keeps well.	BURP RAW SUN THO
YELLOW PE-TSAI LEAF SNIJKOOL			Early boiling greens. Can be used at any stage.	WILL

ORIENTAL CABBAGE
HEADING, SQUAT TYPE

Variety	Days	Size	Remarks	Sources
AICHI HAKUSAI		10-12 lbs.	Plant in July/August.	KIT

◀ ORIENTAL CABBAGE—HEADING, SQUAT TYPE

Variety	Days	Size	Remarks	Sources
CHINA DOLL (hybrid)	60		For spring and fall crops. Tolerance for spring bolting. Green, finely savoyed.	HARR
CHINA KING (hybrid)	80	7-9 lbs.	Club-root-resistant. Extremely vigorous growth.	TER
CHINA PRIDE	68	5½ lbs.	High tolerance to downy mildew, bacterial soft rot and tip burn. Best adapted to cooler temperatures.	RIS STO TWI
CHINESE EXPRESS (hybrid)	62		Dark green, savoyed. Top of head is ruffled. Slow-bolting.	HARR
CHINESE WR 55 (hybrid)		4 lbs.	Vigorous. Resistant to heat and diseases.	POR
EARLY HYBRID G	55		Medium-green, deeply savoyed. Slightly spreading outer leaves. Good variety for spring planting.	HARR
EARLY TOP (hybrid)	50		Heat-resistant. Good salad quality. Mild flavor. Shorter than most varieties. Tolerant to virus and soft rot.	JOH
HYBRID F CHINESE CABBAGE			Spring planting. Firm head.	ARC
KASUMI	64	5 lbs.	Excellent tip burn-tolerant. Sow early or late. Good tolerance to bolting.	STO
KYOTO NO. 3	70-75	15 lbs. 12 in.	Crisp and tender. Wind-hardy and virus-resistant. Sow late summer or early spring.	RED WILL
MATSUSKIMA	85	6-8 lbs.	Japanese variety. Short-season variety. Suited to limited storage.	JOH
NAGAOKA HYBRID NO.2	40	6-8 lbs.	Slow to bolt. Tightly folded heads.	KIT
NAGAOKA HYBRID 50	50	3-4 lbs.	For summer production. Pale green head. Yellow with crispy white interior.	JOH TWI
NAGAOKA PRIDE			Similar to Hybrid No. 2. For summer and early fall sowing.	KIT
NAGAOKA WR (hybrid)	50-60	6 lbs.	Head is well filled and solid. Excellent quality.	FIS KIT LAG MID
NOZAKI EARLY			Light green. Late spring sowing.	ABU FIS
SHUKO	80	7 lbs.	Light green. Resistant to virus, rots and mildew. Tender and succulent.	LEM
SNOW CABBAGE			Withstands temperatures to 20° F. Very green, puckered leaves.	LEM
SPRING A-1 (hybrid)	60-75	3-4 lbs.	Sow in spring. Small, pale green. Slow bolting. Not sensitive to temperature changes.	JOH KIT MID NIC PIN SUN TER WES
SPRINGTIME	60	3-3½ lbs. 10 in.	Slow to bolt.	STO

Variety	Days	Size	Remarks	Sources
SPRING TRIUMPH (hybrid)	70-75	5-7 lbs.	Sow spring or summer.	SUN
SUMMERTIME	70	6-8 lbs. 11 in.	Larger and later than Springtime.	STO
TREASURE ISLAND (hybrid)	85	6 lbs.	Disease-tolerant. Vivid green interior. Grows well under low temperatures.	NIC
TROPICAL DELIGHT (hybrid) (LOUISIANA LETTUCE)	58	3-4 lbs.	Suited to hot weather. Bolts in cool weather. Light yellow-green head. Very uniform.	KIT TWI
TROPICAL PRIDE (hybrid)	50-55	3-4 lbs.	Sow in summer.	SUN
WINTER GIANT	80-85	10 lbs.	Sow in summer.	SUN
WINTER QUEEN (hybrid)	80	7-9 lbs.	Semi-heading type. Sow in early summer for fall harvest. Creamy white center is crisp and tender. Excellent in salads.	VER
WINTERTIME	80	7-9 lbs. 10 in.	Tolerant to wilt. Storage type.	STO
WONG BOK (op)	60-85	5-7 lbs. 10 in.	Completely bland. Sow spring or summer.	ARC COM DEG HUM NIC SEE SUN TSA TWI WES
WR 60 (hybrid)	60	4 lbs. 12 x 8 in.	Very slow bolting. High-yielding. Shows tolerance to mosaic virus, soft rot and mildew.	JOH LED WILL
WR SUPER 90 (hybrid)	90	7 lbs.	Very firm, well-folded, barrel-shaped. Japanese variety. Tolerant to root knot. Ideal for winter storage.	WES

CANTALOUPES
(Cucumis melo cantalupensis)

The cantaloupe (or muskmelon) is an extremely popular vegetable, since the homegrown varieties are generally sweeter because you pick them ripe. Unlike some other fruits, cantaloupes do not increase in sweetness when picked green. The sugar content begins to drop soon after picking.

CULTURE: Plant in rows 1 inch deep, 12 inches apart, with 48 to 72 inches between rows. Or plant in hills, 4 to 6 feet apart each way, with 2 to 3 plants per hill. Later, thin to the strongest two plants. You can also choose from several varieties of bush melons for space-saving gardens.

SEASON: Warm season. 60° F soil temperature or higher.

INSECTS/DISEASES: CUTWORMS: Sevin or diazinon.

MELON APHIDS, PICKLE WORMS, MELON WORMS, CUCUMBER BEETLES, SQUASH BUGS, SQUASH VINE BORERS, STRIPED CUCUMBER BEETLES: Malathion, diazinon, rfotenone or ryania.

ANTHRACNOSE, DOWNY MILDEW: Captan, maneb or zineb.

BACTERIAL SPOT OR BLIGHT: Fixed copper.

POWDERY MILDEW: Karathane.

SCAB: Maneb, captan or zineb.

HARVEST: Cantaloupes are ready to eat when the stems pull off easily (called slipping). If they don't pull off easily, they should stay on the vine. You can also tell when they are ready because the skin begins to look like a cork net and the stem cracks a little way around.

For testing Crenshaw and Persian melons, smell the blossom ends. If they smell fruity and sweet, the melons are probably ripe. Honeydew and Casabas are ripe when the rinds have turned completely yellow.

CANTALOUPES
LARGE

Variety	Days	Size/Flesh	Remarks	Sources
BENDER'S SURPRISE	90-95	10 lbs. 8 x 7 in. Deep orange	Ribbed netting turns a golden tint. Flavor improves after picking.	DEG LET SEE SOU
BIG DADDY (op)	88	14 lbs. 10 in. Bright orange	Lightly netted. Vigorous vine growth. Firm, fine-flavored flesh.	GUR HEN
GIANT HYBRID	80	Up to 18 lbs. Orange	Compact vine has heavy fruit set. Firm, sweet, excellent flavor.	GUR
GIANT PERFECTION (op)	97	14 lbs. 8 in.	Firm flesh. Large seed cavity. Productive and dependable.	HEN SEE
IMPROVED MILWAUKEE MARKET (SCHOON'S HARDSHELL) (NEW YORKER)	90	5-8 lbs. Red-salmon	Extra hard shell. Yellow skin.	BURR DEG LED LET MID RIS WIL
JUMBO		Up to 25 lbs. Orange	Sweet.	GLE
MAMMOTH (GURNEY'S)	95	14-18 lbs. Deep orange	One melon feeds a crowd. Fragrant.	GUR
MINNESOTA HONEY		7-9 lbs. Bright orange	High sugar content. Fusarium-resistant.	GUR
NC CANTALOUPE		20-25 lbs.	Sweet and juicy. Easy to grow.	FAR
OLD TIME TENNESSEE MUSKMELON	90-100	12-16 in. Salmon	Convoluted in shape. Deep creases. Delicious when fully ripe.	LEM SOU WIL
STUTZ SUPREME		5-10 lbs. Orange	Bears until frost. Requires heat to develop full flavor. Tan, smooth rind.	ABU
TURKEY	100	15-18 lbs. 12-16 in.	Slightly netted with light green sutures. Thick, firm flesh.	SOU
WEEK'S GIANT CANTALOUPE		Up to 22 lbs.		LAK

CANTALOUPES—EARLY
TO 80 DAYS

Variety	Days	Size/Flesh	Remarks	Sources
ALAMO (hybrid)	75-80	4-6 lbs. Dark salmon	Heavy producer. Distinct suture and good netting. Tasty and sweet.	WIL
ALASKA (hybrid)	70-80	4½ lbs. 6 x 9 in. Salmon	Medium netting. Pick when netting turns light reddish-brown.	COM GUR LIBE NIC PIN RAW SEED VER VES WILL
BURPEE HYBRID	72	4½ lbs. Oval, deep orange	Heavily netted and ribbed. Small seed cavity.	STO WILL
CANADA GEM (hybrid)	78	Oval, deep orange	Heavy netting. Resistant to powdery mildew and fusarium.	STO

◄

Variety	Days	Size/Flesh	Remarks	Sources
CHACA (hybrid)	75	3-3½ lbs. Salmon	French variety. Distinct flavor. Resistant to powdery mildew and fusarium wilt.	NIC
CHARENTAIS	74-90	3½ lbs. Salmon	French variety. Good flavor.	ECO HER NIC SEE
CHARENTAIS IGOR		Dark orange	French variety. Smooth with light green stripes changing to yellow when fully ripe. Does not slip, must be cut. Do not over-water.	LEM
CHARENTAIS IMPROVED	74	3 lbs. 5½ in. Dark orange	Ridged and smooth. 2½ in. flesh.	SOU STO
DALLAS (hybrid)	75-80	4 lbs. Deep salmon	Slightly ribbed. Good netting. Good disease tolerance. Turns yellow-gold when ripe. Sweet flavor.	WIL
DIXIE JUMBO (hybrid)	78-80	6 x 7 in. Salmon	Heavy netting. Tolerant to powdery mildew and downy mildew. High sugar content.	BURR FAR LAG LIBE POR
EARLIGOLD (hybrid)	73	Round	Fine, dense netting. Cool weather tolerance. Pick when fruit just turns orange.	JOH
EARLISWEET (hybrid)	73-75	5½ x 5½ in. Salmon	Medium netting. Produces where others fail. Resistant to fusarium wilt.	BURR EAR FAR MID NIC RAW STO WIL
EARLY DELICIOUS	75	4-5 lbs. Orange	Good sweet yielder.	SEE
EARLY HANOVER		Globe-shaped	Heirloom seed, almost extinct commercially.	ABU
EASY RIDER (hybrid)	80	3½-4 lbs. 5½-6 in. Deep orange	Thick netting. Juicy. Resistant to fusarium wilt, powdery mildew and crown blight. Tolerant to sulfur applications.	HARR
EMERALD GEM	80	Yellow	Heavily netted. Sweet and productive.	SEE
FAR NORTH	65-70	4-5 in. Salmon	Good short-season variety. Heavily netted rind. Each vine produces 6-8 melons. Large seed cavity.	FAR GLE FUR VER
FLYER (hybrid)	75	Size of a grapefruit	Charentais type. European variety. Light netting. Dark green sutures. Suitable for greenhouse culture. Very productive.	JOH
GAYLIA (hybrid)	65	7-9 lbs.	Very mildew-resistant. Trouble-free. Good flavor and aroma.	THO
GOLDEN CHAMPLAIN	75	3-4 lbs. Salmon	Sparse netting. Resistant to fusarium wilt. Sweet and juicy.	GUR
LAGUNA (hybrid)	77	3 lbs. Deep salmon	Heavily netted, sutureless.	WIL
LUSCIOUS (hybrid)	75	4 lbs. 7 in. Orange	Uniform and vigorous. Resistant to powdery mildew and fusarium wilt.	PAR
MAGNUM 45 (hybrid)	80	Deep orange	Strong growing, disease-resistant. Small seed cavity.	MID POR RIS WIL
MAINROCK (hybrid)	75	6 x 4 in. Salmon	Medium netting. Excellent flavor. Tolerant to fusarium wilt.	BURG FAR JUN

►

◀ **CANTALOUPES—EARLY**

Variety	Days	Size/Flesh	Remarks	Sources
MAXIMUM (hybrid)	80	3 lbs. Salmon	Good netting. Good disease tolerance. Slightly sutured.	WIL
MISSION (hybrid)	80	4 lbs. Deep salmon	Well-netted, sutureless. Stands up to weather stress.	WIL
MONTANA GOLD	60		Short-season variety. Netted. Starts to set with first blossoms. Good flavor.	FIS
PANCHA (hybrid)	80	2 lbs. 6 in. Deep orange	French variety. Sweet. Netted with slight green ribs. Good served as an appetizer, dessert or snack. Resistant to powdery mildew and fusarium wilt.	SHE
PERFECTION (hybrid)	75	4½ lbs. Round, Salmon	Well-netted. Strong rind. Heavy cropper.	STO
PERLITA	80	Round-oval, yellow-orange	Well-netted. Tolerant to downy and powdery mildew. Good flavor.	WIL
SAVOR (hybrid)	75	2 lbs. Deep orange	French Charantais type. Fusarium wilt-resistant.	NIC
SCOOP (hybrid)	61	6 in. Orange	Short-season variety. Thick flesh. Vigorous and heavy-yielding.	PAR
SUMMET (hybrid)	75		Vigorous vines. Heavy netting. Tolerant to fusarium wilt, downy mildew and more races of powdery mildew.	LET STO
SWEET GRANITE	70-80	2-3½ lbs. Orange	Lightly netted. Sure cropper in short-season areas.	ABU ALL GAR JOH PLA
SWEETHEART (hybrid)	65	Oval	Short-season variety. Very vigorous and easy to grow.	THO
SWEETIE (hybrid)	65	Salmon	Highly resistant to melon diseases caused by high humidity.	HEN
SWEET 'N EARLY (hybrid)	75	4½ in. Bright salmon	Corky netting. Small seed cavity. Resistant to powdery mildew. 6-8 fruit per plant. Full flavor.	BURP VES
TEKOS (hybrid)	75-80	3-4 lbs. Salmon	Very productive. Good disease tolerance.	WIL
TOPPER (hybrid)	80	3-3½ lbs. Round, salmon	Sutureless. Good disease tolerance. Very firm flesh.	WIL
ZENITH (hybrid)	80	4-4½ lbs. Round, salmon	Tolerant to fusarium wilt and powdery mildew. Large, vigorous vine. Heavily netted, slightly ribbed.	WIL

CANTALOUPES—MID-SEASON
81-90 DAYS

Variety	Days	Size/Flesh	Remarks	Sources
ALL STAR (hybrid)	88	3½ lbs. Oval, deep orange	Hard, beige rind, with fine netting. Tolerant to fusarium wilt and downy mildew.	HARR

▶

◀

Variety	Days	Size/Flesh	Remarks	Sources
AMBROSIA (hybrid)	86	4-5 lbs. 6-6½ in. Deep orange	Heavily netted. Very sweet, thick flesh and small seed cavity. Resistance to powdery mildew.	ARC BURP DEG LAG LED LET LIBE PAR POR SOU STO WET
BURPEE'S HYBRID	82	4-4½ lbs. 6-7 in. Oval, deep orange	Well-netted. Vigorous vines. Sweet, firm flesh.	ARC BURG BURP EAR LET LET LIBE MEY MID SEED STO WET WYA
CAMEO (hybrid)	80-90	5 lbs. Whitish	Sugar sweet. Good freezer.	THO
CLASSIC (hybrid)	85-87	4-4½ lbs. Salmon	Netted with slight rib. Resistant to powdery mildew and fusarium wilt.	BURR EAR FAR GUR JUN LET LET LIBE MEY MID RIS SEED VER WET WIL
DELICIOUS 51	85	6-6½ lbs. Salmon	Fine netting. Resistant to powdery mildew and fusarium wilt.	ALL BURR EAR GAR HARR JUN LED LET LIBE MID PIN PON SEED SOU STO WILL
EARLY DAWN (hybrid)	82	Oval, deep orange	Fine netting. Resistant to powdery mildew and fusarium wilt.	HARR
EDISTO 47	88	6½ in. Oval, salmon	Heavily netted. Resistant to downy and powdery mildew.	BURR MEY SOU
EXCEL 45 (hybrid)	80-85	3-3½ lbs. Salmon	Disease-tolerant. Slightly ribbed, good netting. Small seed cavity.	WIL
GOLD STAR (hybrid)	87	Oval, deep orange	Heavy netting. Very dependable. Productive over the season. Tolerant to fusarium wilt.	HARR JUN LED
HALE'S BEST	86	6½ in. Oval, orange	Heavy netting. Thick, sweet flesh with compact seed cavity.	ALL BURG HEN HUM LEJ
HALE'S BEST JUMBO	85	4½ lbs. 7½ x 6 in. Deep salmon	Flesh is thick and sweet.	ARC BURG BURR BUT DAN DEG EAR HARR LAG LED LIBE PON POR ROS SEE TWI VER WET WIL WYA
HALE'S BEST NO. 36	85	5½-6 in. Salmon	Medium netting. Thick sweet flesh.	DEG LET POR
HALES BEST NO. 36 IMPROVED	82	Salmon	Solid net. Rich spicy flesh. Not resistant to powdery mildew.	BURR JUN
HALE'S BEST NO. 936	82-87	5-5½ in. Salmon	Heavy netting. Thick flesh, small seed cavity.	MEY
HARPER (hybrid)	85	3½-4 lbs. Deep salmon	Fine netting. Tolerant to fusarium wilt.	HARR LET SEED STO TER TIL WET
HONEY ROCK (SUGAR ROCK)	85	5½ in. Salmon	Heavy netting. Sweet flavor. Tolerant to fusarium wilt.	ARC BURG DEG GUR HEN LET WET WILL
IMPERIAL 45 (HALE'S BEST NO. 45)	87	3½ lbs. 6½ x 5½ in. Bright orange	Firm, sweet flesh, small seed cavity. Resistant to powdery mildew. Solid ribbing.	DEG WIL WYA

▶

◄ CANTALOUPES—MID-SEASON

Variety	Days	Size/Flesh	Remarks	Sources
IMPERIAL 45 S-12	85	Oval to round, orange	Some sutures. Sweet flesh. Powdery mildew-resistant. Adapted to south-western areas of United States.	BURR COM
MAINSTREAM	85	2¾ lbs. Round, orange	High yields. Medium ribbing, good netting. Small seed cavity. Powdery and downy mildew-resistant. Good southeastern United States variety.	BURR
MARATHON	88		Plant Variety Patented.	MID
MARKET STAR (hybrid)	84	5½-6 in. Salmon	Medium netting, light ribbing. Powdery mildew-resistant. Thick, sweet flesh.	LIBE MID
PERLITA	80-88	Salmon	Well-netted. Mildew-resistant.	HARR WIL
PHARO (hybrid)	85	Deep orange	French variety. Fine flavor and aroma. Fine texture. Small seed cavity. Traditionally served with prosciutto. Gray-green rind. Resistant to fusarium wilt and powdery mildew.	SHE
PLANTERS JUMBO	85	4 lbs. Oval, orange	Well-netted. Vigorous vines. Small seed cavity. Resistant to downy and powdery mildew. Good yielder.	BURR MID LIBE WIL
PMR 45 IMPROVED	81	3-3½ lbs. 4½ x 5 in. Deep salmon	Full, high net. Small seed cavity. Juicy. Tolerant to powdery mildew.	HARR
PM RESISTANT NO. 45	85	5¼ x 6 in. Salmon	Well-netted. Firm, fine-textured flesh.	BURR MID WIL
PULSAR (hybrid)	86		Coarse net and deep sutures. Fusarium Race 2- and powdery mildew-resistant.	RIS
RESISTANT JOY N 22 (hybrid)	70	Round	Heavy producer. Good freezer. Total resistance to fusarium wilt and mildew.	THO
RESISTANT 4	50		Heavy net, medium ribs. Thick flesh. Firm and sweet. Resistant to powdery mildew.	NIC POR
ROADSIDE (hybrid)	85-90	7 x 6 in. Orange	Well-netted. Sweet, thick flesh. Resistant to powdery mildew and fusarium wilt.	BURG HEN JUN LET LIBE POR VER
SHIPMASTER	87	Oval, salmon	Plant Variety Patented. Good netting. Small seed cavity.	BURR MID
SIERRA GOLD	85	Nearly round, salmon	Well-netted. Resistant to powdery mildew.	WIL
SUPERSTAR (hybrid)	86	6-8 lbs. Round to flattened, salmon	Deeply ribbed and thickly netted. Thick flesh is very flavorful.	HARR LED WIL
SUPER MARKET (hybrid)	82-90	4½ lbs. 7 x 6 in. Deep orange	High yielder. Well-netted. Resistant to fusarium wilt and downy mildew.	ARC BURR FAR HEN

►

Variety	Days	Size/Flesh	Remarks	Sources
TAM PERLITA		2-3 lbs. Round, salmon	Light netting, light sutures. Resistant to powdery and downy mildew. Excellent flavor.	POR
TAM UVALDE	85-90	Oval-round, deep orange	Strong flavor. Small seed cavity. Well-netted, hard rind. Downy and powdery mildew-tolerant.	HARR MID POR WIL
TANGIERS (hybrid)	82	6 in. Round, deep orange	Best characteristics of honeydew and cantaloupe. Pale lime-colored rind. Strong vines are vigorous and resistant to powdery mildew and fusarium wilt. Good dessert melon.	SHE
TOP NET SR	85	3-3½ lbs. 4½ x 5 in. Deep salmon	Plant Variety Protected. Full net. Holds well. Tolerant to sulfur and heat.	HARR
YELLOWSTONE (hybrid)	80-85	3-4 lbs. Salmon	Good net cover, slight sutures. Good disease tolerance.	WIL

CANTALOUPES—LATE
90 DAYS ON

Variety	Days	Size/Flesh	Remarks	Sources
EDISTO	90-95	5 lbs. Rich salmon	Heavy netting. Tender, but firm flesh. Vigorous vines. Resistant to alternaria, powdery and downy mildew.	BURR DEG PAR WIL
FOUR-FIFTY (GRANITE STATE)	90	Blocky-oval, salmon	Heavy net with moderate ribbing. Large 45 type. Firm, sweet flesh. Tolerant to several strains of powdery mildew.	BURR
HARVEST QUEEN (PRIDE OF WISCONSIN) (QUEEN OF COLORADO)	80-92	6½ x 5½ in. Deep orange	Well-netted. Thick flesh. Resistant to fusarium wilt.	DEG HARR HEN LED LET MEY MID RED RIS SEE WILL
HEARTS OF GOLD (HOODOO)	90-95	3 lbs. 5 x 6 in. Deep orange	Well-netted. Sweet, spicy, fine-grained flesh.	ARC BURR DAN DEG EAR HEN LAG LET MEY SEE WES WET WIL WYA
IMPERIAL NO. 4-50	90	Oval, salmon	Heavy netting. Small seed cavity. Resistant to powdery mildew.	ARC COM DEG FAR GUR HEN JUN LET LIBE MID PON RIS SEED STO TER WIL
IROQUOIS (GIANT EARLY WONDER)	90	7 x 8 in. deep-orange	Coarse netting. Sweet, prolific. Resistant to powdery mildew.	ARC COM DEG FAR GUR HEN JUN LET LIBE MID PON RIS SEED STO TER WIL
ISRAELI (OLD ORIGINAL)	90-95	Oval, creamy	No ribs or sutures. Sparse netting. Yellow-orange rind.	WIL
MAINSTREAM	90	3-4 lbs. Bright orange	Mild-flavored. Slight sutures and netting. Tolerant to downy and powdery mildew.	WIL

◀ ## CANTALOUPES—LATE

Variety	Days	Size/Flesh	Remarks	Sources
MUSKETEER	90	4½ lbs. 7 x 6 in. Orange	Heavy netting.	MEY
RED QUEEN (hybrid)	90	2¼ lbs. Round, orange	Chinese variety. Beige-pink rind. High sugar content. Vigorous vine, great crops.	GLE
SATICOY (hybrid)	84-90	4 lbs. Deep orange	Medium netting. Tolerant to fusarium wilt and powdery mildew.	BURR COM HARR JUN LED LET LIBE MEY MID PAR RIS SEED STO WET WIL
SMITH'S PERFECT	90-95	5½ in. Deep orange	Sparse netting. Well-suited to the South. Small seed cavity. Disease resistant.	POR WYA
TOP MARK	90	6-7 in. Salmon	Well-netted. Sweet, firm flesh, small seed cavity.	BURR HARR ROS WIL
U.C. HONEYLOUPE	92	3-5 lbs. 7 x 6½ in. Salmon	Rind is creamy-white with pale salmon tint when mature. Small seed cavity. Tolerant to verticillium wilt, crown blight and sulphur.	STO WIL

CANTALOUPES

SPACE SAVERS

Variety	Days	Size/Flesh	Remarks	Sources
BUSH MIDGET	60	Salmon	3 foot vine produces many melons. High sugar content.	JUN
BUSH MUSKETEER	90	3-4 lbs. 5½-6 in. Orange	Outstanding performer. Heavily netted. Can be grown in pots and containers. Loads of juicy, sweet fruits.	ARC COM DAN EAR GUR HEN LED PAR PIN SOU STO THO WET
BUSH STAR (hybrid)	88	2-2½ lbs. 4 x 5 in.	Medium netting. Good variety for limited space.	HEN LED LET MID POR
HONEYBUSH	82	2½-3 lbs. Salmon	Productive bush-type cantaloupe grows 5-7 feet in diameter. Grows 3-6 melons. Small seed cavity. Tolerant to fusrium wilt. Ripens down to the rind.	BURR LAG PON
ITSY BITSY SWEETHEART	70	2½ lbs. Round, salmon	Sugar sweet. Heavily netted. Golden rind. Just right for 2 people to share.	GUR
JENNY LIND	75	Flat, green	Baby melon. Sweet flesh. Many melons have a knob on the end.	LED SEE
MINNESOTA MIDGET	60-65	4 in. Salmon yellow	3 foot vines produce small melons with high sugar content and spicy flavor.	BURG BURP EAR FAR GAR GUR PAR PIN SEE THO
SHORT 'N SWEET	90	Round	Bushy growth. Sugar flavor. Resistant to heat, drought and powdery mildew.	PAR

CANTALOUPES
GREEN—FLESHED

Variety	Days	Size/Flesh	Remarks	Sources
BOULE D' OR	120	Pale green	Ripens late September when planted in May. Lightly netted rind. Good winter keeper. Yellowish rind.	LEM
GREEN NUTMEG (EDEN GEM)	63	2-3 lbs. Green	Heavily netted.	JUN SEE SOU VER
ISRAEL (OGEN)	80	Pale green	Wide sutures. Small seed cavity. Sweet and tasty. Pale yellow rind.	ABU LEM PEA THO WIL
ROCKY FORD GREEN FLESH	84-92	2½ lbs. 5 in. Oblong, green	Solid netting. Deep, fine-grain, sweet flesh. Rust-resistant.	ARC BURR DEG HEN MEY NIC POR ROS WES WET WIL WYA
ROCKY SWEET (hybrid)	85	2½-3½ lbs., Globular, green	Sparse netting. Sweet and pleasant flavor. High yields. Outstanding melon.	LED MID WIL

CANTALOUPES
ODD-SHAPED/OTHER TYPES

Variety	Days	Size/Flesh	Remarks	Sources
ANANAS (ISRALEI) (SHARLYN)	100-110	5 lbs. Oblong, whitish-yellow	Slight net. Green rind turns orange beige when ripe. Sweet, juicy and aromatic. Vigorous vine. Tolerant to crown blight.	LEM POR WIL WILL
BANANA	90-95	7 lbs. 18 x 24 in. Salmon pink	Resembles a giant banana. Sweet and spicy. Little or no netting. Yellow rind.	BURG DEG EAR HEN JUN LAG MEY POR ROS SEE VER WIL WYA
BALSAM PEAR [op] (BALSAM APPLE) (BITTER MELON) (FOO GWA)	75-80	2 x 8 in. Light green	Similar to a cucumber. Heavily warted. Grow on a trellis. Should be soaked in salt water to help leach out bitterness before cooking. Grows 10-12 feet. Does best in hot, moist soil as a summer crop.	GLE LAG LEM SEE STO SUN TSA
HONEY GOLD NO. 9	90	10 ozs. Egg-shaped, white	Japanese cantaloupe. Smooth shiny golden yellow skin. Crisp, sweet flesh. Good keeper.	NIC
HONEY GOLD SWEET	90	10 ozs. Egg-shaped	Golden yellow fruit. Flesh is sweet and crisp. Aromatic.	SUN
HONG KING BITTER MELON	80	5 in.	Smiliar to Balsam Pear, but shorter. Dark green.	SUN
MR. UGLY MUSKMELON		Salmon	Italian melon. Deep ribs, big warts and rough all over. Sweet flesh.	GLE
SAKTU'S SWEET	90	11 ozs. Round	Light green rind. Juicy and very sweet flesh.	SUN
TURNER CANTALOUPES			Grows well under marginal conditions. Cross between cantaloupe and persian melon.	ECO
VALENCIA	110	Slightly elongated, almost white	Common in Mediterranean countries. Dark green, tough-skinned. Excellent keeper. Taste blends with other fruit.	LEM

◀ ## CANTALOUPES

Variety	Days	Size/Flesh	Remarks	Sources
VERTE DE TRESTE (I AMERICAIN)		Football-shaped, pale green	Winter keeper. Dark green rind.	LEM

CANTALOUPES
OTHER COLORS

Variety	Days	Size/Flesh	Remarks	Sources
COB MELON		White	Flesh actually melts in your mouth. Old-time melon. Productive vine produces large fruits that are light-dark 'mottled green'.	GLE POR
GOLDEN CRISPY (hybrid)		12 ozs.	Japanese variety. Golden yellow and very sweet. Eat like a pear, skin and all.	GLE VER
GOLDEN PEAR GIANT		4½ x 3½ in. Egg-shaped, white	Flesh is thick, soft, sweet and juicy. Large, productive plant. Golden-yellow rind.	RED
MARBLE WHITE (hybrid)	95	2 lbs. Creamy-white	Reminiscent of honeydew when ripe. Japanese variety. Short, productive vine. Pure white, smooth rind. Withstands heat and drought conditions.	LEM VER
SPEAR		Yellow	Heavily netted. Popular in Maritime Northwest.	ABU
TIGER		Oval, pink	Green rind splashed with yellow.	ECO
YUKI LARGE		1/2 lb. White	Japanese variety. Pure white rind. Distinctly ribbed. Thick sweet flesh with fine aroma.	GLE

CANTALOUPES—HONEYDEW

Variety	Days	Size/Flesh	Remarks	Sources
AFGHANI HONEYDEW		White		ABU
EARLI-DEW (hybrid)	86	2¼-3 lbs. 5-6 in. Green	Short-season variety. High sugar content. Smooth-skinned.	BURG COM FAR HEN JOH JUN LED LET MID NIC PIN PON RAW RIS SEED STO VER WES WET WIL
FRUIT PUNCH (hybrid)	80	6 in. Green	Heavily netted.	PAR
GOLDEN HONEYMOON (GOLD RIND HONEYMOON)	92	Emerald-green	Should be left on vine until fully ripe.	ABU BURR EAR
HONEYDEW (GREEN FLESH)	110-112	6-8 lbs. 7-7½ in. Emerald-green	Prefers a warm, dry climate. Smooth ivory skin, thick juicy flesh.	ARC BURR HARR LAG LET MEY NIC RED ROS SEE WES WYA
HONEYDEW (ORANGE FLESH)	110	5-6 lbs. 7½ x 7 in. Salmon	Small seed cavity. Smooth creamy-white rind when ripe.	BURR HARR
KAZAKH	70	2-3 lbs. Cream	Slightly netted. Orange rind. Has a distinctive flavor.	ABU GUR

▶

◀

Variety	Days	Size	Remarks	Sources
LIMELIGHT (hybrid)	96	7-7½ lbs. Green	Thick, juicy, sweet flesh. Fruit slips from vine when ripe.	BURP
MILKY WAY (hybrid)	80	Pale green	Big yields on wilt-resistant vines. Short-season variety.	GUR
OGEN (hybrid)	80	5½-6 in. Green	Flavor of Anjou pears.	PAR
OLIVER'S PEARL CLUSTER		5 in.	2 foot vine.	SEE
PINEAPPLE		5 lbs.	Pineapple taste. Netted.	PAR
TAM DEW	90-100	6½ lbs. 8 x 6 in. Green	Resistant to downy and powdery mildew. Rind turns ivory when ripe. Good flavor.	PAR WIL
TAM DEW IMPROVED	110	3-4 lbs. 5 x 5 in. Lime-green	Smooth whitish rind. Tolerant to downy and powdery mildew.	HARR
ROCKY SWEET (hybrid)	77	2½-3½ lbs. Green	High sugar content. High yields. Rind turns yellow-orange when ripe. Firm, fragrant flesh.	EAR GUR JUN LET PAR
VENUS (hybrid)	88	5¼ x 5¾ in. Green	Light netting on golden rind. Very sweet. Heavy producer. Thick, juicy flesh. Fruit slips from vine when ripe.	BURP DAN

CANTALOUPES—CASABA-CRENSHAW-PERSIAN

Variety	Days	Size/Flesh	Remarks	Sources
BURPEE EARLY HYBRID (CRENSHAW)	90	Up to 14 lbs. Salmon	No netting. Turns yellowish when ripe.	BURP LET WET
CASABA	120	6-8 in. White	Very sweet. Long keeper. Golden rind.	LAG RED SEE
CRENSHAW	90-110	5 lbs. 6 x 8 in. Salmon	Rough, dark green rind turns yellow when ripe.	ARC BURR DEG EAR GLE GUR LEM RED RIS ROS SEE WES
ESCONDIDO GOLD		Yellow-orange	Casaba-like. Yellow-orange rind. Epicurean melon.	ABU
EARLY HYBRID (CRENSHAW)	88-90	Up to 14 in. Salmon	Vigorous vine grows almost anywhere.	LAG LED
GOLDEN BEAUTY (CASABA)	110-120	6-8 in. Nearly white	Wrinkled, golden skin. Keeps in good condition for months.	BURR HARR LAG POR ROS VER
GOLDEN CRENSHAW	110	6-7 lbs. 8 x 6 in. Pale orange	Tolerant to crown blight. Rind is mottled green and yellow.	HARR MID
HONEYSHAW (hybrid) (CRENSHAW)	75-85	Salmon	Good short-season variety. Free of netting.	LET NIC VER
JAUNE DES CANARIES (YELLOW CANARY) (JUAN CANARY)	105	8-9 lbs. 8 x 6 in. Egg-shaped, pale green to whitish yellow	Casaba melon. Very sweet flesh. Good flavor. Yellow rind.	HARR LEM WIL

▶

◄ CANTALOUPES—CASABA-CRENSHAW-PERSIAN

Variety	Days	Size/Flesh	Remarks	Sources
PERSIAN MEDIUM	95	7-8 lbs. 7 x 7½ in. Deep orange	Heavily netted. Small seed cavity. Flesh is thick, sweet and with a distinct flavor. Grows well in arid areas.	HARR NIC POR SEE
SANTA CLAUS (CASABA)	108	8-9 lbs. 12 x 6 in. White to pale-green	Faint netting. Wrinkled gold and dark-green mottling.	HARR LEM

CANTALOUPES
GREENHOUSE TYPES

Variety	Days	Size/Flesh	Remarks	Sources
HYBRID OKITSU		4-5 lbs. Green	Japanese variety. Beautiful netting. Greenhouse strain that is sweet and has high spicy aroma.	GLE

CANTALOUPES—PRESERVING MELON

Variety	Days	Size/Flesh	Remarks	Sources
AOURI		12 x 4½ in. White	Dark green fruit. Thick flesh.	KIT
MANGO MELON		White	Needs a long, warm season. 13-17 weeks growing time. Good for pies and preserves.	SEE
OSHIRO URI		Long, oval	Light green fruit turns white when mature. Medium thick, crisp flesh.	KIT
PICKLING MELON	73	12 x 3 in.	Good quality pickling melon or for cooking. Rind is bright deep-green with slender stripes.	SUN

CARDOON

Variety	Days	Remarks	Sources
CARDOON		When leaves are nearly full grown they are tied together near the top. Straw piled around the head and earth put against it to blanch Plant in garden from March to May. Needs full sun and moist soil.	RED
ITALIAN DWARF		Produces a very small plant with good stalks.	LEM
LARGE SMOOTH	110	Fine smooth stalk. Requires rich soil. After stalks are blanched steam or boil.	COM DEG LEJ NIC PIN SEE TAY WILL
PLEIN BLANC INORME		Produces a large 3 to 4 foot plant.	LEM
TENDERHEART	140		LAG

CARROTS
(Daucus carota sativa)

Carrots offer the home gardener a tremendous number of choices—so many, in fact, that you can almost select a different kind of carrot for each and every mood. There are long, slender ones; medium, fat ones; short shaped ones; even bite-size midgets just right for parties.

CULTURE: Carrots grow best in stone-free soil. They also need deep porous soil for optimum growth. Open up hard clay to a one-foot depth by spading in quantities of organic matter. As soon as the ground can be worked in spring, sow seed a half-inch deep a half-inch apart in rows one foot apart. Later thin to 2 to 3 inches.

SEASON: Cool.

INSECTS/DISEASES: *APHIDS, CARROT WEEVILS:* Malathion, diazinon, pyrethrum, rotenone or ryania.
  LEAF BLIGHT: Maneb or zineb.
  MOSAICS: Malathion.
  ROOT ROTS: Diazinon.

HARVESTING: Pick carrots when relatively small. Bigger carrots produce woody cores. Carrots can be stored right in the ground until you need them.

CARROTS (GOLD PAK TYPE)
LONG, SLENDER

Variety	Days	Size/Color	Remarks	Sources
APACHE (hybrid)	65	10 in. Dark orange	Contains Super Sweet Gene. Tolerant to alternaria. Very smooth.	STO
GOLD PAK	65	8½ x 1 in. Deep orange	Good quality.	BURP DAN FAR GUR HEN JUN LET MID PON POR SEED TWI
GOLD PAK 28	69-77	10 x 1¼ in. Reddish-orange	Good strain for northern muck soils. Small indistinct core.	JUN MID STO
GOLD PAK 263		Bright orange	Grows well in mineral soils and muckland soil. Good storer.	LET
HICOLOR 9		10-12 in. Deep orange	Primarily for muckland conditions.	LET
HURON (hybrid)	67	10 in. Cigar shape	Super Sweet Gene. Tolerant to alternaria and leafspot.	STO
MOKUM (hybrid)	60	6-10 in. Deep orange	Good sweet flavor. Use for canning or freezing when 6 to 8 inches. Suitable for deep containers. Can be pulled early as a baby carrot.	COO THO
ORLANDO GOLD (hybrid)	65-80	10-11 in. Orange	Bolt-resistant, crack-resistant. Remarkably smooth with no green shoulders. Has small core.	GUR HEN HUM LET MID PIN POR RIS STO WILL
SCARLET WONDER	70-110	12 in. Deep scarlet	Grown for cooking. Sweet and tender.	VER
SWEET-N-CRISP (hybrid)	75	8-9 in. Bright orange	Tastes great cooked. Crisp and good raw. Strong tops.	HEN

CARROTS (IMPERATOR TYPE)
LONG, SLENDER BROAD SHOULDERS

Variety	Days	Size/Color	Remarks	Sources
A PLUS (hybrid)	65-73	7-8 in. Deep scarlet	Sweet flavor. Medium strong tops. Adapted for growth in organic and mineral soils.	JOH LET SEED

183

◀ ## CARROTS (IMPERATOR TYPE)

Variety	Days	Size/Color	Remarks	Sources
ARISTO PAK (hybrid)		8-8 ½ in. Bright orange	Strong 18-20 in. tops. Good color inside and out.	WIL
CANDY PACK (hybrid)	75	8-10 in. Bright orange	Uniform, sweet and tender.	JUN LET
CANUCK (hybrid)	64	10-11 in. Bright orange	Good in northern soil.	STO
CIMARRON (hybrid)		7-9 in. Bright orange	Medium strong tops. Uniform color.	HARR
CRUNCHY (hybrid)	73	9 x 1 ½ in. Bright orange	Very smooth. Moderately resistant to bolting.	BURR
DAGGER (hybrid)		8-10 in.	Smooth, bright, uniform roots.	ARC
DISCOVERY	62	10 in. Deep orange	Strong vigorous tops are tolerant to alternaria.	MID STO
DOMINATOR	63	10-11 in. Intense orange	Slender. Good processor variety.	LED
EL PRESIDENTE		Bright orange	Good fresh-eating carrot.	LET
FANCI PAK	56	11 x 1¼ in.	Resists bolting.	VES
FLAVOR PAK (hybrid)	72	8-9 in.	Uniform size and shape. Good flavor.	PIN
GOLD PRIDE (hybrid)		8-10 in. Bright orange	Cores are indistinct. All-purpose carrot.	HARR
GRENADIER (hybrid)		7-9 in. Bright orange	Vigorous grower adapted for mineral soils.	HARR
HYBRID A-PLUS	75	6-8 in. Bright orange	Delicious, no bitter taste.	GUR JUN LET PAR WILL
IMPERATOR	64-80	10 x 1½ in. Orange-red	Very popular variety.	BURP FAR HUM LAG PIN PON ROS WET WIL WILL WYA
IMPERATOR, KING	64-77	10 x 1½ in. Deep orange	Good interior and exterior color.	MID STO
IMPERATOR, LONG	77	10 x 2 in. Orange	Fine-grained and tender.	SEE
IMPERATOR 58	58-77	10 x 1½ in. Rich orange	Fine-grained, tender. An ideal bunching carrot. Uniform interior color.	ABU ARC BURR LED RAW RIS STO TIL
IMPERATOR 58 IMPROVED	75	10 x 1½ in. Dark orange	Fine flavor. Crisp and coreless. Good cooked or raw.	BURG GUR HARR HEN LET MID
IMPERATOR 408	63	9-10 in.	Not as tapered as other Imperators.	STO
LONG ORANGE	85	11 x 2 in. Deep orange	Fine-grained.	WYA

▶

Variety	Days	Head	Remarks	Sources
LONG ORANGE IMPROVED	88	12 x 1¾ in.	12-18 in. tops.	MEY
PAK MOR (hybrid)		8-10 in. Bright orange	Strong tops. Excellent color.	FAR HARR
SEMINOLE	66	9 in. Dark orange	Contains Super Gene for super sweetness. Multi-tolerance to leaf diseases.	STO
SHORT TOP IMPERIDA	75	10 x 1½ in. Orange-red	Bunching carrot.	WYA
SIX-PAK (hybrid)		7-8 in. Bright orange	Uniform color. Strong tops.	HARR
SIX-PAK II (hybrid)		7-9 in. Deep orange	Medium tops.	HARR VES
SIX PENCE (hybrid)		9-10 in. Bright orange	Medium strong tops. High quality. Good yielder.	HARR
TENDERSWEET	69-80	10 x 2 in. Orange-red	Sweet, tender, heavy producer.	GUR HEN LET
TOP-PAK (hybrid)		7-9 in. Deep orange	Large, strong tops. Very smooth roots.	HARR
VITASWEET 721	72	10 x 1¼ in. Orange	No bitter aftertaste. Smooth skin. Colorful inside and out.	TWI
VITASWEET 771	72	10 in. Orange	18 in. tops. Good color inside and out. Tolerant to alternaria.	TWI
WALTHAN HICOLOR	74-80	10 x 1¼ in. Glossy, deep orange	Free of green shoulders. Tops are short and strong. Grow on deep loose soil.	LET
WOODLAND (hybrid)	56	11 x 1¼ in. Dark orange		MID

CARROTS (DANVERS TYPE)
MEDIUM SLENDER, TAPERING

Variety	Days	Size/Color	Remarks	Sources
CAMDEN (hybrid)	67	8¾ in. Orange	Processing carrot. Can also be used fresh. Smooth interior.	STO
DANVERS	75	7½ x 2 in. Deep orange	Adapted to all types of soils. Very productive. Tender and sweet.	BURG
DANVERS HALF LONG	73-85	8 x 2 in. Deep orange	Tender, sweet, crisp. Excellent quality. Stores well. Widely adapted. Nearly coreless. Suited for heavy soils.	ALL ARC BURP BUT DEG EAR FAR GAR GUR HEN HIG HUM LAG LEJ MEY PAR PIN PON ROS SEE SOU TIL WES WET WILL WYA
DANVERS HALF LONG IMPROVED	75	Bright orange	Produces well in almost any soil. Red core.	COM

◄ ## CARROTS (DANVERS TYPE)

Variety	Days	Head	Remarks	Sources
DANVERS NO. 126 (op)	65-75	6-8 in.	Processing carrot. Outstanding variety in heavier soils. Excellent interior color.	ABU HARR LED LET POR RIS SEED STO VER VES WIL
DANVERS NO. 126 IMPROVED	75	6-8 in. Orange-red	Heavy yields. Smooth skin. Tops are heat-resistant. Excellent storer.	TWI
DESS-DAN (hybrid)	67	7-9½ in. Deep orange	Processing carrot. Half long type. Nice carrot.	JUN STO
PARK'S MUNCHY (hybrid)	70	8 in. Orange-red	Sweet carrot. Retains color when cooked.	PAR
PROCESSOR II (hybrid)	67	9 in. Intense orange	Processing carrot. High quality.	STO

CARROTS (SPARTAN TYPE)
MEDIUM PLUMP, BLUNT END

Variety	Days	Size/Color	Remarks	Sources
ORANGE SHERBERT	60	10 x 1¼ in. Bright orange	Tolerance to blight. Strong dark green tops. Smooth skin.	STO
SPARTAN BONUS (hybrid)	70-77	7 x 2 in. Deep orange	Good quality and flavor.	FAR FIS PAR
SPARTAN DELIGHT (hybrid)	70-75	14 x 1¼ in. Orange		RIS
SPARTAN FANCY 80 (hybrid)	65-67	10 x 1½ in. Deep orange	Good bunching variety. Shows tolerance to cercospora leaf spot.	RIS STO
SPARTAN PREMIUM-80	67	9 in.	Good tolerance to leaf blight and rusty root.	STO
SPARTAN PREMIUM (hybrid)			Good yield. Sweet and crisp.	RAW
SPARTAN SWEET	60	Deep orange	Rich in carotene.	GUR
SPARTAN WINNER (hybrid)		4-6 in.	Sweet and tender. Pull early for baby carrots.	POR

CARROTS (CHANTENAY TYPE)
MEDIUM, PLUMP, TAPERING

Variety	Days	Size/Color	Remarks	Sources
AUTUMN KING			Fine variety for winter storage. Heavy yields.	ECO
AUTUMN KING IMPROVED	70	10 in. Orange	Good flavor. Use fresh, canned or frozen. Large roots. Winter-storage type.	THO

►

Variety	Days	Size/Color	Remarks	Sources
BURPEE'S GOLDINHEART	70-72	5½ x 2¼ in.	Tender, sweet. Good canner or freezer.	ARC BURP DEG FAR
CHANTENAY	68-72	6 x 2¼ in. Bright orange	Tender. Red core.	ALL BURG DEG ECO HER JLH LEJ NIC WET
CHANTENAY IMPROVED	70	7 in.	Red core. Strong grower.	COM LET
CHANTENAY HALF-LONG RED CORED IMPROVED	70	Deep orange	Red core. Use fresh, frozen or canned.	LED
CHANTENAY LONG	68-72	7 x 2 in. Deep orange	Good quality and flavor.	POR VER
CHANTENAY WINTER HARDY			For clay soils. Good keeper.	SEE
EARLY CHANTENAY		Rich orange	Sweet and early.	SEE
GOLD KING	68	7 x 2¼ in. Red-orange	Smooth interior.	RIS
KURODA CHANTENAY	70	8 x 2 in. Deep orange	Large storage carrot. Grows in poorer soil. Good flavor. A fall-harvest carrot.	GAR HIG JOH PLA
RED-CORED CHANTENAY	68-72	6 x 2½ in. Red-orange	Tender, sweet. Retains reddish color when cooked. Solid orange, no lemon-colored core.	ABU DEG FAR FIS GUR HEN JUN LAG MEY PIN PON RAW RIS ROS SEED SOU STO TIL VES WIL WILL
ROYAL CHANTENAY (op)	68-70	6½ x 2½ in. Red-orange	Easily grown. Good flavor. Coreless, smooth roots. Use fresh, canned or frozen. Good variety.	BURP BURR DAN EAR GUR HARR HEN HUM MID PAR SEE STO TER WES WILL
ROYAL CROSS (hybrid)	70	7 x 1¾ in. Orange-red	Vigorous, uniform grower. Good fresh, cooked, canned or frozen.	PAR
SUPREME CHANTENAY RED CORED	70	6½-7½ in. Deep orange	Good flavor. Very smooth skin. Use fresh. Winter storer.	THO

CARROTS (NANTES TYPE)
MEDIUM CYLINDRICAL, BLUNT END

Variety	Days	Size/Color	Remarks	Sources
AMSTERDAM MINCOR	65	5-6 in. Deep orange	Sweet, fine-grained. Never coarse or woody. Does well in almost any kind of soil.	JOH JUN RAW
A-PLUS	65	6-8 in. Dark orange	Has Super Sweet Gene. Fine taste. Has double the amount of carotene.	SEED SOU STO
BERLICUMMER	69	1¾ x 9 in.	Very smooth, straight roots with almost no cracking or splitting. First-rate flavor.	PIN WILL
CARAMBA	75	5½ in. Bright salmon	Dutch variety. Crisp and full-flavored. Pull young for baby carrots. Good juicer.	SHE TER
CHRISNA (hybrid)	70	8 x 1½ in.	10-12 in. tops.	EAR MEY VER WET

◄ **CARROTS (NANTES TYPE)**

Variety	Days	Size/Color	Remarks	Sources
CLARION (hybrid)	60	7in. Orange	Smooth skin. Sweet and aromatic. Short tops. Good eating quality.	JOH
CORELESS AMSTERDAM	55	6-7 in. Salmon-red	Long, sweet and crisp. Dutch variety.	STO
DANRO	70	6-7 x 1½ in. Intense orange	High fiber content. Grows in heavier soils and keeps longer in the soil. Dutch variety.	TER
DUTCH EARLY SCARLET HORN		Deep orange	Heirloom variety. Grows well in mediocre soil. Cover shoulders to prevent greening.	ECO LEM
EAGLE	56	8½ in. Orange	High quality canner and slicer.	STO
EARLYBIRD NANTES	50	7¾ in. Bright orange	Slow bolter. Strong tops.	STO
EARLY NANTES			Almost coreless. Good in heavy soils. Juicy.	ECO
FAKKEL MIX	90	6-7 in.	Dutch variety. For winter eating. Good juicer.	TER
FLAKKEE LONG RED GIANT	65	2 feet	Strong, red-cored carrot. Excellent storer. High-yielding. Good taste.	WILL
HERZ ZENO	85	8-10 in. Orange	A giant of a carrot. Good flavor. Use fresh, canned or freeze. High juice yield.	THO
INGOT	66	9 in. Deep orange	Contains Super Gene. High quality slicer and canner.	STO
JAMES SCARLET INTERMEDIATE			Good exhibitor or cooked. Half-long.	ECO
JUWAROT DOUBLE VITAMIN A	90	5-8 in. Deep red	Full of vitamin A. Excellent juicer. All-purpose carrot. Freeze at 5 inches. Winter storer.	THO
KLONDIKE NANTES	56	7-8 in. Deep orange	High sugar content. Tender. Good fresh or frozen.	STO
LINDORO (hybrid)	63-80	8-10 in. Intense orange	Dutch variety. Big yields. Good uniformity.	PAR TER
LUCKY'S GOLD (hybrid)	70	6-7 in. Deep orange	Half-long type. All-purpose carrot. Exceptionally sweet and flavorful.	JUN
NANDOR (hybrid)	66	8-10 in Orange-red	Coreless. Tender, crisp, sweet and juicy. High yields.	PAR
NANTAISE TIP TOP (NANTES TIP TOP)	73	7 in. Deep orange	Low in fiber. Smooth, crisp and sweet. Adapts well to wide range of soils.	LEJ SHE WILL
NANTES	68-70	6 x 1½ in. Reddish	Crisp carrot. Very flavorful.	LAG LEJ MEY PIN SEED SEE
NANTES EXPRESS	70	6½ in.	Freeze or can when 6-8 inches. Suitable for sowing in cold frame. Good flavor.	THO

►

Variety	Days	Size/Color	Remarks	Sources
NANTES FANCY	65	7 in.	Strong tops. Excellent storer. Adapted to wide range of soils.	JOH
NANTES FRUBUND (FAST CROP)	60	6½ in. Deep orange	Use fresh. Grows well under cold conditions.	THO
NANTES IMPROVED CORELESS	68	Bright orange	Desirable for frame culture. Crisp, tender, with delicate flavor. Small core.	BURR
NANTES SLENDERO	70	6-9 in. Bright orange	Sweet, tender and juicy. Holds well in ground without cracking. Dutch variety.	TER
NANTES STRONG TOP (op)		6 in. Medium-orange	Can be used as a baby carrot. Use fresh or processed. Medium-short tops.	HARR LET TWI
NANTES STUMP ROOTED	69	7 x 1¼ in. Bright orange	High quality. Small tops.	ROS
NANTUCKET (hybrid)		Bright orange	Has short top so it can be cultivated under glass or polythene tunnels. Good color.	SEED
PIONEER (hybrid)	67	8 in. Deep orange	Uniform color. Small tops. Excellent quality. Good yielder.	COM HARR
REDCA	70	6-7in. Orange-red	All-purpose carrot. Can or freeze when 6 inches. Good juice content. No core.	THO
RONDINO	62	7 in. Orange	Medium-size tops. All-purpose carrot. Indistinct core.	JOH
SCARLET NANTES HALF LONG (EARLY CORELESS) (NANTES CORELESS) (op)	68-70	8 x 1½ in. Deep orange	Sweet flavor. Good freezer, cooked or raw. Coreless. Good standard variety. Fine juicer.	ABU ALL ARC BURG BURR COM EAR FAR FIS GAR GUR HARR HEN HIG HUM JOH JUN LED LET MID PAR RIS STO TIL VER WIL WILL
SPECIAL NANTES 616	62	7 in.	Good storage carrot. High quality. Well-colored smooth roots.	STO
SUPER NANTES	62	8 in. Bright orange	Small core. Exceptional color.	STO
TAMINO (hybrid)	90	10 x 1½ in.	Very sweet. Grow in loamy or humusy soils. Will hold all winter in ground without losing quality. Dutch variety.	TER
TOPSCORE	70	6 x 1½ in. Orange	Coreless. Tends to be broader than most Nantes.	PIN
TOUCHON	70-75	7 x 1½ in. Red-orange	Excellent quality.	ABU COO DEG FAR HER LEJ LEM LET NIC RAW SEE STO VES WES
TOUCHON DELUXE	58	7 in. Brilliant orange	Very smooth and uniform.	STO
TOUDO (hybrid)	70	7½ x 1½ in.	Resists splitting. Can be pulled young for baby carrots. Tender, crisp and sweet.	BURP

CARROTS
ROUND

Variety	Days	Size/Color	Remarks	Sources
GOLDEN BALL	58-66	2 in. Golden-orange	Gourmet carrot. Sweet. Does well in shallow soils.	DEG PIN RAW
GOLD NUGGET	71	3 x 2 in. Golden-orange	Top-shaped, golf-ball.	NIC
KUNDULUS	65-71	2 in. Deep orange	Use in difficult soils, window boxes, containers. Use fresh, canned or freeze. Smooth skin.	LAG PAR THO
ORBIT	50	1 in.	Highly tolerant to splitting and yellowing when past maturity.	VER
PARISIAN	60	2 x 1½ in. Deep orange		LEM WILL
PARMEX	50	1 in. Bright orange	Excellent flavor.	GRA JOH
PLANET	55	1½ in. Deep red-orange	French variety. Beet-shaped. Tender and sweet.	COO SEE SHE STO
ROUND			Dutch variety. Looks like oversize radish.	LEJ
SWEET CHERRY BALL	50	1½ in. Orange	No slicing needed. Bite-size.	GLE

CARROTS
SMALL

Variety	Days	Size/Color	Remarks	Sources
AMSTEL	62	4 x 1 in.	Gourmet carrot. Delicious, tender and extra sweet.	HER PAR
BABY FINGER NANTES	50	3 x ¾ in. Rich orange	Good canner and pickler. Tender when young.	STO
BABY LONG	65	6-7 in.	Good color throughout. Smooth skin.	NIC
BABY ORANGE	53	Bright orange	Good processing variety.	STO
BABY SWEET (hybrid)	49	Bright orange	Very smooth skin. Slow to bolt. Rich interior color.	STO
CARROT SUCRAM	70	3-4 in.	Nantes type. Very sweet. Good processing variety.	NIC SEE
EARLY SCARLET HORN		2-6 in.	Useful in greenhouse or outdoors. Excellent flavor. Use canned, fresh, pickled or freeze.	ABU ECO
FINCOR	55		Slow grower for mid-summer plantings.	STO
KINKO 4"	55	4 in. Red-orange	Crisp and sweet. Harvest young. For shallow soils.	GAR JOH SOU
KINKO 6"	50	6 in.	Grows well in adverse conditions. Cone-shaped roots.	GAR HIG SEE

▶

Variety	Days	Size/Color	Remarks	Sources
KINKO CROSS (hybrid)	55	6 in.	An improved strain of Kinko 6".	HIG
LADY FINGER	60-95	5 in.	Sweet. Almost coreless. Gourmet carrot. Plant fairly thick.	BURG FAR LET PLA
LITTLE FINGER	50-65	3½ x ⅝ in. Orange	Nantes-type small gourmet carrot. Small core, extra-sweet taste. Great for container gardening.	BURG COM EAR HUM LAG PAR PIN TIL TWI VER WILL
MINICOR (BABY NANTES)	55	7 in. Orange	Harvest when young. Smooth, rounded tip. Crisp and sweet.	COO GUR HEN HIG JOH JUN LEM RED RIS STO VER
OX HEART (GUERNADE)	70-75	6 x 4 in. Deep orange	Short and fat. Easily dug. Sweet. Heavy yields in thin soils.	ABU DEG GAR MEY RED SEE WILL
SHORT 'N SWEET	68	8½ x 2 in. Bright orange	Good in heavy soils.	BURP FAR LAG
SUKO	55-60	2½ in. Orange	Use where space is limited and in difficult soils. Use fresh, canned or freeze. Tender, crisp and sweet. Does not need thinning for high yields. For container growing.	THO
TINY SWEET	62-65	3 in. Golden orange	Good pickled or cooked.	PAR
VITASWEET 500 (hybrid)	50	5 x ¾ in. Bright orange	Smooth. High yields. Good flavor.	TWI
VITASWEET 750	50-75	5-8 x ⅝ in.	Dual purpose "baby finger". Colorful and sweet.	TWI

CARROTS
UNUSUAL TYPES

Variety	Days	Size/ Color	Remarks	Sources
BELGIUM WHITE	75	White	Very mild flavor. Productive and vigorous.	NIC SEE
INDIAN LONG RED			Very long and tapering. True carrot taste.	GLE
KINTOKI EARLY STRAIN		8 x 1½ in. True red	Japanese variety. Decorative in salads. Tender and sweet.	GLE
KINTOKI REGULAR STRAIN		10 in. Crimson	Fall strain. Japanese variety. Tender.	GLE JLH
KOKUBU	130	2 feet x 1½ in. Deep orange	Japanese variety. Sow in summer.	GLE
RED MUSCADE		1 lb. Lumpy	Heirloom variety. Best planted in late summer. Highly aromatic, thick and juicy.	LEM
SCARLET IMPERIAL LONG	77	3 feet. Salmon-orange	Japanese variety. Crisp and sweet.	GLE
TOPWEIGHT		Orange-red	New Zealand variety. High in carotene. Will stand in soil for 6 months without cracking or splitting.	GLE

CARROTS—FORCING VARIETIES

VarietyDays	Size/ Color	Remarks	Sources	
AMSTERDAM FORCING	72	Deep orange	Stump-rooted.	ABU DEG SEE WILL
MOKUM (hybrid)		6 in.	Good variety for culture under grow tech or plastic tunnels.	SEED

CAULIFLOWER
(Brassica oleracera var. botrytis)

Cauliflower is one of those delicious vegetables that can sometimes be a bit finicky. There are varieties that are from early to late, and a choice of colors.

CULTURE: Start transplants 8 to 10 weeks before you set them out, or buy them from your local nursery. Plant 2½ to 3 feet apart in rows two feet apart. When the cauliflower begins to head you must "blanch" the buds—that is, keep them by turning green from shielding the head from the sun. You do this by pulling a few outer leaves over the head, gathering the tops of the leaves together, and tying them loosely with a string or rubber band. Or you can buy the self-blanching varieties. There is no need to blanch the colored varieties.

SEASON: Cool.

INSECTS/DISEASES: *APHIDS, BLISTER BEETLES, CABBAGE LOOPERS, CABBAGE WEBWORMS, FLEA BEETLES, CABBAGE WORMS*: Malathion, diazinon, pyrethrum, rotenone or ryania.

CLUBROOT: Lanstan.

DOWNY MILDEW, FUNGAL SPOTS: Maneb or fixed copper sprays.

HARVESTING: Pick cauliflower as soon as the heads fill out—otherwise they lose quality.

CAULIFLOWER—EARLY
TO 59 DAYS

Variety	Days	Head	Remarks	Sources
ABUNTIA	45	White	Crisp, medium-large head is of highest quality.	THO
ALERT	52-55	Large	High quality. Very dense head, short-stemmed with large leaves.	GAR HIG JOH PAR STO
ALPHA BALANZA		Large	Slow grower. Dutch variety. Excellent flavor.	TER
ALPHA PALOMA		Large	Dutch variety. Dense head. Excellent flavor.	TER
ALPHA BEGUM		Large	Dutch variety. Excellent flavor.	TER
DWARF ERFURT	50-54	Creamy white	Snowball type. Short-stemmed.	WILL
EARLY LIGHT (hybrid)	58	2 lbs.	Good disease tolerance. Best as fall crop. Widely adapted.	TWI
EARLY ABUNDANCE	47	Extra-large, white	Extra early. Grows vigorously. Fine flavor.	EAR STO
EARLY SNOWBALL (SNOW DRIFT)	55-60	7¼ in. Creamy white	Close, compact head. Standard main crop.	ABU ARC BURG BUT EAR HUM LAG PIN PON POR RAW RED STE
EARLY SNOWBALL A	55	Ivory white	Good head coverage. Short-season variety.	BURR VER WES
EARLY SNOWBALL SELECT	80	Large, pure white	Vigorous and compact. Solid head.	COM
EARLY SNOWFLAKE	30-45	Pure white	Suitable for hot summer sowing.	ROS

◀

Variety	Days	Head	Remarks	Sources
EARLY WHITE (hybrid)	52	9 in. Pure white	Superb quality for freezing, pickling, raw or cooked.	BURP
EXTRA EARLY SNOWBALL	50	Snow-white	Good curd protection. Use for mid-August or early September crops.	SEE STO
PIONEER	65	Large, snow-white	Fine-textured. Firm head. Thrives where cabbage grows. Withstands light frost.	HEN
POLAR EXPRESS	50	2. lbs. Dome-shaped	Tolerance to purple tinge.	STO
RAKET (hybrid)	53	White	Dutch variety. Vigorous, easy growing plant. Use fresh or cooked. Tender and mild.	SHE
SNOWBALL	65	Medium-large	Deep, solid head. Sure header.	ALL DEG LEJ MID WYA
SNOWBALL A IMPROVED	60	Large	Best when planted for fall crop. Good taste and freezing quality.	WILL
SNOWBALL T-3	51		Compact, domed heads.	GAR
SNOWBALL T-4	50	Large, white	Self-blanching. Deep, firm, smooth. Excellent quality and uniformity.	WET
SNOWBALL 16		7-9 in.	Dwarf plant.	DEG MEY
SNOW CROWN (hybrid)	50-68	5-9 in. 2 lbs.	Snowball type. Good fresh or frozen. High yields.	ARC BURP COM DAN DIX EAR FAR HARR JOH JUN LED LEM LIBE MEY MID NIC PAR PIN PON POR SEED STO TER THO TWI VER WILL
SNOW KING (hybrid)	43	5½-9 in.	Snowball type. Erect plant. Heat-tolerant. Good for freezing.	COM FAR GUR HEN JUN LIBE PIN TWI WET WIL WILL
SNOW QUEEN (hybrid)	43	2 lbs. Pure white	Plant during the hottest part of summer for fall harvest.	VER
STOKES EXTRA EARLY SNOWBALL	55-60		Very solid head. Widely adapted to different soils. Good curd protection.	GAR SOU
SUPER SNOWBALL (op) (BURPEEANA) (EARLY SNOWBALL A)	55-60	6½ in. Ivory white	Dwarf plant. Freezes well. Short-season variety.	ALL BURP BURR DAN FAR FIS HEN LED MID PIE TWI WET
WHITE BISHOP	52	2¼ lbs.	Heavy wrapper leaves. Deep heavy head. Harvest in two cuts. Tolerant to purple tinge.	STO
WHITE CONTESSA 62	62	1 lb. White	Stands heat well. Fall crop for the North. Tolerant to downy mildew and black rot. Vigorous, compact plant.	TWI
WHITE KNIGHT	55	2¼ lbs. 6¾ in.	Tolerance to purple tinge. Vigorous self-wrapping leaves.	STO

CAULIFLOWER—MID-SEASON
60 + DAYS

Variety	Days	Head	Remarks	Sources
ALL YEAR ROUND	70	Large	Keeps in good condition for a long time. Good for frame culture. Good freezer.	ECO THO
ANDES	65	6½ in.	Deep head is self-wrapping. Very uniform. Heat- and cold-tolerant.	HIG JOH STO VES
ARAPAHO (op)		Large, white	Excellent head protection. Susceptible to frost damage.	HARR
ARMADO SPRING	220-260		This has several strains. Dutch variety. Over-wintering type. Fine salad quality.	TER
BLUE DIAMOND (op)		Large	Good head protection.	HARR
CANDID CHARM (hybrid)	75	7-9 in. Pure white	High, tightly packed dome. Plant is vigorous. Heavy yields. No purple cast.	HARR HIG LIBE MID TWI
CERVINA	72		High quality. Great self-wrapping.	STO
CLOUD NINE	67		Good bad-weather tolerance. Tolerant to mildew. Erect, self-blanching plant.	STO
DOK ELGON	65		Undemanding and can overwinter. Good freezer.	ECO THO
DOMINANT	68	Large	Excellent variety. Firm white head. Vigorous foliage growth. Extensive root system provides some drought tolerance.	GAR JOH RAW SEE STO VES
DRY WEATHER (DANISH GIANT)	67	2-3 lbs. Snow-white	Needs little water.	DEG
EARLY GLACIER (hybrid)	105	2 lbs. Pure white	Grows in cooler climates. Dome-shaped head. Vigorous growth.	LIBE VES
EARLY MARCH (op)		Large	Well-protected head. Vigorous. Dark green leaves.	HARR
ELGON (hybrid)	60		Widely adapted. High yielder. Vigorous grower. Large, coarse-grained curds. Does well in hot weather.	VER
ENGLISH WINTER (LEAMINGTON)			Sow in early autumn for April-May harvest.	ABU
IGLOO	70	Very white	Well-protected head. Large plant. Widely adapted. Does best when planted for cool-weather harvest.	BURR
IMPERIAL 10-6 (op)		Large, white	Good head cover when tied.	DIX HARR
INCA		2 lbs.	Winter variety. Good frost tolerance. Plant in July for April harvest.	HUM TIL
JURA	120-140	Large	Grows well in maritime Northwest. Well-wrapped heads. Dutch variety.	TER
LATE QUEEN	90	Large	Reliable variety. Fine quality.	THO
LERCERF	68		European variety. Solid, white self-protecting head.	WILL

Variety	Days	Head	Remarks	Sources
LINAS	68		Self-wrapping leaves. Tolerance to riceyness and pinking.	STO
MAJESTIC (hybrid)	66	7-8 in. Pure white	Slightly domed head.	TWI
MONARCH (SNOWBALL)		10 in.	Nice head even under adverse conditions.	DEG
MONARCH 73M (op)		Medium-large, deep white	Uniform maturity.	HARR
NEWTON SEALE	180	Large	Winter and early spring. Frost-resistant. Very white curds.	THO
SELF-BLANCHE (op)	68-71	6½-8 in. White	Self-wrapping variety. Recommended as fall crop only.	ALL BURG DIX EAR FAR FIS GAR GUR HARR HEN LET LIBE MEY MID PON RAW RIS SEE SEED STO TWI WYA
SELF-BLANCHE IMPROVED	72	6-8 in. Pure white	Good head protection. Finely textured.	JUN
SILVER STAR (op)		Large, lumpy	Wavy leaves give excellent heat protection. Large frame. Plant Variety Protected.	HARR
SNOWBALL D (op)	65	6½ in.	Dwarf plant. Heads are well protected.	HARR
SNOWBALL E (op)	58-66	6½ in. White	Performs well in eastern states. Dependable cropper.	TWI
SNOWBALL Y	65-70	6½ in.	Reliable under adverse conditions.	DEG EVA LIBE MEY PER PIE
SNOWBALL Y IMPROVED (op)	68-70	Medium-large, snow-white	Widely adapted. Medium-large plant.	BUR DIX HARR JUN LAG MID RIS WIL
SNOWBALL X	60-64		Similar to Snowdrift. Thick, firm and pure white. Strong outer leaves.	BURR EVE PIE
SNOWBALL 16	70	Snow-white	Dwarf plant.	GUR
SNOWBALL 123 (op)			Deep, compact head. Plant Variety Protected. Easy to tie. Erect foliage.	HARR
SNOWBALL 741	66		Does best as fall crop. Big leaves and vigorous growth.	JOH
SNOW GIANT	110	5 lbs. Snow-white	Vigorous. Grows under adverse conditions. Tall and productive plant. Good quality head.	GLE
SNOW MARCH (hybrid)		Medium, snow-white	Good head protection. Medium-upright plant.	HARR
SNOW PAK (op)	62	White	Plant Variety Protected. Dependable uniform maturity.	LET MID RIS TWI
SNOW WINTER WHITE	180		Cold-tolerant. Easy to grow.	ECO THO
STARLIGHT (hybrid)	85	2½-7 lbs.	Well-adapted variety. Smooth, deep heads. Grows even under adverse conditions. Self-blanching.	TWI

◀ ## CAULIFLOWER—MID-SEASON

Variety	Days	Head	Remarks	Sources
STOVEPIPE	65	White	Good head protection. Heat-resistant.	GUR
TAIPAN	66		High quality. Self-wrapping. Spiral leaf provides good ventilation and curd coverage.	STO
VERNON	75-95		Dutch variety. Deep, smooth curds, almost globe shape. Medium-size plant.	TER
VETCH'S SELF-PROTECTING	80	White	Good leaf protection.	ECO THO
VETCH AUTUMN GIANT		Large	1885 heirloom variety. Large plant.	ABU
WHITE CASTLE (hybrid)	63	7¼ in.	Self-wrapping. Curds are tolerant to purple tinge, internal black speck and hollow stem.	STO
WHITE FOX (WITTE VOS)	68	8 in. Creamy white	Smooth and very uniform. Self-wrapping leaves. High quality. Dutch variety.	PIN SHE STO
WHITE ROCK	69-100	6½ in.	Plant Variety Protected. Good curd protection. Dutch variety.	MID STO TER
WHITE SAILS (hybrid)	68	7½ in.	Excellent heat tolerance. High-yielding. Self-wrapping leaves. Recommended for fall planting only.	STO SOU
WHITE SUMMER	65		Self-wrapping type. Excellent curd protection.	FAR STO
WHITE TOP	70-90		Self-wrapping. Excellent quality. Dutch variety. Strong root system.	STO TER VES

CAULIFLOWER

OTHER COLORS

Variety	Days	Head	Remarks	Sources
BURGUNDY QUEEN (hybrid)	70	6½ in. 19 ozs.	Heat tolerant. Good freezer. Deep purple color.	STO
CHARTREUSE (GREEN BALL)	115	8½ in. Green	Tall, spreading plant. Good freezer.	RAW
GREEN HARMONY (hybrid)	80	Medium, pale green	Chinese call this "Flocoli". No blanching needed. Cross between broccoli and cauliflower.	GLE
ITALIAN PURPLE BRONZE	110			COM
PURPLE CAPE			Treat this one like broccoli. Hardier than the white cauliflowers.	ECO THO
PURPLE GIANT	75	Purple	Spreading giant. Freezes well. Turns green when cooked.	DEG LED SEE WES
PURPLE HEAD	70-110	Purple	Large, compact head. Flavor like broccoli. Good freezer. Turns green when cooked.	BURP JUN WILL

▶

Variety	Days	Size/Color	Remarks	Sources
ROYAL PURPLE HEAD	85-95	Purple	Flavor like broccoli. Good freezer.	FAR
SICILIAN PURPLE	85	Purple	Mild flavor. Good freezer.	ABU NIC
VIOLET QUEEN (hybrid)	60	Purple	Easy to grow. Grown like broccoli, without tying. Use fresh or cooked.	JOH LEM TIL VER

CAULIFLOWER—MINIATURE

Variety	Days	Head	Remarks	Sources
GARANT	82-86		Harvest when head is 1½ to 3½ inches across. Quick-growing, vigorous. Does not mature all at once. Good freezer.	THO
PREDOMINANT	90-94		Harvest when head is 1½ to 3½ inches across. Good freezer.	THO

CELERIAC
(Apium graveolens rapaceum)

Celeriac, a close relative of celery, forms rough, knobby, rounded roots that are peeled and used in soups and stews. The foliage of the celeriac is a beautiful deep green, and the dark green stems are hollow. Sometimes celeriac is called turnip root. Most celeriac varieties are fairly similar.

CULTURE: To grow from seeds, soak seeds first, then plant in flats or peat pots. They germinate in about 10 days. Transplant when seedlings reach about 6 inches high. Work in fertilizer and space 6 to 8 inches apart in rows 24 to 30 inches apart. When the plants are about half-grown, feed them at regular intervals. Make sure celeriac receives plenty of water throughout its growing period.

SEASON: Cool.

HARVESTING: (1) Pull up the plant when the root has swollen to 3 to 4 inches wide and cut off the top; or (2) snip off the side roots and hill the soil over the swollen root as it is beginning to form. This partially blanches it. Harvest when the root is 3 to 4 inches wide.

CELERIAC

Variety	Days	Plant/Roots	Remarks	Sources
ALABASTER	120	Large, thick 4 in. root	White flesh, similar to celery. Good in vegetable soups.	BURP RIC SEE TIL
ARVI	110	Flattened bulb	Vigorous strain. Dutch variety. White flesh doesn't discolor.	TER
CELERIAC (KNOB CELERY)	110-120	Turnip-rooted celery, 2-3 in. across	Stores well. Use fresh, grated, or boiled in stews and soups.	GUR PAR SUN VER WET
DE-RUEIL				LEJ
DOLVI	150	Nearly round roots	Multiple disease resistance and vigor. Fine texture and flavor. Use fresh or cooked.	NIC
GIANT SMOOTH PRAGUE	110	4 in. Smooth root	For use in soups.	COM DEG JUN LED LET MEY PER PIN RAW RED STO WILL
GLOBUS	120		Wide variety of uses.	THO
JOSE	110	Large roots	White interior. Flavorful.	JOH
MAGDENBURGER		Large, white roots	Pure white interior. For use in soups.	LEJ

◀ CELERIAC

Variety	Days	Plant/Roots	Remarks	Sources
MARBLE BALL	110	Large, solid, knobs	Heavy yielder. Free of side shoots. Dark green foliage.	HARR LIBE
MARKET GROWERS CELERIAC	130-150	Small to medium roots	European variety.	LEM
MONARCH	120	Large roots	Firm, white flesh does not discolor.	WILL
PARIS IMPROVED	120	Large, smooth. Harvest when 2 in. in diameter.	Good cooked or raw.	HER
PRAGUE		Large	Larger than Giant Prague.	RIS SEE
PRAGUE MODEL		Large		DEG SEE

CELERY
(Apium graveolens dulce)

Celery is not always easy to grow, but is well worth the try since the root, stalk and foliage can be used in cooking. Celery is a heavy feeder and a heavy drinker.

CULTURE: Plant seedlings outside, leaving 6-8 inches between plants in rows 24 inches apart. If you want to try blanching, place a cardboard collar around each plant two weeks before harvest, then place soil or a heavy mulch around the collar. You can also wrap the plants from top to bottom with heavy brown paper held in place with rubber bands.

SEASON: Cool.

INSECTS/DISEASES: *APHIDS, CELERY LEAF TIERS, CELERY WORMS, BLISTER BEETLES, CABBAGE LOOPERS:* Malathion, diazinon, pyrethrum, rotenone, or ryania.
SNAILS, SLUGS: Slug-Geta.
LEAF BLIGHT, STEM ROT: Maneb or zineb.
MOSAICS: Malathion.

HARVESTING: You can harvest younger stalks when plants are still two to four weeks from maturity. Celery stores well in a cool place. Some gardeners leave fall surplus in the soil during early winter, piling dirt and straw around the stalks to protect against freezing.

CELERY
GREEN

Variety	Days	Size	Remarks	Sources
BISHOP		25 in.	Plant Variety Protected. Dark green. Compact and cylindrical. Tolerates fusarium yellows in some areas.	HARR
BURPEE'S FORDHOOK	130	15-18 in.	Always tender, crisp and juicy. Ideal for fall use and winter storage.	BURP
CUTTING LEAF CELERY	80	Dwarf	Recommended for drying. Leaves are used for flavoring soups and stews. Strong taste.	LEM SEE WILL
DEACON		25 in.	Dark green. Average petiole length is 13 in. Compact and cylindrical. Tolerant to fusarium yellows in some areas.	HARR
FLORIDA 683	120-125	22-24 in.	Excellent heart formation. Mosaic-resistant. 10½ in. petioles.	DEG HAR LET MID STO WIL
FORDHOOK EMPEROR	130	Large	Dark green foliage and thick stalks. Golden heart.	WET
FORDHOOK GIANT	120	Short and stocky	Dark green. Good flavor.	DEG SEE

▶

Variety	Days	Size	Remarks	Sources
FRENCH CELERY DINANT (CHINESE CELERY)	55		Sends out a multitude of narrow thin stalks. Resistant to light frost. Has fuller flavor than most other celery, and can be dried for winter use.	ABU NIC THO
GREEN GIANT (hybrid)	75	Large	Not hardy. Light green, long, thick stems. Vigorous.	THO TWI
GIANT PASCAL (WINTER KING)	134-140	Tall	Stringless, thick stalks. Excellent keeper.	ALL BURG COM DEG LET PON ROS SEE WET
SUMMER PASCAL (TALL FORDHOOK)	115-125	26-28 in.	Extra-thick stems. Vigorous and compact. Resistant to blight.	DEG LIBE MEY PAR
SUMMER PASCAL (WALTHAM GREEN)	120-125	22-24 in.	Full-hearted. Dark green.	DEG LET MEY MID
SUMMIT	100		Fusarium-tolerant. Dark green, medium ribbed, 10 in. petioles.	STO
SUREPAK	100		Medium-green, compact, heavy growth. Ribs average 10-12 in. Good heart formation.	STO
TALL GREEN LIGHT		21 in.	Medium-green, 10 in. petioles. Freedom from chlorosis.	HARR
TALL UTAH	90	23 in.	Large heart, long petioles. Very compact, medium-green plant.	ROS
TALL UTAH 52-70R			Resistant to mosaic and boron deficiency.	HARR LIBE
TALL UTAH 52-70R IMPROVED		24 in.	Dark green 11-12 in. petioles. Very compact habit. Tolerates boron deficiency.	BURP BURR HARR HUM LET MID STO TER TIL TWI
TENDERCRISP	105		Upright, medium-green, large heart.	DAN GUR STO
UTAH (SALT LAKE)	100-125		Stocky, full-hearted. Thick stems.	DEG FAR FIS SEE WILL
UTAH IMPROVED	90			LAG
UTAH 52-70	125-130	24-28 in.	Upright and compact. Tender, yet crisp. Dark green petioles. Excellent quality.	ABU COM HARR JUN LET PAR PIN RAW RIS SEED VES WIL WILL
VENTURA 80	100	28 in.	Tall Utah type. Petioles average 13 in.	JOH LET MID STO
ZWOLSCHE KRUL-CUTTING CELERY	60	2½-3 ft.	Dutch heritage variety. Hardy. Leaves are used like parsley but taste like celery. Stems are thin and hollow. Use in soups and stews.	PIN

CELERY
GOLDEN

Variety	Days	Size	Remarks	Sources
DWARF GOLDEN SELF-BLANCHING	85-100	18-22 in.	Crisp, solid, stringless and compact.	BURR DEG
GOLDEN PLUME (WONDERFUL)	85-118		Self-blanching and stringless.	JUN STO

◄ CELERY

Variety	Days	Size	Remarks	Sources
GOLDEN SELF-BLANCHING (AMERICAN) (FALL DWARF STRAIN)	80-118	20 in.	Compact. Not hardy.	ARC BURP BUT COM EAR ECO FAR HEN JUN LET MEY NIC PIN PON POR RIS ROS SEE TER THO VER WET WILL WYA
GOLDEN TALL SELF-BLANCHING	110-120	20-30 in.	Delicate flavor. Highly disease-resistant. Good keeper.	DEG RED

CELERY
PINK/RED

Variety	Days	Size	Remarks	Sources
GIANT PINK			Stalks are pink to red, redder in winter.	LEM
GIANT RED	120		Cold-hardy. Light green with purple tinge. Put earth up around it and it turns shell-pink.	JLH THO
PINK CELERY	120		English variety. Color remains after cooking.	GLE SEE
RED CELERY	120		Adds color to salads.	GLE PEA SEE

CELERY—ORIENTAL

Variety	Days	Size	Remarks	Sources
CHINESE GOLDEN MEDIUM EARLY	90		Light green leaves with long, hollow stalks. Frangrant aroma.	SUN
CHINESE KAN-TSAI			Long slender stems and strong flavor.	ABU
HEUNG KUNN (CHINESE CELERY)	90		Fragrant, aromatic and delicious; can be grown indoors. Grows best in cool, moist soil.	BAN SUN TSA
KINTSAI ORIENTAL WILD			Widely used in Asian cooking. Has strong, sharp flavor.	LEM

CHARD
(Beta vulgaris cicla)

If you've tried spinach and failed, or if you are just tired of fighting the weather requirements of spinach, you'll want to grow Swiss chard. It can take summer temperatures that would make spinach bolt to seed. Chard is a member of the beet family without the bulbous root. The leaves are cooked and served like asparagus.

CULTURE: Sow seed a half-inch deep in rows 18 to 24 inches apart. Later, thin plants to 12 inches apart. Sow in early spring in cold-winter areas, about two weeks befor the final frost in areas where winter temperatures stay above 25° F, plant in the fall for harvesting the next year. In regions of very mild climate plant almost any time of year.

SEASON: Cool.

HARVESTING: There are two ways to pick chard. You can cut the outer leaves every few days while the plant continues growing. Don't let the old, tough leaves remain on the plant or it will stop producing fresh leaves. You can also cut off the whole plant a couple of inches above the root crowns, in which case the plant a couple of inches above the root crowns in which the whole plant should produce new leaves.

CHARD
DARK GREEN, CRUMPLED

Variety	Days	Stalks/Leaves	Remarks	Sources
BURPEE'S FORDHOOK GIANT	60	White stalks, dark green, savoyed	Heavy yields. Prepare like asparagus.	BURP
DARK GREEN WHITE RIBBED (LARGE WHITE RIBBED) (SILVER RIBBED)	55-60	Broad, white ribs, crumpled dark green	Use the chard leaves and midrib like asparagus.	FAR HARR HUM LAG LED MID RIS
DE LANGUEDOC		Thick, white midribs, curly, dark green	Widely adapted. For year-round planting. Resists bolting.	LEM
DE NICE		Thick white midribs, deeply curled	Grows quickly. Resistant to cold. Bolts with onset of spring.	LEM
DORAT	60	Wide white stalks, pale yellow-green, savoyed	Danish variety. Mild tasting.	TER
FORDHOOK	58	Dark green, savoyed		BUT LET PIN
FORDHOOK GIANT (DARK GREEN LUCULLUS)	50-55	Snow-white midrib, heavily crumpled	Yields until frost.	ABU ALL COM DAN EARL EVA FIS GAR HEN HIG JOH LAG MEY MID PON RAW RED ROS SEE SEED STO TER WES WIL
FRENCH GREEN		Thick, crumpled	Some resistance to heat and cold.	ABU
PAROS	55	Dark green, crinkled	French variety. Sweet and mild. Delicious in stir fry. Won't bolt in hot weather.	SHE
WHITE KING	55	Thick white ribs, dark green, savoyed		STO

CHARD
DARK GREEN, SMOOTH LEAVES

Variety	Days	Stalks/Leaves	Remarks	Sources
FRENCH SWISS CHARD	60	Thick, white stalks, large	Heavy yields. 18 in. plant.	NIC SEE
JAPANESE SWISS CHARD (NIHON)		Thick, light green stalks, broad	Resembles smooth round-leaved spinach.	SUN
LARGE SMOOTH WHITE RIBBED	60	Broad white ribs	Very productive and tasty.	SEE TWI
PERPETUAL	50	Very little midrib	New leaves are produced until fall. Resistant to heat, drought and frost. Very productive.	BURP
GENEVA SWISS CHARD	60	Large ribs	Can withstand severe weather. Can be grown year-round. Tops make delicious greens.	PAR

CHARD
LIGHT GREEN

Variety	Days	Stalks/Leaves	Remarks	Sources
BLONDE A CARDE BLANCHE	50-60	White stalks, crumpled, light green	Heat-resistant. Frost-tolerant.	HER
GIANT LUCULLUS	50	Yellow-green, crumpled	24-28 in. plant.	COM
LUCULLUS	50-60	Large white mid-rib, crumpled	Fine flavor.	ABU ALL ARC BURG EAR EARL FAR GUR JUN LED LET PAR POR RAW RIS SEE SOU THO VES WET

CHARD
RED

Variety	Days	Stalks/Leaves	Remarks	Sources
RAINBOW	60	Red, orange, purple, yellow and white stems	Tender and tasty.	THO
RED BURGUNDY	60	Red stalks, deep maroon leaves	Useful as well as ornamental. Nice Flavor. Yields until frost.	EAR FAR
RHUBARB CHARD	55-60	Crimson stalks, heavily crumpled green leaves	Delicious stalks. Tasty leaves.	ABU ALL BURP COM DEG FIS GUR HARR HUM JUN LAG LED LET PIN PLA POR RAW RIS SEE SOU STO TER THO TIL TWI WES
RUBY RED	60	Red to white stalks, red crumpled	2-24 in. plant.	GAR HEN JOH LEM NIC ROS SEED WET
VULCAN	60	Bright red stems, dark green, savoyed	Exceptionally sweet flavor.	PAR

CHICORY
(Chicorium intybus)

Chicory comes in several forms. The group includes chicorees frisées (curly endives), the escaroles, radicchios, green chicories and Belgian endive (Witloof chicory), the same vegetable being know by names from different countries or regions. Regardless of the different names, chicories share one common characteristic—bitterness. For Europeans, this bitterness is desirable—it adds flavor. However, most Americans find chicories to be too bitter for their taste. Bitterness is increased by hot weather and overlong growing, so try to make allowances for your climate.

CULTURE: Sow seed a quarter inch deep, then thin to 4 to 8 inches apart in rows 18 to 24 inches apart. Treat frisées and escarole as lettuce, but avoid overhead watering. Give plenty of water and nutrients to start, as rapid growth will help keep away excess bitterness. Plant in spring or fall. Allow non-forcing types to mature in place during fall, winter, and early spring. Avoid nitrogen fertilizers, except at first planting. Forcing types require special treatment in order to produce nice heads. They need freezing weather during the fall and winter months. The leaves must be cut off to within one inch of the crown 2 to 3 weeks before the first frost. The roots may then be dug and stored in a cool dark place (45 to 55° F), where they will produce their second growth.

SEASON: Cool.

HARVESTING: Chicoree frisée's leaves are finely cut and used in salads, or serve as individual heads. Escarole is a popular green in Italy and France and used like lettuce. Radicchio is generally a winter crop and provides red-colored leaves to salads. Open-headed green chicories have long, thin strappy leaves, deeply indented or rounded leaves. Each shape has a distinct flavor. Root chicories are grown primarily for the root; they are sliced and cooked, or baked and ground into a coffee substitute.

CHICORY—RADICCHIO

Variety	Days	Remarks	Sources
ADRIA	75	Italian chicory. Crimson heads mature to 5½ in. across and weigh 9 ozs. White veins.	STO
AUGUSTO	70	Italian chicory. Plant mid- to late summer for fall harvest. Burgundy-red head. Frost-tolerant.	JOH
BARBE DE CAPUCIN (BARBA DI CAPUCCINO)		Leaves are long and deeply cut. Force in soil.	LEJ VER
BAXTER'S SPECIAL	65	Italian dandelion. Heavy, thick-leaved.	RIS
CASTELFRANCO	83	Non-forcing radicchio type. Red and white interior, crinkled outer leaves are green tinged with red.	LAG LEM SEE VER
CERIOLO (GRUMOLO)		Dark green heading type resembles lettuce. use whole in salads or serve individually dipped in vinaigrette.	LEM NIC VER
CHIOGGIA	80	Round-headed, turn white with red speckles after they are blanched. Non-forcing radicchio type. Plant in late summer.	LEM NIC RED
CRYSTAL HAT	70	Non-forcing variety. Long oval heads resemble romaine lettuce. Withstands heat and frost. Use as salad greens.	NIC
CURLED LARGE HEAD	90	Summer variety. Leaves and ribs are edible right down to the crown.	HER
DI CHIAVORI		Grown for its root. A long vegetable. Thick-collared, creamy-white. To prepare, scrape and boil root until tender.	LEM
DI TRIESTE		A green cutting chicory. Italian variety. Use leaves when they are 3 to 4 in. Plant in spring or summer.	LEM
EN CORNET D'ANJOU		Broad-leaved heading chicory for spring and fall.	LEJ VER
EN CORNET DE BORDEAUX			LEJ
FINE CURLED LOUVIERS	90	Has indented leaves. Compact, but curled heart. Grows 10 in. across. Yellow-green foliage.	HER LEM VER
FINE MARAICHERE		Matures to size of an open hand. Use in salad when young. Grows 8 in. across.	LEM
FRASTIGLIATA		Open-headed green use chicory. Thin leaves and sharp flavor. Use in salads, stuffings or as cooked greens.	LEM
GUILIO	60-100	Compact plant. Round garnet-colored head with white rib. Resistant to bolting. Does best in mild climates.	JOH LEM SHE VER
IMPROVED SUGAR LOAF	90	Tall, yellowish foliage. Well-formed long heads. Plant in June or July.	HER
MADGEBURG (COFFEE CHICORY) (LARGE ROOTED)	55-100	Large-rooted variety. Roots are long and tapered. Can be ground into coffee substitute. Grows 15 in. tall and the roots are 14 to 16 in.	ABU COM DEG LET RAW RED RIC SEE STO TIL WILL
MARINA	90-110	Large compact bright red heads. Easily grown. Cultivate like a lettuce for autumn and winter production. 10 to 12 oz. heads.	BURP HER
MEILOF		Late forcing variety.	VES WILL
MILANSE	82		LAG

▶

◄ CHICORY—RADICCHIO

Variety	Days	Remarks	Sources
MITADO		Forcing variety. German variety. Sow in May. Lift roots in late autumn.	NIC
PAIN DE SUCRE (SUGARLOAF)		Large 18-20 in. upright plant with twisted head. Mildest of all chicories. Easy to grow. Use in salads, wrapping meats or vegetable combinations.	LEM VER
PALA DI FUOCO ROSSA	80		LAG
PALLA ROSSA		Non-forcing radicchio has dark green exterior leaves and red interior. Pure white ribs.	LEM VER
PAN DI ZUCCHERO	89	Tight yellow-green oblong head.	LAB RED SHE
PONT DE PIERRE		Vigorous European variety. Large roots are pulled in the fall, cut into pieces, dried, roasted until brown and ground up, then used with coffee. Tops are used in salads.	JLH
PRODUCTIVA		Uniform 6 in. heads. Forcing type.	WILL
RADICHETTA (ASPARAGUS) (CATALONGA) (CICCORIA)	52-75	Toothed, curled and green. 1½-3 in. wide tender stalks. Cook like asparagus.	COM DEG GAR HARR LAG LED NIC RED SEE STO VER
RADICCHIO, CESARE	90-110	Non-forcing radicchio. Green outer leaves, red and white heads. Uniform.	HARR LEM SHE
RED TREVISO (ROSSA DI TREVISO)	85	Green leaves with red veins. Heads to 8 in. long and 3 to 4 in. across. Pure white mid-rib. Forcing type.	GLE LAG LEJ LEM NIC RED SEE SHE VER
RONETTE	80	Italian chicory. Closed, rounded intense red head with white veins. 8 ozs.	STO
ROSSA DI VERONA	85	Dark red chicory popular for centuries in Italy. Should be started by July for a fall crop. Slightly bitter, unique delicate flavor.	ABU ECO GAR LAG SEE
ROUGE DE VERONE (VERONA RED) (ITALIAN GREENS)	85	Red-green color. Good for salads. Recommeded for northern gardens. Forcing type.	COM GLE HER LEM NIC SEE THO TWI VER
SAN PASQUALE (ALL SEASONS) (ITALIAN DANDELION)	70	Light green, finely cut. Similar to radichetta. Small and tender.	HARR MEY STO TWI
SELVATICA DE CAMPO		Long, thin leaves and sharp chicory taste. Use in mixed salads, cooked green or in stuffings. Open-headed green chicory.	LEM
SNOWFLAKE (WINTER FARE)	75	No forcing or blanching needed. Grow like lettuce. Very cold-resistant.	THO
SOTTOMARINA		Non-forcing radicchio. Varigated green and red. Loose heads. Plant early spring or late summer.	LEM
SPADONA (LINGUA DI CANE) (DOG'S TONGUE)	85	Plant spring or fall. Cut at about 6 inches.	LAG VER
SUGARHAT	86	Medium green outer leaves. Sweet, tender, yet tangy. Good cooked, or tossed in salads. Elongated heads.	BURP LAG
TONER	130	Easy to grow and to force. Fall harvest, forcing October to March.	JOH

Variety	Days	Remarks	Sources
WITLOOF CHICORY (FRENCH ENDIVE) (LARGE BRUSSELS) (BELGIAN ENDIVE)	70-140	Solid heads, clusters of blanched leaves are 4 to 6 in. long. Sharp flavor is tangy in salads. Forcing variety.	BURP COM DEG HARR IND LAG LED LEM LET MEY NIC PIN RAW RED RIC THO VER WILL
WITLOOF IMPROVED	110	Heads are 5 to 6 in. Broad leaf stalks.	HER SEE STO
ZOOM (hybrid)	110	Belgian endive. Roots may be forced by digging up roots and keeping in dark place 40 to 60° F for second growth. French variety. Forcing hydroponic variety.	HER LEM WILL

CHICORY—ENDIVE
NOT CURLED (ESCAROLE)

Variety	Days	Remarks	Sources
BATAVIAN FULL-HEARTED (DEEP HEART) (ESCAROLE) (FLORIDA DEEP HEART) (WIVOL)	85-90	Slightly crumpled, dark green leaves. 12 in. spreading, white rib. Tender heart.	COM DEG ECO GAR HARR LAG LED LET LIBE MID PIN RAW RIS SEE SEED STO TER TIL TWI
BROAD-LEAVED BATAVIAN	90	Large, broad slightly twisted leaves. 16 in. spread. Full heart.	ALL BURP DEG HARR MEY NIC RIC WET WILL
BROADLEAVED FULLHEART WINTER	95	Extra-large heads. Tie up for tender yellow hearts.	WILL
CORNET DE BORDEAUX		Lobed leaves, but not deeply cut. Grows upright. White-ribbed. Makes excellent wrapping for stuffings.	LEM RED
CUORE PIENO		Broad, pale leaves. Full-hearted.	LEM
GROWER GIANT	70	Long, smooth broad leaf. Well-formed butt. Grows well in muck and mineral soils.	LET
RED		Grow like Belgian Endive. Root stock produce compact, rounded heads of purplish-red foliage.	RIC
SINCO	83	Dark green, broad slightly crinkled leaves. French variety. Folded outer leaves with a closely bunched, well-blanched heart. Tangy flavor.	SHE

CHICORY—ENDIVE
CURLED (FRISEE)

Variety	Days	Remarks	Sources
CRISPY GREEN	93	Curled, moderately cut leaves. Good body, full heart. Slow to bolt. Dark green with pale green midribs.	HARR
DEEP HEART FRINGED	90	Dark curled leaves. 10 to 12 in. spread. Extra-deep heart, well-filled.	DEG
ELODIE	70	Frothy, curled, dense leaves. French variety. Crisp ribs, blanched hearts. Produces over a long season. Crunchy, clean taste.	SHE
FRISAN	98	17 in. head. Well-filled with blanched center. Dark green leaves. Tolerant to bad weather and low temperatures.	STO

◀ **CHICORY—ENDIVE**

Variety	Days	Remarks	Sources
GREEN CURLED (GREEN FRINGED OYSTER) (GREEN CURLED RUFFEC)	90	Finely cut, green curled leaves. 16 to 18 in. spread. Easily blanched. Tangy flavor.	ABU ALL BURG BUT DEG EAR EARL ECO FAR HARR HUM JUN LAG LED LET LIBE NIC POR RED RIS SEE SOU STO TWI VES WET WYA
GREEN CURLED PANCALIER	95	Pink-ribbed. Large plant blanches well with close plantings.	LET
GREEN CURLED PINK RIB	90	18 in. spread.	SEE
NUVOL	50	Wavy dark green broad leaves. Self-blanching. Creamy yellow well-filled heart. Slow bolting. Large head.	JOH
PRESIDENT (GIANT GREEN CURLED)		Large endive with a dense full heart. Withstands adverse weather in the fall.	LET TER
RUFFLE LEAF		Ruffled green leaves. Salad-bowl type endive. Mild flavor. Tender and mild.	GLE
SALAD KING	75-100	Deep green, frilly toothed leaves. 22-24 in. spread. Slow to bolt. Not harmed by light frost.	BURG BURR COM DEG HARR JOH LIBE MEY MID RIS STO

CHIVES
(Allium schoenoprassum)

Chives are a gourmet's delight, with hollow, grass-like leaves that persist in the garden for many years.

CULTURE: You can buy pots of chives from a nursery and separate or you can sow seeds outside in the garden almost anytime, except winter in the North. Chives prefer full sun but will tolerate some shade. Once the plants are established, cut them back regularly to encourage new growth. Lift and divide established clumps every few years in the spring or fall.

HARVESTING: Clip off the leaves whenever you need them.

CHIVES			
Variety	Days	Remarks	Sources
CHINESE CHIVES (HP) (GARLIC CHIVES) (GOW CHOY)		Grows 1-2 ft. Has flat, rather tubular leaf. Ashy gray instead of green. Has slight garlic flavor. Winter-hardy. Needs moist, fairly rich soil.	COO LEM NIC RIC SUN TSA VER WES
CHIVES FRUHLAU (hybrid) (HP)		Grows 6-9 in. More productive than standard chives. Fewer flowers. Can be cut more frequently.	THO
CHIVES GRASS ONION (GARDEN CHIVES)(P)	80	Grows to 1 foot. Grows from seed. Leaves have mild onion flavor. Use in soup, eggs, soft cheese, mashed potatoes. Divide the clump every three years.	ABU ALL ARC BURP BURR COM COO DAN EAR EARL ECO FAR FIS GUR HARR HER IND JLH JUN LAG LED LEJ LEM LET LIBE MID NIC PAR PER PLA RAW RED RIC SEED SHE STO TAY TER THO TIL TWI VER VES WES WILL
GROLAU CHIVES (P)		Grows to 1 foot. Best for indoor growing. Produces well if kept cut. Medium-thick foliage. Good strong flavor.	NIC
SCHNITTLAUCH		Thick tufts, dark green hollow foliage. Cut throughout the summer.	DEG MEY

CITRON

Citron is a round melon that is used primarily for preserving and for making candied peel.

CULTURE: Citron should be isolated from watermelons by five miles. It can contaminate the watermelons. Cultivate like you would cantaloupes.

HARVESTING: Harvest as you would a cantaloupe.

CITRON

Variety	Days	Heads/Plants	Remarks	Sources
CITRON		10 lbs. Clear white	Skin is green-striped. Excellent for pickles. Should not be planted near other melons.	FAR JUN LEM
GREEN SEEDED	98	Round, light green	Use exclusively for preserving.	RAW
RED SEEDED	90-95	10-12 lbs. Light green	Used for preserving. Extremely productive. Small seeds.	GLE NIC SEE STO VES

COLLARDS
(Brassica oleracea acephala)

Collards are rather old as vegetables go, having been used as food for at least 4,000 years. In this country they have long been a Southern favorite. Today, they are rapidly taking their place along with other delicious greens such as spinach, mustard greens and kale (a close relative of collards).

Collards generally resemble a lanky, open-growing cabbage with smooth, dark green edible leaves. They are usually regarded as non-heading, but several types form rather loose heads.

CULTURE: Plant seed outdoors in late spring in cool-summer areas. In other areas plant in mid- to late summer for a fall and winter harvest. The mature plants are frost-hardy. Sow seeds a half-inch deep, 1 inch apart in rows 24 to 30 inches apart. Thin to 18 to 24 inches apart.

SEASON: Cool.

HARVESTING: You can harvest the entire plant, or you can leave the first six to eight leaves to sustain the plant, harvesting the young leaves over a period of time.

COLLARDS

Variety	Days	Remarks	Sources
BLUE MAX (hybrid)	68	Large, blue-green crinkled leaves. Fast grower. Tender, mild and tasty.	POR TWI
CAROLINA		28-32 in. Slightly wavy leaves. Mildew-resistant. Tolerant to wind and cold.	LIBE
CHAMPION	78	34 in. Blue-green. Vigorous grower. Widely adapted.	HARR JOH MEY RIS SOU STO TWI WET
FLORIDA	45	Short-season variety. Vigorous and mildly pungent leaves. Doesn't bolt until August.	GAR
GEORGIA (GEORGIA GREEN) (GEORGIA BLUE) (CREOLE) (SOUTHERN)	70-80	2-3 feet. Non-heading. Blue-green, crumpled leaves with white veins.	BURP BUT DAN DEG EAR LED LET LIBE MEY MID NIC POR ROS SEE TWI WES WET WIL WYA
GREEN BLAZE	79	30-34 in. For southern and warm coastal areas. Bright green, smooth leaves. Non-heading, slow-bolting.	SOU
HEAVI-CROP (hybrid)		Large medium blue-green leaves. Good vigor and yield.	TWI
HICROP (hybrid)	75-80	15 in. Heavy-yielding, slow to bolt. Sweet, mild flavor. Slightly savoyed leaves. Easy to grow.	PAR THO VER

◄ ## COLLARDS

Variety	Days	Remarks	Sources
MORRIS CAROLINA HEADING	80	1½-2 feet. Low-growing, smooth leaf.	MEY
MORRIS HEADING	85	30-40 in. Wavy green, savoyed leaves. Slow to bolt.	DEG POR SOU WET
MORRIS HEADING IMPROVED	85	Slightly savoyed, dark green leaves. Compact heads on short stems.	SEE WYA
SOUTHERN SHORT STEM (NORTH CAROLINA SHORT STEM)	80	2 ft. Will thrive under conditions where cabbage is hard to grow.	SEE
VATES NON-HEADING	55-80	1½-2 feet. Smooth leaf. Will stand light frost.	ABU BURP BURR COM DEG DIX EVA HARR HEN HUM LAG LED LET LIBE MEY MID PIE PIN RIS SEED SOU STO TER TIL TWI WET WIL WILL WYA

CORN
(Zea mays)

What we call corn today is a far cry from the maize that the Pilgrims found the Indians growing when they first arrived in America. Corn loves to crossbreed, and, unlike some plants, every time one kind of corn is crossed with another, you get something in between. The different genotypes can truly be confusing. The heirloom seed is one that is from the original corn plant, saved and replanted, to be saved again and again. The everlasting heritage (E.H.) is a family of hybrids; the genes are the result of a sugary-floury corn cross. The corn has a super high natural sugar content which makes it hold longer before and after picking. With E.H. varieties there is no need to isolate from normalcorn. E.H. is also know as SE (sugary enhanced).

Normal Sugary (su) kernals contain moderate, sometimes varying degrees of sugar. Sugars convert to starch rapidly after being harvested.

Ultra-sweet or Shrunken (sh$_2$) has sugar content sometimes as high as twice as much as that of the normal sweet corn. It is slow to convert to starch after picking. Also known as Supersweet and Extra-sweet corn, this type must be isolated. Cross-pollination will result in tough, starchy kernels.

Corn also comes in many colors, from the standard yellow, to white, blue, and ornamental corn of all shades of the rainbow.

CULTURE: Wait until the soil has warmed to about 60° F. Plant corn in a block of at least three rows—never plant a single row. You can plant early, mid-season and late varieties for a continuous harvest or plant one variety every few weeks until about 85 days before the first frost.

Plant seeds 1 to 2 inches deep, 4 to 6 inches apart, in rows 30 to 36 inches apart, or plant in hills 3 feet apart, four-five seeds per hill. Later, thin to the three strongest plants.

SEASON: Warm.

INSECTS/DISEASES: *CORN FLEA BEETLES, CORN EARWORMS, CUTWORMS, EUROPEAN CORN BORERS, GRASSHOPPERS, LEAFHOPPERS*: Use Sevin, diazinon, pyrethrum, rotenone, ryania.

LEAF BLIGHTS, RUSTS, BACTERIAL WILT: Use maneb, zineb or Sevin.

HARVESTING: You must catch eating-type corn in the milky stage. For best results, take your thumbnail and squeeze a kernal. It should squirt a milky juice. Dent corn usually has two maturity dates given: the first, days to maturity for using as a roasting ear; the second, the number of days to use as cornmeal, grits or hominy.

Popcorn is grown and dried the same way as dent corn. Store kernals in sealed jars for two more weeks from shelling before popping.

For ornamental corn, simply peel back the husks and let the rainbow-colored kernals dry. Use for decoration.

CORN—YELLOW, EARLY				
TO 75 DAYS				
Variety	Days	Plant/Ears	Remarks	Sources
ASHWORTH (op)	69	5 ft. stalks; 6 in. ears; 12 rows	Excellent flavor. Selected from a composite of numerous early varieties.	JOH
AZTED (hybrid)	69	6½ ft. stalks; 7½ in. ears; 14-16 rows	Glossy green husks. Deep, rich golden kernals.	LAG LET MID SEED STO

►

Variety	Days	Plant/Ears	Remarks	Sources
BEACON	69	6 ft. stalks; 8 in. ears; 14-16 rows	High quality. Good flavor, good freezer.	VES WIL
BUTTERVEE	58-73	8-12 in. ears; 12-14 rows	High sugar content. Butter-yellow kernals. Outstanding flavor and tenderness.	GAR STO
CARMELET (hybrid)	58-73	7 ft. stalks; 8-9 in. ears; 12-14 rows	Good husk protection. Good eating quality.	SEED
DAWN (hybrid)	64	5 ft. stalks; 8 in. ears; 12-14 rows	Nice flavor.	VER
DEBUT (hybrid)	71-73	7 ft. stalks; 8 in ears; 16-18 rows	Good seedling vigor in early spring. Very tender and sweet.	JUN LED RIS WET WIL
DEBUTANTE (hybrid)	73	7½ x 1¾ in. ears; 16-18 rows	Medium plants are high yielding and disease-tolerant.	TWI
DORING EARLY (DORINNY)		2-6 ft. stalks	Produces 1 to 3 ears per stalk.	ABU
EARLIBELLE	71	7½-8 in. ears	Bright green husks. High quality corn.	HARR
EARLIGEM (hybrid)	64	7-8 in. ears; 12-16 rows	Excellent early vigor in cold soil. Tender, high quality corn.	SEED
EARLIKING (hybrid)	63-66	5½ ft. stalks; 8 in. ears; 12 rows	High quality corn with scant foliage. Produces few suckers. Excellent for northern gardens.	BURG DEG HUM JOH JUN LET MEY RIS THO TWI
EARLIVEE (hybrid)	63-69	5 ft. stalks; 7 in. ears; 12-14 rows	Large, bright yellow tender kernels. Good flavor. Ears have a little taper.	COM FAR GAR HIG RAW SEED STO TIL VES
EARLY ARTIC (hybrid)	60	5½ ft. stalks; 7½ in. ears; 12-14 rows	Good freezer. Combines earliness and high quality.	DEG THO
EARLY DAWN (hybrid)	62	6-7 in. ears; 8-12 rows	High quality deep-kerneled corn that can be used fresh, canned or frozen.	VER
EARLY GOLDEN GIANT (hybrid)	63	5 ft. stalks; 8 in ears; 14-18 rows	Large ears. Good early main crop.	BURP GUR
EARLY GOLDEN 113	65-68	8-10 in. ears; 12 rows	Good flavor.	FAR
EARLY SUNGLOW (hybrid)	63	4½ ft. stalks; 7 in. ears; 12 rows	Tender and tasty for a long time. Early vigor in cold weather. Tolerant to bacterial wilt.	ARC BURG BURP BURR FIS GUR HUM MEY NIC PAR POR THO TIL TWI VER WET WYA
EARLY SUNRAY (hybrid)	65	7½ in. ears; 12-14 rows	Tender, sweet golden kernels. Attractive husks.	SEED
EXTRA EARLY GOLDEN BANTAM	69-70	5 ft. stalks	Rich, sugary taste. Can be planted close together.	ALL JUN WILL
FOURTH OF JULY (hybrid)	63	7 in. ears; 10-14 rows	Rich golden ears.	EAR
GOLDEN BEAUTY (hybrid)	58-73	5½-6 ft. stalks; 7-8 in. ears	Good for short-season areas. Sweet, tender, golden kernels.	BURG BURR COM DEG FAR FIS GUR HEN PON STO WILL
GOLDEN EARLY MARKET	72	5-6 ft. stalks; 7-8 in. ears; 12 rows	Broad kernels. Sturdy plants.	JOH

◀ CORN—YELLOW, EARLY

Variety	Days	Plant/Ears	Remarks	Sources
GOLDEN SUNSHINE	68	8 in ears; 10-12 rows	Small kernels.	RED
MORNING SUN (hybrid)	72	6 ft. stalks; 7-8 in. ears; 14-16 rows	Large ears have been proven outstanding.	ARC LET
MONTANA BANTAM	65	6-7 in. ears; 8 rows	Delicious flavor and quality. Short-season variety.	FIS
NK 75	65-75	6½ ft. stalks; 7-8 in. ears; 15-16 rows	Good wilt resistance.	ARC MID
NORGOLD	75	7¾ in ears; 16 rows	Good cold-soil vigor. Medium-green husks. Great eating quality.	STO
NORSWEET	69	7¾ in. ears; 16 rows	Dark green husks.	STO
NORTHERN BELLE (hybrid)	74	6 ft. stalks; 14-18 rows	Plump, tightly packed kernels. Heavy yielder.	HARR
NORTHERN SWEET (hybrid)	65-68	8 x 2 in. ears; 12-14 rows	High sugar is retained over a long period after picking.	FAR
NORTHERNVEE (hybrid)	62	7¾ in. ears; 12-14 rows	Excellent early vigor in cold soils. Dark green husks.	PIN SEED STO
NORTHLITE	62	7¾ in. ears; 12-14 rows	Good seedling vigor in cold soils. Ears snap easily.	STO
POLARVEE (hybrid)	52-55	3½ ft. stalks; 6-8 in. ears; 12-14 rows	Cold-resistant. Good short-season variety.	FAR GAR GUR HEN HIG HUM SEED STO THO VES
PRIDE OF CANADA (hybrid)	58	8 in. ears	Sweet, tender golden ears. Excellent flavor.	EAR
ROYAL CREST (hybrid)	60	5½ ft. stalks; 7½ in. ears; 12 rows	Sweet, tender golden kernels. Fine eating quality.	DEG LET
SENECA 60	64		Exceptional quality.	ALL
SENECA HORIZON	65-75	8 in. ears; 14-18 rows	Has good vigor in cool soils. Highly recommended.	ALL BURR GAR HARR LET LIBE MEY MID RAW RIS STO TER TWI VES WET WIL
SENECA STAR	67	8 in. ears	Cold- and drought-resistant.	LIBE
SENSATION 65 (hybrid)	63		Good flavor and tenderness.	LET
APANNCROSS (hybrid)	58	7 in ears; 10-12 rows	Highly resistant to bacteria. Somewhat cold-resistant. Short, stocky plant with ears set low.	BURG
SPARTAN	71	5½ ft. stalks; 8 in. ears; 14-16 rows	New version of Earlivee. Cold-soil tolerant.	GAR LIBE RIS STO
SPRING DANCE	70	7¾ in ears; 16 rows	Good cold-soil vigor. Picks easily. Good taste.	STO

▶

Variety	Days	Plant/Ears	Remarks	Sources
SPRING GOLD	67	7 in. ears; 12-16 rows	Small, tight kernels. Sweet. Yields a large crop.	ABU HARR HUM
SUNBURST (hybrid)	72	6 ft. stalks; 9 in. ears; 14-16 rows	Large ears are sweet, juicy and tender. Seed is not cold-resistant.	MID
SUNBURST IMPROVED (hybrid)	70-72	6 ft. stalks; 10 in. ears; 14 rows	Easy to pick. Good husk protection.	BURR LED RIS STO
SUNDANCE	69	7½ in. ears	Highly refined type. Sweet flavor. Husks have extra long tip cover.	HARR
SUNNYVEE (hybrid)	64	7 in ears; 12 rows	Excellent variety for short-season areas.	RAW STO WET WILL
SWEET STAR	68	8 in. ears; 16 rows	Good sugar content retained after picking.	STO
WASHINGTON	68-72	12 rows	Long, tight husks.	FAR

CORN—YELLOW, MID-SEASON
75 TO 85 DAYS

Variety	Days	Plant/Ears	Remarks	Sources
APACHE (hybrid)	80	7 ft. stalks; 8 in. ears; 16 rows	High-yielding. Bright golden kernels. Tolerant to diseases. Outstanding flavor.	LET
ARTISTOGOLD (hybrid)	85	8 ft. stalks; 9-10 in. ears; 16-18 rows.	High quality. Resistant to earworms, smut and hot weather.	TWI
ARTISTOGOLD BANTAM EVERGREEN	85-90	9 ft. stalks; 10 in. ears; 12-14 rows.	Good wilt resistance.	BURG WIL
BELLRINGER (hybrid)	79	8 in. ears; 16 rows	High quality. Shows tolerance to Stewart's wilt.	HARR
BONANZA	72-83	6½ ft. stalks; 9 in. ears; 16-18 rows.	Good sugar content. High quality corn.	LET ROS WIL
BURPEE'S HONEYCROSS	87	7 ft. stalks; 9 in. ears; 16 rows	High-yielding. Wilt-resistant. Tight husks protect it from earworms and smut.	BURP
CALUMET (hybrid)	82	7 ft. stalks; 12-14 rows.	Long, slender ears. Resistant to earworms.	POR WIL
CANDYSTICK	75-80		Thin cob eliminates cobby flavor when frozen on the ear. 2 or more ears per stalk.	FAR PAR
CARMELCROSS (hybrid)	75	6 ft. stalks; 7½ in. ears; 12-14 rows	Tender, yellow kernels. Top quality and flavorful.	FAR
COMANCHE (hybrid)	72	14-16 rows	Tight, glossy dark green husks. Suited for whole-ear processing. Disease-resistant.	LET
DWARF MINIMAX (hybrid) (MINIMAX)	83	8 in. ear; 16-18 rows	Large, well-covered ears. Sweet and tender.	GUR HEN LED WIL
EARLIGLOW (E.H.)	75	8 in. ears	Excellent holding qualities.	PON WET WILL
EARLY GOLD (hybrid)	75	7 in. ears; 16-18 rows	High quality. Use fresh or processed.	HARR

◀ **CORN—YELLOW, MID-SEASON**

Variety	Days	Plant/Ears	Remarks	Sources
EARLY SUMMER DELICIOUS	78	7 ft. stalks; 8½ in. ears	Excellent quality, heavy yields.	LIBE
ELEPHANT EAR (hybrid)	84	8 in. ears; 18-20 rows.	Extra-deep golden kernels. Tender and sweet.	GUR
GOLD CUP (hybrid)	80	6½ ft. stalks; 8 in. ears; 14-16 rows	Sweet flavor. Productive yields.	HARR
GOLD LADY (hybrid)	82	9 in. ears; 10-12 rows	Small cob. Holds quality over several days after picking stage. Good husk protection.	SEED
GOLD WINNER	79	8 in. ears; 14-16 rows	High yields. Tightly wrapped husks. Good flavor.	HARR
GOLDEN BANTAM (op)	78-83	6½ ft. stalks; 17 in. ears; 8 rows	One of the sweetest yellow corns. Excellent quality canned or fresh. 1902 heirloom variety. Ears should be picked promptly as the milk stage is short.	ABU ALL BURR COM EAR ECO FIS GAR GUR HEN JLH JOH LED LEM PLA RAW RED SOU WES WIL WYA
GOLDEN BANTAM IMPROVED	84	6 in. ears; 10-14 rows	2 ears per stalk. Sweetest corn of all this type.	ABU LET MID NIC RED ROS TER
GOLDEN BEAUTY	75	5½ ft. stalks; 7 in. ears	Excellent flavor. Heavy yield.	LET
GOLDEN CROSS (hybrid)	82	7 ft. stalks; 8 in. ears; 12-14 rows	Good husk protection. Stalk shows to produce suckers.	WET
GOLDEN CROSS BANTAM (hybrid)	80-90	7 ft. stalks; 8 in. ears; 10-14 rows	Resistant to bacterial wilt. Standard hybrid for quality.	ABU BURG BURP BURR COM DAN DEG FAR GUR HEN HUM LED LET MEY PON POR ROS SEED VER WIL WYA
GOLDEN QUEEN (hybrid)	92	9 ft. stalks; 9 in. ears; 14-16 rows	Unsurpassed in quality and flavor.	LED LET MEY PAR SEED TWI WET WYA
GOLDEN SWEET (EH)	87	9 in. ears; 14-16 rows	Disease-resistant. Tender kernels. Has excellent holding ability.	STO
HONEY GOLD (hybrid)	75	7 in. ears; 14 rows	Tops for taste. Above-average germination. Large yields. Widely adapted.	HEN
IOCHIEF (hybrid)	86-93	6½ ft. stalks; 10 in. ears; 14-18 rows	Drought-resistant. 2 ears per stalk.	ARC BURG BURP BURR DEG EAR FAR GUR HEN LAG LET LIBE MEY MID PAR PLA SEED WIL WYA
INCREDIBLE (hybrid)	86-93	8 ft. stalks; 9½ in. ears	First-rate eating quality. Bright yellow kernels.	PIN
JUBILEE (hybrid)	85	5½ ft. stalks; 8½ in. ears; 16-20 rows	Deep, narrow kernels. Good freezer or corn on the cob. Good for cool-season areas.	ALL COM FAR HARR HUM JOH JON LAG NIC PON RIS SEED STO TER TIL TWI VER WET WILL
MAINLINER (EH)	88	9 in. ears; 16-18 rows	Slow to convert sugars to starch. Stays sweet and tender for a long time.	DEG
MERIT (hybrid)	84	8½ ft. stalks; 9 in. ears; 20 rows	Good processor or fresh use. Tight husks.	ARC DEG LET MID PAR POR RIS SEED WET WIL

▶

Variety	Days	Plant/Ears	Remarks	Sources
MEVAK (hybrid)	74	7 ft. stalks; 18-20 rows	Medium-green husks give good ear coverage.	VES
MIDWAY (hybrid)	86	8 ft. stalks; 9 in. ears; 20 rows	Full-season hybrid for processing or fresh use. Excellent yield. Large ears.	DEG
MONARCH ADVANCE (hybrid)	83	7 ft. stalks; 9x2¼ in. ears; 16 rows	Excellent variety.	ROS
NK 199 (hybrid)	84	8 ft. stalks; 8 in. ears; 14-20 rows	For canning or freezing. High-yielding. Grows well everywhere. Excellent flavor.	BURR HEN JUN LET LIBE MEY MID RIS TWI WET
NK 51036	77	7 ft. stalks; 7½ in. ears; 16-18 rows	Very productive. Good frozen or canned.	LET
RELIANCE	76	6 ft. stalks; 8 in. ears; 16-18 rows	Use fresh or processed.	MID
SENECA CHIEF (hybrid)	86	6½ ft. stalks; 8½ in. ears	Highly resistant to bacterial wilt. Use fresh, canned or frozen. Good flavor.	ALL BURR LET LIBE MEY NIC PAR RIS STO WIL WILL WYA
SENECA FEATHER	78	84 in. stalks; 8 in. ears; 14-16 rows	Good flavor. Deep kernels.	WET
SENECA HORIZON (hybrid)	65	5½ ft. stalks; 10 in. ears; 16-18 rows	Short-season variety. Superb eating qualities. Rapid seedling growth.	TWI WIL
SENECA RAIDER	80	9 in. ears	Deep, narrow kernels are crisp and delicious.	LIBE
SENECA SCOUT	82	8 in. ears; 16-18 rows	High-yielding. Tolerant to Stewart's wilt.	LIBE
SENECA SUNLITE	76	9 in. ears; 12-14 rows	Tolerant to Stewart's wilt. Fine quality.	LET
SENECA WARRIOR 225	74	8 in. ears	Well-filled tips.	LET
SLENDERGEM (hybrid)	76	9 in. ears; 10-12 rows	Slender, very small cob. Good seedling vigor in cold soils. Glossy green husks.	SEED
STARLET (hybrid)	75	7½ ft. stalks; 9 in. ears; 16-18 rows	Good eating quality. Medium-golden kernels.	SEED
SUGAR KING	78	7 ft. stalks; 8 in. ears	Excellent quality. Tender and sweet. Deep, narrow, bright yellow kernels.	DEG LET STO
TENDERMOST (hybrid)	80-90	7½ ft. stalks; 8 in. ears; 14-18 rows	Deep yellow kernels. Very sweet. Small cob. Good freezer. Wilt-resistant.	MEY
YELLOW DENT (op)	85	7 ft. stalks; 9 in. ears; 16 rows	Primarily for roasting ears.	HEN PAR POR WIL
YUKON (hybrid)	78	7½ ft. stalks; 9 in. ears; 16 rows	Good hybrid with outstanding flavor. Grows under adverse conditions.	DEG MID RIS STO

CORN—YELLOW, LATE
85 + DAYS

Variety	Days	Plant/Ears	Remarks	Sources
ATLANTIC (hybrid)	90	10½ in. ears; 16-18 rows	Plants stand up well in adverse conditions. Adapted to fall harvest.	HARR

◄ CORN—YELLOW, LATE

Variety	Days	Plant/Ears	Remarks	Sources
CANDYSTICK	90	12 in. ears; 8-12 rows	Extra-sweet and tender. Extra-long holding ability. Ideal for freezing on the cob.	GUR
CELEBRITY	86		A mid-season variety with good holding ability.	WET
COMMANDER (hybrid)	86		Superior quality. High-yielding. Good for freezing or processing.	LET
FLAVORVEE	86	8½ in. ears; 14-18 rows	Vigorous plant. Ears snap easily. Flavor holds well. Good freezer.	STO
GOLDEN QUEEN (hybrid)	88	8 in. ears; 14-16 rows	Dark green husks. Sweet, tender, good quality. High yields. Tolerant to leaf blight.	MID WIL
MEXICAN JUNE (op)	120		Vigorous stalks are drought-resistant. Good husk protection. Disease-resistant. Dependable field corn.	POR ROS
REWARD	95	9 in. ears; 16-20 rows	Many stalks produce 2 ears. Good cold-soil tolerance. Sweet flavor.	TER
SENECA SENTRY	89	8½ in. ears; 16-18 rows	M.D.M. tolerance. Excellent quality.	LET LIBE MID PAR RIS
SENECA 258	85	8½ in. ears; 16 rows	Tolerant to M.D.M.	STO
SOUTHERN DELICIOUS	98	9 ft. stalks; 9 in. ears; 16-18 rows	Good husk protection.	WIL
STYLEPAK (hybrid)	85	8 in. ears; 18-20 rows	Excellent flavor. High yields. Ears snap easily.	STO
TENDERTREAT (E.H.) (hybrid)	93	10 ft. stalks; 9 in. ears; 16-18 rows	Full-season corn.	VER

CORN—YELLOW

SPACE SAVERS

Variety	Days	Plant/Ears	Remarks	Sources
BABY ASIAN (hybrid)		Medium-size stalks	Plant bears 2-3 ears per stalk. Grow as ordinary corn but harvest ears when silks first appear, no later.	LEM
BABY CORN			Not a sweet corn; should be harvested within 5 days of silk appearance. Excellent freezer.	NIC
BUTTER IMPROVED	50-60	26-30 in. stalks; 4 in. ears	High sugar content. Good freezer.	THO
FISHER'S EARLIEST (op)	60	6 in. ears; 10-12 rows	Dwarf plant. Yellow kernels are sweet and tender. Good freezer or canner.	FIS
GOLDEN MIDGET (op)	58-65	3 ft. stalks; 4 in. ears; 10 rows	Sweet, tender kernels. Good freezer. Ideal for small space garden.	ABU ALL BURG FAR GAR GUR LAG NIC PAR PIN RED SEE TIL WILL

CORN—WHITE, EARLY
TO 75 DAYS

Variety	Days	Plant/Ears	Remarks	Sources
AUNT MARY'S (hybrid)	70		White, sweet kernels. More than 1 ear per stalk.	SEE
EARLY LARGE ADAMS	70			WYA
EARLI QUEEN (hybrid)	78	7 ft. stalks; 9 in. ears	Fair wilt resistance.	MEY MID
GLACIER	65		Short-season variety. Delicious flavor.	FIS
HONEY CREAM	60	7 in. ears; 10-12 rows	Delicious, does not become mealy. Well suited for small gardens. Good fresh, frozen or canned.	JUN
PLATINUM LADY (hybrid)	75-85	7 ft. stalks; 8 in. ears; 14-16 rows	Highly recommended. Mostly double-eared. Vigorous, sturdy and drought-resistant.	BURP BURR COM JOH LEM LIBE NIC PIN PLA STO TIL TWI WET
QUICKSILVER (hybrid)	75	7½ in. ears; 14-18 rows	High quality. Good cold resistance.	HARR
SILVER BEAUTY	84	7½ ft. stalks; 8 in. ears; 14-16 rows	Fine-textured kernels.	HEN
SILVER STREAK (hybrid)	81	7 in. ears; 14-16 rows	High yields. Excellent quality. Light green husks.	HARR
SPRING CRYSTAL (hybrid)	66	7½ in. ears; 12-14 rows	Attractive snapped ears. Dark-green husks. Very tender kernels.	SEED STO
SPRING WHITE	66	7 in. ears; 14-16 rows	Small, tight, pure white kernels.	HARR
STAR DUST	66	7½ in. ears; 14-16 rows	Bred to handle early spring conditions.	LIBE PAR
TAIT'S NORFOLK MARKET	75	7 ft. stalks; 10 in. ears.; 12 rows	Small, tight, white kernels. 2 ears per stalk.	WET
TEXAS 17-W (hybrid)			Large grain and high yields. Good for milling, homing or roasting ears.	ROS
WHITE MAGIC (hybrid)	73	7½ in. ears.; 14 rows	Pure white kernels.	HARR VES
WHITE SATIN (hybrid)	73	6½ ft. stalks; 8 in. ears; 14-16 rows	Good wilt resistance.	MEY
WHITE SUNGLOW (hybrid)	68	6½ in. ears	Reliable and very consistent. Short-season variety. Snow-white tender kernels.	GUR RAW VER WET
YUKON	75		White silk on large ears.	MID

CORN—WHITE, MID-SEASON
75 to 85 DAYS

Variety	Days	Plant/Ears	Remarks	Sources
ARCO	84	8 x 1¾ in. ears; 14 rows	Good husk protection. Good freezer.	ROS

▶

◄ **CORN—WHITE, MID-SEASON**

Variety	Days	Plant/Ears	Remarks	Sources
CHALICE	82	7 ft. stalks; 8 in. ears	Dark green husks. Good seedling vigor. Rich flavor.	JOH LED TWI WET WYA
CRYSTAL DELIGHT (hybrid)	84	8 in. ears; 14-16 rows	Good snapped ear. Excellent early seedling vigor.	SEED
LUTHER HILL (op)	84	5½ ft. stalks; 6 in. ears	1902 heirloom variety. Stalks produce some suckers. Lacks the vigor of the other open pollinated varieties.	SOU
MIDNIGHT SNACK	84	5½ ft. stalks; 7½ in. ears; 14-16 rows	Blue-black kernels at full maturity. Creamy white at eating stage.	JOH
SENECA PALEFACE	85	82 in. stalks; 8½ x 1⅝ in. ears	High quality. Pure white kernels have excellent flavor.	TWI
SILVERMINE	82	12 in. ears; 14-18 rows	Heavy yielder. Resistant to worm damage. Heavy, dark green husks. Used for roasting corn.	SOU
SIX SHOOTER	80	10 rows	Has as many as 6 ears per plant. Free of cobby taste.	GUR LAK
SNOWBELLE	78	8 in. ears; 14-16 rows	High quality. Sweet and tender. Creamy textured.	LET MID
TRUCKER'S FAVORITE (op)	78	9 in. ears; 16 rows	Large roasting ears. Hardy variety.	ARC HEN PAR ROS SEE WIL WYA
TRUCKER'S FAVORITE (hybrid)	80	7½ ft. stalks; 9 in. ears	Large, tender and fairly sweet kernels. Vigorous, hardy.	WYA
WHITE KNIGHT (hybrid)	80	6½ ft. stalks; 8 in. ears; 14-16 rows	Good wilt resistance.	LET MEY

CORN—WHITE, LATE

85 + DAYS

Variety	Days	Plant/Ears	Remarks	Sources
COUNTRY GENTLEMAN (SHOEPEG) (op)	73-100	7½ ft. stalks; 9 in. ears	1891 heirloom variety. Sweet, white, tightly packed kernels. Dry grains are thin and narrow. Very flavorful. Good canned or frozen.	ABU ARC BUT GUR HEN LED LEM LET MEY NIC RED SOU WIL
HICKORY KING	85-100	12 ft. stalks; 9 in. ears	Large, flat, white kernels. Used for dry and well-suited for hominy, grits and flour. Not a sweet corn. 2 ears per stalk. Has some tolerance to blights.	ARC GUR HEN RED ROS SEE SOU WET WYA
MEXICAN JUNE	110	Tall	Blue and white kernels. White kernels at eating stage. Roasting ear. Drought- and disease-resistant.	WES
SILVER PAC	86	7½ ft. stalks; 9½ in. ears; 20 rows	Multi-purpose use, fresh, canned or frozen. Cold-tolerant.	LET LIBE
SILVER QUEEN (hybrid)	94	8 ft. stalks; 9 in. ears; 14-16 rows	Good flavor. Germinates slowly in cool soil. Snowy-white kernels. Tolerant to leaf blights and Stewart's wilt. Has some drought resistance.	ALL ARC BURP COM DAN DEG EAR FAR GUR HARR HEN JOH LED LET LIBE MEY MID PAR PON POR RIS SEED SHE SOU TWI VER WET WIL WYA

►

Variety	Days	Plant/Ears	Remarks	Sources
BI-HONEY SUNRISE	70	9 in. ears; 14-16 rows	Gold and white kernels. Ultra flavor corn has less starch. Isolate this variety.	LIBE
BODACIOUS	75		Has the homozygous sugar-enhancer (SE). Exceptionally tender kernels. Holds well after harvest.	LET
BUNKER HILL (hybrid) Sh_2	87	$9\frac{1}{2}$ x 2 in. ears	Ear placement is at hip level. Snaps easily. Medium-green husks, white silk. Tolerant to Stewart's wilt, northern leaf blight and some tolerance to MDM. Good canner and freezer.	STO
BURPEE'S SUGAR SWEET (hybrid)	89	$6\frac{1}{2}$ ft. stalks; 8 in. ears; 16-18 rows	Stays sugary for long time. Glossy yellow kernels. Extra-sweet. Good freezer.	BURP
BUTTERFRUIT BI-COLOR (hybrid)	76	7 ft. stalks	Bi-colored. Heavy yielder.	PAR
BUTTERFRUIT ORIGINAL EARLY	72	5 ft. stalks	Bright yellow kernels. Plant when temperature reaches 75° F.	PAR
COMSTOCK'S PRIDE AND JOY SE (hybrid)	76		Large ear, bi-colored corn.	COM
CRISP 'N SWEET 620 (hybrid)	76		Supersweet yellow kernels. Long holding qualities.	LET
CRISP 'N SWEET 700	76	6 ft. stalks; 8 in. ears; 16 rows	High-yielding corn that requires isolation.	BURR LIBE
CRISP 'N SWEET 711 Sh_2 (hybrid)	85		High-yielding. Large well-filled ears with good tip cover. Resistance to northern leaf blight, tolerance to races of Stewart's wilt and races O and T of southern leaf blight.	LET
CRISP 'N SWEET 720 (hybrid)	87	$9\frac{1}{2}$ in. ears; 20 rows	Holds flavor, sweetness and tenderness for a long time. Resistant to northern leaf blight and tolerates races of Stewart's wilt.	GUR
CRUSADER (hybrid)	72	8 in. ears; 16-20 rows	No isolation required. Has sugary enhancer. Narrow, deep, tender gold kernels.	SEED STO
CRYSTAL BELL (hybrid)	76	7 ft. stalks; $7\frac{1}{2}$ in. ears; 16-18 rows	White, sugary enhancer genes. High quality. Dark green husks.	SEED
CRYSTAL DELIGHT (hybrid)	84	8 in. ears; 14-16 rows	Long flag leaves and good husk protection. High eating quality. Tinge of burgundy on the husk. White kernels.	SEED
CRYSTAL-n-GOLD (hybrid)	74	8 in. ears; 16 rows	Sugar-enhanced bi-colored kernels. Tight husk and good flag leaves. No isolation required.	SEED
DINNER TIME (hybrid) Sh_2	85	7 ft. stalks; $8\frac{1}{2}$ x $1\frac{7}{8}$ in. ears; 16 rows	Excellent tip cover. Supersweet flavor holds for a long time. Good husk protection. High yields.	TWI
DOUBLE DELICIOUS (hybrid)	83		Supersweet golden kernels. Good holding ability. Good seed germination.	GUR
DOUBLE DELIGHT	77	$7\frac{1}{2}$ ft. stalks; 8 in. ears; 16-18 rows	Bi-color with homozygous sugary enhanced (SE) gene. Good holding ability. Isolation is not required.	HEN LIBE NIC RIS

◄ CORN—EXTRA-SWEET/SUPERSWEET

Variety	Days	Plant/Ears	Remarks	Sources
EARLY XTRA-SWEET	85	8 in. ears; 14-18 rows	Yellow kernels with sugary enhancer. Four times as sweet 48 hours after picking. Does not turn starchy. 2 ears per stalk. Good freezing variety. Isolate.	ARC BURP DAN EARL FAR HEN JUN LET PAR PON STO THO TWI VER WET
ESCALADE (hybrid)	84	8 in. ears; 20 rows	Supersweet bi-colored kernels.	HARR
EXTRA EARLY SUPER SWEET (hybrid)			Bright yellow kernels. Isolate.	RAW
EXTRA SWEET 82 (hybrid)	71	14-16 rows	Large ears, extra-sweet and good uniformity. Vigorous. Dark green husks.	LET LIBE TWI
FLAVOR KING (hybrid)	85	8½ in. ears; 16 rows	Supersweet kernels, white silk. Good tip coverage.	STO
FLORIDA STAYSWEET	86	7½ in. ears; 14-18 rows	Good husk protection. Excellent variety.	HARR WIL
GOLD 'N KRYSTAL	85	16-20 rows	SE gene sugary enhancer. Bi-colored. Uniform ears. Shallow kernels. Excellent quality.	LET
GREAT TASTE (hybrid)	85	8½ x 1⅞ in. ears; 18-20 rows	Extra sugary-enhanced bright yellow kernels. Tall plants yield well. Widely adapted. Rust-tolerant. Good flavor.	TWI
GREAT TIME (hybrid)	78	6½ ft. stalks; 8 x 1¾ in. ears	Supersweet yellow kernels. Long holding ability. Light silk. Good disease tolerance, multiple-ear tendency. Widely adapted.	TWI
HONEYCOMB (hybrid)	79	16-18 rows	Excellent quality yellow supersweet kernels. High sugar variety.	BURR LET RIS
HONEY & PEARL Sh$_2$	78	9 in. ears; 16-18 rows	Bi-colored kernels. Sweetness is 200% greater than normal corn.	LIBE
HONEY-RIFFIC	66	8 in. ears; 16 rows	Sugar-enhanced bi-colored kernels. Gourmet in taste. Ears grow high for easy picking.	LIBE
HOW SWEET IT IS Sh$_2$	87	7 ft. stalks; 8 in. ears; 16 rows	2 ears per stalk. Ultra-sweet corn. Retains flavor long after the harvest. Good uniformity. Excellent eating.	ARC BURG BURP DAN EAR FAR GUR HARR HUM JOH JUN LAG LED MEY MID NIC PAR PIN POR RIS STO THO TIL TWI VER WET WIL
ILLINICHIEF	85	8 in. ears; 14-18 rows	Does not turn sugar content into starch as rapidly. 2 or more ears per stalk. Golden kernels are extremely tender.	BURG DEG LET TWI WET
ILLINI GOLD (hybrid)	80-85	8½ x 1¾ in. ears; 16 rows	Easy-to-grow golden corn. Widely adapted. Outstanding flavor.	HARR LEM PAR
ILLINI EXTRA SWEET	85	8 in. ears; 14-18 rows	Ability to hold for days without losing its sweetness. Twice as sweet as normal corn. Good freezer.	ARC BURP EAR FAR GUR HEN JUN LAG LIBE MEY MID PAR POR TWI VER VES WIL
INCREDIBLE	80	7½ ft. stalks; 9½ in. ears; 18 rows	Good tip fill and good eating. Has homozygous sugar enhancer.	LIBE RIS WET
IVORY AND GOLD (hybrid) Sh$_2$	75	6 ft. stalks; 9 in. ears; 16 rows	Good husk cover. Excellent fresh or frozen. Isolate.	HARR LET STO VER

Variety	Days	Plant/Ears	Remarks	Sources
KANDY KORN (EH) (hybrid)	89	8½ ft. stalks; 8 in. ears	High sugar content. Does not require isolation. Heavy yielder. Excellent quality.	ARC BURG BURP BURR EAR FAR FIS HEN HUM JUN LAG LET MEY MID PON SHE STO TIL TWI VER WET WIL WILL WYA
LANDMARK (hybrid)	73	8½ in. ears; 12-14 rows	Excellent yields. Good cold-soil emergence and vigor.	HARR
LIGHTNIN' (hybrid)	87	7½ ft. stalks; 8 x 1⅞ in. ears; 16-18 rows	Delicious pearly white kernels. Excellent husk protection. Widely adapted.	TWI
MAIN TIME (hybrid) Sh₂	82	6 ft. stalks; 7½ x 1⅞ in. ears; 14-16 rows	Bright yellow, ultrasweet kernels. Disease-tolerant.	TWI
MAPLE SWEET	63	7½ in. ears; 14-16 rows	Sugary enhanced gene. Excellent tip cover. Easy to pick.	STO
MERLIN	84	10 in. ears; 20-22 rows	Sugary enhanced gene. Extra-tender. Creamy texture. Good husk color and tip cover in warm soil.	STO
MILK N' HONEY (hybrid) Sh₂	73	8½ in. ears; 14 rows	Bi-color kernels. Good tip cover. Low ear placement. Great texture and flavor.	STO
MIRICLE	78-85	6 ft. stalks; 9½ in. ears; 20-22 rows	Does not need isolation. Usually double ears.	BURP COM EAR FAR LEM LET LIBE MID NIC RIS STO
NORTHERN SUPER SWEET (hybrid) Sh₂	63-75	5 ft. stalks; 9 in. ears; 14 rows	Plant often has 2 ears. Germinates in cool soil. Dark green husks. Isolate.	FAR JOH JUN LET STO
PARAGON	82		Supersweet bi-colored kernels. Good cold-soil emergence. Exceptional eating quality held over a long period of time.	LET
PARTY TIME (hybrid) Sh₂	63	6 ft. stalks; 8 x 1¾ in. ears; 12 rows	Excellent supersweet corn. Holds well on stalk. Medium-green husks. Yellow kernels. Isolate.	TWI
PHENOMENAL (hybrid) Sh₂	85	8½ in. ears; 16 rows	Great-tasting bi-colored kernels. Low ear placement on stalk avoids wind damage. Isolate.	EAR STO
PINNACLE (hybrid) Sh₂	77	8½ in. ears; 14-16 rows	Good germination and vigor. Excellent eating. Yellow kernels.	HARR
SILVERADO (hybrid) SE	79	8 in. ears; 16 rows	White kernels. Good cold-soil emergence and vigor.	HARR
SNOW QUEEN (EH) (hybrid)	87	91 in. stalks; 10 in. ears; 16-20 rows	Does not need to be isolated. Sweet white kernels. Holds well.	FAR HEN LAG PON VER WET
SPRINGSWEET (hybrid) Sh₂	82	9 in. ears; 16-18 rows	Main-season variety for the northeast. Cobs are easily snapped. Medium-green husks. White silk.	STO
STARDUST (hybrid)	70	6½ ft. stalks; 7½ in. ears; 14-16 rows	Sugary enhanced gene. Good vigor. Good husk protection. Excellent flavor.	TWI

◄ CORN—EXTRA-SWEET/SUPERSWEET

Variety	Days	Plant/Ears	Remarks	Sources
STARSTRUCK	81	9 in. ears; 14-16 rows	Bi-colored extra-sweet kernels. Excellent variety for freezing.	JOH
SUGAR BUNS (SE)	65-72	6 ft. stalks; 8 in. ears; 14-16 rows	Gourmet corn. Superb eating. Long picking season. Not necessary to isolate from other corn. Excellent fresh or frozen.	COM LIBE RIS STO TIL
SUGAR DOTS	78-85	7 ft. stalks; 8½ in. ears; 16-18 rows	Husks are deep green splashed red.	LIBE TER
SUGAR LOAF	83	6 ft. stalks; 8 in. ears	Sweet-gene type. Rust resistance, maize dwarf mosaic virus tolerance and northern leaf blight-tolerant. Especially good freezer. Yellow kernels.	LED LIBE MID WET WIL
SUPREME (hybrid) (SE)	71	7 in. ears; 14-16 rows	Very good cold-soil vigor. Yellow kernels have very good sweet flavor. High yields.	HARR
SUMMER FLAVOR BRAND 65 BC	65	6½ ft. stalks; 8 x 1⅝ in. ears; 16 rows	Bi-colored kernels.	TWI
SUMMER FLAVOR BRAND 65 Y	65	6 ft. stalks; 7½ x 1¾ in. ears; 16 rows	Yellow, creamy texture. Does not require isolation, but still suggested.	TWI
SUMMER FLAVOR BRAND 70Y	70	7 ft. stalks; 8 x 1¾ in. ears; 16-18 rows	Yellow kernels.	TWI
SUMMER FLAVOR BRAND 72Y	72	6 ft. stalks; 7½ x 2 in. ears; 18 rows	Yellow kernels.	TWI
SUMMER FLAVOR BRAND 77BC	77	6 ft. stalks; 7½ x 1¾ in. ears; 14-16 rows	Bi-colored kernels.	TWI
SUMMER FLAVOR BRAND 79BC	79	6 ft. stalks; 8 x 1¾ in. ears; 16-18 rows	Bi-colored kernels.	TWI
SUMMER FLAVOR BRAND 79Y	79	6 ft. stalks; 8 x 1⅝ in. ears; 16-18 rows	Yellow kernels.	TWI
SUMMER FLAVOR BRAND 80W	80	8 ft. stalks; 8½ x 1⅞ in. ears; 20 rows	Pure-white kernels.	TWI
SUMMER FLAVOR BRAND 82Y	82	8 ft. stalks; 8½ x 1⅞ in. ears; 20 rows	Yellow kernels.	TWI
SUMMER FLAVOR BRAND 87BC	87	7½ ft. stalks; 8½ x 1⅞ in. ears; 18 rows	Bi-colored kernels.	TWI
SUCRO (hybrid)	90	7 ft. stalks; 9 x 1⅞ in. ears; 16-18 rows	Rich yellow, supersweet kernels. Good yields. Good fresh or frozen.	PIN
SWEET DREAMS Sh$_2$	77	9 in. ears; 16 rows	Supersweet variety for northern areas. Excellent for processing. Low ear placement. Well-filled ears. Isolate.	STO

▶

Variety	Days	Plant/Ears	Remarks	Sources
SWEETIE	81	8 x 1¾ in. ears; 16-18 rows	Yellow kernels. Tolerant to rust. Isolate.	FAR GUR HEN JUN LED LET MID SEED SHE TWI
SWEETIE 70 Sh_2	70	5 ft. stalks; 9 x 1¾ in. ears; 12-14 rows	Short white silk. Yellow kernels. Dark green husks. Fair cold-soil seed vigor. Tolerant to rust, NCL, blight and MDM. Isolate.	STO
SWEETIE 73 Sh_2	73	5 ft. stalks; 8 x 1¾ in. ears; 12-16 rows	Similar to Sweetie 70. Isolate.	STO
SWEETIE 76 Sh_2	76	5 ft. stalks; 8½ x 1⅞ in. ears; 14-18 rows	Similar to Sweetie 70. Isolate. Yellow kernels.	STO
SWEETIE 76 Sh_2	76	8½ in. ears; 16-18 rows	Bi-colored kernels. Good tolerance to northern leaf blight and rust. Short white silk. Use fresh or processed. Isolate.	STO
SWEET TIME (hybrid) Sh_2	82	6½ ft. stalks; 7½ x 1¾ in. ears	Widely adapted. Sweet yellow kernels. Good seedling vigor. Sturdy, disease-tolerant plant. Isolate.	TWI
TENDERTREAT (EH) (hybrid)	95	10 ft. stalks; 9 x 2 in. ears; 16-18 rows	Burgundy color stalk and husk is green and burgundy. Excellent flavor. High sugar content. Retains flavor and quality over long period. Does not require isolation. Yellow kernels.	EAR HEN TWI
TRI SWEET (hybrid) (SE)	65	8 in. ears; 16 rows	Bi-colored kernels. Dark green husks. Low ear placement helps prevent wind damage.	STO
TUXEDO (hybrid) (SE)	67	7½ in. ears; 16 rows	Bi-colored kernels. Low ear placement.	STO

POPCORN

WHITE

Variety	Days	Plant/Ears	Remarks	Sources
BURPEE'S PEPPEY (hybrid)	90	6 ft. stalks; 4 in. ears	Good variety in short season areas. Deep, pointed hull-less white kernels.	BURP
EARLY WHITE HYBRID			Requires full season to mature. Harvest after first frost.	RAW
FARIBO HULLESS WHITE	90-95	4 in. ears	Every kernel will pop. Kernels are long and hull-less.	FAR
JAPANESE WHITE HULLESS	83-95	7 ft. stalks; 4¾ in. ears	Well-filled ears with deep, narrow white kernels.	DEG GUR HLJ LED LET SEE VER WIL
MINIHYBRID WHITE	95-98		Fine flavor, tender and hull-less.	FAR
P304 (hybrid)			Excellent yield, standing ability, popping expansion.	ARC
PEPPY POP (hybrid)	90		Hull-less. Good popping quality.	LAG WILL
POPWHITE (hybrid)	95	6 ft. stalks; 5 in. ears	High-yielding. Hull-less kernels. Pops into beautiful white puffs.	JOH TWI

◀ **POPCORN**

Variety	Days	Plant/Ears	Remarks	Sources
SNOW PUFF WHITE (hybrid)	85	5½ ft. stalks; 5 in. ears	Hull-less. Delicious.	BURG LET
SOUTH AMERICAN GIANT	100		Large-eared. Pops perfectly white.	LET
TOM THUMB (op) (DWARF RICE) (HULL-LESS) (SQUIRREL TOOTH) (AUSTRALIAN HULLESS) (BUMBLE BEE)	85	3½ ft. stalks; 3½ in. ears	Long, narrow, pointed kernels. No hard center when popped. Matures even in far north. 1-2 ears per stalk.	JOH TIL
WHITE CLOUD (hybrid)	110		Almost no waste. 99% small white kernels pop. Excellent eating quality.	VER
WHITE HULL-LESS (hybrid)	85-100	6 ft. stalks; 5 in. ears	Finest and best popcorn you can grow.	ARC HEN RED
WHITE RICE	110		Standard variety used for many years. 2-3 ears per stalk.	MEY

POPCORN

YELLOW

Variety	Days	Plant/Ears	Remarks	Sources
BEST YELLOW A-222 (hybrid)	105		Tastes great, tender and delicious.	HEN
CREME-PUFF (hybrid)	105	8½ ft. stalks	2 ears per stalk. Heavy yields. Excellent popping expansion.	BURP
GOLDEN POPCORN (op)	110	6½ ft. stalks; 8 in. ears; 14-16 rows	Good popper.	RED
HYBRID GOLD	115		Pops to large, flaky, tender kernels. High popping volume.	FAR TWI
IOPOP 12 (hybrid)			Good yield. Hull-less. Widely adapted. Good popping volume.	EAR HARR JUN LET
JAPANESE HULL-LESS YELLOW	110		Fluffy, hull-less popcorn.	GUR
PURDUE YELLOW (hybrid)	110	Tall	Heavy yields. Excellent popping quality.	POR VER WYA
PURDUE 410 (hybrid)	90-105		Widely used for commercial popcorn. A heavy yielder.	ALL BURR GUR LET NIC
ROBUST (hybrid)	100		Highest quality. Vigorous grower. Does well under adverse conditions. Excellent popper.	VER
SOUTH AMERICAN GOLDEN (hybrid)	95	12-15 ft. stalks	3-5 ear per stalk.	GRA
SOUTH AMERICAN (hybrid) (T.N.T.) (LATE YELLOW)	110		Produces heavy ears.	DAN DEG GUR ROS

▶

◄

Variety	Days	Plant/Ears	Remarks	Sources
SOUTH AMERICAN YELLOW GIANT	**105-115**	7 ft. stalks 8 in. ears	Pops to large, flaky, tender kernels of butter-yellow.	ARC GUR LED MEY PAR SEE
YELLOW LADY FINGER		7 in. ears	Heirloom Amish variety. Deep yellow kernels. Short, stocky plants. Excellent flavor. Pretty in dried arrangements.	JLH

POPCORN
OTHER COLORS

Variety	Days	Pods	Remarks	Sources
BLACK POPCORN	100		Be sure to provide ample fertilizer and water as well as sunny location. Black kernels explode into pure white balls.	LEM
CALICO POPCORN	100		Brilliantly colored ears. Easy to grow.	HEN
CAROUSEL	104	5 in. ears	Grows 4-6 ears per stalk. Vividly multi-colored kernels.	NIC
CUTIE POPS	100	5 in. ears	Multi-colored.	PAR STO
MINIATURE INDIAN ORNAMENTAL	100	5 ft. stalks; 4 in. ears	Red and yellow kernels.	PLA SEE
PAPOOSE	100	5 x 1¼ in. ears	Miniature popcorn. Can also be used in floral arrangements. Glossy multi-colored kernels. 2-3 ears per stalk.	TWI
PRETTY POPS	95	6 ft. stalks; 5 in. ears	Multi-colored kernels turn white when popped.	PAR
STRAWBERRY ORNAMENTAL POPCORN (op)	100-110	4 ft. stalk; 2 x 1½ in. ears	Tiny, mahogany-red ears. Use for popcorn or decoration.	ALL ARC BURP FAR GUR HARR HEN HER JLH JUN LED LET LIBE MEY NIC PAR PLA SEE SEED STO VER

CORN—DRY FIELD

Variety	Days	Plant/Ears	Remarks	Sources
AFRICAN ZULU MAIZE			Pure-white, pearl-like kernels. High in starch and sugar. Use fresh when young or dry when mature.	JLH
BEASLEY'S RED DENT	105	9 ft. stalks; 12 in. ears; 16-20 rows	Has excellent resistance to blight and drought. Red kernels. Used for cornmeal.	SOU
BLACK AZTEC (MEXICAN)	90	6½ ft. stalks; 6 in. ears; 8-12 rows	Ancient Mexican corn. Can be eaten as fresh corn when in "milk" stage or leave to dry black and use for cornmeal.	ABC GAR
BLOODY BUTCHER	120	12 ft. stalks	1845 heirloom variety. Red kernels striped with darker red. Dent-type field corn. Fine flavor. Makes very good flour, cornmeal or corn on the cob when young.	JLH

►

◀ CORN—DRY FIELD

Variety	Days	Plant/Ears	Remarks	Sources
BLUE TORTILLA	100	Large ears	Dark blue kernels. Vigorous, drought-resistant plant. Grown for centuries in the Southwest. Grind into blue cornmeal. Ears turn from white to lavender to deep blue. Can be used fresh in lavender stage.	HEN LEM PLA WES
BUHROW'S WHITE DESERT SWEET CORN (op)	70	9 ft. stalks; 9 in. ears	Drought-tolerant.	PLA
HOOKER'S SWEET INDIAN	75-100	4½ ft. stalks; 7 in. ears	Thin ears. White kernels dry to blue-black when mature. Makes sweet cornmeal.	TER
HOPI BLUE FLINT			Grind into meal for tortillas.	SEE RED
HOPI WHITE		8 in. ears; 12 rows	Grind into meal or make into hominy. Soft kernels.	RED
HOPI YELLOW			Grown mostly for eating on the cob, but can be ground into cornmeal.	RED
INDIAN FLINT	105		Hard flint corn used for grinding into cornmeal. Multi-colored ears.	EAR
LONGFELLOW FLIGHT	118	10 ft. stalks; 10 in. ears; 8 rows	Orange kernels.	JOH
MANDAN BRIDE	98	7 ft. stalks; 6 in. ears; 8-12 rows	Multi-colored flint corn. Makes a beautiful ornamental corn that can also be used for cornmeal.	GAR JOH
MINNESOTA #13 (op) (Mellum strain)	112	9 ft. stalks; 8 in. ears	Good yields. For cornmeal. Old time dent strain. Adapted to most of the North.	JOH
MOHAWK WHITE HOMINY (ONENHAKERA)		8 in. ears; 8 rows	Used for corn syrup.	RED
M.S. 722-A	90		Good field corn for early or late planting.	LED
M.S. 747-B (hybrid)	95-110		Good field corn.	LED
M.S. 775 (hybrid)			Field corn. Dual-purpose corn.	LED
NOTHSTINE DENT	100	7 ft. stalks; 8 in. ears	Glossy, yellow kernels with white caps. Short-season dent corn. Heirloom variety.	JOH
PAPAGO CORN	60		Slender, small, cream-colored corn. Drought-tolerant. Grind into corn meal.	PLA
REID'S YELLOW DENT	85-110	7 ft. stalks; 9 in. ears	Dates back to the 1840s. Tolerates heat. Used for cornmeal.	SOU
TEXAS GOURDSEED	120	8 ft. stalks; 18-22 rows	2 ears per stalk. Cream-colored kernels are narrow and easy to hand shell. Susceptible to smut. Does well in clay soils and withstands drought. Great for tortilla flour.	SOU

▶

Variety	Days	Plant/Ears	Remarks	Sources
VIGIRNIA WHITE GOURDSEED DENT	**120**	10 in. ears; 12-18 rows	Excellent resistance to southern leaf blight. Highly productive. 2 ears per stalk. Does well in clay soils and during drought. Susceptible to smut.	SOU
WHITE POSOLE	**100**		Vigorous, drought-tolerant plants. Used for making posole, the hominy of the Southwest.	LEM PLA

CORN—ORNAMENTAL
PARCHING

Variety	Days	Plant/Ears	Remarks	Sources
BLUE SQUAW			Large ears with dark blue kernels. Used for tortillas or decoration.	ROS
FIESTA (hybrid)	102	7 ft. stalks; 10 in. ears	Wide range of colors on each ear.	JOH LET RIS TWI
INDIAN FINGERS	110	7 ft. stalks; 4½ in. ears	Small shiny kernels in an assortment of colors. Very good in floral arrangements.	HARR
INDIAN ORNAMENTAL (INDIAN SQUAW) (CALICO)	110		Large decorative ears in an array of endless color combinations.	ALL ARC BUR BURR DEG FAR GUR HARR HEN LED LIBE MEY PIN POR RIS SEE STO TIL TWI VER WET WIL WYA
LITTLE INDIAN		4½ in. ears	Miniature Indian rainbow corn. Multi-colored kernels.	ARC JUN LAG LEM LET
PENCIL COB			No cob and very deep plump kernels. Very sweet.	JLH WIL
PURPLE HUSK	112		Colored kernels. Purple outer husks.	LET
RAINBOW	112		Strictly decorative. Rich colors. Great for holiday decorating.	BURP GUR LET MID PEA PLA ROS THO TIL WES
SEEDWAY ELITE			Easy to grow. Gaily colored ears.	SEED
STRIPED QUADRICOLOR			Dark green leaves have pink and white bordered stripes. Dries to make colorful ears.	NIC
SYMPHONIE	110	5 in. ears	A true baby Indian corn. Kernels have a wide array of colors.	STO VER

CORN SALAD
(Valerianella locusta)

Corn salad is known by two other names, Mache and Lamb's lettuce. This green is appreciated where fresh salad greens are in short supply. Corn salad is divided into two types, large seeded and small seeded. The large seeded variety is popular in warm climates, and not hardy in cold climates.

It is an immensely tasty vegetable that is rich in vitamins and minerals.

CULTURE: Sow seed a half-inch deep, 4 to 6 inches apart, in 12 to 16 inch rows. It grows best planted in the fall for a quick crop. In milder climates it will grow all winter, if protected with hay or cornstalks.

SEASON: Cool.

HARVESTING: Harvest entire plant or the spoon-shaped leaves when needed.

CORN SALAD
(ALSO KNOWN AS MACHE AND LAMB'S LETTUCE)

Variety	Days	Remarks	Sources
BIG SEED (LARGE-SEEDED DUTCH)		Large leaves are used in salads.	HER JLH NIC RED TER
BLONDE SHELL-LEAVED		Small plant is extremely hardy.	NIC SEE
BROAD LEAVED (WINTER SALAD PLANT)	45-60	Large, thick leaves.	COM DEG LIBE STO TIL
CAVALLO	50	Deep green, fresh-flavored leaf. Very hardy.	THO
COQUILLE DE LOUVIERS (SCALLOP OF LOUVIERS)		Shiny green plant with spoon-shaped leaves.	LEM RED
DUTCH		Large leaves will germinate in the heat. European variety. Piquant flavor.	RIC SEE
FETTICUS	35-60	Mild, slightly nutty flavor. Large, rounded, dark green leaves with smooth edges. Use in salads or steamed.	DEG HEN LEJ
GREEN CAMBRAI	40-45	Large, rounded, dark green, cold-resistant leaves. High yields. An autumn and winter grower.	ABU HER JOH LEM SHE
GREEN FULL HEART (CABBAGE)		Compact plant is cold-resistant. Round, smooth intensely green leaves. Firm heart.	BURP HER RED
GROTE NOORDE	70-80	Dutch variety. Elongated paddle-shaped leaves. Heirloom strain for mild-winter areas. Mild and tender flavor.	SEE SHE
GROTE NOORDHOLLANDSE		Large-seeded. Cannot tolerate frost. Large, bushy leaves.	LEM
LARGE ROUND-LEAVED	60	Mild flavor. Grown for salad use.	GAR LED MEY WILL
MACHE (CORN SALAD) (LAMB'S LETTUCE)	45	Velvety 3 in. long green spoon-shaped leaves have delicate nutty flavor. Grows best in cool weather.	COO ECO HUM PIN VER WET
RONDE MARAICHERE		An heirloom variety. Distinct oval, almost round leaves. Upright growth.	LEM
VERELLA	37-40	Productive. Resistant to cold and mildew.	HER
VERTE DE CAMBRAI	70-80	French variety. Hardy strain. 3-4 in. flat, teardrop-shaped leaves. Fine-textured and deep green. Overwinters well. Very cold-tolerant.	JOH LEM SHE
VIT		Vigorous spring and fall variety. Long, glossy green leaves. Tender, mild and minty flavored. Mildew-tolerant.	JOH

CRESS

Variety	Days	Remarks	Sources
EARLY CURLED	10	Fine flavor. May be cut several times.	ALL
CURLED CRESS		Ready to use when seedlings have 3-4 leaves.	RIC
EXTRA FINE CURLED [A]	45	A quick grower. Finely cut, dark green leaves. Pungent flavor. Grows 8 in. tall.	HARR THO

▶

Variety	Days	Remarks	Sources
GARDEN CRESS (CURLICRESS) (FINE CURLED) (PEPPER CRESS) (LAND CRESS) (MOUNTAIN CRESS)	40-45	Grows to 1 foot. Plain curled leaves. Delicious as sprouts, or in salads or as garnish. Slow to bolt to seed. Pungent flavor.	ABU ALL BURP COM DEG ECO FIS GAR HER JOH JUN LEJ NIC RAW RED SEE SEED SHE STO THO TWI VES WILL
MEGA	50	Big watercress foliage. Cut throughout the summer.	THO
MOSS CURLED	10	Tastes like watercress. Fine-cut leaves resemble parsley. Dwarf, compact growth.	JUN
PLAIN CRESS	40	Fast grower. Unusual sweet-hot flavor. Plant early in a warm spot. During the summer it needs a shady place.	HER RED
TRUE WATERCRESS [P]	50-180	Small oval leaf. Can be grown in shallow water or moist soil. Mild, salty, pungent flavor.	ABU ALL COO DIX GLE JLH LED LET LIBE PAR RIC SUN
UPLAND BROADLEAF CRESS [A] (WINTER CRESS)	60	Broad, bright green leaves. Similar to watercress. Can be grown in any type of soil.	COM DEG HARR HER JLH LED RIC SEE TAY TIL VER WET WYA
WATERCRESS LARGE LEAF	50	Mildly pungent.	SEE STO

CUCUMBERS
(Cucumis sativus)

Cucumbers are members of the same family as melons, pumpkins and squash. The vines for most varieties will spread well over six feet. Each cucumber vine bears both male and female flowers. The first ten to twenty flowers produced on any plant are males. After that there are ten to twenty male flowers for every female. Cucumbers come only from the female flowers, so it takes a while before most vines start to produce.

The modern gynoecious (gyn) varieties have all female flowers. These varieties are popular because they start bearing fruit as soon as the first flowers appear.

Cucumbers come in many shapes, sizes and colors. They are usually divided into two families, white spine and black spine. The spines are minature stickers that protrude from the warts when fruits are young. White spine cucumbers turn creamy white when completely mature. Black spine varieties turn yellowish-orange.

Cucumbers are classified in two categories, slicing varieties and pickling. The slicers are usually long and slender and have a sweet taste. The pickles are shorter, blockier, making them more convenient for whole pickles.

CULTURE: Sow 6 seeds per foot in rows 2 feet apart, ½ inch deep and thin to 6 to 12 inches apart. On hills, thin to 2 to 3 plants per hill, 6 inches apart. To save space try growing vine cucumbers up a fence or on a trellis.

SEASON: Warm.

INSECTS/DISEASES: *APHIDS, SPIDER MITE, SPOTTED CUCUMBER BEETLES, SQUASH BUGS, SQUASH VINE BORERS, STRIPED CUCUMBER BEETLES, SOUTH CORN ROOTWORMS*: Use Malathion, diazinon, pyrethrum, rotenone, Sevin or ryania.

ANTHRACNOSE, DOWNY MILDEW, SCAB: Apply captan, maneb or zineb.

BACTERIAL SPOT, BLIGHT: Use fixed copper sprays.

HARVESTING: Pick cucumbers anytime while they are still green, unless you have the colored variety; then pick according to package instructions.

CUCUMBERS
EXTRA-LONG

Variety	Days	Size	Remarks	Sources
ARMENIAN YARD LONG (SERPENT CUCUMBER)	65-75	3 ft. long	Gray-green color with unique fluting.	ABU BURG BURP GUR HEN KIT LAG LEM NIC POR RED ROS WES WIL

◀ **CUCUMBERS**

Variety	Days	Size	Remarks	Sources
CHINA HYBRID	58	12 x 1½ in.	Dark green, moderately ribbed and high-spined. Few small seeds. Strong vigorous vines need to be trellised.	BURG
CHINA LONG GREEN (JAPANESE CLIMBING)	75	20 x 2 in.	Light green with black spines. For climbing trellis and covering fences.	BURG COM EARL GLE GRA NIC RED STO THO
ENGLISH	66	18 in. straight	European cuke that is a climber and non-bitter. Dark green.	HUM
JUMBO	65	18 x 3 in.	Dark green, nearly black with only a few spines.	DEG GRA
KYOTO		19 x 3 in. to 3 feet	Light green. Excellent quality. For early summer sowing.	LAG SUN THO
SANJIAKU KIURI		2 ft.	Support the vines. Fairly smooth, light green.	KIT
SUYO LONG	61	15 in.	Dark green with white spines. Support the vines. Burpless. Summer planting.	BAN JOH RED SOU SUN
YAMOTO EXTRA LONG	65-75	24 in. straight	Dark green, smooth skin. Crisp and mild flavor.	NIC TSA
ZEPPELIN	67	12 lbs.	Stays firm and juicy.	THO

CUCUMBERS—SLICING
LONG

Variety	Days	Size	Remarks	Sources
AODAI	60	10 x 2 in.	Spineless. Hardy and heat-tolerant. Bright green. Pinch off main stem to encourage prolific bearing.	JLH
GREEN ICE (hybrid)		9 x 11 in.	Strong vigorous vines need to climb. Extra firm. Thin, smooth skin. No bitterness. Small seed cavity.	BURG
JAPANESE HYBRID CLIMBING	58	9 x 3 in.	Black-spined. Crisp and tender. Long-season producer that needs to grow on fence or trellis.	BURG FAR
LONG GREEN	70	10 in.	Dark green. Crisp. Poor appearance but good flavor.	ALL WYA
LONG GREEN IMPROVED [op]	60-70	14 x 2½ in.	Dark green, black-spined. Vigorous vines. Fine producer.	ARC DEG EARL LET MEY RED ROS
MARKETER [op] (EARLY GREEN MARKET)	60-68	10 x 2¼ in.	Dark green, white-spined. Heavy yielder. Good variety for southern gardens.	ARC BURR GUR HEN LED LEJ LET STO WET WIL WYA
PALACE PRIDE (hybrid)		12 in.	Dark green, ridged with white spines. Small seed cavity.	KIT

▶

Variety	Days	Size	Remarks	Sources
PARK'S WHOPPER IMPROVED (hybrid)	55	10 in.	Highly disease-resistant. Sweet and crisp. Female flowers dominate. Strong growing productive vines.	PAR
SOOYOW		12 x 1½ in.	Ribbed and high-spined. Dark green. Almost seedless.	JLH KIT
STREAMLINER (hybrid) [gyn]	60	10½ in.	Medium-green. Thick flesh, small seed cavity. Mosaic- and mildew-resistant.	BURP PIN
SWALLOW (hybrid)	50	12 in.	From Taiwan. Burpless. Hothouse culture or plant outside in warm weather. Provide ample moisture. White-spined. Grow on trellis.	LEM
SWEET SUCCESS (hybrid) [gyn]		14 in.	Thin, smooth skin. No bitterness. Sets without pollination. Burpless. Disease-resistant.	PAR THO VER
THE LONGFELLOW	74	15 x 2½ in.	Dark green, white-spined. Perfectly uniform in size.	DEG

CUCUMBERS—SLICING

MEDIUM

Variety	Days	Size	Remarks	Sources
AMIRA (hybrid)	55	3 in.	Thin-skinned, sweet and crisp. No need to peel. Tolerant to downy mildew, mosaic and powdery mildew.	NIC PAR PIN
AMIRA II	70		Middle Eastern variety. Thin, smooth skin. Fine flavor.	TER
ASHLEY	66	8 x 2¼ in.	Dark green, white-spined. Vines are productive and vigorous. Downy mildew-resistant.	JUN LAG LED LET RIS WIL
BLACK DIAMOND	55	7 x 2½ in.	Heavy producer.	DEG
BURPEEANA HYBRID II [gyn]	55	9 x 2¼ in. Straight	Dark green. Vigorous vine is productive over a long season.	BURP WET
BURPEE HYBRID	60	8 x 2¼ in. Squarish	Dark green, white-spined. Mosaic-resistant, downy mildew-resistant.	ARC LET
BURPEE HYBRID II [gyn]	55	8½ x 2½ in. Straight	Medium seed cavity. Crisp flesh. Productive heavy cropper. Mildew- and mosaic-resistant.	MID RIS
BURPEE M & M (hybrid)	64	8 in.	Dark, glossy green. Crisp flesh. Productive heavy cropper. Mildew- and mosaic-resistant.	BURP
CENTURION (hybrid)	59	8½ in.	Dark green. High-yielding. Scab-, mosaic-, and mildew-resistant.	MID RIS
COMANCHE NO. 7 (hybrid)	70	7½ x 2 in. Slightly tapered	Dark green. Long-season producer. Mosaic- and scab-resistant.	ROS
CONQUEROR	65	Long	Smooth green fruit. Easy to grow, indoors or out. Stands heat well.	THO
CRACKERLEE	65	8 in.	Downy and powdery mildew-resistant.	MID

◄ CUCUMBERS—SLICING

Variety	Days	Size	Remarks	Sources
DASHER (hybrid)	58	8 in.	Dark green, white-spined. Straight, slim.	MEY
DASHER II (hybrid) [gyn]	55-60	8½ x 2¼ in.	Dark green. Highly productive, compact plant. Anthracnose, angular leaf spot, downy, powdery mildew, scab and mosaic resistance.	LET MID POR RIS STO TWI WET
DUBLIN [gyn]	48-65	9 x 2 in.	Dark green. Not tolerant to powdery mildew. Anthracnose-, mosaic- and downy mildew-resistant.	STO
EARLIPIK (hybrid) [gyn]	54	6 in.	Disease resistance. Medium-green with white spines.	FIS
EARLY FORTUNE	58-65	9 x 2½ in. Tapered at both ends	Dark green, with yellow-green stripe. Heavy yielder.	DEG GUR
EARLY GREEN CLUSTER	55	5½ in. Chunky	Smooth medium-green skin.	WYA
EARLY MARKETER (hybrid)	55	9 x 2¼ in.	Very dark green. Mildew- and mosaic- resistant.	BURR HUM
EARLY PRIDE (hybrid) [gyn]	55	8½ x 2 in. Straight	Dark green. Medium-thick flesh. Produces for a long time. Mosaic- and mildew-resistant.	BURP
EARLY SURECROP (hybrid)	58	9 x 2½ in. Blunt end	Dark green. Mosaic- and downy mildew-resistant.	BURR COM GUR HEN JUN LED POR TIL WET WYA
EARLY TRIUMPH	56-62	8 in. Straight	Dark green. Monoecious type. Long season, high-yielding. Disease-resistant.	JOH LIBE PAR PIN
ENCORE (hybrid)	62	Slightly tapered	Dark green, white-spined. Disease-resistant.	HARR
GEMINI (hybrid) [gyn]	61-65	9 x 2½ in.	Pick frequently. Angular leaf spot, anthracnose, mosaic, downy, powdery mildew, and scab resistance.	ALL EAR LED MID WET
GEMINI 7 (hybrid)	60	8 in.	Dark green skin. Excellent quality.	BURR EARL GUR POR RAW VES WIL
GUARDIAN (hybrid)	61	9 in.	Dark green. Good disease resistance.	MID
HIGH MARK II			High-yielding. Dark green. Mosaic- and scab-resistant.	LET
HYLARES	58		Middle Eastern variety. Glossy bright green, smooth-skinned. Juicy and crisp. Mosaic-resistant.	SHE
HY SLICE (hybrid)	54			MID
MARKETMORE	76	8 in.	Dark green. Very productive. Scab-, downy and powdery mildew-resistant.	ALL PON WILL
MARKETMORE 70 [op]	60-70	8½ x 2¼ in.	Dark green skin. Color does not fade in summer. Mosaic- and scab-resistant.	BURP EARL HEN LET PAR TER

Variety	Days	Size	Remarks	Sources
MARKETMORE 76	68	8 in. Straight	Glossy dark green, white-spined. Mosaic-, Scab-, downy and powdery mildew-resistant.	BURR COM DEG FAR FIS CAR HARR HUM JUN LED MEY MID RAW RIS SEED STO TWI VER VES WIL
MARKETMORE 80 [op]	60	9 in.	Dark green. No bitter taste. Scab-, downy and powdery mildew-resistant.	JOH LIBE SOU
MARKETSETT [op]	65	9 in.	Vigorous vines set well even in cool weather. Angular leaf spot, anthracnose, mosaic, scab, downy and powdery mildew resistance.	SOU STO
MEDALIST [op]	63	Blocky	Deep green, white-spined. Mosaic, scab, downy and powdery mildew resistance.	HARR
OLYMPIAN [gyn]	59	7½ x 1¾ in.	Dark green skin. Angular leaf spot, scab, powdery and downy mildew resistance.	WIL
PACER	62	8½ in. Cylindrical	Heavy bearer. Mosaic- and scab-resistant.	HARR
PALOMAR	60-66	9 x 2¼ in.	Dark green. Heavy cropper. Downy mildew-resistant.	DEG
POINSETT	65	8 in. Rounded ends	Heavy yielder, does well in the South. Mosaic- and powdery mildew-resistant.	BUR DEG LAG LET WIL
POINSETT 76 [op]	67	Straight	Highly disease-resistant. Glossy deep green with white spines. Stands up to unfavorable growing conditions.	BURP GUR HARR JUN LIBE MEY MID PAR SOU TWI WET WIL WYA
RAIDER (hybrid)	62		Dark green skin with white spines. Compact, vigorous vines. Heavy uniform yields. Angular leaf spot, mosaic and scab resistance.	HARR VES
ROADSIDE FANCY (hybrid) [gyn]	60	8½ in.	Dark green skin. Heavy yields. Angular leaf spot, mosaic, scab and mildew resistance.	LIBE TER
SCORE (hybrid)			Medium to dark green. Good seedling vigor.	LET
SETMORE 100 (hybrid)	56	Long, slim, straight	Widely adapted. Dark green skin. Angular leaf spot, anthracnose, scab, mosaic, downy and powdery mildew resistance.	TWI
SHAMROCK II [gyn]	55	8¼ x 2½ in.	Dark green skin. Dense small leaf cover. Angular leaf spot, scab, mosaic, anthracnose, downy and powdery mildew resistance.	STO
SLICEMASTER (hybrid) [gyn]	55	Slim	Dark green skin. Angular leaf spot, scab, mosaic, anthracnose, downy and powdery mildew resistance.	STO
SLICE NICE (hybrid) [gyn]	62	Slim	Dark green skin. Anthracnose-, scab- and downy mildew-resistant.	LET LIBE TWI VES
SOUTHERNSETT [op]	63	Long, slim	Dark green skin white spines. High yields. Angular leaf spot, mosaic, scab, downy and powdery mildew resistance.	HARR
SPRINT 440 [gyn]	52	9 in.	Dark green. Angular leaf spot, scab, mosaic, anthracnose, downy and powdery mildew resistance.	STO

◄ CUCUMBERS—SLICING

Variety	Days	Size	Remarks	Sources
STOKES EARLY HYBRID	55	9 in. Cylindrical	Heavy yields. Dark green. Scab, anthracnose, mosaic, angular leaf spot, downy and powdery mildew resistance.	STO
STONO	65	8 x 2½ in.	Vigorous vines producs heavily.	DEG
STRAIGHT EIGHT [op]	60-67	8 in. Blunt	White-spined. Small seed cavity. Very prolific.	ABU ALL BURG BURP BURR DAN DEG EARL FAR FIS GUR HEN LET MEY PON POR RAW ROS STO VER WES WIL WILL WYA
STRAIGHT 9	65	9 x 1½ in.	Dark green skin. Vigorous vines. Downy and powdery mildew-resistant.	EAR LED WIL
SUPERSETT (hybrid)	53	8½ x 2¼ in. Tapered	Smooth. High yielder over a long season. Angular leaf spot, mosaic, anthracnose, scab, downy and powdery mildew resistance.	JOH RIS STO
SURE SLICE (hybrid)	55	7½ in.	Deep green, nearly spineless. Very small seed cavity. Good producer over long season.	DAN
TAMU TEXLONG		9 in. Slender	Dark green. Strong vines. Mosaic- resistant.	POR
TEX LONG	65	9 in.	Very juicy and mild. Downy and powdery mildew-resistant.	WIL
TOP MAKER (hybrid)		7 x 2 in.	Easy to grow, vigorous vines.	GLE
TRIPLE CROWN (hybrid)	54		White-spined. Multiple disease resistance. Good yields.	LET
TRIUMPH (hybrid)	62	8 in. Tapered at ends	Heavy yields from vigorous vines. Mosaic and downy mildew resistance.	FAR MID
ULTRASLICE™ EARLY (hybrid)	56	8½ x 2⅜ in.	Smooth, dark green skin. Good results during stress weather conditions. Angular leaf spot, mosaic, anthracnose, scab, downy and powdery mildew-resistant.	STO
UNIVERSAL (hybrid)	60	9 in.	Smooth, dark green. High yields. Strong vines. Angular leaf spot, anthracnose, mosaic, scab, downy and powdery mildew resistance.	TWI
VICTORY (hybrid) [gyn]	60	8 in. Straight	Dark green. Vigorous vines. Scab, mosaic, downy and powdery mildew resistance.	ARC LAG STO VES WIL
WHITE SPINE IMPROVED	62	9 x 2½ in.	Deep green skin.	ALL WET

CUCUMBERS—PICKLING

Variety	Days	Size	Remarks	Sources
ARMADA (hybrid) [gyn]	50	Medium-long	Dark green, white-spined. High-yielding. Scab, mosaic, anthracnose, angular leaf spot, downy and powdery mildew resistance.	JOH

►

◄

Variety	Days	Size	Remarks	Sources
BEIT ALPHA MR	56	Straight, round ends	Medium-length vine. Uniform size. Medium-green skin, black-spined. Mosaic-resistant.	WIL
BOSTON PICKLING	52-58	6 in.	Rich green. Good quality.	ABU ALL COM LET TIL WIL
BOURBONNE IMPROVED	50	5 in.	European strain. Disease-tolerant.	LEM
BURPEE PICKLER	53		Medium-green skin, black spines. Warted fruit. Mosaic-tolerant.	BURP
CALYPSO (hybrid) [gyn]	56	6 in.	Dark green. High-yielding. Scab, anthracnose, leaf spot, mosaic, downy and powdery mildew resistance.	ALL HARR LET LIBE MID RIS STO TWI VES
CAROLINA (hybrid)	49	Straight, blocky	Medium-sized vigorous vines. Mosaic, scab, anthracnose, downy and powdery mildew resistance.	BURR JUN MID WIL
CHICAGO PICKLING	59	6½ x 2½ in.	Most widely used variety for pickling.	ARC DEG FAR LET ROS WET
CHINA-SCHLANGEN		Up to 20 in. Crooked	Disease-resistant.	WILL
CORNICHON DE BOURBONNE		Slightly curved	Makes tiny sour pickles. French variety. Harvest frequently. High yields. Scab-, mosaic- and powdery mildew-resistant.	COO NIC SHE
COUNTRY FAIR 83 (hybrid) [gyn]	58	7 in.	Non-bitter. Produces seedless fruits if isolated from other cucumbers.	EAR HEN JUN PAR STO
DOUBLE YIELD PICKLING	50		Dark green. Good variety for gherkins. Also for dills.	STO
EARLIPIK [gyn]	54	5¾ x 2½ in. Blocky	Medium-green, white-spined. Scab-, mosaic-, downy and powdery mildew-resistant.	PON
EARLIPAK 14 (hybrid) [gyn]	53	5 x 1½ in. Blocky	Dark green and warted. Fine variety for any type of pickle. Scab-, mosaic-, and powdery mildew-resistant.	BURP
EARLY CLUSTER		Blocky	Medium-green with tender skin and flesh. Vines produce in clusters.	POR
EARLY RUSSIAN	50	5 x 2 in.	Prolific. Small and uniform.	ABU DEG EARL HIG
EDMONSON	70	4 in.	1913 heirloom variety. Resistance to disease, insects and drought. Whitish-green skin.	SOU
EXPLORER (hybrid) [gyn]	50-55	Straight	White-spined. Adapted to moist climates. Vigorous and productive. Angular leaf spot, anthracnose, mosaic, downy and powdery mildew resistance.	WIL
EXPRESS (hybrid) [gyn]	50	6 x 2 in.	Medium-green. Does not become bitter under stress. Anthracnose, angular leaf spot, mosaic, scab and downy and powdery mildew resistance.	WILL
FINE MEAUX	60		For gherkin pickles.	HER

►

◀ CUCUMBERS—PICKLING

Variety	Days	Size	Remarks	Sources
FREMONT (hybrid)			Medium-dark green. Attractive pickles at all stages. Mosaic, mildew, anthracnose and leaf spot resistance.	BURG
GHERKIN	60	2 in. Chunky	Covered with tender spines. Very productive vines.	GUR LET RED TIL
HOKUS ORIGINAL	59		Non-ridged European type. White-spined. Stays solid when pickled. Mosaic- and scab-resistant.	WILL
KATSURA GIANT PICKLING		12½ x 4½ in.	Japanese variety. Light green skin turns almost white. Thick white flesh.	GLE
LEVINA (hybrid) [gyn]	52		Prolific yields even under poor conditions. White-spined, bitter-free. Mosaic-, scab- and powdery mildew-resistant.	VER
LIBERTY (hybrid)	56	Blocky	High-yielding. Black-spined, warted. Weather-tolerant. Widely adapted. Angular leaf spot, mosaic, scab and downy mildew resistance.	BURG BURP COM DAN FAR GUR HUM JUN LAG LED LIBE NIC PAR PIN POR THO TWI WET WYA
MINCU	50	4 x 1¾ in.	White-spined. Compact vines. Heavy cropper.	EARL FAR FIS GUR HEN
MISS PICKLER (hybrid) [gyn] (LUCKY STRIKE)	50	6 in. Blocky	Tremendous yielder. Small seed cavity. White-spined and well-warted.	HEN LET LIBE PIN RIS SEED VER
MORDEN EARLY	50	3 in.	Short vines are very productive. Makes good dills.	EARL
MULTIPIK (hybrid) [gyn]		Long	Medium-green and firm. Strong, vigorous, productive vines.	POR
NATIONAL PICKLING	53	5 x 2½ in. Blunt ends	Dark green skin. All-around pickler. Big yields. Mosaic- and scab-resistant.	DAN DEG EARL FIS GUR HEN JOH JUN LEJ LET PIN RED TIL VER WET WILL WYA
NORTHERN PICKLING	50		Not recommended in areas having mosaic. Scab-resistant.	GAR HIG
OHIO MR 17	57	7 x 2 in.	Dark green skin. High-yielding. Mosaic-resistant.	ARC WILL
PEPPI (hybrid) [gyn]	48	Slightly tapered	Dark green skin. High yields. Scab-, mosaic- and downy mildew-resistant.	FAR STO

▶

Variety	Days	Size	Remarks	Sources
PICAROW (hybrid)	52	Blocky	Small seed cavity. Medium-green skin. Angular leaf spot, scab, mosaic, anthrancose, downy and powdery mildew resistance.	RIS
PICCADILLY (hybrid) [gyn]	56	6 in. Blocky	High yields.	PAR
PICKLE-RIFFIC (hybrid)	50	4½ in.	Heavy yields. Makes good crisp pickles.	HEN
PIK MASTER [gyn]	55	5½ in.	Medium-dark green skin, white spines. Vigorous plant. Mosaic, scab, downy and powdery mildew resistance.	SEED
PIK-RITE [gyn]	63	Blocky	Dark green, white-spined. Short-season variety. Angular leaf spot, anthracnose, mosaic, scab and powdery mildew resistance.	STO
PIONEER (hybrid) [gyn] (MRS PICKLER)	48-55		Medium-green skin, black spines. Short-season variety. High-yielding. Mosaic, scab and powdery mildew resistance.	BURR EAR EARL GUR HIG RAW RIS STO TIL WILL
PRINCE (hybrid)	54	Tapered	Large vine. Medium-green skin, white-spined. Mosaic-, scab-, downy and powdery mildew-resistant.	HARR
PRODUCER	54		White-spined. Tremendous yielder.	LET
REGAL (hybrid) [gyn]	52	Cylindrical, blunt ends	Dark green skin, white spines. Scab, angular leaf spot, anthracnose, mosaic, downy and powdery mildew resistance.	HARR VES
ROYAL (hybrid)	52	Cylindrical	Dark green with white spines. Small vine. Brines well. Angular leaf spot, anthracnose, mosaic, scab, downy and powdery mildew resistance.	HARR
SALADIN PICKLER (hybrid) [gyn]	55	5 x 1¾ in. Curved	Bright green skin. Dutch variety. Fine crisp flavor. Mosaic-, bacterial wilt- and powdery mildew-resistant.	BURP EAR FAR PAR PIN SHE
SALTY (hybrid)	53	5 in.	Dark green, white-spined. Heavy yielder. Good canner. Doesn't hollow. Mosaic-, scab-, downy and powdery mildew-resistant.	STO
SMALL PARIS (VERTE PETITE DE PARIS)	50-60		Harvest this gherkin cucumber when approximately 2 in. long. Short, spiny fruit.	HER LEM
SMR 58	56	6½ x 2½ in.	Medium-green, black-spined. Excellent variety. Mosaic, scab, angular leaf spot, and rot resistance.	ALL BURG BURR EAR GUR HEN HUM JUN LED LET MEY MID NIC PON RIS SEED STO TER WET
SPARTAN DAWN (hybrid)	49	6 x 2½ in.	Black-spined. High yields.	DEG EARL RAW
SPEAR-IT [gyn]	52		Widely adapted. White-spined. Angular leaf spot, anthracnose, scab, mosaic, downy and powdery mildew resistance.	MID STO
SUMPTER	56	Slightly tapered, blocky	Dark green, white-spined. Not bitter. Angular leaf spot, anthracnose, scab, downy and powdery mildew resistance.	SOU

◀ CUCUMBERS—PICKLING

Variety	Days	Size	Remarks	Sources
TRIPLE MECH (hybrid) [gyn]	**52**		White-spined. Compact plant. Anthracnose, scab, mosaic, downy and powdery mildew resistance.	LET TWI
V.I.P. (hybrid)	**50**		Brines well. Heavy producer. Wide disease tolerance.	MID
WEST INDIA GHERKIN (BURR)	**60**	3 x 1½ in.	Light-green skin. Very prolific. Ideal for small pickles or relish.	BURG BURP LEM LET NIC POR
WHITE WONDER	**58**	6 in.	Skin turns ivory-white when mature. Mild flavor. Pickles are small.	GAR LET
WISCONSIN SMR 18	**56**	6 x 2½ in.	Black-spined. All-purpose pickler. Mosaic- and scab-resistant.	GUR LET MID

BUSH CUCUMBERS—PICKLING

Variety	Days	Size	Remarks	Sources
BUSH PICKLE	52	4½ x 1½ in.	Produces normal-size fruit. 20-24 in. compact vines. Use for sweet or dill pickles. Mosaic- and powdery mildew-resistant.	BURP DAN EAR GUR HEN JUN LED LIBE MEY MID PAR PIN SEED
CASCADE (hybrid)	55		Small tidy bush. White-spined.	TER
ZESTY (hybrid) [gyn]			Productive compact vine. Dark green skin, white-spined.	LET

BUSH CUCUMBERS—SLICING

Variety	Days	Size	Remarks	Sources
BURPLESS BUSH	42	12 in.	Dark green skin, spineless. Dwarf plant.	PAR
BUSH CHAMPION	55	11 in. Straight, slender	Short, compact vines. Bright green skin. Perfect for slicing.	BURP DAN LAG NIC PON
BUSH CROP (hybrid)	55	8 in.	Dwarf bush plants are a good container variety.	BURR DAN EAR GUR HEN JUN MEY MID PIN SEED WET
BUSH WHOPPER	55	8 in.	Has no runners.	DEG PAR
PATIO PIC (hybrid)	50-55	6½ in. Straight, blocky	An all-purpose cucumber. Performs well even in hanging baskets. Scab-, downy and powdery mildew-resistant.	ARC FAR GLE GUR HEN HUM LAG PAR PIN THO
POT LUCK (hybrid)	50-55	7 in. Straight	Green skin, white spines. Grows well in containers. Mosaic-resistant.	ALL BURG COM EARL GUR JUN LED LET MEY MID NIC RAW RIS TIL VER WIL
SPACEMASTER	60	8 in. Slender	Big yields in small places. 18-24 in. bush. Adaptable to wide range of climates. Harvest regularly. Disease-resistant.	ALL ARC BURP COM EARL FIS GAR HEN JOH LET PIN PLA POR SOU STO VER WILL

CUCUMBERS—BURPLESS

Variety	Days	Size	Remarks	Sources
ARMENIAN BURPLESS	60	2 ft. x 2 in. Curved	Gray-green skin. Fluted. Best picked when 12 in. long.	EARL
BURPLESS DELIGHT	60		No need to peel. Mild taste.	HUM
BURPLESS HIGH-FEMALE GYN 200 (hybrid)		10 in. Slender	Shiny green skin. Uniform size. Crisp, not bitter. Stands up well in summer heat, but not cold temperatures. Mosaic-, downy and powdery mildew-resistant.	SEED
BURPLESS HYBRID	62	10 in. Curved	Japanese variety. Non-bitter. Downy and powdery mildew-resistant.	ARC BURG BURP COM DEG EAR FAR FIS GUR HEN LED LEJ MID PIN PON POR RIS STO TIL TWI
BURPLESS HYBRID NO. 26	50-70	9 x 1½ in. Straight	Dark green, white-spined. Downy and powdery mildew-resistant.	HARR WET
BURPLESS MUNCHER [op]	65	7 x 2¼ in.	Medium-green skin. Heavy producer.	ALL
BURPLESS TASTY GREEN (hybrid)	62	10 in.	Non-bitter. Crisp and delicious.	LAG THO
BURPLESS TASTY GREEN NO. 26 (hybrid)	62	10 in to 2 ft. Straight	Productive in all climates. Needs no peeling. Grow on stakes or fence.	NIC PAR
EURO-AMERICAN (hybrid)	45	1 ft.	Small seed cavity, thick, juicy, sweet flesh. Bright green skin. Good vigorous vines.	DEG PAR PIN
GREEN KING [gyn]	70	1 ft.	Intensive and prolific cropper. Bacterial wilt-, mosaic-, and powdery mildew-resistant.	TER
GREEN KNIGHT (hybrid)	60	8 in.	Dark green skin is thin. Heat-resistant, vigorous plant. Scab-resistant.	BURP
JET SET (hybrid) (JUNIOR BURPLESS)	59	8 in.	Does well in all climates. High quality. Can eat skin and all.	GUR HEN NIC
JORDAN (hybrid)	50	7 in.	Skin is not bitter. Crisp flesh. Middle East variety. Mosaic-resistant.	LEM
ROLLINSON'S TELEGRAPH	60	18 in. Slim, straight	British variety. Grow on fence or trellis. Dark green skin. Delicate, clean flavor. No need to peel as it is non-bitter.	SHE WILL
SWEET DELIGHT (hybrid)	65	10 x 2 in. Slightly curved	Medium-green, burpless and non-bitter. Mosaic- and scab-resistant.	ROS
SWEET SLICE (hybrid)	62	12 in. Slightly tapered	Dark green skin, white spines. Sweet taste. Bitter-free. Anthracnose, scab, mosaic, downy and powdery mildew resistance.	ALL ARC BURG BURR EARL FAR GLE GUR HARR HEN HER JUN LAG LET LIBE MID PAR SEED STO TWI VER VES WET WIL WILL
SWEET SUCCESS (hybrid) [gyn]	65	12 in.	Dark green skin. Burpless and bitter-free. For indoors or outdoor growing. Trellis culture.	BURP COM DAN HEN JUN LAG LED LIBE MEY NIC PAR PIN POR THO TWI VER WILL

▶

◄ **CUCUMBERS—BURPLESS**

Variety	Days	Size	Remarks	Sources
TASTY GREEN	**60**	10 in.	Smooth, dark green skin. Heavy cropper tolerant to cool soil. Scab-, downy and powdery mildew-resistant.	DEG LAG NIC SEED SUN THO VER VES WILL
TENDERFRESH		7 in.	Nearly spineless. High yields. Disease-resistant. Slicer or pickler.	LIBE

CUCUMBERS

GREENHOUSE TYPES

Variety	Days	Size	Remarks	Sources
AURELIA (hybrid)	64	14 in.	Semi-glossy, shallow ribs. Very good yields. Strong, open growth. Leaf spot- and gummosis-resistant.	JOH
BITSPOT (hybrid)		15 in.	Needs heat for germination. English variety. Bitter-free. Can be grown outdoors as well. Leaf spot- and scab-resistant.	WILL
CORONA (hybrid)[gyn]		16 in.	Slim plant. Does not produce heavy foliage. Good performer in hot or cold weather.	STO
DYNASTY [gyn]	60	Straight	Dark green fruit. Tolerant to scab, anthracnose, angular leaf spot, mosaic, downy and powdery mildew.	TWI
ENGLISH TELEGRAPH		18 in. Slim, straight	Dark green. Bitter-free English variety.	EARL STO
FARBIOLA (hybrid) [gyn]		17 in.	Dark green. No male blooms.	STO
FARIBO (hybrid) [gyn]		15 in.	Used as year-round crop.	STO
FEMBABY (hybrid) [gyn]			Cold-tolerant, disease-resistant. No pollinator needed. Will grow on a window sill facing north.	THO
GELE TROS		Long	Yellow-skinned for greenhouse or outdoors. Old European variety.	WILL
GOURMET (hybrid) [gyn]		16. in.	Bitter-free slicer. Leaf spot- and gummosis-resistant.	BURG POR WIL
GOURMET NO. 2 (hybrid) [gyn]	60	16 in.	Vigorous vines. Sweet flesh. Bright green fruit. Scab- and angular leaf spot-resistant.	NIC
LA REINE [gyn] (THE QUEEN)		17 in. Ridged	Dark green fruit. Bitter-free.	HARR
MAJA (hybrid) [gyn]			Slow-growing. High quality. Open plant.	STO
MILDANA (hybrid) [gyn]	75	14 in.	Cold-tolerant. High quality fruit. Powdery mildew-resistant.	THO
PANDEX (hybrid) [gyn]		17 in.	English variety. Bright green, seedless and bitter-free.	WILL
PETITA (hybrid)	60	8 in.	Dark green, slightly ribbed. High yields. Good staying power. Mosaic-resistant.	JOH

Variety	Days	Size	Remarks	Sources
ROLLINSON'S TELEGRAPH		Long	Dark green. Non-hybrid. Not as high-yielding or disease-resistant.	WILL
SANDRA (hybrid) [gyn]		16 in.	Dark green. Can be grown in any season. No male flowers.	STO
SUPERATOR (hybrid [gyn]		15 in.	Easy-to-prune plant. Produces well. No male blooms. Downy and powdery mildew-resistant.	STO
SUPER SANDRA (hybrid) [gyn]		16 in.	Vigorous plant. Do not use for winter harvest. Powdery mildew-resistant.	STO
TELEGRAPH IMPROVED	62	Long	19th century non-hybrid variety. Early and vigorous. Smooth-skinned.	ABU LAG THO
TOSKA 70 (hybrid) [gyn]		14 in.	Deep-green fruit is bitter-free. Remove the male blossoms.	STO
UNIFLORA D (hybrid)		15 in.	Dark green fruit. Stands up well in hot weather.	THO
VITALIS (hybrid) [gyn]			Finely ribbed, dark green fruit. No male blooms. Gummosis- and leaf spot-resistant.	STO

CUCUMBERS

OTHER TYPES/COLORS

Variety	Days	Size	Remarks	Sources
AFRICAN HORNED (JELLY MELON)			Thorny and filled with greenish-gold gel and lots of seeds. Tastes like citrus. Long keeper. Vigorous climber.	LEM SEE
CRYSTAL APPLE	65	Apple-shaped	Creamy white skin. New Zealand variety. Very prolific.	GLE JLH LEM THO
LEMON	64	3 in. Round	Yellow fruit with flat stem end.	ABU BURP COM COO DAN DEG FIS GAR GUR HEN HUM JUN LAG LEM NIC PLA POR RED ROS SHE STO TER TIL VER WES
LONG WHITE			European variety. White inside and out. Perfect for salads or dill pickles.	GRA LAG
POONA KHEERA		Small	India variety. Smooth, greenish-white skin. May be eaten at all stages. Tender and crisp.	GLE
WHITE WONDER	65	10 in.	Ivory-white when mature. All-purpose cucumber. Vigorous vine.	BURG GLE GUR VER WYA

DANDELION
(Taraxacum officinale)

The dandelion is a tasty green that can be purchased from a number of sources. It has a tangy taste that adds an interesting touch to salads, or it can be cooked and eaten like spinach. The leaves of the cultivated varieties are considerably larger than those of the wild ones.

CULTURE: Dandelion can be blanched to increase tenderness by covering with ventilated, black plastic about halfway through the growing period. Best sown in early spring or fall.

SEASON: Cool.

HARVESTING: Harvest leaves in early spring. Prepare like spinach.

DANDELION

Variety	Days	Size	Remarks	Sources
BROADLEAF	95	18-24 in. across	Large leaves, partially toothed. Dark green and prolific.	NIC
DANDELION			Sharp taste. Can be forced. Plant in late summer for early spring harvest.	COO
GIANT BROAD LEAF	95	Large	Many thick leaves of good substance and quality.	ALL
MONTMAGNY (GREEN IMPROVED)			Thick-leaved with full heart. Use in stir fry, soup or salads.	LEM
THICK-LEAVED	95		Large, thick, dark green leaves are used for boiling or eating raw. Quick-growing.	BURP LAG STO
THICK-LEAVED IMPROVED			Stocky, very broad-leaved plant with white rib. Prepare like spinach.	LED RIC WILL
PISSENLIT IMPROVED	10	8 in.	French strain. Can be forced like chicory. Cook like spinach.	HER

EGGPLANT
(Solanum melongena)

Eggplants grow on tree-like bushes about three feet tall and produce beautiful fruit. The culture of eggplant is somewhat like that of tomatoes. Each plant will produce about twelve fruit. Eggplant comes in many shapes, sizes and colors.

CULTURE: To grow eggplant from seed, place seeds a third to a half-inch deep in peat pots. It takes three weeks for the seeds to germinate and another eight to ten weeks before they are ready to set out. You can save a lot of time by purchasing them from the nursery. Plant the seedlings 25 inches apart in rows 3 feet apart.

SEASON: Warm.

INSECTS/DISEASES: *APHIDS, BLISTER BEETLES, COLORADO POTATO BEETLES, FLEA BEETLES, SPIDER MITES, THRIPS, WHITEFLIES*: Use malathion, diazinon, pyrethrum, rotenone, Sevin or ryania.

TOMATO FRUITWORMS, TOMATO HORNWORMS, CUTWORMS: Use Sevin.

ANTHRACNOSE, EARLY AND LATE BLIGHT: Use maneb or zineb.

HARVESTING: Pick eggplants before they start to lose their glossy shine; after that they become tough. Be sure to keep picking the fruits as they become ready so that the plants will continue to bear.

EGGPLANT

Variety	Days	Size/Color	Remarks	Sources
BEAUTY (hybrid)	65-70	7 x 6 in. Glossy, black	Slightly smaller than Black Beauty. Tolerant to fusarium wilt.	PAR RIS
BLACK BEAUTY	73-80	Dark purple	24-28 in. plant. Creamy flesh with small seed cavity. Mild flavor.	ALL ARC BURG BURP BURR BUT COM DAN DEG EAR EARL GUR HEN HUM JLH JUN LAG LED LEJ LET MEY MID PAR PIN PLA PON POR RED RIS ROS SEE SEED SOU TWI VER WES WET WIL WILL
BLACK BELL (hybrid)	68-70	Round, oval, very glossy	28-30 in. plant. Excellent yields.	MID RIS TWI WET WIL
BLACK ENORMA (hybrid)	75	1½ lbs.	Very prolific, must be kept picked or heavy weight of fruit will knock plant over. 2½ ft. plant.	THO

◄

Variety	Days	Size/Color	Remarks	Sources
BLACK MAGIC	73	Blunt, deep purple	Prolific.	HARR
BLACK PRINCE (hybrid)	62		3 ft. plant. High-yielding. Firm elastic skin.	THO
BURPEE'S HYBRID	70	Oval, glossy, purple	Tall, tree-like plant. Drought- and disease-resistant.	BURP
DE BARBENTANE	70	Dark purple	French heirloom variety. Hardy, but not highly productive.	LEM
EARLY BEAUTY (hybrid)	62	Oval, dark purple	Prolific 25 in. plant.	BURP GUR
EARLY BIRD (hybrid)	67	7 x 6 in. Glossy, purple	Very prolific Black Beauty type.	PAR
EARLY PROLIFIC (hybrid)	75-80	Oval, dark purple	Bushy plants hold fruit well above the ground.	GUR LIBE
EPIC (hybrid)	64	4 x 8¾ in. Deep purple-black	Teardrop-shaped fruit. 36 in. plant. Widely adapted. Resistant to tobacco mosaic.	MID TWI
FLORIDA HIBUSH (HYBUSH) (FORT MEYERS MARKET) (FLORIDA SPECIAL)	83	Egg-shaped, dark purple	Vigorous, tall plant.	LED WYA
FLORIDA MARKET	80	6½ x 9½ in. Oval, dark purple	30-36 in. plant. Productive and resistant to fruit rot.	LED MEY SEE
HYBRID SLICER	68	9 x 2 in. Glossy, dark purple	2 ft. plant.	BURG
IMPERIAL BLACK BEAUTY	80	Egg-shaped, dark purple	18 in. plant.	RIS STO
IMPROVED NEW YORK SPINELESS		Egg-shaped, deep purple	Stalky and quite productive plant.	DEG
MIDNITE (hybrid)	68	Pear-shaped, deep purple	28-30 in. plant.	COM JUN POR RIS
NEW YORK IMPROVED (LARGE PURPLE)	80	Broad, egg-shaped, glossy, purple	Large and uniform. 30-36 in. plant.	SEE

EGGPLANT

LONG, CYLINDRICAL

Variety	Days	Size/Color	Remarks	Sources
AGORA (hybrid)	70	Long	Upright bush with strong stems. Good shelf life. Italian.	JOH SHE
BLACKNITE (hybrid)	61-85	9 x 3½ in. Glossy, black-purple	36 in. plant.	LET RIS STO TWI
CHINESE LONG	125	10 x 1¾ in. Purple	Late Japanese variety. Heavy cropper. Tolerant to diseases.	GLE RED
CLASSIC (hybrid)	76	Long, slim, purplish-blue	Vigorous plant.	DIX HARR PIE

►

◀ EGGPLANT

Variety	Days	Size/Color	Remarks	Sources
DUSKY (hybrid)	56-68	8 x 3½ in. Dark purple	36 in. plant. Tobacco mosaic virus-resistant.	ARC BURG BURP BURR COM EAR FAR FIS HARR HIS LAG LED LIBE MEY NIC PAR PIE PIN RAW RIS STO TER TIL TWI VER VES
EARLY LONG PURPLE	78-80	12 x 4 in. Dark violet	Heavy cropper.	COM LAG SEE SUN WES
EXTRA LONG		12 x 1½ in. Purple	Very long and slender.	SUN
FLORIDA MARKET (COOK'S STRAIN)	82	Long, narrow, glossy, blackish-purple	20-36 in. plant.	BURR LED
FRENCH IMPERIAL (IMPERIAL)	63	10 in. Slender, purple-black	36-40 in. plant. Very productive. Tobacco mosaic virus-tolerant.	STO TWI
ICHIBAN (hybrid)	58-65	Up to 12 in. Purple	More prolific than most eggplants. 36-40 in. plant.	COO HER LAG TSA TWI VER
ICHIBAN IMPROVED				MID
KURUME LONG PURPLE		10 in. Black-purple	Japanese variety. Grows well in warm areas.	GLE
LITTLE FINGERS (op)	68	Long, slender, glossy, dark purple	Grows in clusters on a spreading plant. Oriental type.	HARR
LONG BLACK (hybrid)		8 x 2½ in. Purplish-black	Unusual quality. Tender skin. Japanese variety.	GLE KIT TSA
LONG BRIDGE (hybrid)	85	13 x 1⅓	Chinese variety. Great in stir fry dishes. Thin-skinned. Needs warmth and moisture to grow.	NIC
LONG DARK PURPLE	80	10 x 2 in. Shiny, velvet	22-26 in. plant.	BAN DEG ECO
LONG PURPLE ITALIAN	75	Small, club-shaped		MID
LONG PURPLE VISERBA	78	8 x 3 in. Dark purple	Smooth-skinned.	LET
LONG TOM (hybrid)		7 x 1½ in. Deep purple	Heavy yielder, high quality. Disease-resistant. 40-50 fruit per plant.	POR RIC
MILLIONAIRE (hybrid)		10 in.	Late variety.	KIT LAG
MONEYMAKER (hybrid)	60	Blackish-purple	Very vigorous plant that bears until frost.	WILL
ORIENTAL EXPRESS (hybrid)	58	10 in. Glossy, black	Sets fruit in cool weather as well as when under heat stress. Tender and quick-cooking.	JOH
PRELANE (hybrid)	60	9 in. Violet-black	French variety. Firm, never bitter. Highly productive. Some verticillium tollerance.	NIC SHE
SHORT TOM (hybrid)	60	5 x 2 in.	Very prolific 2½ in ft. plant.	TER THO

◀

Variety	Days	Size	Remarks	Sources
SLICE RITE (hybrid)	74	1 lb. Cylindrical, shiny black	Heavy cropper. Disease-resistant.	DEG
SLIM JIM		Lavender to purple	Great variety for pots. Excellent baby vegetable. Borne in clusters to main stem.	COO
SPECIAL HIBUSH (op)	82	Long, oval, intense black	Sturdy upright plant.	HARR
TAIWAN LONG (hybrid)		7 x ½ in. Purple-black	Plant produces about 45 fruit.	SUN TSA
TYCOON (hybrid)	54-61	8 x 1¼ in. Shiny, purple-black	Oriental type. 36 in. plant. Heavy yielder.	BURR GUR HARR HEN LED MID NIC PAR PIN POR RIS SEED STO TWI
VIOLET LONGUE	65	Long, bright purple	French variety.	HER
VIOLETTA DI FIRENZE		Oblong, very large with grooves, pale violet	Resembles squash. Needs plenty of heat to grow.	COO PIN
VIOLETTA LUNGA		8 in. Deep purple	Italian eggplant. Good slicing variety.	COO

EGGPLANT
SMALL

Variety	Days	Size/Color	Remarks	Sources
BABY WHITE		Quarter-size	Very seedy. Use in stews.	SHE
BABY WHITE TIGER		1½ in.	Bite-size seedy eggplant.	SEE
EARLY BLACK EGG	65-70	4 x 2 in. Shiny black	Japanese variety. Unusually tender and flavorful. Prolific bushy plant.	GAR GLE SOU TER
EMERALD PEARL		¼ in.	Bitter. Used in Asian dishes.	SEE
HITO (hybrid) (HAGURO) (HITOKUCHIMARU)		Oval, pecan-size, dark shiny-purple	Higly prolific.	LEM
JAPANESE EARLY PURPLE		Smallish	European variety.	ABU
JAPANESE PURPLE PICKLING	75	Small	Produces masses of tiny eggplant. Use any pickling recipe.	NIC SEE
MORDEN MIDGET		Small, deep purple	Bush plant.	SOU
RONDE DE VALENCE	75	Dark purple	Pick when the size of a large navel orange or grapefruit. French variety. Not a heavy producer. Requires a hot climate.	LEM
SMALL RUFFLED RED		2 in. diameter	Bitter. Used in Asian cuisine.	SEE
SNAKE EYE		½ in. Green	Not bitter.	SEE

EGGPLANT
NON-PURPLE

Variety	Days	Size/Color	Remarks	Sources
APPLE GREEN		Medium-size, light green	Non-acid. No need to peel.	SEE
BIANCA OVALE		Egg-size, pure white	Good variety to grow in tubs or pots.	COO
BRIDE ASIAN (hybrid)	75	10 x 3 in. Light lavender with white stripes	Strong, compact plant.	LEM
BUSH WHITE (BUSH-L-FULL-O'EGG) (EGG TREE)	90	Egg-shaped	Asian variety. Tree plant bears purple flowers. Low-calorie fruit. Grows on window sill. Needs warmth and well-drained soil.	BAN GLE SEE TSA
CASPER		6 x 2¾ in. Shiny ivory	Snow-white flesh.	SEE STO WES
EASTER EGG (hybrid)	52-65	Egg-shaped, white	Branching 23 in. plant. Little seed development. Pick at 3 in. before they turn yellow.	LEJ PIN TWI VER
FARMER'S LONG ASIAN (hybrid)	65	12 x 2 in. Red-purple	Plant is vigorous and prolific. Pendulous fruit.	LEM
LISTADA DE GANDIA		White with purple stripes	Italian variety.	SEE
LONG WHITE SWORD		2 x 9 in.	Lots of meat.	SEE
LOUISIANA GREEN OVAL		2-4 lbs. Glossy, light green	Mild flavor. 3 ft. sturdy plant. Harvest while eggplant is still glossy.	GLE
PINK BRIDE (hybrid)		8½ x 2½ in., 3-4 oz. Pink-violet with white stripes	Small, compact, strong plant. White flesh is tender.	GLE
PINKY		Enormous, pink-violet	20-24 in. plant. Very mild flavor.	GLE
ROMANESCA (TONDA SFUMATA DI ROSA)		Round, white with pink-purplish blush	Italian variety.	RED
ROSA BIANCO	75	Globular, lavender and white	Meaty Italian type. Difficult to pick.	LEM SEE
THAI (BRINJAL)		Round, lavender	3 ft. tall plant has some thorns. Seedy and bitter. Asian variety. Grow only in warm, moist conditions.	LEM
THAI GREEN		12 in. Light green	Tender.	SEE
WHITE OVAL		White	Pick when 3-4 in. long and still shiny. Mild flavor.	GLE

FLORENCE FENNEL
(Foeniculum vulgare, azoricum)

Florence Fennel is grown for its bulblike base that is formed by the overlapping leaf stalks. The plant itself is an annual that grows to 2½ feet tall. There are actually two kinds of fennel besides Florence Fennel: Common Fennel, (Foeniculum Vulgare), a tall plant resembling dill that is grown for seeds and leaves; and Carosella (Foeniculum piperitum), grown for flavoring.

CULTURE: Sow the seedlings in rows 20 inches apart, then thin to 9 to 12 inches apart. Plant in summer for a fall crop. In regions where the summer remains cool, you may plant in the spring.

As the plant develops its thick base of leaf stalks, pull the soil up around the base to blanch the stalks.

SEASON: Cool.

HARVESTING: Pull the plant from the ground when the bulbous base measures 3 to 6 inches in length.

FENNEL

Variety	Days	Remarks	Sources
BRONZE		Perennial. Grows to 5 ft. Coppery-tinged foliage. Leaf tips are used as garnish. Seeds are used for seasoning.	ABU NIC PIE SEE TAY
CRISTAL		Produces medium-size bulb when mature. Plant during June and July. Recommended where spring is short with hot summers.	LEM
FENNEL FINO		Italian variety. Egg-shaped bulb has a celery-like, nutty anise flavor. Use seeds in cakes and cookies.	SHE
FLORENCE FENNEL (FINOCCHIO) (SWEET FLORENCE)	90	Enlarged, flat, oval leaf. 2½ ft. growth. Anise-like flavor. Used raw, boiled or in salad.	ABU ALL BURP CAP COM DAN EAR GUR HER IND JUN LED LEJ LET LIBE MEY NIC PAR RAW RED RIC SEE SEED SOU STO SUN TAY TER THO TIL TWI VER WES WILL WYA
MAMMOTH		Slow-bolting strain. Fall crop.	HARR
PERFECTION		Large French variety.	THO
REDLEAF FENNEL		Grown as an annual for ornamental and herbal qualities.	COO
SICILIAN FENNEL (WILD FENNEL)		Tender perennial. Large, heavy fleshy variety. Distinctive flavor.	COO DEG SEE
SWEET FENNEL	60	Annual. Fern-like foliage. Young sprouts are used in salads, soups and fish sauces. Seeds are used in baking.	EARL RIC SEE
ZEFA FINO	85	Forms robust, tender bulb. Slow bolting.	JOH

GARLIC
(Allium satium)

Garlic is a strong medicine in any garden. Besides being an essential vegetable in the kitchen, many gardeners believe it can be used to control a wide variety of insects.

There are two basic types: regular garlic bulbs, which contain a number of small cloves, and large garlic bulbs, which have the flavor of regular but none of its pungency.

CULTURE: In very early spring plant garlic cloves, or sets, 1 to 1½ inches deep, 2 inches apart, in rows 12 to 18 inches apart.

SEASON: Cool.

HARVESTING: Dig up the roots when the tops fall over.

GARLIC

Variety	Days	Remarks	Sources
CALIFORNIA WHITE	110	Stores like onions, or may be left in the garden over the winter.	HEN JUN
EXTRA SELECT SETS	100	Grow, harvest and store like onions. Separate cloves before planting.	BURP FIS
FRENCH MILD		Very mild, large bulbs. Very thin skin.	POR
GARLIC SETS		Most pungent flavor of the onion family.	COM EAR EARL FAR FOS GUR MEY RED SUN TAY WILL
ITALIAN TOP SETTING GARLIC		Medium-size bulbs have pungent flavor. Produce clusters of top sets much like Egyptian onion. May take two seasons to produce large bulb with separate cloves.	KAL NIC
ROCAMBOLE (SPANISH GARLIC) (SERPENT GARLIC)		Small cloves.	LEJ PEA RIC SEE SOU
SOCIETY GARLIC		Perennial. 18 in. Excellent border plant. Lilac flowers.	TAY
TRICOLOR SOCIETY		Perennial. 1 ft. Excellent border plant. Pink, white, green leaves with lilac flowers.	TAY
WHITE GARLIC		Add to your favorite recipe.	KAL

GARLIC
LARGE BULBS

Variety	Remarks	Sources
BAVARIAN	Bulbs are large, up to 1 pound. Keeps for a long time.	DEG
ELEPHANT GARLIC	True garlic flavor, but more delicate. Short growing season. Often produces bulb weighing 1 pound, 4 to 5 in.	BURG BURP FAR FIS GUR HEN JUN NIC PAR RIC SEE SOU TAY TIL VER
SILVERSKIN	Very hardy. Strong flavor. Good keeping qualities.	NIC TIL VER

HORSERADISH
(Armoracia rusticana)

Horseradish is a centuries-old, tall, hardy plant native to Eastern Europe that is grown for its pungent root. Grated or shredded, it is added to many foods for flavor.

CULTURE: Cut the tops off square (of any 6 to 9 inch piece of root) and slant the bottom. Set the cuttings 2 to 3 inches below the soil surface, 7 to 9 inches apart, in rows 12 to 18 inches apart. When the leaves are about a foot high, remove all but one or two crown sprouts. Pull the soil back and rub off the side roots.

SEASON: Cool.

HARVESTING: Lift the roots in October or November. Make cuttings from the base of the roots for planting the following spring.

HORSERADISH

Variety	Remarks	Sources
BOHEMIAN HORSERADISH	Roots are large with snow-white flesh. Very hot to the taste.	ALL BURG FAR FOS GUR HEN JUN LED LET PAR TAY
HORSERADISH	Fleshy roots are grated for use as a pungent relish.	PON RIC
HYBRID HORSERADISH	Superior disease resistance. Dig roots during cool weather.	GUR

◀

Variety	Remarks	Sources
MALINER KREN	True Bohemian Horseradish. Vigorous grower with large white roots.	BURP NIC

JERUSALEM ARTICHOKE
(Helianthus tuberosus)

The Jerusalem artichoke is a species of sunflower that grows from 6 to 10 feet high on a single stalk and produces three-inch sunflowers. The round, knobby tubers produced by the roots are starchless. They can either be cooked like a potato or used raw in salads.

CULTURE: Cut the tuber into sections with one to two eyes in each section. Plant early, after danger of heavy frost, 4 inches deep, 1 to 2 feet apart, in rows 2 to 3 feet apart. When the foliage appears, hill the soil up around the plants.

HARVESTING: Dig the tubers about six weeks after the flower petals drop. Store in a cool place. If any tubers are left in the ground, the plant can become a nuisance the following spring.

JERUSALEM ARTICHOKE

Variety	Remarks	Sources
DWARF SUNRAY	5-7 ft. Crisp and tender. No need to peel. This variety flowers frequently.	THO
FRENCH MAMMOTH WHITE	Large knobby roots. Harvest after frost.	ABU SEE
FUSEAU	4 x 1 in. Yam type.	SEE
GOLDEN NUGGET	Looks like a long radish. 2½-3 in. Carrot type.	SEE
JERUSALEM ARTICHOKE (SUNCHOKE)	Tremendous yields of tasty tubers with nutlike flavor. Good in salads, raw, or boiled, baked or creamed. Said to be an excellent dish for diabetics.	BURG BURP COM FAR FOS GUR HEN JUN LED LEJ NIC PAR TAY
SILVER SKINNED	7-9 ft.	THO
SMOOTH GARNET	Ruby and smooth.	SEE
STAMPEDE	90 days. High-yielding strain. Flowers in July. Winter-hardy. Large white tubers often weigh ½ lb.	JOH

JICAMA

Remarks	Sources
Sweet and crisp, an excellent substitute for water chestnuts. Can be eaten raw or cooked. Jicama is a root crop. The plant is 5-6 ft. high. The sandy-colored skin and white flesh weigh 2 to 5 lbs.	BAN LAG LEM RED TSA

KALE
(Brassica oleracea acephala)

A member of the cabbage family that is easy to grow. Cold weather doesn't bother kale at all; in fact, light frost will enhance the flavor.

Borecole or Scotch types have blue or dark green leaves that are tightly curled. Siberian types have smoother, gray-green leaves with frilled edges and a spreading habit. Ornamental kale is deeply curled and ranges in colors from green to white to lavender to red. It makes quite a display in the fall and winter garden.

CULTURE: Sow seeds a half-inch deep, 15 inches apart, in rows 18 to 24 inches apart.

SEASON: Cool.

INSECTS/DISEASES: *APHIDS, BLISTER BEETLES, CABBAGE LOOPERS, FLEA BEETLES, IMPORTED CABBAGE WORMS, STINKBUGS*: Use malathion, diazinon, pyrethrum, rotenone, Sevin or ryania.

FUNGAL LEAF SPOTS, DOWNY MILDEW: Use maneb or fixed copper sprays.

HARVESTING: You can cut the outer leaves as they mature or you can cut the entire plant. Generally, the inside leaves are more flavorful and tender than the outer ones.

KALE—VATES TYPE

Variety	Days	Leaves	Remarks	Sources
BLUE ARMOR (hybrid)	45-75	Deep blue-green	Vigorous uniform plant.	TWI
BLUE CURLED SCOTCH	65	Finely curled, bluish-green	Low, compact plant.	DIX PAR VES
BLUE KNIGHT (hybrid)	55	Curly, deep blue	7-8 in. plant in 45 days. Less yellowing tendency. Suitable for spring and fall harvest.	TWI
DWARF BLUE CURLED VATES (GEM)	55	Finely curled, bluish-green	Low, compact, short-stemmed plant. Can withstand below-freezing temps.	ABU ARC BURP BUT COM DAN DEG EAR HARR HEN HUM JUN LAB LED LEM LET LIBE MEY PIN RAW RIS ROS SEE SEED SOU TIL TWI WET WIL
KONSERVA	60	Broad, tall, dark green	Well-curled with good fall-weather tolerance. 24-30 in. plant.	JOH SOU
SEMI-DWARF WESTLANDSE		Frilly	Excellent flavor.	SEE
SPRUT	65	Curly, deep green	Grows like spinach. 12-15 in. Crisp and tender stems.	THO
TALL GREEN CURLED SCOTCH		Deeply cut, light green	Very tender after exposure to frost.	ABU FAR RAW
VERDURA	60	Dark blue-green	Dutch variety. Sweet flavor. Productive and vigorous.	SHE
WINTERBOR (hybrid)	60	Well curled, blue-green	Good cold-hardiness. Hybrid Vates types.	JOH MEY TER

KALE—SIBERIAN TYPE

Variety	Days	Leaves	Remarks	Sources
BLUE SIBERIAN (SPROUTS)		Frilled, bluish-green	Large, coarse leaves. Grown mostly in the South. Hardy and vigorous. 12-16 in. plant with a 24-36 in. spread.	DEG SEE
CURLED SIBERIAN	60	Curled, bluish-green	Hardy, rapid growing.	MEY
DWARF SIBERIAN IMPROVED	65	Plume-like, grayish-green	12-16 in. plant with 24-36 in. spread. Stands cold well.	TIL
EARLY CURLED SIBERIAN	55	Curled at ends, green	Dwarf spreading plant. Extremely hardy.	WET WYA

Variety	Days	Leaves	Remarks	Sources
HANOVER LATE SEEDLING (LONG SEASONS)	45	Smooth, dark green	14 in. tall.	ABU MEY
HARVESTER L.D.	68	Extra-curled, dark green	Short-stemmed, erect plant. Will hold color through frosty weather.	GAR
KONSERVA L.D.	60	Medium-curled, moss-green	30 in. tall.	GAR HIG
LONGSTANDING (SLOW SEEDING)	75	Smooth	Slow-growing. Hardy variety.	SOU WET
PREMIERE		Scalloped margins, deep green	High-yielding. Main stems remain short.	WET
RUSSIAN RED		Wavy, red-purple, veined	Edible landscape plant.	ABU PEA
SIBERIAN (DWARF GERMAN)	65	Frilled, dark blue-green	14 in. tall. Vigorous, sprawling growth.	ABU COM FIS LAG LET MID PEA TER VER
SIBERIAN IMPROVED	60-70	Frilled, bluish-green	12-15 in. tall. Sprawling and extremely hardy. 36 in. spread.	DAN POR WIL
SPRING (HANOVER) (SMOOTH)	30	Smooth, light green	16 in. tall. Hardy, quick-growing.	ABU RED SOU WET WYA

KALE
OTHER TYPES

Variety	Days	Leaves	Remarks	Sources
CHRISTMAS FRINGED WHITE FLOWERING		Ruffled, green with white center	Japanese variety. Sow in summer.	GLE
HUNGARY GAP			Hardy and very vigorous.	ECO
LACINATO ITALIAN		3 x 10 in. Strap-like, blue-green	Rather primitive open kale. Useful and ornamental. Extremely winter-hardy.	LEM
MARROW STEM GREEN (CHOU MOELLIR)			Grows to 5 ft. Very thick stems. High yields.	ECO JLH SEE
ORNAMENTAL FLOWERING			In early season leaves are green, but in fall they change to cream and red shades.	COO DEG GAR GUR HIG JUN LEM NIC SEE
PENTLAND BRIGG	75	Curled	Very hardy. High yields.	ECO
RAGGED JACK		Red oak-type leaves		SEE

KALE—ORIENTAL

Variety	Days	Leaves	Remarks	Sources
CHINESE KALE (GAI LOHN)	70	Dark green	Broccoli-like vegetable. Grows best in cool weather. 12-14 in. Mildly sweet and crispy.	BAN NIC RIS TSA

◀ **KALE—ORIENTAL**

Variety	Days	Leaves	Remarks	Sources
SEKITO		Carmine-rose fringed	Japanese variety. Loose leaf heads.	GLE
THOUSAND HEADED		Large, green	Large branching type from England. Grows 2-3 ft. Strong-growing late-winter crop.	JLH TER
WHITE FLOWER	70	Smooth and pointed	Thick stem. White flowers. Hardy.	SUN
YELLOW FLOWER	70	Light green	Dwarf plant with yellow flowers. May bolt in cold weather.	SUN

KOHLRABI
(Brassica oleracea)

Often called a turnip cabbage, kohlrabi produces an above-ground 'turnip' in the middle of a profusion of cabbage-like leaves. When the plants are 6 to 8 inches high, the stems begin to swell just above the root line until the bulbs are 3 to 4 inches across. The swollen stem is delicious when eaten young. Cook like you would a turnip.

Kohlrabis are green-white or purple. The flesh of both varieties is whitish.

CULTURE: Sow the seeds two weeks after the average date of the last frost and follow with several plantings two weeks apart. Sow seeds a half-inch deep in rows 18 inches apart, then thin the small plants to 4 inches apart.

SEASON: Cool.

INSECTS/DISEASES: *APHIDS, BLISTER BEETLES, CABBAGE LOOPERS, CUTWORMS, FLEA BEETLES, IMPORTED CABBAGE WORMS, STINKBUGS:* Use malathion, diazinon, pyrethrum, rotenone, Sevin or ryania.

FUNGAL LEAF SPOTS, DOWNY MILDEW: Use maneb or fixed copper sprays.

HARVESTING: Harvest when the 'bulbs' are 2 to 2½ inches in diameter. Beyond this they become hard and have a bitter taste.

KOHLRABI				
PURPLE				
Variety	Days	Leaves	Remarks	Sources
BLUE DANISH L.D.	66		Deep red color.	SOU
EARLY PURPLE VIENNA	60	3 in. Globe	Purplish skin, green-white flesh. Mild, nutty flavor.	ABU ARC BURP COM DAN DEG EAR EARL GAR GUR HEN HUM JLH JUN LAG LED LET RAW SEE SOU STO VES
LAUKO	60		Cold-hardy. Danish variety. Delicate texture. Sweet and rich flavor.	TER
PURPLE DANUBE (hybrid)	46	Round	Color fades when cooked. Bulbs are sweet and crunchy. Fine-stemmed.	JOH LEM
PURPLE DELICACY	70	Globe	Large plant habit. Slow to bolt. For summer to early autumn growing.	VER
RAPID	45	3 in.	15-18 in. plant. Red-purple. Smooth, crisp white flesh. Cook like turnips.	PAR

KOHLRABI
GREEN/WHITE

Variety	Days	Leaves	Remarks	Sources
EARLY WHITE VIENNA	55-60	10 x 2 in. Globe	Light green skin, creamy white flesh. Good freezer variety. Dwarf plant.	ABU ALL ARC BURG BURR BUT COM DAN DEG EAR EARL ECO FIS GAR HARR HEN HUM JUN LAB LED LEJ LEM LET MEY MID NIC PIN PON RAW SEE SEED SOU STO TIL VER WET WYA
GRAND DUKE (hybrid)	50-60	4 in. Semi-globe	White skin. Mild, sweet flavor.	BURP COM EAR FAR GUR HEN JUN LAG LET LIBE MID PIN POR RIS THO
GREEN WALDEMAR (hybrid)	60	Light green	Austrian variety. Smooth skin, short tops. Sweet flavor.	SHE
KOLPAK (hybrid)	38	Round, white	Fine-stemmed foliage. Resists getting pithy. Sweet flavor.	JOH
PEKING	55	Pale green bulbs	Pure white flesh. Fine quality.	SUN
PRAGUE EARLY FORCING			Tender leaves and bulbs.	SEE
PRAGUE SPECIAL	44	Flattened	White skin. European variety. Tender and flavorful.	HARR
VIENNA GREEN SHORT TOP		2-3 in. Globular	Light green skin, white flesh.	RED
WHITE KOHLRABI	55	2½ in.	Nutty-flavored bulbs. White flesh. Bulbs grow well above ground.	GUR
WINNER (hybrid)	60	Round	Light green skin. Japanese variety. Mild, sweet flesh.	TER

LEEKS
(Allium ampeloprasum)

Leeks look much like flattened green onions. They do not bulb, as onions do; the stems simply thicken.

CULTURE: In early spring, sow seeds in a trench and thin to 2 to 4 inches apart in rows 12 to 18 inches apart. The trench is gradually filled as the leeks develop. This blanches the leeks white as they grow. Leeks overwinter nicely if a mulch is used to protect them from consistently low temperatures.

SEASON: Cool.

HARVESTING: For baby leeks, you can plan on 65 days to table. For full-size leeks, 130 or more days.

LEEKS

Variety	Days	Remarks	Sources
ALASKA	105	8 in. broad, dark blue-green foliage is tolerant to freezing temperatures.	STO WILL
ALBERTA	120	Cold-hardy, non-bolting. Will overwinter until late spring. For winter or spring harvest.	NIC

◀ LEEKS

Variety	Days	Remarks	Sources
AMERICAN BROAD FLAG	90-130	Tall, hardy, large-stalked. Strong-growing and productive.	ALL COM EARL
AMERICAN FLAG (GIANT MUSSELBURGH)	120-150	8½ - 9½ in. Grows quickly. For fall or spring planting.	ABU BURG DEG EAR ECO FAR HUM JLH LED LET MEY MID NIC RAW RIS STO TIL WES WET WIL
ARTICO		Dutch variety. Very cold-resistant.	LEJ
AUTUMN GOLIATH		Highly productive variety. For use from September through November. Thick shaft, gray-green leaf, no bulbous base.	ECO
BLUE SOLAIZE	145	19th century French heirloom variety. Very cold-resistant hardy variety. Turns violet during autumn.	COO HER LEM
BROAD LONDON (LARGE AMERICAN FLAG) (LONDON FLAG) (BROAD SCOTCH)	130-150	7½ x 1½ in. Medium-green leaves. Good southern variety. Sweet-flavored.	BURP BURR GUR LAG LEJ PIN VER WYA
CARENTAN WINTER (WINTER GIANT)	95-150	8 x 2 in. stalks. Cold-resistant. For winter and fall use.	ABU HER RED SEE WILL
CATALINA	150	Dutch variety. High-yielding. Blue-green leaves, broad, long erect, non-bulbous shafts. Can be stored right in the ground as winter crop.	RIC SHE TWI
CHINESE LEEKS		Strong-flavored.	RAW SUN
CONQUEROR		Hardy winter strain. Late-storage type. Medium-length thick stalks. Moderate bulbing. Blue-green tops.	HARR SHE
DE CARENTAN		French variety. Fine-textured long stems with blue-green foliage. Grows rapidly. Very productive. Keeps easily in the ground.	SHE
DURABEL		Winter leek. Slow-growing. Mild-flavored and tender texture. Non-bulbous 5 in. shaft. Danish variety.	TER
ELECTRA		Dark blue-green leaves. Good cold resistance. Very dependable variety.	HARR HER
ELEPHANT LEEK	85-150	Large, vigorous variety for fall or winter.	RAW SEE WET WILL
FRENCH SUMMER-KILMA	75	Rapid-growing. Long shaft. For summer and fall use.	RIS SEE WILL
GENNEVILLIERS		European variety. Long slender stems. Dark blue-green upright foliage. Somewhat cold-resistant.	LEM
KING RICHARD	75	Light green leaves. 12 in. tall. Not frost-hardy if heavy.	COO FIS GAR JOH PIN
LEADER	140	Blue-green leaves, long luscious shanks. Vigorous and quick-growing variety.	TWI
LONGINA	102	8 in. Popular storage type. Upright leaves do not trap soil.	STO
MAMMOTH OTINA		Long white shanks.	MID
MOLOS	120	Giant leek. Thick, long white stems with fine flavor.	THO

Variety	Days	Remarks	Sources
MUSSELBURGH IMPROVED	90	Hardy. Fine strain of this variety.	THO
NEBRASKA	90	Fall-winter leek. 10 in. long, smooth, firm stems with little or no bulbing. Good cold and disease resistance.	JOH
PRIZETAKER (THE LYON)	135	Very hardy. Produces tender, solid white stems. Fine flavor.	THO
SPLENDID	95	10 in. Heavy yields. Some frost tolerance. Excellent for dehydration. Danish variety.	STO TER
TITAN SUMMER	70	6 in. stalks. Vigorous growth.	BURP SEE STO
TIVI		Danish variety. Long straight stems, medium-green tops. Autumn harvest.	HARR
UNIQUE	100	8 x 2 in. stalks. Hardy strain for winter storage.	SEE STO
VARNA	105	24 in. shafts above the soil line. Good yields. Late autumn or winter harvest.	NIC
WILD LEEK		Perennial. Germinate irregularly over a year's time. Keep seed flat in a moist, cool spot.	RIC
WINTERRUITZEN		Withstands very cold temperatures. Recommended where temperatures drop below freezing.	LEM

LETTUCE
(Lactuca sativa)

Gardeners today have a lot of choices when it comes to lettuce. Not only is it easy to grow; it comes in all colors, textures and sizes.

CULTURE: Sow looseleaf lettuce a quarter-inch deep. Thin to 4 to 6 inches apart in rows 12 inches apart. Sow other types a quarter-inch deep. Thin to 8 to 10 inches apart in rows 18 inches apart. All lettuce does not thrive in the hot summer, so plant in early spring and early fall or buy a variety that does well in summer.

SEASON: Cool.

INSECTS/DISEASES: *APHIDS, CABBAGE LOOPERS, CORN EARWORMS, LEAFHOPPERS:* Use malathion, diazinon, pyrethrum, rotenone, Sevin or ryania.

SLUGS AND SNAILS: Use Slug-Geta or a dehydrating agent.

EARWIGS: Use a commercial earwig bait.

BACTERIAL LEAF SPOTS, DOWNY MILDEW: Use fixed copper spray, maneb, or zineb.

DAMPING OFF: Treat soil with captan.

HARVESTING: Pull the entire plant for romaine, butternut and head lettuce. Harvest looseleaf lettuce leaves individually as you need them. Some varieties are quicker to bolt to seed than others.

CRISPHEAD LETTUCE—ICEBERG TYPES
LARGE

Variety	Days	Leaves/Color	Remarks	Sources
ANTINA	55	Medium-green with bluish-red edging	French variety. Can be harvested as a looseleaf or left to mature. Slow to bolt.	SHE
AVONCRISP			Resembles Webb's Wonderful.	THO
BALLADE	80	Bright green	Globe-shaped head. Slow-bolting. Heat-resistant.	VER

◄ **CRISPHEAD LETTUCE—ICEBERG TYPES**

Variety	Days	Leaves/Color	Remarks	Sources
BOGATA	55	Glossy green, slightly frilled, light brown edges	French variety. Can be harvested young as a looseleaf. Plant in the spring.	SHE
BURPEE'S ICEBERG	85	Light green, heavily savoyed	Vigorous and hardy. Crisp, tender silvery-white hearts.	BURP
CALMAR	95	Dark green	White-seeded. Resistant to downy mildew. Adapted to cool, humid coastal areas. Excellent quality.	VES
CANASTA	50	Bright green, puckered, red—tinged	French variety. Crisp, cream-colored heart. Tip burn, bottom rot and bolt resistance.	JOH
CYBELE BATAVIAN		Red ruffled	For fall or spring planting. Good flavor. Begins to fade with summer heat.	LEM
DELMAR		Dark green	Plant Variety Protected. Resistant to downy mildew, tolerant to tip burn.	HARR
EARLY GREAT LAKES	70	Dark green	Extra good quality. Resistant to tip burn and heat.	FIS GUR
EL TORO	75		Performs well under cool, wet and hot, dry conditions. Crisp, well-filled heart.	HARR THO
FROSTY M.I.	98	Dark green	Light frost-tolerant.	STO
GREAT LAKES	90-100	Bright green, large, erect outer leaves	Resistant to tip burn, sunburn and heavy rain. Slow to bolt to seed.	ALL ARC BURP COM DAN DEG EAR FAR HEN HUM LAG MEY NIC PIN PON THO TIL WES WET WYA
GREAT LAKES 118A	78		Thrives under most adverse conditions. Crisp, tender, solid heads.	BURG
GREAT LAKES 118	85	Glossy, dark green outer leaves	White-seeded. Shows resistance to tip burn. Suited for summer harvest in cool western coastal areas.	DEG LET
GREAT LAKES 407	100	Bright green	Resistant to tip burn, sunburn and heavy rain.	DEG
GREAT LEAKES 659-G (MESA)	80	Extra-fringed, dark green	Firm heads with good tip burn tolerance.	BURR LED LIBE MID POR RIS ROS TWI WILL
GREAT LAKES 6238 M.I.	94	Medium-green	Fall variety. Large, solid head.	STO
GREENFIELD		Dark green	Medium-large core. Mosaic virus-resistant. Tip burn-tolerant.	HARR
GREEN LAKE M.I.	88	Light green	Tolerance to bolting, root rot, tip burn and rib light.	STO
ICEBERG (GIANT CRYSTAL HEAD)	85	Wavy, light green, tinged with brown	Hearts are crisp. Does well in spring and summer. Slow to bolt.	ALL BURG COO DEG EARL FAR GUR HEN LED LEJ LET MEY PON ROS SUN THO WET WIL WILL

►

Variety	Days	Leaves/Color	Remarks	Sources
ICEBERG IMPROVED			Summer variety.	ARC
IMPERIAL NO. 847	83	Dark green	New York type for hot weather. Heads well in mid-summer.	COM
ITHACA (IMPROVED ICEBURG)	60-72	Frilled, glossy green	Resistant to tip burn and brown rib. Slow to bolt to seed.	ARC COO FIS GAR GUR HARR HEN JOH LIBE MID RAW SEED STO TIL VES WILL
ITHACA MTO	72	Medium-green, fringed	Very uniform. Grows in upland and muck soil. Resistant to tip burn and brown rib.	TWI
KING CROWN	75		Up to 8 in. heads. Widely adapted. Good tip burn resistance.	JOH
MARMER	75		Good greenhouse variety.	THO
MESA 659 M.I.O.		Medium-dark green	Grown as summer and fall crop where bolting and tip burn are a problem.	HARR LET PIE SEED
MISSION	74		The 6-8 in. head is protected by long, thick outer leaves.	PAR
MONTELLO		Glossy green	Good tip burn resistance. Tolerant to bolting and corky root.	HARR RAW
MONTELLO M.T.O.	75	Dark green	Round head with flat bottom. Slow to bolt in hot weather. Widely adapted. Resists splitting.	HARR JUN LIBE MID RIS TWI
MORANGOLD		Medium-dark green	Plant Variety Protected. Tolerant to downy mildew and tip burn.	HARR
MORANGUARD		Medium dark-green	Moderate tip burn tolerance. Adapted to California's San Joaquin Valley desert.	HARR
NEW YORK (WONDERFUL)	70-80		3-4 lbs. Solid head. Good quality.	DEG PIN SEE
NEW YORK NO. 12	75	Bright green	Solid heads. Will do well in well-drained soil most anywhere.	DEG EARL HEN
OSWEGO	80-85	Medium to dark green	Very slow to bolt to seed. Does well in northern muck soils. Good tolerance to tip burn.	RIS
PENNLAKE M.I.	88		White-seeded. Solid head.	STO
PREMIER GREAT LAKES	80	Medium-green, no fringed margins	Resistant to tip burn and heat.	STO WILL
QUEEN CROWN	65		Up to 2 lb. heads of excellent flavor. Susceptible to tip burn.	RAW VES
ROSA	75	Red	6 in. head. Crisp, sweet flavor. Easy to grow.	PAR
SALINAS (SALADIN)	85	Dark green	Head is slow to develop. Resistant to tipburn and downy mildew.	HARR TER THO

◄ CRISPHEAD LETTUCE—ICEBERG TYPES

Variety	Days	Leaves/Color	Remarks	Sources
SALINAS R-100		Dark green	Adapted to California's San Joaquin Valley desert. Tolerant to tip burn and downy mildew.	HAR
SEAGREEN		Dull green	Resistant to big vein and tip burn.	HARR
SOUTH BAY M.I.	**90**	Dark green	6 in. firm head. Widely adapted. Resistant to tip burn; corky root-tolerant.	HARR STO
VAN MOR		Dark green	Plant Variety Resistant. Fair tip burn resistance.	HARR
VANGUARD	**90-199**	Dull dark green	Large core. Adapted to west coast and central valley of California.	PAR
WEBB'S WONDERFUL	**85**	Wrinkled	Tight, crisp head. Distinct flavor. Good in wet and dry summers. Slow to bolt to seed.	ECO THO
WINTER MARVEL		Clear green, slightly wavy	Sow in the fall. Hardy to temperatures of 18° F. Fine flavor.	ABU
YUMA		Dark green	Cold and moderate tip burn resistance.	HARR

CRISPHEAD LETTUCE—ICEBERG TYPES
MEDIUM

Variety	Days	Color/Leaves	Remarks	Sources
ALL-YEAR-ROUND	72	Pale green	Crisp and tender. Sow in spring or late summer.	ABU FAR LEM RED SEE THO
BATAVIA BORD ROUGE	59	Crumpled, dark green, tinged deep red	Bitter, but mellows to a nut-like flavor. Stands about 45 days before bolting.	PIN
CAL K-60		Medium-dark green	Plant Variety Protected. Resistant to downy mildew. Good tip burn resistance.	HARR
DOREE DE PRINTEMPS		Bright green	French variety. Plant in spring and fall. Tender leaves.	LEM
EMPIRE		Medium-green	Fair tip burn resistance. Slow-bolting.	HARR
GLOIRE DE DAUPHINE		Bright green with tines of red	Plant in spring or fall.	LEM
HANSON HEAD	80	Yellow-green, frilled	Medium core. White-seeded. Tolerant to tip burn.	DEG SEE
MINILAKE	80	Dark green	Solid and uniform in size.	BUT STO
RED GRENOBLAISE (RED GRENOBLE)		Light green, red-tinted	Does well in warm or cool weather. Good flavor.	COO LEM
REINE DES GLACES (ICE QUEEN)		Deep color, deeply cut lacy leaves	Crisp and good.	COO LEM

CRISPHEAD LETTUCE—ICEBERG TYPES
SMALL

Variety	Days	Color/Leaves	Remarks	Sources
AVENUE	50	Bright glossy green	Mild and juicy. Heat-resistant. Easy to grow. Spring, summer or fall crop.	JOH
EMPIRE	80	Yellow-green	Round, compact. Black-seeded. Suitable for warm weather and northeastern area.	MEY
MINETTO	80		Very firm, compact head. A dependable header. Resistant to tip burn. Crisp and tasty.	BURP

LETTUCE—BUTTERHEAD/BIBB TYPES
LARGE

Variety	Days	Color/Leaves	Remarks	Sources
AUGUSTA 68	75	Medium green	Extra-large head without virus. Resistant to bolting.	HER PAR
AVON DEFIANCE		Dark green	Solid hearts. Stands well. High resistance to mildew. Sow in summer.	ECO
BEN SEMEN	70	Deep green	Heat and bolt resistance. Large, compact head.	GLE
BIG BOSTON	79	Wavy, slightly brown edges, yellow center	Hard head. Superior quality.	ALL COM DEG LED POR
BRUNE D'HIVER	56	Smooth, fan-shaped, green with bronzy-red edges	French heirloom variety. Halfway between bibb and romaine in shape. Recommended for cool-season growing.	ABU COO SHE
BUTTERCRUNCH	55-75	Smooth, dark green	Tolerant of heat. Slow to bolt. Black-seeded.	ABU ALL ARC BURG BURP BURR BUT COM COO DAN DEG EAR EARL ECO FAR FIS GAR GUR HARR HEN HUM JUN LAG LED LET LIBE MEY MID NIC PAR PON POR RAW RED RIS SEED STO TER THO TIL VER WES WET WIL WILL WYA
BUTTERCRUNCH M.I.O.	65		Long-standing. Centers blanch to creamy white.	LET
BUTTER KING	70-85	Wavy	Israeli variety. 12-13 oz. head. Does well even in hot weather.	EARL SEE
CAPITANE	62		Dutch variety. Large, buttery flavored leaves. Vigorous grower. Bolt-resistant.	SHE SOU
CINDY	57	Light green	12-14 in. heads. No bitterness. Vigorous head is held well above soil line.	PAR TER
CITATION	74	Frilly, light green	Conical blanched heart. Slow-bolting.	TER
DOLLY	57		Long-standing. Resistant to tip burn. Creamy white interior with tender texture.	VES

LETTUCE—BUTTERHEAD/BIBB TYPES

Variety	Days	Color/Leaves	Remarks	Sources
HANSON	80	Frilled, light yellow-green	Hardy, broad and thick. Winter-hardy.	SOU WET
HILDE	65	Yellowish-green	High quality.	WILL
KAGRAN SUMMER	54	Light green	Heat-resistant. Large head is slow to bolt to seed. Does not tip burn. German variety.	HIG JOH LEM PIN PLA SEE
KWIEK			Large, quick-growing forcing variety.	COO
MAGNET		Pale green	Forcing variety resistant to adverse conditions.	COO
MANTILIA	60	Green	French variety. Disease-resistant. Heat-tolerant, slow-bolting, easy to grow.	SHE
MAY-QUEEN	60		Good for early sowing or for greenhouse culture.	WILL
MEDIA	50	Bright green, slightly curled	French variety. Summer variety. Slow to bolt. Disease- and tip burn-resistant.	NIC
MERVEILLE DES QUATRES SAISONS (MARVEL OF 4 SEASONS)	50-72	Wavy, ruby-red-tipped leaves	Slow to bolt. Good-tasting. Tight-folded green hearts. Forms rosettes of radiant colored crispy leaves. Dutch variety.	COO HER LEM PIN RED SHE TER
MIRENA	65	Medium green	Slow to bolt. Resistant to lettuce mosaic and mildew diseases.	WILL
NANCY	58	Glossy, medium-green	Well-packed heart. Resistant against rot, mosaic virus, and 9 races of mildew. For spring or fall crops.	JOH
ORFEO KAGRANER SOMMER	58	Light yellow-green	German variety. Slow to bolt. Extremely heat-tolerant.	COO GUR HER WILL
PATTY	65	Wavy, light green	Well-folded hearts. Resistant to mildew and tolerant to botrytis. For spring and fall crops.	JOH
PRADO			Fast-growing for late spring. Resists bolting during hot spells.	COO
PRIMA		Bright, clear green	French butterhead. Full heart.	LEM
RED BOSTON	68	Red-tinged	Green heart.	STO
RED BUTTERHEAD	58	Red	Heirloom variety from Marbury, Yugoslavia. 8 in. across with yellow interior.	SOU
RIGOLETTO		Green	Dutch variety. For summer growing.	COO
SUMMER BOSTON	70	Light yellow-green	For summer harvests. Very slow to bolt to seed during hot weather. High quality. Well-folded leaves.	STO
VALDOR		Deep green	Firm head. Very cold-hardy.	COO

Variety	Days	Size	Remarks	Sources
WHITE BOSTON (SUMMER UNRIVALLED)	66-76	Smooth, wavy, bright green	Free from bottom rot, tip burn. Compact heads. Unbeatable for forcing.	DEG RIS SEE STO WILL
WINTER DENSITY		Green	Very hardy variety. Semi-cos resembling fall buttercrunch.	COO
WINTER MARVEL		Pale green	Winter-hardy. Sow in fall, harvest early spring.	COO

LETTUCE—BUTTERHEAD/BIBB TYPES
MEDIUM

Variety	Days	Color/Leaves	Remarks	Sources
APOLLO			Short-day lettuce for winter culture.	WILL
ARTIC KING			Adapted to growing from early fall through winter.	COO
BABYLON	55	Red	Heat-resistant. Well-folded. Crisp and tender.	VER
COBHAM GREEN		Dark green	Solid hearts stand well. Excellent flavor.	ECO
CRISP AS ICE (CONTINUITY) (HARTFORD BRONZEHEAD)	65-70	Wavy, dark green overlaid with red-brown	Very hardy. Buttery, sweet flavor. Great hot-weather variety. Fine quality.	COM COO ECO GUR LET NIC
DARK GREEN BOSTON	80	Smooth, dark green	Uniform and dependable under various conditions. Can be grown in spring or fall.	BURR HARR LAG LET LIBE MEY MID
DARK GREEN BOSTON M.I.	68			LET
DARK GREEN BOSTON M.I.O.	68	Dark green	Similar to White Boston.	LET
DELTA			Quick-growing forcing lettuce.	COO
DEER TONGUE (MATCHLESS)	80-90	Triangle shape, rounded tip, green	Stands heat well. Compact, upright growth. 8 in. across. Slow to bolt to seed.	ABU GAR
HILDE	79		Crisp salad lettuce.	THO
KINEMONTPAS		Pale green	Standard summer lettuce in France. Slow-bolting.	COO
MAY KING	65	Light green, fringed brown	Creamy yellow interior. Can be used for greenhouse forcing.	COO DEG ECO SEE
MESCHER	50	Green ringed with red	Dates back to the 1700s. Best grown in cool weather. Excellent flavor and appearance.	ABU SOU
NORTH POLE	50	Light green	Compact head is cold-resistant. Winter-hardy. Bolts during summer.	COO NIC
PIRAT (BRAUNER TROTZ KOPE)	55	Savoyed, medium-green overlaid with soft brick-red	Well-adapted to growing throughout the season. Bolt-resistant. European variety.	COO JOH

◀ **LETTUCE—BUTTERHEAD/BIBB TYPES**

Variety	Days	Color/Leaves	Remarks	Sources
RADIAN		Pale bronze	Good cold tolerance. Adapted for fall crops in the north.	COO
SWEETIE	70		Easy to grow. Plant bears all season.	GUR
TANIA		Wavy, dark green	Plant Variety Protected. Resistant to downy mildew. Does best in cool weather.	HARR
VAD D'ORGE		Pale green	Early fall butterhead. Soft buttery taste.	COO
VOLUMA		Green	Dutch variety. Wide disease resistance. Smooth texture.	COO

LETTUCE—BUTTERHEAD/BIBB TYPES
SMALL

Variety	Days	Color/Leaves	Remarks	Sources
AKCEL		Deep green	Good French forcing variety for early baby lettuce.	COO
ATTRACTIVE (UNRIVALLED)			6 oz. heads. Brittle, golden-yellow heart. Few outer leaves. White-seeded. Long-standing. Can be sown anytime.	ECO
BIBB (LIMESTONE) (KENTUCKY)	60-70	Smooth, waxy-green	Black-seeded. Bolts in hot weather.	ALL ARC BURG COO DAN DEG LED LET MEY MID NIC PAR PON POR WET WIL
BIBB SLOW BOLTING	75	Dark green	Black-seeded. Withstands hot weather.	COM
DIANA			French variety. Compact head. Delicate flavor. Plant in spring or fall. Cooler climates can harvest in summer too.	LEM
FLORI BIBB	58	Medium-dark green	Slow to bolt to seed.	MID
MIGNONETTE BRONZE	65	Frilled, medium-brown, with dark green tinge	Slow to bolt. Blanches white. Black-seeded.	LEJ SEE
MIGNONETTE GREEN	65	Deep green	Black-seeded. Grown mostly in tropical climates.	LEM NIC SEE
PERELLA GREEN			Italian lettuce.	LEM
PERELLA RED			Italian variety. Hardy performance and good taste. For fall, spring or early summer planting.	LEM
ROUGETTE DU MIDI (RED MONTPELIER)		Bronze-red	Needs lots of water. Tasty leaves from small to mature stage. Great as a baby lettuce. Not for summer planting.	COO LEM
SUMMER BIBB	60-70	Wavy, medium-dark green	Black-seeded. Vigorous grower. Slow to bolt to seed. Firm interior. Ideal for summer conditions.	FIS HARR LET LIBE MID RIS TWI

LETTUCE
SPACE SAVERS

Variety	Days	Color/Leaves	Remarks	Sources
LITTLE GEM MINI ROMAINE		Bright green, slightly wavy	Thick and crunchy. 5-6 in. tall. Head grows rapidly. Well-balanced flavor. Moderately frost-tolerant.	COO SHE
SUMMER BABY BIBB	60	Green rosettes, teardrop-shaped leaves	Petite head. Sturdy, vigorous grower under a variety of conditions. Nice flavor.	SHE
TOM THUMB	65	Tennis-ball size, medium-green, crumpled	Centers are blanched creamy white. Buttercrunch type.	COM DEG EARL FAR GUR HIG LAG LED PAR PIN SEE SOU THO TIL VER

LETTUCE
GREENHOUSE

Variety	Days	Color/Leaves	Remarks	Sources
CAPITAN	62		Use year-round for greenhouse or hydroponic culture.	STO
DIAMANTE		Dark green	For winter production. Large heads are produced even under cold conditions. Do not heat above frost protection at night.	JOH
GRAND RAPIDS FORCING (WASHINGTON STRAIN)	45	Curled green	Loose leaf variety.	STO
OSTINATA	60		Best Boston type for summer greenhouse or hydroponic cultures.	STO
SALINA		Dark green	Sow January through August. Compact head. Bolt-resistant. Mild, non-bitter flavor.	JOH
VALDOR		Green	Winter lettuce. Used mostly in greenhouses. Good resistance to botrytis (gray mold).	ECO
VASCO		Bright green	Can be grown outdoors for mini head. Mild flavor. Resists bolting.	JOH

LOOSELEAF LETTUCE

Variety	Days	Color/Leaves	Remarks	Sources
ARTIC KING	80	Light green	White-seeded. Early-winter variety. Does not stand heavy frost. Small.	THO
BIONDO A FOGLIE LISCE		Smooth	Quick-growing, tender leaves. Can be cut several times.	COO
BRONZE ARROWHEAD		Arrow-shaped, overlaid with magenta		SEE

▶

◀ **LOOSELEAF LETTUCE**

Variety	Days	Color/Leaves	Remarks	Sources
BLACK-SEEDED SIMPSON	45	Light green, frilled, outer leaves	Center leaves blanch almost white.	ABU ALL ARC BURG BURP BUT COM COO DAN DEG EAR FAR FIS GAR GUR HARR HEN JOH JIN LAG LED LEJ LET LIBE MEY MID NIC PAR PIN PLA POR RAW RED RIS ROS SEED SOU STO TIL TWI VER VES WES WET WIL WYA
CRISPY SWEET	40	Crinkled	Everbearing, cut and come again habit. Fast-growing, upright plant.	PAR
CURLY OAKLEAF (FEUILLE DE CHENE) (FOGLIE DI QUERCIA)			Used solely as a cutting lettuce. Will form head at maturity if thinned.	COO
DEEP RED		Savoyed, dark green, bronze-red tinge	Plant Variety Protected. Does not stand up under hot-weather conditions.	HARR
DUNSEL	35	Round, yellow-green	European variety. Very tender. Pick leaves after 3-5 weeks of sowing. Plant early spring.	WILL
EARLY CURLED SIMPSON	45	Crumpled, light green	White-seeded. Slow to bolt in hot weather.	ARC EAR HEN LAG LED
EARLY PRIZEHEAD	45	Curled and crumpled, bright green, shaded brownish-red	Large, tender loose head. Excellent flavor.	EAR
FLAME		Deep red, frilled	Slow-bolting.	HARR
GOOSE		Heavy	Very winter-hardy.	SEE
GRAND RAPIDS (BURPEE'S GREENHART)	45	Frilled, light green	Resistant to mildew and tip burn. Slow to bolt to seed.	ARC BURG DEG EAR EARL FAR HARR HEN JUN LAG LED LET MEY MID PIN RAW RIS SE TWI VES WET WYA
GRAND RAPIDS T.B.R.	45	Light green, deep-cut frilly edges	Special tip burn-resistant strain. Recommended for hot beds, greenhouses and outdoor planting.	BURR LET LIBE MID
GRAND RAPIDS T.B.R.-M.I.O.	45	Deep green	Good tolerance to tip burn under glass or outdoors.	LET STO
GREEN ICE	45	Savoyed with fringed margins, dark green	Used over a longer period of growing season than most leaf lettuces.	BURP COM LED PAR
GREEN WAVE	45	Frilled	Heat-resistant Grand Rapid type. Vigorous and disease-resistant.	VER
LINGUE DE CANARINO		Pale green, rounded oak leaf-like	The name means canary-colored tongues. Very mild and delicious in the spring. Edible all year.	PIN

▶

Variety	Days	Color/Leaves	Remarks	Sources
LOLLO BIONDO		Ruffled, bright green	Cut leaf by leaf rather than entire head.	COO LEM
LOLLO ROSSO	75	Very frilly, magenta with light green	Plant either spring or fall. A cutting lettuce.	COO LEM SHE TWI VER
OAK LEAF	38-50	Medium-green	Leaves look like oak leaves. Does not become bitter in hot weather. Long-standing variety.	ABU ALL ARC BURG BUT COM DEG EAR FAR GAR HEN HIG JOH LED LEM LET LIBE NIC PIN PLA PON POR RED SEE SEED SHE SOU WES WET WILL
PRIZEHEAD (JUNG'S ALL CREAM)	47	Wrinkled, medium-green, with reddish tinge to leaf edges	A bunching sort. Sweet and tender. Good quality.	ABU ALL ARC DEG EARL FIS GAR GUR HARR HIG JOH LET LIBE MID PLA RAW RED RIS SEED TIL VER
PRIZEHEAD M.T.		Red		MID
RED FIRE	45	Savoyed and frilled, intense red	Easy to grow. Very productive. Crisp and tender.	VER
RED GRENOBLE		Green, tinged magenta	Cold-hardy.	SEE
RED HEAD M.I.O.	50	Medium-red, crumpled and frilled	Takes heat stress. Yellow-green interior.	LET
RED OAK LEAF		Deeply indented, deep red	Grow in full sun.	LEM
RED RAPIDS	48	Savoyed, bright red	Loses color as leaves become over-mature.	STO
RED SAILS	45	Heavy crinkled, deep red-bronze	Slow to bolt to seed. High quality.	ALL BURP BURR COM COO EAR HARR HIG HUM JOH LIN LAG LED LET LIBE MEY NIC PAR PIN POR SEED SOU STO TER TIL TWI VER WET WILL
RED SALAD BOWL	50	Deep maroon, deeply lobed	Very slow-bolting. Blanched interior.	BURP COO HEN HIG JOH LEM LIBE VER VES
ROSSA DI TRENTO		Savoyed, red tipped	Italian cutting lettuce. Can be grown year round in mild climates.	COO
ROYAL OAK LEAF	50	Dark green, oak-like	Heat-tolerant. Thick midribs. Tender and tasty. Plant Variety Protected.	BURP COO LAG
RUBY	47-65	Frilled, bright green with intense red	Sweet and crisp.	ARC BURP COM COO DAN DEG EAR GUR HUM JLH JUN LAG LED LEJ LET LIBE MID PIN PLA PON POR RIS ROS SEE STO WES WIL WILL

◄ **LOOSELEAF LETTUCE**

Variety	Days	Color/Leaves	Remarks	Sources
SALAD BOWL	45	Waved, light green	Black-seeded. Deeply lobed, giving it an endive appearance. Slow to bolt. Stands heat well.	ABU ALL ARC BURP BURR BUT COM COO DAN DEG EAR EARL ECO FAR FIS GAR GUR HARR HEN HIG HUM JOH JUN LAG LED LET LIBE MEY NIC PAR PIN PON POR RIS SEE SEED TER THO TIL VER WET WIL WILL WYA
SLOBOLT LEAF	45	Purplish-red, crumpled and frilled	Lasts entire summer season without bolting to seed. Black-seeded. For greenhouse culture also.	COM EARL FAR HEN LET LIBE MID SOU STO TER
SUPER PRIZE	45	Red-tinged	Good bolting tolerance. Harvest outer leaves throughout the summer. Loses red color when over-mature.	STO
SWEETIE	45	Rich green	Large upright plant.	HEN LET LIBE
TANGO	45	Dark green, deeply cut, pointed	Uniform plant forms tight, erect rosettes. Tender and tangy.	BURP
WALDMAN'S DARK GREEN GRAND RAPIDS M.I.O.	45-50	Deep green, wavy	Resistant to tip burn. Longer, darker green than other Grand Rapid types.	GAR HARR JOH LET LIBE MID RIS STO

ROMAINE LETTUCE

Variety	Days	Shape/Leaves	Remarks	Sources
BALLON		Tall	For summer or fall. Late-bolting. French variety. Heat-tolerant.	COO HER SEE
COSMO	65	11 in. Savoyed, bright green	For spring and fall crops only.	JOH SOU
CRAQUANTE D'AVIGNON (CRAQUERELLE DU MIDI)		Deep green	A semi-romaine. Cold-resistant but also slow to bolt. Plant spring, summer or fall.	COO LEM
CRISP MINT (ERTHEL)	65-80	Rippled, savoyed	Excellent mildew and virus resistance.	THO
DE FRONTIGNAN		Bright green	Extremely hardy. Slow to bolt. Plant spring, summer or fall.	LEM
DE MORGES BRUAN		Bronze-tinted	Looser leaves and thinner ribs than most romaines.	LEM
GREEN TOWERS		Dull gray-green, slightly savoyed	Large, full-bodied heads.	HARR
LITTLE GEM (SUGAR COS)	70	6 x 4 in. Glossy green.	The heart is a mass of crisp, crunchy, blanched leaves with delicious, sweet flavor.	ALL DEG ECO TER THO
LOBJOIT'S GREEN COS (DARK GREEN COS)	55-70	12 in. Dark green	Excellent quality. White-seeded. Hard in texture. Crisp, sweet and firm. Does well in the summer.	ALL DEG ECO HIG

▶

Variety	Days	Shape/Leaves	Remarks	Sources
PARIS WHITE COS (TRIANON) (VALMAINE) (ROMAINE)	70-83	10-12 in.	Crisp, sweet, yet piquant flavor. Widely grown in the North.	BURP BURR BUT DAN DEG EARL FAR FIS GUR HARR HUM JUN LET LIBE NIC PAR RAW SEE STO SUN TER VER VES WES WILL
PARRIS ISLAND COS (PARIS ISLAND)	70-75	8-9 in. Dark green	Crisp texture. Mild flavor.	COM EAR GAR HARR HIG JOH LAG LED LET LIBE MEY MID PIN RED RIS SEE SEED STO TIL TWI VER WIL
ROMANCE	75	Large	Heads fold well. Crisp centers. Fast-growing. Virus- and mildew-resistant.	SHE THO
ROUGE D'HIVER (RED WINTER)		Bronze to deep-red; broad, flat leaves	European heirloom variety. Easy to grow. Cold- and heat-resistant. Give plenty of water. Grows quickly.	COO LEM PEA SEE SHE
SIGNAL		Tall, dark green	Good outer leaves for head protection. Good quality.	MID POR
SIGNAL ROMAINE M.T.O.				MID
ST. ALBANS ALLHEART		Tall, dark green	English variety. White-seeded. Tender, crisp heads. Excellent flavor.	JLH
SUCRINE		Green	Semi-romaine with loose leaves. Crisp, sweet flavor. Resistant to cold. Plant fall or winter.	LEM
VALMAINE	75	Dark green	Tolerant to mildew.	WILL
WALLOP	80	1½ lbs.	Cross between crisp head and cos. Crisp, tasty, sweet. Upright habit.	THO
WINTER DENSITY	60	10 in.	White-seeded. Round top, well-formed leaves. Creamy white interior. Cold-resistant. Late-bolting in summer.	ABU ECO GAR JOH SEE

MUSTARD
(Brassica juncea)

Mustard greens have been popular in the South for years. It is a fast-growing vegetable under fertile conditions, and the plants live for several months. Cool weather improves the flavor. In hot weather the peppery flavor becomes especially strong. There are two types to choose from, plain leaf and curled. The Asian mustards are distinct from the leafy cabbage types, yet their leaves are used in the same way. Mustard is another cut and come type of green. Cut what you need and new ones appear to replace them.

CULTURE: Sow seeds as soon as the soil can be worked in the spring. Plant seeds a half-inch deep, 1 to 2 inches apart, in rows 18 inches apart. Thin plants to stand 4 to 6 inches apart. The plants thrive in cool weather and quickly go to seed in the heat of summer.

SEASON: Cool.

INSECTS/DISEASES: See Kale.

HARVESTING: Young leaves are mixed in green salads. Cut individual leaves or the whole plant.

MUSTARD
CURLED

Variety	Days	Leaves	Remarks	Sources
BURPEE'S FORDHOOK FANCY	40	Deeply curled, fringed, dark green	Mild flavor. Slow to bolt to seed.	BURP DEG SEE
GREEN WAVE	45-55	Edges are finely cut; ruffled, dark green	Used for southern 'greens'.	COM DEG EAR EARL GAR GUR HIG JOH LAG MEY MID PIN RIS SEED STO TER
GIANT RED		Large, savoyed, maroon with chartreuse undersides	Japanese variety. Winter-hardy, slow to bolt to seed. Plant early spring or late summer.	LEM
HORNED MUSTARD		Frilled, bright green	Japanese variety. Semi-heading. Each stem flares into a horn, opening the plant into a leafy bush. Used in stir-fry or surrounding meat dishes. Easy to grow in warm, but not hot weather.	LEM
KYONA (MIZUNA)	40	Deeply cut, frilled	Japanese variety. Narrow white stalks. Ornamental and edible. Grow for spring or fall.	HIG LEM LET SEE
MIIKI PURPLE		Deep purple	Japanese variety. Clear peppery taste. Can be grown out for boiling greens. Cut at 1-6 in. Ornamental.	COO
MIIKI GIANT		Large and wavy green	Asian variety. Thick midribs. Veins tinged with red. Use in pickle or cooking. Plant early spring or late summer. Easy to grow. Good variety for southern warm areas.	GLE LEM TER
OLD FASHION (HEN-PECKED)	40	Long and ruffled	Fine quality.	WET WYA
OSAKA PURPLE MUSTARD	80	Fringed, purplish-red	Very mild flavor.	GLE SEE
SOUTHERN GIANT CURLED	40-60	Wide, crumpled, bright green	Large, moderately broad leaves. For spring or fall planting. 18-24 in. spread. Slow to bolt to seed.	ARC BURR DEG JUN LED LET MEY MID PAR POR RIS SEE TIL TWI WES WET WIL WYA

MUSTARD
PLAIN

Variety	Days	Leaves	Remarks	Sources
BAN SIN		Short, thick, flat, wide petals	Relatively short plant. Tender, crisp tasty large heads. Good for frying, cooking or pickling.	GLE
BURGONDE	85		Makes good brown mustard, mild or hot, from dried seed pods.	PIN
FLORIDA BROAD LEAF	43-50	Broad, smooth, with flattened greenish-white rib	Leaves are easy to work with as greens. 16-22 in. spread.	ARC BURR COM DAN DEG FIS LAG LEJ LET MEY MID POR RED RIS ROS SEE STO TWI VER WET WIL WYA

Variety	Days	Size	Remarks	Sources
KOMATSUNA LATE		Round, broad, dark green	Bolts mid-May. Japanese variety. Upright plant. Stems are delicate, tender and sweet.	TER
SAVANNAH (hybrid) (TENDERGREEN IMPROVED)	25-40	Smooth, thick, dark green	Large vigorous plant. Narrow, cream-colored ribs.	HARR LED PAR VER
SLOBOLT	40	Smooth, dark green	Long-standing. Slow-bolting.	MID RIS
TENDERGREEN (MUSTARD SPINACH) (KOMATSUMA)	34-40	Large, broad, thick, dark green	Rapid growing. 16-22 in. spread. Well-suited to the South.	ABU ALL ARC BURG BURP COM DAN DEG EAR FAR GLE HEN LAG LET MEY RIS ROS SEE SUN TER WES WET WIL WYA
TENDERGREEN II (hybrid)	48	Thick, glossy, dark green	Vigorous plant. Slow to bolt. High-yielding.	TWI

OKRA
(Abelmoschus esculentus)

Okra, a member of the Hollyhock family, is another long-time southern favorite. The long pod is cut and used as soup stock, with seafood and in other types of cooking. Okra pods grow on large, erect, bushy plants with tropical looking leaves. If your garden will grow sweet corn it will grow okra. Okra, too, now comes in an array of sizes and color.

CULTURE: Okra requires a warm and long growing season. 4 months of very warm weather is recommended. Soak the seeds in water for 24 hours before planting. Plant a half-inch deep, in rows 36 inches apart, after the soil has warmed to at least 75 degrees. Thin plants to 15 inches apart.

SEASONS: Warm.

INSECTS/DISEASES: *CORN EARWORMS*: Use Sevin or ryania.
ANTHRACNOSE, LEAF SPOTS, RUST: Use maneb or zineb.
POWDERY MILDEW: Use Karathane or sulfur.

HARVESTING: Once the pods form, cut them when only 2 inches long; that's when they are the most tender. Pods left on the plant will become tough and stringy and will shorten the picking season.

OKRA
GREEN, FULL-SIZED

Variety	Days	Pods	Remarks	Sources
ANNIE OAKLEY (hybrid)	48-52	Long, slender	3-4 ft. tall plant. Compact, uniform plant. Spineless pods. Keep picking pods to encourage production.	BURP BURR GUR HEN JOH LED LET POR RIS TWI WET WIL
CLEMSON SPINELESS	55-60	6-9 in. Rich green, slightly grooved	4-5 ft. plant. Very heavy yielder.	ARC BURG BURP BURR COM DAN GUR HARR HEN JUN LAG LED LEJ MID NIC PAR PIN POR RED ROS SEE VER WES WET WIL WYA
CLEMSON SPINELESS 80	55	Medium-green	4-5 ft. plant. Spineless pods. High-yielding.	EAR MID RIS TWI
EMERALD GREEN VELVET		7-9 in. Medium-green, smooth, with some ridging	6-9 ft. plant. Leaves have a grayish cast.	DAN HEN LET TWI WYA

◀ **OKRA**

Variety	Days	Pods	Remarks	Sources
EVERTENDER	50	5-7 in. Green	Disease-resistant.	GLE SOU
GREEN VELVET SPINELESS	60	7 in. Light green	5 ft. plant is vigorous, heavy yielder.	POR
LOUISIANA GREEN VELVET	60	6-7 in. Velvety-green	6 ft. plant is branching type.	HEN LEM
PARK'S CANDELABRA BRANCHING	50-60		4-6 spikes per plant. Open habit.	PAR
PENTAGREEN			Japanese variety. High-yielding. Short-season variety. Does well in fertile soil.	WILL
PERKIN'S LONG POD		7-8 in. Dark green, ribbed	Medium-tall stalks are heavy producers.	POR WET WIL
PERKIN'S MAMMOTH	60	8-9 in. Brown-green, ribbed	6-12 ft. plant. Pods retain their tenderness and color.	SEE
PERKIN'S SPINELESS	53	6-9 in. Ribbed	4½-7 ft. plant. Leaves are lobed.	DEG MEY
VINING GREEN			Grows on trellis, fence or ground. Edible in its early stage.	PET

OKRA
SPACE SAVERS

Variety	Days	Pods	Remarks	Sources
CEE GWA (CHINESE OKRA)	90	6-8 in. Green	Summer crop that is delicately sweet, tender pods. Eat raw or cooked.	STO
DWARF GREEN LONG POD	50	7 in. Dark green, ribbed	2½-3 ft. plant. Prolific.	ALL ARC BURG COM DEG EAR EARL FAR GUR HARR HEN LET MEY POR RIS ROS SEE WET WIL WYA
DWARF STALKED LONG GREEN PROLIFIC	55	7-8 in. Dark green	3 ft. plant. Vigorous.	LED
EMERALD	56-58	Round, dark green	6-7 ft. plant. Spineless pods. Prolific. Pick pods when young.	BURP BURR DEG HARR LED POR SEED WIL
LEE	50	6-7 in. Bright green	Space-saving 3 ft. plant. Open habit. Spineless pods.	HEN PAR POR WIL
PERKIN'S DWARF SPINELESS	53	7 in. Dark green	3½ ft. plant.	BUT WYA
TENDER POD (hybrid) (LADIES FINGERS)	48-54	Harvest by 2½ in.	Bushy and compact plant. Plant in sunny location. Will crop best when nights are not cold.	THO

OKRA
OTHER COLORS

Variety	Days	Pods	Remarks	Sources
BLONDY	50	Harvest before 3 in.	3 ft. plant. Short-season variety. Spineless pods.	COM EAR GUR HEN JUN LET POR TWI
BURGUNDY	60	Red	3½ ft. plant. Ornamental as well as useful. Produces well even in cooler weather.	VER
RED OKRA	60	Red	5-6 ft. plant. Unusual and delicious.	DEG GUR HEN PAR PET ROS SEE SOU WES
RED VELVET		Red, slightly ribbed	Tall red stalks with red-ribbed leaves. Good producer of good quality pods.	LAG LEM POR
RED WONDER		Long	Pods are tender to maturity.	GLE
STAR OF DAVID	61	5-9 in. But harvest when small	Israeli variety. Unbranched 8-10 ft. stalk. Keep well-picked. Purple on top of leaf petioles and major leaf veins.	SOU
WHITE VELVET	60	6-7 in. Smooth, velvety, white	5 ft. plant. Prolific.	DEG ROS SEE

ONIONS
(Allium)

Onions are really quite easy to grow and are a large family to choose from. Onions come in all shapes, sizes and shades of browns, whites and reds, not to mention the green onions called scallions. There are even onions that multiply or grow on top of a mother plant.

CULTURE: Onions can be grown from sets or from seed. Sow seeds a quarter-inch deep in rows 12 inches apart. Thin the rows to 4 inches apart (you can pick and eat the pulled onions), then let the bulbs develop.

Plant seedling purchased from the nursery 1 inch apart, then to 2 to 3 inches apart.

Sets, which are tiny bulbs, are the best way to grow onions. Plant the sets 1 to 2 inches apart and harvest green onions until the plants are spaced 2 to 3 inches apart. Let the remaining bulbs develop to maturity.

SEASON: Cool.

INSECTS/DISEASES: *ONION, MAGGOT, ONION THRIPS, WIREWORMS*: Use diazinon or malathion.

DOWNY MILDEW, TIP BLIGHT: Use maneb or zineb.

BACTERIAL SOFT ROT: Treat soil with diazinon before planting.

HARVEST: When the tops of the ordinary bulbs (not scallions) begin to dry and yellow, bend them over to a nearly horizontal position on the ground or break them off. This will divert all growing energy to the bulbs. When all the tops are dead, dig the bulbs up and let them dry on top of the ground for a few days, then store them in a dry, frost-free place. Harvest green onions as needed.

ONIONS—GLOBE
RED

Variety	Days	Scales/Flesh	Remarks	Sources
BENNY'S RED (BENNIES RED)	112	Bright red, pink to white flesh	Large onion. Short-term storer.	BURR HARR MID PIE STO TER TWI VER WES
BIG RED (hybrid)	110	Dark red, white flesh	Relatively free of double centers. Good storage qualities.	TWI
CARMEN (hybrid)	108-155	Deep blood-red scales, bright pink flesh	Stores well. Spanish cross.	PIN STO THO
MOUNTAIN RED	100	Deep red, white flesh	Mild flavor. Keeps well.	FIS

◄ ONIONS—GLOBE

Variety	Days	Scales/Flesh	Remarks	Sources
RED BARON (hybrid)	110	Dark red, red flesh	Southport Red Globe type. High percentage of single centers.	RIS
RUBY		Red	Pungent, and good quality.	COO LET
SOUTHPORT RED GLOBE	100-113	Deep red scales, pink-tinged, white flesh	Standard red onion. Short-term storage. Heavy-yielding. Pungent flavor.	ABU DAN DEG ECO FAR GUR HARR HEN HUM JOH JUN PIE PIN RAW SEED STO TIL WILL
TANGO (hybrid)	108	Glossy red scales, pink flesh	Similar to Carmen. Good tolerance to weather stress. Long-day type. Mild flavor, firm and crisp texture. Stores well.	PAR STO
SOUTHPORT RED GLOBE	100-113	Deep red scales, pink-tinged, white flesh	Standard red onion. Short-term storage. Heavy-yielding. Pungent flavor.	ABU DAN DEG ECO FAR GUR HARR HEN HUM JOH JUN PIE PIN RAW SEED STO TIL WILL
TANGO (hybrid)	108	Glossy red scales, pink flesh	Similar to Carmen. Good tolerance to weather stress. Long-day type. Mild flavor, firm and crisp texture. Stores well.	PAR STO

ONIONS—GLOBE
WHITE

Variety	Days	Scales/Flesh	Remarks	Sources
LANCASTRIAN (FOOTBALL ONION)		Yellowish-white scales, white flesh	Can grow up to 7 lbs. Great storer.	THO
SOUTHPORT WHITE GLOBE	110	Clear white scales	Long-day type. Medium-large, high globe shape. Fairly mild flavor. Not as good a keeper as the colored Southport Globes.	BURR DEG HARR JUN LED LET PIN PON RIS SEE
WHITE SWEET KEEPER			Average 1/2 to 3/4 lb. Frostproof. Sweet, mild, firm flesh. Good keeper.	MID PIN
WHITE SWEET SLICER			Often weighs 1 lb. Fine-grained, sweet mild flesh. Good storer.	GUR

ONIONS—GLOBE
YELLOW/BRONZE

Variety	Days	Scales/Flesh	Remarks	Sources
AILSA CRAIG	110	Golden-straw scales	A large round bulb. Mild, long-keeping. Spring or autumn sowing.	ECO THO
AUSTRALIAN BROWN		Chestnut brown scales, Lemon-yellow flesh	Flattened globe, medium size. Does best in cool coastal climate of central California. Extremely pungent flavor.	LAG
AUTUMN GLO (hybrid)			Long storage type. Uniform, medium-size bulbs.	FAR
AUTUMN SPICE (hybrid)	95-100	Dark yellow scales	Medium size bulb. Pungent, hard flesh. Long-day type. Noted for its uniformity and long storage qualities.	EARL RAW VES

Variety	Days	Size/Color	Remarks	Sources
AUTUMN SPICE (hybrid)	95-100	Dark yellow scales	Medium size bulb. Pungent, hard flesh. Long-day type. Noted for its uniformity and long storage qualities.	EARL RAW VES
AUTUMN SPICE IMPROVED	98		20% larger than regular Autumn Spice. Good variety where muck is not too deep.	STO WILL
BEDFORDSHIRE CHAMPION		Brownish scales, white flesh	Very old, established variety. Long keeper.	ECO
BINGO	100	Bronze scales	Long storage type. Extra-hard flesh. Refined neck.	STO
BROWN BEAUTY (hybrid)	110	White flesh	Large globe, modification of Brigham Yellow. Mild flavor.	MID
BROWN BEAUTY '80 (hybrid)	105	Yellow scales	3 x 4 in. Up to ¾ lb. Mildly pungent. Good keeper.	PIN
BUCCANEER IMPROVED (hybrid)		Bronze scales	An Eastern type. Long-term storer.	HARR
BURPEE'S YELLOW GLOBE (hybrid)	102	Golden-yellow scales, yellow flesh	3½ in. across. Long storer.	BURP
CANADA BRONZE	96		Long storage life. Excellent skin, thin necks.	STO
CANADA MAPLE (hybrid)	98		Extra-hard long storer. Excellent yields in deep muck.	STO
CHIEFTAIN (hybrid)		Yellow scales	Mildly pungent. Western type. Short storer.	HARR
COOPER GEM (hybrid)	93	Brownish scales	Round, medium-size onion with firm flesh.	TIL
COPRA (hybrid)	111	Dark, heavy yellow scales	Dutch variety. Long storage type. Vigorous tops, well-defined necks.	JOH SEED STO
CYPRUM	110	Copper scales	Must be grown in deep muck soils to encourage heavy yields. Blocky high globe.	STO
DANVERS YELLOW GLOBE	110	Coppery yellow scales, white flesh	Medium-large and solid.	LET
DOWNING YELLOW GLOBE (TRAPP'S)	112	Dark yellow scales	Long-day type. Medium-size. Hard flesh, pungent flavor. Excellent long storer that does best in north-central growing states.	LET RIS SEE SEED
EARLY SHIPPER (hybrid)	90		Will store as well as other hybrids. Has small, well-matured neck. Large bulbs.	RIS
EARLY YELLOW GLOBE	100	Deep yellow scales, clear white flesh	Long-day type. Mild flavor, good keeper. Heavy-yields of 2½ in. onions.	ABU COM DEG FAR GAR HARR HUM JOH JUN LET PIN PON RIS SEED STO SOU TER VER
ESKIMO (hybrid)	85	Light bronze scales	Flattened globe. Short-storage life. Short-season variety. Good resistance to botrytis. Tolerance to basal rot.	HARR STO TWI
EXPRESS YELLOW (hybrid)	250		August sown variety. Lift bulbs in June and July.	THO

ONIONS—GLOBE

Variety	Days	Scales/Flesh	Remarks	Sources
GOLDEN BALL	105		Plant from middle to late spring. Good yields. Long-storage type.	THO
GOLDEN CASCADE (hybrid)	120		Firm, crisp, sweet and mild. Excellent storer.	NIC
GOLDEN MOSQUE	105		Almost round at maturity. Good variety grown from sets.	STO
HUSTLER (hybrid) (2610)		Bronze scales	Flattened globe. Medium-long storage ability.	HARR
KODIAK (hybrid) (D5537P)		Bronze scales	Deep globe. Very uniform. Good yielder. Long-term storer.	HARR
MR. SOCIETY (hybrid)			From globe to thick flat shape. Firm, sweet, juicy flesh. Can be stored up to five months.	EAR
NORTHERN OAK	108	Oak-colored scales	Long-day type. Large storage onion. Shows tolerance to fusarium and some strains of pink root.	STO
NORSTAR (hybrid)	80	Light bronze scales	Short-storer. Short-season variety. Long-day type. Good resistance to botrytis and tolerant to basal rot.	HARR STO TWI
NUTMEG (hybrid)		Bronze scales	Early storer for muck-growing areas.	HARR
ODORLESS LIME (ODOURLESS) (NO TEARS)	95	Straw-colored scales, white flesh	Lime-green tops. Absolutely odorless.	GUR THO
PROGRESS (hybrid)		Bronze scales	Heavy yields. An eastern type. Medium storage life.	HARR
PRONTO S			Pink root-resistant. Medium to large bulbs.	LET
RIJNSBURGER	110	Straw-colored scales, white flesh	A heavy cropper.	THO
RUSSET (hybrid)	105	Medium-bronze scales	Long-term storer for short-season areas.	STO
SENTINEL (hybrid)		Bronze scales	Excellent uniformity of size. Long-term storer.	HARR
SIMCOE (hybrid)		Golden-bronze scales	Long-day type. High globe bulbs for muck-lands of the North. Hard flesh is pungent. Storage type.	TER
SOUTHPORT YELLOW GLOBE	115	Bright golden-yellow scales, creamy white flesh	Long-day type. Strong flavor. Deeply globular with broad shoulders. Good keeper.	COM
SPARTAN BANNER (hybrid)		Bright yellow scales	Long-day type. Very productive storage onion. High globe shape.	FAR HARR RIS
SPARTAN BANNER '80 (hybrid)	114	Bronze scales	Long-term storage onion. Similar to Spartan Banner.	HARR RIS

Variety	Days	Scales/Flesh	Remarks	Sources
SPARTAN SLEEPER (hybrid)	110	Yellow scales	Excellent long-term storer. Tolerance to fusarium wilt. Perfect cooking onion.	GUR JUN STO
STOKES EXPORTER II (hybrid)	100		Fusarium-tolerant. Recommended long-storage type.	STO
SUPER APOLLO	98	Dark bronze scales	Long-day storage type. Good quality and high yields. Medium-hard, pungent flesh with small tight necks.	TWI
SUPER SLEEPER (hybrid)		Bronze scales	Yields well. An eastern type, long-term storage onion.	HARR
SUPER SPICE II (hybrid)	95		Heavy scales. Improved version of Super Spice. Long storer.	STO
SWEET WINTER	340		Grow from onion sets, overwintering type. Short storage life.	HEN STO
TAMARACK II (hybrid)	94		Long-term storer.	STO
TARMAGON (hybrid)	76		Short-storage onion.	STO
TITAN (hybrid) (D55SS)		Bronze scales	For use in western areas. Medium storage life.	HARR
TOPAZ (hybrid)	105	Yellow scales	Firm, pungent flesh. Adapted for mineral or muck soil.	LET
TRAPP #6 (hybrid)	106	Light bronze scales	Long storage type.	RIS
TRAPP #8 (hybrid)	108	Deep bronze scales	High quality storage type. Tolerant to fusarium plate rot.	RIS
TURBO	100	Amber scales	Dutch variety sets. Long keeper. Excellent flavor. Highly resistant to bolting.	THO

ONIONS—GLOBE, SPANISH
YELLOW-BROWN

Variety	Days	Scales/Flesh	Remarks	Sources
BURPEE'S SWEET SPANISH (hybrid)	110	Light yellow scales, white flesh	Huge, globular, mild-flavored onion.	BURP
BRONZE WONDER (hybrid)	115		High-yielding. Tolerant to pink root. Average keeper. Single heart, mild flavor.	MID
BURRELL'S YELLOW VALENCIA	115	Deep bronze scales	6 in. full globe bulbs. Keeps well and withstands thrips. Vigorous tops are slow to ripen.	BURR
EARLY YELLOW SWEET			3-4 in. Top quality. Very sweet. Not a long keeper.	TER
FIESTA (hybrid)	110		Long-day type. Medium to large onions that store well. Small necks firm, pungent flesh.	ARC EARL GUR HEN LED RAW RIS SHE
GRANADA (hybrid)	110	Yellowish-brown scales	Long-day type. Resistant to bolting and pink root. Adapted for mineral or muck soils.	LET

◀ ONIONS—GLOBE, SPANISH

Variety	Days	Scales/Flesh	Remarks	Sources
GRINGO (hybrid)	105	Copper scales	Long-day type. Medium-large, deep globe with thick scales.	STO
HYBRID SPANISH 720	115	Dark brown scales	Large size. Good storer. Produces well in all types of soils.	RIS
HYBRID SWEET SPANISH	110		Big, crisp, sweet, mild slicer. Long keeper.	EAR
MAGNUM (hybrid)		Yellow scales	Large round bulbs. Thick, sweet, moderately pungent. Fairly good keeper.	TER
NORTHSTAR (hybrid)	86	Light brown scales, white flesh	Bred for northern, cool regions. Shows resistance to botrytis and white rot. Mild flavor. Good keeper.	VES
RINGMAKER (hybrid)	118	Yellow scales	3-4 in. diameter. High percentage of single centers. Mild flavor.	JOH STO
RIVERSIDE (op)	115		Used principally for starting in the greenhouse in February and March. Large onion with good keeping qualities.	STO
SPANISH BEAUTY (hybrid)		Copper scales	Short-storage type. Large. Tolerant to pink root.	HARR
SPANISH MAIN (hybrid)	115	Dark copper scales	Firm flesh. Good storer.	WIL
SWEET SANDWICH (hybrid)	110	Yellow scales	Hard storage onion. Mild flavor.	BURP COO EAR GUR JOH JUN PIE POR RIS STO THO WET WYA
SWEET SPANISH YELLOW COLORADO NO. 6	115	Bronze scales	4 in. diameter. Thrips-resistant. Best keeper of the Spanish types.	BURR MID
SWEET SPANISH YELLOW UTAH JUMBO	110-130		6 in. diameter. Large, jumbo onions that are mild, sweet and have excellent flavor. Limited storage time.	BURG BURR DEG EARL GUR LAG LET MID PON ROS SEE SEED WILL
YELLOW SKIN (hybrid)			Large, round-globe shape. Mild, sweet flavor.	BRO EAR PAR STE
YELLOW SWEET SPANISH (hybrid) (PRIZETAKER)	110	Light yellow-white flesh	Long-day type. Mild, sweet flavor. Good keeper. Withstands unfavorable growing conditions.	ALL ARC BRO BURG BURP BUT DEG EAR EVA FAR FIS GUR HARR HEN JUN LED MEY MID PIE POR RED RIS TIL TWI VER WES WET WYA

ONIONS—SPANISH

WHITE, RED

Variety	Days	Scales/Flesh	Remarks	Sources
AVALANCHE (hybrid)		Bright white scales	Large bulbs. Small necks, firm flesh. Fairly pungent flavor. High quality.	BURR
RED MAC (hybrid)			Tasty and mild. One center slice is enough for a hamburger.	PAR

Variety	Days	Scales/Flesh	Remarks	Sources
RINGMASTER WHITE SWEET SPANISH	110		High percent of single centers. Pine root-resistant. Large, uniform bulbs.	BURG LET
SWEET SPANISH UTAH (JUMBO WHITE)	110	White scales	4 in. diameter. Thrips-resistant. Not a storage onion.	BURG BURP BURR MID RIS TER TEX
WHITE SWEET SPANISH (hybrid)	110		Large globular shaped. Mild, firm flesh. Limited storage. Spring-sowing. Northern area variety.	ARC BRO BURP DEG EAR EARL FIS GUR HARR HEN JUN LAG LED LET NIC PIN RIS ROS STE STO TEX TIL TWI WES WILL

ONIONS
FLAT, RED

Variety	Days	Scales/Flesh	Remarks	Sources
FLAT RED		Red scales, white flesh	4 in. diameter. Sweet and mild. Does not store well.	JUN
RED CREOLE	95		Short-day type. Flesh is firm and very pungent. Bulbs are small, thick and flat. Good keeper.	DEG
RED WETHERFIELD	103	Deep red scales, white flesh	Long-day type. Excellent keeper. Large and flat. Mild flavor. Can be grown from sets.	ALL COM DEG EARL FOS RIS SEE
STOCKTON EARLY RED			Excellent hamburger onion. Sweet flavor. Large flat size.	LAG MID

ONIONS
FLAT, YELLOW

Variety	Days	Scales/Flesh	Remarks	Sources
BUFFALO (hybrid)	88	Yellow scales	Summer harvest onion. Short-term storer. High percentage of single centers.	JOH SEED
EBENEZER	105	Yellow-brown scales, yellowish-white flesh	3 in. across. Mild flavor. Keeps in good condition until spring. Can be grown from sets.	DAN GUR NIC PAR RIS SOU
GIANT ZITTAN		Golden-brown scales	For autumn or spring sowing. Long keeper.	ECO
RELIANCE		Yellow scales	Semi-flat. Vigorous grower. Winter-hardy. For spring or summer sowing.	ECO
SENSHYU		Yellowish-brown scales	Japanese onion. Mild flavor. Heavy yielder. For late sowing. Takes 10-11 months to fully mature.	ECO
STUTTGARTER		Dark yellow scales	Large. Excellent keeper that can be grown from sets.	BURG COM FOS JUN SEED VES WILL
SWEET WINTER	95	Light yellow scales	Plant Variety Protected. 4 in. diameter. Extremely sweet and mild. Will store through summer into fall. Survives 20° temperatures. Widely adapted. Resists bolting.	PAR TER

◄ ONIONS

Variety	Days	Scales/Flesh	Remarks	Sources
WALLA WALLA	**125-300**		Sweet and large. Mild and juicy. Not for storage.	ABU COO EARL FIS GUR HEN HUM JOH LAG LEM NIC PIN RAW SEE TIL
YELLOW ROCK		Bronze scales	Seed set variety. Flattened. Heavy yielder and an excellent keeper.	RIS
YELLOW VERTUS			Large, flat. Good storer.	HER

ONIONS
FLAT, WHITE

Variety	Days	Scales/Flesh	Remarks	Sources
WHITE CREOLE		White scales	Pungent, for dehydration. Medium storer.	HARR
WHITE EBENEZER	100	White scales	Long-day type. Used almost entirely as a dry onion set. Then planted and used as a green onion.	RIS WET

ONIONS—GRANEX
THICK, FLAT

Variety	Days	Scales/Flesh	Remarks	Sources
GRANEX WHITE (hybrid)	105-175	Clear white flesh	Short-day type. Mild flavor. Crisp, firm flesh. Spring or fall sowing. Grown mainly in the South.	POR TEX WIL
GRANEX YELLOW (hybrid)		Yellow scales	Firm, mild flesh. Very short storage life.	BURP HARR PAR PIE POR TEX
GRANEX YELLOW PRR (hybrid)		Yellow scales	Firm, mild flesh. Pink root-resistant. Short storage life.	HARR
VIDALIA	110		Short-day variety. Widely adapted to most any climate. Extremely sweet and mild.	BRO EVA GUR HEN LEJ POR STE

ONIONS—GRANO
TOP-SHAPED

Variety	Days	Scales/Flesh	Remarks	Sources
NEW MEXICO YELLOW		Light yellow scales	Flesh is soft and mild. Foliage is somewhat resistant to thrips.	LEM WIL
RED GRANO PRR	90	Dark red scales	Medium-size. Will store up to 3 months. Resistant to pink root rot.	ROS
TEXAS EARLY GRANO 502 PRR		Straw-colored scales	Jumbo size. Soft, mild flesh. Short storage life. Pink root-resistant.	HARR
TEXAS EARLY YELLOW GRANO 502	168	Yellow scales	Flesh is soft with mild flavor. Short storage life. Resistant to thrips and pink root.	PIN POR

►

Variety	Days	Size/Color	Remarks	Sources
TEXAS GRANO 1015Y		Yellow scales	Plant Variety Protected.	POR TEX WIL
UNO GRANDE PRR		Straw-colored scales	Short storage life. Pink root-resistant.	HARR
YELLOW GRANO		Straw-colored scales, white flesh	Large, mild onion.	ROS

ONIONS
SPINDLE-SHAPED

Variety	Days	Scales/Flesh	Remarks	Sources
ITALIAN RED (TORPEDO)	95-115	Purplish-red scales, red flesh	Grown mainly in central California. Non-bolting. Unexcelled in mildness and sweetness. Short storage life.	COO GUR HEN LAG THO
ITALIAN BLOOD RED BOTTLE	120		Large onion with spicy, tangy flavor.	NIC
OWA SLICER	100	Gold scales, white flesh	Danish variety. Crisp and sweet, delicate flavor. You get exactly ten 2 in. slices per bulb. Excellent keeper.	GUR SEE

ONIONS—BERMUDA

Variety	Days	Scales/Flesh	Remarks	Sources
CALIFORNIA EARLY RED		Red scales, white flesh	Large and sweet. Stores well.	POR
CRYSTAL WHITE WAX (ECLIPSE) (1-303)	95	White scales, white flesh	Short-day variety. Medium-size and flat. Mild taste. Plant in spring or fall. Little or no bolting. Grown mainly in the South.	BRO BURP DEG FAR GUR HEN MID PIE POR RIS ROS SEE TEX
MISS SOCIETY (hybrid)		White flesh	Medium-large. Mild, sweet. Dependable yielder. Good keeper. Mature onions weigh about 1/2 lb. Can also be used as scallions.	EAR
RED BURGUNDY (HAMBURGER ONION)	95		Plant in spring or fall. Soft, mild flesh. Short storage life. Mostly grown in the South.	ARC BRO BURG BURP DEG EAR FAR GUR HEN NIC PIE POR PON STE WIL
RED MAC	110	Red scales, white flesh	Sweet flavor. Medium to large size. Exceptionally mild. Crisp texture. Best eaten fresh.	HEN
WHITE BERMUDA	92-185	White scales, white flesh	Not hurt by frost or freeze. Mild flesh. Thick, flat shape.	ARC DEG EAR FAR FOS HEN LAG LET MEY VER WIL
WHITE SKIN HYBRID			Very mild taste.	BRO BURP STE
YELLOW BERMUDA	92-185	Straw-colored scales	Short-day type. Medium-size. Mild, juicy flesh. Plant in spring or fall. A southern onion.	BURP DEG LET POR TEX

ONIONS—BUNCHING/SCALLIONS

Variety	Days	Remarks	Sources
ANNUAL GREEN BUNCHING		Long, white, single, thick stems. Mild, sweet flavor.	EARL STO
BELTSVILLE BUNCHING	65	Slight bulbing. Winter-hardy. Plant in spring or fall.	LET SEE STO TWI VES
EARLY RED	60-70	Light green leaves. Grows in clusters of 2-3 stalks, 12-14 in. long. Good in salad, stews or soups.	HER
BROOKS P.R.R. BUNCHING		White Libson type. Pink root-resistant.	MID
EVERGREEN HARDY WHITE	65	Winter-hardy bunching onion. Little or no bulbing. Handle as a perennial by dividing the clumps.	GAR JOH SOU
EVERGREEN LONG WHITE BUNCHING	65-120	Long, silvery-white stems. Pungent stalks will not bulb, but divide continuously from the base.	ABU BURG BURP DAN DEG FIS HIG HUM JLH PAR PIN RED SEE SUN TWI WIL WILL
HE SKI KO EVERGREEN (LONG WHITE BUNCHING WELSH) (NEBUKA)	60-80	Perennial, non-bulbing. Continues to grow and divide at the base. Winter-hardy. White pungent flesh.	ALL BRO COO FAR GUR HEN KIT LAG LEG LET NIC RAW RIC SEE VER WILL
ISHIKURA LONG	65	Japanese type. Blue-green leaves. Thick, cylindrical, non-bulbing stalks. Tops stay upright. Generally winter-hardy.	GLE HARR JOH SEE STO THO
JAPANESE BUNCHING (HARDY WHITE BUNCHING) (WHITE SPANISH)	70	Hardy green scallion. Does not form bulbs. Multiplies several stalks per plant.	COM COO HARR MID NIC STO WET
KUJO MULTISTALK	70	Produces 2 or more scallions per plant. Winter-hardy. Attractive, mild, bunching onion.	JOH SEE
KINCHO		Long, slim, pure white, non-bulbing stems.	HARR STO
KINCHO III		Slightly longer white shanks than Kincho.	HARR
KUJYO REGULAR STRAIN	120	Japanese variety. Very hardy. Sow in summer or fall.	RED
LONG WHITE SUMMER BUNCHING		Improved Nebuka type. 6-7 in. white shafts, non-bulbing. Tolerant to fusarium and pink root.	STO
LONG WHITE TOKYO BUNCHING	95	Single-stalked. Summer to winter crop. 16-18 inches.	COM HARR MEY MID NIC RIS STO SUN TWI
PERFECTO BLANCO		Long, clear-white stalks are slow to bulb. Selection of White Sweet Spanish used for green bunching.	LED
PERENNIAL BUNCHING		Divides continually at the base to form new shoots throughout the growing season. Winter-hardy. Small, white, mildly pungent shoots.	EARL
PURPLETTE		Red-skinned green onion.	SEE
RED BEARD	60	Japanese variety. A red green onion. Vigorous variety. Mild and crisp.	SHE

Variety	Days	Remarks	Sources
RED WELCH BUNCHING		14 in. tall red non-bulbing onion which grows in clusters.	VER
SOUTHPORT WHITE GLOBE	65	Most popular strain of Southport White Globe. Sweet and mild. Excellent green bunching.	HARR MID STO
TSUKUBA		Heat-resistant. Sow in mid-spring for summer use. High-yielder. Straight green leaves, pure white shafts.	LEM
WHITE BUNCHING	40	14-18 in. white tender stalks. Stands heat well. Not recommended letting it grow to maturity of 3 in. diameter.	ALL EAR DEG HEN
WHITE LISBON (IMPROVED GREEN BUNCHING)	60	Foliage resistant to heat and cold. Crisp and moderately mild. Holds freshness after being pulled.	ECO FAR HARR LEM LET MID RIS ROS SEE SHE STO THO WILL
WHITE SPEAR BUNCHING	60	Long, slender, pure white, mild and tender. Tops are blue-green and hold well. Very slow to bulb even in hot weather.	MID
WHITE SWEET SPANISH BUNCHING		Used for bunching or stripping. Slow to bulb. Mild flavor.	BURR HARR MID SEED STO TIL
YAKKO SUMMER	100	Sow late spring. Stands summer heat well.	RED

ONIONS—EGYPTIAN AND MULTIPLYING

Variety	Remarks	Sources
EGYPTIAN TREE TOP (PICKLE ONION) (SALAD ONION) (WINTER ONION)	24-36 in. tall. Top sets ½ in. diameter while the bottom onions are 1 in. in diameter. Multiplies at the top, divides at the bottom. Plant anytime. Very hardy.	ABU COM DEG LEJ NIC SEE SOU THO
McCULLAR'S WHITE TOP SET	Heirloom variety from Missouri. Fast top growth. Excellent cold hardiness, excellent keeping qualities. Very prolific. Use larger bulbs for eating, smaller bulbs for planting.	SOU
MORITZ EGYPTIAN	Heirloom variety from Missouri. Red-purple bulbs. Good yields.	SOU
OLD FASHIONED (POTATO ONION) (HILL ONION)	The largest multiplier. Multiplies in soil only. Does not go to seed. Can be planted in spring or fall. There are yellow, red or white varieties, all similar.	SOU

ONIONS
OTHER TYPES

Variety	Days	Remarks	Sources
FOOTBALL ONION	110	Good storer. Sweet-flavored. Averages 5 lbs.	LAK THO

PICKLING ONIONS

Variety	Days	Remarks	Sources
BARLETTA (WHITE PEARL)	70	Small, round bulbs.	EARL FIS GLE JLH LEM SHE STO WILL

◀ PICKLING ONIONS

Variety	Days	Remarks	Sources
CRYSTAL WAX PRR		Plant Variety Protected. Matures in August. Small, pearly white bulbs. Thin, tender skin. Resistant to pink root. Ideal for pickling and canning.	TER
WONDER OF POMPEII (POMPEII PERLA PRIMA)	100	Very small, round, excellent pickler.	NIC SEE STO
PURPLETTE	60	Purple-red. Turns pastel pink when cooked or pickled. Can be harvested as baby bunching onion with purple-pearl ends.	HIG JOH
QUICK SILVER PEARL	56	White bulbs. Round bulbs grow to ping-pong ball size with extra thin necks. Excellent quality fresh, canned or frozen.	HIG JOH
REINA RONDELLA	75	Improved Silver Queen. European strain. Clear white skin. Bulbs are round with waxy appearance.	STO
SILVER QUEEN	80	Fast-maturing white pickling onion. Round bulbs have a waxy appearance desired for pickling.	EARL
SNOW DROP		Excellent pickling qualities. Small, white, globe-shaped. Plant thickly and pull when still small.	EARL
WHITE PORTUGAL (SILVERSKIN)		Flat white mild-flavored onions for pickling or early green onions.	ARC DAN HARR LAG STO THO

ORIENTAL GREENS

Variety	Days	Remarks	Sources
BAYAM	30	Resembles spinach. Stands extreme heat. Tender and tasty. Easy to grow.	THO
BIG TOP (hybrid)	30	Spinach-like leaves. Cut back when 15-18 in. tall.	THO
CHOP SUEY GREENS (GARLAND CHRYSANTHEMUM) (SHUNGUKI) (SHINGIKU)	35	Large leaf or small leaf varieties. Dark green, aromatic leaves are used in cooking when 4-5 in. tall. Yellow flowers. Harvest frequently. Doesn't like heat. Grows bitter if allowed to flower.	BAN COO ECO GAR JOH KIT NIC PIN SEE SUN TER THO TSA VER WIL
ENTSAI GREENS	60	Mild, long leaves and 12 in. stems are easily grown and used in salads and stir-fry dishes. Not frost-hardy.	VER
HINN CHOY (CHINESE SPINACH)	40	A vegetable green unique in taste. Small fuzzy paddle-shaped leaves. Tangy flavor.	TSA
KINTSAI	60	Quick grower. Celery flavor. Slender, dark green stems and celery-like leaves.	VER
LATE KOMATSUNA		Japanese variety. Upright, dark green, round, broad leaves. Sweet, delicate, tender stems.	TER
NAROVIT	45	High-yielding cross between Chinese cabbage, kale and turnip and is grown for its tops. Use boiled, fresh or in stir-frys.	VER
NIPHON (JAPANESE SWISS CHARD)		Resembles smooth round-leaved spinach. Light green stalks, broad, deep green leaves.	SUN

▶

Variety	Days	Remarks	Sources
ONG CHOY (DRY WATER SPINACH)	65	Tropical semi-aquatic vegetable. Sweet and crispy. Hollow stems and long, pointed, green leaves. A summer crop.	TSA
ORIENT SPINACH (hybrid)	45	Vigorous, smooth dark green leaves. Heat-tolerant.	SUN
PURPLE TSE TAI		Spicy-flavored purple green. Grow in spring or late summer. Quick to bolt.	PIN
RED GIANT MUSTARD	90	Large, deep purplish-red savoyed leaves with white midrib. Tender and mildly pungent. Winter-hardy and slow-bolting.	ABU SHE VER
TSOI-SIM	60	Multi-purpose green. Whole plant is edible. That includes the flowers. Tender, bright green leaves on fleshy stems. Quick grower.	VER

ORIENTAL MUSTARD CABBAGE
GREEN STALKS

Variety	Days	Leaves/Stalks	Remarks	Sources
AOTAKANA				KIT
CHINESE TSAI SHIM		Leaves and stalks are light green	Flowering stalks are used as vegetable. Heat-resistant. Harvest when flowers begin to open.	SUN VER
DAI GAI CHOY (INDIA MUSTARD) (BRASSILA JUNCEA VAR RUGOSA)	65	Broad, thick stems and leaves	More mustardy taste than Gai Choy. Grows best in humid climate with lots of moisture.	BAN TSA
GAI CHOY (INDIA MUSTARD) (BRASSICA JUNCEA VAR FOLIOSA)	45		Pungent mustard flavor. Use both stem and leaves. Fast-growing in cool moist areas.	BAN TSA
HAKARASHINA				KIT
KWAN-HOO CHOI	50	Dark green leaves, light green stems	Resistant to heavy rainfall and heat. Best grown in summer and early fall.	JLH
MEI QING CHOI (hybrid)	45	Green petioled	Upright, compact plant. Widely adaptable. Grows well under cool temperatures. Slow to bolt. Tender leaves.	HARR JOH PAR SHE STO THO VER
NAMFONG (BRASSICA JUNCEA)	35-50		Non-heading chinese variety. 12-18 in. tall. Full-flavored summer mustard.	NIC

ORIENTAL MUSTARD CABBAGE
WHITE STALKS

Variety	Days	Leaves/Stalks	Remarks	Sources
AKA TAKANA		Dark purplish-red leaves; white ribs	Pungent flavor.	KIT
BOK CHOI (BOK CHOY)	45-60	Thick green leaves; broad white stalks	Plant resembles swiss chard. Plant in late summer for a fall crop.	COM GUR NIC SEE STO SUN WES

◀ ORIENTAL MUSTARD CABBAGE

Variety	Days	Leaves/Stalks	Remarks	Sources
CHINESE FLAT CABBAGE	40	Deep green leaves	Medium-size plant. Sow in spring or fall.	SUN
CHIN KANG	45	Green leaves	Small erect plant. Sow in spring.	SUN
FLOWERING PURPLE PAK-CHOI (HON TSAI TAI GREENS) (CHINESE TSAISHIM)	50		Yellow flowering. A vigorous cool weather plant. Harvest the flowering stalks like broccoli.	ABU NIC SUN VER
GREEN-IN-SNOW			Sow late summer. A Chinese mustard that withstands cold. Excellent greens in late fall.	RIC SEE SUN TER THO
HIROSHIMANA	75	Loose dark green leaves; wide midrib	Japanese variety. Resembles chard. Unique flavor. Use steamed or pickled. Sow in late summer.	JLH
HUNG CHIN	35	Light green leaves	Medium-size plant. Loose shape. Sow spring or fall.	SUN
JAPANESE WHITE CELERY MUSTARD	50	Thick light green leaves; spoon-shaped leaves	Sharp flavor. Cooked as greens or stir fry. Cold-resistant. Slow-bolting. Sow spring or summer.	NIC SUN WILL
JAPANESE WHITE PAC CHOI	60	Deep green, spoon-shaped leaves	Has good cold resistance. Similar to Taisai.	LEJ
JOI-CHOI (hybrid)	45	Dark green leaves; white stalks	Cold- and heat-tolerant. Slow to bolt. Erect plant.	HARR JUN STO TER VER
KWAN-HOO CHOI	60		Loose head. Grow in mid-summer to early fall. Heat-resistant.	RED
LEI-CHOI	47	Green leaves; white celery-like stalks	10-14 erect stalks, 8-10 in. long. Slow-bolting. Easy to grow. Plant Variety Protected.	BURP HARR LAG LED LIBE SEE SHE SOU THO TWI
MARUBA SANTO	50	Loose, light green leaves; white ribs	Grows best in cool weather. Mild, tender greens. Fast-growing.	JLH
MIZUNA (KYONA)	40	White stalks with deeply indented leaves	High resistance to cold. Japanese greens. Use like lettuce in winter salads. Mustard-like flavor.	ABU BURP COO GAR HIG JOH NIC PAR PLA RED SHE TER THO
NAN FOON	50	Dark green leaves; 1½ in. white stalks	Non-heading. Chinese variety. Flavorful.	RED
OSAKA PURPLE LEAVED	80-150	Purplish-red leaves; white ribs	Very large leaves are 20 in. and round. Easy to grow.	RED SEE
PAK CHOI (op) (SHAKUSHINA)		Smooth, rounded green leaves; white stems	Bolts easily on exposure to cold temperatures.	ABU BAN BURP DEG HUM LEM LIBE PAR PLA POR RED STO TER TIL VER WILL

◀

Variety	Days	Vines/Pods	Remarks	Sources
PAK CHOI, BOK CHOI (BRASSICA CHINENSIS VAR CHINENSIS)	50-65		Outer leaves and stalks are tangy. Gentle hint of mustard flavor. Grows best in cool, moist soil.	ABU GAR JOH NIC TIL
PAK CHOI, CHOY SUM (BRASSICA PARACHINENIS, BAILY)	60		Leaves are smaller and heart (sum) is dominant. Slightly sweeter than Bok Choy. Grows best in cool, light, well-drained soil.	BAN GAR NIC
PAK CHOY (hybrid)	30	Smooth, round white stems	Thick stalks. Slow to bolt. Easy to grow.	VER
PRIZE CHOY	50	Dark green leaves; white stems	Large, tender spoon-shaped leaves. Thick rounded celery-like base. 15-18 in. tall. Good quality. Slow-bolting.	HIG JOH
ROUND LEAVES SANTUNG	35	Deep green leaves	Large erect plant. Sow in the fall.	SUN
SANTO FRILLED			Japanese variety that bolts May 1 from February planting. Non-heading mild-sweet flavor.	TER
SANTOH ROUND LEAVED	50	Broad green leaves; white stalks	Fast-maturing. Spicy, celery-like stalks. Excellent raw or cooked. Easy to grow.	LEM TER VER
SHANGHAI PAC CHOI	40-50	Light green leaves	Dwarf plant. Very heat-resistant. Suited to mid summer growing. Sow spring or fall.	GAR NIC SUN
SPOON CABBAGE	45	Green leaves	Large erect plant. Sow in the spring.	SUN
SPOON PAK-CHOI		Dark green leaves; white stalks; form dense clumps	Better in warm climates, less tendency to bolt to seed.	GLE SEE
TAISAI	45-55	Bright green leaves; white ribs	Used at any point of maturity.	FIS LEM NIC RED TER
TAH TSAI	50	Deep green leaves	Winter-hardy. A tasty addition to soups, meat or vegetable dishes.	HIG VER
TATSOI	45	Dark green leaves	Small leaves are spoon-shaped. Thick rosettes. Slow to bolt. Tender. Long harvest period.	JOH PEA
TOKYO BEAU (hybrid)		Shiny dark green leaves; white stalks	Vigorous and cold-hardy. Forms rosettes. Japanese variety. Sweet, not hot, flavor.	TER
WHAT-A-JOY	45	Glossy dark green leaves; wide white stalks	10-12 in. plant with 10-12 in. spread. 10-12 erect stalks per plant. Easy to grow.	TER
WHITE STALKED	45	Green leaves	Medium-erect plant. Sow spring or fall.	SUN

PARSLEY
(Petroselinum crispum)

Parsley is a favorite with gourmet cooks because it makes a delicious garnish for salads, soups and similar dishes. A cut and come again plant. Parsley does well in the garden or in pots on a windowsill. Parsley varieties grow either leaves that are deeply curled and cut...flat, cut or plain...or as parsley for roots.

CULTURE: Soak seeds overnight before planting. Then sow ½ inch deep, 3 to 6 inches apart, in rows 12 to 18 inches apart. Parsley seeds take at least three weeks to sprout and when they do they grow slowly. If your winters are mild, parsley will live, then shoot up seed stalks when the days grow long and warm.

SEASON: Cool.

HARVEST: Snip parsley in the morning before the oils have evaporated. Pinch off old outer stems and leave the new center growth to replace the pulled leaves. Small bunches can be hung upside down in the shade to dry and used as parsley flakes.

PARSLEY
CURLED

Variety	Days	Leaf/Color	Remarks	Sources
AFRO	80	Dark green, tightly curled	Very distinctive leaf held upright on long strong stems.	SHE THO
BANQUET	76	Deep green, tightly curled	Danish variety. Weather-tolerant. Grows erect.	HARR
BRAVOUR	75	Dark green, finely curled	Long, stiff stems. Tolerant to cold. Resprouts after cutting.	COO STO
CLIVI	65	Deep green, very curled	Dwarf, neat and prolific. Base leaves do not turn yellow.	THO
COMPACT CURLED	70	Dark green, tightly curled	10 in. plant.	PAR
CURLINA	72	Dark green, triple curled	Globe-shaped 6½ in. plant. A mini parsley.	STO
CURLY PARSLEY	12-21		1 ft. plant. Use as garnish or in cooking.	HER
DARKI	77	Dark green, tight, heavy curled	Excellent cold-weather tolerance.	STO
DECORA		Deep green, heavy curled	Best suited for growing in warm climates.	COM LAG RIC
DECORATOR	75	Dark green, curled	Extra-dense tops. Strong, stiff stems. Does not wilt as fast as other varieties.	TWI
DEEP GREEN	70	Dark green, densely cut	Erect.	FAR LED LET RED
DWARF TRIPLE CURLED	70	Dark green, finely curled	Vigorous, pretty and flavorful.	WIL
EMERALD (EXTRA CURLED DWARF)	85	Dark green, finely cut and curled	Compact plant.	NIC
EVERGREEN (DOUBLE CURLED)	70	Deep green	Frost-resistant.	ALL APP BURR DAN
EXOTICA		Deep green, curled	Grows vigorously even in cool weather.	RIC

▶

Variety	Days	Vines/Pods	Remarks	Sources
FOREST GREEN	70	Dark green, densely curled	15 in. tall.	HARR HIG JOH LET NIC RIS SEED SOU RAW VER
GREEN VELVET	80	Deep green, fully curled	Strong stalks.	THO
IMPROVED MARKET GARDENER'S	76	Extra dark green, double curled	Uniform curl. Less tendency to turn yellow.	TWI
JAPANESE PARSLEY (MITSUBA)	90	Heart-shaped	Grows 2 ft. tall. Unique flavor, tender leaves.	ABU KIT NIC RIC WILL
MOSS CURLED (CHAMPION) (TRIPLE CURLED)	75	Very dark green, closely curled	12 in. high. Very compact and productive.	ABU ARC BURR COM DEG EAR EARL FAR FIS GAR GUR HEN LAG LED LEJ MEY PER POR STO TER TIL TWI VER WILL WYA
NEW DARK GREEN	75	Emerald green	Very dwarf and compact. Withstands winter better than most.	THO
PARAMOUNT	85	Dark green, densely triple-curled	Extra fancy 12 in. tall plant. Stout stems	DEG PAR
PERFECTION	75	Deep green, densely curled	Holds its color in summer and winter.	ECO
UNICURL	73	Dark green, finely curled	Leaves curl in instead of out. Tolerance to fall rust.	STO

PARSLEY
PLAIN LEAF

Variety	Days	Leaf/Color	Remarks	Sources
DARK GREEN ITALIAN	72	Heavy, glossy green	Celery-like leaf. Erect, vigorous. Strong flavor.	GAR HARR LEM MID RAW RIC SEED TER TIL
FLAT LEAF			Strong parsley flavor.	SEE
GIANT ITALIAN (CATALOGNA) (CELERY PARSLEY)	85	Plain green	3 feet tall. Strong flavor.	ABU COO DEG LAG LEM MEY NIC RED SEE
PLAIN LEAF (COMMON) (ITALIAN) (FRENCH) (SINGLE) (SHEEPS)	75	Dark green	Rich flavor.	ABU ALL APP BURP BURR BUT CAP COM ECO FIS HER HIG JLH JOH LED LEJ LET NIC PER PLA RIC RIS SHE SOU TAY THO TWI VER WET WILL WYA

PARSLEY
LONG-ROOTED

Variety	Days	Size	Remarks	Sources
EARLY SUGAR	78	Wedge shaped	Looks like a Chantenay carrot. High in sugar content. For use in heavy soil.	STO

◀ **PARSLEY**

Variety	Days	Size	Remarks	Sources
HAMBURG LONG-ROOTED (TURNIP ROOTED) (PARSLEY FOR ROOTS) (PARSNIP-ROOTED) (THICK-ROOTED)	90	6 x 2 in.	Parsnip-like roots are white. Used for flavoring soups and stews.	BURP DEG EARL HARR JLH JUN LAG LED LET MEY MID NIC RAW RED RIC RIS SEE SOU STO THO TWI WILL
SHORT SUGAR	95	4 in. Stumpy	Old world-type grown for its flavorful root. White roots store easily. Tops are also flavorful.	JOH
TOSO	95	7 x 1½ in.	Flavor is similar to parsnips.	TER

PARSNIPS
(Pastinaca sativa)

The parsnip is a root crop that can try your patience since it needs a long growing season. It is one of the hardiest of root vegetables and actually improves in flavor after exposure to frost. The parsnip remains a minor vegetable, but is unsurpassed in flavor when pan-fried or pureed.

CULTURE: Sow seed a half-inch deep in rows 3 feet apart. Thin to 5 inches apart. In cold areas, plant seed in late spring, let it grow all summer, and harvest in the fall. Leave the excess in the ground to be dug as needed. In mild-winter climates, sow in the fall and harvest in the spring. Parsnips must have a loose soil worked to a depth of 18 inches.

SEASON: Cool.

HARVEST: Dig the roots, don't pull them up. You can also leave them in the ground over-winter. In spring store what roots you haven't used in peat or sand.

PARSNIPS				
Variety	Days	Size	Remarks	Sources
ALL AMERICAN (HARRIS MODEL)	95-145	12 x 3 in.	White. Fine quality.	COM DEG EAR FIS GAR HARR HEN HUM LET RAW ROS STO VES
AVONRESISTER	110		Space saver variety if you thin out to 3 in. Most resistant to canker.	THO
COBHAM IMPROVED MARROW	120		English variety. Half-long, tapered smooth white roots. High sugar content. Resistant to canker.	JOH
GLADIATOR (hybrid)	105		Smooth white skin. True parsnip flavor. Canker-resistant.	THO
HARRIS EARLY MODEL	100	10 x 3½ in.	White skin. Smooth roots with superior flavor.	BURR DEG EARL HARR HIG JUN MID SEE SEED TER TWI VES
HOLLOW CROWN	95-130	12 x 2¾ in.	White skin on long smooth roots with broad shoulders. Fine-grained.	ABU ALL ARC BURG BURP DAN DEG EARL FAR LAG LEM MID RED SEE SOU VER WILL WYA
IDEAL HOLLOW CROWN	130	14 x 2½ in.	Creamy white smooth-textured skin.	BUT

▶

Variety	Days	Size	Remarks	Sources
IMPROVED HOLLOW CROWN	95	10 x 3 in.	White skin.	LED LET MEY
IMPROVED STUMP ROOTED		8 x 3 in.	White skin. Sweet, fine-textured.	JUN
JUNG'S WHITE SUGAR			White skin. Half-long, stocky form, heavy at the shoulders. Fine-flavored.	JUN
LONG WHITE			Large, smooth and sweet.	TIL
OFFENHAM			Thick fleshy roots. Good freezer. Suited for a wide range of soils.	ECO
TENDER AND TRUE	102		Reputed to be the longest, best-flavored. No hard core. Good resistance to canker.	ECO THO
WHITE MODEL	100		White, smooth skin.	FAR PIN RIS

PEAS
(Pisum sativum)

Peas are always star performers in the garden. They come up right away, bloom fast and produce quantities of food within 60 to 70 days. Peas are a cool-season crop that thrive in soil and air filled with cool moisture. Peas can tolerate some frost early in the season, but they prefer a mild climate.

CULTURE: Be sure to add bonemeal to the soil as peas thrive with an addition of phosphorous and calcium. Peas grow well only from seed planted in the spot where they are going to remain. In the spring, as soon as the ground can be worked, plant the seeds 2 inches deep, 2 inches apart, in rows 18 to 30 inches apart. Make subsequent plantings five to ten days apart, for a continuous crop.

SEASON: Cool.

INSECTS/DISEASES: *PEA APHIDS, PEA WEEVIL:* Use malathion, diazinon, pyrethrum, rotenone or ryania.
DOWNY MILDEW, ANTHRACNOSE: Appy maneb, zineb or fixed copper during wet period.
POWDERY MILDEWS: Apply karathane or sulfur.

HARVEST: Pick off all the pods as they mature in order to keep the plants producing vigorously. It is best to harvest only in the morning, this seems to preserve the flavor. Shell the peas (if they are shell peas) and store in the refrigerator. Snap peas need no shelling.

PEAS—BUSH
TO 24 IN.

Variety	Days	Vines/Pods	Remarks	Sources
ARISTAGREEN	66	20 in. vine; 6-8 peas per pod	Highly productive. Widely adapted. Tolerant to adverse growing conditions. Multiple pod set, up to 5 per stem. Good quality.	WILL
AURORA	69	3-4 in. pods	Resistant to common wilt and powdery mildew. Excellent variety for cool climates. Short-season variety.	HUM
BLUE BANTAM	64	18 in. vine; 4 in. pods	Heavy yields. Long-bearing. Use fresh or frozen.	NIC
BURPEEANA EARLY	63	18-24 in. vine, 3 in. pods; 8-10 peas per pod	Sweet, tender peas that retain color and flavor when quick frozen. All-purpose pea.	BURP WET
CORVALLIS	65	2 ft. vine	Sometimes grows to 3 ft. Mosaic- and virus-resistant. Sow in spring.	NIC TER

◄ **PEAS—BUSH**

Variety	Days	Vines/Pods	Remarks	Sources
DWARF TELEPHONE (DAISY)	70-76	20 in. vine, 2 in. pods; 9 peas per pod	Vigorous grower. Does well in cooler climates. Hardy upright	ALL VER
FELTHAM FIRST	58	18 in. vine, 3½ in. pods	Heavy producer.	ECO THO
FREEZER 69	69		Heavy yielding. Tender, sweet peas are good for canning, fresh or frozen use.	EARL
FROSTY	62	24-28 in. vine	High-yielding. Sets double pods. Peas are dark green. Wilt-resistant. Good fresh or frozen.	EAR FAR HARR MEY RAW WET
GREATER PROGRESS	62	18 in. vine, 4½ in. pods; 7-9 peas per pod	Very dependable and productive.	HARR SEED TWI VES
GRENADIER	61	14-17 in. vine, 4½ in. pods; 7-10 peas per pod	Plump pods are easy to shell. Productive. Resistant to powdery mildew. Good for fall crop.	BURP TER
HOLLAND CAPUCIJNERS	85		Dutch variety soup pea. Compact plants red with violet, red and pink flowers. Large wrinkled brown-gray peas are cooked whole.	JOH
HUNDREDFOLD (BLUE BANTAM) (LAXONIA)	63	18 in. vine; 8 peas per pod	Good freezing variety.	ALL DEG NIC TIL WET
HURST BEAGLE	55	18 in. vine, 3½ in. pods; 6-8 peas per pod	Wrinkled pea. Sweet and juicy. Good freezer.	THO
JUNG'S HONEY SWEET	73	18 in. vine; 8-10 peas per pod	Heavy bearer.	JUN
KELVEDON WONDER	65	18 in. vine, 3 in. pods	Wrinkled peas. Use fresh or canned. Cold-tolerant vines.	ECO LEM THO
KNIGHT	61	20 in. vine	Resistant to mosaic virus, powdery mildew and common wilt. Double-pod set.	EARL HARR HIG JOH LED PAR MEY RIS VES WET
KOSTA	60	24 in. vine	Good quality. High yielder. Ripens slowly.	VER
LACY LADY	55	18 in. vine, 3 in. pods	Semi-leafless variety. Produces many tendrils. Pods are produced in pairs near the top of the plant.	EAR FAR HEN VER WET WILL
LAXTONIAN	62	16-18 in. vine; 8-10 peas per pod	Hardy Marrowfat variety.	DEG GUR
LAXTON'S PROGRESS (MORSE'S PROGRESS NO. 9) (PROGRESS NO. 9) (EARLY GIANT) (BIG DAKOTA)	60	15-20 in. vine, 4½ in. pods; 7-9 peas per pod	High resistance to fusarium wilt.	ALL ARC BURP BURR COM DEG EAR EARL FAR GUR HEN JUN LED LEM LET MEY PAR RAW TIL VER WET WIL WILL
LAXTON'S PROGRESS IMPROVED	55	16-18 in. vine, 3½ in. pods; 7-9 peas per pod	Good main crop variety.	SEE STO

▶

◄

Variety	Days	Vines/Pods	Remarks	Sources
LAXTON'S SUPERB (EARLY BIRD)	60	24 in. vine, 3½ in. pods; 7-9 peas per pod	Semi-wrinkled pea.	ARC MEY WET
LITTLE MARVEL	62	18 in. vine, 3 in. pods; 7-9 peas per pod	Sweet and tender. Heavy yields. Good freezer.	ABU ALL ARC BURG BURP BURR DAN DEG EAR EARL FAR GUR HARR HEN HUM JUN LAG LED LET MEY MID PAR PIN PON POR RAW RED RIS SEE SEED STO THO TIL VER WET WIL WILL
MAESTRO	57	24-30 in. vine, 4 in. pods	Multiple disease resistance. Vigorous vines bear well over extended picking season.	EAR FIS GAR HEN HIG JOH JUN LET PAR TER TIL
MONTANA MARVEL	64	18 in. vine, 3½ in. pods; 8-9 peas per pod	Excellent freezer variety.	FIS HIG
NOVELLA	57	20 in. vine	Semi-leafless. Self-supporting tendrils mean no staking. Pods form at top of the vine. Good freezer variety.	ALL EAR EARL GUR HUM JUN LET NIC PAR POR SEE SEED STO THO WET
NOVELLA II	64	2 ft. vine, 3 in. pods	Semi-leafless freezer variety. Powdery mildew-resistant. Easy to shell. Good quality for fresh or frozen use.	JOH
OLYMPIA	62	16-18 in. vine, 4½ in. pods; 8-9 peas per pod	High percentage of double pods. Resistant to mosaic viruses and powdery mildew.	FAR HUM RAW SEED STO
PARSLEY PEA		2 ft. vine	Tendril-less. Resembles curled parsley.	PEA
PATRIOT	65	18-22 in. vine, 4 in. pods; 9-10 peas per pod	Medium-size peas retain flavor and firm texture after freezing.	HEN PAR STO VER WET
PETIT PROVENCAL	58	18-20 in. vine	French original petit pois. Harvest when young for best quality. Excellent table or frozen pea.	COO VER
PRECOVIL	60	2½ in. pods	French variety. Tiny sweet peas. Pick when young. Resistant to fusarium wilt and top yellow.	SHE
PROVAL	60	16 in. vine	Very productive. Good variety for cold-frame production.	HER
RAISIN CAPUCIJNERS		24 in. vine	This type of pea is grown for dry use. Plant early. Harvest when vines are dry. Large brownish peas for winter use.	WILL
ROUND GREEN	55	24 in. vine	Round green peas for dry use. Good soup bean. Strong variety.	WILL
SPARKLE	55-60	15-24 in. vine, 2½ in. pods; 7-9 peas per pod	Good freezer pea.	ALL COM FAR HARR HEN JOH LED MEY RAW SEED TER VES
SUNSET WONDER	64	24 in. vine, 5 in. pods; 10-12 peas per pod	Resistant to fusarium wilt.	EARL

►

◄ PEAS—BUSH

Variety	Days	Vines/Pods	Remarks	Sources
TWIGGY	68	24 in. vine, 3½ in. pods	Similar to Novella and Lacy Lady. Lots of tendrils for self-support.	FIS PIN
VEDETTE			Good all-purpose, very sweet pea. Remains sweet even under hot conditions. Use fresh, canned or frozen.	LEM
WAVEREX			West German variety. Grows well in cool climates. Pick when young, at 1/6 in. diameter. Staking required.	ECO LEM THO
WINFRIDA	100	15 in. vine	Wrinkled pea. Extremely cold-tolerant. Heavy crop potential. Good freezer variety.	THO

PEAS—BUSH
25 + INCHES

Variety	Days	Vines/Pods	Remarks	Sources
ALASKA (EARLIEST OF ALL)	56	26 in. vine, 2½ in. pods; 6-8 peas per pod	Heavy yields. Main variety for split pea soup. Resistant to fusarium wilt.	ARC BURG BURP BURR BUT DAN DEG EAR FAR FIS HEN HUM JOH LET MEY PAR PIN SEE VER WET WIL
ALMOTA	60	34 in. vine	Extremely disease-resistant. Very reliable producer. Use fresh, canned or frozen.	VER
EXTRA EARLY ALASKA	51	30 in. vine	Can be used as fresh or dried pea.	GUR HEN WYA
BLUE POD CAPUCIJNERS		4 ft. vine	Produces a heavy crop of grayish peas. For use as a dry pea.	SEE WILL
BOLERO		26 in. vine	Double- and triple-pod set. High yields. Resistant to fusarium wilt. Freezer type.	LET
EARLY FROSTY	64	28 in. vine, 4 in. pods; 7-8 peas per pod	Use fresh or frozen.	ALL BUT COM EAR TIL TWI
EARLY MARKET	58	36 in. vine, 5 in. pods; 7-9 peas per pod	High quality, heavy yielder. Peas retain their bright color when cooked.	FAR
EARLY MAY	55	3 ft. vine	Quick-growing. Heavy yielder. Succeeds in adverse weather. Yellow round-seeded type can also be used as a dry pea.	WILL
FRIZETTE	65	3 in. pods; 6-7 peas per pod	French variety. Stands cold weather well. Harvest these 'petit pois' when young. Real gourmet pea.	SHE
FROSTIRAY	55	2½ ft. vine; 8-9 peas per pod	2 pods per stem. Resistant to fusarium wilt. Easy to pick. Baby-pea type and very sweet.	WILL
GIANT STRIDE	73	28 in. vine, 5 in. pods; 8-10 peas per pod	Good freezer and canner.	BURG

►

◄

Variety	Days	Vines/Pods	Remarks	Sources
GREEN ARROW	62-70	28 in. vine, 4 in. pods; 9-12 peas per pod	High yields of very sweet peas.	ABU ALL BURP COM EAR EARL FAR FIS GAR GUR HARR HEN HIG HUM JOH JUN LAG LET MEY NIC PAR PIN PON POR RAW RIS STO TIL TWI VER VES WET WILL WYA
HOLLAND BROWN			Not for shelling green. Let ripen on the vine and thresh. Cook like dry beans. Old Dutch variety.	FIS
HOMESTEADER	67	2½ ft. vine, 3¼ in. pods	Vigorous and productive. Good canner and freezer.	EARL
HURST GREEN SHAFT	100	28 in. vine, 4½ in. pods; 9-11 peas per pod	Double-podded variety. Super-yielding.	THO
HYALITE	68	30 in. vine, 3½ in. pods	Dark green peas. Excellent for freezing.	FIS
ICER NO. 93	74		Half-dwarf vigorous vines. Heavy producer of large pods. Sweet and tender.	TIL
LINCOLN	66	3 ft. vine, 3 in. pods; 9 peas per pod	Not as disease-resistant as some newer varieties. Heirloom variety. Good fresh or frozen.	COO
MIRAGREEN	70	48 in. vine, 8-10 peas per pod	Very hardy. High sugar content.	JUN
MULTISTAR	70	4-5 ft. vine, 3 in. pods	Space saver with heavy yields. Heat-tolerant. Medium-small, sweet peas.	JOH THO
NIPPON KINUSAYA	50	Tall vine	Oriental variety. Light green pods. Sweet peas.	RED
ONWARD	72	30 in. vine	Reliable pea variety.	THO
PERFECTION DARK-GREEN	67	30 in. vine, 3 in. pods; 5-7 peas per pod	Good freezer variety.	GUR HEN TER
SIERRA MADRE DEL SUR			Mexican variety. Small-podded and sweet. Use either fresh or dried. Good soup pea. Plants resist aphids.	RED
SPRING	57		Good variety for freezing.	LET
THE PILOT		4 ft. vine	Large, deep green, pointed pods. Sow in spring or autumn. Hardy variety.	ECO
THOMAS LAXTON	65	3 ft. vine, 3½ in. pods; 7-9 peas per pod	High quality all-purpose pea. Grows well under wide variety of conditions.	ALL DEG GAR HEN HIG JOH MEY PIN POR VER VES WET WIL WYA
THOMAS LAXTON IMPROVED	62	36 in. vine, 3½ in. pods	Similar to Thomas Laxton but earlier.	LET
TITANTIA	65	28 in. vine, 11 peas per pod	Wrinkled pea. Double pods. Ideal for freezing.	THO

►

◀ PEAS—BUSH

Variety	Days	Vines/Pods	Remarks	Sources
TRIO	74	32 in. vine	Multi-podded variety. Extra high sugar content.	THO
VICTORY FREEZER	65	30 in. vine, 3½ in. pods	Excellent quality. Use fresh, canned or frozen. Heavy yields. Fusarium wilt-resistant.	GUR HEN
WANDO (MAIN CROP)	68	2½ ft. vine, 2½ in. pods; 7-8 peas per pod	Tolerant of dry, hot weather.	ABU ALL ARC BURG BURP COM DEG EAR EARL FAR GAR GUR HARR HEN HIG JOH JUN LAG LED LEM LET MEY PIN PLA PON POR RAW SEE SEED SOU TWI VER WES WET WIL
WORLD'S RECORD	58	28 in. vine, 4 in. pods; 7-9 peas per pod	Improved Gradus type. Good freezer.	ALL

PEAS

EXTRA-TALL

Variety	Days	Vines/Pods	Remarks	Sources
ALDERMAN (TALL TELEPHONE)	75	4-6 ft. vine, 5 in. pods; 8-9 peas per pod	Holds color well in cooking.	ABU ALL COM DAN ECO FAR GUR HUM LAG LED LET PIN RAW SEE SEED TER TIL VER WES WET WYA
FREEZONIAN	60	2½ ft. vine, 3½ in. pods; 7-8 peas per pod	Good variety for quick freezing and canning. Vigorous, wilt-resistant vines.	ALL ARC BURG BURP BURR DEG FAR HARR LED LET SEED WET WYA

PEAS—EDIBLE-PODDED

Variety	Days	Vines/Pods	Remarks	Sources
AGIO	58	24 in. vine	Double-podded variety. Good freezer. Crisp and sweet. Heavy producer. Good greenhouse variety.	THO
ASPARAGUS PEA	50	12 in. vine	Harvest pods at 1 in. or they develop fiber.	THO
BAMBY		Bush	French variety. Pods remain tender after peas have formed.	PAR LEM
BLIZZARD	63	30 in. vine, 3 in. pods	High quality, determinate pea. Pods are tender.	PAR
BURPEE'S SWEET POD SUGAR PEA	68	4 ft. vine, 4½ in. pods	Wilt-resistant. Can be prepared like snap peas and should be picked when peas are just visible.	WET
CAROUBEL		Vining	French edible-podded. Vigorous and well-adapted to warmer climates. Late producer.	LEM
CAROUBY DE MAUSSANE		3 ft. vine	Sugar-sweet pod. Snow-pea type.	ABU COO KIT

▶

Variety	Days	Vines/Pods	Remarks	Sources
DWARF GREY SUGAR	65	2½ ft. vine, 3 in. pods	Pick peas when still slender.	ABU COM DAN DEG EAR EARL FAR FIS GUR HEN JLH LET MEY MID PAR POR RED RIS ROS SEE SOU VER WES WET WILL WYA
DWARF WHITE SUGAR (CHINA SNOW)	50-65	30 in. vine 2½ in. pods	Pick pods when young. An Oriental delicacy.	ABU EAR EARL KIT TER
EARLY SNAP	58	24 in. vine, 3 in. pods	Heavy producer. Resistant to mosaic. Fleshy-podded variety.	FAR HARR HEN LET SEED
EDIBLE POD	65	Bush 3 in. pods	Tender, fleshy edible pods. Light green, curved pods.	ALL
GIANT DWARF SUGAR	65	2 ft. vine, 4 in. pods	Heavy producer. Fiber-free and tender if picked in slender stage.	WILL
HENDRIKS	60	3 ft. vine, 2½ in. pods	Does well in summer. White flowers. Very sweet taste, good raw or cooked.	SEE WILL
LITTLE SWEETIE	60	16 in. vine, 2½ in. pods	Non-fibrous peas with high sugar content. Can be harvested over a long period.	STO
MAMMOTH MELTING SUGAR	75	5 x 7/8 in. pods	Pods can be prepared like snap beans.	ABU ARC BURP COM DEG GUR HARR LAG LEM PAR RED SEE VER WYA
NORLI	50-58	1½ ft. vine, 2½ in. pods	White-flowered. Very sweet, crisp pods. Dutch variety. Prolific. Good freezer.	SEE SHE WILL
OREGON SUGAR POD	68	28 in. vine	High percentage of two pods. Resistant to pea enation virus.	ABU ARC DAN HIG HUM KIT LAG LED PLA RAW SEE SEED SUN THO TIL TWI VES WES
OREGON SUGAR POD II	68	28 in. vine, 4 in. pods	Multiple disease resistance. Tender, crisp and sweet. Stringless. Good freezer.	ABU BURP GAR HARR JUN MID NIC RIS TER VER
OSAYA ENDO		Pole type		KIT
POIS MANGETOUT GRACE	65		Harvest when young and peas are just visible.	HER
REMBRANDT	100	4 ft. vine, 5 in. pods	Sweet when picked immature. Indeterminate vines. Dutch variety. Long-season producer. Remains sweet even when large.	TER
SNAPPY	63	6 ft. vine, 4¾ in. pods	Plant Variety Protected. Resistant to powdery mildew. Thick, fleshy pods. Vines need support. Vigorous and productive.	BURP
SNOWBIRD	58	18 in. vine, 3 in. pods	Short-season variety. Space saver. For fall crop. Heavy yielder. Double and triple clusters.	BURP
SNOWFLAKE	58-72	2½ ft. vine, 4 x 1 in. pods	Dark green, straight, flat pods. Harvest when peas just begin to show, and while pods are still flat. Mild flavor. Resists powdery mildew.	JOH LED LET PLA WET

◀ **PEAS—EDIBLE-PODDED**

Variety	Days	Vines/Pods	Remarks	Sources
SNOW PEA (SUGAR PEA) (HO LOHN DOW)		Large pods		PON STO
SUGAR ANN		18 in. vine	Similar to Sugar Snap. Plump edible pods. Good compact space-saver variety.	ABU BURG BUT EAR EARL FAR FIS GAR GUR HARR HIG HUM JOH LED LET MEY NIC PIN PON POR RAW RIS SOU STO SUN TER THO TWI VER VES WET WILL
SUGAR BON	57	24 in. vine, 3 in. pods	Plant Variety Protected. Pod and pea are similar to Sugar Snap.	BURP COM HEN MEY PAR POR SUN TWI WIL
SUGAR DADDY	74	30 in. vine	Plant Variety Protected. Stringless snap pea. Compact plants are easy to pick.	BURP COM GUR HARR HEN HUM JUN LAG LED MEY NIC PAR POR RIS SEED STO TWI VER
SUGAR MEL	60-68	24 in. vine, 3 in. pods	Produces the largest pods of all the snap peas. Heavy cropper. Heat-tolerant. Resistant to powdery mildew.	BURR FIS GUR PAR PIN SHE SUN
SUGAR POP	60	18 in. vine, 3 in. pods	Resistant to powdery mildew and pea leaf roll. Excellent raw or frozen. Stringless snap pea.	PAR
SUGAR RAE	73	24-30 in. vine	Plant Variety Protected. Pods are similar, but more slender than Sugar Snap.	HUM LED MEY SOU WIL
SUGAR SNAP	70	6 ft. vine, 3 in. pods	Plant Variety Protected. Fleshy round, sweet edible pods. Plant early for highest yields.	ABU ALL ARC BURG BURP BURR BUT COM DAN DEG EAR EARL ECO FIS GAR HARR HEN HIG HUM JOH JUN KIT LAG LED LEM LET MEY MID NIC PAR PIN PLA POR RAW RED RIS ROS SEED SOU STO SUN TER THO TIL TWI VER WES WET WIL WILL WYA
SWEET SNAP	66	34 in. vine, 3 in. pods	Top yielder. Fiberless. Resists mildew and legume yellow virus. Vines need no support.	ARC DEG HEN LAG RAW VER WYA

COWPEAS
(Vigna sinensis)

Although they are called "peas", cowpeas are really more like beans in cultural requirements. There are several distinct types of pea, of which blackeye, crowder, and cream are the best known.

CULTURE: Plant 1½ to 2 inches deep, 2 to 4 inches apart, in rows 2½ to 3½ feet apart.

SEASON: Cool.

HARVEST: Harvest and shell peas before the pods turn yellow, or let the overly mature pods dry and shell the seeds.

SOUTHERN BLACKEYED PEAS

Variety	Days	Pods	Remarks	Sources
BIG BOY	60-65	10½ in. pods	Light green peas of excellent flavor. Easy to shell. Top quality.	POR WIL

▶

Variety	Days	Vines/Pods	Remarks	Sources
BLACKEYE SOUTHERN PEAS (COWPEAS)	60-85	6-8 in. pods	24 in. tall vigorous vines. Use green in summer, dried in winter.	BURG COM GUR HEN LAG LEJ MEY MID ROS VER
BLACKEYE NO. 5	95	6-8 in. pods	Vines are very prolific. Drought-tolerant. Excellent quality.	EAR LED LEM LET PAR POR WIL
CALIFORNIA BLACKEYE	75	7-8 in. pods	Use fresh or dried. Vigorous, heavy-yielding vines. Resistant to pea diseases.	PAR
CALIFORNIA BLACKEYE NO. 5		6-8 in. pods	Semi-spreading. Resistant to pea diseases. Use fresh or dried.	BURR WYA
EXTRA EARLY BLACKEYE	50	Straight	Bears a heavy, early crop.	DEG
MAGNOLIA BLACKEYE			Very high-yielding. Of excellent quality for canning or freezing.	PAR
QUEEN ANNE (BLACK EYE BEAN)	56-68	7-9 in. pods	Bushy, compact plant. Good canner or freezer. Large, smooth-skinned beans. Disease-resistant.	MEY SOU TWI VER WET WYA
RAMSHORN	60	7-9 in. pods	Wilt-resistant. Heavy yielder.	ARC WET

COWPEAS
CROWDER TYPE

Variety	Days	Pods	Remarks	Sources
BLACK CROWDER	70	12-15 peas per pod	Bush-type plant. Prolific yielder.	WET WIL
BLACKEYED CROWDER			Good producer. Fine flavor.	POR
BLACKEYE WHITE CROWDER		6 in. pods	Small seeds are white with small blackeye.	WIL
BLUE GOOSE (GRAY CROWDER) (TAYLOR)	80		Vine grows to 3 feet.	MEY WET WYA
BROWN-EYED SIX WEEKS	65		Small brown-eyed white peas.	WYA
BROWN CROWDER	74-85		Cream-colored seed turns brown when cooked. Vine type. Good producer. Fine flavor and quality.	ARC GUR HEN MID POR WET WIL WYA
BROWN SUGAR CROWDER	85-90	9 in. pods; 8-12 peas per pod	30 in. plant.	MEY
CALICO (HEREFORD) (POLECAT)			Seed is maroon, red and white. Good flavor.	POR SOU
COLOSSUS	75-80		Easily picked and shelled. Good producer.	POR WET WYA
CRIMSON (ARKANSAS)	75	6-7 in. pods	Erect Purple Hull type. Light brown, medium-size peas. Bush type. Excellent fresh, canned or frozen.	VER
KNUCKLE PURPLE HULL			Semi-vining. Very prolific.	POR WET WIL WYA

◀ COWPEAS

Variety	Days	Pods	Remarks	Sources
MISSISSIPPI CREAM			Large, plump off-white seeds with a dark eye.	WIL
MISSISSIPPI PURPLE HULL	70		Vigorous and healthy. Bright purple pods when mature, green when young. Good green or dry.	PAR WYA
MISSISSIPPI SILVER	64-70	6½ in. pods	Low, bushy plant. Prolific. Adapted to South or East.	EAR LAG LEM LET PAR POR RIS SOU TWI VER WET WIL WYA
PINKEYE PURPLE HULL	50-85	6-7 in. pods	18-24 in. plant. Often produces two crops. Good freezer. Excellent flavor.	HEN LAG RIS TWI VER WET WIL WYA
PURPLE HULL CROWDER	74		Freezes well. Heavy producer. Easy to shell.	ARC DEG GUR MID POR
TENNESSEE WHITE CROWDER	65		Vining type. Round seed with a light brown eye. Dark green pod at maturity stage.	WIL
WHITE PURPLE HULL	85	Purple	Large, plump, off-white seeds. Pole type. Good freezer.	PAR VER WIL

COWPEAS
CREAM

Variety	Days	Pods	Remarks	Sources
CREAM			Very sweet flavor.	POR
CREAM 8		Kidney-shaped	Bush-type plant.	WIL
CREAM 12		Round	Bush-type plant.	WIL
CREAM 40		6-8 in. Kidney-shaped	Orange-eyed seeds. Semi-bush.	WIL
ZIPPER CREAM			Off-white seed, small darker eye. An old-time favorite.	HEN POR

COWPEAS
OTHERS

Variety	Days	Pods	Remarks	Sources
BIG BOY	80	7-8 in. pods	Creamy seed with brown eye, but cooks up white. Large, prolific vine.	PAR VER
CORONET			A cross between a Pinkeye Purple Hull X and Iron Cowpea. Tolerant to bean and cucumber mosaic.	WIL
DIXIELEE	65	8 in. pods	An edible pod pea. Highly productive. For canning or freezing.	WIL WYA
WHIPPOORWILL	82		Old standard variety. Tall plant.	LAG POR WIL
WHITE LADY			Very prolific. Tiny, delicate bean.	WIL

PEPPERS, HOT
(Capsicum annuum)

Hot peppers have a wide range of hotness. Actually, there is no sure way to predict the hotness of any individual pepper, although each variety has its own range.

Usually the smaller the pepper, the hotter. Climate also affects hotness. Peppers grown in cool, moist climates are milder than the same variety grown in a hot, dry area.

When full size, the mature pepper will have reached maximum hotness. Most peppers are harvested at this stage. If left on the vine, most varieties will turn slowly red and become sweeter.

Hotness is concentrated in the interior veins, or ribs, near the seeds. Yellow or orange veins usually indicate that the pepper will be extra-hot for its variety.

CULTURE: See planting instructions under Peppers, Sweet.

SEASON: Warm.

INSECTS/DISEASES: See Peppers, Sweet.

HARVEST: Clip off peppers as soon as they turn a mature color. When growing hot peppers for dry storage, let them turn red before picking. Don't rub your eyes since the juice of the pepper is very irritating.

HOT PEPPERS
LONG, TAPERING

Variety	Days	Size/Color	Remarks	Sources
ANAHEIM CHILI (CALIFORNIA LONG GREEN) (CALIFORNIA CHILI)	80	8 x 1 in. Green to red when ripe	2 ft. high plants. Mildly pungent. Used extensively in the South and California.	ABU COO DEG GAR HEN HIG HOR JLH LAG PEP PIN PLA POR RED SEE SHE TER WES WIL
ANAHEIM IMPROVED	78			MID
ANAHEIM M	80	7 x 1¾ in. Green to red when ripe	Hot, medium flesh. 28-34 in. plant.	VER
ANAHEIM TMR 23	77	Long, tapered; green to red when ripe	Pungent, medium-thick walls. Good dried or fresh.	BURP NIC TWI
ANAHEIM TMR	70-80	Green to red	Used for canning, drying or frying. Mildly pungent.	BURR GUR PAR
BLACK DALLAS		5 in. Green and black to red when ripe	Hot. Large plant.	PET
CAYENNE LONG RED SLIM	70-75	6 x¾ in. Slim, pointed, wrinkled; green to red when ripe	20-24 in. plant is strong and spreading. Can be used for processing, drying and sauce.	ABU ARC COO EAR EARL GAR GUR HEN HIG HOR LAG LEJ MEY MID PAR PEP PIN PLA PON POR RED RIC RIS SHE TER TIL VER WES WET WIL WILL WYA
CAYENNE LONG THICK RED	70-74	7 x 2¼ in. Bright red when ripe	24 in. plant.	DEG HARR LED MID NIC PEP PIE RIS STO
CHIMAYO	95	Thin, curved; green to red when ripe	American southwest variety. 24-30 in. plant. Mild flavor when green; hot in red stage.	LEM PEP PLA SOU
DE COMIDA		4-6 in. Glossy red	Rather hot. Used in making 'mole'. Dries well.	RED
EASTER ROCKET	65	5 x 2 in. Ripens to red	Fine hot variety. Short-season variety.	PEP TER VES
ESPANOLA IMPROVED	70	Small point; red when ripe	Short-season variety. Medium walls. Uniform, heavy producer.	PLA ROS

◄ HOT PEPPERS

Variety	Days	Size/Color	Remarks	Sources
GOAT HORN	70	5 x 1 in. Green to cherry-red when ripe	Often curled and twisted. Easily dried.	SUN
GUAJILLO		4½ x 1¼ in.	Very hot. Good for drying. Mexican variety.	RED
HOT PORTUGAL	64	6 in. Pointed; ripens to bright red	Fiery-hot flesh.	GAR HARR PEP STO TER
HUNGARIAN WAX SHORT (RAINBOW WAXED)	60	Blocky; yellow to red	Thick-meated. Medium-hot. Heavy yields.	LAG LET WILL
HUNGARIAN YELLOW WAX (CAYENNE LONG THICK YELLOW) (BULGARIAN BANANA)	60-65	6 x 1¼ in. Light yellow to red when ripe	14-22 in. plant is moderately bushy. Medium-hot. Good type for pickling. Use fresh or canned.	ARC BURG BURP BURR COM DEG DIX EAR EARL GAR GUR HARR HEN HIG HOR JOH LED LEJ LET MEY MID NIC PEP PIE PIN POR RAW RIS SEE SEED STO TER TIL TWI VER WET WIL
LONG RED CAYENNE	70-75	5 x ½ in. Pointed; waxy yellow to bright red	Very hot variety.	ALL BURG BURP COM DIX LET PEP PET TWI
LONG RED MARCONI		5 x 1 in. Horn-shaped; red when ripe	European variety. Hot.	PEP RED
LONG THICK RED	60	4 in.	Very hot.	STO
LOUISIANA RED CAYENNE	52-70	5 x ¾ in. Green to red when ripe	A favorite hot variety used for canning, drying or as pickles.	PEA PEP
MEXICAN NEGRO		6 x 1½ in.		RED
MIRASOL		5 x 1 in.	Very hot! Name means 'It follows the sun'.	PEP RED
MULATO				SOU
NEW MEXICO CHILI	75	5 in. Green	Extra-hot. Use for chili rellenos.	LEM PEP RED
NEW MEXICO NO. 6		8 x 2 in. Bluntly pointed; green to red when ripe	Dries dark red to maroon. Mildly pungent.	PLA ROS
NEW MEXICO R NAKY	80	Medium-size	Mild chili. Excellent for cooking and drying.	HOR PLA POR
NEW MEXICO SANDIA		6-7 in. Green	Pungent. High yields. Sets fruits under hot growing conditions.	PEP
NU MEX BIG JIM (SLIM JIM) (NEW MEXICO BIG JIM)		8-12 in. 4-6 ozs.	16-24 in. plant. High yields of fleshy fruit. Good canner.	BURG BURR GRA GUR HOR MID PEP PLA POR ROS THO WES
NUMEX SIX		6 x 1½ in.	Mild to medium-hot.	WES
PASILLA		Long, slender; green to red to brown-black	Hot. Mexican variety. Used dried and toasted in sauces.	HOR

►

◄

Variety	Days	Vines/Pods	Remarks	Sources
PEPPERONCINI	65-75	5 in. Fiery red	Mildly hot. Southern Italy variety. Good pickler. Trim upright bushes.	HOR LEM LET NIC PEP PET POR SEE STO
PRETTY RED (hybrid)		6 x 1½ in. Green to red when ripe	Very pungent. Heat- and wet-tolerant.	GLE
RING OF FIRE	60	4 in.	Very hot and pencil-thin.	PEP SEE STO
ROUGE LONG (LONG RED) (GUINEA PEPPER)		5 x 1 in. Red when ripe	Ranges from mild to hot when ripe. Old 1500s European variety.	RED
ROMANIAN WAX		5 in. Tapers to a point; bright yellow to red when ripe	Medium-hot. Compact, vigorous plant.	HARR
SANDIA	80	Green to red	A very hot chili. A standard for hot-chili lovers.	BURR PLA ROS WES
SMALL RED CHILI	75	5½ x 2½ in. Pointed	Medium walls.	MEY WET
SUCETTE DE PROVENCE		Thin	Mediterranean variety. Hot.	LEM PEP
SUREFIRE (hybrid)			Vigorous growth under marginal conditions. Hot, thick, juicy walls.	TER
TABICHE	48	5 x ⅞ in.	From the Zapotec Indians of Mexico. Mildly hot.	RED
TORITO (hybrid)			Plants bear early. Good cool-summer grower.	COO
YUNG KO		Long, curved; dark green to red when ripe	Taiwan variety. Hot. Use fresh or dried.	HOR
ZIPPY (hybrid)	57	6 x ⅝ in.	Zesty, but not fiery hot. Plants bear until frost if kept picked. Can be dried for winter use.	BURP

HOT PEPPERS
CYLINDRICAL

Variety	Days	Size/Color	Remarks	Sources
ANCHO (POLANO)			36 in. plant. Great chili relleno.	GUR HOR LEM PEP RED SHE
ANCHO 101		Black-green to brown-red when ripe	Medium-hot. Used fresh, dried, powdered or for stringing.	POR
COLLEGE 64L		Medium-size; green to red when ripe	Mild. Use fresh for chili rellenos, roasted and peeled or dried and powdered.	HOR
COLORADO		Large	There is a Colorado mild and a Colorado hot. Use fresh or dried.	HOR

►

◀ **HOT PEPPERS**

Variety	Days	Size/Color	Remarks	Sources
DE ARBOL		2½ x ⅜ in.	Very hot. Known as 'Tree Chilis'. Does not seem to upset the stomach.	RED
EARLY JALAPENO	63	3 x 1½ in.	Extremely productive. Very hot with smooth thick walls.	GAR HIG HUM JOH JUN MID SHE TER TIL
HADES HOT	75	4 x ⅜ in. Green to red	Ornamental, bushy, small-leaved plant. East Indian variety.	PEP STO
JALAPA (hybrid)	65	2½ x 1 in. Blunt tip; green to red	High-yielding. Hot and spicy.	PIN TWI VER
JALAPENO	72-80	3½ x 1½ in. Green to red	Hot, thick walls. 26-36 in. plant. Popular pickler.	BURR COM COO DEG EAR FIS GLE GUR HEN HOR LAG LED LET MID NIC PEP PET PIN PON POR RED ROS SEE SOU STO WES WET
JALAPENO IMPROVED	75			MID
JALAPENO L	75	Blocky, short; dark green to red	Wildly hot pepper great for salsas. Develops thin, dry lines at full maturity.	LEM
JALAPENO M	75	3½ x¼ in. Dark green to red	Best pepper grown for dried hot-pepper seasoning.	ARC BURP HARR MEY PAR PIE PLA RIS TWI VER WIL WYA
PEPERONE SIGARETTA		Thin, green, cigarette-shaped	Especially grown for pickling in vinegar.	RED
PIQUIN	80	3 in.	Often seen growing in pots. Chilis grow erect from the top of the plant. A very hot, prolific pepper.	PLA
PUYA (SPUR)	60-70	3½ x 1 in.	Name means 'spur of the rooster'. 2 ft. plant. Very hot chili. Grows tapering and upward.	RED SUN
RELLENO	75	6½ x 2½ in. Green to red	Mildly hot. Can be used for stuffing.	GUR HEN PEP
SERRANO	75	2 x 2½ in. Dark green, tinged orange	Hot, hot, hot.	COO GUR HEN HOR LEM MID PAR PEP PIN POR RED RIS SHE THO WIL
SUPER CHILI (hybrid)	75	2½ in.	24 in. plant. Ideal for container, patio or windowsill. Hot chili.	VER
TAM MILD JALAPENO	65-70	3½ x 1½ Dark green to red	Blunt ends. 22-24 in. plant. Mildly pungent, medium-thick walls.	BURR EAR GUR HEN HOR LEM MID NIC PAR PEP TER TWI WIL
TAM MILD JALAPENO 1			Mild. Medium-tall plant. Virus-resistant. Easy to grow.	POR
YATSUFUSA		3½ in.	Japanese variety.	NIC RED

HOT PEPPERS
MEDIUM AND SMALL, TAPERING

Variety	Days	Size/Color	Remarks	Sources
FRESNO	78	2½ x 1 in. Green with a trace of red	24 in. high plant. Very pungent.	GUR HOR LAG PEP POR
PETER PEPPER		4 in. Green to red	Excellent pickler when green.	GLE
POINSETTA PEPPER		3 in.	Hot. Upright clusters on compact plant. Beautiful foliage. Lots of peppers.	PET
PURPLE PEPPER		1 in. Purple to red	Hot. Purple plants, purple peppers.	PET
RED CHILI	70-85	3 x ½ in. Green to red	18-20 in. plant. Very pungent chili used for drying or sauce.	ARC BURG DEG GUR HARR HEN LED LET PEP POR RED RIS TER
SANTAKA		3 in. Deep scarlet	Japanese variety grown in China. Very hot chili used for powder.	PEP RED
TABASCO	90-120	Greenish-yellow to scarlet	Super hot, hot.	PEP
TAI HOT		1½ in. Green to red	Chilis grow upright on bush. Asian pepper is medium-hot. Needs warm days and nights.	LAG LEM PEP PIN

HOT PEPPERS
YELLOW, WAXY

Variety	Days	Size/Color	Remarks	Sources
CALORO TMR	75	2½ x 1¼ in. Yellow-orange and waxy when mature	24 in. plant. Medium-hot chili.	HOR PEP
CASCABELLE		Long; yellow to orange	2 ft. vigorous plant.	LEM
FLORAL GEM GRANDE	75	1 x 2½ in. Yellow to red when ripe	20-24 in. plant. Use fresh, pickled or canned	HOR LAG MID PEP
GOLDSPIKE (hybrid)	75	2½ x 1½ in.	32-36 in. plant. Use for freezing or pickling.	HOR
KARLO	55	Pointed; yellow to red	Semi-hot.	HIG JOH PEP
ROUMANIA BLOCK TYPE MILD HOT	65	4 x 2½ in. Stubby; yellow to red	Medium-hot chili. 22-24 in. plant. Good canner.	HOR MID NIC RIS
SANTA FE GRANDE	75	3½ x 1½ in. Yellow to orange-red at maturity	25 in. plant. Use canned, fresh or pickled.	BURR GUR HOR MID PEP WES WIL
SZENTESI SEMI-HOT	60	4½ in. Lime-green to yellow-orange	Medium-hot. For indoor or outdoor growing.	STO
YELLOW SQUASH HOT		2 in. across. Golden-yellow	Very hot. Extremely productive.	POR

HOT PEPPERS
ROUND AND CLAW-LIKE

Variety	Days	Size/Color	Remarks	Sources
CHEROKEE			Hot. Small and round like a cherry.	PET
HABANERO		Yellow, wrinkled	Mexican variety. Hot. Grows best in warm, moist conditions.	LEM PEP POR
HOT APPLE	70	2½ x 1½ in. Butter-yellow	Semi-hot. Globe Cheese type.	STO
LARGE RED CHERRY	75	1¼ in. Green to red	Medium-hot. Primarily for canning and pickling.	BURP COM DEG EARL EVA GUR HARR HOR LAG LED LET MEY MID NIC PEP STO
PEQUIN		½ x ¼ in.	A wild chili that grows on a 4 ft. bush.	PLA RED
SMALL RED CHERRY	80	1 x¼ in. Green to red	18-20 in. plant. Very pungent chili used for pickling.	LET MID PEP PIN POR SEED VER
TEPIN		¼ in. Round	Hottest pepper known. Pods are dried for cooking. Southwest variety.	RED
TOKANOTSUME		2 x ¼ in. Small, narrow	Extremely hot variety that takes time to mature. Old-fashioned Japanese variety.	HOR PEP RED
VENEZUELAN PURPLE		¼ in. Purple to red	Leaves, stems, flowers and immature fruit are all purple-colored. Extremely hot.	RED

PEPPERS, SWEET
(Capsicum frutescens)

Peppers originally came to the attention of the Western world when explorers tasted the native American chili and mistook it for the spice 'pepper,' one of the trading spices from the Orient. The various sweet and hot peppers native to the 'New World' are related to the tomato and eggplant.

CULTURE: You can start peppers from seed or from plants purchased from a local nursery. If you are going to use seed, start them indoors in peat pots, two to four seed planted a half-inch deep in each. Do this about ten weeks before all danger of frost will be over, when you can plant outdoors. Plant pepper plants in the garden 18 to 24 inches apart, in rows 24 to 36 inches apart. Peppers like temperatures above 60 degrees and below 80 degrees. When the temperatures are out of this range on both sides, fruits do not seem to set well.

SEASON: Warm.

INSECTS/DISEASES: *APHIDS, BLISTER BEETLES, COLORADO POTATO BEETLES, CUTWORMS, FLEA BEETLES, LEAFHOPPERS, PEPPER WEEVILS AND GRUBS, THRIPS, TOMATO FRUITWORMS, TOMATO HORNWORMS, WHITEFLIES:* Use malathion, diazinon, pyrethrum, rotenone, Sevin or ryania.
ANTHRACNOSE, LEAF SPOT, EARLY BLIGHT: Use maneb, zeneb, nabam.

HARVESTING: Pick the bell peppers when they are firm and crisp. If green peppers are left on vine they will slowly turn red and become sweeter.

SWEET PEPPERS
BLOCKY GREEN

Variety	Days	Size	Remarks	Sources
ACE (hybrid)	60		3-4 lobes. Deep, glossy green.	ALL PEP PIN STO
ARGO (hybrid)	74	6½ x 5 in.	4 lobes. Extra-thick flesh. Heavy cropper.	GUR NIC POR RIS STO

◄

Variety	Days	Size	Remarks	Sources
BELL BOY (hybrid)	63-70	3¼ x 3½ in.	Glossy green to red at maturity. All-purpose pepper. 24 in. plant. Tolerant to tobacco mosaic virus.	ARC BURP COM EAR FAR GUR HEN JUN LAG LED LET MEY MID PEP PIN RIS SEED STO VER WET WIL
BELL CAPTAIN	72	Slightly elongated	Mosaic-resistant compact plant. 4 lobes. Thick, dark green walls.	LED LET MID PEP RIS STO TWI
BELL TOWER (hybrid)		Large, deep blocky	Green to red. 3-4 lobes. Large, sturdy vigorous plant with good foliage cover. Tobacco mosaic virus-resistant. Tolerant to potato Y virus.	HARR POR
BIG BELLE		4½ x 3¼ in. Blocky	4 lobes. High yields.	HEN LET
BIG BERTHA	70	6½ x 4 in.	3 lobes. Jumbo green pepper that turns red early. Thick walls. Tobacco mosaic virus-tolerant.	GRA GUR HEN JUN LAK LED LET MEY PAR POR RIS STO THO TWI VER WET
BLOCKY BELL (hybrid)	70	4 x 4 in.	18 in. plant. Heavy producer. 4 lobes. Sweet and crunchy. Tobacco mosaic virus-tolerant.	PAR
BULL NOSE (LARGE BELL) (SWEET MOUNTAIN)	55		Deep green to red. Pungent flavor.	ABU DEG PEP RED WET
BURPEE'S BELLRINGER	75	3½ x 4½ in.	Glossy green to red. 4 lobes with extra-thick walls. Heavy cropper.	EAR
BURPEE'S TASTEY (hybrid)	70		Dark green to scarlet when mature. 3 lobes, medium-thick walls. Sturdy spreading plant.	BURP
CADICE		Large	French variety. Thick flesh. Does well in cool areas. Vigorous grower. Green to crimson red. Sweet flavor.	PEP SHE
CALIFORNIA WONDER	75	4½ x 4 in.	Big, thick-walled stuffing pepper.	ALL ARC BURG BURP BURR COM DAN DEG DIX EAR EARL FAR FIS GUR HEN HUM LED LEJ LET MEY NIC PEP PIE PIN PON POR RED RIS STO TIL VER WET WIL WYA
CALIFORNIA WONDER 300 TMR	71	4 in.	Emerald-green. 24-28 in. plant.	HARR MID SOU TWI
CALWONDER	63	4 in.	Green to bright crimson. 3-4 lobes. Thick walls. Dwarf plant. Heavy producer.	ALL HARR MID
CANAPE (hybrid)	60	2½ x 3½ in.	3 lobes. Green to red. 20-25 in. plant. Heavy yields.	HARR NIC
CHINESE GIANT		6 x 5 in.	Dark green to brilliant cherry color. Sweet flesh.	GLE
CRISPY (hybrid)	70	2½ x 3½ in.	3-4 lobes. Green to red. Thick, sweet walls.	BURP

►

SWEET PEPPERS

Variety	Days	Size	Remarks	Sources
EARLIRED			Extremely early bell type.	SEE
EARLY BANQUET (hybrid)	65-72	4 x 3 in.	3 lobed, medium-size walls. 24-26 in. plant. Resistant to tobacco mosaic virus. Semi-con-centrated fruiting habit.	SEED
EARLY BOUNTIFUL (hybrid)	58-65	2¾ x 3 in.	Dark green to red. Tolerant of mosaic. Upright plant.	NIC
EARLY CALIFORNIA			Sweet and mild.	SEE
EARLY CALWONDER	70	4 x 4 in.	Green to red. Vigorous, compact plant bears 12 peppers.	COM DEG JUN WILL
EARLY CANADA BELL	67	4 x 4 in.	26 in. plant. Extra-thick walls. Tolerant to tobacco mosaic.	STO
EARLY NIAGARA GIANT	65	4½ in.	Green to red. 3-4 lobes with thick walls. 24 in. plant. Sets well during cool summers.	GAR STO
EARLY PROLIFIC (hybrid)	57		Short-season variety. Good drying pepper.	COM DAN THO WILL
EARLY THICK SET	48		4 lobes, thick walls. Borne in clusters of 12 or more. Vigorous plant. Green to scarlet red. Excellent quality.	PAR
EMERALD GIANT	74	4½ x 3¾ in.	4 lobes, thick walls. Vigorous plant is mosaic-tolerant.	BURR DEG LET MEY MID PEP PIE RIS TIL
FOUR CORNERS	71	5 in.	4 lobes. Thick walls. Tobacco mosaic virus-resistant.	LET PEP STO
GATER BELLE (hybrid)		4 x 3¾ in.	24-26 in. plant. High yields. Bright green. 3-4 lobes. Tobacco mosaic virus-resistant.	WET
GEDEON (hybrid)	78	Extra-large	Great stuffing pepper. Thick walls.	BURP
GIANT ACE (hybrid)	78		18-22 in. plant. 4 lobes. Very productive.	MID
GRANDE RIO	66	4 x 3½ in. Blocky	Thick walls. Dark green to red. Upright, vig-orous plant with good foliage cover. Resis-tant to tobacco mosaic virus.	HARR
HYBELLE (hybrid)		Blocky	3-4 lobes, thick walls. Glossy green to red. Large, vigorous upright plant. Tobacco mosaic virus-resistant.	HARR
JUPITER (op)	66	4½ in.	Dark green to red. Very thick walls. Dense bushy plant gives good protection from sun scald.	MEY MID PEP RIS STO TWI
KEYSTONE RESISTANT GIANT	70-80	4½ x 3½ in.	4 lobed, thick walls. Tolerant to tobacco mosaic virus.	ARC BURR DEG DIX HARR HEN LET MID PEP POR RIS SOU TER WET WIL WYA

Variety	Days	Size	Remarks	Sources
KEYSTONE RESISTANT GIANT NO. 3	73		4 lobes. Very thick, sweet walls. 28 in. plant.	MEY MID PIE
KING OF THE NORTH (RUBY KING)	57-65	6 x 3½ in.	3 lobes. Takes cold well. Mildly sweet.	ABU GUR PEP SEE
LADY BELL	68	4 in.	3-4 lobes. Good stuffer. Compact plant.	DIX HARR LED PIE
LINCOLN BELL	68	4 in.	Very dark green. 3-4 lobes, thick walls. Sets well in cooler weather.	STO
MA BELLE (hybrid)	62	4 in.	Thick walls. Tobacco mosaic virus-tolerant.	FAR PEP PIE RIS STO
MARTINDALE	63	3½ x 3½ in.	3-4 lobes. Good yields. Tobacco mosaic virus-tolerant.	STO
MERCURY TMR	75	4½ in.	Dark green. 4 lobes. Compact plant. Sets well in hot, dry weather.	MID PEP RIS
MERRIMAC WONDER	68	3½ x 3½ in.	Green to red. 4 lobes. Short-season variety. Sets in cold weather.	JLH PEP SOU
MEXI BELL (hybrid)	70		First bell pepper with mild chili flavor. 3-4 lobes. 26 in. upright plant has good leaf cover. Sweet flesh. Seeds and ribs have the chili flavor. Tolerant to tobacco mosaic virus.	JUN LET VER
MICHIGAN WONDER	68	4½ x 3½ in.	Green to red, extremely thick flesh. Good flavor and yields.	BURG
MIDWAY	70	4½ x 4½ in.	Green to red. 3-4 lobes. Mild, sweet flavor. Thick walls. 18-24 in. plant. Mosaic-tolerant.	COM DIX HARR LET PEP RIS SOU
NEW ACE (hybrid)	68	3½ x 4 in.	Short-season variety. Short, sturdy plant. 3-4 lobes. Medium-thick walls. Good freezer.	BURP VES
OZARK GIANT	68		4 lobes. Thick walls.	PEP SEE
P 342 (hybrid)	72	4½ x 4½ in.	4 lobes. Dark green to yellow-golden. Mild and sweet.	LED
PARK'S WHOPPER IMPROVED	71	4 x 4 in.	4 lobes. ¼ in. thick walls hold up well for cooking and stuffing.	PAR
PICK ME QUICK	65		Firm and meaty. Withstands cool springs and hot summers.	GUR
PIP	75	Blocky	4 lobes. Dark green to scarlet.	LET
PERMAGREEN			Deep green pepper that retains its color when mature.	FAR SEE
PRO BELL 11	72		4 lobes. 26 in. plant. High yields. Tobacco mosaic virus-resistant.	TWI
PURPLE BELLE (hybrid)	72	3½ x 3½ in.	Green to deep purple to red. 4 lobes. Compact plant.	BURP PAR

◀ **SWEET PEPPERS**

Variety	Days	Size	Remarks	Sources
QUARDRATI D' ASTI RED			Italian variety. 3-4 lobes. Superb flavor.	LEM PEP
RINGER (hybrid)	62	Slightly elongated	Firm, 3-4 lobes. Dark green to red. Good foliage cover. Resists tobacco mosaic.	JOH
RUBY GIANT	72	5 x 3½ in.	Large plant. Thick flesh. Green to red.	DEG EARL SOU
SHAMROCK (hybrid)		Medium to large	4 lobes. Glossy green. Resistant to tobacco mosaic virus.	POR
SLIM PIM	65	4 in.	Produces immense crop of little peppers. All-purpose variety.	DEG PEP POR
STADDON'S SELECT (MISSILE)	72		4 lobes, thick walls. Dependable.	GAR FIS JOH MID PLA RAW SEE SOU STO TER VES
TITAN	80		4 lobes, thick walls. Yolo type. Mosaic-resistant.	HOR
TOKYO BELL (hybrid)	57	Medium to large	Sturdy plant grows clusters of peppers. Dark green to red. Stays mild and sweet.	EAR
TWIGGY	75		Huge yields. Fruits form on top of the plant.	THO
VALLEY GIANT (hybrid)		Large	4 lobes. Thick walls. Tobacco mosaic virus-resistant.	DAN MID PEP TWI
VIOLETTA (hybrid)			Dutch variety. True purple to lustrous red. Turns green when cooked. Compact plant.	COO LEM
WORLD BEATER	74		Sweet. Green to red.	BURG DEG
YOLO WONDER	77	4 x 4¾ in.	4 lobes, thick walls. Good processor type. Mosaic-tolerant.	ARC DEG ECO GUR LEJ MID PEP POR STO
YOLO WONDER IMPROVED	77			LAG
YOLO WONDER B	77	4 x 4 in.	4 lobes. Dark green thick walls. Mosaic-resistant.	BURR HARR PIE WIL
YOLO WONDER L	75	4 x 3¾ in.	Taller than Yolo Wonder B. Resistant to mosaic.	BURR DIX JUN LET PON RIS TWI WET
YOLO WONDER L IMPROVED	75	Extra-large	Dark green to red. 3-4 lobes.	HARR LED

SWEET PEPPERS

RED

Variety	Days	Size	Remarks	Sources
EARLIEST RED SWEET			Standard lobe shape. Bright red. Fruit is not uniform.	RAW

▶

Variety	Days	Size	Remarks	Sources
EARLY RED SWEET	55	3 x 4 in.	Fiery red. 3-4 lobes. Small plant.	STO
ITALIAN RED MACARONI		12 x 3 in.	Sweet. Ripens to bright red.	ABU COO
PETER PIPER (hybrid)	57	4 in.	Bright red. 11-12 fruit per plant.	FAR
SHEPHERD	68	7 in.	Pointed. Thick walls. Strong, bushy plant.	LET
STOKES EARLY (hybrid)	60		Red. 3-4 lobes. Short-season variety.	STO
SUPER SET	64	4 x 5 in.	Early red variety. Compact plant. Medium-thick walls.	STO
VINEDALE (hybrid)	60-65	4 x 2 in.	Pointed. 3-4 lobes. 14 in. plant.	MID STO

SWEET PEPPERS

LONG

Variety	Days	Size	Remarks	Sources
CORNO DI TORO RED		8 in.	Red version of yellow variety. Great in pickling marinade. Heirloom variety.	COO LEM
CORNO DI TORO YELLOW		8 x 1½ in.	Called the bull's pepper. Not real sweet, but distinctly peppery.	LEM
EARLY SWEET BANANA	65	6 x 1¾ in. Tapered	Pale, waxy yellow fruit.	GAR STO VER
GIANT YELLOW BANANA	60	7 in.	Hungarian variety. 26 in. plant. Hybrid-like yields. Thick flesh.	STO
HUNGARIAN YELLOW WAX	65	6 x 1½ in. Tapered	Waxy yellow. 18-20 in. plant.	DEG EARL HEN PEP
ITALIA	55	8 x 2½ in.	Similar to Corno di Toro. Green to dark crimson red. Easy to grow. Full of flavor.	JOH PEP
ITALIAN SWEET	60	6 x 2½ in. Tapered to blunt end	Sweetest of all peppers. Deep green to bright red. Dwarf upright plants. Space saver.	BURG DEG HOR LAG LET PAR PEP SOU TER
JIMMY NARDELLO				PEP
LAMUYO (hybrid) (ROUGE ROYALE)		8 in.	3 lobes. French variety. Green to red. Mild, sweet flavor.	LEM
LONG GREEN FUSHIMI		6 in.	Japanese variety. Bright glossy green. Tall, vigorous plant. Very prolific.	LEM PEP
LONG SWEET BANANA (SWEET HUNGARIAN)	58-70	6 x 1½ in.	Yellow to red. 18-22 in. plant. Medium-thick walls. Use fresh or for pickling.	ABU ARC BURP BURR BUT COM DAN DEG EAR GUR HARR HOR HUM LAG LED LET MID NIC PAR PEP PIN PON POR RIS SOU STO TWI WET WILL WYA
MARCONI YELLOW		12 x 3 in.	Italian variety. 3 lobes. Large plant.	COO

◀ **SWEET PEPPERS**

Variety	Days	Size	Remarks	Sources
MIDAL (hybrid)	73	8 in. Oval	Cream-colored. Very tall plant is vigorous. Turns reddish-orange at full maturity.	PIN
MILD CALIFORNIA		6 x 1½ in. Wrinkled	Paprika pepper grown for dehydration when in red stage. 30-36 in. plant is upright and spreading.	VER
MOGDOR (hybrid)		Long, 8 ozs; slightly pointed	Good yellow color. Mild, sweet, thick and meaty. Extremely prolific plant.	LEM
PAPRIKA PEPPER	80		Flat, thin-fleshed, 2-celled pepper. Red when ripe. Excellent drying variety.	LEM NIC PEP POR SEE SOU
SUPER SHEPHERD	68	7½ in. Tapered	Thick flesh, dark red color. Distinct sweet, juicy flavor. Good processor and freezer.	LET PEP STO
SWEET SPANISH	68	Long	French variety.	HER PEP
TA TONG		Elongated	Fine, sweet flavor. Taiwan variety. Dark green to red.	HOR
TOP BANANA (hybrid)	65	5 x 1¼ in.	Very sweet, vigorous and productive. Medium-thick walls.	JUN LED PIN POR TER THO TWI
TRITON	70		Space-saver variety. Grow in 6 in. pot. Highly productive. Good freezer.	THO

SWEET PEPPERS

SPACE SAVERS

Variety	Days	Size	Remarks	Sources
PARK'S POT HYBRID	45		A 10-12 in. plant that bears heavy crop.	PAR
PARK'S TEQUILA SUNRISE		4-5 in.	12-14 in. plant, 12 in. wide. Peppers are deep green to warm golden orange.	PAR
TRITON	70		Grows in 6 in. pot. Highly productive. Good freezer.	THO

SWEET PEPPERS

YELLOW/ORANGE

Variety	Days	Size	Remarks	Sources
BUTTER BELLE	70	2½ x 2¾ in.	12 in. plant is vigorous and heavy-yielding. 3-4 lobes. Extra-thick flesh. Butter-yellow color.	STO
CAL WONDER GOLDEN	75	3½ x 3½ in.	Medium-thick walls. Upright plant.	BURP LET PEP RIS WET
CUNEO (op)		Size of a softball and pointed	Bright yellow. Italian variety.	LEM PEP
GARDEN SUNSHINE		Large	Yellowish-green. Excellent quality. Bushy plant. Mild flavor.	GLE PEP
GIANT SZEGEDI	70	5 x 3 in.	Similar to Yellow Romanian.	PEP STO

Variety	Days	Size	Remarks	Sources
GOLD CREST (hybrid)	62	Medium-large	3-4 lobes. Dark glossy green turns golden yellow. Resistant to fruit rot, spot and rus-setting. Very sweet taste.	JOH PEP
GOLDEN BELL (hybrid)	65	4 x 3½ in.	Golden color when mature. 3-4 lobes. Compact, vigorous, high-yielding plant.	EARL HARR LET MEY MID PIN POR SEED TER VER TWI WIL
GOLDEN PEPPER P-324 (hybrid)		Medium	Short-season variety. 3-4 lobes. Dark green to golden yellow.	TIL
GOLDEN SUMMER (hybrid)	67	4 x 3½ in.	4 lobes. Soft lime-green to rich golden yellow. Vigorous plant has lush foliage and resistant to tobacco mosaic virus.	COO EAR GUR HEN JOH LAG PAR PEP RIS
GOLDIE	60	2¼ in.	16 in. plant. 3-4 lobes. ¼ in. sweet flesh.	STO
GOLD STAR	70		For greenhouse or frame growing. Superb quality. Good drying variety. Sweeter than reds.	THO
GYPSY (hybrid)	65	4¼ x 2¼ in.	16-20 in. plant. Sweet Italian type. Short-season variety. Thick, pale yellow walls.	BURG BURP COM DAN EAR FAR FIS GUR HARR HIG JUN LED LEM LET MID NIC PAR PEP PIN POR RIS STO TER THO TIL TWI VER WILL
HERCULES YELLOW GOLDEN	79		Large, sweet and mild.	PEP
HONEYBELLE (hybrid)		Slightly elongated	3-4 lobes. Thick walls. Green to golden yellow. Large, vigorous plant. Resistant to tobacco mosaic virus.	HARR
ITALIAN GOLD	68		Flesh is thick. Plants are short and bushy with 6 to 8 pendant fruit per plant. Space-saver variety. Ripens yellow to gold to orange to red.	STO
KARLO	50		Yellow Romanian type. Sets well in cool weather. Good stuffing pepper.	GAR PEP
KEY LARGO (hybrid)		7 x 2½ in.	Yellow-green to orange-red. Medium-large plant. Good foliage cover. Cubanelle type.	HARR
KLONDIKE BELL	72	4½ in. Square	Can be grown outside or in a green-house. Ripens dark green and turns gold. Tobacco mosaic virus-tolerant.	STO
PETITE SIRAH (hybrid)		3 in. Conical	For making sweet pickled peppers. Sets under cool conditions.	TER
QUADRATI D' ASTI YELLOW			Italian variety. Usually 4 lobes. Superb flavor. Deep gold color.	LEM
QUADRATO D' ORO (hybrid)			Dutch variety. Golden. Productive and disease-resistant plant. Good leaf coverage.	PEP SHE
SUMMER SWEET 860 (hybrid)	86	4½ x 3½ in.	Medium-green to yellow. 4 lobes.	PEP PIE TWI
SUMMER SWEET 820 (hybrid)	86	4½ x 4½ in.	22 in. plant. TMV- and PVY- resistant. 4 lobes.	TWI

◀ SWEET PEPPERS

Variety	Days	Size	Remarks	Sources
SUPER STUFF	67	6 x 3¾ in.	Deep Butter Belle type. Good stuffer. 3-4 lobes. ¼ in. thick flesh. Good greenhouse variety.	STO
SWEET PICKLE	65	2 in. Oval	12-15 in. plant. Perfect for pickled peppers. Thick walls, sweet and tasty. Turns from yellow to orange to red to purple.	PAR PEP SEE
SWEET ROMANIAN YELLOW	67-80	4 x 2½ in.	Waxy yellow. 22-24 in. plant.	HOR LET
WONDER GOLD	55		Glossy green to golden yellow. 3-5 lobes. 20 in. plant. Short-season variety.	PEP
YELLOW BELLE	65	3½ x 3 in.	Turns bright red if left to mature. 4 lobes, medium-thick walls. Mild flavor.	JUN LET STO

SWEET PEPPERS
HEART- OR TOMATO-SHAPED

Variety	Days	Size	Remarks	Sources
BURPEE'S EARLY PIMENTO	68	2½ x 3½ in.	Heart-shaped. Heavy walls.	BURP
CANADA CHEESE	75	2 x 1¼ in.	Ripens green to red. Excellent for pickling. A miniature red pimento.	STO
CHERRY		1½ in. Round	Red. Sweet, non-pungent. Use for salads, canning or stuffing to serve as appetizers.	GLE
EARLY SWEET PIMENTO	73	2½ x 3 in.	Flat, tomato-shaped. Mild and sweet.	SEE
GAMBO	90	2½ x 4 in.	Pimento type. Excellent pickling type. Flat globe, mostly four lobes. Rich deep red color. Crisp and sweet. Medium-tall vigorous plant.	GLE PEP SEE
LIPSTICK	53	5 in. Tapered to blunt point	Dark green that ripens to glossy red. Thick flesh. Nice cooked or in salads or for roasting. Dependable heavy yields.	JOH PEP
PIMENTO (PERFECTION)	65-80	3 x 2½ in.	Dark green to red when ripe. Smooth, heart-shaped. Thick walls are sweet and flavorful.	ABU ARC COM DEG HARR HOR LAG LEM LET NIC PEP PIN POR ROS SOU WET
PIMENTO L	75	3½ in.	Dark green to deep red. Heart-shaped. Concentrated fruit.	RIS SEED WIL
PIMENTO SELECT	73-75		Heart-shaped, dark green. 33 in. plant. Peppers have thick walls.	GUR HEN PAR PEP
SUNNYBROOK (TOMATO PEPPER) (CHEESE) (SWEET SQUASH)	65-73	2½ x 3¼ in.	Deep green to red. Tomato-shaped. 23-28 in. upright plant. Mild flavor.	MID STO
SUPER RED PIMENTO	70	5 x 3¼ in.	Flat-shaped pimento type. Ripens green to red. Tobacco mosaic virus-tolerant.	STO

Variety	Days	Size	Remarks	Sources
SWEET SPANISH		1 x 2 in.	Very old variety. Mild and good for stuffing.	RED
YELLOW CHEESE PIMENTO	73		Ripens green to yellow to orange. Large squash-shaped fruit.	PEP SEE STO

SWEET PEPPERS
OTHER TYPES/COLORS

Variety	Days	Size	Remarks	Sources
ACONCAGUA	75		Frying type. Yellow to green to red.	GLE HOR PEP SEE
ALBINO PEPPER		Bell-shaped	White to red. Space-saver variety. Extra-dwarfed bush.	GLE PEP SEE
CANAPE (hybrid)	51	2 x 2½ in.	Sets well under cooler temperatures. Heat and drought-tolerant. 3 lobes. 20 fruits per plant. Medium-thick walls.	VER
CHERRY SWEET (RED CHERRY SWEET)	78	1 x 1½ in. Round	20 in. plant. Perfect pickler. Use red or green.	BURG BURP BURR DEG GLE GUR HARR HEN HOR LAG LED LET MID NIC PEP POR RIS SEE STO TER
CHOCO			Pimento type, chocolate-colored. Good stuffer.	GLE PEP
CHOCOLATE BELL (hybrid) (SWEET CHOCOLATE)	75	4½ in.	Dutch variety. Not a true hybrid. Turns tan, dark brown to red. Very rare seed.	STO
CUBANELLE	66	2 x 2½ in.	Yellow-green to red. Italian type. Medium-thick walls. Excellent fryer.	BURR COM DIX GAR GLE HARR HOR LET PAR PEP PIN POR RIS SEE SEED STO TER
CUBANELLE IMPROVED	68		Frying type. Bright waxy yellow-green to red. Snappy flavor.	TWI
FRY KING (hybrid)	63	¾ in. Tapered to blunt tip	Cubanelle type. Yellow-green. 18 in. plant. Thick, sweet flesh.	TWI
LORELEI PURPLE BELL			Dutch variety. Deep purple exterior, green interior. 4 lobes. Sturdy plant.	PEP SHE
PURPLE BELL	68	4½ in. Blocky, square	European variety. 4 lobes. Bushy compact plant. Keep fruit well protected from sun. Green to purple to blood-red. Tobacco mosaic virus-tolerant.	STO
SUPER SWEET CHERRY	75	1¾ in.	Red to green. Good crack tolerance. Tobacco mosaic virus-tolerant.	STO TWI

POTATOES
(Solanum tuberosum)

The potato, a member of the same family as the tomato and the eggplant, is one of the most popular dinner-plate vegetables grown today. Potatoes are basically tubers grown underground at the end of short stems.

You have many choices in colors and shapes.

CULTURE: You can either purchase potato seed or buy certified seed potatoes. Cut pieces about 1½ inches square with one good eye per piece. Sow seed pieces with the cut side down, 4 inches deep, 12 inches apart, in rows 24 to 36 inches apart. When the plants are

5 to 7 inches high, scrape the soil from between the rows and hill around the plant. Cover the stems with soil (potatoes exposed to light turn green).

SEASONS: Potatoes prefer long, cool seasons with temperatures that seldom rise above 65 degrees.

INSECTS/DISEASES: *APHIDS, COLORADO POTATO BEETLES, CUTWORMS, FLEA BEETLES, LEAFHOPPERS,*

SPIDER MITES: Use Sevin, malathion. pyrethrum, rotenone or ryania.

WHITE GRUBS: Use diazinon as soil treatment before planting.

LATE BLIGHT, EARLY BLIGHT: Apply maneb or zineb.

HARVESTING: Dig early varieties when flowers form on the plants. For later varieties, yellowing and dying vines indicate that tubers have reached maturity. Store in a cool, dark place.

POTATOES
RED

Variety	Days	Color/Shape	Remarks	Sources
BISON		Light reddish skin, pale yellow flesh; round	Mid-season variety. Medium-size tuber. Good yields. Good resistance to late blight and scab.	HEN
Mc NEILLY		Red skin, light yellow flesh	Sets potatoes all season. Excellent keeper. Everbearing variety.	HEN
NORLAND		Oblong	Shallow eyes. Good yields.	BURG EAR EARL FAR FIS FOS GUR HEN JUN TIL WET
RED PONTIAC		Red, round	Heavy yields. Shallow eyes.	BURG BURP EAR EARL FAR LED PAR
RHINERED		Red, round	Mid to late variety. Adaptable to most soils. Resistant to scab and verticillium wilt.	JUN
RUBY CRESCENT		Deep pink skin, yellow flesh	Fingerling type. All-purpose variety.	SEE
SANGRE	107	Red, 3 in. Round	Good keeping qualities.	PAR
VIKING (hybrid)	70	Red skin	Jumbo-size potatoes. Very prolific. Drought-resistant. Good boiling potato.	EAR EARL GUR

POTATOES
WHITE

Variety	Days	Color/Shape	Remarks	Sources
CHIPPEWA	110	Oblong	Good short-season variety. Shallow eyes.	LED
CRYSTAL (hybrid)		White skin, white flesh	Reliable and disease-resistant. All-purpose potato.	GUR
GREEN MOUNTAIN		White flesh	Dependable old-timer.	LED SEE
IRISH COBBLER	100	Round	Eyes are strong and deep-set.	GUR LED
KATAHDIN	110	Glossy white skin	Shallow eyes.	LED MEY
KENNEBEC	115	Smooth	Great yields. Shallow eyes. Vigorous vines.	BURG BURP EAR EARL FOS GUR HEN JUN LED MEY TIL
NORCHIP		Smooth	Ideal for chips and potato dishes.	FOS

Variety	Days	Color/shape	Remarks	Sources
SEBAGO	110	Oval	Blight-resistant. Stores for long periods. Heavy yields.	FOS
SUPERIOR		Smooth, oval	Shallow eyes. Does not gray or discolor after cooking.	DIX FAR JUN LED
WHITE COBBLER		Smooth, oval; light skin, white flesh	Early variety. Adapts to almost any growing conditions. All-purpose potato.	BURP HEN PEA
WHITE ROSE		Long and flattened	Early variety. Does not store well.	TIL

POTATOES
RUSSET

Variety	Days	Color/Shape	Remarks	Sources
BUTTE		Long; brownish skin, white flesh	Late variety. Russet-shaped tubers. Good baker, boiler or for frying. Good disease resistance.	GUR HEN
LEMNI RUSSET		Oblong; white flesh	Seldom knobby.	EARL
MAYFAIR		Creamy buff skin	Medium-large tubers. Shallow eyes. High yields.	EAR
NETTED GEM			Late variety. Excellent keeper. Good baker.	TIL
NORGOLD RUSSET		Golden netting, white flesh	Early variety. Scab-resistant.	BURG FAR FOS GUR HEN MEY WIT
RUSSET BURBANK		Oblong; white flesh	Late variety. Good all-purpose potato.	EARL FIS FOS HEN PAR
RUSSET CENTENNIAL	120	Brown skin, white flesh	Known as a white baking potato.	PAR

POTATOES
OTHER COLORS

Variety	Days	Color/Shape	Remarks	Sources
ALL BLUE POTATO		Blue skin, blue flesh	Has good flavor baked or boiled. Good yields.	GUR SEE
BENTJI		Waxy yellow skin, yellow flesh	Early to mid-season variety. 1910 variety. Virus-free. Good yielder. Widely adapted. Good keeper.	EARL SEE
FINGERLINGS		1 in. Yellow skin, yellow flesh	Boil with jackets on.	JUN
GERMAN YELLOW		4 x 1 in. Yellow skin, yellow flesh	Unique texture and flavor.	GAR
LADY FINGER		5 x 1 in. Golden brown skin, yellow flesh	Fingerling type. Good fried or in salad. Good yields.	GUR

◀ **POTATOES**

Variety	Days	Color/Shape	Remarks	Sources
PURPLE		Dark purple skin, purple with white veins inside	Lightens when cooked. Good flavor.	GAR
PURPLE PERUVIAN				PEA
URGENTA		Red skin, yellow flesh	Sold as 'new potatoes'.	SEE
YELLOW FINN		Yellow flesh	Good for boiling or baking.	SEE TIL
YUKON GOLD		Yellow flesh	Early to mid-season variety. All-purpose variety. Good yields. Keeps well.	EARL

POTATOES
TRUE POTATO SEEDS

Variety	Remarks	Sources
DESIREE	Plant late spring, harvest mid-August. Red skin.	THO
EXPLORER	120 days. Medium-size tubers with white skin and white flesh. Adaptable and disease-resistant.	GUR HUM PIN
TRUE POTATO SEEDS		DAN THO
HOMESTEAD (hybrid)	90 days. 4 in. tubers. Grows big potatoes and continues to grow larger into the summer.	PAR

PUMPKINS
(Cucubita maxima)

Nearly everyone loves pumpkins. They're great for canning, for pies or for Halloween jack-o-lanterns. The majority of the pumpkins are the vining type, with vines that spread as much as 20 to 25 feet. Some varieties, however, are called bush and require much less space. Pumpkins vary greatly in size and shape, from the huge varieties weighing in at over four hundred pounds, to the very small hand-size types.

CULTURE: Start from seeds as soon as the ground warms up in the spring. Transplanting sets pumpkins back. Plant seeds 1 to 1½ inch deep, 24 to 36 inches apart, in rows 72 to 120 inches apart. Or plant in hills, three seeds per hill, 5 feet between hills. When the plants are about 2 inches high, remove all but the one strongest plant from each hill.

SEASONS: Warm.

INSECTS/DISEASES: See Squash, Summer.

HARVESTING: When the pumpkin is ready to pick the skin darkens and becomes tough, and the vines dry up. Cut pumpkins before a heavy frost, leaving 3 to 4 inches of stem on the pumpkin.

PUMPKINS
EXTRA-LARGE

Variety	Days	Size/Shape	Remarks	Sources
ATLANTIC GIANT	115-120	400 plus pounds	Bright orange rind. Small seed cavity. Thick and meaty.	FAR GLE GUR HEN JUN LAG LED NIC RAW SEE STO TIL VES VER WIL

▶

◀ **PUMPKINS**

Variety	Days	Size/Shape	Remarks	Sources
BIG MAX	120	100 lbs. 70 in.	Pink-orange skin. Fruit are flattened round. Yellowish-orange flesh.	ALL ARC BURG BURP BURR COM DAN EAR EARL GRA GUR HARR HEN LAG LED LET MEY MID PIN PON POR RIS SEE STO TWI WET WIL WILL
BIG MOON (op)	120	Over 200 lbs.	Plant Variety Protected. Produces 1 to 2 huge pumpkins per vine. Medium-orange rind with a slightly rough texture. Thick flesh is light orange. Brown seeds.	GUR HEN HUM JUN LAG LET MID PAR POR RIS TWI VER WET
HUNGARIAN MAMMOTH	120	Up to 200 lbs.	Creamy white to slight orange. Ridged texture. Round to slightly oblong.	LET
JUMBO	110	75-100 lbs.	Sweet, fine-textured flesh. Excellent quality for pies and canning.	BURG
KING OF GIANTS	120	Up to 200 lbs.	High quality.	DEG
MAMMOTH KING (POTIRON)	120	100 plus lbs.	Orange-salmon skin, orange flesh.	EARL LET
MAMMOTH ORANGE GOLD	110	20 x 20 in. 80 lbs.	Thick orange meat. Matures firm and smooth.	ECO NIC ROS WET WIL WYA
SHOW KING (ARTHUR VESEY'S)	100	400 lbs.	Yellow meat. Orange, yellow or gray-blue rind.	GUR THO
THE GREAT PUMPKIN	120	100 lbs. 35 in. diameter	Easy to grow. Pinky-orange rind, thick sweet orange meat.	SHE

PUMPKINS
MEDIUM-LARGE

Variety	Days	Size/Shape	Remarks	Sources
CONNECTICUT FIELD (SOUTHERN FIELD) (LARGE YELLOW) (BIG TOM)	120	25 lbs. 10 x 14 in.	Flattened at ends. Deep orange rind, orange-yellow flesh.	ALL ARC BURP BUT COM DEG EAR FAR HARR HEN HIG HUM JOH JUN LAG LED LET MEY MID PON RAW RIS SEED SOU STO TWI VES WILL
ETEMPES		30 lbs.	A pre-1855 heirloom French variety. Great pie-making pumpkin.	PEA
HALF MOON	115		Pumpkin of the Connecticut Field class.	LAG LET MID RIS TWI
HOWDEN'S FIELD	115	Round, ridged	Extra-thick flesh.	HARR TER WIL
PANKOW'S FIELD	120	20-30 lbs. 13-16 in.	Orange rind, yellow-orange meat.	HARR VES
WINTER QUEEN (LUXURY)	110		Closely netted yellow rind. Best keeper.	DEG JUN

PUMPKINS
SMALL

Variety	Days	Size/Shape	Remarks	Sources
AUTUMN GOLD (hybrid)	90	10 lbs.	Short-season variety. Vigorous, medium-sized vine produces 3 fruit. Bright orange even in the immature stage.	ARC BURP BURR COM GUR HEN HUM JOH JUN LET NIC PAR POR STO TIL TWI VER VES WET WILL
BABY PAM	100	5½ in. across	10-12 in. vines. Bright orange inside and out. Hardy.	GUR MID
EARLY SWEET (SUGAR PIE)	90-110	6-8 lbs. 9 x 8 in.	Dark orange rind, orange flesh.	DEG GUR LEJ LET
IDAHO GEM	80		Heirloom variety. Tolerates cool weather. Not large.	HIG
JACK O' LANTERN (HALLOWEEN)	115	10 lbs. 9 x 8 in.	Medium-orange rind. Firm, even-textured flesh.	ABU ALL ARC BURG BURP BURR COM DAN DEG EAR EARL FAR FIS GUR HUM LAG LED LEJ LET MEY MID PIN RIS ROS SEED STO TIL TWI VER WES
NAKED SEEDED	110		6-8 ft. vines. Abundance of shell-less seeds.	COO PLA
OMAHA	79	4 lbs.	Orange. Prolific.	SEE
SMALL SUGAR PIE (BOSTON PIE) (NEW ENGLAND PIE)	110	8 x 10 in. Round, ribbed	Meaty, sweet, fine-grained. For general use.	ABU ALL ARC BURP BURR COM DAN EAR EARL FAR HIG JOH LAG LED MEY MID NIC PLIN PLA PON POR RAW RED RIS ROS SEE SEED SOU STO TIL VER VES WES WET WIL WILL WYA
SPOOKIE	105	6 lbs. 6 x 6 in. Round	Dark orange rind. Orange-yellow flesh. Fine-textured flesh.	HARR MID PIN SHE
SUBAG BABY	95	8 x 3½ in.	Heirloom pie pumpkin. Distinct ribbing. Prolific yields on long, disease-resistant vines.	SOU
TRICK OR TREAT	105	10-12 lbs. 11 in. diameter	Medium-ribbed fruit. Thick orange meat. Excellent flavor. 5-6 ft. vines. High yielding. Hull-less seeds can be eaten raw or whole.	BURG FAR HEN JUN LED PIN SEED WET
TRIPLE TREAT	110	8-10 in. 6-8 lbs.	Deep orange flesh. Hull-less seeds can be eaten raw or roasted.	BURP JUN LAG TWI
YOUNG'S BEAUTY	112	8-9 lbs. 7½ x 8 in. Globe-shaped	Deep orange rind. Moderately ribbed.	HARR MID RIS

PUMPKINS
SPACE SAVERS

Variety	Days	Size/Shape	Remarks	Sources
BUSH FUNNY FACE (hybrid)	90	10-15 lbs.	Vigorous upright semi-bush. Good pie variety. 5 ft. vine.	ARC BURG HEN LAG LED LET MID POR RAW SEED TWI VES WET WIL

◄

Variety	Days	Size	Remarks	Sources
BUSH SPIRIT (hybrid)	100	10-15 lbs. 12 in. diameter	4 ft. semi-bush plant takes up little space. Thick, golden yellow meat makes great pies.	BURG BURP COM EAR GUR HEN JUN LED LET MID NIC POR STO TER WET

PUMPKINS
SPECIAL TYPES

Variety	Days	Size/Shape	Remarks	Sources
BEZEN CHIREMEN	110	7 x 4 in.	Japanese variety. Dark green, very heavily ribbed and warted rind. Deep yellow flesh with tinge of green. Good for stuffing. Thrives under wide variety of growing conditions.	JLH
CINDERELLA	95	10 in. Globe	Bright orange rind. Grow in well-drained soil.	BURP
CUSHAW, GREEN STRIPED	110	10-15 lbs. 18 x 10 in. Crook neck	Whitish-green with darker green stripes. Thick cream-colored flesh. Good baker.	ABU ARC GUR HEN LED LET MEY MID POR RED RIS ROS SEE SOU WET WIL WYA
DICKINSON	115	12-16 lbs. 18 x 4 in.	Buff-colored rind, slightly furrowed. Sweet orange meat. Used for pies or canning.	WET
GOLDEN CUSHAW	118	12-18 lbs. Curved neck	Golden yellow rind. Popular for baking as it is an all-purpose pumpkin.	DEG MEY SEE
JACK BE LITTLE	95	2 x 3 in.	Deep orange. Small enough to hold in the palm of your hand. Deep orange flesh. About 10 fruit per vine. Let thoroughly ripen on the vine. When stem is dry, pick and little pumpkins will last up to 12 months.	ARC FAR JOH JUN LAK LED LEM LET MEY MID PAR POR RIS SEE SEED TIL TWI VER WIL
JACKPOT (hybrid)	100	10-15 lbs. 10-12 in.	Glossy yellow-orange rind. Orange-yellow meat. Compact vines are very productive. Heavy-yielding.	HARR
KENTUCKY FIELD (LARGE CHEESE)	110		Flat, buff-colored rind. Very meaty. Keeps well.	DEG
LADY GODIVA (STREAKER)	110	6 lbs. 8 in.	Green and yellow striped rind. Seeds are eaten raw or roasted.	GLE WILL
LITTLE LANTERN	100	5 x 5½ in.	10 ft. vines. Deep orange meat. Slightly ribbed.	STO
MINI JACK	100	3-6 in. Round	Bright orange pumpkin used mainly for decoration.	ROS
MUNCHKIN	110	3-4 in. diameter	Deep orange rind. Hard, ridged shell. Sweet meat interior. Bake or use as containers for soups and stuffings.	HARR LAG SHE
MUSQUEE DE PROVENCE		Convoluted, flat	French variety. Good storer. Buff-dark orange rind. Tasty meat for pies.	LEM
ORANGE HOKKAIDO (UCHIKI KURI)		10 lbs.	Orange-red rind. Clear yellow meat has nutty flavor.	ECO
PHOENIX (hybrid) (PAPAYA PUMPKIN)			Japanese pie pumpkin. Tasty cooked. Has papaya shape. Few lateral shoots.	GLE NIC

►

◄ PUMPKINS

Variety	Days	Size/Shape	Remarks	Sources
ROUGE D' ETAMPES	120	20 lbs. Flattened	French heirloom variety. Red rind with roughly pebbled texture. Long, trailing vines. Color of pumpkin fades with sun exposure.	LEM
SWEETIE PIE	110	5 ozs. 3 x 1¾ in.	Chinese stock seed variety. Deeply ribbed like an old-fashioned flat pumpkin.	COO STO
TRIAMBLE	120	15 lbs.	Three cornered-shaped pumpkin. Slate-gray, thick, tough rind. Sweet firm deep orange meat. Excellent keeper.	GLE
WHANGAPAROA CROWN			Hard gray rind. Excellent storer. Small seed cavity. Solid, deep orange flesh.	GLE
WHITE CHEESQUAKE			1824 variety. Creamy white rind. Orange meat. Productive and quite hardy.	LEM

RADISHES
(Raphanus sativus)

The radish is a rather spectacular, quick-maturing, here-today-gone-tomorrow plant. Some mature in as few as 18 days.

Radishes are easy to grow. There are two main kinds of radishes—the ordinary, small, quick-spring radishes most of us visualize when we think of radishes, and the longer-maturing, larger, fall-winter types. These are known as Oriental varieties. Radishes come in all shapes and colors and add a great deal of color to salads.

CULTURE: For spring radishes, sow seed half-inch deep in rows one foot apart; thin to 1 to 2 inches apart. Sow seed as early in the spring as the soil can be worked. Repeat at 10-day intervals until early summer. Sow again about a month before frost.

For winter varieties, sow seed a half-inch deep in rows one foot apart; thin to 3 inches apart. Fall and winter varieties need cool weather at the end of their growing seasons. Sow seeds in early summer for fall in mid-summer for late fall.

SEASON: Cool.

INSECTS/DISEASES: *FLEA BEETLES, ROOT MAGGOTS:* Use malathion, Sevin, pyrethrum, rotenone or ryania.

DOWNY MILDEW, FUNGAL LEAF SPOTS: Spray with maneb or fixed copper sprays.

HARVESTING: Pull as needed. If left, they become pithy.

RADISHES
ROUND, RED

Variety	Days	Size/Color	Remarks	Sources
BELLE GLADE	23	Bright red	Mild. Resistant to fusarium wilt. Tolerant to black root/black scurf disease complex. Plant Variety Protected.	HARR
CAVALIER	21-24	Oval, red	Uniform, crisp, mild. Forcing type.	FAR MID
CAVALRONDO	24	Oval, brick-red	Greenhouse or spring forcing type.	HARR
CHAMPION	25-28	Round, bright scarlet	Seldom pithy. Does well in hot weather.	ARC BURG COM DAN EAR EARL FAR FIS GAR GUR HARR HEN HIG HUM LED LET MEY MID PAR POR SEE SEED STO VES WET
CHERRY BEAUTY (hybrid)	24	Bright cherry	Snow-white interior. Slow to turn pithy.	TWI

◄

Variety	Days	Size/Color	Remarks	Sources
CHERRY BELLE	22-24	¾ in.	Resembles a crisp cherry.	ABU ALL ARC BURG BURP BURR COM DAN DEG EAR EARL ECO FAR FIS GUR HARR HEN HUM LAG LED LEJ LET MEY NIC PIN PON POR RAW SEE SOU STO TIL VES WET WIL WILL WYA
CHERRY BELLE SHORT TOP	21	Round, red	Does well in nearly all type of soils.	MID
COMET	25	1 in. Cherry red	Short tops, white flesh. Good forcing variety.	EARL HUM LET MID SEE SEED STO
CRIMSON GIANT (BUTTER) (SILVER DOLLAR)	29	1½ in. Crimson	Solid white flesh is firm, crisp and mild. Grows large without getting pithy and hollow.	ALL ARC BURP DAN DEG FAR GUR HEN LEJ LET POR RED SEE TIL WES
DANDY	23	Round; deep scarlet	Resistant to cracking. Short tops. Crisp white flesh. Yellows-resistant.	BURR
DELTA RED			Resistant to club root. Crisp, firm, mild flesh.	VES
EARLY SCARLET GLOBE MEDIUM TOP (VICKS)	24-30	Bright scarlet	Crisp, white flesh.	ABU ALL BURG BURR BURR BUT DAN DEG FAR HUM JUN LEJ MEY MID SEE SEED TIL WET WIL WILL WYA
EARLY SCARLET GLOBE SHORT TOP	24	Round	Bright and attractive.	ARC COM DEG EAR
FANCY RED	25	Globe; bright red	Medium top. Plant Variety Protected. Resistant to fusarium yellows. Tolerance to black root and root scruf.	HARR
FANCY RED II	25	Globe; bright red	Larger tops than Fancy Red.	HARR
FUEGO	24	2¾ in. Deep scarlet	Tolerant to fusarium, black root and rhizoctonia scruf.	MID RIS STO
GALA	26	Round; scarlet red	Dutch variety. Crisp, white flesh. Resistant to splitting and sponginess.	SHE
GALAHAD	20		Tolerant to club root.	STO
GERMAN GIANT (PARAT)	29	Size of baseball	German variety. Slightly pungent.	GLE GUR HEN
INCA	27	Round; crimson	Mid-summer variety. Resists pithiness.	JOH PAR SOU WET WIL
MARABELLE	23	Medium-size; round	Short tops. Can be grown outside or in greenhouse.	JOH
RED BALL (ROODBOL)	24		Dutch variety. Mild, sweet flavor. Does not go woody or pithy. Widely adapted.	SHE
RED BARON	24	Round; scarlet	Very sweet, crisp and mild flesh. Crack- and disease-resistant. Tolerates cool growing conditions.	HEN RIS
RIBELLA	25	Round	Refined Cherry Belle. Medium tops. Resists pithiness.	JOH TER

►

◄ RADISHES

Variety	Days	Size/Color	Remarks	Sources
S RED BOY	25	Sparkling red	Short tops. Spicy, crisp white flesh.	FAR HARR MID RIS STO
RED DEVIL	24	Bright red; dime-size	Mild, pungent flesh.	TWI
RED DEVIL B	23	Round to olive-shaped; deep red	Short 3-5 in. tops.	WIL
RED KING	25	Bright red	Plant Variety Protected. Resistant to fusarium yellows and club root.	HARR
RED PRINCE (PRINZ ROTIN)	25	Globe	Stands longer than most. Tasty.	DEG HEN JUN LED RIS THO
SAXA	18	Bright scarlet	Short tops. Mild, crisp flesh. Well adapted to greenhouse growing.	DEG GUR THO
SAXAFIRE	21	Oval; bright red	Tops are very short. Club root-tolerant.	STO
SCARLET CHAMPION		Large, red	Grows best in spring or late summer. Dutch seed.	TER
SCARLET GLOBE	24	1 in. Scarlet	Medium-size tops. Crisp, tasty flesh. Good forcer as well as for outdoor growing.	LAG PON RIS
SCARLET GLOBE SPECIAL	23	Scarlet	Strain of Scarlet Globe.	STO
SCARLET KING	30	Red	Variety for late spring.	TER
SCARLET KNIGHT	22	Bright red	Medium-size tops. Resistant to fusarium yellows. Plant Variety Protected. Tolerant to black root and root scruf.	HARR TWI

RADISHES
LONG, RED

Variety	Days	Size/Color	Remarks	Sources
LONG BRIGHTEST		Long, tapered	Mild white flesh.	POR
LONG RED ITALIAN	35-45	12 in. Bright crimson	Mildly pungent white flesh.	LEM

RADISHES
WHITE TIP

Variety	Days	Size/Color	Remarks	Sources
COPPER SPARKLER (NATIONAL)	25	Round; bright pink with white tip	Good keeper.	HER
CERISE	20-30	Round; bright red	Grows rapidly. European strain.	LEM
D'AVIGNON	25	Long, slender	French variety. Tapered to a point.	JOH

►

Variety	Days	Size/Color	Remarks	Sources
EARLY SCARLET WHITE TIP	24	Round	Short tops. Crisp and tender flesh.	ALL LAG
EIGHTEEN DAY		Red shaft, white tip	Not for mid-summer. Half-long French Breakfast type.	COO HER
FLAMBO		Bright rose, white tip	Strain of Flamboyant.	LEM
FLAMBOYANT	28	3 in. Cylindrical	French variety. Short tops. Crisp, juicy and mild.	HER SHE
FLAMIVIL	27	Cylindrical	French variety. Looks like it's been dipped in milk.	JOH
FRENCH BREAKFAST	23	1¾ in. Rose-scarlet, white tip	Short top. White flesh. Pull when young.	ALL ARC BURP COM DEG EARL FAR FIS GUR HEN JUN LAG LED LET MEY NIC PIN PON POR RAW ROS SEE SEED SOU STO TER THO TIL WES WET
GREEN MEAT CHINESE	50-60	3-4 in.	Chinese variety. Hot. Deep lime-green interior.	LEM
LONG SCARLET AMIENS	22-24	Long, straight	Unusual summer type.	HER
MARTIAN	25	White tip	Similar to French Breakfast in shape. Green shoulders.	STO
OLIVA	25	1½ in. Crimson, white tip	French Breakfast type. Resistant to pithiness.	LEM
PONTVIL	24	Oblong	Stays crisp, sweet and firm.	THO
RED MEAT CHINESE	50-60	1¼ in. White, tinged purple	Chinese variety. Red flesh. Hot taste.	LEM
SCARLET GLOBE WHITE TIP	26		Does not become hollow or pithy.	ARC WYA
SEZANNE	20-30	Round; white topped, pale magenta	European strain.	LEM
SPARKLER (EARLY SCARLET TURNIP) (BRIGHTEST WHITE TIP)	25	1¾ in. Scarlet, white tip	White flesh has a snappy flavor.	BURP BURR DEG EAR EARL ECO FAR FIS GAR GUR HEN JLH JUN LAG LEJ LET MEY NIC POR ROS SEE SEED VER WES WET WIL WILL

RADISHES

ALL WHITE

Variety	Days	Size/Shape	Remarks	Sources
BURPEE WHITE	25	3 x 1 in. Round	Mild and crisp flesh.	BURP EARL JUN LAG
CANDELA DE GHAICCIA		6 in.	Italian variety. Crisp texture, mildly pungent.	LEM

◀ **RADISHES**

Variety	Days	Size/Color	Remarks	Sources
CRYSTAL WHITE	30	Tapered	Very crispy. Resistant to fusarium wilt.	HARR
HAILSTONE	30	Round	Large. Crisp and sweet.	ARC BURG FAR FIS GAR HEN
SILVER DOLLAR	27	Round	Extra mild, pure white flesh.	EAR
SNOW BELLE	30	Round	Plant Variety Protected. Smooth white skin. Tangy flavor.	EAR GUR POR STO TIL TWI VES WET
WHITE BALL (WHITE PEARL)	25		Never gets pithy.	DEG
WHITE GLOBE (GIANT WHITE GLOBE) (GIANT HAILSTONE) (MAMMOTH)	28	6 in. Round	Early, sweet, tender white flesh. Will grow in any climate.	HEN LET SEE THO VER
WHITE ICICLE	30	5 in. Long	Great flavor. Mid-season variety. Standard long white type.	VER WES
WHITE PRINCE	28	Round	Very short tops. Good holding ability.	GUR
WHITE ROUND			Stays sweet, crisp and edible over a long period of time.	POR

RADISHES

OTHER COLORS/TYPES

Variety	Days	Size/Color	Remarks	Sources
EASTER EGG (hybrid)		Red, pink, white, purple and violet	Firm, crisp, tasty. Fast-growing and long-standing.	BURP COM EAR EARL GUR HEN HIG HUM JOH JUN LET NIC PAR PIN POR TIL VER WES WET WILL WYA
FRENCH GOLDEN	60	Light golden	Distinctive, piquant flavor.	NIC
MUNCHEN BIER	67	24 in. tall	Grown for seed pods, eaten raw, steamed or stir-fried.	THO
NAVET	30	9 in. Pink with white tip		SEE
PINK BEAUTY	27	Large	Short top. White flesh.	EAR GLE GUR HEN
RAVE D'AMIENS	30	4 in. Scarlet	Crisp and tender. Slow to mature.	THO
RAINBOW MIX		White, pink, carmine, scarlet, lilac-purple	Crisp and tasty. Radishes do not mature all at once.	THO
VALENTINE	25	Round; green and white	Interior turns red at maturity.	STO
VIOLET DE GAURNAY		Dark violet	French heirloom type. Pure white flesh. Pungent. Fall variety.	COO

RADISHES—ORIENTAL
SPRING

Variety	Days	Size/Color	Remarks	Sources
APRIL CROSS (hybrid) (DAIKON)	63	15 x 2 in. Tapered, white	For early spring sowing. Doesn't become pithy. Slow-bolting. Has the pungency of a winter radish.	NIC PAR THO TSA VER
OMNY (hybrid)	48	16 in. White	Japanese variety. Juicy, crisp white flesh. Can withstand cold temperatures. Easy to grow.	SHE
MINO EARLY (op)	58	16 x 2 in. White	White flesh. Sow in the spring.	SUN
MINO SPRING CROSS (hybrid)	55	16 in. White	Mildly pungent white flesh. Sow in spring or fall. Bolt-resistant.	JOH SUN WILL
SHUNKYOH SEMI-LONG	35	5 in. Red	Mainland China variety. Sow early spring or fall. Crispy white flesh.	VER
TOKINASKI (op) (ALL SEASONS)	45-80	15 x 2 in. 2 lbs.	Very pungent. Cold- and heat- resistant. Can be sown anytime except for months where daytime temperatures drop to freezing.	LEM NIC PIN RED SEE SUN

RADISHES—ORIENTAL
SUMMER

Variety	Days	Size/Color	Remarks	Sources
MINO SUMMER CROSS (hybrid)	45	18 x 2½ in. White	White flesh is mildly pungent. Sow in the spring.	SUN
MINOKUNICHI IMPROVED	55	24 x 2¼ in. Tapered, pure white		RED
MINOWASA DARK GREEN-LEAVED		24 x 2 in. White	Mildly pungent flavor. Heat- and disease-resistant.	RED
MINOWASE DAIKON	60	24 x 3 in. White	Japanese variety. Has a mild, delicate flavor.	GUR
MINOWASE SUMMER CROSS NO. 1	50	2ft. x 1½ in. White	Excellent resistance to virus and soft rot. Grows vigorously during summer. Fine quality.	GLE
OSAKA SHIJUNICHI	50	10 x 1¾ in. White	Vigorous grower in hot weather.	RED
SUMMER CROSS HYBRID	45	18 x 2 in. White	Japanese type. Crisp, firm texture. Piquant flavor. Never woody. Tolerates heat. Disease-resistant.	HEN
SUMMER CROSS NO. 3 (hybrid)	55	Tapered, white	Sow late spring and summer planting.	JOH
WHITE AND LONG	55	16 x 2 in. White	White flesh. Sow either spring or fall.	SUN

RADISHES—ORIENTAL
WINTER

Variety	Days	Size/Color	Remarks	Sources
AWA PICKLING	80	18 x 3 in. White	Selected for pickling.	RED

325

◀ RADISHES—ORIENTAL

Variety	Days	Size/Color	Remarks	Sources
BLACK SPANISH ROUND	55	3½ in. Black skin; globular	Crisp, solid white pungent flesh. Strong tops. Bulbs store well. Matures in cool weather.	FAR GUR JLH JUN LEM LET LIBE SEE STO VER WES WILL
BLACK WINTER ROUND	55	Deep black skin	Italian variety. White flesh. Sow in July and August. Crisp and pungent.	GLE
CALIFORNIA WHITE MAMMOTH	60	8 x 2 in.	Crisp, mild flavor.	EAR FAR SEE
CELESTIAL WHITE WONDER	60	8 x 3 in. White	Crisp, white mild flesh.	LET NIC
CHINESE ROSE (CHINA ROSE)	52	6 x 2 in. Rose to light pink	Crisp white flesh is very pungent. Old variety that dates way back. Sow in fall.	EAR GUR HEN JUN LET PIN SEE SOU STO SUN VER
CRIMSON AND LONG (op)	90	11 x 2 in. Red	White flesh. Sow in fall.	SUN
GREEN SKIN AND RED FLESH (op)	55	5 x 4 in. Green	Red flesh. Sow in fall.	SUN
LONG BLACK SPANISH	55	10 in. Cylindrical; black skin	Crispy, zesty-flavored white flesh.	LET NIC SEE
MISATO ROSE-FLESH	65	4 in. diameter White skin, green shoulders	Chinese variety. Unique red flesh. Stores well.	VER
MIYASHIGE	78	17 x 2½ in. White	Sow August through early September. Solid crisp, pungent roots.	HIG JOH NIC RED
NERIMA LONGEST	90	30 x 3 in. White	Flesh is not juicy and can be dried after harvest. Firm and tender texture.	RED WILL
OHKURA	75	15 x 3½ in. White	Mild flavor. Good keeping quality. Resistant to virus disease. Quick to grow. Sow in late summer and early fall.	JLH RED
SAKURAJIMA	150	25-100 lbs. Globe-shaped	Japanese variety. White flesh. Fine quality.	GLE GUR NIC
SHANTUNG GREEN	50	10 x 2 in. Green	Green flesh. Sow in fall.	SUN
SHOGOIN LARGE ROUND	65-85	5½ in. Round; white	Sweet and good for boiling.	NIC RED
TAMA HYBRID	70	18 x 3 in. White	Japanese variety. Tender and crisp. Uniform, vigorous grower. Excellent keeper.	VER
WINTER KING (op)	55	16 x 2 in. White	White flesh. Chinese variety. Sow in the fall.	SUN

RHUBARB
RED

Variety	Stalks	Remarks	Sources
CANADA RED	Deep red; extra-heavy	Temendous yields. Very tender and juicy.	ARC EAR FAR FOS GUR HEN LED

▶

Variety	Stalks	Remarks	Sources
CHERRY RED	Large, cherry-red outside, greener inside	Fine quality. Tender and juicy.	BURG GUR HEN PAR
CRIMSON RED	Large; crimson red	Heavy producer of large tart juicy stalks. Always tender.	GUR PON TIL WYA
McDONALD'S	Brilliant red	Excellent flavor. Tender skin makes peeling unnecessary. Sauces and pies become a rich pink.	BURP
STARKRIMSON		Exclusive Stark Bros. variety.	STA
STRAWBERRY	Rosy-red	Mild flavor. Stalks cook up well.	TIL
VALENTINE	Deep red	Good in pies or stewed.	EAR SEED THO

RHUBARB
GREENISH

Variety	Stalks	Remarks	Sources
FLARE	From green to red	Tender, juicy stalks. Good producer.	GUR HEN
GIANT VICTORIA		Produces lots of big, juicy stems.	EAR RED
VICTORIA	Broad, thick; green-shaded red	Pleasant, tart flavor. Heavy yielder.	ARC BURP DAN DEG EARL FOS HEN HUM LAG LED PAR ROS VER WET

RUTABAGA
(SWEDE TURNIP)
(Brassica napobrassica)

Rutabagas are closely related to turnips, but they are larger, have smooth, waxy leaves and develop much more slowly than turnips. In addition, rutabaga roots are chockful of vitamin A and can be stored for long periods of time. There is a variation in skin color among varieties—yellow-purple top to white-red top to all-red. The flesh can be yellow or white.

CULTURE: Sow seeds a half-inch deep in rows 15 to 18 inches apart. Thin in stages to about 8 to 12 inches apart. Sow seeds in June or July so the roots develop in cool weather.

SEASON: Cool.

INSECTS/DISEASES: See Kohlrabi.

HARVESTING: Pull and top rutabagas before roots are injured by extreme cold. If well mulched, rutabagas can be stored in the ground and dug as needed.

RUTABAGA (SWEDE)

Variety	Days	Stalks	Remarks	Sources
ALTASWEET	92	7 in. diameter	Canadian variety. Cross between Laurentian and McComber. Deep yellow flesh is very sweet to the taste.	STO TER
AMERICAN PURPLE TOP	88-90	Purple tops, buttery-yellow globes	Sweet, fine-grained, light yellow flesh. Good winter keeper. Plant like you would turnips.	ALL BURR DEG EAR ECO FIS GUR HARR HEN HUM JUN LAG LET MEY NIC PON POR RIS ROS SEE TIL TWI WIL WYA
BEST OF ALL		Up to 6 in. diameter. Purple top	English variety. 18 in. tall. Mild, creamy yellow flesh. Tender texture.	TER
BURPEE'S PURPLE TOP YELLOW	90	Deep purplish above, yellow below	Fine-grained yellow flesh. Cooks to bright orange. Good keeper for winter storage.	BURP

◀ RUTABAGA (SWEEDE)

Variety	Days	Stalks	Remarks	Sources
CANADA GEM			Short-season variety. Extremely hardy.	SEE
CHAMPION PURPLE TOP	90		Reliable and widely grown. Good freezer.	THO
FORTUNA CERTIFIED			Similar to York. Good tolerance to storage rot.	STO
IMPROVED AMERICAN PURPLE-TOP YELLOW	90	4-5 in. diameter	Short-neck strain. Yellow flesh is solid and sweet. Fine keeper when mature.	COM FAR VER WET WILL
LAURENTIAN CERTIFIED NO. 1			Is recommended for commercial growers.	STO
LAURENTIAN NECKLESS (LAURENTIAN)	90	Purple tops; globe-shaped	Rich yellow flesh. Free of excess rot. Good keeper.	ABU DEG EARL FAR GAR HARR JOH JUN LED MID PIN RAW SEE STO WILL
LONG ISLAND IMPROVED	90	Purple-red above, yellow below	Yellow flesh is fine-grained, firm, crisp and sweet.	SEED
WILHELMSBURGER GELBE (WILHELMBURGER GREEN TOP) (PANDUR)	85	Pink top	Cold-hardy. Fiberless. Short-season variety. Good storer. Good freezer.	RAW THO
YORK SWEDE CERTIFIED			Laurentian type. Club root-tolerant.	BUT RAW VES STO

RUTABAGA
OTHERS

Variety	Remarks	Sources
COLBAGA	Cross between Chinese cabbage and rutabaga. Purple tops, white below the soil. White flesh. Grow and store like a rutabaga. Good keeper.	FIS

SALSIFY
(VEGETABLE OYSTER PLANT)
(Tragopogon porrifolius)

This vegetable got its nickname, 'oyster plant,' because that's what it tastes like. Gourmets love it. In appearance, salsify resembles a long, skinny parsnip. It is a long-season vegetable that takes up to 150 days to grow.

CULTURE: As early as possible in the spring, work the soil to a depth of 18 inches. Sow the seeds in rows 12 to 15 inches apart. When the plants are 2 inches high, thin to 3 inches apart. Since it is a long-season crop, you can make better use of space byplanting it with fast-maturing vegetables such as lettuce, radishes or spinach.

SEASON: Cool.

INSECTS/DISEASES: See Lettuce.

HARVESTING: Dig, do not pull the roots. Damaged roots will bleed and lose their flavor. Roots can be mulched and left in the ground to be used during winter.

SALSIFY (VEGETABLE OYSTER PLANT)

Variety	Days	Roots	Remarks	Sources
ANNUAL BLACKROOTED		8-10 in. Black	Creamy white interior. Plant in rich deeply worked soil.	WILL
CREAMY WHITE		8 x 1½ in. Dull white	Mild oyster-like flavor. Thick and smooth.	FIS

▶

Variety	Days	Size	Remarks	Sources
FRENCH BLUE-FLOWERED		9 x 1½ in. White	The flavor is improved by frost.	LEM
GIGANTIA	120	Black	Danish variety.	JOH
LONG BLACK (BLACK GIANT RUSSIAN) (SCORZONERA)	120-140	Black	Very hardy. Purple flowers. Considered by some to be better than the white variety.	DEG GUR LEM NIC RED SEE THO
MAMMOTH LONG ISLAND				COM
MAMMOTH SANDWICH ISLAND	120-140	6-8 in. Long, thick; dull white	Roots can be stored in moist sand in cool areas.	ABU ALL ARC BURG BURP BURR DEG EAR EARL FAR HEN JUN LAG LED LET MEY MID NIC PIN RAW ROS SEED STO THO VER WILL WYA
MAMMOTH SANDWICH ISLAND IMPROVED	120	Long, slender; white	Delicious baked or creamed.	GUR
WHITE FRENCH		White	Has oyster flavor. Good in soup. Easy to grow. Good all winter.	TIL

SEAKALE
(CRAMBE)

Seakale is a perennial that lasts 10 years. Harvest in the third year. The delicacy is the blanched stalks.

SEAKALE (CRAMBE)

Variety	Days	Remarks	Sources
LILY WHITE	270	Sow in the open in spring. Harvest second-year shoots like asparagus. Small, crisp heads that snap off when bent. Delicious.	ECO THO

SHALLOTS

Variety	Remarks	Sources
BAVARIAN BROWN SHALLOT	Bavarian variety. Medium-brown scales, yellow interior. Average 1½-2½ in. bulbs. Good flavor. Medium-pungent.	SOU
CREAM SHALLOT	Virginia heirloom variety. Produces shallots up to 3½ in. Pale yellow flesh. Drought-tolerant and high yields.	SOU
DRITTLER WHITE NEST ONION	1885 Arkansas heirloom variety. Widely adapted. White shallot.	SOU
DUTCH YELLOW	Will often keep for 12 months. Mild flavor.	SOU THO
FRENCH SHALLOTS	Plant in spring or fall. Multiplies in soil. Used in French cuisine.	JOH NIC SOU VER WILL
FROG LEGS SHALLOTS	One shallot multiplies into a cluster of over 15.	LEJ
GIANT RED	Mild, spicy, yet sweet. Stores through winter and spring.	THO
GREY SHALLOT	Considered true shallot in France.	LEJ

◀ SHALLOTS

Variety	Remarks	Sources
SANDER'S WHITE MULTIPLIER	Heirloom Missouri variety. Large bulbs up to 1¾ in. Pure white, sweet and mildly pungent.	SOU
SHALLOTS (YELLOW MULTIPLIER SETS)	Good keepers. Hardy everywhere. Mild, onion-like flavor.	BURG COM EAR FAR GUR HEN JUN LEJ MEY POR RED TAY WILL

SPINACH
(Spinacia oleracea)

Spinach is probably America's favorite green. Although spinach is fast-growing, it can't take long days or hot temperatures. A few warm days and it starts to go to seed. Spinach is somewhat difficult to grow, but worth it.

For hot-summer areas there are spinach substitutes that grow under conditions where spinach would be otherwise impossible.

CULTURE: Sow seeds half an inch deep, 2 inches apart, in rows 18 inches apart. After seedlings have begun to grow, thin to 8 inches apart and feed with a high nitrogen fertilizer. Plant seeds in early spring and in early fall. Make successive plantings 10 days apart.

SEASON: Cool.

INSECTS/DISEASES: *APHIDS, LEAF-MINERS:* Use malathion, diazinon, pyrethrum, rotenone or ryania.
CERCOSPORA LEAF SPOT, DOWNY MILDEW: Use maneb or zineb.
SPINACH BLIGHT: Spray with fixed copper.

HARVESTING: You can pick the outer leaves individually as needed. When the first flowers start to form, pick the entire plant.

SPINACH
SAVOYED, UPRIGHT

Variety	Days	Leaves	Remarks	Sources
AMERICA	50	Glossy, dark green; heavily savoyed and crumpled	Slow to bolt. Heavy yields.	ARC BURR COM EAR GUR LED SEED SOU STO TIL TWI
BLOOMSDALE	48	Thick, twisted, crumpled	Heavy yields. Excellent canned or fresh. Slow to bolt.	ARC DEG EAR EARL FIS HARR HUM LED LEJ MEY PIN PON POR ROS TER WILL WYA
BLOOMSDALE LONG STANDING	39-48	Very crinkled; glossy, dark green	Slow to bolt. Heavy yields. Thick-textured.	ABU ALL ARC BURP BURR BUT DAN DEG FAR FIS GAR GUR HEN HIG HUM JLH JOH JUN LET NIC PAR RAW RED RIS SOU STO TIL TWI VER WES WET
BOUQUET		Crumpled; dark green	Stands longer than other varieties.	TIL
COLD-RESISTANT SAVOY	45	Well-savoyed	For fall planting. Tolerant to heat. Cold- and blight-tolerant.	SEE SOU STO
EARLY HYBRID # 30	40	Well-savoyed; glossy, dark green	For spring planting. Excellent for freezing. Large, stocky plant.	VES
HYBRID 178		Dark green	Large, erect fall variety.	HARR
HYBRID 612 SAVOY	40	Deeply savoyed; dark green	Erect. Fall variety.	MEY

Variety	Days	Leaves	Remarks	Sources
HYBRID 621	39	Dark green	Erect. For spring or fall planting.	MEY
IRON DUKE (hybrid)	50	Very crinkled; dark green	High yields. Tolerant to white rust.	POR VER
ITALIAN SUMMER (hybrid)		Green	High-yielding. Sturdy, erect plant. Bolt-resistant. Short-season variety. Good freezer.	SHE
KENT (hybrid)	39	Dark green	Large plant. High-yielding. Good tolerance to blight and blue mold.	LET
KING OF DENMARK	46	Dark green; crumpled	Broad and rounded leaves. Good canner. Hardy and good quality.	ALL EARL SEE THO
NIZ 82-10 (hybrid)		Dark green	Dutch variety. Thick, bushy plant. Resistant to mildew. Slow-bolting.	RAW
NORFOLK		Well-crinkled; green	Canadian variety. Hardy strain. Sow in the fall.	ABU
SAVOY 612 (hybrid)	39	Deeply savoyed; dark green	Fall and winter variety. High-yielding. Use fresh or frozen.	HARR
SAVOY SUPREME	45-50	Well-savoyed; dark green	Fall or early spring variety.	MEY
TYEE (hybrid)	41		Indeterminate growth. Bland flavor. Heavy yields. Good bolt resistance. Tolerant to race 1 and 3 of downy mildew.	BURP BURR HARR HEN HIG HUM JOH PIN RIS SOU STO TER VES WET
VIENNA (hybrid)	45	Heavily savoyed; dark green	Medium-large erect plant. For spring or fall planting.	HARR MEY PAR RIS TWI
VIRGINIA SAVOY YELLOWS RESISTANT	39	Massive, thick, heavily crumpled	Very hardy. Grows vigorously in late fall, but cannot be sown at other seasons without going to seed.	COM LET SEE
WINTER BLOOMSDALE	45	Dark green	Blight-resistant. Hardy enough to winter over from fall sowing. Slow to bolt.	BURP DEG HARR LET MID SEED TIL

SPINACH

SEMI-SAVOYED

Variety	Days	Leaves	Remarks	Sources
AVON (hybrid)	44	Large; dark green	Quick-growing, vigorous and slow to bolt.	BURP HEN
CHESAPEAKE (hybrid)	45	Medium-large		POR WET
CHINOOK (HYBRID NO. 7 IMPROVED)		Large; dark green	Upright habit. Downy mildew-resistant. Best sown early spring. Good freezer.	TIL
EARLY HYBRID NO. 7	45	Large; dark green	Upright habit. Resistant to downy mildew. Good canner and freezer variety.	COM DEG EARL FAR GUR LED MID NIC RIS WET WILL
GIANT WINTER	45	Medium-green	Cold-hardy.	ABU SEE WILL
INDIAN SUMMER (hybrid)	39	Dark green	Excellent flavor. Upright habit. For spring or fall planting. Tolerant to mosaic virus and downy mildew.	JOH MID

Variety	Days	Size	Remarks	Sources
MARJORE (hybrid)		Dark green	Widely adapted. Slow-bolting. Use fresh or for processing.	POR
MELODY (hybrid)	42	Dark green	Large plant is resistant to mosaic and powdery mildew. Heavy yields. Vigorous and fast-growing.	BURG BURP COM EAR FAR FIS HARR HIG JUN LEM LET MEY MID NIC PAR PIN POR RIS SEED STO THO TWI WILL
OLD-DOMINION	40	Medium savoyed	Medium-size. Fall and winter variety.	WET
PACKER (hybrid)	37	Dark green	Large, erect plant. Fast-growing. Heavy-yielding.	LET
SHAMROCK		Dark green	High yields.	MID
SKOOKUM	41	Large, round; dark green	Resistant to blue mold. Vigorous and high-yielding.	TWI
SPUTNIK (hybrid)	60	Dark green; slightly savoyed	Plant from early spring to late summer. Mildew-resistant.	COO

SPINACH
SMOOTH, ERECT

Variety	Days	Leaves	Remarks	Sources
BAKER (hybrid)	41	Dark green	Summer type in California. Fast-growing. Resistant to downy mildew.	HARR
BENTON NO. 2 (hybrid)	45		Semi-heat-tolerant. Virus- and downy mildew-tolerant. Bush-form plant. Thick, broad leaves have long stems. Hardy.	VER
HYBRID 424	40	Large; dark green	Highly resistant to blue mold.	HARR WILL
MARATHON (hybrid)	39	Large, heavy, rounded; dark green	Long-standing. High-yielding. Slow-bolting. Vigorous upright plant.	LET
MAZURKA (hybrid)		Large; dark green	Mild, slightly sweet flavor. Slow-bolter even in hot summer weather.	TER
MEDIANA		Dark green; broad	Plant Variety Protected. Heat- and cold-tolerant. Spring variety. Resistant to blue mold.	GUR HEN MID
NOBEL GIANT (LONG STANDING QUADRAY) (GIANT THICK LEAVED)	46	Huge, thick, smooth, pointed with round tip; dark green	Enormous yields. Large plants. Vigorous.	ARC BURR DEG HEN ROS SEE SOU TIL
NORDIC (hybrid)		Deep vibrant green	Dutch variety. Long-standing, slow-bolting. Good fresh or cooked. Resistant to downy mildew.	SHE
OLYMPIA	46	Deep green	For spring and summer sowing. Slow-bolting. Erect plant. Highly tolerant to downy mildew. Heavy yields. For fresh, frozen or canned use.	STO

Variety	Days	Leaves	Remarks	Sources
POPEYE'S CHOICE (hybrid)	50	Very large; medium-green	Stands for long period without bolting to seed. Excellent flavor.	VES
ROUND		Large, round	Mild and sweet. Summer variety. Keep well moist or it tends to run to seed.	ECO
ST. HELEN'S (hybrid)	38	Medium-dark green	Hardy overwintering variety. Erect growth. Very resistant to mildew. Bolts under hot temperatures.	HARR TIL
SUZAN (hybrid)		Dark green	Japanese variety. Suited for early spring and fall culture. Viroflay type. Tolerant to some mildews. Smooth seeds.	LEM
USHIWAKAMARU		Medium-green; broad	Fall variety. Fast-growing. Resists bolting. Erect plant. Spiny seeds.	LEM
VIROFLAY 90 (RESISTOFLAY)	45		Large, erect. Good resistance to downy mildew. Fall variety.	HER LAG
VITAL-R	45	Fleshy	Resistant to all known forms of blue mold. For spring and fall crops.	WILL
WOLTER		Almond-shaped; medium-green	Dutch variety. High-yielding. Grows rapidly. Good disease resistance. Strong flavor.	SHE

SPINACH—ORIENTAL
PRICKLY-SEEDED VARIETIES

Variety	Days	Leaves	Remarks	Sources
BROADLEAVED SUMMER	45	Smooth; medium-green	Prickly-seeded. Quick-grower. Birds do not eat this seed.	ECO SEE WILL
MUNSTERLANDER	55	Arrow-shaped; flat	German strain. Resistant to summer heat and can take frost.	RED
SOHSHU (EARLY AUTUMN)	40	Smooth; green	Grows rapidly. Tolerant to summer heat. Sow between May and October. Tender.	RED
UJO	45	Smooth	Large plant. Resistant to hot weather. Excellent flavor.	RED

SPINACH—ORIENTAL

Variety	Days	Leaves	Remarks	Sources
ORIENT SPINACH (hybrid)	45	Smooth; dark green	Vigorous. Heat-tolerant. Resistant to disease.	SUN

SPINACH SUBSTITUTES

Variety	Days	Leaves	Remarks	Sources
CLIMBING SPINACH (HINCHOY) (BASELLA RUBRA)	70	Red	Use fresh or boiled. Unusual, quick-growing vine. Grow on trellis or fence.	GLE
MALABAR SPINACH (BASELLA ALBA)	70	Large, glossy; bright green	Quick-growing. Takes little growing space if trained on fence.	GLE NIC PAR RED THO

◀ **SPINACH SUBSTITUTES**

Variety	Days	Leaves	Remarks	Sources
MOUNTAIN SPINACH (GERMAN SPINACH) (ORACH)			Can grow to 9 feet if not clipped. For specific colors see below.	RED SEE
MUSTARD SPINACH (TENDERGREEN) (KOMATSUNA)	35	Long, tender, glossy; dark green	Mild taste of mustard.	KIT NIC RED ROS
NEW ZEALAND SPINACH	70	Small leaves are brittle; green	Strong heat-resistant plant. Nice spinach flavor.	ABU ARC BURP BUT COM DEG EAR EARL ECO GAR HEN HIG HUM JLH JUN LAG LED LET MEY MID NIC PIN POR RAW RED SEE SEED SOU STO THO TIL VER WES WET WILL WYA
ORACH, GREEN (MOUNTAIN SPINACH)			An annual. Sometimes mistaken for Lamb's Quarters. Harvest over a long period of time. Will reach 6 ft. tall if left uncut.	ABU COO GAR PIN
ORACH, RED			Annual. Red-purple variety. Popular as a garnish. Does not lose color when cooked.	ABU COO GAR PIN SEE
ORACH, YELLOW			Annual. Bright golden seed heads.	COO
PERPETUAL SPINACH			Biennial. Heavy producer through heat and cold. A refined variety of chard, but fine-textured leaves resemble spinach.	COO
TAMPALA SPINACH (FORDHOOK)			Tastes like an artichoke. Cooks fast.	BURP
TETRAGONE CORNUE			A New Zealand spinach that needs lots of water.	HER

SQUASH, SUMMER
(Cucurbita pepo)

Summer squash is fast-growing and produces an abundance of thin-skinned fruits; it grows primarily on bushy, compact plants that take up less space than winter squash. Summer squash types include Bush Scallop, Straightneck, Crookneck and Zucchini.

CULTURE: Squash is a heat-lover, and should not be set outdoors until night-time temperatures regularly stay above 55° F.

Plant bush varieties 2 feet apart in rows. If you plant in hills, allow three plants each. Maintain 4 feet from the center of one hill to the next.

Plant vine types in rows 5 feet apart. If planted in hills, plant three plants each and allow 8 feet between hills. Vining squash can also be planted against a fence and trained to grow on it, this saves a lot of space.

SEASON: Warm.

INSECTS/DISEASES: *APHIDS, CUTWORMS, SPIDER MITE, SPOTTED CUCUMBER BEETLE, SQUASH BUG, SQUASH VINE BORER, STRIPED CUCUMBER BEETLE:* Use malathion, Sevin, diazinon, pryethrum, rotenone, kelthane or ryania.

ANTHRACNOSE, CHOANEPHORA FRUIT ROT, DOWNY MILDEW, GUMMY STEM BLIGHT, SCAB: Apply catan, maneb, zineb, copper fungicides or ziram.

BACTERIAL SPOT OR BLIGHT: Apply fixed copper sprays.

POWDERY MILDEW: Apply karathane or sulfur 7 to 10 days apart.

HARVESTING: Summer squash should be picked when they are young and tender. The seeds should be undeveloped and the rind soft. Summer squash is too old for eating if your thumbnail doesn't pierce the skin readily with little pressure. Let winter squash mature fully on the vine until the skin is very hard.

SUMMER SQUASH—SCALLOP

Variety	Days	Size/Color	Remarks	Sources
BENNING'S GREEN TINE	54	Disk-shaped, scalloped; pale green	Tender and flavorful.	FIS GAR GUR HEN LAG LEM MEY RED TER WET
EARLY WHITE BUSH (WHITE PATTY PAN)	54	8 x 3 in. Scalloped; pale green	Flesh is milk-white and flavorful.	BURP BURR DAN DEG EARL FIS LED LET MEY NIC POR RIS ROS SOU TIL WET WIL WYA
GOLDEN BUSH		Large, scalloped; golden yellow	Distinctive flavor. Vigorous bush.	SEE
MAMMOTH WHITE BUSH	60	Thick, scalloped; creamy white		ARC
PATTY GREEN TINT (hybrid)	50	White, tinted green	Plant has open habit. Good yields.	HUM SEED
PATTY PAN (hybrid) (EARLY BUSH SCALLOP)	50	Scalloped, flattened; pale green	Flesh is pale green, meaty and tender.	BURG BURP BURR ECO SEE WES
PETER PAN (hybrid)	52	4 in. across. Medium-green	Semi-bush. Excellent quality. Vigorous. Weather-resistant plant with open habit.	FAR HARR LAG NIC PAR POR STO TWI VER WET WIL WILL
SCALLOPINI (hybrid)	50	Scalloped; bright green	Can be eaten raw or cooked. Cross between scallop and zucchini. Compact bush plant.	ARC BURG DAN FIS JUN LAG LEJ NIC PIN POR SEED STO TER
SUNBURST (hybrid)	53	Pick when 3 in. across; bright golden yellow	Bushy. Productive. Good raw or cooked.	BURP COM COO DAN EAR HARR JOH JUN LAG LEM NIC PAR PIN POR SEED SHE TWI VER
WOOD'S EARLIEST PROLIFIC		White	Very prolific.	SEE
YELLOW BUSH SCALLOP		Flattened; yellow	Bush type.	ABU LET POR SEE

SUMMER SQUASH—STRAIGHTNECK

Variety	Days	Size/Color	Remarks	Sources
BABY STRAIGHTNECK	51	Harvest at 6 in. Butter-yellow	High yields.	STO
BUTTERSTICK (hybrid)	50	Golden	Best when picked small. Creamy-white flesh has firm texture. Prolific plant.	BURP
EARLY PROLIFIC STRAIGHTNECK	50	Harvest at 4 x 1/4 in. Creamy yellow	Heavy yields. Bush-like plant.	ALL ARC BURP BURR COM DEG FIS GUR HARR HEN LED LET MID PLA RIS ROS TER VER WET WIL WYA
EARLY YELLOW		Creamy yellow	Bushy, spreading plant. Pale yellow, crisp tender flesh.	POR
GOLDBAR (hybrid)	50	Harvest at 6 in.	Compact, open bush. Heavy yields.	COM EAR JUN LET MEY MID PIN POR RIS TWI WET WIL WYA

SUMMER SQUASH—STRAIGHTNECK

Variety	Days	Size/Color	Remarks	Sources
GOLD CREST (hybrid)	50	Creamy yellow	Compact bush. Excellent quality.	PIN
GOLDEN GIRL (hybrid)	50	Buttery yellow	Prolific. Bears over a long season.	HARR
MULTIPIK (hybrid)		7 in. Tapered; glossy yellow	Vigorous, productive plant. Resists mosaic virus.	HARR POR
SENECA BUTTERBAR (hybrid)	50	3 in. diameter	Solid flesh. Open habit, compact bush-type plant. Space-saver variety.	PAR TWI VER
SENECA PROLIFIC		Creamy yellow	Heavy production over long season.	BURR HARR JOH LED LET MID PAR RIS TWI WET WIL
SMOOTHIE	47	Golden yellow	Sets well. Good yields. Compact plant.	TWI
SUPERPIK (hybrid)	50	5-7 in. Tapered; glossy yellow	Good yields. Resists greening.	HARR
VALLEY GOLD (hybrid) (SUNRISE STRAIGHTNECK)	48		Use as a baby squash or harvest as standard. Very productive.	LEM

SUMMER SQUASH—CROOKNECK

Variety	Days	Size/Color	Remarks	Sources
BUTTER SWAN	50	6-8 in. Light yellow	Bushy space-saver variety. Open habit, short stems. Excellent flavor.	PAR
DAYTONA (hybrid)	41	Harvest when 5-6 in. Yellow	Creamy-yellow flesh. Vigorous, semi-open plant.	GUR
DIXIE (hybrid)	45	Yellow	Compact plant. Prolific yields.	PAR POR WIL
DWARF SUMMER CROOKNECK	50	Harvest when 3 x 10 in. Orange-yellow	Heavy yields of warted fruit.	BURR VER
EARLY GOLDEN SUMMER CROOKNECK	48-53	Harvest at 3 x 10 in. Bright yellow	Meaty texture. Bush type.	ABU ALL BURP COM DAN DEG GAR HEN HIG HUM LED LET PAR POR RED RIS SOU VER WET WIL WILL WYA
GIANT CROOKNECK	55	Finely warted; golden yellow	Salmon-yellow flesh. Grows large if left.	TIL
GOLDEN CROOKNECK	53	Harvest at 4-6 in. Bright yellow	Very prolific. Heavy yields. Orange-salmon flesh. Bush type.	ARC
GOLDIE (hybrid)	53	3-5 in. Bright yellow	Strong disease resistance. Semi-open plant. Nutty sweet flavor.	MID PIN SHE TWI WET
PIC-N-PIC (hybrid)	50	Golden yellow	Wart-free. Productive, open habit. Harvest when small.	BURP
SUMMER CROOKNECK	48	4-6 in. Yellow		MEY MID TER
SUNDANCE (hybrid)	50	Bright yellow	Flesh is creamy white.	BURG COM LAG LET NIC PAR SEED STO TWI WET WIL

◄

Variety	Days	Size/Color	Remarks	Sources
TARA (hybrid)	51	5-6 in. Golden yellow	Good yields. Easy to pick.	HARR
YELLOW SUMMER CROOKNECK IMPROVED	55	Light lemon-yellow		EARL JOH SEE

SUMMER SQUASH—ZUCCHINI
GREEN

Variety	Days	Size/Color	Remarks	Sources
AMBASSADOR (hybrid)	55	7-8 in.	Good yields over a long season.	COM EAR LET MEY MID PAR PIN RIS TWI
ARLESA (hybrid)	48	Harvest under 5 in. Glossy green	French variety. Delicious when picked young. Quick-growing, open habit.	SHE
ARISTOCRAT (hybrid)	48	8-10 in. Glossy green	Single-stemmed. Good yields.	COM EAR HER HUM JUN LAG NIC PAR THO WET
BLACK BEAUTY	58	6-8 in.	High yields. Greenish-white flesh.	ARC GAR RIS TER TIL WIL
BLACKJACK	55		Open bush.	ARC GUR
BLACK MAGIC (op)	55	Glossy black-green	Easy separation from plant. Produces uniform fruit.	GUR HEN JUN VER WET WILL
BLACK ZUCCHINI	52-62	6-8 in.	Bush type. Greenish-white flesh.	ALL BURG BURR DEG EARL FIS GUR HIG JOH LED LET MEY MID PIN RED SEE WES WET WYA
BUCCANEER (hybrid)	48	Rich green	Plant has an open habit.	JOH
BURPEE'S FORDHOOK	57	8-12 in.	Creamy-white flesh. Freezes well. Vigorous bush-like plant.	BURP PON
CHEFINI	51	7-8 in. Glossy dark green		FAR GLE LAG MID POR RAW
CLASSIC (hybrid)	52	Waxy medium-green	High yields. Compact, open bush.	MID RIS
DARK GREEN ZUCCHINI	50-60	6-7 in.	Bushy plant.	ABU DAN GAR PAR WILL
DIPLOMAT (hybrid)	53	7-8 in.	High yields.	LEJ
ELINI	48	Medium-green	Strong plant is fairly compact. Recommended for eastern and southern gardens.	TWI
ELITE (hybrid)	48	6-8 in. Glossy dark green	Abundant yields. Prolific, vigorous plant.	HARR VER
FLORINA (hybrid)	50	4-6 in.	Flowers stay attached for a long period. Compact bush.	COO
GENIE (hybrid)	50	7-8 in. Medium-green	Well-adapted. Large plant. High yields.	HARR

►

SUMMER SQUASH—ZUCCHINI

Variety	Days	Size/Color	Remarks	Sources
GREEN MAGIC (hybrid)	51	Deep, glossy green	Very vigorous and productive. Open habit and spineless.	VER
JACKPOT (hybrid)		Long; medium-green	Open plant. High yields.	FIS LEM
NAPOLINI (hybrid)	48	7-8 in. Dark green	Tolerant to cucumber mosaic virus.	HARR
PARK'S GREEN WHOPPER	48	Dark green	Good producer over long season.	PAR
PRESIDENT (hybrid)	47	Dark green	Highly productive. Easy to harvest. Adapted to field or greenhouse.	MID POR SEED WIL
RICHGREEN (hybrid)	50	Dark green	Exceptional yields. Bushy plant. Good vigor. Open habit.	BURP VES
ROMANO BLOSSOM (hybrid)			Italian variety grown for its blossom. Good for stuffing.	LEM
RONDE DE NICE	45	Up to 5 in. Round; pale green	French variety. Very vigorous. Quick-growing plant.	LEM
SARDANE (hybrid)	48	Deep dark green	Italian variety. Large blossoms make good stuffers. Good taste. Bushy plant is very productive and high-yielding.	SHE
SENATOR (hybrid)	47	Nearly straight	Prolific, heavy yields.	POR SEED WIL
SENECA (hybrid)	47	Dark green	Does well from Florida to the North. Tremendous yields.	LED LET MEY MID NIC RIS TWI WET WIL WYA
SENECA GOURMET (hybrid)	46	2 x 8 in.	High yields. Upright, bushy plant.	BURR LET MEY PAR TWI WIL
SMALL GREEN ALGERIAN (op)	50	Short, rounded; light green, with gray-green spots	North African strain. Bears over a long period of time.	LEM
SUPER SELECT	48	7-8 in. Dark green	High yields. Upright plant with good leaf cover. Mildew-resistant.	STO
VICEROY (hybrid)	52	Medium-green	Open, semi-sprawling plant. Very productive.	MID RIS
ZUCCHINI SELECT	47	6 in. Medium-green	Downy and powdery mildew-resistant. Compact, open plant.	STO

SUMMER SQUASH—ZUCCHINI
DARK GREEN STRIPES (COCOZELLE TYPE)

Variety	Days	Size/Color	Remarks	Sources
CASSERTA	50	Light green, striped dark green	Bush-type. Abundant yields.	DEG LET RIS

Variety	Days	Size/Color	Remarks	Sources
COCOZELLE BUSH (ITALIAN VEGETABLE MARROW) (LONG GREEN BUSH)	60-65	14 x 5 in.	Greenish-white flesh. Pick young for best flavor.	ALL COM ECO GAR GUR HEN HIG JOH LED NIC PLA SEE STO THO VER VES WET WIL WILL
COUSA (hybrid)	51	3-5 in. Pale greenish white	Lebanese zucchini. Compact bushy plant. Easy to pick. Great for Middle Eastern cooking.	STO
CUCCUZZI (LONG COCOZELLE) (GUINEA BEAN) (CLIMBING SQUASH)		Pick when 6-15 in.	Grows quickly. Eat at immature stage. Edible gourd.	GRA LED LET MID
CUCUZZI CARAVASI	65	To 4 ft.	An edible running gourd.	COM
GREEN COCOZELLA	60	16 x 4 in.	Popular Italian strain.	DEG
GOURMET GLOBE (hybrid)	55	Round; light and dark green stripes	Rich flavor. Very productive bush. Can be stuffed, steamed, fried or boiled.	DAN EAR LAG PAR SHE THO WET
LONG GREEN STRIPED	68	Dark green, light green stripes	European type. Very vigorous and prolific. Easily grown marrow for fence or trellis.	THO

SUMMER SQUASH—ZUCCHINI
OTHER COLORS

Variety	Days	Size/Color	Remarks	Sources
AUSTRIAN BUSH	50	White	Stands dampness.	SEE
BLONDY (hybrid)	40	Harvest at 2-4 in. Creamy green	Superb flavor. Good freezer variety. Creamy-white flesh. Almost every flower is female.	THO
BURPEE GOLDEN	54	Glossy, bright golden yellow	Distinctive zucchini flavor.	BURP DEG THO
CASERTA	52	5-6 in. Gray	White interior. Semi-open bush.	LAG
CEREBERUS BUSH	55	6 in. Dark green when young, lighter when mature		NIC
EL DORADO (hybrid)	49	7-8 in. Deep orange-yellow	High yields.	HARR
ENGLISH VEGETABLE MARROW	60	20 x 6 in. Creamy white	English favorite. Bush type.	EARL VES
FRENCH WHITE BUSH	50	3-5 in.	French variety. Firm-meated with few seeds. Vigorous plant.	NIC
GREY (SLATE)	61	7 in. Gray green, mottled dark green	Medium to large plant.	GAR GUR HEN HIG LAG MID SOU TER WIL
GREYZINI (hybrid)	55	Gray	Bush type. Excellent vigor.	ARC COM FAR LAG PIN STO WYA
GOLDEN ZUCCHINI		Bright golden	Yields less than other types of zucchini.	SEE

◀ SUMMER SQUASH—ZUCCHINI

Variety	Days	Size/Color	Remarks	Sources
GOLD RUSH (hybrid)	52	4-8 in. Glossy golden	Small plant is open. Heavy producer.	BURR COM COO EAR EARL GUR HUM JOH JUN LAG LED LET MEY MID NIC PAR PON POR RAW RIS SEED STO THO TIL TWI VER WET WIL WILL
LONG WHITE VEGETABLE MARROW	60	7 in. White	English variety. Pale green interior, tinged white. Closed habit.	RAW
ONYX (hybrid)	43	Harvest at 2-4 in. Onyx-like color	Good fresh, frozen or canned. Compact bush is immensely productive.	MID THO
ROCKY GOLD (hybrid)	55	Bright yellow	Prolific plant with open habit. Baby squash are full golden yellow.	FIS LEM VES
WHITE LEBANESE	45-55	Pale green, almost white	Delicate flavor. Very popular variety in the Middle East, Italy, Britain and Mexico.	LEM

SUMMER SQUASH
SPACE SAVERS

Variety	Days	Size/Color	Remarks	Sources
BUTTER SWAN	50	6-8 in. Light yellow	Crookneck type. Bushy compact plant grows to 3 to 4 ft. across. Open habit.	PAR
GOLD SLICE (hybrid)	48	Golden yellow	Crookneck. Tolerant of cooler soils. Pick regularly.	VES
GREEN MAGIC (hybrid)	48	Dark green	Zucchini. Compact 18 in. plant. Heavy yielder.	PAR VES
PARK'S CREAMY HYBRID	48	6-8 in. Creamy yellow	Straightneck. 18 in. plant. Prolific over a long season. Withstands extremes of temperatures.	PAR
ROUND ZUCCHINI (RONDE DE NICE)	45	Round	European variety. Bush plant. Harvest from 1 in. diameter to tennis-ball size.	COO EAR GAR LEM

SUMMER SQUASH
OTHER TYPES

Variety	Days	Size/Color	Remarks	Sources
BUTTERBLOSSOM (hybrid)	45		Bears enormous numbers of large, firm male flowers which are used for stuffing. Keep fruit picked to stimulate new flower growth.	COO VER
COSTA ROMANESCA		8 in. to 2 ft. Long and fluted	Italian variety. Remains tender even when they reach maturity. Usually fried whole with flower attached.	RED
HUICHA	90	8 in. Light green	Vines grow 40 feet long with leaves 2 feet across. Old Mexican variety.	RED
LAGINARIA LONGISSIMA	65		Vining Italian variety. Full rich flavor when picked half ripe. Allow vine to climb.	NIC SEE

Variety	Days	Size/Color	Remarks	Sources
ROYAL KNIGHT	55	Light green, slight tinge of yellow	Bottle-shaped with slightly crooked neck.	FAR
TATUMA		Pear-shaped; green	Buttery, nutty flavor. No peeling necessary. Mexican variety. Vining.	HOR POR WES
TETSUKABUTO (hybrid)		8 in. round. Glossy green	Japanese variety. Deep orange flesh. Flavor like yams. 50 or more fruit per vine.	GLE
VEGETABLE MARROW			Vining English variety.	SEE

SQUASH, WINTER
(Cucurbita marima, pepo, mixta, maschata)

This variety comes in such a profusion of types and shapes that you may want to try them all. Some resemble a giant banana, others are acorn-shaped, heart-shaped, often with other forms thrown in. Winter squash has more flavor than summer squash and can be stored for later use.

Winter-fall squash grows slowly on large, runner-type vines (a few now have bush varieties), takes up a lot of space, has hard, thick shells, and should be left on the vine until fully ripened.

CULTURE: See Squash, Summer.

SEASONS: Warm.

INSECTS/DISEASES: See Squash, Summer.

HARVESTING: See Squash, Summer.

WINTER SQUASH—ACORN

Variety	Days	Size/Color	Remarks	Sources
BUSH TABLE QUEEN (ACORN BUSH)	82	4 x 5 in. Deeply ribbed, green	Orange flesh. Semi-bush is extremely productive.	ABU ALL BURP BURR DAN DEG TER WES
CHESTNUT	105	Dark green	Very large. Prolific. Orange-yellow flesh. Good storer.	SEE
EARLY ACORN (hybrid)	75		Semi-bush. 5 medium-large fruit per plant.	BURP
EBONY (IMPROVED TABLE QUEEN)	85	5 x 6 in.	Heavy yields. Stores well.	BURR BUT COM GUR HIG JOH LAG LED LET PIN RIS SHE
FISHER'S EARLY ACORN	85	8 x 6 in. Dark green, sharp ridges		FIS
FORDHOOK ACORN			Popular variety of the 1920s.	SEE
GOLDEN ACORN		Yellow	Semi-bush vine. Some leaves show orange color.	ABU
JERSEY GOLDEN ACORN	50-60	Golden	Plant Variety Protected. Eat when young as a summer squash or let mature as winter squash. Semi-bush plant. Light orange meat.	BURP BURR COM COO FAR FIS GAR GUR HEN HIG JOH LAG LEM LET MID NIC PAR PIN PON POR RIS SEED SOU STO TWI VER VES WILL
ROYAL ACORN (MAMMOTH TABLE QUEEN)	82	6 x 7 in. Dull dark green	Turns dull orange after being stored.	BURR DEG LET PON STO TIL TWI VER WYA

WINTER SQUASH—ACORN

Variety	Days	Size/Color	Remarks	Sources
WHITE SWAN ACORN	90	6 x 5 in. Creamy white	Pale yellow flesh is sweet and smooth. Plant Variety Protected. Young 3 in. squash can be eaten as summer vegetable. Heavy-yielding vine type.	STO
TABLE ACE (hybrid)	78	4½ x 5½ in. Black-green	Semi-bush type. Bright orange flesh.	ARC COM GUR HARR HEN JUN LAG LET MID PAR POR RIS STO TWI WET
TABLE KING	75	6 x 5 in. Dark green	Bush acorn. Hard-ribbed. Meaty, thick golden flesh. Good space-saver variety.	VER
TABLE QUEEN (ACORN) (DES MOINES)	85	4½ x 5 in. Ribbed	Trailing vines. Light yellow flesh. Good baker.	ABU ALL BURG BURR DEG EAR EARL FAR FIS GUR HARR HUM JUN LED LET MEY MID NIC PIN PLA PON RED ROS SOU STO TER TIL WIL WILL
TAY BELLE (hybrid)	70	Green-jet black	Table Queen class of squash.	LET

WINTER SQUASH—BUTTERCUP
FLATTENED GLOBE/TURBAN-SHAPED

Variety	Days	Size/Color	Remarks	Sources
BUTTERBALL HYBRID	90	Round, slightly flat on bottom; green	Medium-orange flesh is thick and dry. Fine-textured, sweet flavor.	VER
BUTTERCUP	105	4-5 lbs. 4½ x 6½ in. Dark green rind, silvery white stripes	Thick orange flesh. Cooks dry and sweet. Keeps well in storage.	ABU ALL BURG BURP BURR COM DAN DEG EAR EARL GAR GUR HARR HEN HUM JOH JUN LAG LET MID NIC PIN PON RAW RED RIS SEE SEED STO TER TIL TWI VER VES WILL
GOLDEN DEBUT (hybrid)	105	2-3 lbs. Oblate green to orange when mature	Orange Butterball type. Edible skin after boiling. Very vigorous. Moist yellow flesh. Good keeper.	VER
HOME DELIGHT (hybrid)	100	Dark green	Plant produces a few lateral shoots. Dry yellow flesh. Good quality and flavor.	VER
HONEY DELIGHT	95	2-4 lbs. Forest-green with moss-green stripes	Japanese 'Kabocha' type. Rich orange meat cooks up dry, flaky and very sweet. Stores well.	JOH
KINDRED	80	Bright yellow	Deep orange flesh. Bush type.	LET STO
MOOREGOLD	90	7 x 5 in. Bright orange	Bright orange flesh. Vigorous vines. Long keeper.	JUN SEE
PERFECTION	85	3¼ lbs.	Golden flesh.	STO
SWEET DUMPLING	100	4 in. Teacup shape; ivory with dark green stripes	Very sweet, tender orange flesh. Requires no curing. Suitable for stuffing. Stores 3 to 4 months. Medium length vines.	JOH LEM SHE TIL VER

Variety	Days	Size/Color	Remarks	Sources
SWEET MAMA (hybrid)	85	Dark gray-green	Short vines. Medium-thick flesh, smooth texture. Keeps well.	BURP FAR NIC PAR POR RAW STO TWI VER VES
SWEET MEAT		10-14 in. 6-12 lbs. Slate gray	Vigorous grower. Firm, sweet interior meat. Stores well.	ABU GAR HARR HIG HUM LAG LEM RIS TER TIL
ZUCCA MARINA DI CHIOGGIA		Dark green with lighter streaks	Italian variety. Covered with large knobs and protuberances.	RED

WINTER SQUASH—BUTTERNUT
BOTTLE-SHAPED

Variety	Days	Size/Color	Remarks	Sources
BABY BUTTERNUT		6-7 in.	Egg-size seed cavity. Deep yellow flesh.	FAR
BURPEE'S BUTTERNUT	85	10 x 5 in. Buff-colored	Orange flesh is dry, fine-textured. Nut-like flavor.	VER WILL
BUTTER BOY (hybrid)	80	2¾ lbs.	High quality. Extra-sweet, nutty flavor. Rich reddish-orange flesh. Stores well.	BURP
BUTTERNUT	90-100	5 x 12 in. Creamy brown	Bright orange, dry flesh.	ALL ARC BUT DEG EARL HUM LEJ LET MEY POR RED WES WET
BUTTERNUT WALTHAM	85-95	3½ x 9 in. Creamy tan	Small seed cavity. Deep orange flesh. Good keeper.	ABU BURG BURP BURR DEG EAR FAR GUR HARR HEN JOH JUN LAG LED LET MID PIN PLA PON RAW RIS ROS SEE SEED SOU STO VER WIL WILL WYA
HERCULES BUTTERNUT	82-110	7½ x 4½ in.	Rich orange flesh. High yields of long lasting fruit.	DAN DEG GUR LET MID SEED
PONCA	85-110	8 x 12 in. Creamy tan	Small seed cavity.	BURR JOH MID RIS SEE SEED SHE TER VER

WINTER SQUASH—HUBBARD

Variety	Days	Size/Color	Remarks	Sources
AUTUMN PRIDE	100	15-20 lbs. Faintly ribbed; golden	Fairly compact growth habit. Each plant produces 2-3 squash. Orangish flesh.	PIN
BABY BLUE HUBBARD (SILVER BELL)		Light blue	Orange flesh. High quality. Good keeper.	ABU FAR GAR SEE
BABY GREEN HUBBARD	100	5-6 lbs.	Good keeper.	FIS
BABY HUBBARD (KITCHENETTE)	100	5-6 lbs.	Yellow-orange flesh. Good yielder.	STO
BLUE HUBBARD (NEW ENGLAND)	120	15 lbs. Bluish-gray	Bright yellow-orange flesh is fine-grained. Good keeper.	ALL BURP COM DEG FAR HARR HUM JOH JUN LED LEJ LET MID RIS SEED STO TER VER

◄ WINTER SQUASH—HUBBARD

Variety	Days	Size/Color	Remarks	Sources
GENUINE HUBBARD (TRUE HUBBARD)	110-115	10 x 12 in. 12 lbs. Dark bronze-green	All-purpose squash. Deep yellow-orange flesh. Fine-grained, sweet and dry.	ABU BURP ROS SEE
GOLDEN HUBBARD (RED HUBBARD)	100	10 x 9 in. Reddish-orange with grayish stripes; slightly warted	Deep yellow-orange flesh. Fine-grained. Good canner and freezer.	ALL GAR LET PON RIS SEE SEED STO TIL VER
GREEN HUBBARD	100	9 x 14 in. Oval, pale green	Moderately warted.	ABU ALL EARL LET RED SEED TIL TWI VER WET
GREEN HUBBARD IMPROVED	95-100	9 x 14 in. Bronzy-green; warted	Orange-yellow flesh is thick and dry.	LEM PON STO WILL
LITTLE GEM	80	3-5 lbs.	Miniature Golden-Hubbard type. Thick, dry, fine-grained flesh. Good storer.	GLE RAW SEE TER VES
MOUNTAINEER	90	Small	Montana variety. Fast-maturing.	HIG
SUGAR HUBBARD		15 lbs. Blue-green	Good fresh-market type.	ABU
WARTED HUBBARD (CHICAGO)	110	12 lbs. 10 x 15 in. Dark slate-green; heavily warted	Orange-yellow flesh. Good keeper.	BURR DEG JUN LET MID RAW RIS STO VES

WINTER SQUASH

SPACE SAVERS

Variety	Days	Size/Color	Remarks	Sources
BURPEE'S BUTTERBUSH	75	1¾ lbs.	Plant grows 3-4 feet long and bears 4 or 5 fruit. Deep reddish-orange meat. Excellent winter keeper.	BURP PIN STO
BUSH BUTTERCUP	88	Round	Thick orange flesh.	ALL FIS
BUTTERBALL (hybrid) (SAKATA)	95	5-6 lbs.	Short vines. Heavy in starch and sugar, low in moisture. Tastes like sweet potatoes. Good keeper.	NIC
BUTTERNUT BUSH		10-12 in.	Rich orange meat. Small seed cavity.	TIL
EARLY BUTTERNUT (hybrid)	75		Bush. Short-season variety. Rich orange flesh. Good keeper.	ARC COM DEG EAR FAR GUR HARR HEN JUN LET MID NIC PAR PIN ROR RIS SEED STO TWI VER WET WIL
EMERALD	90	Gray-green	Turban type. Thick orange flesh. Excellent keeper.	JUN VES
GOLD NUGGET		1-2 lbs. Red-orange with faint stripe	True bush plant. Fruit is round to round oblate. Thick, deep orange meat is fiber-free. Small seed cavity.	DEG HARR HIG JOH SEE TIL VES
SEMI-BUSH BUTTERCUP		3-5 lbs.	1 in. flesh.	SEE
TABLE KING	70-80	5 x 6 in. 1½ lbs. Dark green	Acorn squash. Golden-yellow flesh. Small seed cavity. 6-8 plants per bush.	BURP GAR EAR FAR HARR LED RAW SEED STO TWI VER VES

WINTER SQUASH
OTHER TYPES

Variety	Days	Size/Color	Remarks	Sources
BLUE BANANA (GRAY BANANA) (GREEN BANANA)	105-120	24 x 6 in. Greenish-gray	Heavy cropper. Sweet flesh is used for pies.	JUN ROS SEE TIL
BOSTON MARROW	100	7-10 in. 20 lbs. Bright orange	Yellow flesh. Heavy yields.	LED MEY SEE
CHILACAYOTE (CUCURBITA FICIFOLIA)	130	15 lbs. Greenish-yellow	Mexican variety. Perennial in tropical and subtropical locations. Usually baked with brown sugar and cinnamon.	LEM
CHIRIMEN		Very dark green and bumpy	Japanese squash. Productive and trailing. Use the dry yellow meat for authentic Japanese cuisine. Nice flavor.	LEM
DELICA (hybrid)	85	Flat globe; dark green	Thick yellow meat. Excellent quality and fine flavor. Good storer. Grows well under a variety of conditions.	VES
DELICATA	100	8 x 3 in. Creamy yellow with dark green stripes	Sweet potato squash. Robust vines are high yielding. Very sweet and tasty orange flesh. Stores well.	ABU GAR JOH LET NIC PLA SEE STO
FUTTSU EARLY BLACK		Flat globe; warted	Japanese variety. Very sweet, fine-grained flesh.	RED
GOLDEN DEBUT (hybrid)	105		Orange Butterball type. Sweet flesh and edible skin after boiling. Good keeper.	VER
GOLDEN DELICIOUS	103	6-7 lbs. Bright orange	Golden flesh. Good keeper. Good canner and freezer.	ALL GUR HARR LET STO VER
GOLD NUGGET	85-95	Deep golden orange	Bush-type vine grows 18 in. 6-12 fruit per plant. Golden orange flesh. Good flavor and texture. Good keeper.	GUR JOH STO
GOLDPAK BANANA	110	8-10 lbs. Pink	Prolific variety.	SEE
GREEN DELICIOUS	103	8 x 10 in. Dark green	Bright orange flesh.	ALL LET STO
GREEN HOKKAIDO	98	Round and ribbed; slate-green	Japanese variety. Yellow flesh is thick and fiberless. Not a high yielder.	JOH PEA
HOME DELIGHT (hybrid)	100		Early Butterball type. Flavorful dry yellow flesh. Lateral shoots for easy cultivation and harvest.	VER
HUNGARIAN MAMMOTH	110-120	378 lbs. is the record	For pies or competition.	GRA GUR LET NIC STO
KUTA	42	6 in. Light green	Crisp and smooth. Can be used raw or cooked. Low in calories, fats and carbohydrates. Rich in protein, vitamins and minerals.	PAR POR
MARBLEHEAD YAKIMA		8-25 lbs. Nearly round; gray-green	1896 heirloom variety. Fine flavor. Good keeper.	ABU

▶

◀ WINTER SQUASH

Variety	Days	Size/Color	Remarks	Sources
NAKED SEEDED PUMPKIN SQUASH		4-6 in. Round	Resembles a mini 'Jack O' Lantern'. Contains loads of 'naked' hull-less seeds that can be eaten raw or toasted.	STO
ORANGETTI (hybrid)	85	2½ lbs. Deep orange	True spaghetti squash but deep orange and semi-bush. Fruit should be left to fully ripen on the vine. Low in calories and easily digested.	LET MID PIN TWI VER
PINK BANANA JUMBO	105	Up to 30 x 7 in.	Thick yellow-orange flesh. Limited storage.	BURG BURR GAR GLE GUR HEN LAG LET MID POR SEE WIL
RED KURI (ORANGE HOKKAIDO) (BABY RED HUBBARD)	92	5-8 lbs. Bright red-orange. Teardrop-shaped	Japanese variety. Smooth-textured flesh. High-yielding.	JOH SEE
SANTO DOMINGO SQUASH	90	12 lbs. Pale yellow, striped green	Sweet pale-yellow flesh. Drought-tolerant. When picked young can be eaten like a summer squash. Keep in cool, dry place.	PLA
SHOW KING		Orange, yellow or blue	Resembles a giant pumpkin. (See pumpkin section.) Creamy-yellow meat.	EARL VES
TARAHUMARA SQUASH	75-80	Round, with a neck striped white and green	Traced back to the Indians of Mexico. Huge vine. Let fruit dry on vine until hard and warty. Flesh is sweet and mild.	PLA
TAHITIAN MELON SQUASH	85-220	Up to 40 lbs.	Very high sugar content. So sweet you can eat it like a melon. Rampant vines need a fence or trellis.	ABU GUR HEN LAK POR SEE THO WES
TURKS TURBAN	110	8 x 10 in. Striped and spotted	Varied, rich colors make for a good decoration squash.	BURP BURR COM DEG HARR JUN LAG LED MEY MID POR RIS TWI WET WIL WYA
VEGETABLE SPAGHETTI	100	Yellow; oblong	Harvest in the fall. Excellent substitute for spaghetti. Low in calories and fat.	ABU ALL ARC BURP BURR BUT COM DEG EAR EARL ECO FIS GAR GLE HARR HEN HIG HUM JOH JUN LAG LED LET MEY MID NIC PIN PLA PON POR RAW RED RIS SEE SEED SOU STO SUN TER THO TIL VER WES WET WIL WILL

SWEET POTATOES
(Ipomoea batatas)

The sweet potato is a sprawling morning glory of tropical origin. It withstands hot summers well and needs a lot of space to grow. You can plant vining or bush varieties.

CULTURE: Start sweet potatoes from plants. Plant in light, sandy, warm, not-too-fertile soil 9 to 12 inches apart in rows 3 feet apart. Dangers: too-fertile soil produces all top; heavy soil produces long and stringy tubers; too much water makes the roots elongated.

SEASONS: Warm.

INSECTS/DISEASES: *SWEET POTATO WEEVIL:* Use Sevin, malathion or rotenone.
   LEAF SPOTS: Apply maneb or zineb 10 days apart.

HARVESTING: Dig the tubers when the foliage begins to yellow. Dry them in the sun for several hours, then cure them for about a week at 80 to 85º F. Store them at 55 to 60 degrees.

SWEET POTATO PLANTS

Variety	Color	Remarks	Sources
ALL GOLD	Golden yellow	Good storing variety. Vining.	FAR FRE MAR
CENTENNIAL	Bright copper	90 days. Uniform, medium-size. Deep orange flesh. Fine texture. Good storer. Vining.	BURP EAR FRE GUR HEN JUN MAR PAR POR STE VER
COPPERSKIN			FRE MAR
GEORGIA JET	Red	90 days. Short-season variety. Deep orange flesh.	EAR FRE HEN JUN MAR STE VER
GEORGIA REDS	Red	Heavy yields. Stores well. Vining.	FRE
GOLD RUSH			FRE MAR
JASPER			FRE MAR
JEWELL	Bright copper	100 days. Good keeper. Deep orange flesh has fine texture.	DIX FRE GUR HEN JUN MAR POR STE
NANCY HALLS	Light	Yam of the 1930s and 40s. Yellow flesh. Good baker.	FRE MAR STE
NEW GOLDEN JEWELL	Bright copper	Deep orange flesh. Highest yields. Vining.	MAR PAR STE
OLD KENTUCKY WHITE	Buff	Buff flesh.	SEE
PORTO RICO	Pale yellow	Space-saver bush type. Deep orange flesh. High sugar content.	FAR FRE HEN MAR PAR POR STE VER
RED NUGGET			FRE MAR
RED YAM			MAR
ROSE CENTENNIAL			FRE MAR
TRAVIS		Small plants, big potatoes.	STE
VARDAMAN	Golden yellow	100 days. Bush type. High yields. Deep orange flesh.	EAR FRE GUR HEN JUN MAR PAR STE VER
WHITE YAMS (CHOKER) (POPLAR ROOT) (SOUTHERN QUEEN) (TRIUMPHS) (WHITE BUNCH)	White	White flesh. High sugar content. One of America's oldest varieties. Vining.	FRE MAR STE
YELLOW YAMS	Yellow		FRE MAR

TOMATOES
(Lycopersicon esculentum)

What would a garden be without the king of vegetables, the tomato. Nothing tastes as good as the vine-ripened fruit just picked. Basically, there are two vine types: *DETERMINATE* (called bush tomato), where the terminal bud sets fruit and stops stem growth, and the plant is self-topping and does not need staking; and *INDETERMINATE*, where the terminal bud does not set fruit, and the vine can grow indefinitely until killed by frost. Most of the indeterminate varieties must be trained on stakes or enclosed with wire cages.

Plant breeders have gone wild with tomatoes and, as a result, you can now buy every shape, size, color, and disease-resistant variety imaginable.

Most people see red when they think of tomatoes, but there are various shades of red. Pink tomatoes are generally milder in taste, while the purplish-pink tomatoes are called blue.

Orange, yellow and white tomatoes are mild in flavor and have long been considered low in acidity. However, tests show that color has very little to do with acidity. Then there are the green tomatoes and even a striped one called Mr. Stripey.

There are also special types of tomatoes: tree, potato and husk tomatoes.

CULTURE: To start from seeds, plant the seed a quarter-inch deep in compressed peat pots or other containers. After the weather has warmed up, plant the seedlings outdoors, 18 inches apart in rows 30 to 36 inches apart.

When you buy the plants from the nursery, bury the plant so that half to three-quarters of the stem as well as the root ball is below the soil level. Roots will form along the stem. For long-stemmed plants, plant the root ball on its side so the stem is almost horizontal, then bend the stem so only the bushy part appears above the ground.

Tomatoes like the sun, moderate moisture and a well-balanced fertile soil. Apply fertilizer at transplant time and again when plants bloom.

SEASON: Warm.

INSECTS/DISEASES: *APHIDS, BLISTER BEETLES, COLORADO POTATO BEETLES, CUTWORMS, FLEA BEETLES, LEAFHOPPERS, TOMATO FRUIT WORMS, TOMATO HORNWORMS, THRIPS, WHITE FLIES:* Use Sevin, malathion, diazinon, pyrethrum, rotenone, roryania.

ANTHRACNOSE, EARLY BLIGHT, GRAY LEAF SPOT, LATE BLIGHT: Use maneb, zineb or fixed copper.

BACTERIAL SPOT, SEPTORIAL LEAF SPOT: Use fixed copper fungicides.

HARVESTING: Tomatoes are best harvested when they reach their full color. They may also be picked when they show only a tinge of red. To continue the ripening process, store them in a warm, dark place.

TOMATOES

LARGE

Variety	Days	Fruit	Remarks	Sources
ABRAHAM LINCOLN	70	1¼-3 lbs. Dark red	Very few seeds. Bears until early frost. Solid meat.	GRA
BEEFEATER (hybrid)	85	Up to 2 lbs.	Should be staked. Almost seedless.	GUR STO
BEEF HYBRID VF	76	Large	Extra-firm for slicing. Large enough to cover a big, big burger.	GUR HEN
BEEFMASTER VFN (hybrid)	80	2 lbs. Oblate; deep red	Beefsteak type, but more tolerant to cracking. Indeterminate vine.	ALL ARC BURG COM HARR HEN LAG LED LET MEY MID PAR PIN POR RIS SEED VER
BEEFSTEAK (CRIMSON CUSHION)	80-90	Large, oblate	Indeterminate plant.	ALL ARB BURG DEG LAG LEJ LET MEY MID NIC PIN RAW RED SEE WET
BEEFSTEAK PLUS VF (hybrid)		Extra-large	Determinate plant. Jointless. Good flavor.	LET
BETTER BOY VFN (hybrid)	70	1 lb.	Indeterminate plant. Disease-tolerant. High yields all season.	ALL ARC BURP BURR COM DEG DIX GUR HEN JUN LED LEJ LET MEY NIC PAR PIE PIN PON POR RIS STO TWI VER WET WIL WILL
BIG BOY (hybrid)	80	2 lbs. Semi-globe; bright red	Indeterminate plant. Heavy bearer. Fairly dense foliage and vigorous vines.	ARC BURG BURP DEG EAR EARL FAR HEN JUN LAG LED LEJ LET MEY MID PAR PIN SEED STO TWI WYA
BIG PICK (hybrid) VFFNT	80	Large	Indeterminate vines need staking. Keeps bearing all season. Disease-resistant.	HEN MID PAR STO

►

Variety	Days	Fruit	Remarks	Sources
BRAGGER VF (hybrid)	75	2 lbs. Deep red	Determinate plant. Resistant to cracking and splitting.	ARC DEG FAR HEN MID PAR
BURGESS COLOSSAL (choices of red, golden, crimson and yellow)	90	Up to 2½ lbs. 6 in. across. Deep-flat	Indeterminate plant. Heavy foliage.	BURG
BURGESS STUFFING	78	3¼ x 2¾ in. Lobe-shaped	Unique. Small core, easily removed for stuffing. High yields.	BURG
BURPEE'S BIG EARLY (hybrid)	62	Up to 1 lb. Bright scarlet	Indeterminate plant. Heavy foliage. Good crops all season.	ARC BURP LED LET MEY MID
BURPEE'S BIG GIRL VF (hybrid)	78	1 lb. Bright red	Crack-free. Indeterminate plant.	ARC BURG BURP LED PIE PON WET WYA
BURPEE'S SUPERSTEAK VFN (hybrid)	80	1-2 lbs. Flat-round	Extra meaty. Rich, full-flavored. Healthy productive plant is resistant to wilts and root knot nematodes.	BURG BURP
CLIMBING TOMATO		5 x 3 in. Crimson red	Grows rapidly up to 18 feet. Good slicer and canner.	FAR GUR LAK
DELICIOUS	77	Up to 2 lbs.	Small seed cavity. Little cracking. Nice quality, flavor.	ARC BURP COM DAN GUR LAG LED LET MID RAW SEE
DOMBITO (hybrid)		11 ozs. to 2 lbs.	Thick, meaty walls. Few seeds. Highly disease-resistant.	THO
EARLY GIANT (hybrid)	65	Bright red	Bears fruit until October.	EARL LET WET WIL
GIANT BELGIUM		2-4 lbs. Dark pink	Non-acid. Makes a sweet dessert wine.	GLE GRA
GIANT KING (hybrid)		Scarlet	Few seeds. Plants grow vigorously even under adverse conditions.	FAR
GIANT TREE	90	1½ lbs. Oblate; crimson	Italian potato-leaf type. Low in acid. 10-12 ft. vine. Indeterminate.	WYA
HEAVY WEIGHT VF IND (hybrid)	70 from transplant	To 1½ lbs. Deep globe	Smooth, firm, juicy fruit. Ripens even during cool summers.	NIC
JUMBO (hybrid)	80	Up to 2 lbs. 4½ x 3¼ in. Dark red	Medium-tall vines with good foliage cover.	GRA
LADY LUCK (hybrid)	78	Up to 1 lb.	Prolific plant resistant to fusarium wilt, verticillium and tobacco mosaic virus. Rich, fruity flavor. Well adapted to any area.	BURP
MAMMOTH WONDER	75	1½ lbs. Globe; deep scarlet	Crack-resistant. Extra-firm. Good producer.	BURG
MEXICAN RIBBED		To 2 lbs. Ruffled	Hollow for stuffing.	SEE
PARK'S WHOPPER VFN (hybrid)	75	4 in. across. Red	Heavy yields.	LAG PAR
PONDEROSA RED	90	Up to 2 lbs. Deep red	Large plant.	DEG JOH LED LET SEE TWI VER WET

◄ TOMATOES

Variety	Days	Fruit	Remarks	Sources
RED HEART (hybrid)	72	1 lb. Rich red	Few seeds. Vigorous vines. Good cropper.	EAR
SUPER BEEFSTEAF VFN	80	17 ozs. or more	Prolific, vigorous plant. Flavorful meaty fruit.	BURP DAN LAG PON TWI
SUPERSTEAK VFN (hybrid)	80	1-2 lbs. Flat, round; red	Disease-resistant plant. Extra-meaty. Full rich flavor. Indeterminate plant.	DAN
SUPER 23 (hybrid)		3/4 lb. Deep globe; scarlet red	Very firm with thick walls. Highly productive. Indeterminate plant.	DEG
TRIP-L-CROP	85	6 in. across. Crimson	12-25 ft. high vine is indeterminate. Good canner or slicer.	ARC BURG HEN POR
ULTRA BOY VFN (hybrid)	72	1 lb. Deep globe	Indeterminate plant.	STO THO
WONDER BOY VFN (hybrid)	68-80	1 lb.	Indeterminate plant. Strong vine produces good quality fruit.	ALL BURR COM DEG MEY MID RIS WIL

TOMATOES—EARLY

UP TO 70 DAYS

Variety	Days	Fruit	Remarks	Sources
ALICANTE (op)		Medium	Good flavor. High quality. Heavy cropper.	THO
ALISA CRAIG (op)		Medium deep red	Fine cropper. Good size and shape.	ECO THO
AMATEUR (op)			Sturdy, dwarf plant. Needs little staking. An old favorite.	ECO
ANGORA	68	Medium brilliant red	Has grayish-white fuzz on stems and leaves. Determinate growth. Very mild flavor.	GLE
BASKET VEE	70	9 ozs.	Free of cracking or catfacing. Ripens from inside first. Verticillium-tolerant.	STO
BENEWAH (op)	60		Spreading determinate habit. Vigorous with good foliage. Short-season variety.	GAR
BIG SET VFN (hybrid)	65	8-9 ozs.	Determinate plant does not need staking. Fruit sets well under adverse conditions. Disease-tolerant.	TWI
BETTER GIRL VFN (hybrid)	68	7 ozs.	Determinate, productive plant.	MID
BONNER IDAHO (op)	58	3 in.	Heavy producer. Large, determinate plant. Short-season variety.	GAR GRA
BONNY BEST (hybrid)	70	5-8 ozs. Slightly flattened	Indeterminate. Short-season variety. Use only as an early transplant variety.	ABU ALL DEG HIG JOH MID NIC PIN SEE SOU WILL
BOUNTY WR	65	Globe shape; red	Heavy producer.	EARL

Variety	Days	Fruit	Remarks	Sources
BRANDYWINE (op)	74	10-12 ozs. Dark reddish-pink	1885 Amish heirloom variety. Potato leaf type. Not disease-resistant, but flavor is gourmet quality.	SOU
BURPEE'S EARLY PICK VF (hybrid)	62	1/2 lb. Bright scarlet	Old-fashioned flavor. Widely adapted. Recommended for the west coast of United States. Bumper crops all summer.	BURP
BURPEE'S VF (hybrid)	72	Medium rich red	Indeterminate. Crack-resistant. Heavy yields. Strong, wilt-resistant plant. Suitable for greenhouse forcing.	BURP DEG MID
BUSH BEEFSTEAK	62	8 ozs. Rich red	Compact, bush plant. Few seeds. Grows well under adverse conditions.	STO
CABOT		Medium brilliant red	Short-season variety. Dwarf, open habit plant.	RAW VES
CAVALIER VENT (hybrid)	71	12 ozs. Deep globe	Good tolerance to cracking.	PIN STO
CELEBRITY VFNT (hybrid)	80	7-12 ozs. Globe	Strong determinate plant. Good disease tolerance. Crack-resistant fruit is all-purpose variety.	ARC BURG BURP BURR COM DAN EAR EARL FAR HEN JOH JUN LAG LED LEM LET MEY MID PAR PIE PIN POR RAW RIS STO THO TWI VER WET WIL WILL WYA
COLDSET	68	5-6 ozs. Blood-red	Indeterminate. Short-season variety. Canning variety.	GUR SOU STO
CRIMSON SPRINTER	71	5 ozs.	Indeterminate plant. Good canner.	EARL
CURABEL (hybrid)		Medium-large	Disease-resistant plant. Short-jointed, open habit.	THO
DEL ORO (hybrid)		Medium; deep round	Processing tomato. Strong, determinate vine. Peels well.	HARR
DORADO (hybrid)		Medium-large; deep round	Canning tomato. Determinate vine. Not for whole peel.	HARR
DOUBLERICH	60		Contains as much vitamin C as citrus.	BURG
EARLIANA (hybrid)	66	6 ozs. Deep oblate; scarlet	Indeterminate plant.	ABU ALL ARC FAR
EARLIBRIGHT	60	6 ozs. Crimson	Good canning variety. Determinate bushy plant. Short-season variety. Fruit is firm with pleasing flavor.	JOH STO
EARLIROUGE	63	6½ ozs.	Determinate. Verticillium-tolerant. Good canner. Ripens from the inside. Easy to peel.	ABU HIG JOH PLA
EARLY CASCADE VF (hybrid)	52	4-6 ozs.	Very disease-resistant. Sweet flavor.	ALL FAR GUR HEN HUM JOH LED LET NIC POR SEE VES WILL WYA
EARLY GIRL (hybrid)	62	5 ozs.	Indeterminate. Good foliage protection. High yields. Resistant to cracking.	ALL ARC BURG BURP DEG EARL GUR HEN HUM JUN LAG LET MEY NIC PAR PIE POR TIL VER WET

◄ TOMATOES—EARLY

Variety	Days	Fruit	Remarks	Sources
EARLY HI-CRIMSON (hybrid)	65	3½ in. Double-red	Short-season variety. Semi-determinate plant.	FIS
EARLY PICK (hybrid)	52	4-6 ozs. Deep oblate	Large, indeterminate plant. Verticillium wilt-resistant.	LAG PIE
EARLY SET (hybrid)	60	3 in. Globe	Vigorous, indeterminate vine. Disease-resistant.	FIS HARR
EARLY TEMPTATION (hybrid)		2-3 ozs.	Dwarf growth. Hardy and vigorous. Short-season variety.	VES
FANTASTIC (hybrid)	72	8 ozs. Deep globe; red	Indeterminate. Can be used for greenhouse forcing in short-season areas.	ARC BURG BURR COM EARL FAR FIS GUR LET MEY MID PIN POR RIS SEED STO TER TWI WIL
FIREBALL	64	5 ozs. Deep oblate	Determinate plant. Short-season variety. Sparse foliage.	ALL DEG GAR LET STO TIL WILL
FIRECHIEF VF (hybrid)		Medium; deep oblate	Determinate. Jointless fruit.	HARR
FRESH PAK VFN (hybrid)		Large globe	Determinate, compact plant. Good foliage cover.	HARR
GURNEY GIRL VFNT (hybrid)	75	Round	Indeterminate plant. Disease-resistant. Sweet, juicy fruit.	GUR
HARBINGER (op)		Medium	Indeterminate plant. Good cropper. Fine flavor. An old variety.	ECO
HEARTLAND VFN (hybrid)		8-10 ozs. Oblate	Self-supporting 4 ft. plant. Heavy foliage. Nice quality fruit. Good producer. Disease tolerance.	ARC POR VER
HIGHLANDER VF	68	5 ozs. Globe; bright scarlet	Determinate. High yielder. Good fresh or canned.	BURR
HYBRID MASTER NO. 3	60	7 ozs.	Stakes well. Also for greenhouse culture.	WILL
HYBRID NO. 31		Medium	Determinate habit. A short-season variety with pleasing flavor.	VES
JACKPOT VFN (hybrid)	68	9 ozs.	Determinate plant. Good leaf coverage. Tolerant to blossom end rot.	JOH MEY POR STO WIL
JOH BAER	72	Globe; scarlet-red	Good producer.	ALL
JUNG'S WAYAHEAD		Scarlet	Determinate growth.	JUN
JUNG'S WAYAHEAD IMPROVED	63	Scarlet; almost round	Heavy bearer. Determinate.	JUN
MANITOBA	60	6½ ozs.	Short-season variety. Good yields. Good fresh or canned.	EARL STO
MARMANDE VF	65	Oblate; slightly ribbed.	French variety, recommended for coastal areas. Indeterminate.	COO HER SHE

◄

Variety	Days	Fruit	Remarks	Sources
MARMANDE SUPER (op)		Large; irregularly shaped	Determinate bushy habit. Fleshy, full-flavored fruit. Can also be grown under glass.	ECO
MORCROSS SURPRISE (hybrid)	70	Flattened	Indeterminate. Crack-resistant. Tolerant to fusarium wilt.	ARC
MOIRA	76	6 ozs. Round	Determinate. Short-season variety. Dependable under adverse conditions.	HIG JOH STO
MONEYMAKER		Medium globe	Excellent flavor. Vigorous plant.	EARL
MORETON (hybrid)	70	Slightly flattened; brilliant red	Bears over a long season. Good quality.	HARR
MUSTANG (hybrid)	65	Medium; red	High yields. Good flavor.	EARL
NEW YORKER	60	3-5 ozs. Bright scarlet	Determinate. Short-season variety. Fruits set under cool conditions.	BURP DIX GAR HARR PIE SEED STO VER
OREGON SPRING		Large	Almost seedless. Good flavor. Short-season variety. Determinate.	NIC TER
OUTDOOR GIRL (op)	58	Medium	Thin skin. Hearty, robust plant. Heavy cropper. Determinate plant.	ECO THO
PARK'S EXTRA EARLY	65	Dark red	High yields.	PAR
PERON (SPRAYLESS TOMATO)	68	Scarlet red	Disease- and crack-resistant. High in vitamin C.	GLE SEE
PLAINSMAN	65	5 ozs. Globe; vivid red	Indeterminate. Heavy yields. Good quality. Does well in dry climates.	POR
PRAIRIE FIRE (op)	53	3 in.	Short-season variety. Compact, determinate plant. Good foliage cover.	GAR
PRESIDENT VFNT (hybrid)	75	Large; deep globe	Excellent yields. Good foliage protection.	EAR MID RIS
PUSA RUBY		Medium; deep red	East Indian variety. Good disease resistance. Good keeping qualities.	GLE
QUEBEC 5			Requires staking. Excellent-tasting tomatoes.	RAW
QUICK PICK (hybrid)		Medium	Heavy producer. Blemish-free.	DAN EAR PAR TIL
QUINTE (EASY PEEL)	70	7 ozs.	Small core. Crimson interior and exterior. Skin peels easily. Verticillium-tolerant plant.	STO
RED EXPRESS VFN (hybrid)	61	8 ozs. Deep globe; bright red	Vigorous bushy plant. Fruit has green shoulders.	STO
RED QUEEN VFNR (hybrid)	78	6½ ozs. Globe shape	Plants are strong, disease-resistant and heavy-yielding. Good foliage cover.	DEG
REVOLUTION (hybrid)	62	Medium-large; deep globe	Compact, determinate plant. Highly productive. Widely adapted. Disease-resistant.	TWI
ROCKET (op)	50	2 ozs. 2 in. across. Medium-red	Short-season variety. Short plants are loaded with small fruit. Slightly acid.	EARL GAR STO

►

TOMATOES—EARLY

Variety	Days	Fruit	Remarks	Sources
ROCKY MOUNTAIN (hybrid)	60	3 in. Scarlet red	Determinate bush type. Short-season variety. Thick, meaty interior. Sets even in cool weather.	FIS
RUSHMORE VF (hybrid)	66	Dark red	Bred to withstand cool springs and hot summers. Good disease resistance and leaf cover.	GUR
SANTIAM		4-5 ozs.	30-in. determinate plant. Produces mostly seedless tomatoes. Slightly acid.	NIC POR TER
SALTSPRING SUNRISE (op)		Small to medium; red	Short-season variety from the Gulf Islands of British Columbia, Canada.	ABU
SCOTIA	60	4 ozs. Red	Determinate. Short-season variety. Sets fruit in cool weather.	RAW STO VES
SIBERIA (op)		Small to medium	Cold-tolerant short-season variety. Doesn't have much flavor when grown under high temperatures.	ABU HIG HUM PLA SEE SOU
SIOUX	70	Globe; Deep red	Indeterminate. Crack-free. Small seed cells. Non-acid. Medium foliage.	DEG MID
SPRING GIANT VFN (hybrid)	70	10 ozs. Deep globe; bright red	Determinate bush. High yields.	EAR FAR JUN POR ROS SEED WIL
SPRINGSET VF (hybrid)	65	6 ozs.	Determinate plant. High yields. Crack-resistant. Vigorous, open vine.	ALL COM HARR LED PIN RAW RIS SEED STO
STARFIRE	56	½ lb. Round; deep red	Determinate. Not inclined to sun scald.	EARL GAR STO WILL
STAR PAK VFN (hybrid)		Large globe	Indeterminate. Firm structure.	HARR
STOKES EARLY (hybrid)	54	4 ozs. Rich red	Produces good quantities. Excellent early staker.	STO
STOKES PAK VFN (hybrid)		9 ozs.	Good tolerance to gray wall, blotchy ripening, gray leaf spot and stem canker. Easy to pick.	STO
STRIPED CAVERN (op)		8 ozs.	Firm, blocky fruit. Thick and meaty. Can be harvested and stored for 4 weeks. Great stuffing tomato.	THO
SUMMER DELIGHT (hybrid)	75	8-12 ozs.	Small, compact determinate plant is resistant to verticillium and fusarium wilts. Very meaty fruit.	BURP
SUMMER FLAVOR BRAND 2000 VF (hybrid)		Large; deep globe	Extra-compact plant has concentrated quantity of fruit.	TWI
SUMMER FLAVOR BRAND 4000 VF (hybrid)		Medium-large; deep globe	Determinate plant. Fruit holds up well.	TWI
SUPER FANTASTIC FVN (hybrid)		Medium-large	Indeterminate plant. Popular variety of meaty, flavorful fruit.	POR

Variety	Days	Fruit	Remarks	Sources
SUPER SIOUX	70	Oblate	Indeterminate. Does well in hot, dry areas.	ARC BURR DEG EAR HOR POR WIL
SURPRISE VF (hybrid)	65	Globe	Indeterminate. Crack-resistant.	DEG EAR MID
SWIFT	54	2¾ ozs. 1¾ in. Deep globe; brick-red	Free of cracking. Sets fruit at low temperatures. Small bushy plant. Short-season variety.	EARL STO
TERRIFIC VFN (hybrid)	70	10 ozs. Oblate	Indeterminate. Strong plant, good foliage cover. Vigorous producer.	MID POR WIL
THE JUICE VF (hybrid)	65	6-8 ozs.	Perfect for making tomato juice. Bushy, compact plant. Big yields.	HEN LET
THESSALONIKI	68	Baseball-size; red	Greek variety. Disease-resistant.	GLE
TOMATO 1 PB-NW	60	Medium	Potato leaf foliage. Indeterminate. Skin is a little tough.	HUM
TOMATO NO. 670	65	Scarlet red	Determinate plant. Excellent canner. Resists sunburn and cracking.	GLE
ULTRA GIRL VFN	56	9 ozs.	Semi-determinate. Tolerance to cracking.	STO
VALERIE VFN (hybrid)	65	8 ozs. Globe	Determinate plant. Smooth, firm fruit.	HARR MID
VALIANT	70	8 ozs. Globe	Indeterminate. Fair foliage cover.	ALL BURG COM DEG MEY
WILLHITE'S 101 VFN (hybrid)	70	6-7 ozs. Deep oblate	Bush type.	WIL
WILLHITE'S 202 VFN (hybrid)	72	7-8 ozs. Deep oblate	Strong determinate plant.	WIL

TOMATOES—MID-SEASON
71 TO 80 DAYS

Variety	Days	Fruit	Remarks	Sources
ACE 55 VF	80	Bright red	Semi-determinate plant. Widely adapted. Heavy bearer all season.	BURP LAG LED MEY WIL WYA
ACE 55 VF IMPROVED	80	Large; scarlet red	Resistant to wilts and stem canker. Adapted to stake or bush culture.	ROS
ACE ROYAL	80	Large; red	Determinate, medium-large growth. Thick-walled. Soft core.	RIS
ALL STAR (hybrid)	72	7 ozs. Globe	Determinate, medium-size plant. Widely adapted. Highly disease-resistant.	MID TWI
AVALANCHE (hybrid)	77	Medium	Indeterminate plant. Resistant to fusarium wilt and cracks.	ARC DEG HARR MID
BIG PICK VFN (hybrid)		Large; round	Indeterminate vine should be staked. Resistant to tobacco mosaic virus.	DAN
BIGSET VFN (hybrid)	75	9 ozs. Oblate	Determinate. Resistant to cracking. Sets under adverse conditions.	FAR LAG POR RIS VES

TOMATOES—MID-SEASON

Variety	Days	Fruit	Remarks	Sources
BIG SEVEN VFN (hybrid)	77	Large; deep globe	Indeterminate plant is disease-resistant.	TWI
BLAZER (hybrid)		Deep oblate	Determinate, vigorous, disease-resistant plant has a heavy set. Widely adapted. Resistant to verticillium, fusarium and alternaria.	HARR POR
BONNEYVEE (hybrid)	71	6½ ozs.	Firm, crack-tolerant fruit. Good canner, ketchup or fresh use. Herbicide-tolerant.	STO
BREAK O'DAY WR	73	Globe shape	Cold-resistant.	ARC
BURPEE HYBRID VF	72	8 ozs. Rich red	Indeterminate. Heavy foliage cover. Resistant to cracking and catfacing.	MEY MID
CAMPBELL 19 VF	75	8-10 ozs.	Bush plant.	STO
CAMPBELL 1327 VF	75	10 ozs. Oblate	Determinate. Good foliage cover. Crack-resistant canning tomato.	BURR DIX GUR HARR LED LET MEY MID PIE RIS STO TWI WIL
CARMELLO VFNT (hybrid)		Large	French variety with exceptionally fine flavor. Crack-resistant.	SHE
CHAMPION VFNT (hybrid)		Medium-large	Good flavor and color.	ARC LAG NIC POR VER
CHEROKEE VF	80	Large, slightly flattened; red	Indeterminate vine. Firm meaty interior.	WYA
DUKE (hybrid)	78	Large	Highly productive. Multiple disease resistance. Concentrated fruit set. Jointless fruit.	RIS TWI
FLORAMERICA (hybrid)	80	16 ozs. Flattened globe; deep red	Tolerant to 16 tomato diseases. Determinate plant.	ALL ARC BURG BURP BURR COM FAR HEN JUN LAG LED LET MEY MID PIE PIN POR RIS STO TWI VER WET WIL WILL WYA
FREEDOM (hybrid)	75	Large	Large determinate plant. Picks stem-free. Widely adapted. Keeps well after picking. Sets well under adverse conditions.	POR TWI
GLAMOUR	77	6-8 ozs. Deep oblate	Indeterminate. Solid, crack-resistant.	BURG DEG HARR LET SEE SEED STO WILL
HARRIS MORAN 3075 (DIEGO)		Medium; deep round	Processing tomato. Determinate compact plant. Plant Variety Protected. Disease-resistant.	HARR
HARVESTVEE VF	75	9½ ozs.	Good tolerance to catfacing, blossom end rot and blotching ripening. All-purpose tomato. Peels easily.	STO
HAYSLIP (op)	72	Large	High disease resistance. Tolerant to blossom end rot, black shoulder, catface and cracking.	TWI
HEAVYWEIGHT (hybrid)	80	8 ozs. Globe	Indeterminate growth. Resistant to alternaria stem canker, stem phylium verticillium wilt and fusarium wilt.	LED PIN RIS

◀

Variety	Days	Vines/Pods	Remarks	Sources
HEINZ 1350 VF	75	6 ozs. Slightly flattened; bright red	Determinate. High-yielding. Canning tomato. Crack-free.	BURP DEG DIX HARR LED LET MID PIE PON SOU STO TER WILL
HEINZ 1370	75		Canning variety. Interiors develop slowly. Fusarium-tolerant.	MID STO
HEINZ 1409	74			MID
HEINZ 1439 VF	72		Excellent vine cover. Tolerance to cracking. No green shoulders.	BURR HEN MID PAR SEED STO
HEINZ 1765 VF	73	9 ozs. Globe	Very firm fruit. Good tolerance to cracking.	STO
HEINZ 2653 VF		2-3 in. Heart-shaped; red	Canning variety. Very productive.	TER
HE-MAN (hybrid)	75	Large; deep red	Few seeds, little or no cracking.	DAN EAR HEN
HERMITAGE VF (hybrid)	80	8 ozs. Deep globe	Prolific, medium, determinate plant. Jointed fruit.	BURR
HOMESTEAD FWR		Bright red	Semi-determinate plant. Good producer.	LEJ POR
HOMESTEAD 500 F	77	Slightly flat; medium to large	Determinate plant. Good foliage cover.	MID WIL
HYBRID 980 VF	75	8 ozs. Deep oblate	Well-suited for staking.	LET
HY X	67	Medium; bright red	Determinate. Resistant to disease. Does well in semi-arid regions.	HEN
INDEPENDENCE VF (hybrid)	73		Determinate, medium-size plant. Thick walled. Light green shoulders. Good flavor.	TWI
LORISSA VFNT		Deep red	French variety. Semi-determinate plant is vigorous grower.	SHE
LUCKY DRAW VF (hybrid)		Medium to large	Very productive, moderately large plant. Crack-resistant fruit.	POR
MARGLOBE	75	10 ozs.	Determinate. Heavy foliage cover.	ALL BURG BURP COM DEG GLE HEN JOH LEJ LET MEY MID WES WIL WYA
MARGLOBE VF IMPROVED	75	Oblate	Determinate plant. Crack-resistant fruit.	ARC ROS SOU TWI WET
MARGLOBE SELECT	77	Medium globe shape	Still used in many gardens.	LED
MARGLOBE SUPREME F	73	Large, globe; red	Small seed cavity. Fruit ripens evenly and crack-free. Heavy cropper. Vigorous plant.	DEG PAR
MARION FWR	78	Large; deep red	High yields.	WYA
MARVEL	70	Large; slightly flat	High quality. Keeps well.	HER
MEATY MARGLOBE	78	6-7 ozs.	Thick and meaty. Small seed cavity. Resistant to fusarium wilt.	BURR

▶

◄ TOMATOES—MID-SEASON

Variety	Days	Fruit	Remarks	Sources
MONEYMAKER		Medium	Mild flavor. Outstandingly reliable.	THO
MONTE CARLO VFN (hybrid)	75	9 ozs. to 1 lb. Globe	Indeterminate plant needs staking.	FAR LET MID STO
MOUNTAIN PRIDE VF (hybrid)	77	Medium to large; deep oblate	Determinate. Flavor is somewhat acid. Widely adapted.	DIX LET MEY MID PIE RIS STO TWI WYA
MURRIETA VF		Medium to small; deep globe	Easy-to-peel processing tomato. High solids, low pH and medium viscosity. Determinate plant.	HARR
NEPAL	80	12 ozs. Globe; deep red	Indeterminate. Himalaya Mountain variety. Intense flavor. High yields. Disease-resistant.	JOH
NUMBER 95 (op)		Square, round	Hard, non-juicy canning tomato. Determinate, compact 3 ft. diameter plant.	TER
OLE VF₁F₂ (hybrid)		Large globe	Excellent flavor. Recommended variety for Florida. Determinate plant.	HARR
OPAL'S HOMESTEAD		Large; red	Old Kentucky strain.	ABU
PEARSON A-1 IMPROVED	80	Deep globe	Indeterminate. Resistant to fusarium wilt. High quality.	BURR ROS WIL
PEELETTE		Deep round globe	Peeling processing variety. Large, strong determinate vines.	HARR
PIK-RED VFN (hybrid) (RED PAK)		Large globe; brilliant red	High quality tomato. Solid, meaty fruit. Sturdy, compact vine adapted to ground or cage culture.	DIX HARR HUM LED PIE TIL WIL
PIRATE VF (hybrid)	76	6-8 ozs. Globe to oblate	Determinate. Extra-firm, flavorful. Jointless and free of cracking. Resistant to stem canker and leaf spot.	JOH
POLE KING V F₁F₂ (hybrid)			Sets fruit in adverse weather. Firm thick-walled, green-shouldered fruit. Vigorous plant.	TWI
PORTER'S PRIDE (IMPROVED PORTER)		Medium; scarlet	Indeterminate. Vigorous and productive.	POR WIL
PORTER		Medium; red	Produces in any kind of soil. Not affected by hot, dry weather. Does not crack or sunburn.	POR WES WIL
PRESIDENT VFN (hybrid)	74	Large	Determinate bush is vigorous and disease-tolerant.	FAR POR RIS
PRITCHARD (SCARLET TOPPER)	75	Large globe; scarlet red	Determinate. Adapted to heavy soils. Thick-walled, small core and seed pockets. Good foliage cover.	SOU
RED CHAMPION (hybrid)	70	Medium	Disease-resistant. Heavy bearer.	HEN
RED ENSIGN (hybrid)		Medium to large	Comes into full production quickly. Fine flavor. Heavy crop of firm-fleshed fruit. Resistant to all strains of cladosporium.	THO
RED EXPRESS 238 VFN (hybrid)	74	8-10 ozs. Red	Determinate. Firm and smooth. Good shelf life.	JOH

Variety	Days	Fruit	Remarks	Sources
RED KING	73	6 ozs. Deep globe	Compact determinate vine. Disease-resistant. Crack-free. Good eating quality.	TWI
RUSHMORE VF (hybrid)	66	Medium; slightly flattened	Determinate. Highly productive.	STO
RUSSIAN RED	74	Medium; round	Determinate. Heavy foliage cover. Tolerates lower temperatures.	GLE
RUTGERS IMPROVED VF	73		Ripens from inside out. Small seed cavity. Few seeds. Good cropper. Good canner.	WET
SAINT PIERRE	80	Large	Very popular French variety.	HER
SHOW ME (hybrid)	72	7-8 ozs.	Firm, crack-resistant plant.	ARC EAR MID
STOKESDALE	72	Large; rich red	Heavy yields. Vigorous vines are productive.	WIL
SUMMER FLAVOR BRAND 5000 V F_1F_2N (hybrid)		Large; oblate	Strong, determinate vine. Fruit is firm, thick-walled.	TWI
SUMMER FLAVOR BRAND 6000 V F_1F_2 (hybrid)		Large; deep globe	Determinate vine. Jointless fruit. Very flavorful.	TWI
SUMMERTIME IMPROVED FN		Medium; round	Heat-resistant. Determinate, compact plant. Resistant to blossom end rot and fruit cracking.	POR
SUNNY V F1F2S A (hybrid)		Medium to large	Plant Variety Protected. Very productive compact, determinate plant. Crack-resistant.	POR
SUPER BUSH VFN (hybrid)	68	Large	38 x 36 in. plant. Bears over long season.	EAR SEED
SUPERCROSS TMV C (hybrid)		Medium; deep scarlet	An abundant producer. Non-green back.	THO
SUPERSONIC B V F_1F_2 (hybrid)		Large; slightly flattened globe	Indeterminate vine. Good crack resistance.	HARR
SUPERSONIC VF	79	Large; flattened globe	Indeterminate. Big, leafy plant.	ARC HARR WIL
SUPER STANDARD BONNY BEST	71		Pre-1934 variety. Produces pretty good crop by today's standards.	STO
SUPER STOKESDALE	74	10 ozs. Globe; bright red	Good crack tolerance. High crimson interior. Fusarium-tolerant.	STO
SUPREME	75			MID
TANGO VFTM (hybrid)	70		Plenty of yields on vigorous plant.	HER
TIP TOP	74	3 ozs. Top-shaped	Can also be used as a paste tomato. Borne in large clusters.	PIN
TROPIC VF	80	Large; deep red	Determinate. Adaptable to greenhouse culture.	MID POR SOU
URBANA	78	Scarlet	High yields.	JUN

◄ ## TOMATOES—MID-SEASON

Variety	Days	Fruit	Remarks	Sources
UC 82 VF	72	2 ozs. Square	Sturdy determinate plant. Processing variety. Outstanding yields.	BURR
V.F. 134 1-2		Small; square, round	Determinate plant. Firm fruit has high viscosity. Resistant to cracking and alternaria stem canker.	HARR MID
V.F. 145 B-7879	74			MID
VINERIPE VFN (hybrid)		Large; flattened	Determinate vine. Jointless firm fruit. Good variety for the Northwest.	HARR
WALTER	79	7 ozs. Dark red	Compact determinate plant. Fusarium-tolerant. High yields of crack-resistant fruits.	LET MID SOU TWI WIL
WEST VIRGINIA	70	8 ozs. Globe	Highly productive. Good foliage cover. Crack- and wilt-resistant.	BURG
WEST VIRGINIA 63	70	6-8 ozs.	Indeterminate. Mature fruit tends to drop from vine. Good disease resistance.	SOU
WILLAMETTE		Medium; red	Short-season variety.	ABU NIC
WISCONSIN CHIEF (WISCONSIN 55)	72	Medium; oblate	Semi-determinate.	JUN

TOMATOES—LATE

Variety	Days	Fruit	Remarks	Sources
ADVANTAGE VF		Medium; deep globe	Processing variety. Plant Variety Protected. Not for peeling. Jointless.	HARR
BRIMMER	100	Often 2½ lbs. Pink/purple	Old Virginia variety. Indeterminate. Meaty with few seeds. Low acid with high sugar content. Recommended for Piedmont and coastal mid-Atlantic areas.	SOU
CAL ACE VF	85		Determinate. Sets well under adverse weather conditions. Superior to other Ace varieties.	BURR HARR LAG
CARDINAL	80	Medium	Indeterminate. Pre-1879 variety. Widely adapted from north to south.	SOU
DAD'S MUG	85	Large	Few seeds. Tasty.	SEE
EARLYPAK NO. 7	81	2¾ x 2½ in. Globular; bright scarlet	Determinate. Good foliage cover. Good canning tomato.	BURR
FLORA DADE VFN (op)		Medium; deep globe	Determinate plant. Firm, jointless fruit.	BURR DIX HARR MID RIS TWI
FLORADEL	85	Large; slightly globe; medium-red	Indeterminate. Resistant to cracks and diseases.	POR
HOMESTEAD 24	83	Medium-large; deep globe	Determinate. Fruits set under wide range of conditions.	ARC BURG WET WIL WYA

►

◀

Variety	Days	Fruit	Remarks	Sources
INDIAN RIVER	85	Globe; scarlet	Indeterminate. High yields under warm, humid conditions. Disease-resistant.	BURG RED
J. MORAN	95	Large	Good canner.	BURR MID
LIBERTY ASVF (hybrid)	80	Medium to large	Strong, determinate plant. Widely adapted. Jointless, green-shouldered fruit. High yields.	TWI
LONG KEEPER	78	Golden red	Flesh is medium-red color. Stays fresh for 6 to 12 weeks.	ARC BURG BURP COM COM FAR HEN HIG LAG LED PIN PON RAW TER WILL
MANALUCIE	87	Medium-large; deep globe	Indeterminate. Tolerant to blossom end rot, leaf mold, early blight and fusarium wilt.	RIS
MANAPAL	85	Medium-large; globe	Determinate. Adapted to hot, humid climates. Disease-resistant. Good foliage cover.	DEG POR
MOUNTAIN PRIDE VF (hybrid)		Large; deep globe	Determinate plant with dark green foliage. Very firm fruit.	HARR JOH
PEARSON	80	Large	Determinate vine. Fruit may have green shoulders. Canning variety.	LEM
RAMAPO VFR (hybrid)		Large; flattened globe	Indeterminate, for ground or stake culture.	DEG HARR LED MID
RUBY (hybrid)	100	Bright red	California variety. Although determinate, plant is gangly. Good flavor. Color even all the way through.	LEM
RUTGERS VF (hybrid)	90	6 ozs. Oblate	Indeterminate. Highly resistant to cracking.	ARC BURG BURP COM DEG DIX EAR FAR GLE HEN JLH LAG LEJ LET MEY MID PIE POR ROS SEE TWI VER WIL WYA
RUTGERS CALIFORNIA SUPREME	73	8 ozs. Dark red	Especially recommended for southern gardens.	PAR
RUTGERS SELECT	80	Globular; dark red	Thick-walls, small seed cells. Used for canning or fresh. Large plant with vigorous foliage.	LED RIS
RUTGERS 39 VF (op)		Medium; flattened globe	Compact, determinate vine. An Improved Rutgers with disease resistance.	HARR
SEPTEMBER DAWN	85	Large	Resistant to fusarium and cracking.	HARR
STONE	81	7 ozs. Slightly ridged and flattened	Indeterminate. Pre-1913 introduction. Uniform ripening. Vigorous vines are highly branched. Good drought resistance.	SOU
SUPERSTEAK VFN	80	Large; flat, round	Indeterminate plant.	PIE
TROPIC	80	Medium-large	Good flavor and quality. Resistant to fusarium and verticillium wilt and gray leaf spot. Well adapted to southern states and greenhouses.	BURP

TOMATOES

PINK

Variety	Days	Fruit	Remarks	Sources
ARKANSAS TRAVELER (ARKANSAS PINK)	76	6-8 ozs. 3-4 in.	Indeterminate. Good flavor and disease resistance. Recommended for disease-prone areas.	SOU
BRADLEY	80	Pink	Fusarium-resistant. Good foliage cover.	MID
BRIMMER	83-100	2½ lbs. Purplish-pink	Must be staked. Has no core and very few seeds. Good slicer.	SOU
DUTCHMAN		Large; oblate; purple-pink	Non-acid.	GLE
DWARF CHAMPION	73	5 ozs. Rose-pink	24 in. potato leaf foliage. Low acid.	STO
EARLY DETROIT	78	Large; globular; purple-pink	Bush plant.	.STO
FIREBIRD V F₁ TMV (hybrid)	76	8-10 ozs. Pearly-pink	Deep red interior. Vigorous indeterminate vine. Very pretty tomato.	JOH
GERMAN JOHNSON (GERMAN JOHNSON PINK)	76	¾-1 lb. Pink-red	Indeterminate heirloom variety from Virginia. Productive plant. Good slicer or canner.	SOU
GIANT ITALIAN POTATO LEAF	82	Large	Non-acid pink strain.	LET
HOLMES MEXICAN TOMATO	75	3 lbs. Pink	Sub-acid. Vigorous grower.	HOL
MISSION DYKE	70	Medium-pink	Determinate. Vigorous. Disease- and drought-resistant.	GLE
MORTGAGE LIFTER	79	2½ lbs.	Indeterminate. Very productive. Bred in Virginia.	GLE SOU
OLYMPIC	76	Pink	Tolerant to fusarium wilt. Short-season variety. Little or no cracking.	STO
PINK DELIGHT (hybrid)	70	4 in. Round; pink	Red flesh, few seeds. Good cropper.	ARC
PINK GIRL (hybrid)	71	8 ozs. Deep globe	Widely adapted. Indeterminate stake tomato. Excellent tolerance to cracking.	BURG BURP EAR GUR HEN LET MID STO TWI WET
PONDERHEART		Semi-globe	Japanese variety. Non-acid.	GLE
PONDEROSA (BEEFSTEAK PINK)	83-95	2 lbs. Oblate; purplish-pink	Indeterminate. Rather rough.	ARC LED MID NIC POR RIS STO VER WIL WILL
PORTER IMPROVED	78	Small; pink	High-yielding even under high temperatures and low humidity.	LET
TAPPY'S FINEST	77	14-16 ozs. Somewhat flattened; pink-red	Indeterminate. Heirloom West Virginia seed originally from Italy. Small core, fine flavor. All-purpose variety. Heavy producer.	SOU
TOMBOY	66	1 lb. Pink	Red flesh, few seeds. Non-acid. Good slicer, canner or for ketchup.	ARC EAR
WATERMELON BEEFSTEAK	75	2 lbs. Oblong; pink	Purplish-red flesh. Non-acid.	GLE

TOMATOES
ORANGE-YELLOW-GOLD

Variety	Days	Fruit	Remarks	Sources
BURPEE'S JUBILEE	72	3¼ x 2¾ in. Golden orange; deep globular	Sub-acid. Indeterminate. Heavy yields.	BURP
CARO RICH	80	4-6 ozs. Carrot-colored	Distinctive flavor. Very low acidity. Too late for north to grow.	STO
D. JENA LEE'S GOLDEN GIRL	80	Yellow-orange	Indeterminate 1929 heirloom variety. Good flavor.	SOU
GOLD DUST	60	Round; golden yellow	Small, determinate plant. Good yielder.	FIS
GOLDEN BOY (hybrid)	80	Globe; golden yellow	Indeterminate. Low in acid.	ARC COM HEN JUN MID PAR PIN RIS TWI VER WET WIL
GOLDEN DELIGHT	65	3-5 ozs. Butter-yellow	Crack-resistant. Low acidity. Mild flavor. Dwarf compact plant.	RAW SEE STO TER VES
GOLDEN GIANT	90	1½ lbs.	Yellow flesh. Low acidity.	GUR
GOLDEN PONDEROSA (RAILROAD STRAIN)	78	Over 1 lb. Rough; yellow-golden	Heirloom seed propagated and traded by employees of the C & O Railroad in West Virginia before 1940. Best suited to cage culture. Not tolerant to foliage diseases.	SOU
GOLDEN QUEEN	83	4-6 ozs. Waxy yellow	Mild, non-acid. Late August yields.	SEE STO
GOLDEN SUNRAY (op)	80	Yellow globe	Resistant to fusarium wilt. Crack-free. Beautiful and delicious.	TWI
GOLDEN SUNRISE	78	Butter-yellow	Indeterminate. For greenhouse or outdoor culture.	ECO SOU THO
GOLDIE HUSK	75	Slightly flattened; golden apricot	Non-acid. Vigorous vines. Clean sweet flavor. Can be eaten raw, frozen, canned or in preserves.	GLE JOH
HY-TOP (hybrid F-2)	64		Big yields of meaty, beefy tomatoes.	GUR
IDA GOLD	59	2 ozs. Carrot-orange	Short-season variety. Determinate. Low acid.	HIG JOH SEE
JUBILEE (ORANGE JUBILEE) (GOLDEN JUBILEE)	80	½ lb. Globe; orange-yellow	Indeterminate. Non-acid. Sweet and extra juicy.	ALL ARC DEG EAR HEN MID NIC PON RIS TIL WES WET WIL WILL
LEMON BOY (hybrid)	82	8-10 ozs. Bright yellow	Indeterminate, big, healthy plant. Good quality fruit.	EAR GUR HEN JOH NIC PAR STO TWI VER
MANDARIN	75	Orange	Japanese variety. Acid-free. Big cropper.	EAR
MANDARIN CROSS (hybrid)	90	9 ozs. Orange-yellow	Low acid. Stake or ground support.	GLE LEM
MOON GLOW	72	Medium-size globe with blunt point; orange-yellow	Non-acid. Keeps indefinitely.	GLE

▶

◀ **TOMATOES**

Variety	Days	Fruit	Remarks	Sources
OLD GERMAN		Over 1 lb. Yellow with red center	Heirloom variety from Virginia. Very tasty. Few seeds. Not a heavy producer and does not tolerate drought.	SOU
ORANGE QUEEN	65	4-6 ozs. Bright orange	Low acidity.	STO
PERSIMMON		Very large; deep orange	Heirloom variety. Indeterminate.	SEE
PINK GRAPEFRUIT	60	Yellow	Pink flesh. Mild flavor.	GLE
PONDEROSA YELLOW	78	Orange-yellow	Mild flavor. Non-acid.	SEE
RUFFLED YELLOW		Yellow; accordion-shaped	Hollow for stuffing.	GLE SEE
SUNRAY V F_1F_2 (op)	80	3 in. across. Deep globe; orange-yellow	Prolific, compact indeterminate plant.	ARC EARL GLE HARR LED LEJ LET MEY MID SEED VER
TAXI	64	Taxi-cab yellow; baseball-size; slightly oblate	Determinate, compact vine doesn't need staking. Small stem scar. Easy to grow. Attractive and fine-flavored fruit.	JOH
VALENCIA	76	8-10 ozs. Round; bright orange	Maine heirloom variety. Meaty. Few seeds. Indeterminate.	JOH

TOMATOES
CONTAINER VARIETIES

Variety	Days	Fruit	Remarks	Sources
BASKET KING (hybrid)	55	1¾ in. Round	A thin-skinned, sweet good flavor. Sturdy, cascading branches. Good variety for hanging baskets.	BURP
BETTER BUSH VFN (hybrid)	72	3-4 in. diameter	3 x 3 ft. plant is stocky and compact. Meaty, juicy tomatoes are high in sugar content.	PAR
BROOKPACK	55	8-9 ozs. Flattened globe; bright red	Strong, dwarf, compact plant holds fruit off the ground. Cold-resistant.	EARL
BURPEE'S PIXIE (hybrid) (PIXIE)	52	1¾ in. Scarlet	14-18 in. plant. Dark green foliage. Strong and stocky. Determinate.	ALL ABU BURP DAN HIG LAG PON THO
BUSH BEEFSTEAK	65	8 ozs. Red	Strong, vigorous dwarf plant. Crack-resistant fruit. Good flavor. Rich red interior.	EARL WILL
EARLY SALAD (hybrid)	45	1½ in. Bright red	6-8 in. plant. Produces until frost. Can freeze these little ones.	BURG
EARLY SET	60	3 in. Round	Determinate compact plant. Short-season variety.	FIS
ELDELROT		Medium	European variety. Bush type. Fruit does not keep well in wet weather.	ABU
EPOCH	80	Large	Determinate plant. Fruit borne in clusters. Crack-free.	JUN

◄ Variety	Days	Fruit	Remarks	Sources
EROS		Medium; red	East German variety.	ABU
FLORIDA PETIT (op)	59	1½ in.	Fruit grows on top of the foliage. Can grow plant in a 4 in. pot.	THO
GERMAN DWARF BUSH	45	2 in. red	Small, rugged plant resists 28 degrees cold.	GLE
GOLDEN PYGMY		Size of a marble; yellow	12 in. high plant. Slightly acid, but excellent flavor. Will bear until frost.	LEM
IRION		Cherry-size	Bush plant.	ABU
NORTHERN LIGHT	55	2 in. Red	Short-season variety. 14-18 in. plant, with potato leaf foliage.	FIS
PATIO VF (hybrid)	50-70	2 in. 4 ozs. Deep oblate; red	24-30 in. plant is determinate but should be staked.	ARC COM DEG EARL LAG LED LET MID NIC RIS SEED STO VER WET WILL WYA
PATIO PRIZE (hybrid)	52	5 ozs. Red	Strong, dwarf, potato leaf plant.	BURR DAN EAR MID PIN STO
PRAIRIE FIRE	52	3 in. Extra-red	Short-season variety. Dwarf plant.	FIS
PRESIDENT VFNT (hybrid)	68	Large	Determinate bush. Good quality fruit.	LET
PRESTO	60	Round; bright red	Small open vine bears over long season.	HARR
RED ALERT (hybrid)	65		Short-season variety. Good for container gardening. Small, bush is heavy bearer.	LEM
RED LIGHTNING	55	2½ in. Scarlet red	Short-season variety. Compact, determinate plant.	FIS
RED ROBIN	55	1 in.	6 in. dwarf pot plant with no disease resistance.	STO
SANTA CRUZ 22 VF		3-4 ozs. Elongated	From Brazil. Determinate. Adapted to hot, humid conditions.	SOU
SIBERIA	48	3-4 ozs.	2½ ft. plant sets fruit at low temperatures. About 60 fruit per plant. Excellent taste.	WET
SMALL FRY VFN (hybrid)	65	1 in. Round; red	Determinate. Heavy cropper. Large cherry type.	ARC BURG COM EAR HARR JUN LED LET MID POR SEED STO TER WET
STAKELESS BUSH	78	8 ozs. Deep red	18 in. plant has dense foliage to prevent sun scald. Tolerance to fusarium.	BURR LAK STO TWI
STOKESALASKA	55	1¾ ozs.	18 in. bush-type plant. Short-season variety. Easy to peel, thin-skin.	STO
STUPICE			Short-season variety. Potato leaf type. Good yields.	ABU
SUBARTIC CHERRY		Small	300 fruit per plant. Bush variety. Grows low and spreading.	THO

◀ TOMATOES

Variety	Days	Fruit	Remarks	Sources
SUPER BUSH (hybrid)	63	6 ozs.	16 in. plant is sturdy and thick stems hold the fruit off the ground. High quality tomato.	DAN PIN WET
TOMATO NO. 506	62	Brilliant red	18 in. plant. Drought-resistant. Yields well in poor soil. Crack- and sunburn-resistant. Fruit will not rot.	GLE
TOY BOY VF (hybrid)	68	Ping-pong size	24 in. plant. Fruit set quickly. Determinate. Grows indoors with plenty of light.	LET POR STO
URBIKANY			Very compact plant.	ABU

TOMATOES
SMALL-FRUITED

Variety	Days	Fruit	Remarks	Sources
BASKET PAK	76	1½ in. Rich red	Indeterminate. Bears heavily all season.	LAG
BAXTER'S BUSH CHERRY	65	1 in. Round; red	Bushy, determinate plant grows to 4 ft. Heavy cropper.	BURP
CAMP JOY		1½ in.	Full tomato flavor. Produces over a long season. Strong growing vines should be staked.	SHE
CHEERIO	65	Medium-large cherry; bright red	Determinate, compact plant. Tolerates cold and adverse weather conditions.	JOH
CHERRY CHALLENGER (hybrid)	55	Large; round; red	Determinate, compact plant. Disease-tolerant. Crack-resistant.	TWI
CHERRY ELITE (hybrid)	77	1¼ in.	Similar to Cherry Grande with better crack tolerance.	STO
CHERRY FLAVOR	65	1 oz. Round; red	15-20 blossoms per cluster with excellent fruit setting. Indeterminate plant with high disease resistance. Easy to grow. High sugar content.	TWI
CHERRY GRANDE (hybrid)	55-74	1¼ in. Red	Vigorous determinate plant with broad foliage. Heavy sets.	RIS STO TWI VER VES
CHERRY SUPREME (hybrid)		1 in.	Heavy yields of sweet juicy fruit. Large indeterminate plant.	LET
CURRANT DROPS		Pea-size	Indeterminate plant. Spread cloth under plant and shake.	SEE
CURRANT HOLDS		Pea-size	Indeterminate plant.	SEE
EARLY CASCADE (hybrid)		2 in. Heart-shaped; red	Indeterminate vine should be pruned or staked.	TER
EARLY CHERRY		1½ in. Bright red	Ripens around July 20th. Determinate plant yields about 30 days before harvest declines.	TER
EARLY TEMPTATION (hybrid)	50	2-3 ozs.	Dwarf growth. Short-season variety. Firm-flesh, smooth-skinned fruit.	VES

◀

Variety	Days	Fruit	Remarks	Sources
GARDENER'S DELIGHT (SUGAR LUMP)	50	Bite-size	Best if staked. Very sweet. Good cropper.	BURP COO ECO GAR JOH JUN PAR SEE THO
GEM STATE	58	2 ozs. Red	Space-saver potato leaf plant does not sprawl. Determinate. Heavy yields.	HIG JOH SEE
GLACIER	54	2 in.	Spreading determinate plant. Sweet fruit.	GAR PLA RAW
GOLD NUGGET	50	Golden yellow	Almost seedless fruit. Small 24 in. plant. Mild flavor.	FIS NIC SEE TER
GREEN GRAPE		1 in. Greenish-yellow	Easily cultivated bush tomato.	LEM
KOOTENAI	70	2 x 3½ in. Red	Stocky, determinate plant. Canning type. Fruit tends to crack.	SEE TER
LOOMIS POTATO LEAF CHERRY		Cherry-size; red	Vine looks like a potato plant. Very productive massive vine. Fine flavor.	GLE
MINIBEL	65	2 in. Bright red	Attractive basket plant. High yields of thin palatable skin tomatoes.	PAR
OREGON ELEVEN		2 in.	Peaks fast and quits producing by September. Fruit tends to crack.	TER
PARTY		Cherry-size	Sweet and prolific.	SEE
PINK CHERRY		¾ in. Round; pinkish-red	Highly productive plant with good fruit settings.	GLE
PIPO		2 ozs.	Produces 4 heavy trusses.	THO
PRINCIPE BORGHESE			Determinate Italian drying cherry tomato.	COO
PURPLE CALABASH		Small; purple-pink	Mostly a novelty. Of poor quality.	GLE SEE
RED CHERRY, LARGE	70	Half-dollar size	Indeterminate. Sweet and mild.	ABU ARC BURG BUT EAR GLE GUR HARR HUM LAG LED LET MID NIC RIS TER WES WIL
RED CHERRY, SMALL	72	⅞ in.	Indeterminate. Disease-resistant.	ALL BURG BURP COM DAN DEG GLE HARR LET MEY PIN PON POR RED ROS SOU STO
RED PEACH		Small		STO
RED PEAR	73	1 in. Pear-shaped	Clusters bear over a long season. Good preserving tomato. Disease-resistant.	BURG COO GUR HARR HEN LEM LET SEE STO
RED PLUM		Scarlet; plum-shaped	Good preserving tomato.	BURG GLE LEM LET MID SEE STO
RED ROBIN	55	1 in.	Super-dwarf 6 in. high plant. No disease tolerance. Mild flavor.	STO
SANDPOINT	70	Cherry-size	Very prolific.	SEE
SPRINTER (hybrid)		2 in.	3 ft. diameter determinate plant. Non-juicy firm-flesh sauce tomato. Short-season variety.	TER

▶

TOMATOES

Variety	Days	Fruit	Remarks	Sources
SPRINT	59	2 ozs. Round; red	Healthy, indeterminate plant. Sparse foliage. Disease-tolerant. Short-season variety.	JOH
STARSHOT	55	2 in. Round; red	Bushy, verticillium-tolerant plant. Low acid.	STO
SUB-ARTIC CHERRY	45	1¾ in.	Heavy yields. Grows under adverse conditions. Averages 300 fruit per plant. Low spreading growth. Short-season variety.	PLA THO
SUB-ARTIC DELIGHT	48	2 ozs.	Short-season variety. Dwarf plant. Fruit borne in clusters.	WILL
SUB-ARTIC MAXI	64	3 ozs. Bright red	Milder flavor than other Sub-Artics. Short-season variety.	GAR EAG HIG HUM JOH PIN RAW STO
SUB-ARTIC PLENTY	62	1⅞ in. 2 ozs.	Determinate. Widely adapted. Short-season variety.	GUR JOH THO
SUNDROP	76	1⅞ in. Globe; deep orange	Meaty, firm and sweet. Crack-resistant. Holds well late into the season.	BURP
SWEET CHELSEA VFTMV (hybrid)	67	1 ozs. 1¾ in. Cherry-red	3 ft. vines should be staked or cages. Sets fruit on lateral branches. Crack-resistant. Harvest from August to frost.	STO VER WILL
SWEETIE (op)		Small; round; red	Very productive. Indeterminate. Tomatoes are borne in large clusters. Sugary flavor.	BURG FAR HEN HUM RAW SEE TER
SWEET 100 (hybrid)	65	Cherry-size; red	Grows in clusters. Indeterminate. Will produce until fall. My personal favorite.	ALL ARC BURP COM COO DAN EARL GRA GUR HARR HUM LAG LEM MEY MID PAR PIN POR SEED STO TIL TWI VER WET WILL
WHIPPERSNAPPER	52	1 in. Oval; pinkish-red	Determinate plant. Do not prune or stake. Numerous side branches. Fruits are full of flavor.	GAR HIG JOH
YELLOW CHERRY		Small; light yellow		SOU STO
YELLOW MARBLE		Marble-size	Indeterminate plant has very sweet fruit.	SEE
YELLOW PEACH		Light yellow	Use fresh or in preserves.	STO
YELLOW PEAR	70	1 x 2 in. Pear-shaped; bright yellow	Indeterminate. Preserving type. Wonderful taste. Grows in clusters.	ABU ALL ARC BURG BURP COO DEG EAR EARL GLE GUR HARR HEN HIG HUM JLH LAG LEM LET MEY MID PIN POR NIC SEE SHE SOU STO WET WILL
YELLOW PING PONG		Ping-pong size; golden	Indeterminate plant.	SEE
YELLOW PLUM	78	2 x½ in. Plum-shaped	Indeterminate plant. Favorite for canning whole.	ABU BURG DEG GLE GUR HARR LAG LED LEM LET MID SEE STO

TOMATOES—FOR PASTE

Variety	Days	Fruit	Remarks	Sources
BELLSTAR	74	4-6 ozs.	Compact plant. Easy-peeling fruit. Good flavor. Use for paste, sauce, juice or salad tomato.	GAR JOH STO
CHICO	75	Pear-shaped	Determinate plant. Heat-resistant. High in acid. Solid meat.	GUR
CHICO III (CHICO GRANDE IMPROVED)		Large; red	Fusarium wilt-resistant. Large plum type. Determinate plant.	JUN LED TER TIL
CRIMSONVEE VF	72	Medium; deep square; dark crimson	Determinate, upright, bushy plant. Excellent crack tolerance. For ketchup, concentrated strained products, stewed or whole cooked.	STO
EARLY PEAR (hybrid)	66	2-3 ozs.	Compact vine requires little space. Canning tomato. Tomatoes produce heavy harvest all at once. Most are ripe before you start picking. Verticillium wilt-resistant.	HEN RIS VER
GRINTA (hybrid)		3½ x 2 in.	Italian variety. Acid flavor, great for sauces and canning. Very meaty, heavy and seedless.	LEM
GS-12 (hybrid)	65	2-3 ozs. Globe	Determinate plant. Multi-use for canning or table. Verticillium wilt-resistant.	VER
HEINZ 2653 VF	68	3 ozs. Red	Often ripens entire crop on vine. Very firm. Compact plant.	JOH
HUNGARIAN ITALIAN		Medium	High quality. Very prolific.	SEE
LAKETA		Long, pointed; blood-red	Solid like a lemon. Non-acid and sweet.	GLE
LA ROMA VF (ROMA HYBRID)	62	3-4 ozs.	Very productive and vigorous.	COM
MACERO II VF		Large, elongated; Pear-shaped	Processing variety that peels easily. Excellent foliage cover.	HARR
MAMA MIA				LAG
MARMANDE (VLEESTOMAAT)	60	Flat; scarlet red	French variety. Suited for paste and sauces. Good flavor. Semi-determinate plant. Sets well even under cool conditions. Very prolific.	SHE WILL
MILANO (hybrid)		Plum type; red	Italian variety. Good for making sauces, canning whole or making paste. Will cook down in half the time required for all other types.	SHE
NAPOLI VF	76	2½ ozs. Elongated; bright red	Compact, determinate.	DEG GLE
NOVA	70	2 ozs. 3 x 1¼ in. Elongated; deep red	Susceptible to early blight. Some tolerance to fusarium. Roma paste type.	ABU GAR HIG JOH SEE STO
NEW ZEALAND PEAR		Size and shape of Bartlett pear	Indeterminate plant should be staked.	SEE

▶

◀ **TOMATOES—FOR PASTE**

Variety	Days	Fruit	Remarks	Sources
PRINCIPE BORGHESE		2 ozs. Plum shape, pointed ends	Italian variety used for drying. Very meaty with little juice or seeds. Indeterminate vine needs support. Good processer too.	PIN
ROMA VF	76	3 in. Elongated, pear-shaped	Determinate plant. Heavy foliage cover. Tremendous crops.	ALL ARC BURG BURP BURR COM DAN DEG DIX EAR EARL FAR GUR HARR HEN HUM LAG LED LEJ LEM LET MID NIC PAR PIE PIN RIS SEE SEED SOU STO TWI VER WET WIL WILL WYA
ROPRECO			Plant runs 4 ft. in diameter and does not need staking. Good yields. Nice paste type.	TER
ROYAL CHICO VFN	80	3½ ozs. Bright red	Determinate, compact plant. Good paste tomato recommended for mid Atlantic and South.	LET MID SOU
SAN MARZANO	80	Pear shape	Indeterminate plant. Drier than others. Intense flavor.	ABU BURG BURP BUT COO GLE LET PIN POR ROS STO TER WES WILL
SQUARE PASTE TOMATO	74	2 in. Square-round; Crimson red	Ripens all at once. Verticillium wilt-tolerant.	GRA STO
SUPER ITALIAN PASTE		4 x 6 in.	Indeterminate. Good paste variety.	SEE
SUPER ROMA VF		Plum shape	Bred for ketchup, tomato juice, or soup-making. Thick, juicy and nearly seedless. Disease-resistant . Heavy cropper.	THO
VEEPICK VF	73	3¼ x 2 in. Elongated, flat-sided, blunt-ended	Skin peels easily.	STO
VEEROMA VF	72	Medium-red	Crack-resistant. Roma type. Good variety for ketchup, paste, or whole packed.	STO
YELLOW BELL	60	3 x 1½ in. Creamy yellow to yellow	Indeterminate. Rare Tennessee heirloom variety. Excellent paste tomato. Heavy yields.	SOU

TOMATOES

GREENHOUSE, FORCING

Variety	Days	Fruit	Remarks	Sources
BUFFALO (hybrid) TMV V_2 C_5		10 ozs.	Vendor type, no green shoulders. Fair taste. Vigorous tall vine.	JOH STO
CARUSO (hybrid) TMV VF_2 C_5			Short, medium plant. Sets and yields under cooler greenhouse temperatures. Open plant. Fair taste.	STO
DANNY (hybrid)		3 ozs. Bright scarlet	High yields. Almost completely resistant to cracking and splitting. Barely affected by cool nights. Vigorous, tall, open plant. Resistant to fusarium 1 and 2, leaf mold races A, B, C, D and E and tobacco mosaic.	JOH

Variety	Days	Fruit	Remarks	Sources
DOMBELLO (hybrid)		10 ozs. Deep oblate; deep red	Very good flavor. Few cracks or blossom end problems. Resistant to TMV, leaf mold, A-E, V, F 1 and 2, nematodes.	JOH
DOMBITO (hybrid) TMV, C_2 mosaic, F_2 fusarium		5-7 ozs.	Fair tolerance to cracking. Bland taste.	STO
DOMBO (hybrid) (JUMBO)		8 ozs.	Produces 12 clusters of fruit. Tolerant to verticillium, F 2 fusarium and nemotodes, but not to some mosaic or leaf mold.	HARR JOH STO
MICHIGAN-OHIO (hybrid)	78	Medium-large; globe; red	Fusarium wilt-tolerant.	BURG
MOTO RED	70	Medium	Determinate 24-30 in. plant. Sets fruit well under condition of high heat.	SOU
OHIO WR 13 TMV		Large	Good crack resistance.	STO
ONTARIO PINK 774 (hybrid)		Rich rose-pink	Immune to all races of leaf mold and tobacco mosaic. Sets freely at 55° F/13° C night temperatures.	STO
ONTARIO HYBRID RED 775		8 ozs. Round	Sets fruit at lower temperatures. Immune to all races of TMV and leaf mold. Fruit ripens from the inside out.	STO
SIERRA (hybrid)		5½ ozs. Deep oblate	Resistant to fusarium 1, leaf mold A, B and C and tobacco mosaic. Flavorful, high quality fruit.	JOH
TROPIC VF	82	10 ozs. Deep globe	Indeterminate. Good tolerance to some leaf molds, verticillium and fusarium race 1. Fruit has prominent green shoulders.	LAG SOU STO
TRUCKCROSS 533 (hybrid)		8 ozs.	Indeterminate. Tolerant to leaf mold and fusarium wilt.	BURR LET POR WILL
VENDOR VF		8 ozs. Deep globe; bright red	Semi-compact plant. Uniform ripening. Some tolerance to leaf mold and tobacco mosaic. Excellent flavor.	EAR JOH SOU WILL
VENDOR VFT		6 ozs.	Tolerance to verticillium, fusarium and tobacco mosaic. No green shoulders.	STO
VISION (hybrid)		6 ozs. Deep globe	TMV-VF_2 C_5 resistant. No green shoulders. Tall plant with open habit. High quality. Fair taste.	STO

TOMATOES
OXHEART

Variety	Days	Fruit	Remarks	Sources
GIANTISSIMO	85	2½ lbs. Heart-shaped	Indeterminate. Nice stuffer. Solid interior with thick, firm walls. Few seeds.	NIC
OXHEART PINK	90	Up to 2 lbs. Pink	Indeterminate open vine.	BURG COM DEG FAR LEJ LEM LET MID PON
OXHEART RED (op)	90	1 lb. Red	Indeterminate vine. Fruit has few seeds.	ARC GLE HEN

TOMATOES
WHITE

Variety	Days	Fruit	Remarks	Sources
SNOWBALL	78	Nearly white	Almost pure white flesh. Has few seeds.	HEN
WHITE BEAUTY	84	Ivory-white	Paper-white flesh. Sub-acid. Good slicer, canner or juicer.	BURG GLE GRA GUR
WHITE WONDER	85	Creamy white	Creamy white flesh. Good white slicer. Low acid.	JUN

GROUND CHERRY TOMATOES—TOMATILLO

Variety	Days	Fruit	Remarks	Sources
GROUND CHERRY (STRAWBERRY) (MEXICAN HUSK) (TOMATILLO)	70	2¼ in.	Sweet flavor. Good for pies and preserves. Turns yellow when ripe. Thin, papery husks.	ABU ARC FAR HOR JOH LEM PLA PON RED SEE STO VER
SUGAR CHERRY		Pale yellow	Fruit are similar to medium-size tomatoes. Sweet taste. Encased in loose, papery husk. Heavy cropper. Good in pies or jam when stewed.	THO
TOMATILLA DE MILPA	70	Nickle-sized; purple-tinged	Sharp flavor. Paper husks completely enclose the fruit.	LEM RED VER
TOMATILLO RENDIDORA		Yellow-green; golf-ball size	Sweet acidic flavor. Upright plant but branches become prostrate when loaded with fruit.	LEM
YELLOW HUSK	85	Cherry-size; deep golden yellow	Very sweet. Heat- and drought-resistant. Extremely prolific. Good for preserves and jams. Thin, papery husk.	COM DEG FAR FIS GLE GUR JUN

TOMATOES
OTHER VARIETIES

Variety	Days	Fruit	Remarks	Sources
BULL SAC TOMATO			Mild, few seeds. Very productive large plant.	PET
COSTOLUTO GENOVESE (RIBBED GENOVA)		3 in. Slightly ribbed; scarlet	From northern Italy.	RED
EGG TOMATO		Chicken-egg size	Solid red flesh. Non-acid. Keeps indefinitely.	GLE
EVERGREEN TOMATO	70	Green when ripe	Low in acid.	GLE SEE
HOLLOW			Smooth, hollow. Great stuffer. Mild taste.	GRA
LIBERTY BELL		Bell-shaped	Red stuffing tomato. Non-acid. Small seed core.	GLE
RED TAMARILLO		Purplish-red	Same as yellow tree tomato except flesh is red.	GLE
STUFFING TOMATO	78		Similar to a bell pepper in shape and hollowness. Holds shape well during cooking.	HER PET

◄

Variety	Days	Fruit	Remarks	Sources
TIGERELLA (op) (MR. STRIPEY)		Medium-size; red and yellow stripes	Tangy flavor. Nice eye appeal.	THO
TREE TOMATO (STANDARD YELLOW)		Plum-shaped; yellow-orange	12 ft. trees. Yellow flesh has mild flavor.	GLE LAK
ZAPOTEC RIBBED		3½ in. Deep ribs, scarlet	Variety grown by the Zapotecs of southern Mexico.	RED

TURNIPS
(Brassica rapa)

Turnips are hardy vegetables with rough-textured, somewhat hairy foliage. The roots are fast-growing and become pithy in a fairly short time. Some varieties are ready for harvest in less than a month.

There is a wide choice in turnip varieties. While some types are grown for the root, others are grown strictly for the greens.

CULTURE: Sow seeds a half-inch deep in rows 15 to 18 inches apart. Thin the seedlings to 3 to 5 inches apart. In the north, sow as early in the spring as the ground can be worked. Plant again in mid-summer for fall harvest. In mild-winter areas, plant in fall for winter harvest. Generally, fall-planted turnips have a better flavor than spring-planted.

SEASONS: Cool.

INSECTS/DISEASES: *APHIDS, BLISTER BEETLES, CABBAGE LOOPERS, CUTWORMS, FLEA BEETLES, IMPORTED CABBAGE WORMS, STINKBUGS:* Use Sevin, malathion, diazinon, pyrethrum, rotenone or ryania.

DOWNY MILDEW, FUNGAL LEAF SPOTS: Use maneb or fixed copper sprays.

HARVESTING: Pull turnips when they are about 2 to 2½ inches in diameter. They become pithy if left in the ground much beyond this size. Despite their liking for cool weather, turnips are not frost-hardy.

TURNIPS
WHITE

Variety	Days	Shape/Color	Remarks	Sources
ALL SEASONS	28	Globe; white	White flesh. Stays sweet even in hot weather.	DEG SEE
EARLY WHITE GLOBE	60	Globe; snow-white	White flesh. Use when young and tender. Can be eaten raw or cooked.	DEG
GILFEATHER	80		Heirloom Vermont variety. Delicate, unexpected sweetness. Green tops resemble kale.	GIL THO VER
JUST RIGHT (hybrid)	60	6 in. across. Globe; white	Fine quality. Sow only for fall crop. Bolts easily. Glossy tender greens in 28 days.	ARC BURG DEG EAR GRU HARR LET TWI WET WIL WYA
PETITE WHITE (hybrid)	30	Small; white	Winter-hardy.	VER
PRESTO	30	Small; pure white		DEG NIC SEE
SAKATA'S FOLIAGE TURNIP (SHOGIN IMPROVED)	70	6 in. roots	Excellent quality. Tops grown for greens. 30 days for greens.	SUN
SHIRO	45	Egg-size	Used both for greens and roots.	PAR
SHOWTOP (hybrid)	55	Semi-globe; white	Can be used for roots and tops. Good hybrid vigor. Strong, large, dark green broad leaves.	TWI

►

◀ **TURNIPS**

Variety	Days	Shape/Color	Remarks	Sources
SNOWBALL	40	Globe; snow-white	White flesh. Good cooked or raw.	EARL ECO LET RED THO
TOKYO CROSS (hybrid)	35	6 in. Semi-globe; white	Good resistance to virus.	ARC FAR HEN JUN LAG LED LET PAR POR STO THO TWI VER WET WILL
TOKYO MARKET	50	Flattened roots; white	Japanese variety. For spring or fall sowing.	GLE HARR KIT MID NIC
TOKYO TOP (hybrid)	50	3 in. across	Disease-resistant. Sweet, pure white flesh.	MEY
VERTUS	60	White	Grows fast. Use when young.	HER
WHITE EGG	55	2 in. Egg-shaped; pure white	Quick growth. Winter variety.	COM DEG SEE TIL WET WYA
WHITE KNIGHT (hybrid)	60	Semi-globe; pure white	Vigorous variety.	RIS WYA
WHITE LADY (hybrid)	35	2½ in.	20 in. plant, some bolting tolerance. High quality green tops.	EAR GUR STO
WHITE TOKYO	25	Marble-size; pure white	Easy to grow. Keep weed-free. Mild and sweet, tender and juicy.	LEM
YORII SPRING	38	Small, flattened; white	Sweet. Large yield of greens.	GAR HIG JOH

TURNIPS

PURPLE-TOP

Variety	Days	Shape/Color	Remarks	Sources
DE NANCY	42	Deep violet necks, creamy white bottoms	French variety. Crispy, good flavored flesh. Pick when young and tender.	SHE
EARLY PURPLE-TOP MILAN	45	4 in. across. Flattened roots; white skin, purple top	Flesh is white.	COM
HINOA KABU PICKLING		Bright purple and white; elongated	Usually fermented and pickled. Also makes a good baby turnip. Plant in early spring or fall.	LEM
PURPLE-TOP WHITE GLOBE	55	5 in. across. Bright purple top, creamy white bottom	Pure white flesh. Fine-grained. Keeps well throughout the winter. Heavy yielder.	ABU ALL ARC BURG BURP BURR BUT COM DAN DEG EAR EARL FAR FIS GAR GUR HARR HEN HIG HUM JOH JUN LAG LED LEJ LET MEY MID PIN PLA PON POR RAW RIS ROS SEE SEED SOU STO TER TIL TWI VER WES WET WIL WILL WYA
ROYAL CROWN (hybrid)	52	Purple top, white globe	Extremely good vigor. Uniform attractive root.	GUR LED LET MEY MID PIN RIS

◀ | Variety | Days | Shape/Color | Remarks | Sources |
|---|---|---|---|---|
| ROYAL GLOBE II (hybrid) | 50 | Globe; purple top | Bright glossy green tops. High quality turnip. | POR TWI |
| SHORT TOP | | Purple top, white globe | 16-18 in. tall. | LET |
| STRAP LEAF PURPLE-TOP FLAT | | Flat shape | White flesh. | FAR LET SOU TIL |

TURNIPS
OTHER COLORS

Variety	Days	Shape/Color	Remarks	Sources
AMBER		6 in. Yellowish	Yellow flesh. Fall variety.	MEY POR ROS SEE WET
DE MILAN (MILAN EARLY RED TOP)	35	Rosy-red top, white globe	Use as a baby vegetable. Quick-growing. French variety. Thrives in cool weather.	LEM SHE
GOLDEN BALL (ORANGE JELLY)	60	4 in. across. Yellow	Sweet, yellow flesh. Fine-grained.	ABU EARL ECO LAG NIC RAW WILL
LARGE YELLOW GLOBE	70	Light yellow	Reliable winter keeper.	COM
OHNO SCARLET	55	Red	White flesh. Red-veined greens.	JOH SEE
SCARLET BALL	30	Semi-globe; slightly flattened; deep scarlet	Japanese variety. White flesh. Looks like a beet. Red-veined foliaged.	GLE NIC
TURNIP LONGUE DE CALURIE	55	Elongated; black	French variety. White flesh.	SEE

TURNIPS—FOR GREENS ONLY

Variety	Days	Remarks	Sources
ALL TOP (hybrid)	50	For greens only, does not make root. High yields. Large, broad, smooth green leaves on sturdy green stems.	PAR RIS TWI
SEVEN TOP (WINTER GREENS)	45	Roots are tough and woody. Quick growth of tasty turnip greens. For spring or late summer.	COM DEG HARR LED LET MEY MID RIS SOU TWI WET WYA
SHOGIN	70	18-20 in. tops. Globe-shaped roots. Upright foliage is highest class of greens.	DEG LAG LEJ LET POR RED ROS STO TER TWI VER WES WET WIL
TURNIP TOPS GREEN		Smooth green leaves. Cut at 6 in. stage. Will grow back for later cuttings.	WILL
TYFON		For greens. Cross between turnip and Chinese cabbage. Heat-tolerant and winter-hardy. Mild flavor. Resists bolting.	MID

WATERMELON
(Citrulus lanatus)

Watermelons once required a long, hot growing season and lots of space to bring the melons to maturity. And that's still true of some varieties, but the icebox types have changed all that for many gardeners. With bush varieties now on the market, you can find many of your favorite long-growing kinds in a more compact form, with shorter growing spans. However, if you want to show off or to win blue ribbons, try the giant varieties. There are many shapes and sizes to choose from, and several different colors of flesh.

CULTURE: Start indoors in peat pots six or eight weeks before you intend to plant outside. When the weather warms up, set out transplants 12 to 18 inches apart in rows 4 to 6 feet apart. Or plant in hills, three plants to a hill, with 8 feet between hills (less for the smaller varieties).

SEASONS: Warm.

INSECTS/DISEASES: See Cantaloupe.

HARVESTING: To test watermelons, there is nothing like thumping them. The ripe ones have a dull, rather than a sharp sound. This test is best left for early morning. Once the watermelons get hot late in the day, the bong sound gives way to a dull thud. You should also look at the discolored spots on the melon bellies where they touch the ground. If the melons are ready, these spots have turned from white to a pale yellow.

WATERMELON
ICEBOX TYPE

Variety	Days	Size/Shape	Remarks	Sources
BABY FUN (hybrid)	82	Medium, slightly oval	Compact vines tolerate fusarium wilt. Extra-sweet.	JUN
BLUE BELLE (hybrid)	75	Round oval	Widely adapted. Tough rind. Good tolerance to race 1 fusarium wilt.	RIS
BURPEE'S FORDHOOK (hybrid)	74	12-14 lbs. Nearly round	Bright red flesh. Dark glossy green rind. Delicious flavor.	BURP
BURPEE'S SUGAR BUSH	80	6-8 lbs.	Bright scarlet flesh. Sweet and juicy. Medium-green rind. Only needs about 6 sq. feet of growing space per plant.	BURP LAG
BUSH SUGAR BABY	80	8½-10 in. 8-12 lbs. Oval	3½ ft. vines. Sweet, bright scarlet flesh. Firm texture. Medium-small seeds.	BURP HEN
FAMILY FUN (hybrid) (EARLY MIDGET)	88	Slightly oblong	Dark green rind, red flesh. Small dark seeds.	NIC TWI
GARDEN BABY (hybrid)	75	Round, dark rind	Determinate and very compact vine. 2-3 melons per vine.	FAR JOH LET PIN RIS TIL VER WILL
GOLDEN MIDGET	65	8 in.	Green rind turns golden-yellow when ripe. Red flesh, black seeds.	DEG
HOPI WATERMELON (op)	100	3-4 lbs. Round	Exceptionally sweet, full-flavored yellow flesh. Takes less water.	PLA
LUCKY SWEET (hybrid)	70	12 lbs.	Sets fruit under low temperatures. Vivid red flesh. Dark green rind with dark tiger stripes.	VER
MICKYLEE	78	4-12 lbs.	Plant Variety Protected. Gray-green rind is hard and tough. Vigorous vine is tolerant to anthracnose and fusarium wilt. Small black seeds.	WIL
MINILEE	78	8-15 lbs.	Plant Variety Protected. Tough rind and red flesh with firm texture. Few seeds. Vigorous vine. Tolerant to anthracnose and fusarium.	WIL
NEW HAMPSHIRE MIDGET	68	4-6 lbs. 7 x 6 in.	Striped, dark green. Red flesh, black seeds. Heavy-yielding.	ALL DEG FAR LET SEE VER VES WILL
PETITE SWEET	71	8 lbs. Round	Bright pink-red flesh. Green rind. Brown seeds. Extra-high sugar content.	FAR GUR LET

◀

Variety	Days	Fruit	Remarks	Sources
SUGAR BABY	73-90	10 lbs. 8 in. Round	Dark green rind. Crisp, sweet dark red flesh. Few seeds.	ABU ALL ARC BURG BURP BURR BUT COM DAN EAR EARL FIS GAR GUR HARR HEN JOH JUN LAG LED LET MEY MID PAR PIN PLA PON POR RAW RIS SEED SOU STO TER VER WET WIL WILL WYA
SUGAR DOLL (hybrid)	72	8-10 lbs.	Sweet red flesh. Very prolific.	LED LET MID RAW RIS TWI
SWEET BABY (hybrid)	86	12-15 lbs. 8½ x 9 in.	Dark green rind. Bright red flesh. Compact vines are tolerant to fusarium wilt. Small seeds.	HARR SHE TWI
SWEET TREAT (SWEETHEART)	85	9-14 lbs.	Bush-type vine 5 ft. long. Bears 2 melons per vine. Light green rind with dark stripes. Scarlet flesh has little fiber and medium-size seeds.	BURP
YOU SWEET THING (hybrid)	70	12-13 lbs. Round	Striped. Rose-colored flesh. High sugar content.	NIC PAR SEED

WATERMELON
OBLONG, GREEN RIND

Variety	Days	Size/Shape	Remarks	Sources
CANDY RED		40 lbs.	Australian variety. Deep red flesh. Resists hollows.	GLE
CONGO	90	30-40 lbs. Blocky	Bright red flesh is sweet and crisp. Highly resistant to anthracnose. Gray-white seeds.	ARC BURR DEG GUR HEN LET MEY SEE WET WIL WYA
FAR NORTH	70	6-8 lbs.	Bright red flesh, black seeds. Cross between Sugar Bush and Peacock. Short-season variety.	FIS
FAMILY FUN (hybrid)	80	13-15 lbs.	Red flesh. Tough rind. Tolerant to fusarium wilt, anthracnose and mildew.	GLE
KLECKLEY SWEET (MONTE CARLO)	87	25-40 lbs. Square ends	Bright scarlet flesh. Broad, solid heart.	DEG RED
KLECKLEY SWEET IMPROVED (WONDER MELON)	85	Long	Thin green rind. Bright red flesh.	COM LET WYA
KLECKLEY SWEET NO. 6	85	Cylindrical	Wilt-resistant. Sweet, crisp, bright red flesh. Tender, dark green rind.	ARC ROS
KLECKLEY SWEET NO. 6 IMPROVED	88		Wilt-resistant vines. Rich red flesh.	WET
KLONDIKE	78-90	20-25 lbs.	Extra-sweet deep red flesh. Heavy yielder.	BURG
KLONDIKE PEACOCK EBONY	90			LAG
KLONDIKE PEACOCK IMPROVED	90	20-22 lbs. Rounded to blocky	Particularly adapted to the Southwest. Thin, tough rind. Bright orange-red flesh.	ROS

▶

◄ **WATERMELON**

Variety	Days	Fruit	Remarks	Sources
KLONDIKE STRIPED BLUE RIBBON	85	Medium; oblong	Light green rind. Red flesh. Tolerant to fusarium. Small seeds.	VER
KLONDYKE WILT RESISTANT NO. 6	85	35 lbs. Long	Dark green rind.	DEG MEY
NORTHERN SWEET (4TH OF JULY)	68	15 lbs.	Crisp, sweet, deep red flesh.	ABU BURG GUR HEN
PEACOCK WR-60	88	20-25 lbs.	Bright red flesh, almost black seeds.	WIL
PEACOCK WR-124 (op)	82	15 x 10 in. 22 lbs.	Orange-red flesh. Tough green rind. Tolerant to fusarium wilt. Heavy foliage cover.	HARR
ROYAL CHARLESTON (hybrid)	84	20-25 lbs.	Sweet, red flesh with few seeds. Tolerant to fusarium, anthracnose and mildew. Tough rind.	ARC BURR JUN POR TWI WIL
ROYAL PEACOCK (hybrid)		25-30 lbs.	Dark green rind. Orange-red flesh.	POR
STOKES SUGAR (hybrid)	70	15 lbs.	Deep rose flesh. Heavy-yielding vines.	STO
STONE MOUNTAIN (op)	85-90	30-40 lbs. Oval	Originated at the base of Stone Mountain Confederate Memorial in Georgia. Dark, green medium-thick rind. Scarlet flesh, few seeds.	SOU
STONE MOUNTAIN NO. 5	85-95		Resistant to fusarium wilt.	SOU
SUMMER FESTIVAL (hybrid)	88	15 lbs. 12 x 15 in.	Pink-red flesh, small black seeds.	FAR HARR NIC
SWEET MEAT (hybrid)	73	10-12 lbs. Blocky	High sugar content. Brown seeds.	EAR FAR
SWEET MEAT II (hybrid)		10-12 lbs. Oblong, blocky	Strong productive vines are fusarium wilt-resistant. Dark green-striped melons.	POR RIS
TOM WATSON	90	35-40 lbs. 22 x 12 in.	Bright, deep red flesh. Large brown seeds.	WIL

WATERMELON

OBLONG, GRAYISH SKIN

Variety	Days	Size/Shape	Remarks	Sources
CALHOUN GRAY	85	20-25 lbs. 10 x 24 in.	Bright red flesh. Fusarium wilt-resistant.	TWI WIL
CHARLEE	87	23 lbs. 17 x 18 in.	Plant Variety Protected. Red flesh, large black seeds. Tolerant to fusarium wilt, anthracnose, powdery mildew and mosaic virus.	TWI
CHARLIE L (hybrid)	81	22-27 lbs. Oblong	Light green rind with slight dark green veins. Deep red flesh. Good resistance to fusarium wilt and anthracnose.	TWI
CHARLESTON 76 (op)	85-90	25-35 lbs. 25 x 10 in.	Tough gray-green rind. Bright red flesh. Resistant to fusarium wilt and anthracnose. Tolerant to sunburn.	HARR

Variety	Days	Size/Shape	Remarks	Sources
CHARLESTON GRAY	85-90	20-40 lbs.	Solid red flesh. High quality. Tolerant to anthracnose and fusarium wilt. Relatively free of hollow heart.	ARC BURP BURR DAN DEG GUR HEN JUN LAG LED LEJ MEY POR RIS ROS SEE STO VER
CHARLESTON GRAY NO.5	90	30-40 lbs.	Resistant to anthracnose and fusarium wilt.	BURG DIX LET TWI WET WIL
CHARLESTON GRAY 133	85		More wilt-resistant and uniform shape than the original.	BURR MID TWI WIL WYA
CHUBBY GRAY	90	28-30 lbs. Blocky, oblong	Plant Variety Protected. Gray rind. Black seed. Firm red flesh.	WIL
PRINCE CHARLES (hybrid)	82	20-30 lbs. Blocky, oblong	Tough gray-green rind. Fusarium tolerant. Bright red flesh.	EAR RIS TWI

WATERMELON

OBLONG, GREEN STRIPES

Variety	Days	Size/Shape	Remarks	Sources
ALLSWEET	90-104	25-40 lbs.	Bright red flesh. High sugar content. Tolerant to fusarium wilt and races 1 and 3 of anthracnose.	BURG GUR LED LET MEY MID POR RIS STO TWI WIL
AU JUBILANT	95	25-30 lbs. Oblong	Plant Variety Protected. Jubilee type. High disease resistance. Sweet, juicy, red flesh.	BURR LET TWI WIL
AU PRODUCER (op)	90	25 lbs.	Beautiful pink-red flesh. High resistance to fusarium wilt, downy mildew and anthracnose race 1.	LED LET TWI WIL
CALSWEET	92	25-30 lbs. Blocky, oblong	Plant Variety Protected. Intense red flesh. Dark seeds. Resistant to fusarium wilt.	MID TWI WIL
CANADA SUPERSWEET (hybrid)	70	22 lbs. Oblong	Short-season variety. Fusarium-tolerant.	STO
EARLY CANADA	75	10-15 lbs. 10 x 12 in.	Red flesh, small, reddish-brown seeds. Short-season variety.	EARL GUR
EARLY KANSAS (HUTCHINSON STRIPE) (KANSAS SWEET) (RED RUSSIAN) (WITCHITA RED SEEDED)	85	30-40 lbs. 13 x 15 in.	Red flesh. Medium-thick rind.	DEG FAR
FAMILY FUN (hybrid)	80	13-15 lbs. Oblong	Sweet, vivid red flesh. Small brown seeds.	WIL
FLORIDA GIANT				MEY
GARRISON	85-90	34-45 lbs. 12 x 24 in.	Deep red flesh, tan seeds with dark tips. Resistant to anthracnose.	HEN MID RIS SEE TWI WIL
IOPRIDE	90	20-25 lbs. Blocky	Fine quality. Deep red flesh with light to dark tan seeds. Good keeper.	GUR MID RIS WIL
JUBILEE	95	25-40 lbs. 13 x 24 in.	Bright red flesh, dark seeds. Heavy yielder. Resistant to race 1 anthracnose.	BURG DEG HARR LED LET MID POR RIS WET WIL WYA
JUBLIEE REGISTERED			Produces with Florida Foundation Seed.	BURR MEY

◀ ## WATERMELON

Variety	Days	Size/Shape	Remarks	Sources
KLONDYKE SUGAR	90	25 lbs.	Scarlet-red flesh is high is sugar content.	FAR DEG
LONG CRIMSON	85	25-28 lbs. Blocky, oblong	Plant Variety Protected. Bright red flesh is firm and sweet. Coal-black seeds.	WIL
MIRAGE (hybrid)	85	25-30 lbs. Oblong	Sweet, deep red flesh. Superb eating quality. High yields. Tolerant to fusarium wilt.	WIL
NORTHERN DELIGHT (hybrid)	75	12-15 lbs. Oblong	Great taste.	STO
OASIS (hybrid)	91	15 x 9 in. 25 lbs.	Tough rind. Intense red flesh. Tolerant to fusarium wilt and resistant to anthracnose.	HARR
RATTLESNAKE	90	22 x 10 in.	Bright rose flesh.	GUR
ROYAL CRIMSON (hybrid)	85	20 lbs. Deep round	High yields. Some fusarium wilt tolerance.	RIS
ROYAL JUBILEE (hybrid)	90	25-30 lbs. Well rounded	Resistant to fusarium wilt. Medium-small seeds.	BURR HARR POR RIS
ROYAL SWEET (hybrid)	85	20-25 lbs. Oblong	Bright red flesh, small dark seeds. Resistant to fusarium wilt.	MID RIS TWI WET WIL
ROYAL WINDSOR (hybrid)	80	20-30 lbs.	Dense, bright red flesh.	TWI
SWEET FAVORITE (hybrid)	64	20 lbs.	Best oblong variety for northern cool areas. Vigorous, highly productive. High sugar content.	BURP COM EAR JOH PAR STO TWI WILL
SWEET MEAT (hybrid)		20-25 lbs. Long, blocky	Sweet, meaty, crisp crimson-red flesh. Small brown seeds.	ARC TER
SWEET MEAT II (hybrid)		10-12 lbs. Oblong, blocky	Firm, bright red flesh. Strong productive vines are fusarium wilt-resistant.	POR
SWEET PRINCESS	90	25 lbs. Oblong	Deep pink-red flesh. Exceptionally small seeds. Tough, thick rind. Some wilt and anthracnose tolerance.	WET WIL WYA
TOP YIELD (hybrid)	82	20 lbs.	Bright red, firm, juicy flesh. Small seeds. Resistant to anthracnose and fusarium wilt.	SEED TWI

WATERMELON
ROUND, GREEN

Variety	Days	Size/Shape	Remarks	Sources
ASAHI MIYAKO (ASAHI SUGAR)	80	12-15 lbs. Round, flattened	Japanese variety. Dark green rind. Very sweet flesh.	GLE LEM
BLACK DIAMOND (CANNONBALL) (FLORIDA GIANT) (SHIPPER)	92	40-60 lbs.	Deep red flesh. Large seeds are dark brown. Very tough rind.	ARC BURG BURR DEG GUR HEN JUN LED LET MID PAR PON RIS ROS SEE TWI VER WET WIL WYA

▶

◀

Variety	Days	Size/Shape	Remarks	Sources
BLACK DIAMOND YELLOW BELLY	90	30-40 lbs. 17 x 19 in.	Bright red flesh, black seeds. Yellow belly.	BURR EAR MID POR
BLACKSTONE	89	25-30 lbs.	Heavy yielder. Seeds stippled black.	GUR RIS WIL
CRIMSON DIAMOND	85		Plant Variety Protected. Cross between Black Diamond and Crimson Sweet. Seeds are small black.	WIL
FORDHOOK (hybrid)	75	12-14 lbs. Nearly round	Bright red flesh with few seeds.	ARC
KING WINTER KEEPER	80-90	20 lbs. 8 x 12 in.	Bright red flesh. Vigorous spreading vines. Sweet flesh. Can be stored for several months.	JUN VER
LEDMON	85	Almost round	Flesh is red, crisp and sweet. Thin rind.	WYA
VERONA	80	30-40 lbs.	Medium-rose flesh, black seeds. Disease-resistant. Black Diamond type.	WIL

WATERMELON
ROUND, STRIPED GREEN

Variety	Days	Size/Shape	Remarks	Sources
BABY FUN (hybrid)	82	15 lbs.	Crimson Sweet type. Fairly compact vine. Sweet flavor.	PIN
BIG CRIMSON		30 lbs.	Plant Variety Protected. High-yielding.	WIL
CARMEN (hybrid)	86	25 lbs.	Fine red flesh. Dark seeds. Good sunburn resistance. Resistance to fusarium wilt and anthracnose race 1.	TWI
CRIMSON SWEET	80	25 lbs.	Dark red flesh. Vigorous vines are resistant to fusarium and anthracnose.	ABU ARC BURG BURP BURR DEG EAR FAR GUR HARR HEN HUM JUN LAG LED LET MEY PIN PON POR RIS SOU STO TER TWI WET WIL WYA
CRIMSON TIDE (hybrid)	84	22-26 lbs.	Resistant to fusarium, tolerant to anthracnose. Bright red flesh is crisp and sweet.	MID
DIXIELEE	90	20-30 lbs.	Red flesh. Tough rind. Vigorous vine.	TWI WIL
DIXIE QUEEN (hybrid)	90	30-50 lbs. 12 x 15 in.	Deep red flesh. Tolerant to fusarium wilt.	ARC BURG BURP EAR EARL FAR GUR HEN JUN LED MEY POR RIS SEE WET WYA
EARLY NORTHERN SWEET	78	10-12 lbs.	Dark red flesh. Pick when ripe or it becomes stringy.	FAR
RED BEAUTY (hybrid)		20 lbs.	Firm, highly palatable red flesh. Very tough rind. Brown seeds. Not wilt-resistant.	WIL
RUBY RED (hybrid)		22 lbs.	Red flesh. Black seeds. Not tolerant to wilt.	WIL
SUGARLEE		Medium	Tough rind. Firm, sweet red flesh. Black seeds. Holds and keeps well.	WIL

WATERMELON
ROUND, OTHER COLORS

Variety	Days	Size/Shape	Remarks	Sources
ICE CREAM (PEERLESS)	75		White-seeded. Sweet white flesh. Heirloom variety.	RED
WINTER MELON	78	10 lbs.	Pale yellow when ripe. Bright red flesh.	FAR GUR SEE SOU
WINTER QUEEN BLACK SEEDED	90	15 lbs.	Greenish-white rind. Deep red flesh. Grown for storing and use during fall and early winter months.	BURR MID NIC

WATERMELON
GIANT

Variety	Days	Size/Shape	Remarks	Sources
COBB GEM	100	130 lbs.	Grayish-black rind, red flesh.	FAR GLE GUR HEN SEE WIL
MOUNTAIN HOOSIER	85	75-80 lbs. Oblong	Dark green rind, deep red flesh. White seeds are slightly black on rim and tip.	SOU WIL
WEEKS NC GIANT	90	197 lbs.	Striped rind.	FAR LAK
WHITE-SEEDED WATSON	95	100 lbs.	Shiny blue-green rind, red flesh.	WIL

WATERMELON
SPACE SAVERS

Variety	Days	Size/Shape	Remarks	Sources
BUSH BABY (hybrid)	80	8 lbs. Round oval	Dwarf, determinate plant. High in sugar, low in fiber, juicy pink flesh. Light green-striped rind. Vigorous and prolific.	PAR
BUSH CHARLESTON GRAY	90	10-13 lbs.	Bush-type plant grows about 3-5 ft. in diameter. Deep red flesh has sweet flavor. Disease-resistant.	EAR LET PAR TWI WET
BUSH JUBILEE	95	13 lbs.	Bush variety. Resistant to anthracnose and fusarium wilt.	EAR GUR HARR HEN LED LET PAR PON POR TWI VER WET WYA
GOLDEN MIDGET	65	6-7 lbs.	Skin turns golden when ripe. Bush type is compact and suited for small gardens and containers. Strawberry-red flesh has high sugar content.	THO
SUGAR JADE (hybrid)		16 lbs.	2 ft. vine. Jade-green rind, rich, deep red flesh is juicy and crisp. High in sugar content. Smells like wine.	THO
SUGAR BUSH	80	6-8 lbs.	Takes 6 sq. ft. to grow a 3½ ft. vine. Bright scarlet flesh, sweet and juicy.	DEG

WATERMELON
YELLOW OR ORANGE FLESH

Variety	Days	Size/Shape	Remarks	Sources
BLACK DIAMOND YELLOW BELLY	90	60-70 lbs.	Just like the red-fleshed variety.	ROS WIL
DESERT KING YELLOW	85		Yellow rind, yellow flesh. Will not sunburn. Grayish-black seeds.	WIL
GOLD BABY		5-6 lbs.	Creamy yellow flesh is very sweet. Light green rind with dark stripes. Prolific and easy to grow.	GLE
GOLDEN HONEY LONG	90	20 lbs. Oblong	Dark green-striped rind, golden-yellow flesh. Light tan seeds.	POR ROS
GOLDEN HONEY SWEET	80	Oblong	Mottled green-striped rind, golden-yellow flesh.	DEG LAG
GOLDEN MIDGET		3-4 lbs.	Yellow flesh.	SEE
HONEY CREAM (hybrid)	65	3-4 lbs. Round	Yellow-orange flesh.	ROS
KAHO	85	3 lbs. Oval	Pale green rind has dark stripes. Orange-yellow flesh is juicy and rich-flavored.	JLH RED
MOON AND STARS		40 lbs.	Dark green rind has yellow splashes for stars and larger splashes for moons. Speckled. Great melon.	SEE SOU
MOON AND STARS NO.2		40 lbs. Round	White-seeds. Very sweet flesh.	SEE
ORANGEGLO	50	50 lbs.	Orange flesh. Cream-colored seeds.	WIL
PINEAPPLE (hybrid)	74	4 lbs. Oblong and ribbed	Orange flesh. Big leaves protect fruit from sunscald.	GUR
TENDERSWEET ORANGE	90	35-50 lbs. 18 x 12 in.	Orange flesh, white seeds.	BURR GLE HEN POR ROS WIL WYA
TENDERSWEET YELLOW	80	30-40 lbs.	Dark green rind, golden-yellow flesh.	GUR
WILHITE'S TENDERGOLD	80	22-28 lbs.	Dark green-striped rind. Sweet yellow flesh. Black seeds.	WIL
WILHITE'S YELLOW FLESH BLACK DIAMOND	90	60-70 lbs.	Yellow flesh. Small, grayish-black seeds. Thin, glossy dark green rind is also tough.	WIL
YELLOW BABY (hybrid)	70	10 lbs. 7 in. diameter	Bright yellow flesh. Small seeds. Icebox type.	ARC BURP HARR LEM PAR STO
YELLOW CRIMSON	80	Round, striped	Plant Variety Protected. Yellow flesh, black seeds.	WIL
YELLOW DOLL (hybrid)	75	5-8 lbs. Round	Crisp, yellow flesh. Small black seeds. Semi-compact vines.	BURG EAR HEN JUN LED LET MID NIC POR RIS TER TWI VER WIL

WATERMELON
SEEDLESS

Variety	Days	Size/Shape	Remarks	Sources
BURPEE HYBRID SEEDLESS (TRI X-313 HYBRID)	80	10-15 lbs. Oval	Striped rind, solid-red flesh. A few soft white seeds. Healthy, disease-resistant vines.	BURP HARR HEN LET MID PAR WIL
GIANT JUBLIEE SEEDLESS	90	30 lbs.	Solid, seedless melon. Sugar-sweet scarlet flesh. Plant next to seed-bearing variety.	GUR HEN
GURNEY'S SEEDLESS	85	24 lbs. Oval	Striped rind, red flesh. A few undeveloped seeds.	GUR
HYBRID SEEDLESS	80	20-24 lbs. Oval	Striped rind, crisp sweet flesh.	BURG FAR
TRI X-313 IMPROVED (hybrid)	90	15-20 lbs.	Sweet crisp red flesh. Vigorous vines resistant to anthracnose.	TWI
SEEDLESS	80	10-15 lbs.	Deep red flesh.	LAG
SUMMER FESTIVAL (hybrid)	91	15 lbs.	Firm, sweet, deep rose flesh. Disease-resistant, vigorous vines.	LET
SUPER SEEDLESS	90	20 lbs.	Red flesh with absolutely no seeds.	EAR
SUPERSWEET SEEDLESS (hybrid)	85	15 lbs. Round	Stiped rind, red flesh up to the rind.	PAR
TRIPLE X SUPERSWEET		Round; medium	Striped rind. Seedless. Exquisite sweet flavor.	POR
TRIPLE SWEET SEEDLESS (hybrid)	80	12-20 lbs. Oval	Striped rind. Produces melons even in short-season areas.	BURP HEN LED LET MID POR TWI

WATERMELON
EDIBLE SEEDS

Variety	Days	Color/Shape	Remarks	Sources
KILY EDIBLE SEEDED (hybrid) (WANLI)	80	Globe-shaped	Grown for its large, very thick seeds. Eat seeds like squash seed. Roast or dry them. Vigorous, disease-resistant vine.	GLE

HERBS

Herb	Growth	Sources
ANGELICA [HB] Known as 'Holy Ghost' herb. Flavoring for fish and for liquors. Stems are used for candying. Thrives in moist, rich soil, partial shade.	3-6 feet	ABU EARL ECO HARR JLH JOH LEJ NIC PER RIC SEE STI TAY THO VER
ANISE [B] 75 days. Use fresh leaves in salad and as a garnish. Seed is flavoring for bread, cookies, stews. Slow-growing. White flowers. Does not transplant well. Requires sunny, fairly dry, sandy, medium-rich soil.	2 feet	ABU ALL CAP COM DAN DEG EARL ECO GUR HUM IND JLH JOH JUN LAG LED LEJ LET LIBE MEY NIC PIN PON RAW RED RIC SOU STI STO TAY THO TIL WET WIL WILL WYA
BASIL, ANISE Sweet anise flavor. Purple foliage.		HIG RED RIC SHE
BASIL, SWEET [A] All basils have clove-like flavor and spicy odor, some more pungent than others. Use leaves fresh or dried in Italian tomato paste, all tomato dishes, salads, pea soup and omelets.	2 feet	ABU ALL APP ARC BURP BURR CAP COM DAN DEG EAR EARL ECO FIS GAR GURR HARR HIG HEN HER HUM IND LIBE MEY MID NIC PAR PER PIN PON RAW RIC RIS SEE SOU STI SUN TAY TER THO TWI VER VES WILL WYA
BASIL, CAMPHOR [TP] Commercial source of camphor. Strong camphor color. Used to relieve stomach ache and colds.	5 feet	RIC
BASIL, CINNAMON [A] Spicy cinnamon scent. Pink flowers and shiny green leaves. Use in jelly, chutney, fruit salads, sweet and sour dishes, rib and chicken marinades.		ABU LAG PAR PIN SEE SHE SOU
BASIL, DARK OPAL [A] Purplish-bronze foliage with small lavender-white flowers. A spread of 12 inches. Leaves can be used dried, or fresh in salads or seasoning. 7-10 days.	To 2 feet	ABU CAP COM DEG EARL GLE GUR HEN HER JLH JUN LAG LIBE LAG LEM NIC PIN RED RIC SEED SHE SOU STI TAY VER WET WILL WYA
BASIL, DWARF (BUSH BASIL, SMALL LEAVED) Grown in pots it makes a fine house plant, emitting a pleasant perfume when leaves are touched.	6 inches	DEG ECO LEJ RED RIC THO WILL
BASIL, EAST INDIAN [TP] Large, hearty type with felt-like gray-green leaves. Strong clove scent and spicy flavor.	5 feet	RIC
BASIL, FINVERT		LEM
BASIL, GENOVESE (GENOVA) Bright green, slightly wrinkled leaves. Intensely sweet-scented.		RED SHE
BASIL, GREEN BOUQUET Round, bushy plants have miniature full-flavored leaves 1/4 to 3/4 inches long. Use fresh or dried. Perfect for pots, edging, or borders. Indoors, put on a sunny windowsill for year-round herb.	12 inches	BURP THO
BASIL, GREEN BALL		STO
BASIL, GREEN BUSH Small leaves and white flowers. Some have a lemon odor.	12 inches	ABU CAP COM HEN JLH LEJ NIC THO VER
BASIL, GREEN RUFFLES Fragrant, ornamental leaves are green serrated and savoyed. Slightly more subtle flavor, but larger leaves than Sweet Basil. For all culinary uses.	24 inches	BURP SLA PIN RIC STO

◀ **HERBS**

Herb	Growth	Sources
BASIL, HOLY Heady, deep spicy clove scent when crushed.	10 inches	ABU GLE NIC PAR SOU
BASIL, LARGE GREEN Big producer of culinary leaves.	10 inches	NIC
BASIL, LARGE-LEAVED ITALIAN [A] 85 days. Rich flavor for all Italian dishes, especially pesto. Popular variety.	2 feet	COM HIG LAG LEM PAR PLA RED SEED SHE STO TIL
BASIL, LEMON [A] Intense lemon fragrance. Spreading gray-green plants. Nice in potpourris, herb teas and cold drinks.	18 inches	ABU BURP COM GAR LAG LIBE PAR PIN RED RIC SEE SHE SOU
BASIL, LETTUCE LEAVED [A] Used as "greens" by some. Very large crinkled leaf, sometimes 6 inches in length. Twice the amount of fragrance.	To 24 in.	ABU BUT CAP COM DEG JLH NIC RED RIC SEE SHE
BASIL, LICORICE Like strong licorice candy. Pale violet flowers.		ABU PAR PIN
BASIL, MAMMOTH [A] Leaves the size of an adult's hand. Good flavor and fragrance.		RIC
BASIL, MEXICAN [A] 60 days. Purple-tinted thick leaves with cimmamon scent.		RED
BASIL, NAPOLETANO A European varieity of basil.		RED
BASIL, PICCOLO Small, fine ¾ inch leaves that are very fragrant. Best variety for growing in pots.	10-12 in.	NIC PAR RED RIC SHE
BASIL, PURPLE RUFFLES Large, heavily ruffled and fringed purple-back leaves, pinkish-purple flowers. Flavorful leaves are fine for herb vinegars, garnish. Tends to germinate and grow slower than other basils.	18-24 in.	BURP COM EAR HUM NIC PAR PIN RIC SEE STO TWI WET
BASIL, SPICE [A] Strong spicy fragrance and flavor.		RIC
BASIL, SPICY GLOBE A spread of 12-18 inches. Narrow leaves and inches delicate white flowers. Looks as if it's been sheared. Use with all tomato dishes.	6-8 in.	LAG PAR RIC SEE
BASIL, SWEET FINE [A] Taller version of bush basil. Fine leaves, compact habit.	16 inches	RIC
BASIL, THAI Green leaves with purple flowers and stems. Good in southeast Asian cuisine.	24 inches	NIC
BASIL, WILD [P] Has faint thyme-like odor. Makes a good cordial tea.		RIC
BAY (SWEET BAY, LAUREL) [P] Excellent in meat dishes and sauces with tomatoes, soups, stews.	30-40 ft.	ABU BAN CAP LEJ NIC PER RIC TAY

▶

◀ | Herb | Growth | Sources
---|---|---

BLUE POPPY SEED
Does not contain dream-inducing stuff. Used for cakes, bread, mixed vegetables, salads.

Sources: DEG

BORAGE [A]
Does not transplant. Gray foliage and blue flowers that can be candied. Leaves flavor salads, lemonade, cooling drinks. Faintly aromatic. Attracts bees. Requires dry, poor soil, sun. High in potassium. Water moderately. Also known as 'herb of gladness'. 80 days.

Growth: 2-4 feet

Sources: ABU ALL BURP BURR CAP COM DAN DEG EARL ECO GAR HARR HEN HIG HUM IND JLH JOH JUN LED LEM LET LIBE MEY NIC PAR PIN RAW RED RIC SEE SHE SOU STI STO TAY TER THO TWI VER WET WILL WYA

BURDOCK
Edible roots used in Oriental dishes and baked beans.

Growth: 2 feet

Sources: ABU RED SEE VER

BURDOCK, GIANT

Sources: ABU

BURDOCK, TAKINOGAWA LONG (GOBO)
Standard variety in Japan.

Sources: ABU JOH RED SUN

BURNET, GARDEN (BURNET SALAD, PIMPERNEL) [P]
Does not transplant. Cut back leaves when 4 inches high for constant supply in salads. Cucumber-flavored leaves used in vinegar, French dressing, dips, iced drinks, herb butter. Plant in dry, poor, sandy soil in sun.

Growth: 2 feet

Sources: ABU CAP COM DAN DEG ECO GAR HER IND JLH LAG LEJ NIC PIN RED RIC SEE STI TAY TER THO TIL WYILL

BURNET, SAXIFRAGE [P]
Young leaves have a cucumber odor and are used in salads, to flavor beer, wine and ales.

Growth: 1-2 feet

Sources: RED

CARAWAY [B]
Seeds produce in second year. Tea from seeds. Also use in rye breads, cheese, German sauerkraut, crackers, apple pie. Leaves are used in soups and salads, roast pork and vegetable dishes. Likes dry, light soil and sun. 70 days.

Growth: 2 feet

Sources: ABU BURP BURR CAP COM DAN DEG EAR ECO GUR HARR HIG HUM JLH JOH JUN LAG LED LEJ LIBE MEY NIC PIN PON RAW RED RIC SEE SOU STI STO TAY THO TIL VER WET WILL

CARDAMON [TP]
Fragrant leaves. Used in cookies, Indian curries and pastries.

Sources: RIC

CAROB [TP]
Source of commercial chocolate substitute. Dark green leaves. Fine specimen plant for sunny window or greenhouse.

Sources: RED RIC

CATNIP (CATMINT) [P]
Heart-shaped grayish-green leaves. Use fresh or dried. For tea or seasoning. Sow seed in sun or partial shade in sandy, rich soil. Grows vigorously and is fine for containers.

Growth: 2 feet

Sources: ABU ALL APP ARC BURP BURR CAP EOM DAN DEG EAR EARL GAR GUR HARR HEN HER HUM IND JLH JOH JUN LAG LED LEJ LET LIBE MEY NIC PAR PIN RAW RED RIC SOU STI TAY THO TIL WET WILL WYA

CATNIP, LEMON

Sources: ABU

CHAMOMILE (CAMOMILE) [A]
Aromatic daisy-like yellow flowers are used for tea, making perfumes and hair rinse. Needs consistent water and well-drained soil.

Growth: 1½ ft.

Sources: ALL BURP CAP COM DAN DEG EARL GUR HIG IND JOH LAG LEJ LIBE NIC PAR STI TAY TER THO WET WILL

CHAMOMILE, GERMAN [A]
Steep white and yellow flowers in hot water to make a fruity-tasting tea. Famous for its curative properties. Do not cover seed as it needs light to germinate. Grow outdoors.

Growth: 12-15 in.

Sources: ABU APP ECO GAR HER PIN PLA RAW RED RIC SEE SOU TAY

CHAMOMILE, ROMAN [P]
Yellow flowers. Strong scent. Used for tea. Plant in light shade to sun in average soil. Keep watered.

Growth: 12 inches

Sources: ABU COM ECO GAR PAR PIN NIC RED RIC TAY

CHERVIL [A]
Parsley-flavored leaves. Used as a garnish, in soup, egg dishes or salads. Old cure-all for hiccoughs. Does not transplant. Plant in light, moderately rich, well-drained soil, partial shade. 80 days.

Growth: 2 feet

Sources: ABU ALL CAP COM DAN DEG EARL ECO GAR HER IND JLH JOH LAG LED LEJ LEM NIC PIN RAW RED SEE SHE STI TAY TER THO TIL VER WILL ▶

◄ HERBS

Herb	Growth	Sources
CHERVIL, CURLED [A] Finely cut, bright green leaves used in soups, fish sauce, vegetables, egg and cheese dishes. Licorice flavor.	1 foot	BURP JLH LEM PAR RED RIC
CHIA		HOR PLA
COMFREY [P] Leaves are used in tea or fruit juice. Also cooked as a vegetable. Roots are used like salsify or parsnip.	4 feet	ABU FAR FOS GUR PER RED RIC STI TAY THO
COMFREY, RUSSIAN BROADLEAF [P] Mature leaves are used for tea. Young leaves for salads.	1 foot	HEN NIC RIC THO
CORIANDER (CILANTRO, CHINESE PARSLEY, YUEN SAI) [A] Pungent leaves are used fresh or dried in many recipes from China, Mexico and Spain. For soups, stuffings, cheese spreads. Dried, powdered seeds are used in sweet breads, cakes, pickles, and curry powder. Sow in the spring. Harvest leaves as needed, gather seeds in late summer. 45 days. Lacy white flowers. Plant in well-drained, rich soil, consistent watering.	2 feet	ABU ALL BAN BURP CAP COM DAN DEG EAR EARL ECO FIS GAR HARR HER HIG HOR HUM IND JOH LED LEJ LEM LIBE MEY NIC PAR PIN PLA RAW RED RIC RIS SHE SOU STI SUN TAY TER TIL TSA TWI VER WET WYA
CORIANDER, VIETNAMESE [TP] Grow this perennial indoors in good light.		RIC
COSTMARY (BIBLE LEAF) [P] Crushed leaves are used in ale, salads, meats, poultry, fish chowder and soup. Pioneers put the leaves in their books to deter silverfish. Seldom sets seeds.	2-4 ft.	CAP LEJ NIC RIC STI TAY
CUMIN [A] Used extensively in Indian, Mexican and Middle Eastern cooking. Requires long growing season to produce seeds. White flowers.	6-12 in.	ABU COM ECO JLH LEM NIC PAR PIN RED RIC THO WILL
CURRY PLANT [P] Has strong curry scent. Gray foliage with yellow flowers.	4 feet	RIC TAY
DILL [A] The stems, head and foliage are used for flavoring tuna and chicken salads, pickles, kraut, steaks, chops and many other foods. A vigorous, upright plant with blooms in compact heads. Grows easily in sunny, well-drained soil.	2 feet	ABU APP ARC BURP CAP DAN EARL ECO GAR GUR HER HIG IND LAG LEJ PAR PER PIN PON RED SHE STO TAY THO VER WYA
DILL, BOUQUET [A] Same as above. Yellow, umbrella-shaped flowers, lacy pale green foliage. 70 days.	3 feet	ABU ALL BURG BURR COM DEG EAR FAR FIS GLE HARR JOH JUN LED LEJ LEM LIBE MEY MID NIC PLA POR RAW RIS ROS STI TAY THO TIL TWI VES WIL
DILL, DUCAT Vigorous, upright plant with larger flower heads than Bouquet dill.	3 feet	HARR
DILL, INDIAN [A] Pungent bitter variety. Grown in India and Japan. Essential ingredient in curry powders.		RIC
DILL, MAMMOTH (LONG ISLAND MAMMOTH) Same uses as for other dills. Pink flowers.	2½ ft.	ABU BUT COM HUM JUN LED LEJ LEM MID NIC RIC RIS SEED SOU TER WILL
DILL, SARI		THO
DILL, TETRAPLOID [A] Bushier and more vigorous than standard varieties. Dark leafy green leaves. Late-blooming. Best strain for dillweed.		RIC

◄ | Herb | Growth | Sources |
|---|---|---|
| **DITTANY OF CRETE [P]**
Used like Oregano and in tea. Chartreuse and pink flowers.
Plant in full sun. | 6 inches | LEJ RIC TAY |
| **ELECAMPANE**
Brilliant daisy-like flowers, violet-scented. Roots are used for
candy and liqueurs. Tolerates light shade and rich soil. | 6 feet | ABU NIC RED TAY THO |
| **EPAZOTE (WORSEED GOOSEFOOT, MEXICAN TEA) [A]**
Pungent culinary herb whose leaves are used to season Mexi-
can bean dishes and sauces. Plant in full sun and rich soil. | 4 feet | NIC PLA RED RIC TAY |
| **FENUGREEK [A]**
Maple-flavored seeds are used in cookies, cakes, syrups, curry
powders, tea or sprouted for use in salads. Clover-shaped
leaves. | 2 feet | ABU COM JLH JOH LEJ LEM PIN RAW RED RIC TAY |
| **FOOT**
Excellent in bean dishes. | 2 feet | TAY |
| **GERANIUM, APPLE**
All scented geranium leaves are used for vinegar, flavoring jel-
lies, sandwiches, potato salad, cakes, fruit salad, stewed fruit,
punch, tea, wine, sachets and potpourri. | 3-4 feet | CAP PAR RIC |
| **GERANIUM, COCONUT [TP]**
Has coconut scent. Self-sows. Small dark leaves on compact, but
trailing plant. Good for hanging basket. | CAP RIC | |
| **GERANIUM, CINNAMON** | | PAR |
| **GERANIUM, LEMON**
Strong scent of lemon is very fragrant. Tiny crisped leaves. Stiff
upright habit. | | CAP PAR RIC TAY |
| **GERANIUM, LEMON ROSE** | | TAY |
| **GERANIUM, LIME [TP]**
Excellent lime scent. Small deep green leaves. | | CAP RIC TAY |
| **GERANIUM, NUTMEG**
Spicy nutmeg scent. Dainty plant. | | CAP PAR RIC |
| **GERANIUM, OAKLEAF** | | CAP |
| **GERANIUM, OLD SPICE** | | CAP |
| **GERANIUM, ORANGE** | | CAP |
| **GERANIUM, PEPPERMINT [P]**
Velvety leaves have strong peppermint scent. | 3-4 feet | PAR RIC TAY |
| **GERANIUM, ROSE [P]**
Delicate rose fragrance. | 3-4 feet | RIC TAY |
| **GERANIUM, STRAWBERRY** | | CAP |
| **GINGER [TP]**
Fresh roots are used in dishes of meat, poultry and fish, while
ground dried ginger is used in baking and puddings. | | RIC |
| **GINGER, WILD**
Edible aromatic root. Grows well in moist, shaded places. | | NIC |

►

HERBS

Herb	Growth	Sources
GINGER ROOT		SUN
GINSENG The root has a human shape and is dried and eaten. The leaves are brewed for tea. Grows in any type of soil.	18 inches	LEJ PAR RIC THO
GINSENG, SIBERIAN [P] This is the variety used by Russian cosmonauts and athletes to improve endurance.		RIC
GOOD KING HENRY [P] Shoots are gathered when 5 inches high and peeled, boiled and eaten like asparagus. Young leaves are prepared like spinach. Said to be good remedy for indigestion.		ECO RIC
GOTU KOLA [TP] Said to have rejuvenating properties. One or two fresh leaves chopped daily in salads or liquified in juice is said to be enough. Culture in humus rich soil where humidity is high. Avoid direct sunlight.		RIC TAY
HOREHOUND [P] Flavors beef stew, braised beef, cakes, candies and teas.	2 feet	ABU BURP CAP COM DAN DEG ECO HEN IND JLH JOH LAG LED LEJ LET LIBE MEY NIC PAR RIC STI TAY THO TWI WET WILL
HOREHOUND, GREEK [TP] Decorative herb with crinkled, white-woolly leaves.		RIC
HYSSOP (BEE PLANT) [P] Aromatic foliage but bitter taste. Used in tea. Grows in light, well-drained, warm soil in sun to partial shade.	2-3 feet	ABU CAP COM DEG ECO GAR IND JLH JOH LEJ NIC PAR PIN RED RIC STI TWI WILL
HYSSOP, ANISE (LICORICE MINT) [P] Dried leaves are used for seasoning and tea. Violet flowers attract bees. Prefers full sun, well-drained loam and moderate watering.	3-5 feet	ABU GAR HER HIG NIC PIN RIC SEE SHE TAY
IBOSA Leaves used between meats in shish kebabs and barbecue meats. Likes shade.	1 foot	TAY
JOSEPH'S COAT (CHINESE SPINACH)		TAY
LEMON BALM [P] Heart-shaped leaves are delightfully lemon-scented. Use in drinks, desserts and herbal potpourris. Plant in dry soil and partial shade.	1-2 feet	APP BURP CAP COM DEG ECO GAR GUR HARR HEN HIG IND JLH JOH LEJ NIC PER PIN RAW RIC SOU STI TAY THO WET WILL
LEMON GRASS [P] Delicious in iced tea. Strong taste and smell of lemon.	18 inches	TAY
LEMON VERBENA [P] Fresh leaves are used in tea, fruit salads, jam, jelly and cold drinks. Semi-deciduous. Lemon fragrance.	3-4 feet	NIC RIC TAY
LICORICE [P] Used in tea or chew on the stick. Pale blue flowers.	6 feet	TAY
LOVAGE [P] Can be used as a celery substitute. Use fresh leaves in split pea soup, tea, potato salad, sauces, stews and salads. Rich, moist soil should be dug deeply to produce a fine handsome plant.	2-6 feet	ABU CAP COM GAR HER IND JLH JOH LAG NIC PER PIN RAW RED RIC SEE STI TAY THO VER WILL
MARJORAM, CREEPING GOLDEN [A] Use the same as you would Sweet Marjoram. Yellow flowers.	8 inches	TAY

◀ Herb	Growth	Sources
MARJORAM, SWEET [TP] Highly aromatic leaves are used in sauces, soups, salads, salad dressings, brown gravy, egg dishes, tomato and potato dishes. Also used in vegetables, especially with eggplant, summer squash and zucchini. 70 days.	2 feet	ABU ALL APP BURP CAP COM DAN DEG EAR ECO GAR GUR HARR HEN HER HIG HUM IND JLH JOH LAG LED LEM LET LIBE MEY NIC PAR PIN PON RAW RED RIC RIS SEED SHE SOU STO TAY TER THO TIL TWI VER VES WET WIL WILL WYA
MERCURY		THO
MINT [P] Excellent in mint jelly, custards, ice cream, fruit juices, mint sauce, tea, stewed pears and salads.	To 2 feet	MEY THO WYA
MINT, APPLE [P] Has a pleasant fruity aroma, soft green leaves.	18 inches	CAP HEN IND LEJ NIC RIC STI TAY
MINT, AUSTRIAN [TP] Flavor is reminiscent of spearmint. Essential seasoning for ravioli-like Austrian dish, 'Topfen Nudeln' stuffed with mashed potatoes and cottage cheese.		RIC
MINT, BALM Has strong scent of winter savory.	18 inches	COM LAG PAR TAY
MINT, CORSICAN (JEWEL MINT, CREME DE MENTHE) [P] Used mostly as a ground cover. Can be used as you use other mints and in tea.	1-2 inches	LEJ NIC TAY
MINT, CURLED Used for flavoring and in beverages.	To 3 feet	ALL CAP LAG TAY WILL
MINT, ENGLISH [P] Dark green leaves have fresh fragrance. Use in mint jelly, peas, carrots, potatoes, mint julep or tomato sauce.	3 feet	RIC TAY
MINT, GINGER [TP] Gold-flecked leaves have a fruity fragrance and a hint of ginger taste.		RIC
MINT, GRAPEFRUIT [TP] Has a spearmint flavor with an extra-strong fragrance of grapefruit.		RIC
MINT, JAMAICAN [TP] Bushy plant with small bright green leaves and strong peppermint aroma.		RIC
MINT, LAVENDER Spicy lavender-scented with smooth oval leaves. Stems, veins and back of green leaves are dark-purple.	1-2 feet	NIC
MINT, LEMON [B] Leaves make a fine tea. Excellent in fish dishes. Purple flowers are also edible and attracts bees.	2-3 feet	ABU PER PLA NIC RED
MINT, LIME [TP] Taste of lime.		RIC
MINT, MOUNTAIN [TP] Use like peppermint. Excellent bee plant. Has menthol fragrance.		RIC
MINT, ORANGE BERGAMONT (OSWEGO TEA, BEE BALM) [P] Leaves make a fragrant tea with the flavor of mint and citrus. Bright red flowers attract bees and hummingbirds. 14-21 days.	30 inches	ABU HER IND JLH NIC PLA RIC SEE TAY ▶

◀ HERBS

Herb	Growth	Sources
MINT, ORANGE Special orange fragrance used in fruit punches and teas.	30 inches	CAP LEJ RIC STI TAY
MINT, PENNYROYAL [P] Used in tea but can be toxic in large amounts. Dies back in winter. Plant in fairly rich moist soil and shade.	1 foot	ABU CAP COM ECO HIG IND JLH JOH LAG LEJ NIC PAR PIN RED RIC SEE SOU TAY
MINT, PEPPERMINT [P] Used as a garnish in drinks and other foods. Grown for its essential oil present in all plant parts.	30 inches	ABU CAP COM EAR EARL ECO HARR JLH JOH LAG LED LEJ LIBE NIC PAR RAW RIC SEE SOU STI STO TAY THO VES WET WILL
MINT, PINEAPPLE [P] Pineapple aroma. Use in tea. Some white variegated foliage.	1-2 feet	CAP LET NIC RIC STI TAY
MINT, ROMAN [TP] Used widely in cooking. Minty odor reminiscent of menthol, spearmint and pennyroyal.		RIC
MINT, SILVERMINT [P] Refreshing spearmint odor.		LEJ RIC
MINT, SPEARMINT [P] Flavoring for drinks, mint jellies, sauces and mint juleps. Sow in rich moist soil, partial shade to full sun. 80 days.	3 feet	ABU APP BURP CAP COM DAN ECO GUR HARR HEN HUM JLH JOH JUN LAG LED NIC PAR PER RAW RIC SEE STI STO TAY WET WILL
MINT, SPEARMINT IMPROVED [TP] Also known as 'Kentucky Colonel' mint. Hybrid of applemint. Has wonderful fruity spearmint aroma and flavor.		RIC
MINT, STONE		LEJ
MINT, THE BEST [P] Narrow green leaves have spearmint flavor.	3 feet	TAY
MINT, VARIEGATED SCOTCH Mild spearmint aroma. vivid gold and green variegated foliage.	1 foot	NIC
MINT, WATERMINT	2 feet	TAY
MINT, WHITE PEPPERMINT	2 feet	TAY
MINT, WILD BERGAMONT		ABU
MUSTARD, BLACK [A] Dark-brown seeds are yellow inside and very strong-flavored. They are ground and blended with vinegar to made mustard. Young leaves make peppery cooked greens. Easily grown in any soil in full sun.	3-10 ft.	RED
MUSTARD, WHITE [A] True companion to curled cress for salads and sandwiches. Whole seeds are used to season pickles, sausages and sauerkraut. Also can be prepared into condiment from ground mustard seeds.		RIC
NASTURTUM [A] Unripe seeds can be used in place of capers in homemade pickles. Spicy leaves and flowers can be added to salads. Plant in full sun.		BUT CAP COM DEG EAR FAR GAR HEN HER HUM IND JUN LET NIC PLA POR RAW RED RIC SEE SEED SHE SOU STO TER THO VER WILL WYA
NETTLE, STINGING Can be cooked as greens or made into beer.	3-5 ft.	ABU IND LEJ RIC SEE TAY WILL

▶

Herb	Growth	Sources
NIGELLA (LOVE-IN-A-MIST) [A] Finely divided leaves create a mist surrounding blue flowers. Seeds are used in curries and bread.		RIC
OREGANO [TP] Leaves are used in sauces, soups, meats, fish, game, poultry, stews, vegetables, Italian and Spanish dishes and vinegars.	2 feet	ABU ALL APP ARC BURP COM DAN DEG EAR EARL ECO GUR HARR HEN HUM IND JLH JOH JUN LAG LED LEJ LET LIBE MEY NIC PAR PIN PLA RAW RED SEED STI STO TAY TER TIL VES VER WET WIL WILL WYA
OREGANO, CRETAN [TP] Also called Pot Marjoram. Strong-flavored form of oregano.		RIC
OREGANO, CUBAN [TP] Almost round leaves with small shallow rounded teeth on edges. Pleasant odor when brushed against.		RIC
OREGANO, GOLDEN [P] Golden foliage. Mild oregano flavor.		RIC
OREGANO, GREEK [P] Trim to encourage growth. Leaves used fresh or dried, in sauces and soups. True oregano. Plant in full sun in well-drained soil. 90 days.	30 inches	ABU GAR HER HIG LEM PIN PON RIC SEE STO TAY
OREGANO, MEXICAN [TP] Heat-tolerant and easier to grow than regular oregano, with sharper flavor.		PAR RED RIC
OREGANO, SYRIAN [TP] Strong spicy flavor.		RIC
PERILLA, GREEN (SHISHO) [A] Green cinnamon mint-scented leaves are used in Japanese and Korean cookery.	3 feet	BAN LEM NIC RIC SUN TSA
PERILLA, PURPLE (BEEFSTEAK PLANT, AKA SHISO) [A] Young leaves are used in Japanese cooking. Large purple leaves are crinkly and pungent. 50-60 days.	3 feet	BAN NIC RED RIC SUN TSA
PERILLA, RED (SHISHO RED) [P]		LEM PIN
POKE (POKEROOT) [P] Young shoots are used in salads. Stems in biscuits.	6-10 ft.	ABU RIC SEE TAY
POPPY, HUNGARIAN BLUE-SEEDED		ABU
PURSLANE (CARTI-CHOY) [A] Salad herb. Used in stir-frys also. Plants that run to seed are pickled in salt and vinegar for winter salads. 60 days.	6 inches	ABU ECO LAG NIC TER THO
ROCKET SALAD (ROQUETTE, RUCOLA, ARUGULA) [A] Plant of the mustard family. Cook and serve like spinach. Peppery pungent taste flavors salads. Leaves are ready to use at 2-3 inches. Best sown in open ground in spring or early autumn. 43 days.	2 feet	ABU CAP ECO GAR HARR HER HIG JLH LAG LEM LET LIBE NIC PAR PEA PIN RED RIC SEE SHE THO TWI VER WILL
ROSE, WILD [P] Fruits (rosehips) are used in preserves, sauces and tea. Fresh petals are used to garnish salads and fruit cups. Dried petals give bouquet to teas. Pink flowers with delicate fragrance.		RIC
ROSELLE [TP] Lemony flavor and beautiful ruby color. Refreshing in tea hot or iced. Also used for preserves, wine or a sour relish similar to cranberry sauce. Requires a long hot growing season.		RIC

◀ HERBS

Herb	Growth	Sources
ROSEMARY [P] Dark green needle-like foliage is used for seasoning beef, chicken, pork, lamb, veal, sauces, sandwich spreads, herb butter and stew. Used in iced drinks, chopped in biscuits, fried potatoes, stuffings, jellies. blue flowers. Lime should be dug into the soil several times a year. 85 days.	30 inches	ABU ALL APP BURP CAP COM DAN DEG EARL ECO GUR HARR HER HEN IND JLH JUN LAG LED LEJ LEM LET LIBE MEY NIC PAR PER PIN RAW SOU STI STO TAY THO TIL VER WET WILL WYA
ROSEMARY, BENEDEN BLUE [TP] Medium-blue flowers.	4 feet	RIC TAY
ROSEMARY, LOCKWOOD [TP] Bright blue flowers. Trailing habit.		RIC
ROSEMARY, MAJORCA Sharp sweet fragrance. Pink flowers on tree-like plant.	2-4 ft.	NIC RIC
ROSEMARY, PINK [P] Pink flowers.	3 feet	TAY
ROSEMARY, SANTA BARBARA [P] Light blue flowers.	2 feet	TAY
ROSEMARY, SEVERN SEAS [TP] Light blue flowers on trailing plants.		RIC
ROSEMARY, TRAILING (CREEPING ROSEMARY) [P] Same uses as for common rosemary. Creeping habit aids in soil retention.	1 foot	NIC
ROSEMARY, TUSCAN BLUE [P] Light blue flowers.	5 feet	TAY
ROSEMARY, WOOD [P] Dark blue flowers.	3 feet	TAY
RUE (GALEGA, HERB OF GRACE) [P] Aromatic blue-green plant used to flavor cheese. Use sparingly in sandwiches, cottage cheese, vegetables, eggplant, asparagus, potatoes, peas and sauces. Grows best in sun.	3 feet	ABU CAP COM DEG ING JLH JOH LEJ LEM NIC PAR PER PIN RED RIC TAY THO VER WILL
SAFFLOWER (FALSE SAFFRON) [A] Dried orange flowers are used as substitute for saffron. Used for dyes, cosmetics and food coloring. Oil from the seed used much like olive oil. Leaves are used for flavoring.	3 feet	ABU CAP COM GUR LAG LEJ NIC PAR VER
SAFFLOWER, EVERLASTING Deep orange petals.	2½ feet	NIC
SAFFRON Used as flavoring and for coloring.	24 inches	DEG SEE
SAGE, BROAD LEAVED (GARDEN) [P] Pleasant aromatic leaf used in poultry, soups, stews, stuffings, sausage, brown gravy, roast meats, port, cottage cheese, stewed tomatoes, lima beans and eggs. Plant in full sun, average soil. Silvery gray-green foliage and lavender flowers. 75 days.	2 feet	ABU ALL APP ARC BURP BURR CAP COM DAN EAR EARL ECO FAR FIS GAR GUR HARR HEN HER HIG HUM IND JLH JOH JUN LAG LEJ LEM LET LIBE MEY MID NIC PAR PER PIN PLA PON RAW RIS SEE SEED SHE SOU STI STO TAY TER THO TIL TWI WYA
SAGE, CLARY Gives muscatel flavor to wine.	2 feet	ABU IND JLH NIC RED SEE STI WILL

▶

Herb	Growth	Sources
SAGE, DWARF [P] Small leaves, violet-blue flowers that attract bees.	18 inches	LEJ SEED TAY
SAGE, GOLDEN [P] Golden variegated leaves.	18 inches	RIC TAY
SAGE, HOLT'S MAMMOTH Best used as a culinary herb.	2 feet	NIC
SAGE, PINEAPPLE [P] Fragrant pineapple odor. Scarlet flowers that attract bees and hummingbirds.	3-6 ft.	CAP LEJ NIC RIC TAY
SAGE, PURPLE [P] Good culinary variety. Soft purple foliage.	2 feet	NIC PER RIC TAY
SAGE, VARIEGATED (TRICOLOR) [P] Flowers vary from white, pink, purple to red. For culinary use.	2 feet	NIC PER TAY
SAVORY, SUMMER [A] Has white and purple flowers and small aromatic leaves. Use in bean dishes, stuffing, rice, soups, sauces, gravies, stews, chicken and tea. Plant early in the spring in a sunny location. 60 days.	To 2 feet	ABU ALL BURP BURR CAP COM DAN DEG EAR EARL ECO GAR GUR HARR HER IND JLH JOH JUN LAG LED LEJ LEM LET LIBE MEY NIC PAR PER PIN PON RAW RED RIC SEE SEED SOU STI STO TAY TER THO TIL TWI VER WET WILL WYA
SAVORY, TRAILING WINTER (CREEPING WINTER) Bright green leaves and white flowers. Similar in use to Winter Savory.	6 inches	JOH NIC RIC
SAVORY, WINTER [P] Shrubby evergreen. Use in beans, stuffing, poultry and meats.	To 2 feet	ABU ECO GAR LAG LEJ LEM NIC PAR PER PIN RAW RIC SEE STI TAY THO VER WILL
SESAME [A] Roasted seeds add nutty flavor to breads and buns. Also good in green salads and with butter. Needs a long growing season.		RIC
SESAME, BENNE Seeds are used in breads, confectionary, and pastries. Leaves are used for tea.	3 feet	ABU DEG NIC PIN TIL VER
SMALLAGE Wild species of celery. Slender stalks and fine leaves. Powerful taste and aroma.		GLE
SORREL, BELLEVILLE [P] Hardy productive herb. Fast grower. Large 3 inch leaves are used for cream of sorrel soup. Drought-resistant.		LEM RED
SORREL BROAD LEAVED BLOND LYON [P] Slightly acid-tasting leaves give zest to salads and soup. Very broad leaves. Slow to bolt to seed.	4 inches	ABU JOH LEM NIC PAR RIC SEE VER
SORREL, FRENCH [P] Mildly sour and lemony flavor. Used in soups, salads, cooked as greens or added to other greens, especially spinach.	3 feet	CAP ECO GAR JLH LED LEJ NIC PER SHE TAY TER THO
SORREL, GARDEN [P] Oblong rosettes and succulent leaves grow about 5 inches long. Used for soup and salads.	3 feet	BURP EARL HER HIG LAG PIN SOU THO WET WILL
SORREL, NOBEL [P] Leaves are larger, broader and more succulent than other varieties.		RIC

HERBS

Herb	Growth	Sources
SORREL, PATIENTA [P] Leaves grow to 1 foot long. Young leaves are used for cooked greens.	6 feet	RED
SWEET CICELY [P] Sugar saver. Sweet, anise-scented leaves and stalks (fresh or dried) are added for flavor to sweets and desserts. Seeds will not germinate unless fresh. Best sown in autumn, seedlings appear in spring.		ABU CAP ECO LEJ NIC RIC TWI
TARRAGON, FRENCH [P] Flavoring for soups, fish sauces, salads, dressings, beef, poultry, game, eggs, vegetables, cheese spreads, tartar sauce, herb butter and tarragon vinegar.	30 inches	ALL CAP GUR HEN LEJ NIC PAR PER RIC STI TAY THO WYA
TARRAGON, MEXICAN [P] Leaves have a distinctive tarragon flavor and can be used as a substitute for such. It is known as Sweet Marigold. Can be added to salads, vinegars or seasoning for chicken. Can also be used as a tea.	1 foot	RED RIC
TARRAGON, RUSSIAN [P] Less aromatic than the French varieties. Pleasing flavor for salads and vinegar. Does not set seed. 90 days.	2½ ft.	COM EARL JLH LAG PIN RIC STO VER WILL
THYME, BROAD LEAVED (COMMON) [P] Strong aromatic aroma. Used as dried herb in vinegar, egg dishes, meat and fish sauces, cooked with vegetables. Plant in light, sandy soil. 85 days.	1 foot	ABU ALL APP BURP COM DAN DEG EAR EARL ECO FAR GAR GUR HARR HUM IND JLH JUN LAG LED LET LIBE MEY NIC PIN PON RAW RED RIS SEE SEED SHE STI STO TER TIL TWI VER WET
THYME, CARAWAY [P] Has red-tinted stems and dark caraway scented leaves. Pink flowers. Used to season 'Baron of Beef'.	3 inches	CAP LEJ NIC RIC TAY
THYME, COCONUT [P] Dark green foliage with pink flowers.	3 inches	TAY
THYME, CREEPING [P] Forms a mat of rosy-purple flowers. Bee plant.	6 inches	CAP NIC RAW RED TAY TWI WILL
THYME, DOONE VALLEY LEMON [P] Gold variegated creeping form of lemon thyme. Use in salads and tea drinks. Protect in the winter.		RIC
THYME, DWARF		LEJ
THYME, ENGLISH [P] Mauve flowers. Used in pork, veal, soups, stuffing, clam and fish chowders.	1 foot	CAP HIG LEM NIC PAR RIC TAY THO
THYME, FRENCH [P] Used in French cuisine. Narrow leaves with pink flowers on trim upright plant. Do not over-water.	1 foot	CAP LEJ LEM NIC PER RIC STI TAY
THYME, GERMAN WINTER		HER SOU WILL WYA
THYME, GOLDEN LEMON [P] Lemon-scented leaves of golden and green variegation. Uses and culture are the same as for lemon thyme.	18 inches	CAP NIC RIC TAY
THYME, GOLDEN CREEPING	3 inches	LEJ STI

Herb	Growth	Sources
THYME, LEMON [P] Lemon-scented leaves make a delicious tea. Use in soups and salads. Mild flavor.	1 foot	LEJ NIC RIC STI TAY
THYME, NUTMEG [P] Small leaves, trailing type. Aroma and flavor of nutmeg.		RIC
THYME, OREGANO Glossy dark leaves have the aroma of Greek oregano.	1 foot	NIC
THYME, SCARLET		CAP
THYME, SILVER [P] Silver foliage. More ornamental than culinary.	18 inches	RIC TAY
THYME, WILD (MOTHER OF THYME) [P] Creeping plant with purple flowers. Low creeper that perfumes the air when stepped on. More for use as a medicine than culinary.	4 inches	ABU APP CAP LEM PAR RIC TAY
VALERIAN [P] Large clusters of fragrant white flowers. Dried root is used to make a soothing tea. Partial to full sun in well-drained moist soil.	6 feet	ABU HIG IND NIC RIC TAY
VALERIAN, RED [P] Fragrant red flowers. Young leaves are eaten in salads or cooked as greens. Roots are used for soups.		ECO RIC
YARROW, MACE [TP] Has spicy aroma reminiscent of the true mace. Leaves are used to flavor soups and salads.		TAY
YERBA BUENA [P] Excellent minty tea or mixed with other herbs.	6 inches	TAY
YERBA MATE [TP] Makes a mate tea more stimulating than coffee or tea but contains little caffeine.		RIC

Indexes

[Illustrations indicated by italics.]

A. BY FIGURE NUMBER

B. ALPHABETICAL LISTING